Social Psychology:

Concepts and Applications

A STUDENT STUDY GUIDE

A study guide has been developed to assist students in mastering the concepts presented in this text. It reinforces chapter material presenting it in a concise format with review questions. An examination copy is available to instructors by contacting West Publishing Company. Students can purchase the study guide from the local bookstore under the title *Study Guide to Accompany Social Psychology: Concepts and Applications*, prepared by Dudley Campbell.

Social Psychology:
Concepts and Applications

Louis A. Penner

University of South Florida

WEST PUBLISHING COMPANY

St. Paul   New York   Los Angeles   San Francisco

PHOTO CREDITS: p. 2: Mary Evans Picture Library/Photo Researchers, Inc. p. 5: Hazel Hankin/Stock, Boston. p. 7: Smolan/Stock, Boston. p. 16: Jeffrey Myers/Stock, Boston. p. 19: Dan S. Brody/Stock, Boston. p. 25: Peter Simon/Stock, Boston. p. 31: Robin Laurance/Photo Researchers, Inc. p. 36: Dean Abramson/Stock, Boston. p. 40: Bohdan Hrynewych/Stock, Boston. p. 42: Jerome Wexler/Freelance Photographers Guild. p. 54: Jeff Albertson/Stock, Boston. p. 60: Gellner/Freelance Photographers Guild. p. 63: Teri Stratford/Photo Researchers, Inc. p. 72: Centers for Disease Control, Atlanta, GA. p. 75: S. Dinicins/ Photo Researchers, Inc. p. 80: Arthur Tress/Photo Researchers, Inc. p. 83: Jean Claude Lejeune/Stock, Boston. p. 89: Elizabeth Crews/Stock, Boston. p. 93: Dr. Gordon Gallup. p. 98: John Running/Stock, Boston. p. 113: Arthur Grace/Stock, Boston. p. 120: Stock, Boston. p. 124: Peter Southwick/Stock, Boston. p. 128: AP/Wide World Photos. p. 129: AP/Wide World Photos. p. 134: Michael Hayman/Stock, Boston. p. 141: Ellis Herwig/Stock, Boston. p. 151: Barbara Alper/Stock, Boston. p. 159: © Jim Shaffer. p. 164: © Chris Grajczyk. p. 183: Steve Skloot/Photo Researchers, Inc. p. 189: Bob Krueger/Photo Researchers, Inc. p. 193: Bell Aircraft Corp./AP/Wide World Photos. p. 202: Stock, Boston. p. 205: Victor Friedman/Photo Researchers, Inc. p. 208: Arthur Grace/Stock, Boston. p. 213: Ed Lattau/Photo Researchers, Inc. p. 217: Suzanne Szasz/Photo Researchers, Inc. p. 226: Jean Claude Lejeune/Stock, Boston. p. 229: Thomas Hollyman/Photo Researchers, Inc. p. 238: Ellis Herwig/Stock, Boston. p. 244: Alice Kandell/Photo Researchers, Inc. p. 256: Bob Combs/Photo Researchers, Inc. p. 260: AP/Wide World Photos. p. 277: Copyright © by Universal Pictures, a Division of Universal City Studios, Inc. Courtesy of MCA Publishing Rights, a Division of MCA Inc. p. 289: Jan Lukas/Photo Researchers, Inc. p. 293: Robert McKeever/Photo Researchers, Inc. p. 299: AP/Wide World Photos. p. 302: Charles Gatewood/Stock, Boston. p. 306: Charles Gupton/Stock, Boston. p. 313: Jeffrey Blankfort/Jeroboam. p. 317: W.D. Zehr/Freelance Photographers Guild. p. 321: Charles Pereira/AP/Wide World Photos. p. 330: George Malave/Stock, Boston. p. 346: AP/Wide World Photos. p. 350: Susan Woog Wagner/Photo Researchers, Inc. p. 352: Michael Hayman/Photo Researchers, Inc. p. 366: Steve Skloot/Photo Researchers, Inc. p. 369: © Chris Grajczyk. p. 378: Jan Lukas/Photo Researchers, Inc. p. 383: Jane Scherr/Jeroboam. p. 389: Mary Evans Picture Library/Photo Researchers, Inc. p. 393: Margaret Bourke White/AP/Wide World Photos. p. 402: Cary Wolinsky/Stock, Boston. p. 411: Hans Jordan/Freelance Photographers Guild. p. 419: U.S. Department of Transportation Ad Council. p. 424: Photoworld, Division of Freelance Photographers Guild. p. 445: Jeff Albertson/Stock, Boston. p. 450: Barbara Alper/Stock, Boston. p. 456: AP/Wide World Photos. p. 463: W.A. York/Freelance Photographers Guild. p. 468: Max Halberstadt/ARCHIV/Photo Researchers, Inc. p. 475: Jeffrey W. Myers/Stock, Boston. p. 488: Ellis Herwig/Stock, Boston. p. 501: J. Berndt/Stock, Boston. p. 508: Suzanne Szasz/Photo Researchers, Inc. p. 512: National Portrait Gallery, Smithsonian Institution, Washington, D.C. p. 519: Ulrike Welsch/Stock, Boston. p. 525: Peter Menzel/Stock, Boston. p. 539: Copyright © by Universal Pictures, a Division of Universal City Studios, Inc. Courtesy of MCA Publishing Rights, a Division of MCA Inc. p. 552: Christopher Brown/Stock, Boston. p. 556: Christian Poveda/Stock, Boston. p. 564: Barbara Alper/Stock, Boston. p. 574: Elizabeth Hamlin/Stock, Boston. p. 580: Gregg Mancuso/Stock, Boston. p. 592: Christopher Morrow/Stock, Boston. p. 602: Arthur Grace/Stock, Boston. p. 610: AP/Wide World Photos. p. 616: Owen Franken/Stock, Boston. p. 621: Charles Gatewood/Stock, Boston. p. 628: Ed Lettau/Photo Researchers, Inc. p. 631: Gary Wolinsky/Stock, Boston. p. 635: William Tou/Freelance Photographers Guild. p. 644: Ellis Herwig/Stock, Boston. p. 656: Katrina Thomas/Photo Researchers, Inc. p. 663 top and bottom: Ellis Herwig/Stock, Boston.

The author is grateful for the granting of permission to reprint or reproduce the following: Excerpt from Mock Segregation Real For Some by J. Brown. Copyright © 1985, The Atlanta Journal-Constitution. All rights reserved.   Excerpt from The Sixteenth Round by Rubin "Hurricane" Carter. Copyright © 1974 by Rubin "Hurricane" Carter. Reprinted by permission of Viking Penguin Inc.   Article about Robert "Shorty" Henderson. Copyright © 1984, United Press International.   The Value Survey. Copyright © 1967, 1982 Milton Rokeach. Reprinted by permission of Halgren N.W., Pullman, WA.   Figure 10-5 From: The elaboration model of persuasion by R.E. Petty and J.T. Cacioppo, in L. Berkowitz (Ed.), *Advances in experimental social psychology* (Vol. 19), New York: Academic Press, 1985.   Figure 11-8, From: Dentist's behavior management as it affects compliance and fear in pediatric patients by B. Melamed and Associates. Copyright © 1983, Reprinted by permission of American Dental Association.   Excerpt from *Thy Neighbor's Wife* by Gay Talese. Copyright © by Gay Talese. Reprinted by permission of Doubleday and Company, Inc.   Figure 12-6, From: Effects of isolation and communication on cooperation in a two person game, by Harvey Wichman. Copyright © 1972 by Wadsworth Inc. Reprinted by permission of Brooks/Cole Publishing Company, Monterey, CA.   Figure 12-10, From: Why men rebel by Ted Robert Gurr. Copyright © 1970 by Princeton University Press, Princeton, NJ.   Figure 13-3, From: Cross modality matches by Latané and Hawkins, in *Perception and Psychophysics*, 1976 (Vol. 20).   Figure 14-8, From: Personal space by Robert Sommer. Copyright © 1969, by Prentice Hall, Inc., Englewood Cliffs, NJ: Figure 14-10a and 14-10b, From: Architecture and social behavior by A. Baum and S. Valins. Copyright © 1979 by Lawrence Erlbaum Associates, Hillsdale, NJ.

Cover art: Maurice Prendergast. *May Day in Central Park.* 1901. Watercolor on paper. 14½ × 21⅝ inches. Collection of Whitney Museum of American Art. Purchase, by exchange. Acq. #48.19.

COPYRIGHT © 1986 By WEST PUBLISHING COMPANY
        50 West Kellogg Boulevard
        P.O. Box 64526
        St. Paul, MN 55164-1003

All rights reserved

Printed in the United States of America

Library of Congress Cataloging-in-Publication Data

Penner, Louis A., 1943–
  Social psychology.

  Bibliography: p.
  Includes index.
  1. Social psychology. I. Title.
HM251.P412 1986   302   85-26540
ISBN 0-314-93405-7
1st Reprint—1987

To: Kathy, Charlie, and Jerry.

Contents in Brief

ONE   AN INTRODUCTION TO SOCIAL PSYCHOLOGY ———————————— 2

TWO   RESEARCH METHODS IN SOCIAL PSYCHOLOGY ———————————— 36

THREE   PERSONALITY CHARACTERISTICS AND SOCIAL BEHAVIOR ———————— 80

FOUR   SOCIAL COGNITION ———————————————————————— 120

FIVE   SELF-PERCEPTION AND PRESENTATION ———————————————— 164

SIX   INTERPERSONAL ATTRACTION: LIKING AND LOVING ———————————— 208

SEVEN   AGGRESSION ———————————————————————— 256

EIGHT   PROSOCIAL BEHAVIOR ————————————————————— 306

NINE   ATTITUDES AND BEHAVIOR ———————————————————— 352

TEN   ATTITUDE CHANGE ————————————————————————— 402

ELEVEN   SOCIAL INFLUENCE ———————————————————————— 456

TWELVE   INTERDEPENDENT SOCIAL BEHAVIOR ———————————————— 508

THIRTEEN   GROUP PROCESSES ———————————————————————— 564

FOURTEEN   ENVIRONMENTAL INFLUENCES ON SOCIAL BEHAVIOR ——————— 616

Contents

Preface   xii

ONE   AN INTRODUCTION TO SOCIAL PSYCHOLOGY   2

Prologue   3

Social Psychology Today   6
Social Psychology Defined   6   •   What Social Psychologists Do   9   •   Where Social Psychologists Work   11   •   How Social Psychologists are Trained   11   •   Social Psychology and the Other Social Sciences   12   •   Social Psychology and Other Branches of Psychology   13

Topic Background: Social Psychology in the Classroom   8

The Shaping of Modern Social Psychology   14
Philosophers   14   •   Sociologists   16   •   Experimental Psychologists   17   •   Social Psychology and History   18

Explanations of Social Behavior   20
The Party   20   •   Learning Orientation   22   •   Cognitive Orientation   26   •   Symbolic Interaction Orientation   30   •   Biological Orientation   33

Topic Background: A View from the Top   28

TWO   RESEARCH METHODS IN SOCIAL PSYCHOLOGY   36

Prologue   37

Research in Social Psychology   39
Operationalization: From the Abstract to the Concrete   40   •   Relationships between Variables   44

The Experimental Approach   45
Laboratory Experiments   46   •   Validity of Laboratory Experiments   51   •   The Value of Laboratory Experiments   57   •   Field Experiments   57   •   Quasi-Experiments   58

Topic Background: Understanding Interactions   49
Research Highlight: Does Television Cause Crime?   59

The Descriptive Approach   62
Surveys   62   •   Observational Methods   66   •   The Approaches Compared   70   •   The Ethics of Research   71

Topic Background: The Correlation Coefficient   65
Research Highlight: Do It Yourself: Class Projects in Social Psychology   68
Applications: Program Evaluation   75

THREE   PERSONALITY CHARACTERISTICS AND SOCIAL BEHAVIOR _____ 80

Prologue   81
The Socialization Process   82
  Psychoanalytic Theories   83   •   Cognitive Developmental Theories   86   •   Social Learning
  Theories   88   •   Development of Self-concept   90
Research Highlight: Self-concept in Chimpanzees   91
Sex Differences in Social Behavior   93
Personality Characteristics and Social Behavior   99
  Trait Approach   99   •   Situationist Approach   102   •   Trait Rebuttal   104   •
  Interactionist Approach   109   •   A Concluding Comment   110
Topic Background: Predicting Behavior the Easy Way   101
Applications: Personality Characteristics and Heart Disease: A Modern Problem   112

FOUR   SOCIAL COGNITION _____ 120

Prologue   121
Forming Impressions of Other People   123
  Physical Appearance   123   •   Impression Formation   127   •   Social Schemata   131
Research Highlight: And She Bakes Cookies at Christmas Time   133
Attribution Processes   136
  Covariation Model   137   •   Correspondent Inferences Model   138   •   Causal Schemata
  Model   140   •   Accuracy of the Models   140   •   Attributions About Success
  and Failure   141
Accuracy of Social Cognitions   143
  Motivational Bias   143   •   Information-Processing Bias   145   •   Is It Human to Err?   151
Research Highlight: Reconstructing the Past   148
Applications: Social Cognitions and the Legal System   154

FIVE   SELF-PERCEPTION AND PRESENTATION _____ 164

Prologue   165
Self-perceptions   168
  Bem's Self-perception Theory   168   •   Schachter's Two-factor Theory of Emotions   172   •
  Self-awareness Theory   175
Research Highlight: Don't Be So Shy   173
Self-attributions   179
  Belief in Self-attributions   181   •   Reactions to Self-attributions   181   •   Effects of
  Individual Differences in Locus of Control on Self-attribution   184
Impression Management   188
  Tactics of Impression Management   193   •   Individual Differences in Impression
  Management   196
Topic Background: Impression Management among Airline Pilots: The Right Stuff   192
Applications: Self-perceptions and Health   201

SIX   INTERPERSONAL ATTRACTION: LIKING AND LOVING _____ 208

Prologue   209
Loneliness and Affiliation   212
  Loneliness   212   •   Affiliation   215   •   Development of Social Relationships   218

Friendship Formation   222
    Propinquity   222   •   Similarity   224   •   Reciprocity   228   •   Theories of Friendship
    Formation   228
Romantic Attraction   233
    Dating: Choosing a Romantic Partner   234   •   Passionate Love and Liking   237   •
    Marriage   243
Research Highlight: The Social Lives of Attractive and Unattractive People   236
Topic Background: Love and Marriage: The Latest Fad?   241
Applications: Sexual Attitudes and Behavior   248

SEVEN   AGGRESSION ──   256

Prologue   257
Theories of Human Aggression   261
    Instinctual Theories   261   •   Frustration-Aggression Hypothesis   266   •   Social Learning
    Theory   268
Topic Background: The XYY Syndrome   265
Specific Acts of Aggression   272
    Angry versus Instrumental Aggression   272   •   Instigators of Angry Aggression   273   •
    Situational and Environmental Influences on Angry Aggression   276   •
    Effects of Alcohol and Other Drugs on Angry Aggression   281
Topic Background: Are Guns a Menace? Ask Harry   278
Research Highlight: Temperature and Aggression: Beyond the Laboratory   282
Control of Aggression   285
    Reducing General Aggressive Tendencies   285   •   Controlling Specific Acts of Aggression   290
Applications: Sexual Assaults and Violence Against Women   297

EIGHT   PROSOCIAL BEHAVIOR ──   306

Prologue   307
Why Do People Help?   310
    Biological Viewpoint   311   •   Social Learning Viewpoint   313   •   Classical Conditioning
    and Empathic Responses   313   •   Reconciling the Biological and Social Learning
    Viewpoints   319
Research Highlight: Something Good about Television   316
When Will People Help?   320
    Stage 1: Physiological Arousal   322   •   Stage 2: Labeling the Arousal   323   •   Stage 3:
    Evaluating the Consequences of Helping   326
Topic Background: One Man's Best Friend   326
Individual Differences in Helping   333
    Temporary States and Helping   334   •   Personality Characteristics and Helping   336
Topic Background: A Full-time Helper   337
Applications: Heroes and Helpers   343

NINE   ATTITUDES AND BEHAVIOR ──────────────────────────────────────   352

Prologue   353
Nature of Attitudes   355
    Structure of Attitudes   355   •   Measurement of Attitudes   358

Topic Background: Randomized Response Technique   364
Formation and Function of Attitudes   368
   Formation of Attitudes 368 • Function of Attitudes 374
Research Highlight: Democracy for Sale   371
Research Highlight: Hearing What You Want to Hear   376
Attitudes and Behavior   379
   Theoretical Explanations 380 • Other-Variables Explanation 382 • Moderator-Variable
   Explanation 384 • Methodological Explanations 385
Applications: Prejudice: The Problem and a Remedy   388

TEN   ATTITUDE CHANGE _____ 402

Prologue   403
Persuasive Message   406
   Source Characteristics 407 • Message Characteristics 414 • Source versus
   Message 420
Research Highlight: The Illusive Sleeper Effect   413
Research Highlight: The More Persuadable Sex?   422
Active Participation   424
   Theory of Cognitive Dissonance 426 • Alternative Explanations of Cognitive Dissonance
   Effects 434 • Value Confrontation Procedure 438 • Attitude Change and Behavior
   Change 440
Research Highlight: Working Off the Pounds   430
Research Highlight: Too Much of a Good Thing?   436
Applications: Beyond the Laboratory: Influencing Attitudes and Behaviors   444

ELEVEN   SOCIAL INFLUENCE _____ 456

Prologue   457
Individual Influence   459
   Attributes 460 • Tactics of Social Influences 472
Topic Background: I'm Not Good to Kill That Man   461
Topic Background: The Boy Will Come to Nothing   467
Research Highlight: Door-in-the-Face Technique   476
Group Influence on the Individual   478
   Sherif's Research 478 • Asch's Research 479 • Conformity 481 •
   Nonconformity 487 • Individual Differences in Reactions to Group Pressure 489 •
   Deindividuation 492
Research Highlight: A Voice in the Wilderness   489
Applications: Medical Regimens: Just What the Doctor Ordered   497

TWELVE   INTERDEPENDENT SOCIAL BEHAVIOR _____ 508

Prologue   509
Social Exchange   513
   Social Exchange Theory 513 • Bargaining 516
Research Highlight: Consumer Protection   521
Conflict in Social Exchanges   524
   Zero-Sum Conflict 524 • Nonzero-Sum Conflict 524 • Reducing Interpersonal
   Conflict 527

Contents

Topic Background: And the Winner Is . . . 532

Justice and Fairness 535
Equity Theory 536 • The Allocation of Resources 545 • Procedural Justice 549

Topic Background: Arabia's New Solomon 537
Topic Background: Equity Theory at the Ballpark 543
Research Highlight: And Justice for All 545
Applications: Civil and International Conflict 551

THIRTEEN GROUP PROCESSES 564

Prologue 565
Nature of Groups 567
Group Formation 568 • Group Structure 569 • Group Processes 574

Topic Background: Measuring Group Interaction 575
Group Performance 577
Group Influences on the Individual 577 • Individual Versus Group
Performance 582 • Improving Group Performance 595

Research Highlight: Were the Beatles Social Loafers? 585
Topic Background: An Exercise in Group Problem Solving 590
Leadership 597
Trait Approach 598 • Leader Behavior Approach 599 • Contingency
Approach 601 • Social Interaction Approach 603

Applications: Decision Making in Actual Groups 606

FOURTEEN ENVIRONMENTAL INFLUENCES ON SOCIAL BEHAVIOR 616

Prologue 617
The Urban Environment 620
The Effects of Urban Living on Social Behavior 621 • Environmental Stressors and
Urban-Nonurban Differences 623 • In Defense of Urban Living 631

Research Highlight: Reducing Noise in Schools 629
The Presence of Others 633
Personal Space 633 • Territoriality 640 • Crowding 641

Research Highlight: Personal Space of Violent Prisoners 638
Topic Background: Home Sweet Home—Maybe 642
The Built Environment 650
Building Design and Social Relationships 651 • Interior Design and Social
Behavior 653 • Built Environments and Reactions to the Presence of Others 657 •
The Built Environment and Crowding 658

Topic Background: Public Housing: A Good Idea Gone Bad 661

References 668

Name Index I1

Subject Index I8

Preface

I had two goals as I wrote this book. The first was to make my writing as clear and straightforward as possible. Social behavior and its causes is a complex topic; the theories and research which address social behavior are rarely simple. But I felt that complex and difficult concepts could be presented in a comprehensible manner. At the same time, I did not hesitate to present more than one possible explanation of a social phenomenon or suggest that the solution to a social problem is simply not yet known. While I wanted readers to comprehend the material in this book, I did not want them to think that understanding human social behavior is an easy task. Indeed, I wanted them to get some sense of what so fascinates me and other social psychologists—the difficult search for answers to complex questions about social behavior.

The second goal was to make the material as interesting as possible. To achieve this end, I tried to avoid taking myself and the field of social psychology too seriously, and I made liberal use of examples based on both historical events and my own personal experiences; they illustrate the relevance of social psychology to people's lives, and some you actually may find entertaining.

FEATURES OF THIS BOOK

This book contains several features that I believe serve my goals. There is a "Prologue" to every chapter presenting a detailed description of a social psychological study. The prologues are intended to pique your interest in the chapter topic and to illustrate how research in social psychology is conducted. The criteria for selecting a particular study were either that it played a role in the development of an important research area, illustrated a basic aspect of social behavior, or raised questions that were addressed in the chapter. Instructors who have a laboratory component in their courses may wish to have their students actually conduct some of these studies.

To aid comprehension, all important terms are presented in **boldface** type and are accompanied by a brief definition. In most instances, this definition is presented in the margin of the text, next to the boldfaced term, so you do not need to refer to a dictionary. Terms that are not as important, but worthy of notice, are presented in *italics*. At the end of each major section, there is a brief summary. These are intended to give an overview of the material just covered and to provide a bridge to the next section of a chapter.

All the chapters, except the first and the last ones, conclude with a section on applications of the concepts presented in the chapter. Chapter one does not have an "Applications" section because it is an introductory chapter; chapter fourteen primarily concerns applications of basic social psychological concepts to environmental psychology, and it did not seem appropriate to divide it into a concepts and an applications section. In some instances, an applications section involves attempts to better understand an important aspect of people's daily lives; in other instances, it involves attempts to solve current social problems. Not all social psychological theory and research is directly applicable to real-world problems—much of social psychology involves basic, nonapplied research, but the applications sections were included to heighten awareness of social phenomena in the world and the potential of social psychology for understanding these phenomena.

I expect that many instructors will choose to present the material in a different order from that of the book, so I tried to make each chapter self-contained. Students without any prior courses in psychology should read chapters one and two before any of the other chapters—they cover the basics of theory and research—but other than that, the chapters can be presented in any order an instructor desires. In those instances where a discussion includes terms from an earlier chapter, the terms are either redefined or the reader is referred back to an earlier chapter. The book's length should make it appropriate for either a semester or quarter system.

I need to make brief mention of sexism in language and the way I attempted to deal with this issue. The problem concerns the gender of personal pronouns; when discussing the actions of an unspecified person, do you use a masculine or feminine pronoun? Some writers attempt to solve this problem by saying "he or she" and "him or her," but, personally, I find this practice distracts me from the material. My solution whenever possible was to avoid singular pronouns and use gender-neutral plurals ("they" and "them" rather than "his" and "her," for instance). When I could not avoid singular pronouns, I used masculine pronouns in the odd-numbered chapters and feminine pronouns in the even-numbered chapters. If, despite this, there is lingering sexism in the language used in this book, I apologize; it occurred without my awareness.

Writing this book has been a personal and professional learning experience for me, and I am grateful for that. It gave me a chance to rediscover social psychology from a student's perspective. The book gave me the opportunity to read those articles I'd just been "too busy" to read, to explore areas of contemporary social psychology with which I was not familiar, and to more fully investigate other areas. Writing this book caused me to remember why I decided to become a social psychologist twenty years ago. Social psychology is an exciting, important, vital field that is relevant to our day-to-day lives. I hope the book conveys the vitality of social psychology and my enthusiasm for the study of social behavior. If it does, then perhaps the time, effort, and occasional agony of the last two-and-a-half years have been worth it.

I would appreciate any comments you might have about the book. You can write to me c/o the Psychology Department at the University of South Florida, Tampa Florida, 33620.

ACKNOWLEDGMENTS

The writing of a textbook is a long, arduous process, requiring long periods of solitude; there were, however, many people who aided me in the completion of this project. The following people acknowledged have earned my sincere thanks.

First, thanks go to Gary Woodruff, who read the early drafts of the book and made extremely valuable suggestions on how the book could be modified and improved. I am grateful to Gary for his enthusiasm, intelligence, and perserverance. I also want to acknowledge the considerable contribution made by my Developmental Editor, Phyllis Mueller. Phyllis was involved in the book from the beginning and was central to its completion. It was a pleasure to work with her. Her good humor, reliability and professionalism made my job much easier. Peter Marshall played a smaller but nonetheless very important and valuable role in the completion of this book. I also want to thank Katherine Teel, the style editor who worked with me on the earlier versions of the book. She made the book more readable and understandable, but allowed me to say what I wanted to say. Deanna Quinn, the Production Editor, did an excellent job with the design of the book and directing the artwork in it.

The principal authors of chapters thirteen and fourteen, Paul Spector and Paul Greenbaum, were cooperative and professional collaborators. I think their chapters provide good evidence of their talents as writers and scholars. I am also grateful to Sandy McIntire and Barbara Grosslight for their work on the instructor's manual. I reviewed and edited all their work, but the quality of what they produced made my job very easy.

Jerry and Rose Lee Smith were instrumental in the production of the book. Jerry introduced me to the world of word processing and to my trusty Kaypro. Rose Lee took my handwritten pages and put them on the diskettes with diligence and skill. Later Peggy McPherson performed the same task, with the same level of competence. Jane Duke and Margo Berk did excellent jobs in proofreading the galleys and catching errors.

I am especially grateful to the people who reviewed earlier versions of this book. Almost without exception, their reviews helped me to improve the book. If the book has shortcomings, they occurred in spite of, not because of, the reviewers. While all of the reviewers have my thanks, I would like to give special notice to Frank Dane of Clemson University, whose careful, thoughtful, and constructive comments were invaluable in the completion of this book, and to Dudley Campbell, Los Angeles Pierce College, who also wrote the Student Study Guide. The reviewers are: William Ford, Bucks County Community College; Ron Rogers, University of Alabama; Charles Turner, University of Utah; Frederick Meeker, California Polytechnic State University—Pomona; Linda Marshall, North Texas State University; Frank Dane, Clemson University; Stephen Fugita, University of Akron; Dudley Campbell, Los Angeles Pierce College; James Phillips, Oklahoma State University; Jack Forthman, San Antonio College; Valerie Melburg, Westfield State College; Robert Cramer, California State University—San Bernadino; Gene Indenbaum, State University of New York—Farmingdale; Robert Massey, St. Peter's College; Frances Hill, University of Montana; John Berg, University of Mississippi; Melton Strozier, Houston Baptist University; Guillarne Leary, Southern University in New Orleans; and Mike Lupfer, Memphis State University.

Jim Davis, Milton Rokeach, and Bibb Laten'e have contributed greatly to my professional development. Jim and Milt were my masters and doctoral advisors, and I appreciate what they taught me and continue to teach me about social psychology through their research and writings. Bibb hosts the Nags Head conference series that I have attended for the last few years. I know this book benefitted from what I learned and the people I met at Nags Head. My colleagues and friends in Tampa, especially Max Dertke, Dave Eberly, Ellis Gesten, Jim Jenkins, Bill Kinder, Ed Levine, and Duane and Sydney Schultz, gave me support and encouragement throughout the long process, and I thank them for it.

My parents gave me love, support, a desire for knowledge of the world around me, and a sense of concern for the things I saw. I am grateful for these gifts . . . and for my brother and sister. My brother, Jerry, has been my role model. Watching him taught me to be intellectually curious and to continually question the quality of my own ideas, as well as those of others. I thank him for this and for being a caring, sensitive, and loving brother who was always there when I needed him. There were times when his support was the only thing I could be sure of.

My son, Charlie, had only a little to do with this book, but he has had much to do with making my life full. I couldn't ask for a better son and companion. He has my love and respect and I take great pride in the things he has accomplished and the kind of person he is. My wife, Kathy, has been my best friend, my exercise instructor, my teacher, and my confidant for the last four years. She suffered the role of an author's "widow" without complaint and was unfailing in her support of my efforts. She is the "Unit Director" of my heart, and she has and always will have my love. If there are times when my behavior communicates something else to Kathy or Charlie, I hope they will read this and be reminded of how I really feel.

Chapter One

An Introduction to Social Psychology

Prologue

Norman Triplett. (1897). The Dynamogenic Factors in Pacemaking and Competition. *American Journal of Psychology*, **9**, 507–533.

Background

In 1897, psychology was still in its infancy and the establishment of social psychology as a formal discipline was still several years away. Norman Triplett, a graduate student at the University of Indiana, published the first article describing a social psychological experiment. Evidently, Triplett was a great fan of bicycle racing and was interested in what influenced how fast a rider pedaled. He examined the records of over 2,000 "racing wheelmen, all ambitious to make records," and he found an interesting difference in their times. Racers who competed alone with the clock took over half a minute longer to complete a mile than did racers who had another rider pace them while they competed with the clock, or racers who competed with another rider only. Some theorists believed that this difference was due to the pacer or competitor reducing the rider's wind resistance. Triplett proposed a more psychological explanation. He believed that "the bodily presence of another rider [arouses] the competitive instinct . . . releasing or freeing nervous energy for him that he cannot himself release." Triplett conducted the following experiment to test his idea.

Hypothesis

Triplett hypothesized, or predicted, that people who raced alone against time would go slower than people who raced against a competitor.

Subjects

The subjects were 40 children ranging in age from 9 to 17.

Procedure

To eliminate the possibility that differences in wind resistance would be responsible for any speed differences he found, Triplett conducted a special kind of race. A small flag was attached to a fishing line, which was connected to a fishing reel. The children were to move the flag as fast as possible over a distance of about 20 yards by turning the handle of the fishing reel. After the children were given a few minutes to familiarize themselves with the equipment, the races began. Sometimes the children raced alone against the clock, and other times they competed with another child. Triplett recorded the time it took the children to complete the "course" under these two conditions.

Results

Triplett found that most of his subjects were faster when they were competing with someone than when they were alone. Since he had eliminated the physical effects of wind resistance, he concluded that a psychological factor was responsible for their improved performance.

Implications

By contemporary standards, Triplett's theory, methods, and means of analysis were rather primitive. But he had done something no one had ever done before: He had shown that a social psychological factor—the presence of another person—could affect people's behavior. This process is at the core of social psychology. This chapter describes what social psychology is and how it has grown and changed since the time of Norman Triplett.

With the possible exception of insects, human beings are the most social animals on earth. During a typical day, most college students spend from 65 to 75 percent of their waking time in the company of other people (Deaux, 1978; Latané and Bidwell, 1977). The behavior of others has an effect on people even when they are alone. The news on radio or television influences people's attitudes, and the commercials people see or hear influence the style of clothes they wear and the kinds of products they buy. People's beliefs about the world around them are influenced by social factors. For example, most criminologists think that economic problems, such as unemployment, force people to commit crimes. Television, however, portrays most criminals as either emotionally disturbed or pathologically greedy (Haney and Manzolati, 1981). When Haney and Manzolati asked about the causes of crime, people who watched a lot of television (four or more hours per day) were more likely than people who watched relatively little television to see mental problems and greed as the primary causes of crime.

Not only is much of what humans think and do influenced by other people, but humans dislike being alone and actively seek the company of other people. Studies that have investigated the effects of long periods of solitude have found that social isolation can result in extreme anxiety and, sometimes, hallucinations (Suedfeld, 1974). People need people. Humans devote large amounts of time, effort, and money to meeting other people, as is evidenced by the large number of people who frequent singles' bars or use dating services. People even use the latest technological advances—like the computer—to make social contacts. For example:

> Guy Barudin and Julie Lewin, students at Princeton University, began using the university's main computer last year to exchange electronic mail. "Every few days I'd write her a little note, and when I'd log on there would usually be a note for me," Mr. Barudin recalled. "It was just chit-chat."

Personal computers have become a phenomenon of interest to social psychologists because many college students are using their computers to make social contacts with other students.

Over time, the letters became increasingly personal, and the two students, who had been casual friends for several years, developed a romantic relationship.

"We had never really talked to each other," said Miss Lewin. "We started writing letters and then flirting in the letters. I don't think we could have done that in person. The computer bridged the gap." (*New York Times*, 1983)

Human social behavior is endless in its variations, as the following examples show.

The Daubs of La Luz, New Mexico, had tried for 12 years to have a baby. When the blessed event finally took place, they named their child Zip Ah Dee Doo Daub.

Shortly before Sally Ride became the first American woman to go into space, a *Time* magazine reporter asked her, "Do you expect to weep if there are problems on the mission?"

In California, a clothing manufacturer produced a line of custom-tailored tuxedos for infants. The prices began at $200.00. Satin diapers were extra.

A man in Canada, concerned about burglars breaking into his home, kept a pistol on the nightstand next to his bed. Very late one night, the phone—which was also on the nightstand—rang. In the darkness, the man mistook his gun for his telephone. He picked up the pistol, said hello into the handle, pulled the trigger, and blew a sizable hole in his skull.

A college professor and his family sold their $100,000 farm, their two new cars, and most of their other possessions. They used all the proceeds to purchase food for starving children in Haiti. They also promised that they would give 25 percent of their future earnings to the children.

In the winter of 1981, an Air Florida plane crashed into the Potomac River. When a rope was thrown from a rescue helicopter to one survivor floating in the icy water, he tied the rope to another victim of the crash, who was pulled to safety. He repeated this act twice. Finally, the man was unable to stay afloat, and he drowned.

This chapter introduces social psychology, the field that studies similar as well as less dramatic aspects of human social behavior. The first section describes the discipline as it is today; the second section describes the ideas and events that shaped contemporary social psychology. The third section presents the major theoretical orientations that social psychologists use to explain social behavior.

SOCIAL PSYCHOLOGY TODAY

Someone who was asked to describe the experiment that began this chapter might say that it demonstrated how the presence of other people—a social stimulus—affected the children's behaviors. This explanation comes quite close to the definition of social psychology used in this book.

Social Psychology Defined

No single definition of social psychology is accepted by everyone. Indeed, some psychologists have claimed that the field is so broad and varied it "defies meaningful definition" (Seidenberg and Snadowsky, 1976, p. 3). Still, a definition of social psychology is needed. In this book, **social psychology** is defined as the branch of psychology that engages in the "scientific study of individual behavior as a function of social stimuli" (Shaw and Costanzo, 1982, p. 4).

This definition states that social psychology is scientific, which means that it uses objective, systematic procedures to investigate the phenomena in which it is interested. Social psychologists may sit in the proverbial armchair and come up with ideas about social behavior, but their musings must be subjected to careful and extensive testing before they will be accepted by other members of the discipline.

The definition also states that social psychology concerns individual behavior. Most, if not all, social psychologists attempt to understand and explain the social behavior of individuals, not the social behavior of large groups or institutions. Thus, the *unit of analysis* in social psychology is the individual. This can be explained with an example of how a topic is studied. Social psychologists and other social scientists have recently become interested in the fear of crime among the elderly. (The elderly are less likely to be victimized by a criminal than are people in any other age group, yet

Advertisers use social stimuli such as the people pictured on these billboards to sell their products.

they are more afraid of crime [Foelker, 1985].) This topic could be approached in a number of different ways. Other social scientists might look at the percentages of young and old people who fear crime or they might examine geographic differences in the fear of crime among the elderly. Social psychologists would collect data from a large number of elderly individuals, put their responses together, and try to identify what causes members of this group to fear that they will be victims of crime.

Finally, the definition says that social psychology studies behaviors caused by **social stimuli.** These stimuli include the actions of other people and the things created by them; for example, a hug from your mother and a letter from her are both social stimuli.

Shaw and Costanzo (1982) proposed that research on social stimuli falls into three broad areas. The first is ''social influences on individual processes'' (p. 5). These phenomena are not necessarily social in nature, but

Social stimuli: things that either directly or indirectly involve other people.

are influenced by social stimuli. For example, reading this book is not a social activity. But it becomes a phenomenon of interest to social psychologists if you read this book because your parents won't pay your tuition if you get an F in the course, or if you stop reading it because your roommate demands that you go out for a drink instead. Social influences on individual processes have a long history in social psychology, dating back to Norman Triplett's study presented in the prologue.

The second class of phenomena identified by Shaw and Costanzo is "shared individual processes" (p. 5). These may not be directly caused by social stimuli, but are social in origin. The language you speak and the attitudes you hold are shared individual processes. Consider your attitude toward some inanimate object, say, the nuclear freeze. The nuclear freeze is not a social stimulus, but your attitudes toward it result from discussions with other people, the attitudes expressed by your parents, and other social stimuli.

Topic Background

Social Psychology in the Classroom

Learning about social behavior is an activity that need not be restricted to social psychologists and other social scientists. Many school teachers conduct lessons for their students on the causes and consequences of prejudice. The following "experiment" is based on an exercise developed about 20 years ago by Ms. Jane Eliot, a third-grade teacher. Ms. Eliot wanted to show her third graders how it felt to be the target of prejudice, so she divided her class into blue-eyed and brown-eyed children. She then implemented "laws" which made children in one group the victims of prejudice and discrimination. As this newspaper article suggests, similar procedures are quite effective in helping children learn about one aspect of social behavior, racial and ethnic prejudice.

He was a second-class citizen, separated from other children in school and scorned by his teachers and classmates.

As he passed a group of other students in the hall, one of them spat on him.

For the child, the segregation experiment at Sandy Springs Middle School had become too real. He tore off the armband marking him as different and refused to participate in the experiment further.

A teacher told him that he could remove his armband, but blacks, Jews and others enjoy no such luxury.

The incident was part of an experiment conducted at the overwhelmingly white school on the birthday of Dr. Martin Luther King Jr. to illustrate to the children what it's like to suffer discrimination.

Seventy-five students—blacks, whites, and Orientals—volunteered to wear white armbands marking them as Yooups (YOu are one of the grOUP) and undergo all manner of prejudice.

They entered through separate doors, drank from separate water fountains, used segregated restrooms, sat in the back of the class and occupied a segregated section of the cafeteria.

For students too young to remember legalized segregation, it was an eye-opening experience. As the day wore on, the Yooups' attitudes changed noticeably.

"They became quieter as if they wanted to be less noticeable, but their armbands made them noticeable," said David Rector, the teacher who devised the experiment. "They were scared. They began to ask more questions about the problem of being physically hurt or verbally abused."

Teachers were assigned roles of liberals, bigots or sympathizers who were afraid to get involved, according to Rector.

"It's terrible," said Brant Petree at the end of what had been a long day of wearing the armband. "Everybody makes fun of you. It makes you feel bad, hurts your feelings."

"It was real hard work," said student John Tyson. "Some of us aren't used to being told to sit in the back of the room, line up last, eat a different dessert, getting snapped at by the teachers. We should get extra credit for this." (Brown, 1985)

The final category is "group interaction" (p. 6). These phenomena occur when a person interacts with other people, and they occur only in response to the actions of other people. Your behavior during a late-night "bull session" with friends or in a committee meeting provides an example of this kind of behavior. Group interaction is the most purely social phenomenon of the three discussed.

What Social Psychologists Do

According to the latest statistics compiled by the American Psychological Association, approximately 4,500 men and women in North America identify themselves as social psychologists (American Psychological Association Directory, 1986). It is difficult to determine the exact number of social psychologists outside of North America, but the number is probably between 1,500 and 2,000.*

Social psychologists can be found in a wide variety of settings; however, most work at a college or university and engage primarily in two activities— teaching and research. Since most readers already probably have a good idea of what a teacher does, the focus here is on research. Research is an

---

*Some of the reasons for the large concentration of social psychologists in North America are discussed in the section on the history of social psychology, later in this chapter.

activity in which a person asks questions about the nature or characteristics of some phenomenon. Social psychologists engage in two kinds of research: basic and applied.

Basic Research

The defining characteristic of *basic research* is that it is motivated by a researcher's desire to learn more about a phenomenon of interest or to test a theory about the cause of the phenomenon. Researchers conduct basic research because they believe that it will contribute knowledge to their scientific discipline. Although basic research sometimes produces results that are of practical value, it should not be evaluated on this basis. Any science, be it social psychology or plant biology, needs to conduct basic research to continually increase its understanding of the phenomena it studies, or it will become stagnant and die.

Applied Research

In *applied research,* the primary motivation is to provide an answer or solution to a practical problem. Applied research sometimes contributes to a basic understanding of a phenomena or to the development of a theory, but this is not the major reason it is conducted, and it should not be evaluated on this criterion. Applied and basic research differ most in these contrasting purposes.

Applied research has a long history in social psychology, but over the last 10 to 15 years, social psychologists have become increasingly involved in it. Perhaps the major force behind this increase has been society's demand for social relevance in research. It has been argued that social psychologists should use their research expertise to address the needs and problems of contemporary society. Also, in recent years, the federal government has reduced the amount of money available for basic research and increased the funds for applied research. In addition, social psychologists have themselves realized the need to address practical problems in research.

Many social psychologists conduct both applied and basic research. For example, yesterday I spent most of the day designing a study to investigate individual differences in social behavior. Tomorrow I will spend most of my time designing a study to investigate people's ability to identify different company trademarks. The impetus for the first activity was my desire to test a specific theory about the causes of helping behavior. The impetus for the second activity was a lawyer's request that I provide expert witness testimony in a forthcoming lawsuit.

Presently, a large number of social psychologists engage in a specific kind of applied research called evaluation research, or **program evaluation.** The social psychologist is asked to scientifically determine if a program (for example, Head Start) works (Kidder, 1981). The techniques the evaluator uses to answer these questions are quite similar to those used to answer basic research questions. The results of evaluation research, however, are used quite differently. The administrators of the program usually use them

Program evaluation: a type of applied research in which the researcher determines if a program is attaining its stated goals.

to modify the way in which the program operates. In some instances, government officials use the results to decide whether or not they will continue to provide funds for a program.

Where Social Psychologists Work

Most social psychologists are employed in psychology departments at colleges or universities, but they can also be found in many other settings. I recently conducted an informal survey and found the following: Within universities, social psychologists are in the departments of aging, communication, criminal justice, home economics, marketing, management, political science, social work, and sociology, and in the schools of architecture, law, and medicine. Outside of universities, social psychologists can be found in the Food and Drug Administration; the National Bureau of Standards; the departments of Education, Labor, and Defense; insurance companies; airlines; manufacturing companies; public opinion polling firms; advertising agencies; hospitals; and private psychiatric institutes. And this is only a partial listing. Perhaps the major reason social psychologists work in so many different settings is that their knowledge and skills can be used in a variety of different areas. For example, a social psychologist with expertise in interpersonal attraction might be used by a department of aging to teach about and do research on social relationships between elderly people and their children. (See chapter six.) Similarly, a social psychologist with expertise in the causes of racial and ethnic prejudice might be used by the Department of Education to work out a school integration plan. (See chapter nine.)

How Social Psychologists are Trained

Despite the diversity of settings in which social psychologists work and the variety of activities in which they engage, they do share one characteristic—the training they receive. Most social psychologists have earned a doctorate, or Ph.D., in psychology. A doctorate is a postgraduate degree which typically takes five to seven years to earn. The Ph.D. degree indicates that a social psychologist has demonstrated the ability to conduct objective, scientific research. Social psychology graduate students must successfully complete advanced courses in all areas of psychology, but they concentrate on courses on different aspects of social psychology and ways of doing research on social stimuli. They must also complete an original piece of research, a doctoral dissertation, which is formally evaluated by their professors. This dissertation may be the only formal research requirement for social psychology graduate students, but research is stressed continually throughout their graduate education. Most students have participated in several research projects before they complete their training. The emphasis placed on research in their graduate training partially explains why social psychologists place such a high value on research and spend so much of their time doing it.

Social Psychology and the Other Social Sciences

Given the diversity of the phenomena social psychologists study and the wide range of places in which they are employed, it may not be clear how social psychology differs from other social sciences. The three other social sciences most similar to social psychology are anthropology, political science, and sociology. In what ways does social psychology differ from these?

This is not a simple question to answer. In practice, there is often little difference between the activities of social psychologists and the activities of anthropologists, political scientists, and sociologists. I have collaborated with people from all three disciplines and have found that our research interests were similar and that we often used similar means to investigate the phenomena of interest. Further, social psychology has always drawn heavily from these three disciplines and they have had a tremendous influence on the development and shaping of present-day social psychology. Contemporary researchers in social psychology often look to the other social sciences for a better understanding of the phenomena they study. For example, a social psychologist who is interested in attitude change might use the work of political scientists on how political attitudes are changed.

The major difference between social psychology and these other disciplines is in their focuses of interest. Social psychology concentrates on the behavior of the individual in response to social stimuli; the other disciplines study either groups of individuals or institutions (Shaw and Costanzo, 1982). For example, suppose an anthropologist, a political scientist, a sociologist, and a social psychologist are all interested in aggression among teenagers. The anthropologist's focus of interest is typically on an entire culture, so he might study the techniques different cultures use to cope with aggression among their adolescents. The political scientist concentrates on political systems and institutions within a culture; thus, he might study the legislation passed to deal with adolescent aggression. The sociologist's level of analysis, or focus of interest, is typically on groups within a culture, so he might look at the difference between the incidences of violent crimes among black teenagers and among white teenagers. The social psychologist, however, would focus on the factors which might cause aggression in the typical adolescent.

A secondary difference between the disciplines is in the research procedures they use. Social psychologists tend to use an experimental approach to the study of social behavior, as Triplett did in the experiment in the prologue. Triplett systematically manipulated or changed the factor of interest, whether the children competed with the clock or with another child. Scientists in the other disciplines tend to use a descriptive approach—instead of changing a phenomenon of interest, they study and describe it as it presently exists. Both approaches are valid ways to gain an understanding of social behavior.

Social Psychology and Other Branches of Psychology

Social psychology is related to other fields of psychology in a number of ways. First, a wide variety of psychologists often use social psychological theory and research to better understand the nonsocial phenomena they study. For example, a developmental psychologist who is interested in language acquisition may turn to the social psychological literature on parent-child interactions. A clinical psychologist who is interested in what makes group psychotherapy effective may turn to the social psychological literature on group influences on the individual. An industrial/organizational psychologist who is interested in how job satisfaction affects worker productivity may turn to the social psychological literature on attitudes and behavior.

Second, a number of social psychologists have interests that cut across different branches of psychology. For example, some of the research presented in chapter three was conducted by developmental social psychologists interested in the social aspects of human sex role development. Some social psychologists study social factors that contribute to the development of depression and other mental problems. And some social psychologists study social factors in industrial settings.

Not only does social psychology give to the other branches of psychology, but it receives as well. Much of the current theory and research on how people process information about social events is based on experimental psychologists' work on how humans process complex information from their environment. Social psychological theories of attitude acquisition, aggression, and helping draw heavily from the work of experimental psychologists interested in learning. And many of the personality variables that social psychologists use in their research were first studied by clinical and developmental psychologists.

So, while the primary focus of interest in social psychology—social stimuli—distinguishes it from other branches of psychology, the overlap between the branches is considerable. Social psychologists help other psychologists to understand the phenomena they study, and are helped by them.

SUMMARY

Social psychology is a branch of psychology that attempts to scientifically study individuals' responses to social stimuli. The topics studied by social psychologists are extremely diverse, ranging from individual differences in social behavior to the ways large organizations operate. One characteristic most social psychologists share is an interest in research. The two kinds of research they conduct are basic and applied. The goal of basic research is to test a theory or to acquire knowledge in the field; the goal of applied research is to find a solution to a practical problem. Because of the diversity of their interests, social psychologists can be found in a wide range of university departments and in an even wider range of nonacademic settings. To become a social psychologist, a student completes five to seven years of graduate study, which typically leads to the Ph.D. degree. The heavy emphasis on research in social psychologists' education usually leads them, irrespective of where they work, to continue to do research after they obtain their doctorates.

Social psychology shares an interest in social behavior with anthropology, political science, and sociology. But whereas these other disciplines focus their interest on large groups of people, social psychology focuses on the individual. Since so much of human behavior is social in character, social psychology overlaps a great deal with other branches of psychology. The areas with which it has most in common are clinical, developmental, experimental, and industrial/organizational psychology. Contemporary social psychology is a broad field which uses scientific methods to gain a basic understanding of social behavior and to seek solutions for practical problems.

THE SHAPING OF MODERN SOCIAL PSYCHOLOGY

The previous section gave an overview of contemporary social psychology. This section discusses the factors that have shaped social psychology into its present form. Just as we can often better understand the behavior of adults if we know something about their childhood and their parents, so we can better understand contemporary social psychology if we know about its past. For example, as you read this book, you may notice the tremendous emphasis social psychologists put on using laboratory experiments to study and understand social behavior; to understand why this is so, it is necessary to look at the roots of modern social psychology.

Social psychology as a formal discipline is less than 80 years old; however, its origins go back at least 2,000 years (Allport, 1968; Sahakian, 1974). Many different people were involved in the history of social psychology, but all shared an interest in understanding and explaining human social behavior. Three disciplines appear to have contributed the most to the development of social psychology: philosophy, sociology, and experimental psychology. In addition, certain historical events helped to shape social psychology.

Philosophers

There is little question that modern social psychology has its roots in philosophy. As Gordon Allport pointed out, until 125 years ago "all social psychologists were . . . philosophers and many philosophers were social psychologists" (1968, 5). The earliest philosophical writings about social behavior came from Aristotle and Plato. Even 2,400 years ago, people disagreed about the causes of social behavior. Plato believed that biological factors (instincts, inherited characteristics) were responsible for social behavior, while Aristotle believed that environmental factors (how people are brought up, what culture they live in) were responsible for the same behavior. This "nature versus nuture" controversy still persists.

Until the eighteenth or nineteenth century, most philosophers concerned with social behavior took a biological approach to it. One famous writer of the sixteenth century, Nicolo Machiavelli (1469–1527), saw humans as naturally deceitful, treacherous, and murderous (Sahakian, 1974). Consequently, in his book *The Prince*, Machiavelli advised the rulers of Italy to use any means at their disposal to obtain power. Religious, moral values might get someone into heaven, he thought, but they were not what determined social behavior.

In the eighteenth and nineteenth centuries, two changes occured in philosophers' writings about social behavior. The first was the idea that a single underlying mechanism may be responsible for all social behavior. The second was the emergence of theories proposing that social behavior is almost entirely learned.

Hedonism

In the late 1700s, Jeremy Bentham (1748–1832), an English philosopher, proposed that human behavior is motivated and controlled by **hedonism,** and that social behavior can be explained by the selfish self-interests of humans. This idea had been proposed long before Bentham, but he first suggested it as an explanation for social behavior.

Hedonism: the desire to achieve pleasure and avoid pain.

Although Bentham's proposal is almost 200 years old, it finds expression in contemporary social psychology. Several of the learning theories presented in the following pages are based on the idea that social behavior is controlled by the rewards and punishments that a person receives. In many respects, Bentham's ideas were the precursors of B. F. Skinner's behavioristic approach to human behavior, and they appear to have strongly influenced Freud's theories of human behavior (Schultz, 1981).

Bentham's ideas about hedonism also reflect the political climate that prevailed at the time they were proposed. Late-eighteenth-century England was in the midst of the Industrial Revolution. One of the less pleasant aspects of the Industrial Revolution was the wholesale exploitation of unskilled workers. Proponents of hedonism argued that there was nothing wrong with employees exploiting the workers because they were doing this to maximize their own pleasure by accumulating wealth. Many of those who adopted Bentham's ideas argued that this was the "natural order" of things. The compatibility of Bentham's theory of social behavior and the events of the time illustrates that theories of social behavior are often influenced by the society in which a scientist lives (Allport, 1968).

Imitation

About 100 years after Bentham, Gabriel Tarde (1843–1904), a philosopher and criminologist, put forth the principle of imitation. As the result of his work in criminology, Tarde came to the conclusion that criminal behavior is primarily the product of suggestion and *imitation:* People become criminals because they have been influenced by other criminals (Sahakian, 1974). Tarde soon extended his analysis to all social behavior. According

The concept of imitation proposed by Gabriel Tarde over 100 years ago may explain recent social phenomena such as the Cabbage Patch Doll craze.

to him, imitation is the "elementary social phenomenon" (1899, 56). Tarde believed that most of human social behavior is acquired by observing others and subsequently imitating their behavior. Tarde's ideas shifted the study of human behavior away from a focus on a biological cause and the simple desire to achieve pleasure and avoid pain—toward social causes.

Modern-day remnants of Tarde's ideas surface several times in this book. Current theories of observational learning propose ideas very close to those of Tarde. Also, the research on conformity and social influence appears to address some of the same issues as Tarde did 100 years ago. (See chapter eleven.)

Sociologists

It is dangerous to credit any one individual with the founding of a science, but most historians attribute the founding of sociology to August Comte (1798–1857). Comte's contribution to social psychology was his belief that one could scientifically study social phenomena. He believed that the study of social behavior was the "true final science" (Allport, 1968). The field Comte founded made significant contributions to contemporary social psychology.

Today, social psychology and sociology are two different fields. At the turn of the century, however, most of the people interested in social behavior were sociologists. In fact, although a psychologist conducted the first social psychological experiment, one of the first two textbooks in social psychology was written by a sociologist (Ross, 1908). Sociologists like Gustav Le Bon, Emile Durkheim, and Max Weber all made significant contributions to social psychology.

The greatest impact on contemporary social psychology may have come from the sociologist George Herbert Mead and his colleagues at the University of Chicago. Mead's primary contribution was to emphasize that one cannot understand individuals without understanding their social environment. These ideas stimulated many psychologists and sociologists to systematically study how social variables influence human behavior. Mead died over fifty years ago, but his theories are still used to explain social behavior.

Experimental Psychologists

By the middle of the twentieth century, social psychology had changed in two related ways. First, whereas most earlier writings about social behavior had come from Europe, now social psychology became centered in the United States. Second, there was a shift in the manner in which social behavior was investigated. In the eighteenth and nineteenth centuries, few people conducted experiments on social phenomena; after the 1950s, the experiment became the primary means of investigation. Before 1950, less than 30 percent of the articles published in the leading social psychological journal were based on experiments; in 1979, the figure was almost 90 percent (Higbee, Millard, and Folkman, 1982).

Most historians credit Norman Triplett, the author of the experiment in the prologue, with the first true social psychological experiment.* However, Triplett's work did not immediately lead to a rash of experimental research on social behavior. It was not until the 1930s that experiments became common among social psychologists in the United States. There are number of reasons for the eventual popularity of the experiment, including the development of objective measures, the positivist philosphy, and Gestalt psychology.

Development of Objective Measures

Conducting a valid experiment requires the objective measurement of whatever the researcher is studying. Until the 1920s, most psychologists believed that social phenomena could not be objectively measured. They argued, for example, that scientists could not conduct experiments on attitudes because attitudes could not be directly observed or measured. In the 1920s and 1930s, psychologists developed techniques that enabled them to accurately and objectively measure phenomena such as attitudes or interpersonal attraction. Social psychology could then use this technology to conduct experiments.

Positivist Philosophy

The experimental approach to the study of human behavior had always been popular among American psychologists (Schultz, 1981), but in the 1920s and 1930s, American psychology came increasingly under the influence of a philosophy of science called **positivism.** It was argued that theories in a science must be proven or disproven by empirical findings be-

Positivism (or empiricism): the argument that for a science to be valid it must be based on observable, objective findings rather than on speculations.

---

*Some argue that the first social psychological experiment was one done on hypnosis by James Braid in 1842 (Murphy, Murphy, and Newcomb, 1937).

cause science is based on objective, empirical (observable) findings from experiments. This philosophy was developed by people interested in sciences such as physics and chemistry. But it was soon accepted by people in the social sciences. Thus, if social psychology was to be a "true" science, like physics and chemistry, it had to be based on empirical findings from experiments.

Gestalt Psychology

Today, most people associate the word *gestalt* with a kind of psychotherapy. Originally it was used to describe a branch of experimental psychology that studied perception. Gestalt psychology had its origins in Germany. Most of its leaders were professors at German universities, and many were Jewish. When Hitler came to power in the 1930s and they were forced to flee their homeland, many came to the United States. Possibly because of what they had experienced in Germany, a number of the gestaltists became interested in social psychology. They approached the study of social behavior in the same manner as they had approached the study of perception—by conducting experiments. As the influence of the gestaltists in social psychology grew, so did the popularity of the experimental approach to the study of social behavior.

Social Psychology and History

No science exists independently of the world around it, and this is especially true of social psychology. Mundane, everyday events influence the theories and topics that social psychologists study. Basically, two historical events appear to have influenced contemporary social psychology more than any others: World War II and the student activism in the 1960s and 1970s.

World War II

Hitler's campaign against Jews resulted in large numbers of gifted European psychologists immigrating to the United States and turning their attention to social behavior. The war also had other effects on social psychology. During World War II, the United States government first began spending large amounts of money for social psychological research. The two specific topics that attracted the most interest were attitudes and group behavior. The government supported research on attitudes because it had a need to keep civilians' morale high in the face of war-caused hardships (shortages of meat and other foods). It also had a need to keep soldiers' morale high to reduce high desertion rates and to overcome resistance to the integration of black soldiers and white soldiers into the same units (Cartwright, 1979). The military's interest in group behavior came from its desire to improve its ability to find and train leaders (officers) and to help combat units to function more efficiently.

Another effect of the Second World War was to increase the amount of research on ethnic and racial prejudice. A major social psychological study of the late 1940s was an attempt to identify the personality characteristics of a person who would be sympathetic to nazi ideology (Adorno, Frenkel-Brunswick, Levinson, and Sanford, 1950). The impetus for this research was concern over whether a nazilike campaign of anti-semitism could occur in the United States.

In summary, the Second World War produced a migration of social psychologists to North America, caused people to become more aware of the effects of social factors on human behavior, and provided dramatic illustrations of the need to understand the social causes of human behavior.

Student Activism of the 1960s and 1970s

Another major historical event that influenced social psychology was the student activism of the late 1960s and early 1970s. This had two effects on social psychology. First, while concern with social problems has a long history in social psychology, it was in the late 1960s that a large percentage of social psychologists began to specifically address social problems. Social psychologists (many of whom were involved in civil rights campaigns and antiwar activities) began to question the relevance of their work to the problems they saw in the world around them, and they greatly increased the amount of applied, or "action," research they conducted. Second, some of the political movements that became prominent in the 1960s raised social psychologists' awareness of social phenomena they had previously ignored. For example, I went to graduate school in the late 1960s. I cannot recall reading one study on sexism or sex role stereotyping. Certainly these phenomena existed at that time, but until the feminist movement made people aware of the problems women confront in contemporary society, there was little interest in this issue among social psychologists, especially

The political activism of the late 1960s and early 1970s caused some social psychologists to become more interested in real world problems and made others aware of social phenomena which previously had been ignored.

male social psychologists. Today, several journals are devoted almost solely to studies of sexism and sex role stereotyping. The political activism of the '60s and early '70s continues to influence contemporary social psychology.

The impact of historical events on contemporary social psychology provides another illustration of the point that science in general, and a science like social psychology in particular, does not exist in a vacuum. The events that occur outside of the laboratory may have a significant positive or negative effect on the type of research that is conducted.

SUMMARY

Social psychology is a young science—it began less than 80 years ago— but it has a long history. People have been thinking and writing about social behavior for a least 2,500 years. Contemporary social psychology owes debts to many disciplines, but to three in particular: philosophy, sociology, and experimental psychology. The philosophers were the first to write about social behavior and the first to propose theories about the causes of social phenomena. Their concepts of hedonism and imitation appear to have had the greatest influence on contemporary social psychology. The sociologists stressed the importance of social stimuli as determinants of social behavior and aroused interest in how these social stimuli might be systematically studied. The experimental psychologists provided social psychologists with a methodology to study social behavior—the experiment. While some may argue that contemporary social psychology relies too heavily on experiments, the fact remains that most contemporary social psychologists use experiments to investigate social phenomena.

Certain historical events have also shaped contemporary social psychology. World War II resulted in large amounts of governmental support for social psychological research. The political activism that swept college campuses in the 1960s resulted in an increased interest in applied, socially relevant research and in social phenomena, which had largely been ignored by social psychologists.

EXPLANATIONS OF SOCIAL BEHAVIOR

The goal of contemporary social psychology is to explain, understand, and predict social behavior. Social psychologists rely on theory and empirical research to achieve this goal. This section introduces explanations of social behavior which are based on four general theoretical orientations: learning, cognitive, symbolic interactionism, and biological. To do this, I want to take you to a party.

The Party

It's Saturday night and a classmate has invited you to a large, informal party. You put on your jeans and a flowered shirt and head out. When you arrive, you discover you don't know many of the people there, so you decide to find a seat and watch what is going on. As you move toward a chair, a large man runs into you. "Get out of my way," he yells. "I've got to get a drink, now." You carefully move to the nearest corner and sit down.

The first thing that catches your eye is a group of males gathered around an extremely attractive female. This amuses you because you know her, and while she is beautiful, what little personality she has is quite unpleasant. An Hispanic man asks her if she would like a sip of his beer. "Are you kidding?" she replies. "I don't drink from the same cup as a wetback." Poor guy that ends up with her, you think.

Next you notice a man and a woman standing off to the side of the dance floor. Their nonverbal behavior fascinates you. They pretend they are not aware of one another, but clearly they are: He moves toward her, but when she looks at him he backs away; she looks at him, but when he notices this she pretends she is looking at a couple next to him.

Your attention is distracted by some loud voices and laughing. You see a man telling a story that has everyone in stitches. You think to yourself, jeez, I wish I could be that at ease at a party.

Over at the door, a disabled person has just entered in a wheelchair. His chair gets caught in the leg of a table. You expect someone to help him, but the student struggles alone for several minutes and frees himself.

Just then a fight breaks out near the refreshment table. Two men are yelling at one another. One of them shouts, "I don't have to take that crap from you," and throws beer on the other. This doesn't surprise you because you know the man and he is always getting into arguments.

All of a sudden, someone taps on your shoulder. It's the host. He's wearing a three-piece suit and acting in a very formal manner. This surprises you since he usually wears jeans and a T-shirt. He welcomes you to the party and tells you the music is about to begin. He also says that he is quite upset by the unruly behavior of the other guests. This too surprises you; at your last party, he got drunk and started a fight.

The music starts and couples begin to dance. You watch one person teaching another the latest dance step for a few minutes. First, the "teacher" performs the step; the "student" watches and attempts to imitate what he has seen.

Then something else catches your attention. It is two men dancing together. Some people seem oblivious to this, others turn away—but several men standing on the edge of the dance floor begin to laugh and hoot at the two male dancers.

Finally, you decide to stop watching the party and become a part of it. However, being a good social psychologist, you make mental notes of the things you have seen.

Pick one of the social behaviors you have seen and try to explain it. Why did the men cluster around the attractive but unpleasant woman? What factors controlled the behavior of the man and the woman who kept moving toward and away from one another? Why didn't anyone help the disabled person? What caused the fight? How can you account for the

Hypotheses: statements about the expected relationship between two or more things.

host's unusual behavior? Why did people react as they did to the two men who danced together? Such questioning is the first task that confronts social psychologists. The next step in explaining social behavior is to construct a theory.

A theory is a set of statements about the nature of a phenomenon or set of phenomena. These statements lead to **hypotheses** about the phenomena. For example, if you believe that the men clustered around the woman because of her physical appearance, you have made a hypothesis: Physical attractiveness leads to social popularity. Just as this hypothesis was based on something you observed, theories are based on observable facts. In addition, they are based on ideas that go beyond the facts. Sometimes these ideas are the results of "hunches" a scientist has, but more often they result from a general theoretical orientation. Most of the theories in this book began with the observation of some social phenomenon, but general theoretical orientations like those described in this section provide the framework for developing a full-fledged theory.

Learning Orientation

The learning orientation proposes that social behaviors are acquired in the same manner as any other behaviors; they are learned. Further, it proposes that the same factors responsible for the learning of a behavior determine whether or not people will engage in that behavior. For example, learning theorists would argue that children learn to be helpful, at least in part, because they are rewarded for helping, and that they engage in helping when it is rewarding to do so. Learning theorists propose several different mechanisms whereby learning takes place, including classical conditioning, instrumental conditioning, drive reduction, and observational learning.

Classical Conditioning

The *classical conditioning* process was first identified by the Russian scientist Ivan Pavlov. He proposed that certain stimuli cause automatic or unlearned responses when they are presented to a living thing. For example, when the stimulus food is presented to a dog, the dog automatically salivates. No learning or conditioning is needed for this to happen because food is an *unconditioned* (unconditional) *stimulus* and salivation is an *unconditioned* (unconditional) *response*. If some other stimulus (a light, for instance) is presented just before the food several times, the dog will begin to salivate at the sight of the light—the dog will learn to associate the light with the food. The light becomes a *conditioned stimulus* (a learned stimulus), and the salivation in response to the light is called the *conditioned response* (learned response).

The classical conditioning of human social behaviors involves processes more complex than those just described. One process is called *higher order conditioning*. In it, a previously conditioned stimulus is used to condition a person to some new stimulus. For example, the word *bad* initially has no meaning to a child. But if parents repeatedly pair the word with a negative event, such as slapping the child's hand, the child will soon develop a

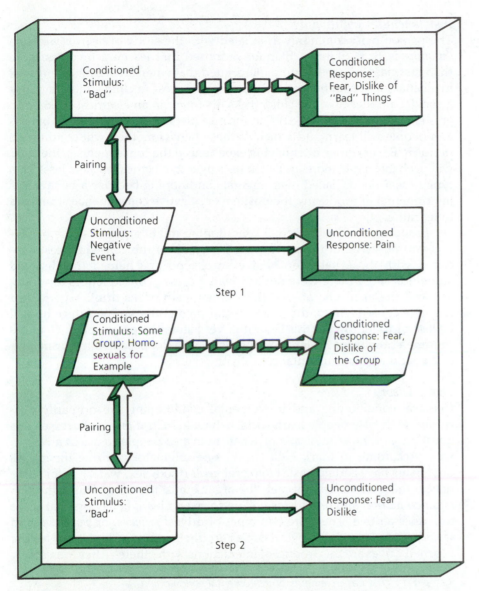

Figure 1-1. *How higher order classical conditioning can produce negative feelings toward members of some group.*

negative reaction to the word *bad*. (See figure 1-1.) Staats and Staats (1958) demonstrated that if words such as *bad* are paired with people's names or nationalities, subjects will develop negative feelings toward these names or nationalities.

This may explain one thing you observed at the party. For many of the party goers, the concept of homosexuality and homosexual activities may have been paired with negative adjectives, such as *bad, dirty,* or *sinful.* Thus, their reactions to the two males dancing together was negative.

Instrumental Conditioning

The person most commonly associated with the study of *instrumental conditioning* is B. F. Skinner. Skinner proposed that learning involves more than just classical conditioning. He argued that when an organism engages in a behavior, it experiences certain consequences—a child smiles and gets a cookie; another time the child sticks his finger in an electrical socket and gets shocked. (See table 1-1.) These consequences determine what behaviors people will learn and which of these behaviors they will continue to perform. For example, after having experienced the consequences, the child will probably smile more and stick his finger in electrical sockets less. This type of learning is called instrumental conditioning because a behavior is instrumental in producing the positive or negative consequences that lead to learning.

Proponents of instrumental conditioning might argue that the behaviors you observed at the party were the result of the consequences associated with those behaviors. For example, no one helped the disabled student because there were not adequate positive consequences for doing so. And the man who offered the woman a sip of his drink experienced negative consequences; thus, one would predict that in the future he will be less pleasant toward this beautiful, yet bigoted, woman. Later chapters present a number of explanations of social behavior based on the principles of classical and instrumental conditioning.

Drive Theory

Classical conditioning and instrumental conditioning are primarily concerned with how people learn social behaviors. *Drive theory* addresses this question as well as the issue of what motivates people to act in a certain way. According to Clark Hull (1943), one originator of drive theory, all organisms have certain basic biological *needs* (food, sex, water). If for some reason these needs are not met, the organism is activated. This activation is called a *drive*, and organisms will perform and learn behaviors that serve to reduce a drive. There are two types of drives: *primary*, or *biological*, and *secondary*, or *learned*. Biological drives are the product of biological needs. Learned drives are the product of interactions with others—they are usually

Table 1-1. The basic elements of instrumental conditioning

Step 1: Person engages in some behavior
      Examples
a)   A child smiles
b)   A man offers a woman a drink

Step 2: The behavior produces some consequence
      Examples
a)   The parent gives the child a cookie
b)   The woman insults the man

Step 3: The consequence affects future behavior
      Examples
a)   The child smiles more often
b)   The man interacts with the woman less often.

Children and adults learn many behaviors through the observation of other people.

social in character and involve behavior in a social context. Examples of secondary, or learned, drives are drives for wealth and for social acceptance. Just as people will perform and learn behaviors that reduce biological (unlearned) drives, so will they perform and learn behaviors that reduce learned drives.

Recall the person at the party who was looking for a drink and almost knocked you over. His behavior can be viewed as an attempt to reduce his thirst drive. Another event at the party that can be explained by drive theory is the fight. According to drive theory, being attacked or insulted creates an aggressive drive in people, and aggression occurs because it serves to reduce this drive. (See chapter seven for a more detailed explanation of aggression.)

Observational Learning
The three learning processes examined thus far implicitly assume humans learn social behaviors only through their own direct experiences. They ignore the possibility that humans might learn from watching the behaviors of others. Proponents of *observational learning,* such as Albert Bandura and Richard Walters (1963), proposed that humans learn many social behaviors by observing the actions of other people. (This idea is similar to Tarde's idea of imitation, discussed earlier). Thus, the actions of people's parents, teachers, and friends provide examples of social behaviors which people imitate and perform.

Observational learning is no different from the dance lesson at the party. In practice, however, it is usually a more subtle process which may have long-lasting effects on a person's social behavior. Bandura and Walters (1963) have shown that children can learn to be aggressive by simply observing aggressive behavior in others (called models). So, for example, the aggressive behavior of the two men who were fighting and yelling at the party may have been due, at least in part, to past exposure to aggressive models. Theories of how humans become socialized place considerable importance on observational learning. (See chapter three.)

Before proceeding to the next orientation, a brief digression is in order. Do not be concerned that different theories are used to explain the same behavior. The goal here is to explain the various orientations to social behavior. At this point, the question of which one is "better" or "more correct" is irrelevant. Later in the book, the relative abilities of these orientations to explain social behavior are considered.

Cognitive Orientation

The four learning theories share a very significant characteristic: They focus on the stimuli that cause people to act and the responses people make, and they place relatively little emphasis on what happens inside the individual (Shaw and Costanzo, 1982). A pure learning theory orientation to social behavior leads to the conclusion that things such as ideas, feelings, and beliefs are irrelevant to the understanding of social behavior. It is this position that psychologists with a cognitive orientation object to strongly. They argue that to understand and explain social behavior, social psychologists must learn about the **cognitions** people hold and examine how people organize, structure, and use the cognitions. Accordingly, cognitive psychologists focus on what goes on inside the person. They do not deny that learning processes affect social behavior or that external stimuli help determine social behavior, but they feel that the key to understanding social behavior lies in an understanding of how people perceive and process these stimuli.

The basic difference between cognitive orientations and learning orientations to social behavior has been stated by Fritz Heider. He contrasted his viewpoint with that of B. F. Skinner (a proponent of instrumental conditioning):

> Skinner treats human beings as guided and determined by habit. I think that in part humans are creatures of habit, but there is another [more important] part. Humans are also creatures of reason and thinking. (Cited in Evans, 1980, p. 17)

It has been argued that social psychology is the most cognitively oriented of all the areas of psychology (Schultz, 1981). The influence of cognitive theory on social psychology is largely attributable to the Gestalt psychologists who emigrated from Germany to the United States in the 1930s.

Gestalt Psychology

Gestalt psychology began as a protest movement against a school of thought in early psychology. Many early psychologists believed that conscious experience could be best understood by breaking it down into its

Cognitions: beliefs, ideas, or thoughts that people have about themselves and the world around them.

Figure 1-2.   An example of the Gestalt principle of proximity; things that are close together in time or space tend to be perceived together. Thus the circles are seen as three columns rather than one large collection.
Source: Schultz (1981).

component parts, just as the properties of a chemical compound are understood by breaking it down into its component chemicals. The gestaltists argued, however, that the "whole is different than the sum of its parts," and that conscious experience is more than the simple sum of the things which make it up (Schultz, 1981). The reason why the whole is different, according to the gestaltists, is because humans order and organize the stimuli they receive from the outside world. For example, look at figure 1-2. What do you see?

In all probability, you see three columns of circles rather than a large collection of circles. You see columns because you perceive things that are close together in space as belonging together; you organize and give meaning to such stimuli. The key concept here is organization. People organize the stimuli they receive so that they are meaningful.

When the gestaltists came to America, they applied the same principles they had used in their studies of perception to their studies of social behavior. Fritz Heider (1958), an influential Gestalt psychologist, proposed that humans organize and give meaning to their social world, and that the manner in which they organize their cognitions about social stimuli, in turn, affects their social behavior. The gestaltists focused their attention on the processes people use to do this. For example, if Heider were looking at the party, he would probably be interested in why you assumed that the person telling the jokes was confident and self-assured; he would want to know what people's assumptions were about the two men dancing together, and what led people to conclude that they were homosexuals. The gestaltist would look at causes and consequences of these phenomena.

Today, few if any social psychologists would identify themselves as Gestalt psychologists. But because of people like Heider, the gestalt orientation still exerts a great influence on social psychological theory and research. Many of the attribution theories (see chapter four), the theories of interpersonal attractions (see chapter six), and the attitude change theories (see chapter ten) are based on the principles put forth by Gestalt psychologists.

Field Theory

The *field theory* of social behavior is the product of one man, Kurt Lewin (1890–1947). It represents Lewin's attempt to integrate principles of Gestalt psychology with certain concepts from mathematics and physics. Field theory's impact on social psychology has been immense but indirect; it is not so much the theory itself as the ideas associated with it that have influenced social psychology.

Life space: the sum of all the events that determine a person's behavior at any given moment.

One important term in this approach to social behavior is **life space** (Lewin, 1936). According to Lewin, if one can understand a person's life space, one can understand the person's social behavior. A person's life space is determined first by the objective characteristics of the situation the person is in and second by the person's perception of that situation. In other words, factors inside and outside people determine their behavior. Lewin put this quite succinctly when he stated that behavior (B) is caused by both the person (p) and the environment (e): B = f(p,e).

Lewin believed that past experiences influence social behavior indirectly by altering how people perceive and react to the stimuli in their present situation. Lewin's emphases on the present and on the situation led many of his students (who are some of the most influential contemporary social psychologists) to focus their attention on how situational factors—rather than personality characteristics or past behaviors—affect social behavior.

Lewin proposed that two aspects of a person's life space will most affect that person's behavior: force and tension. A *force* causes people to move toward or away from something (Franklin, 1982). When forces oppose one another, *tension* occurs and people are motivated to act. In Lewin's view, it is a desire to reduce tension rather than learned habits which motivates most human social behavior.

Consider the couple at the party who moved toward and away from one another. The field theorist would focus on the aspects of the situation that produced their ambivalent behavior. What forces caused them to approach; what forces caused them to withdraw? How did they finally resolve the tension this situation created? (See the chapters on attitude change, groups, and environmental influences on social behavior for explanations of social behavior derived from field theory.)

Topic Background

A View from the Top

This chapter presents an overview of what social psychology is like today, how it got there, and the theories social psychologists use to explain social behavior. Two of the people who have played major roles in the development of the field are Leon Festinger and Fritz Heider.

Leon Festinger   Leon Festinger was born in 1919. He did his undergraduate studies at the City College of New York and received his doctorate from the University of Iowa in 1942. Although Festinger took no undergraduate or graduate courses in social psychology, he is considered by his colleagues to be the most important living social psychologist (Lewicki, 1982). Among his many contributions to the field are pioneering work on how groups function and the development of the theory of cognitive dissonance. (See chapters nine and ten on attitudes and attitude change.) While Festinger's theories still exert a powerful influence in social psychology, he left the field in 1964. He is presently conducting research on the physiology of perception at the New School of Social Research in New York.

The major influence on Festinger's ideas about social behavior was Lewin. Festinger went to the University of Iowa because Lewin was there, and he later followed Lewin to the Massachusetts Institute of Technology. Because of Lewin, Festinger's orientation to the explanation of social behavior is a cognitive one. Here are some of Festinger's thoughts on the causes of social behavior and how one should study them.

On the contribution (or lack thereof) of the behavioristic or learning orientation to social psychology:

> The tradition of behaviorism that dominated much of American psychology also had its impact on social psychology. One consequence of this impact was avoidance of concern with "inner" experience, such as cognition and affect, and a taboo on theorizing about matters that were not directly measurable. [But] the problems with which social psychology dealt were a bit too complex for the straightforward application of stimulus-response theorizing. (Festinger, 1980, p. 246–47)

On the contributions of the cognitive orientation (especially those of Lewin) to social psychology:

> Kurt Lewin and his co-workers . . . changed something . . . brought something new and original into the field. The orientation of Kurt Lewin and those around him was drastically at odds with behaviorism. The theoretical ideas were primarily about internal states: goals and aspirations that people and groups have; how people evaluate themselves; cognitions about others; processes of self-persuasion. (Festinger, 1980, p. 238)

On how he developed his theories of social behavior:

> I have always thought . . . that if the empirical world looks complicated, if people seem to react in bewilderingly different ways to similar forces, and if I cannot see the operation of universal underlying dynamics—then that is my fault. I have asked the wrong questions; I have, at the theoretical level, sliced the world up incorrectly. The underlying dynamics are there, and I have to find the theoretical apparatus that will enable me to reveal these uniformities. (Festinger, 1980, 246)

On criticisms of his theories:

> I have never been bothered by any of the criticisms of my work. I have felt that some of them were rather useless, but that is the prerogative of other people. There should be criticism in science. When something is published, one imagines that it is not perfect; one imagines that others will criticize it; one hopes that the criticism will be constructive, leading to improvement. (Evans, 1980, p. 134)

Fritz Heider   Fritz Heider was born in Vienna, Austria, in 1896. He received a Ph.D. in philosophy from the University of Graz in 1920. After receiving his doctorate,

Heider went to the University of Berlin, where he worked with the founders of Gestalt psychology and Lewin. He immigrated to the United States in the 1930s, and from 1947 until his retirement he taught at the University of Kansas. When a group of social psychologists were asked to name the people who had made the greatest contribution to the field, only Festinger and Lewin were named more often than Heider. Perhaps Heider's major contribution was his book, *The Psychology of Interpersonal Relationships*, published in 1958. This book contains relatively few empirical findings, but it presents a large number of well-thought-out theories and predictions about why humans act as they do. Since the book's publication, literally thousands of experiments have been conducted to test the ideas presented in it. In the quotations presented below, Heider talks about the roles of theory and empirical research in social psychology.

On the relationship between theory and science:

It is not very fruitful to make empirical studies without having cleared up one's concepts, which are the tools so to speak, with which we think about things. There are many cases in the history, not especially of psychology, but of physics and chemistry, in which the important breakthroughs came about not through empirical investigation but through an analysis of concepts. For instance, our life is now very much dependent on what's going on in nuclear physics, on atomic energy and atom bombs and so on. That did not come from empirical investigations. Einstein sat down and thought through Newton's concepts and found some logical incompatibilities. He sat there in his study and came to conclusions that became terribly important for our understanding of the physical environment. Einstein's theories did not come from experimenting. (Evans, 1980, p. 15)

On how social psychologists should learn about social behavior:

I feel that many psychologists develop a kind of encapsulated system. They read other psychologists' work and use their results as the empirical background for their theories. Now, for me the empirical background is not from reading psychological papers, but it is first of all from one's own experiences, in talking with other people and so on, and from reading literature. The empirical background should not be just the latest psychological experiments. That's kind of an incestual and very restricted way to develop knowledge. At least the same importance should be given to life experiences. You should keep going back to life and not to the laboratory for fresh insights in psychology. (Evans, 1980, pp. 22, 23)

On criticisms of his theories:

I think the main one was that my theories were often described as simply being "common sense," but I can't say that it troubled me . . . If they want to call my ideas "common sense," so be it. (Evans, 1980, p. 23)

Symbolic Interaction Orientation

The symbolic interaction orientation to social behavior has been more influential in sociology than in social psychology. However, its impact on contemporary theories of social behavior has been so great that it merits

According to the symbolic interactionists, this punk rocker's self-concept may be influenced by other people's reactions to him.

inclusion here. Further, in recent years, an increasing number of social psychologists have proposed specific theories of social behavior that have their roots in *symbolic interactionism*.

The development of this orientation is most often attributed to George Herbert Mead (1863–1931). The basic premise of symbolic interactionism is that the individual and society are inseparable and interdependent; one cannot be considered without the other (Schlenker, 1980). According to Mead, other people shape how individuals see themselves and how they act in social interactions through the use of symbols—"mental representations of objects and events with agreed upon social meanings" (Schlenker, 1980, p. 26). For example, we all know that a smile indicates positive feelings and a frown indicates negative feelings. We have learned the meanings of these nonverbal expressions (symbols) from society (other people).

In a social interaction, symbols from the environment and from the behavior of other people determine our actions. However, the meaning of a symbol depends to a large extent on the situation in which it occurs. For example, a smile given by someone at a party has a quite different meaning from a smile given by someone trying to look at your answer sheet during a test.

Society does more than teach the symbolic meaning of objects and actions. It also teaches what kind of people we "are." Put another way, the reactions of other people to our appearances and actions have a strong impact on the way we see ourselves. For example, imagine that people make oinking sounds every time you approach them. According to symbolic interactionism, you would come to see yourself as someone who has piglike qualities. You would "know" this because society has taught you the symbolic meaning of oinking sounds. Cooley (1922) called this process of others' behaviors determining a person's self-view the "looking glass self"—we see ourselves as others see us. Thus, the woman who received all the attention at the party probably saw herself as quite attractive.

Two contemporary theories that are derived from the symbolic interaction approach are self theory and role theory (Schlenker, 1985).

Self-Theory

Self-theory proposes that people's conceptions of themselves, which come largely from their interactions with others, provide a framework people use to organize and understand the information they receive from the world around them. Information that is consistent with or relevant to one's self-concept usually has more influence than information that is inconsistent or irrelevant. Self-theory also proposes that people attempt to manage the impressions they make on others by presenting favorable images of themselves to others. Thus, the self-theorist might view the glib joke teller's behavior at the party as an example of impression management. (See chapters three and five for more detailed information about self-theory.)

Role Theory

The term *role* comes from the theater. When actors play a role, they do what the script says their character is supposed to do. Similarly, a role is the behavior people perform when they hold a certain position in society. For example, giving lectures, writing examinations, and grading examinations are behaviors performed by a person who holds the position of college professor. However, one significant difference exists between the roles actors play and the roles people play in their day-to-day lives: Actors stop playing their roles when the audience goes home; "real people" play their roles even when no one else is around.

Three things are primarily responsible for the behavior of people in a certain position. The first is what others have taught them about which behaviors are appropriate for that position. The second is whether they accept this and thus act in a manner consistent with the appropriate role. And the third is that society has expectations about which behaviors are and are not appropriate for different positions. If people deviate too far from these, society will force them back into the appropriate behaviors. While others' expectations are sometimes the main determinant of behavior, more commonly the actors' own expectations determine their behavior.

The same person may simultaneously hold several different positions. For example, I hold the positions of father, husband, son, and college professor. My behavior varies as a function of which position is most important at a particular time. To demonstrate how role theory works, return to the party one last time. Remember the host's behavior? Role theory would argue that his behavior reflects his view of how someone who occupies this position should act. When he holds a different position (that of a guest at a party), he might act quite differently. (See chapters eleven and thirteen on social influence and groups for more about role theory.)

If taken too literally, role theory may appear to be an unrealistic way of explaining human behavior. We know that people do not systematically consider the positions they hold and then carefully decide on the appropriate behaviors, but this is not what role theory proposes. Rather, it argues that through our interactions with others we learn what behaviors are appropriate and inappropriate in certain circumstances, and we then act accordingly.

Biological Orientations

The final general orientation to human social behavior differs radically from those covered so far. It is the biologically based orientation of *sociobiology*, which proposes that a substantial portion of human social behavior is genetically determined (Barash, 1977; Wilson, 1978). Sociobiologists propose that evolution and natural selection do more than determine what physical characteristics are passed from one generation of a species to another—they determine what social behaviors are passed on as well. The members of a species who engage in social behaviors that increase their chances of survival are more likely to live long enough to reproduce and pass these genetic tendencies on to their offspring. The sociobiologists point to the numerous examples of inherited social behaviors among animals. Bees instinctively do a special dance when they find a food source; wolves instinctively live in packs; and dogs seem to innately know which territories belong to them and which do not.

The sociobiologists claim that a number of complex human social behaviors may have similar origins. Aggression, for example, was probably an adaptive characteristic among early humans. Thus, some contemporary human aggression may be the result of human genetic heritage. The sociobiologist might propose a genetic explanation for the fight at the party. Another social behavior that interests the sociobiologist is an act of altruistic self-sacrifice, such as risking one's own life to save another person. Learning theory, it is argued, cannot explain such an action because there are no positive consequences for acting this way, but genetically determined altruistic tendencies can.

The sociobiological explanation of human social behavior is a relatively recent addition to the general orientations that underlie social psychology, but it is gaining influence. (See chapters seven and eight on aggression and helping for sociobiological explanations of these behaviors.)

SUMMARY

Social psychology is a science, and an integral part of any science is theory. Most theories in social psychology are derived from three general orientations. The learning orientation proposes that learning principles can explain how people develop certain behaviors and why they display these behaviors in social interactions. Proponents of the learning orientation propose four related theories of how learning occurs: classical conditioning, which looks at how people learn to associate one stimulus with another; instrumental conditioning, which looks at how the consequences of a behavior can influence learning; drive theory, which looks at what motivates people to learn and perform behaviors; and observational learning, which proposes that people learn a great many social behaviors by observing and imitating the behaviors of others.

The cognitive orientation approaches social behavior from a different perspective. Rather than focusing on what happens in people's environment, it concentrates on how people process and organize external stimuli. The basic premise of the cognitive orientation is that humans are rational, thinking creatures who try to make sense out of their social world. The two cognitive theories that have most affected social psychology are Gestalt psychology and field theory. The former attempts to identify the way in which people organize and process their cognitions. The latter provides a way of understanding how people's environment influence their social behavior.

Symbolic interactionism places a greater emphasis on society than do either of these orientations. It argues that society teaches individuals how to view themselves and the world around them. The clearest expressions of this orientation can be found in self-theory and role theory. Self-theory concerns the social origins of the self-concept and how the self-concept affects social behavior. Role theory concerns how people learn the roles that go with the social positions they occupy and how these roles affect social behavior. Finally, the biological orientation proposes that humans are genetically predisposed to engage in certain types of social behaviors.

Chapter Two

Research Methods in Social Psychology

Prologue

Robert B. Cialdini, Richard J. Bordon, Arvil Thorne, Marcuse R. Walker, Stephen Freeman, and Lloyd R. Sloan. (1976). Basking in Reflected Glory: Three (Football) Field Studies. *Journal of Personality and Social Psychology,* **34,** 366–375.

Background

The primary focus of this chapter is a review of the methods used by social psychologists to acquire knowledge and test theories of social behavior. This study by Robert Cialdini and his colleagues illustrates some of these methods. The researchers were interested in a phenomenon they called basking in reflected glory—associating oneself with a person or group who achieved success. In the first study reported in this article, Cialdini and his associates looked at the tendency of college students to bask in the reflected glory of their school's football team. The researchers placed observers in classes held on the Monday morning after a school's team had played a game. The observers counted the number of students who wore apparel identifying them with their school or its football team, such as sweatshirts with the school name or mascot on them. Cialdini and his associates found many more students wore such apparel after wins than after losses. In the experiment described here, the researchers investigated whether people bask in reflected glory as a means of improving their image with someone else.

Hypotheses

Two hypotheses were made. The first was that students would more closely identify with their school team after a win than after a loss. The second was that this tendency would be greater when students had a need to bolster their image in the eyes of another person.

Subjects

The subjects were 173 students at a university with a nationally ranked football team.

Procedure

The students received a phone call from a person who claimed to be conducting a survey of college students. The caller asked students to answer six factual questions about their campus. Some of the students were told they had correctly answered only one of the six questions; others were told they had correctly answered five of the six questions. (In fact, both groups of students had correctly answered the same number of questions.) Then, both groups of students were asked to describe the outcome of a game their school's football team had recently played. The caller recorded how many students used the word *we* to describe the team's performance as the measure of basking in reflected glory.

Results

When the team had won the game, 32 percent of the students used *we* to describe the outcome of the game; when the team had lost the game, only 18 percent of the students used *we* to describe its outcome. The first hypothesis was supported. The second hypothesis was also supported. (See figure 2-1.) Students who had been successful (who thought they had answered five questions correctly) should have had no need to improve their image in the caller's eyes and, thus, should not have displayed greater identification with a team win than with a team loss—and there was essentially no difference among successful students. But students who had been unsuccessful (who thought they had answered only one question correctly) should have had such a need and, thus, should have shown greater identification with a team win than with a team loss. This is what was found. Among unsuccessful students, the percentage who said *we* when describing a win was almost three times as great as the percentage who said *we* when describing a loss.

Implications

This study adds something to social psychologists' knowledge about a phenomenon called impression management. (See chapter five.) It shows one tactic people use to improve the image they present to others and a reason why they use it. However, the study's primary implication for this chapter is that it illustrates the methods used by researchers to go from an abstract idea or theory about social behavior to an objective test of that idea or theory.

This chapter describes the specific techniques used by social psychologists in their research and the relative strengths and weaknesses of these techniques. The chapter begins with discussions of why research is so important in social psychology and of how research develops from a general idea about social behavior into a study that tests this idea. The second section discusses one method of conducting research, the experimental approach; it presents the basics of designing, conducting, and interpreting the results of an experiment. The third section presents the other major method of conducting research, the descriptive approach. These three sections are followed by an applications section, containing an illustration of how research methods can be used to determine if programs intended to help people are, in fact, achieving their goals.

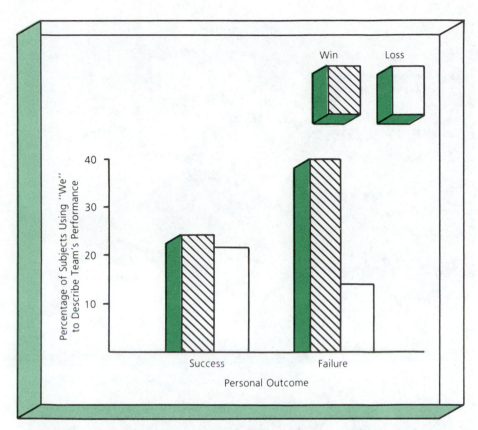

Figure 2-1. *When subjects had experienced success, they did not "bask" in the performance of their school's football team; when they had experienced failure, they did by using "we" to describe a team win.*
Source: Cialdini et al. (1976).

RESEARCH IN SOCIAL PSYCHOLOGY

As part of their scientific activities, social psychologists propose general theories and specific hypotheses derived from these theories. For example, Cialdini and his associates made a hypothesis, or prediction, in their experiment. This hypothesis seems reasonable, but science requires more than ideas which seem reasonable. It requires objective, empirical tests of whether an idea is correct. While theories are crucial to a science, they cannot be directly tested. Theories make statements about the nature of abstract entities called constructs which cannot be directly observed or measured. To determine the value of a theory, researchers develop hypotheses based on the theory and then test the hypotheses. To test a hypothesis derived from a theory, researchers must translate the constructs the theory contains into observable, measurable entities. This section describes the principles and procedures which guide this process.

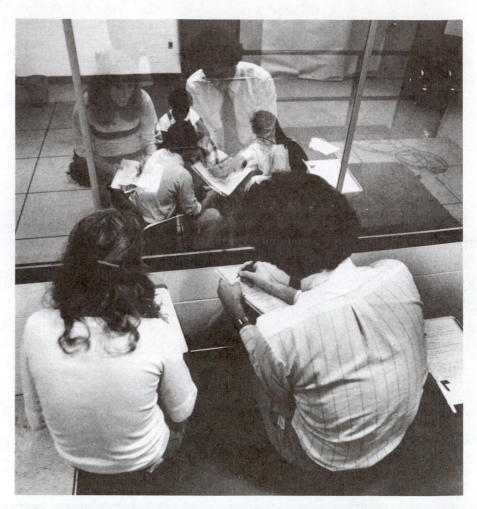

Social psychologists test hypotheses about social behavior by translating abstract concepts into entities that can be observed, measured, and recorded.

Operationalization: From the Abstract to the Concrete

While most theories are concerned with the nature of abstract ideas or concepts, they are expressed as statements about relationships between **variables.** Some examples of variables are sex—people can be male or female; intelligence—people can differ in how intelligent they are; beauty—people and things can differ in how beautiful they are; status—people can have high or low status; and social class—people can belong to the upper, middle, or lower social class.

Variables are useful in everyday conversations, but they are often too abstract to permit the testing of a hypothesis. Therefore, abstract variables are translated into concrete, variables which are directly observable and

Variables: any characteristic of a person, place, event, or thing that can have more than one value.

measurable by a process called **operationalization.** For example, to translate intelligence into a measurable entity, researchers develop an intelligence test which produces a score; to operationalize beauty, researchers have a number of people rate a person or thing in terms of attractiveness. This process can be illustrated by the prologue; basking in reflected glory is a variable; people can bask a little, a moderate amount, or a great deal. Using the process of operationalization, Cialdini and his associates translated this variable into whether students used the word *we* to describe the football team's performance. The researchers could then test their ideas about when and why people bask in reflected glory.

Operationalization: the development of procedures or operations that permit the observation or measurement of a variable.

Operational Definitions

Suppose you have decided to conduct a study similar to the one presented in the prologue; you are interested in what factors affect school spirit at your university. You operationalize school spirit as how much a student donates to the campus scholarship fund. You do not find that donations increase after a win in football, but you do find that the average donation made by seniors is much less than that made by freshmen. Thinking about this, you say to a friend: "You know, the seniors at this school have no school spirit." But your friend replies: "Are you nuts? They are the first ones to throw garbage at the visiting teams." Between the two of you, there is a breakdown in communication because school spirit has very different meanings to you and your friend.

This same problem exists in science. Many of the variables social psychologists study are vague and subject to alternative meanings. Just as you and your friend need a way to clearly communicate with one another, so do researchers. They cannot test and evaluate one another's ideas unless they know what a person means by the terms she uses. Social psychologists solve a large portion of this problem by using **operational definitions.** For example, you could have prevented any misunderstanding between yourself and your friend by saying, "I operationally defined school spirit as the average contribution seniors made to the campus scholarship fund over the last three months." Your friend may not agree that this behavior reflects the variable, but she knows what you mean by school spirit. Researchers use operational definitions to effectively communicate with one another. A researcher in Nome, Alaska, knows exactly what some term means to a researcher in Key West, Florida. This enables the former researcher to see if the findings obtained by the latter are replicable (repeatable).

Operational definitions: definitions of variables in terms of the operations or methods used to measure them.

One common type of operational definition is the **scale.** A scale with which you are already familiar is the Fahrenheit scale, which translates the variable temperature into something observable (the reading from a thermometer) and increases the precision in a discussion of temperature. For example, if I call my brother who lives in Chicago and tell him it is cold today, he might think I am talking about subzero weather. However, since I live in Florida, I may be talking about weather that is balmy by Chicago standards. If, on the other hand, I say it is 52 degrees Fahrenheit today, he knows exactly what I am talking about. Similarly, social psychologists

Scale: a measurement that describes how people or things differ on a variable of interest.

A thermometer translates the variable, temperature, into something observable and measurable—the Fahrenheit scale.

use scales to more precisely describe how people differ on a variable they are studying.

Scales can describe two general kinds of difference between people, events, or things. The first is categorical, or qualitative, differences; for example, differences in marital status. A *nominal scale* is used to describe such differences. Often researchers give numbers to the categories on a nominal scale—1 = married, 2 = single, 3 = divorced. These numbers simply reflect the categories; they say nothing about the relative amounts of the variable people possess (one person cannot be three times as divorced as another). Numbers are used primarily because they can be read and stored more easily by computers than can words. In addition to marital status, other variables for which social psychologists use nominal scales are places of residence (home, apartment), race, religion, sex, and occupation.

The second way people or things can differ on a variable is quantitatively—in terms of the amount of the variable they possess. An *ordinal scale* is used to describe these differences. Examples of variables that are described by ordinal scales are anxiety, intelligence, and sociability. We can talk about one person being more or less anxious (or intelligent, or sociable) than another; thus, in an ordinal scale, the numbers assigned to people or things have meaning. They indicate the relative amount of the variable that the person or thing possesses. Social psychologists often construct ordinal scales to measure differences on variables such as attitudes or personality characteristics. To measure attitudes, they ask people a series of questions about their feelings on a particular issue and combine their answers into a total score. Differences in total scores reflect differences on their attitudes on that issue.

Reliability and Validity

Operationalization of variables does not by itself ensure the appropriate test of a theory. Once researchers have operationalized a variable, they must carefully examine the procedures they have used by asking themselves if the procedures produce data that are reliable and valid.

Reliability   Think of what the word *reliability* means to you. When we say that people are reliable, we mean they are consistent, dependable, and stable. When we say that a measure is reliable, we mean exactly the same thing. How can a researcher determine if a procedure is reliable? One way is to determine if it is stable across time. The formal name for this is *test-retest reliability*. The same characteristic is measured at two different times and the researcher determines if the two measurements are the same or different. If they are the same, they have good test-retest reliability. A second way of determining the reliability of a measure is to compare one person's ratings of the variable of interest with the ratings of another person. If the two consistently agree, one can have confidence in the reliability of the measurements. This technique is called *interjudge reliability*.

Reliability only concerns whether your measurement is consistent; it does not speak to the question of whether it actually represents or reflects the construct or concept contained in the theory of interest. The question of whether the meausre reflects the construct of interest is addressed by the concept of construct validity.

Construct Validity   A measure that is a faithful reflection of the construct it is supposed to represent has *construct validity*. For example, researchers may predict that people are more sociable at the beginning of an academic term (because they do not need to study) than halfway through the term. They may decide to use the amount of beer consumed in local bars as the measure of sociability. They may therefore obtain sales records from the local bars of the first week and the eighth week of the term. Since most businesspeople keep good sales records, this measure would be reliable. But does it really reflect sociability—would it be construct valid? Greater beer drinking during the first week of a term could reflect the effects of the weather (it may be hot at the beginning of the term) or attempts to reduce beginning-of-the-term jitters. Later in the chapter, the methods researchers use to determine whether their measures are construct valid are explained.

Relationships between Variables

The primary activity of research is to examine the relationship between variables—or more precisely, to examine the relationship between differences on variables. The first step in doing this is to make a prediction about the relationship, which is called a *hypothesis*. Researchers usually make one of three kinds of hypotheses about the relationships between variables: null, noncausal, or causal.

Null Hypotheses

In a *null hypothesis*, the researcher proposes that two variables are unrelated; differences between people or things on one variable are totally unrelated to differences on the other. One kind of null hypothesis is that the relationship between two variables is *spurious*. This means that the two variables are related, but their relationship is due to a third, external variable. For example, there is a relationship between the temperature in Tokyo and the number of ice-cream cones sold in Topeka, Kansas, However, this relationship reflects the effects of a third variable, the sun's heat. A researcher could not learn anything about why people in Kansas eat ice-cream cones by studying the temperatures in Japan.

Noncausal Hypotheses

In a *noncausal hypothesis*, a researcher predicts that two variables are related—differences on one variable go along with differences on the other—but does not predict which variable causes the other. For example, some researchers are interested in the relationship between education and income. They predict that education and income are related, but do not state which causes which because they recognize that while better-educated people earn more money, it is also true that wealthier people can obtain more education. They predict a noncausal, or *nonfunctional*, relationship. Another illustration of a nonfunctional relationship is that between violent television and aggression in children. The more violent television shows children watch, the more aggressive they are (although this relationship is not very strong). Does this mean that media violence causes aggression? Not necessarily. It is possible that aggressive children like to watch violent television shows. Without further study, one must conclude that while the relationship is real, one does not know the causal relationship between the variables.

Causal Hypotheses

In a *causal hypothesis*, researchers predict a causal, or *functional*, relationship between variables. A functional relationship exists between two variables when they are related and one variable causes the other. Consider the relationship between heart rate and exercise. We know that when people exercise, their heart rates increase. We also know that people do not go out and exercise when their heart rates increase. Consequently, a causal hypothesis about the relationship between these variables can be made: Exercise causes people's heart rates to increase. In the earlier experiment, a football team's performance could have affected how fans dressed a few days later, but the way fans dressed could not have affected the team's performance in a game that took place several days earlier. Therefore, the researchers made a causal hypothesis: The football team's performance affected the way fans dressed a few days after the game.

The quality of a research project depends a great deal on the quality of the hypotheses a researcher makes. If they are ill considered, trivial, or not capable of being tested, the research is of little value no matter how precisely it is done. Good research depends on more than scientists' abilities to measure variables in a reliable and valid manner; it also depends on intelligent and creative hypotheses. As McGuire (1973) has observed, the most important thing an aspiring researcher can be taught is to make good hypotheses.

SUMMARY

One major purpose of research is to test hypotheses derived from theories. Since theories deal with relationships between abstract variables, it is difficult to conduct objective, empirical tests of hypotheses derived from them unless the variables in a theory are translated into observable, measurable entities through the process of operationalization. One aspect of operationalization is the operational definition, in which variables are defined in terms of the operations used to measure or produce them. Often variables are operationally defined by scales describing how people or things differ on the variable. There are two major types of scales: nominal, which describe categorical, or qualitative, differences on a variable; and ordinal, which describe difference in the amount of a variable a person or thing possesses. After a variable has been operationally defined, the reliability and validity of the measures used must be considered. A measure is reliable if it is consistent, dependable, and stable. A measure is valid if it is a faithful representation of the construct described by a theory.

There are three types of relationships between variables which can be predicted. In a null hypothesis, it is predicted that there is no relationship between the variables. In a noncausal hypothesis, it is predicted that variables are related, but no statement is made about their causal relationship. And in a causal hypothesis, predictions are made that the variables are related and that one of them causes the other.

THE EXPERIMENTAL APPROACH

Most research in social psychology attempts to test hypotheses about the causal relationships between variables. Usually this is done using the experimental approach. Experiments come in all shapes, sizes, and varieties, but they all have one characteristic in common: they test a hypothesis by causing a change in one variable and seeing if this produces a change in another variable. This section examines the procedures used to conduct laboratory experiments and discusses the validity and value of laboratory experiments.

Laboratory Experiments

Among social psychologists, the experimental approach most often involves a laboratory experiment. The following material takes you through a laboratory experiment step by step and explains how this process works.

Step 1. Making a Hypothesis

First, it is necessary to make a prediction about the relationship between two or more variables. This experiment will test a hypothesis which comes from the research on helping: people who see themselves as similar to another person will help that person more than will people who see themselves as dissimilar to that person, or similarity causes helping.*

Step 2. Defining the Variables

Immediately, the problems discussed in the previous section raise their ugly heads. For example, similarity is an abstract term, as is helping. These terms must be operationalized. The first stage in this process is to generate a conceptual definition.

Initially, similarity is defined as the belief that another person shares similar interests, hobbies, attitudes, likes, and dislikes. This leads to the operationalization of perceived similarity as the knowledge that another person agrees with or shares 80 percent of a subject's interests, hobbies, and so on. Perceived dissimilarity is the knowledge that another person agrees with or shares 20 percent of a subject's interests, hobbies, and so on.

The construct of helping is also operationalized, beginning with a conceptual definition: Helping is doing something that benefits another person at some cost to the helper. This conceptual definition is operationalized in the following way: One person receives electrical shock while another watches; at some point in the experiment, the observer is asked if she is willing to take the other person's place and receive the shock. It is made clear that the more shock the observer agrees to take, the less shock the other person will receive. Helping is operationally defined as the number of shocks the subject is willing to take for the other person.

In this experiment, perceived similarity is the **independent variable.** It is manipulated independently by the experimenter. Helping is the **dependent variable.** The purpose of this experiment is to determine if changes in the independent variable (perceived similarity) cause changes in the dependent variable (helping the other person).

Step 3. Designing the Experiment

The first consideration in designing an experiment is how many conditions it will have. The term *condition* refers to the manner in which the independent variable is manipulated. If the independent variable is given to one group of subjects and withheld from another group, the experiment

Independent variable: the variable in an experiment that is manipulated by the experimenter and is not affected by what the subjects say or do.

Dependent variable: the variable in an experiment that changes as a function of changes on the independent variable; it is affected by the independent variable.

---

*This experiment is partially based on a study by C.D. Batson and his associates (Batson, Duncan, Ackerman, Buckley, and Birch, 1981).

Table 2-1. *Design of Study*

Group	Independent variable	Dependent variable
Experimental	Similar confederate	Number of shocks
Experimental	Dissimilar confederate	Number of shocks
Control	No specific information about confederate	Number of shocks

has two conditions. The condition in which subjects are given the independent variable is called the *experimental condition;* the condition in which the subjects do not receive the independent variable is called the *control condition.* To see if the independent variable has any effect on the dependent variable, the experimental subjects' scores on the dependent variable are compared with the control subjects' scores. All experiments involve a comparison between subjects in at least two different conditions. In this study, there are three conditions: (1) subjects are told they are similar to the confederate; (2) subjects are told they are dissimilar to the confederate; (3) subjects receive no specific information about their similarity or dissimilarity to the confederate.

The first two conditions are called experimental conditions because different levels of the independent variable are used in them. The third one is called the control condition because the independent variable will not be administered in it. A control condition will be used because it provides a baseline against which the effects of the independent variable on the dependent variable can be compared. Other than this difference, the procedures in the three conditions are identical. Chance, or luck, decides which condition a subject is in. (See table 2-1 for the design of this study.)

Step 4. Conducting the Experiment

The experiment begins with a subject and another person filling out a similarity questionnaire. The subject thinks the other person is also a subject, but she is an accomplice, or *confederate,* of the experimenter. After the questionnaires are done, the experimenter takes them into another room, supposedly to score them. However, the experimenter instead uses this time to complete another questionnaire for the confederate. In the similar condition, 80 percent of the confederate's answers are made to match those of the subject; in the dissimilar condition, 20 percent of the confederate's answers are made to match those of the subject. The experimenter then returns to the room and gives each subject a questionnaire to examine. In the similar and dissimilar conditions, the subjects are given the questionnaires supposedly filled out by the confederate; in the control condition, subjects are given their own original questionnaires. The independent variable of similarity/dissimilarity is thus manipulated.

After the subjects examine the questionnaires, a rigged drawing is held, which results in the confederate always being the person who receives the shocks. She and the subject are told that she will receive 50 shocks. The confederate is taken into another room, and the subject watches her over a closed circuit television system. In fact, the subject sees a prerecorded videotape of the confederate pretending that she is receiving shock. The same tape is used in all three conditions, making the experiment consistent, or reliable, across all three conditions.

After the confederate has received 15 shocks, she begins to complain that the shock is quite painful. After 22 shocks, she says she does not think she can continue. The experimenter goes into the subject's room and asks her if she is willing to take the confederate's place and if so, how many of the remaining 28 shocks she will take. It is made clear that the more shocks the subject takes, the less the confederate will receive. The dependent measure is the number of shocks a subject agrees to take. After this is obtained, the experiment ends.

Step 5. Debriefing the Subject

Debriefing is a term taken from the military. It originally meant interviews that were conducted with soldiers after they had returned from a mission. In this laboratory experiment, the debriefing has three purposes. First, it is used to check on the effectiveness of the manipulation of similarity. Second, it is used to question the subjects about their perceptions of the experiment; did the subjects understand the instructions, were they suspicious, how did they feel during the experiment, what did they think was the purpose of the experiment, and so on. Finally, the debriefing is used to tell the subjects the truth about the experiment. The experimenter fully explains the deceptions used, probes for any discomfort that may have occurred, and attempts to alleviate it. In studies like this, subjects are debriefed because it is required by law and because researchers have an ethical and moral responsibility to do so.

Step 6. Comparing the Subjects

After a sufficient number of subjects have been tested in each of the three conditions, the experimenter compares their scores on the dependent variable. In this experiment, the hypothesis is supported if the number of shocks subjects in the similar condition were willing to take is greater than the number of shocks subjects in the dissimilar or control conditions were willing to take.

Statistical significance: an estimate of the likelihood that differences between scores are due to luck or change.

To determine this, the experimenter would probably compute the mean or average score in each condition and then use a statistical test to compare the averages. In this case, the statistical test would be an *analysis of variance*. The results of this test would tell the experimenter about the **statistical significance** of the differences between the means. Most researchers conclude that differences are real and meaningful if an estimate indicates a likelihood of no more than five in one hundred that the differences found are due to luck or chance. This is called the .05 level of significance.

It is good to remember that a statistical test compares the typical (mean or median) scores of groups of people. A significant difference does *not* mean that every person in one group has a score that is significantly different from the scores of people in another group. There are usually differences between the scores of members of the same group (this is called *variance*, or *variability)*, and often some of the scores in one group are the same as scores in another group. When you read statements in this book such as "women are shorter than men," do not become concerned if you are an exception to this general statement. It refers to a measure of central tendency (mean, median, or mode), and people vary or deviate from the central tendencies of the group they belong to.

Topic Background

Understanding Interactions

In most social psychological experiments there are at least two independent variables. To understand the results of these experiments, you need to understand interactions between variables.

Deborah Richardson and Jennifer Campbell (1982) were interested in how certain variables might influence people's reactions to a rape. There were two independent variables in this study: the role of the person in the rape (attacker or victim) and whether a person was drunk or sober. Each subject read one of four descriptions of a rape, which represented all possible combinations of the two independent variables. (This is called two-by-two *factorial design.)* The descriptions were as follows:

1. Attacker drunk–victim sober

2. Attacker drunk–victim drunk

3. Attacker sober–victim drunk

4. Attacker sober–victim sober

After reading the descriptions, the subjects rated how much blame should be placed on the victim and how much should be placed on the attacker. The ratings of blame were the dependent variable.

The analysis of the dependent variable produced a significant difference. As you might expect, the subjects blamed the attacker more than the victim. This is called a *significant main effect*—the role of a person in the story (attacker versus victim) significantly affected the subjects' ratings.

Richardson and Campbell also found a *significant interaction*, which means that the effects of one variable depended on the effects of the other variable. The easiest way to understand an interaction is to see a picture of it. The following figure shows the interaction these researchers found.

Note that the subjects blamed the attacker less when he was drunk than when he was sober, but their ratings of the victim's blame were unaffected by whether she was drunk or sober. Thus there was an interaction between the two independent variables.

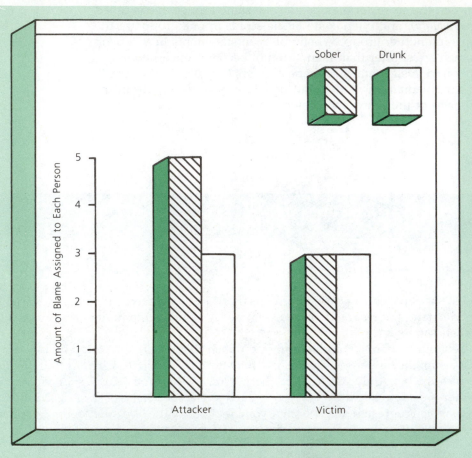

This interaction shows that the drunk/sober variable only affected ratings of the attacker. He was blamed less when he was drunk than when he was sober; blame of the victim did not change. (Note: Data have been modified to illustrate this interaction.)
Source: Richardson and Campbell (1982).

Richardson and Campbell also asked their subjects to rate how responsible each of the two people was for what had happened. The analysis of this dependent variable produced another kind of interaction, as shown in the following figure.

This interaction indicated that the attacker was seen as less responsible for what happened when he was drunk than when he was sober. But the victim was seen as more responsible for what happened when she was drunk than when she was sober.

One final point: Often studies find significant main effects and significant interactions. This is what Richardson and Campbell found on both of their dependent variables. How does one interpret this? One can conclude that overall, the independent variables produced significant differences between the subjects and also that the independent variables affected one another.

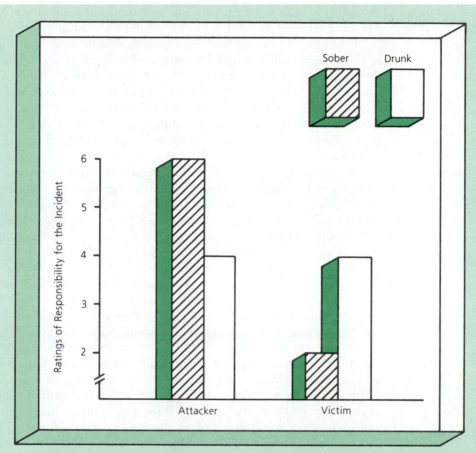

This interaction shows that the drunk/sober variable affected responsibility ratings differently for the attacker and the victim. The attacker was seen as less responsible when drunk than sober; the victim was seen as more responsible when drunk than when sober. (Note: Data have been modified to illustrate this interaction.)
Source: Richardson and Campbell (1982).

Validity of Laboratory Experiments

Assume that a statistical test indicates there are statistically significant differences between the groups in an experiment, and that those differences support the hypotheses. The researcher's job is not yet completed, for the validity of the experiment must now be considered. There are three aspects of validity: internal, construct, and external.

Internal Validity

An experiment is *internally valid* if the independent variable and the independent variable alone is responsible for differences between the subjects on the dependent variable (Campbell and Stanley, 1966). For example, if subjects in the similar condition helped more than subjects in the dissimilar, or control, condition, and this was due to the manipulation of the independent variable, similarity, the experiment would be internally valid.

One threat to the internal validity of this experiment is that the subjects in the three conditions may have differed on certain characteristics before the experiment began. For example, all of the subjects in the similar condition could have been planning careers as social workers and could thus have been more helpful to begin with. Subject characteristics such as age, race, sex, and mood can have a dramatic effect on social behaviors, and researchers must try to equalize these characteristics across the conditions of an experiment.

Random assignment: the placement of subjects in different conditions of an experiment on the basis of chance.

A procedure called **random assignment** is a simple and powerful way to reduce this threat to internal validity. For example, in the preceding experiment, the experimenter randomly assigned subjects to each condition. She placed three slips of paper in a cup. Before an experimental session began, she picked one of the slips; if it had a 1 on it, the subject in that session would be in the similar condition; if it had a 2 on it, the subject would be in the dissimilar condtion; if it had a 3 on it, the subject would be in the control condition. By assigning subjects on the basis of chance, the subjects in the three conditions of the experiment were made comparable; this procedure should have prevented the subjects in the three conditions from differing in any systematic way.

Random assignment is a vital part of experiments. Although Cook and Campbell (1979) call the first usage of random assignment in an experiment a "great breakthrough", its purpose is often misunderstood. Many people think that random assignment ensures that the selection of subjects for an experiment will be random and, thus, the subjects are a representative sample of some larger group of people. This is wrong! Random assignment does nothing to ensure that subjects are representative of some larger group; its sole purpose is to reduce the probability that subjects in different conditions of an experiment are different before the independent variable is manipulated. This makes it easier for the researcher to conclude that any differences between subjects on the dependent variable are due to differences on the independent variable. (The procedure used to obtain a representative group of subjects is called random sampling and is discussed later in this chapter.)

Two other things were done to increase the internal validity of this experiment. First, in the debriefing, the experimenter determined if the subjects had, in fact, seen the confederate in the similar condition as more similar to themselves than had the subjects in the other two conditions. Second, with the exception of the similarity manipulation, the subjects' experiences in the three conditions were virtually identical. Any differences other than those specifically manipulated (perceived similarity–dissimilarity) were controlled or eliminated. The key to internal validity is the control of variables other than the independent variable which could produce differences on the dependent variable.

Construct Validity

Construct validity is quite similar to internal validity and many of the things which could jeopardize an experiment's internal validity could also jeopardize its construct validity. According to Cook and Campbell (1979), the two types of validity differ only in the following respect: internal validity concerns whether events or things other than the independent variable could cause changes in the dependent variable; construct validity concerns whether the independent and dependent variables are faithful reflections of the constructs of interest. Several things can threaten an experiment's construct validity, including demand characteristics, evaluation apprehension, and experimenter effects.

Demand Characteristics   Thus far, you have seen this experiment from the experimenter's point of view. Now consider a subject's perspective. Social psychologists use the same general experimental procedures as do psychologists who conduct experiments on pigeons or rats, but humans are quite different from these animals; humans are bright, thinking creatures who live in a rich environment. Unlike the rat whose sole concern is the food pellet at the end of a maze, human subjects often try to figure out why the experimenter is conducting an experiment: Why are they telling me about how similar I am to the other subject? Why is this person being shocked? Why am I being asked to take her place? They may form hypotheses about the purpose of an experiment and about how the experimenter expects them to act. If a subject's behavior reflects these hypotheses rather than the independent variable, the experiment is not construct valid. **Demand characteristics** (Orne, 1969) are the information upon which subjects base their hypotheses about the purpose of an experiment and about what the experimenter expects from them.

> **Demand characteristics:** rumors about an experiment, its setting, the instructions an experimenter gives, how the experimenter acts, and the experimental procedure itself.

Demand characteristics are a source of problems in the laboratory experiment, but they can also be used to explain some interesting social phenomena, such as the effects of placebos on people's behavior. A *placebo* is a substance that has no pharmacological effect, but is believed to have effects by the person taking it; for example, a sugar pill that people believe will make them sleep is a placebo. In a 1971 study, Jones gave real and placebo marijuana cigarettes to a group of experienced marijuana users. The placebo joints smelled and tasted like marijuana but did not contain tetrahydrocannabinol (THC), the psychoactive agent in marijuana. Subjects rated the quality of the marijuana they had smoked on a scale of 0 to 100, where 100 represented "the best grass you have every smoked." Much to Jones's surprise, the placebo received an average rating of 57, while the real marijuana received a rating of only 66. However, subjects who had colds were not fooled by the placebo joints—evidently because they could neither smell nor taste the marijuana and, thus, these demand characteristics were absent for them.

Evaluation Apprehension   One specific kind of demand characteristic is subjects' belief that, in general, one purpose of an experiment is to evaluate their mental health, moral character, and intellect (Rosenberg, 1969). *Evaluation apprehension* occurs when subjects become apprehensive about the supposed evaluative aspects of an experiment and modify their behavior to present themselves in the most favorable light. Therefore, their behavior is not due to the variables of interest, but to their desire to look good in the eyes of the experimenter.

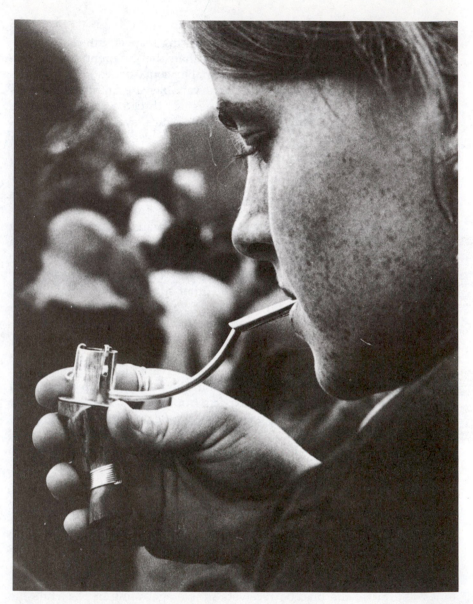

Some research suggests that part of the effects of marijuana may be due to the placebo effects created by the way it tastes and smells.

Experimenter Effects   Rosenthal (1966, 1969) has argued that experimenters can often unintentionally communicate to their subjects how they expect them to act. If this occurs, the observed behavior is not reflective of the construct of interest but of *experimenter expectancies*. A study by Rosenthal and Fode (1963) illustrated this threat to construct validity. Students were recruited to serve as experimenters in a study. Their task was to show a series of pictures of people's faces to a group of subjects and have the subjects rate those pictures on a scale from -5.00 to $+5.00$. A

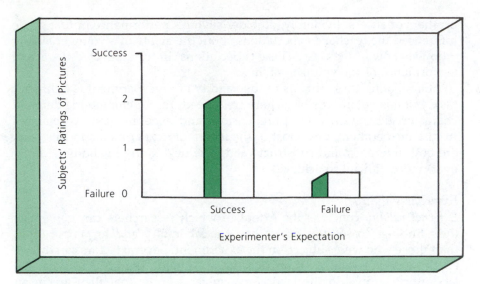

Figure 2-2. *Subjects' ratings of objectively neutral pictures were influenced by the experimenter's expectations of how the subjects should rate the pictures*
Source: Rosenthal and Fode (1963).

−5.00 rating indicated that the person pictured was a failure; a +5.00 rating indicated that the person pictured was a success.

Rosenthal and Fode deceived their "experimenters" in two ways. First, they did not tell them that the pictures had been previously rated and had received an average rating of 0.00. Second, they told half their experimenters to expect that the people would be rated as successes. Each experimenter then showed the pictures to a group of subjects. The people were rated as significantly more successful by the subjects who had an experimenter with a success expectancy than by subjects who had an experimenter with a failure expectancy. This was because the experimenters' expectations influenced the subjects' ratings.

Experimenter effects, like demand characteristics, have implications beyond the social psychological experiment. For example, it has been demonstrated that a teacher's expectancies about a student's ability may influence how the student actually does in school (Rosenthal and Jacobson, 1968). Seaver (1973) was interested in how a teacher's experiences with a student might impact the performance of the student's younger brother or sister.

Seaver's subjects were two groups of first graders. Children in one group had the same teachers as had their older brothers or sisters when they were in first grade; children in the other group also had older siblings in the same school, but their older siblings had had different first-grade teachers. Seaver found that among children who had the same teachers as their older siblings, there was a strong relationship between their performance in first grade and their older brothers' or sisters' performance. This was not true among the children whose teachers had not taught their older brothers or sisters. Evidently, an older sibling's performance in first grade influenced the teacher's expectations about the ability of a younger sibling who was now in the class. These expectations, in turn, affected the actual performance of the younger sibling.

Eliminating these threats to the validity of an experiment is a difficult task, but it is not impossible. There are procedures for eliminating demand characteristics, evaluation apprehension, and experimenter expectancies from an experiment, and most of the laboratory experiments in this book are both internally and construct valid. The next kind of validity is, however, more difficult to achieve.

External Validity

External validity concerns the extent to which researchers can generalize their findings to settings other than the laboratory and to people other than those who were subjects in the experiment. Several factors can threaten the external validity of an experiment. One is the artificiality of the laboratory setting. In the laboratory, subjects know that they are in an experiment and are being observed. This knowledge can produce behaviors that do not exist in the real world, behaviors which are merely laboratory artifacts.

Another factor that can threaten the external validity of a laboratory experiment is the manner in which the variables of interest are operationalized. To make an experiment internally valid, experimenters attempt to create *experimental realism;* they arrange the situation so that subjects will take the independent variable seriously and will be affected by that variable. The independent variable is operationalized in a clear and unambiguous manner (Aronson and Carlsmith, 1968). Critics argue that as the result of creating experimental realism, the experimenter may sacrifice *mundane realism*, or the extent to which an event in an experiment approximates that event in the real world.

The laboratory experiment used as an example here illustrates the difference between the two types of realism. Similarity is manipulated in a clear and unambiguous fashion, and it is the only thing about a subject's relationship to the confederate that is manipulated—everything else is carefully controlled. Think about how many times you have received information about another person in this manner. A very rare occurrence has been created, one that is lacking in mundane realism. In their day-to-day lives, people do not learn about others through their responses to questionnaires, but through interactions with them and through the opinion of others. It is almost impossible to think of a circumstance in the real world where information about similarity-dissimilarity is presented in as precise a fashion as it is in this experiment. Thus, the variable manipulated in the laboratory may bear little resemblance to the variable as it exists in the real world.

Finally, the type of subjects used in an experiment may severely threaten the generalization of its findings. The majority of subjects are college students, who may be quite different from the general population. Further, the subjects in a typical laboratory experiment have usually volunteered to be in the study, and volunteers are often quite different from nonvolunteers. For example, volunteers are more intelligent, are less conventional, are more sociable, have a greater need for approval, and come from a higher social class than nonvolunteers (Rosenthal and Rosnow, 1975). The simple fact that a group of subjects differs from the general population in certain ways does not make an experiment externally invalid. For example, if one's interest is in how quickly the pupil of the eye dilates in response to a bright light, the characteristics of the subjects used would probably not make any difference. But if the variables of interest might be affected by subjects' characteristics, there is good reason to question the external validity of a laboratory experiment.

The Value of Laboratory Experiments

As you might expect, laboratory experiments have been strongly criticized on the grounds that they are not externally valid and, thus, might not constitute an appropriate means to study social behavior (Gergen, 1978; Gilmour and Duck, 1980). Defenders of the laboratory experiment argue that these criticisms are based on a misunderstanding of the purpose of a laboratory experiment (Berkowitz and Donnerstein, 1982; Mook, 1983). According to them, the purpose of the laboratory experiment is to test theoretical predictions about the relationships between constructs. It is not to determine the frequency with which these relationships might occur in the real world. Further, even relationships that occur rarely in the real world are worthy of study. Proponents feel that experiments further the knowledge of these phenomena, and that this is the true purpose of research.

It is also argued that if one is interested in real-world phenomena, the laboratory experiment is often the best means to begin an investigation. The first step to the understanding of a complex social behavior is to study it under carefully controlled conditions. This gives the researcher the knowledge needed to understand these phenomena as they exist in nature. Proponents of this position point out that many of the natural phenomena scientists now understand were first identified and studied in the laboratory.

Finally, defenders of the laboratory experiment argue that it is impossible to make a blanket statement about the generalizability of findings obtained in a laboratory. Empirical research must be done to determine if an experiment's findings are externally valid. In other words, let the facts decide whether one can generalize from a particular procedure with particular subjects to different procedures with different subjects. In support of this position, it is noted that some laboratory findings that were originally considered nongeneralizable have been found to be quite generalizable (Berkowitz and Donnerstein, 1982).

Field Experiments

Since there are questions about the value of laboratory experiments, many social psychologists also conduct **field experiments** to study social

Field experiments: experiments conducted in natural settings.

behavior. The logic and philosophy in field experiments are exactly the same as in laboratory experiments. The constructs are operationalized, the independent variable is manipulated, the subjects are randomly assigned to different conditions, and differences on the dependent variable are examined. As in the laboratory experiment, the crucial question is whether the independent variable and only the independent variable is responsible for the differences found in the dependent variable.

But in the field experiment, the subjects are not aware that they are in an experiment. They are studied as they go about their daily lives. As an example of this consider a fictional field experiment on the relationship between similarity and helping. As shoppers leave a department store in a large mall, they come upon a person whose shopping bag has just broken and whose purchases are strewn all over the parking lot. Similarity is operationalized as racial similarity. The effect of this variable on helping is determined by having a black confederate and a white confederate play the role of the distressed shopper and recording whether a potential helper is of the same race as the confederate. The dependent variable, helping, is measured by a hidden observer recording whether or not subjects help the confederate.

A field experiment has several advantages over a laboratory experiment. Field experiments are not affected by demand characteristics and evaluation apprehension, and most importantly, the artificiality which is part of most laboratory experiments does not exist in the field experiment. But this is achieved at some price. Field experiments are difficult and expensive to conduct. Whereas it might take two weeks to conduct a laboratory experiment, it could take two months to conduct a field experiment on the same topic because the staging of the experiment requires the co-ordination of several people's activities. In addition, researchers have less control over the independent variable in field experiments. How do they know, for example, that all the people who did not help saw the confederate? How do they control for people being late for an appointment or being afraid to stop in the parking lot of a shopping center? In other words, how does the researcher know that the behavior the subjects display is the result of the independent variable? What researchers may gain in mundane realism, they may lose in internal validity. As the former increases, the latter usually decreases.

Quasi-Experiments

Random assignment enables researchers to eliminate many alternative explanations of their results because it essentially equalizes the subjects in different parts of an experiment. But when the independent variable is a naturally occurring event, a researcher usually cannot randomly assign subjects to the different parts of an experiment. Because subjects are not randomly assigned to the different conditions of the experiment, it becomes more difficult to determine if the independent variable alone is responsible for differences on the dependent variable—if the experiment is internally valid. In such cases, researchers often conduct **quasi-experiments** (Cook and Campbell, 1979).

In a quasi-experiment, researchers cannot control who receives the independent variable, but they can control how and when the dependent variable is measured. By taking a number of different measurements at different points in time, researchers can use the quasi-experiment to test hypotheses about the relationships between variables in the real world.

For example, the first study on basking in reflected glory was a quasi-experiment. Whether a football team won or lost a game on the Saturday before a class was not a random event. To reduce the likelihood that an unknown factor, such as the weather, would affect students' dress, Cialdini and his associates observed the dress of students at eight different universities after several games. In almost every instance, more students wore university-related apparel after a win than after a loss. The likelihood that such consistent differences in the way students dressed were due to factors such as differences in the weather is very small.

Quasi-experiments: experiments, usually conducted in nonlaboratory settings, in which subjects cannot be randomly assigned to different conditions.

Research Highlight

Does Television Cause Crime?

Many people believe that watching violent television programs can increase the tendencies of viewers to commit violent crimes. Karen Hennigan and her associates (Hennigan, DelRosario, Heath, Cook, Wharton, and Calder, 1982) used a quasi-experiment to investigate the effects of television on another kind of crime, larceny (shoplifting, pickpocketing, bicycle stealing). According to Hennigan and her associates, there are three reasons to suspect that television might increase the incidence of this type of crime. One, it may stimulate people's desires for products they cannot afford. Two, since most characters on television are presented as wealthier than the typical viewer, viewers may come to feel deprived and want to reduce their deprivation. And three, there is so much crime shown on television that some viewers may come to feel crime is a commonly used way to obtain things people want.

To test their hypothesis about the effects of television Hennigan and her colleagues needed to compare people who were exposed to television to people who were not. They could not use random assignment to do this, but they were able to take advantage of a naturally occurring event and to conduct a quasi-experiment.

In the late 1940s, a large number of businesses received licenses to operate television stations. By 1949, the number of stations had grown so rapidly that the Federal Communications Commission (FCC) became alarmed and placed a ban on all new licenses. Since television was in its infancy at this time, many communities were left

A family watching television in the early 1950s. Hennigan and her associates used a quasi-experiment to determine the effects of the introduction of television into American homes.

without a station. This decision created an experimental group (communities who were receiving television in the early 1950s) and a control group (communities who were not).

The dependent variable was the crime records kept by the police departments in the communities. First, the researchers looked at the frequency of larceny among the communities that had television stations. They found that after television was introduced in these areas, larceny increased significantly. Then they looked at the larceny rates during the same period of time in the no-television communities. No comparable increase was found.

Since television was not randomly assigned to the various communities, other factors could have been responsible for the differences between them. For example, television could have been introduced first to urban areas, and the no-television communities could have been in rural areas. Since crime rates differ between rural and urban areas, this might explain the difference the researchers had found.

In 1953, the FCC removed its ban. This created the possibility of seeing if the effect found with the early-television communities was repeated in the late-television communities. Hennigan and her associates found that when television was introduced to these communities, larceny also increased significantly; during this time period in the early-television communities, the larceny rate stayed the same. In other words, in two separate areas, at two different points in time, the introduction of television was followed by an increase in the rate of larceny. These findings make it quite reasonable to conclude that television has an effect on larceny rates. And this conclusion is reached without the benefit of random assignment.

SUMMARY

Causal relationships between variables are studied with the experimental approach, in which experimenters manipulate or change one variable (called the independent variable) and examine whether this causes changes in another variable (called the dependent variable). The most common setting for an experiment is a laboratory.

Researchers compare differences between subjects in the different conditions of an experiment and determine whether or not they are statistically significant. They also consider three aspects of the validity of an experiment. Internal validity concerns whether the independent variable and the independent variable alone is responsible for differences on the dependent variable. The biggest threat to internal validity is that subjects in the different conditions of an experiment may differ from one another in ways that affect their scores on the dependent variable. The technique used to address this threat is called random assignment. Since the independent and dependent variables are supposed to faithfully reflect the constructs of interest, researchers must also be concerned with an experiment's construct validity. Several things can threaten the construct validity of an experiment, including demand characteristics, evaluation apprehension, and experimenter expectancies.

Finally, researchers must be concerned with the external validity, or generalizability, of a laboratory experiment. Laboratory experiments have been strongly criticized for producing findings that are not generalizable beyond the laboratory. Because of this concern, researchers also conduct field experiments.

A field experiment is conducted in a natural setting. Variables are manipulated and behavior is observed, but the subjects are not aware that they are in a study. In these studies, researchers hope to obtain behaviors that are more natural and thus more generalizable. Researchers who conduct research in natural settings are often unable to randomly assign subjects to different conditions of an experiment. When random assignment cannot be used in an experiment, a quasi-experiment is conducted. In quasi-experiments, internal validity is achieved by obtaining multiple measurements of the dependent variable and using these to exclude alternative explanations of differences between the subjects on the dependent variable.

THE DESCRIPTIVE APPROACH

There are two major differences between the descriptive approach and the experimental approach. First, variables are manipulated in the experimental approach, but are not manipulated in the descriptive approach; instead, already existing differences in variables are examined. This leads to the second difference: As a rule, the descriptive approach is used to study noncausal, or nonfunctional, relationships because usually variables must be manipulated to study a causal relationship. This section examines two methods researchers use to gather information in descriptive studies—surveys and observational methods.

Surveys

The goal of surveys is to determine the frequency of a phenomenon among a large group of people. This is the technique public opinion polling firms use to determine such information as whom people will elect in a presidential election or what people's attitudes are toward abortion. When social psychologists conduct a survey, their purpose is usually to use the data on the frequency of a phenomenon to investigate the relationship between variables of interest. For example, if researchers are interested in the relation between religious affiliation and racial prejudice, they might conduct a survey to determine the percentage of Catholics, Protestants, and Jews who favor busing children to achieve racially integrated schools.

Just as there are steps when conducting an experiment, so there are steps when conducting a survey.

Step 1. Selecting a Sample

The goal of surveys is to accurately describe the characteristics of a large group of people, but the cost and time of collecting information from every person in the group, called a *population,* is usually prohibitive. Therefore, survey researchers usually collect the needed information from a **sample** (Warwick and Lininger, 1975). A culinary example illustrates how a sample can be used to make statements about the characteristics of a population.

Sample: a segment of a population which is studied to make inferences about the characteristics of the total population.

Imagine that you are interested in determining the quality of the food at a restaurant that has a very large menu. All the meals on the menu comprise the population of food in this restaurant. (In the terminology of survey research, the meals would be called *units* or *elements*.) You could spend four to six weeks ordering every meal on the menu. But this would be very expensive and could have dire consequences for your stomach. A much more reasonable strategy is to order a small number of meals and to generalize from this sample to the total menu.

Random sampling: a procedure for selecting a sample in which every element (person) in a population has the same chance of being in the sample and for selecting elements (people) for inclusion on the basis of chance.

There is a problem in this strategy. How will you know that the few meals you have eaten are representative of the total menu? In survey research, this problem is solved by a technique called **random sampling.** Random selection does not mean some haphazard procedure of selection. Rather ramdom sampling involves a precise procedure which ensures that the odds of one person being selected are no greater or no less than the odds of any other person being selected. If true random sampling procedures are used, one should obtain a sample that is representative of the total population. The more people there are in the sample, the more representative it will be—so long as the sampling procedure is truly random.

Return to the restaurant for a moment. Imagine that there are 200 meals on the menu. You number them from 1 to 200 and use a computer program to select the numbers from 1 to 200 in a random order. You order the meal represented by the first number (say, 27) the first day, the meal represented by the second number (say, 112) the second day, and so on until you have eaten 10 meals. Since all meals have an equal chance of being among the numbers selected by the computer, there is no bias in the selection of your sample. This way, the 10 meals you eat will give you a good idea of what the rest of the food on the menu is like. If you eat 20 meals, the sample could be even more representative of the total menu, and you will be even more sure about the quality of the food you did not taste.

In actual surveys, the elements are people rather than meals, and researchers work out very precise strategies to select samples of people who are representative of the populations from which they have been drawn. These samples do not have to be very large to enable researchers

In surveys, researchers use interviews to collect information on people's attitudes, opinions, and behavior.

to make inferences about a population. For example, firms interested in whom people will vote for in a presidential election can get very accurate estimates of the voting behavior of sixty or seventy million people from a sample of less than 2,000 individuals. They use a very complex procedure, but the basis of it is random sampling. (Do not confuse random sampling with random assignment, which is used in experiments to equate subjects in the different conditions of an experiment.)

Step 2. Collecting the Information

Two techniques are used for collecting information in a survey: interviews and questionnaires. An **interview** (Cannell and Kahn, 1968) can involve a conversation that is unstructured and freeflowing or structured. In structured interviews, the interviewer has a very specific set of questions to ask and goes from one question to another until all have been answered. Although an interview is described as a conversation, it is a conversation with very specific purpose—to get reliable and valid information from the interviewee. Thus, before an interview is conducted, researchers spend considerable time and effort on the structure of the interview and the questions contained in it.

Traditionally, survey interviews were conducted face to face. In recent years, an increasing number are being conducted over the telephone. Telephone interviews are now popular because almost everyone has a telephone (which eliminates most bias in the selection of a sample) and because it costs much less to interview someone over the phone than to go to a person's home for the interview. One popular and economical technique presently used for telephone interviews is called *random digit dialing*. A computer is given all the three-digit prefixes in a geographical area; it then randomly selects the last four digits in telephone numbers and dials those numbers. This technique produces representative samples at a cost lower than that of face-to-face interviews (Dillman, 1978).

The **questionnaire** eliminates the need for an interviewer. Because there is no interviewer to explain or clarify the questions, great care must be taken in the preparation of a questionnaire. Clear, concise instructions must be written and questions that are confusing or likely to be misunderstood by the subjects must be eliminated. Researchers should also avoid questions that would bias people toward a certain answer—for example, the question "You do believe pornography should be made illegal, don't you?" should not be used because it almost forces a person to answer yes. Also, the researcher must be alert for questionnaires that appear to be carelessly filled out and answers that appear to reflect a **response set** (Rorer, 1965). For example, a person who answers yes to 90 percent of the questions is probably showing a response set. And finally, because there is no interviewer to "ease" the person into sensitive or embarrassing areas of questioning, these types of questions are best avoided in questionnaires. Despite these problems, questionnaires provide an inexpensive and usually valid way of collecting information, and they are used in many surveys.

Interviews and questionnaires also have other uses in social psychology. For example, much of what is known about the relationship between

Interview: a method of data collection in which a researcher engages a person in a conversation.

Questionnaire: a method of data collection in which people are presented with a written set of questions and asked to answer them on their own.

Response set: a tendency to answer all questions a certain way irrespective of the content of the questions.

personality characteristics and social behavior is based on information gathered from questionnaires. (See chapter three.) In experiments where the variable of interest is a characteristic of the subjects, a researcher may use a questionnaire to obtain information about this characteristic. Also, in many studies, the dependent variable is subjects' answers to a questionnaire. For example, researchers who investigate different technqiues of changing people's attitudes often use an attitude questionnaire as the dependent variable.

Step 3. Analyzing the Results

After a survey is completed, researchers need to describe the relationships that have been found. Say a group of researchers is interested in the relationship between income and people's sense of control over their lives. (Both of these variables could be measured by using an ordinal scale.) The researchers will probably not be able to determine the causal relationship between these two variables because the amount of money people earn could affect their feelings about how much control they have over their lives, or the amount of control people feel they have over their lives could affect how much money they earn. A researcher can, however, describe how strongly these two variables are related by using a *correlation coefficient*.

Topic Background

The Correlation Coefficient

To determine the degree to which two variables are related, or vary together, researchers compute a statistic called the correlation coefficient. The relation between two variables can be positive—high scores on one variable can be related to high scores on the other variable; it can be negative—high scores on one variable can be related to low scores on the other variable; or it can be nonexistent—scores on one variable can be unrelated to scores on the other variable. The figure below on the left illustrates a perfect positive correlation between people's weight and the number of calories they consume each day; the more they weigh, the more calories they consume. The center figure illustrates a perfect negative correlation between people's weight and the speed with which they run a mile; the more they weigh, the slower they run a mile. The figure on the right describes a nonexistent correlation between weight and grades in college; the amount people weigh is unrelated to their college grades.

If two variables are perfectly negatively related, the correlation coefficient is -1.00; if they are perfectly positively related, the correlation coefficient is $+1.00$; and if there is absolutely no relationship between the two variables, the correlation coefficient is 0.00. Thus, correlations cannot be larger than $+$ or -1.00 or smaller than 0.00. Note that a negative correlation is just as strong as a positive correlation; they differ only in how the two variables are related.

Although the figures present two perfect correlations of 1.00, in practice correlations of this size are rare. Correlations of less than 1.00 can still provide valuable information about the relationship between two variables. For example, the correlation between how much people weigh and how fast they can run a mile is probably no more than .50, but knowing how much people weigh gives you some basis to predict how fast they will run a mile. Colleges and universities use tests that correlate imperfectly with grades to decide which students they will admit.

The final thing that one must remember about the correlation coefficient is that it indicates how strongly two variables are related, not which variable causes which. Causal relationships cannot be inferred from a correlation coefficient.

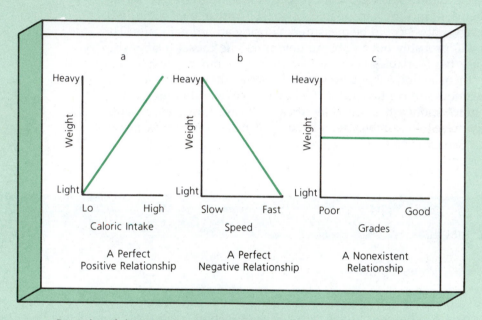

Examples of three possible kinds of relationships between two variables.

Observational Methods

Researchers can learn a great deal about social variables by observing *natural social behavior*. Three characteristics distinguish natural social behavior from behavior obtained in a typical experiment: (1) it is not created for the sole purpose of conducting research, (2) it occurs within a natural setting (for instance, a class or a student union), and (3) it will happen whether or not a researcher is present (Tunnell, 1977).

The major advantage to studying natural social behavior is that this approach may help researchers avoid the problem of **reactivity.** Reactivity

Reactivity: the process in which measuring a variable causes changes in that variable.

is a problem in all sciences, but is of special concern in the social sciences because of the kind of variables social scientists study (Webb, Campbell, Schwartz, Sechrest, and Grove, 1981). For example, people in interviews may not express their true attitudes, or people in experiments may not act the way they would normally act because of evaluation apprehension or experimenter expectancies. Problems such as these have led many social psychologists to argue that at least some of the discipline's research efforts should be devoted to observations of natural social behavior through field studies, content analysis, archival studies, or simple observation.

Field Studies

The *field study* is a technique popular with anthropologists and also used by social psychologists. The researcher observes and records people's daily behavior and does as little as possible to disturb or change the way the subjects behave. In field studies, researchers can observe and record behavior from a distance or they can be *participant observers*. Participant observers join the group and take part in its activities. One classic example of a field study done by social psychologists is an investigation of a religious cult whose members believed that the world would end on a specific date and that they would be saved by people from outer space (Festinger, Riecken, and Schachter, 1956). The researchers posed as people who accepted the cult's doctrine, and they observed the members' reactions when the appointed day of destruction came and went and their extraterrestrial friends did not appear.

Content Analysis

Researchers can also examine the records people leave behind. Ever since humans first made markings on a cave wall, they have been leaving records of what they thought and did. Today it is possible to obtain a permanent copy of almost anything a person says or writes. This can take the form of books, letters, newpaper or magazine articles, political speeches, movie or television scripts, or popular song lyrics. *Content analysis* involves systematically observing, coding, and analyzing these written or verbal communications. It can be used to better understand a phenomenon of interest or to test a prediction from a theory.

Rokeach, Homant, and Penner (1970) used content analysis to determine the authorship of a set of historical documents—the Federalist Papers. The Federalist Papers were several articles written in the late eighteenth century. Their purpose was to persuade citizens of the United States to support the ratification of the Constitution. The authors of most of these articles are known, but the authorship of some is disputed. Some people attribute them to James Madison; others attribute them to Alexander Hamilton. Rokeach and his associates compared the values emphasized in articles known to be written by Hamilton and those known to be written by Madison to the values emphasized in the disputed articles. This comparison disclosed a much greater congruence between the values emphasized by Hamilton and those found in the disputed articles than between Madison's values and those of the disputed papers. Thus, it was concluded that

Hamilton was the author of the disputed papers. This conclusion has been supported by other independent analyses of the Federalist Papers (for example, Mosteller and Wallace, 1963).

Lau and Russell (1980) used content analysis to test a theory of how people explain their successes and failures. According to this theory, people attribute their successes to personal characteristics and their failures to factors beyond their control. The documents that were content analyzed were interviews with athletes that appeared in the sports pages of daily newspapers. The authors analyzed the explanations athletes gave of why their team had won or lost a game. Consistent with the theory, it was found that the athletes tended to attribute their wins to personal characteristics and their losses to factors beyond their control.

Archival Studies

The researcher can also study the records that accumulate over time, or historical documents. One valuable source of information is government records. These were used by Grush (1980) to determine whether the amount of money candidates spend in an election affects their chances of winning. Candidates for the presidency of the United States are required by law to report how much they spend, and Grush was able to obtain copies of these reports from the Federal Elections Commission. He computed the correlation between how much money a candidate spent in a specific state and how many votes the candidate received. The more candiates spent, the more likely they were to be elected.

Simple Observation

Finally, social psychologists often conduct studies by simply making a hypothesis and testing it by observing a specific behavior that occurs in the real world. The first study described in the prologue used simple observation to test the hypothesis concerned with basking in reflected glory. Cialdini and his associates simply observed the manner in which students dressed after a win and after a loss.

Research Highlight

Do It Yourself: Class Projects in Social Psychology

Recently I gave my students the task of picking a social phenomenon, formulating a hypothesis about the variables that might affect it, and testing the hypothesis by making observations of natural social behavior. Following are brief synopses of some of their studies.

The Eating Habits of Normal and Obese College Students Stanley Schachter (1971) has proposed that there may be differences in the factors that influence the eating habits of normal and obese people. He has suggested that people of normal weight eat in response to internal cues (for example, stomach contractions), while obese people eat in response to external cues (for example, the sight of food, the time of day). Maria Teresa Bajo and Lynn Carmichael attempted to test this hypothesis by observing the kinds of choices normal and obese college students made at vending machines. The students had their choice of two machines: a candy machine which clearly displayed the type of food a purchaser would get, and an ice-cream machine which displayed only the names of the possible choices.

Two hypotheses were made. First, it was predicted that the obese people would use the candy machine more than would the normal people. Second, obese people would use the machines more during mealtimes than would normal people. The first hypothesis was not supported; the two groups used the machines an equal amount. The second hypothesis was confirmed. Obese and normal people did not differ in how much they used the machines during nonmealtimes, but during mealtimes the obese people used them significantly more often than did the normal people. This finding was consistent with earlier research (Schachter and Gross, 1968), which has shown that obese people's eating behaviors are influenced by the time of the day (specifically, mealtime) rather than whether they are hungry.

Seating Position and Exam Grades   Many instructors believe that their better students tend to sit toward the front of the room. Cindy Maederer and Mary Blair Young decided to objectively test this belief. Their subjects were students in an introductory psychology class. They observed where the students sat and obtained (with the students' consent) their scores on eight quizzes they had taken. Then Maederer and Young correlated where students sat in the class (first row, second row, and so on) with their average grades on the quizzes. The correlation was small, but statistically significant. The nearer students sat to the instructor, the higher were their grades.

Sex Role Stereotyping in Magazines   This study involved a content analysis of the advertisements people read. In recent years, there has been a dramatic increase in the number of women who have entered the business world. As a result, there are now some magazines targeted at the working woman. Jean Carsten, Barbara Grosslight, and Ruth Moscowitz wondered whether the advertisements that appear in these magazines reflect a new view of women or reflect traditional sex role stereotypes about the interests of men and women.

To investigate this question, the researchers obtained a random sample of ads from men's and women's business magazines. Then they compared these ads on the types of product they were selling and the way the products were sold. Sixty-seven percent of the products advertised in the men's business magazines were intended for business use; 18 percent of the products advertised in women's business magazines were intended for business use. Also, less than 1 percent of the men's advertisements concerned products that would enhance the user's personal appearance, but almost 30 percent of the women's advertisements had this purpose. And most (90 percent) of the men's advertisements used a sales pitch that pointed out the objective benefits of the product (increased profits, increased efficiency); most women's advertisements appealed to the user's vanity or need for status. In short, the men's advertisements were rational and logical; the women's were irrational and emotional. There may be a new woman in the work force, but the ads she reads have not changed.

The Approaches Compared

You have read about a number of different ways of conducting social psychological research. This section compares them in terms of their ability to produce findings which are internally valid and findings which are externally valid. Then the ethical considerations which underlie all kinds of research are presented.

Internal Validity

A study is internally valid if the researcher can conclude that changes in one variable are due to changes in another variable. The laboratory experiment is the best means to establish the internal validity of a relationship because the researcher can control or eliminate things other than the independent variable which might have an impact on the dependent variable. This can also be done in a field experiment, but it is often a very difficult task. The descriptive approaches, as a rule, provide the least internally valid results because they take place in natural settings, where it is often difficult to control for or eliminate differences between people on variables other than the ones in which the researcher is interested.

Consider a survey in which a positive relationship is found between income and a sense of control—the more money people earn, the greater a sense of personal control they have. Without further study, one cannot exclude the possibility that a third variable (age, for instance) is responsible for the positive relationship; as people become older, both their income and their sense of control may increase. Another example is the study of explanations athletes give for wins and losses. Athletes are not randomly assigned to teams, so one cannot exclude the possibility that athletes who are picked by winning teams give more internal explanations of their behavior than do athletes picked by losing teams. The results of this study may reflect the characteristics of the athletes on different teams rather than the effects of winning or losing.

This does not mean that descriptive approaches are worthless. There are techniques for increasing the internal validity of a descriptive study. For example, in the study on income and sense of control, groups of people can be matched or equated on the variable believed to be responsible for the differences between them (age). If the differences in sense of control still exist between people with different income levels, the third variable can be excluded as the cause of the differences. Even in cases where matching and other comparable techniques cannot be used, a simple description of a noncausal relationship often aids in the understanding of social phenomena.

External Validity

External validity refers to the generalizability of the results a researcher obtains. In general, descriptive studies produce more externally valid results than do laboratory experiments because most descriptive studies observe natural, everyday behaviors. Subjects in descriptive studies are not aware that they are being observed and they are more likely to be representative of a general population than are subjects in a laboratory experiment because a major concern in many descriptive studies (such as surveys) is to collect information from people who are representative of a larger group.

This does not mean that descriptive studies are always externally valid and laboratory studies are always externally invalid. Whether a study is externally valid is an empirical question; the facts determine whether a finding is generalizable. One must objectively determine if a result obtained in the laboratory can also be found in the field; similarly, one must objectively determine if a result obtained with one set of subjects in a descriptive study can be generalized to another set of subjects.

There is no one best way to study social behavior. Experimental methods are strong where other methods are weak, and vice versa. The most appropriate way to investigate a phenomenon of interest is to use as many different approaches as possible. If these different approaches converge and all produce the same results, one will probably have a good understanding of the phenomenon of interest.

The Ethics of Research

Thus far, only passing attention has been given to ethics in social psychological research. This does not reflect the importance of this issue to social psychologists. The organization to which most social psychologists belong, the American Psychological Association, publishes a book for its members entitled *Ethical Principles for Psychologists*. This book sets forth the principles that are supposed to guide psychologists in their research; failure to follow these principles can lead to public censure and dismissal from the organization. Further, many graduate programs provide courses on ethical standards for psychologists. The ethics of research are complex, and involve questions about deceiving, harming, and invading the privacy of subjects.

Deception
In the laboratory experiment on similarity, the subjects were deceived. The experimenter lied to them about how similar they were to the other person, did not tell them that she was a confederate, and led them to believe that she was being shocked. Is this ethical? Deception is considered by most researchers to be an undesirable practice, but not automatically an unethical one. In some instances, it provides the only means possible for the investigation of a phenomenon of interest (Kidder, 1981). The crucial question about an experiment that employs deception is the extent to which it harms subjects.

Harm
Many experiments, even those which do not involve deception, use procedures that might cause some harm to subjects. Usually, the harm involves creating stress or embarrassment or making subjects do something that would reflect badly on them (such as stealing or hurting another person). If there is a possibility of harm, the researcher must carefully weigh the

benefits to science against the costs a subject might pay. This is an extraordinarily difficult judgment to make. Decisions that appear to be ethical at the time they are made may look quite unethical in retrospect.

For example, in the 1930s, the United States Public Health Service decided to conduct a long-term study on the degenerative effects of syphilis. The researchers believed that the results of such a study would be of considerable scientific value and might contribute to finding a cure for this disease. They identified a group of syphilitic black men, living in a rural part of Alabama, and kept careful records on them over a 30-year period. During this time, a cure for syphilis was found—but because they did not want their study "contaminated," the researchers did not provide their subjects with the cure. On several occasions, they actually prevented the men from taking the drug which would have cured their syphilis or at least stopped its spread in the community. As a result, many of these men's wives were infected and their children were born syphilitic. This study has been compared to the experiments conducted in Hitler's death camps (Jones, 1981).

Few social psychologists have conducted studies as dramatically harmful as this one, but they still must be concerned about the ethics of their research. Certain practices are required to ensure that subjects are not abused when they participate in research. If a university receives federal

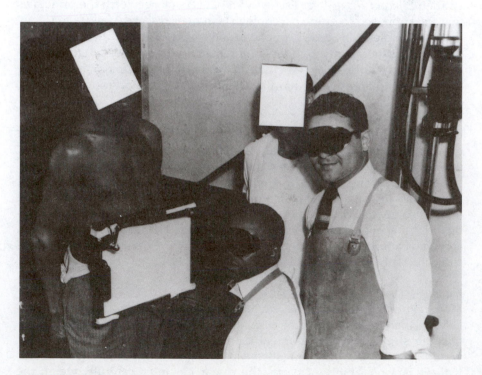

Some of the victims of the Tuskegee syphilis experiment. Many of them and their families suffered because the researchers prevented them from receiving treatment for their illness.

funds, it must have an internal review board which evaluates the ethics of all experiments conducted on its campus; without the approval of this board, an experiment cannot be conducted. Also, subjects must be given an *informed consent* form before they participate in an experiment. This form tells the subjects what to expect from the experiment and whether they will experience any psychological or physical distress as the result of participation. The form also makes it clear to the subjects that if they refuse to participate, they will not be penalized in any way. In most experiments, it is required that subjects read and sign this form before they can take part in the study.

When an experiment is over, the experimenter must *debrief* the subjects. At this time, the experimenter tells them the full truth about the experiment and addresses any problems the experiment might have caused. Any university which receives federal funds is required to provide both informed consent and a debriefing to the subjects who participate in experiments.

Invasion of Privacy

In a laboratory experiment, subjects are aware that they are in a study, they know they will be observed, and they have the right to refuse to participate. In many descriptive studies and field experiments, however, people are not aware that they are in a study. Is this ethical? There is no simple answer to this question. A researcher who conducts this kind of study must do a cost-benefit analysis. There are no laws against observing people without their awareness, but researchers must carefully consider what they plan to do. In general, the more public the behavior of interest, the less of an ethical problem there is in observing it. If the behavior is quite private and personal, however, researchers must think very carefully before they decide to observe it. After all, psychologists have no more right to invade a person's privacy than do any other members of society.

SUMMARY

In the descriptive approaches, no attempt is made to change or modify the variables of interest; as a result, a descriptive approach usually tests noncausal hypotheses. The survey is a descriptive approach that attempts to determine the frequency of a phenomenon in a large group of people by collecting information from a representative sample of those people. The technique used to obtain a representative sample is called random sampling. The two methods used to collect information in a survey are the interview and the questionnaire. A statistic called the correlation coefficient is used to describe the relationships found in a survey.

Another descriptive approach to studying social behavior is to simply observe it. There are several ways of doing this. One is a field study, in which the researcher observes the natural behavior of a group of people over a period of time. Content analysis and archival studies examine the records people have made of their actions. In content analysis, the researcher analyzes what people have said or written; in archival studies, the researcher analyzes historical records. Finally, the researcher can simply observe whether a group of people engage in a certain behavior.

The major disadvantage of a descriptive approach is that it is usually more difficult to establish the internal validity of a relationship in a descriptive study than in an experimental study. However, the results of a descriptive study are also usually more generalizable than are those obtained from an experiment, especially a laboratory experiment.

Irrespective of the approach used, researchers must consider the ethics of their study. Ethical problems arise in laboratory experiments because subjects may be deceived or harmed in some way. In a study conducted in the field, there is the additional ethical issue that subjects may not be aware they are in a study and thus cannot give their consent to be in it. Researchers must carefully weigh the benefits that might result from a study against the costs to the people being studied and whenever possible must attempt to eliminate or reduce these costs.

Applications

Program Evaluation

Every year, federal, state, and local governments spend millions, if not billions, of dollars on programs that provide services to the public. These programs range from providing federal support for the treatment of people suffering from kidney failure (the government spends over seventy million dollars a year on this) to providing free meals to disadvantaged elderly people. In the late 1960s and early 1970s, government agencies began to formally require that such programs be evaluated. This gave rise to a tremendous increase in the number of people who were program evaluators. Many social psychologists were employed in this capacity because the techniques they had developed to study social behavior were also amenable to the evaluation of programs.

Service programs do not exist in a well-controlled laboratory setting, but in the real world; thus, many things other than the services a program provides could produce changes in a person's behavior—and these changes could mistakenly be attributed to the program. In other words, it is often difficult to determine if a program alone is responsible for changes in the people it serves. This is the issue of internal validity. In a laboratory experiment, the researcher controls or eliminates these other factors by randomly assigning people to different conditions of the experiment. In the

In recent years, it has become clear that the elderly can be helped to lead active and productive lives. Program evaluation is used to determine the effectiveness of programs designed to do this.

real world, this is often difficult or even immoral and unethical. If a government agency decides to do something about a group of elderly people who are slowly starving to death by providing them with three free meals a day, the agency cannot test if this will improve the health of the elderly by choosing, on a random basis, half of these people to be in an experimental group (to receive three meals) and the other half to be in a control group (to receive no meals). What is a valid and reasonable procedure in the laboratory becomes cruel and inhuman in the real world.

Therefore, techniques that can produce internally valid findings without the use of random assignment, such as quasi-experiments and other field research techniques, are used to evaluate programs. This section presents the evaluation of an actual program. The primary purpose is to describe how the principles and methods presented in this chapter were utilized in an applied research project. Therefore, only the results of the evaluation that serve to illustrate these are described.

The program of interest was designed to serve elderly individuals who either had been institutionalized for psychiatric reasons or were in danger of being institutionalized. The rationale underlying this program was that if these people could be taught certain basic skills in areas such as personal care and social communication, they could avoid long-term institutionalization and live in the community (Patterson, Dupree, Eberly, Jackson, O'Sullivan, Penner, and Kelly-Dee, 1982). The program served 50 to 60 clients at a time. When this evaluation was conducted, the program had been in operation for about four years and had provided treatment to about 400 people.

PROCESS EVALUATION

In the early stages of evaluating a program, it is necessary to conduct a *process evaluation*, in which the evaluator compiles a detailed description of how the program is presently functioning and determines whether the program's operation matches an agency's description of how the program is supposed to function (Rutman, 1977). In this program, the major component was a series of classes which attempted to teach the clients various personal care and social skills; therefore, it was necessary to observe how these classes were conducted. In addition, the staff members who ran these classes were interviewed, the records they kept of the clients' performances were examined, and the clients' activities over the course of a day were recorded.

Once these data had been obtained and analyzed, a meeting was set up between the evaluators and the administrators of the program. The information that had been collected was given to the program administrators and suggestions for changes in the program were made. One major suggestion was that the operation of classes and the records of clients' performance be made more objective and standardized. This would make the program more efficient and provide the groundwork for an evaluation of the effects of the program on its clients. It would also reduce the problem of evaluating a program in which staff members performed the same function in very different ways, which is like conducting an experiment in which several experimenters operationalized the independent variable in different ways.

It takes a long time to describe a complex program with a large number of staff members and clients, and it takes even longer to implement changes that make the program amenable to evaluation. In this instance, the process took almost two years.

OUTCOME EVALUATION

The purpose of an *outcome evaluation* is to determine if a program has achieved its goal (Rutman, 1977). Most programs have both short- and long-term goals. In this program, the short-term goal was for the clients to learn the skills taught in the classes. The long-term goal was to enable the clients to live in the community rather than in an institution.

The manner in which evaluation of short-term goals is carried out can be illustrated by looking at how one of the classes in this program was evaluated. The class addressed personal hygiene skills, such as bathing, nail care, and hair care. These are important skills for the elderly—failure to keep clean may cause others to avoid them and thus reduce desired social contacts; failure to trim toenails properly can result in gangrene and other health problems. The first step in the evaluation of this class was to develop a scale that reliably and validly measured the skills taught, to be used as the dependent variable in the investigation of the class's effects on the clients. A scale was developed that had both of these characteristics (Patterson, Penner, Eberly, and Harrell, 1983).

The easiest way to investigate the effects of the class would have been to have randomly assigned people to a personal hygiene class or to no class (a control group) and to have compared the two groups' scores on the scale after several weeks. But this would have endangered both the psychological and physical health of members of the control group. Therefore, random assignment was not possible and, instead, a quasi-experiment developed by Campbell and Stanley (1966) was used.

In the first part of this quasi-experiment, clients' personal hygiene skills were measured when they entered the program and then a second time after several weeks of training. A significant improvement in their hygiene skills was found, but several factors other than the training could have produced this. For example, an external event such as an increase in social security benefits could have improved the clients' moods and thus increased their concern with personal appearance. Or perhaps the teachers of the classes were biased in their posttraining ratings of the clients.

To eliminate the first possibility, exactly the same procedure was used with a group of clients who entered the program several months later. Again, a significant improvement was found. Since these were different people, in the program at a different time, this second finding greatly reduced the probability that some specific event, external to the training, was responsible for improvement in either group of clients. To control for the possibility of teacher bias in the posttraining measure, independent ratings of the clients' personal hygiene skills were obtained from someone who was not involved in the class. It was found that the more a client improved in the class, the more the independent rating increased. Basically the same procedures were used to evaluate the other classes. Clients showed significant improvement in every class. The program had achieved its short-term goals.

The evaluation of whether the program had achieved its long-term goal—to prevent institutionalization among its clients—involved several different studies, only one of which is described here. It was decided to determine the percentage of program "graduates" who were living in the community after treatment and compare this to the percentage among people who were similar to the clients but had not participated in the program.

A large number of the program's clients had transferred there from a state mental hospital. Participation in the program was voluntary, and clients at the hospital had to give their permission to be transferred. Many refused to do so. These people made up the comparison group. The following types of information were collected about each of them: nature of disorder, length of hospitalization, age, race, sex, marital status, and date of refusal to be transferred. Then a group of the program's clients were selected who were similar to the refusal group on these characteristics. This procedure was intended to serve the same purpose as random assignment; to equalize the two groups on factors other than the variables of interest.

The major comparison made was the percentage of refusers who were still in an institution two years after the date of refusal versus the percentage of program clients who were still in an institution two years after the date they had agreed to enter the program. Among the refusers, 80 percent were still in a psychiatric institution. Among the clients who entered the program, 79 percent were living in the community. This comparison suggested that the program was achieving its long-term goal.

At least partly because of the positive results of this evaluation, this program's treatment procedures have been implemented at several other institutions, with considerable benefit to their elderly mental health clients. This case study of a program evaluation illustrates that the value of the principles and procedures discussed in this chapter is not limited to basic research. The research methods utilized by social psychologists in basic research can be used to solve real-world problems.

Chapter Three

Personality Characteristics and Social Behavior

Prologue

John B. Pryor, Frederick X. Gibbons, Robert A. Wicklund, Russell H. Fazio, and Ronald Hood (1977). Self-focused attention and self-report validity. *Journal of Personality,* **45,** 513–27.

Background

This chapter concerns the role social experiences play in the development of personality characteristics and the effects differences in personality characteristics might have on social behavior. Almost all social psychologists would agree that social experiences during childhood and adolescence play an important part in the shaping of personality. Fewer would agree that differences in people's personality characteristics produce differences in their social behavior. Those who question whether personality characteristics are a major cause of social behavior point out that information about people's personality characteristics does not very accurately predict how they will act in social situations; the correlation between personality characteristics and actual behavior is generally .30 or less. Pryor and his colleagues believed that under certain circumstances the relationship could be much stronger than this correlation suggests. They conducted the following study to investigate one such circumstance.

Hypothesis

It was hypothesized that if subjects became more introspective and focused their attention on themselves, the ability to predict their social behavior from their personality characteristics would improve greatly.

Subjects

The subjects were fifty-four male students attending the University of Texas at Austin.

Procedure

In the first phase of this study, each subject filled out a 16-item questionnaire concerned with how sociable he was. The independent variable, self-focus, was manipulated by placing a mirror in front of half the subjects while they filled out the scale. The mirror was used because other researchers had found that when people see themselves in a mirror, their tendency to focus on and pay attention to themselves as opposed to things around them increases.

A few days later the subjects returned to the laboratory, supposedly to take part in an experiment on manual dexterity. A subject and an attractive female student (a confederate) were told that it would be a few minutes before the experiment began and were asked to wait together in a small room. The confederate had been instructed not to speak until the subject spoke to her. The subject's behavior toward the woman was observed and scored in two ways: (a) the confederate rated how sociable he was and (b) an observer recorded the number of words he spoke to the confederate. These two scores reflected the dependent variable, sociability.

Results

Correlations were computed between each subject's score on the sociability questionnaire and his scores on the two dependent variables. The correlations between scores on the sociability questionnaire and scores on both dependent variables were much greater when the mirror had been present than when it had been absent. Put in terms of the hypothesis, the presence of the mirror when the subjects filled out the questionnaire increased their self-focus and attention and, thus, increased the predictability of their social behavior from their personality characteristics.

Implications

This study and others conducted at about the same time rekindled interest among social psychologists in the role of personality characteristics in the determination of social behavior. Their findings indicated that it might be unwise to totally discount personality characteristics in the study of social behavior; under certain circumstances and among certain people, personality characteristics are reflected in social behavior. This research and the effects of a mirror are examined more fully later in this chapter.

Socialization process: the process wherein humans are taught about themselves and the world around them.

This chapter covers two separate, yet related, topics. The first part examines the **socialization process,** which has two general effects on people. First, it teaches them a set of socially accepted ways of thinking and acting and a common set of guidelines for their social behavior; this is called *social development*. At the same time, since the socialization process is not exactly the same for any two individuals, it can produce differences between people. This is called *personality development*.

The second part of this chapter is primarily concerned with the issue addressed in the chapter experiment. To what extent are differences in people's social behavior due to differences in their personality characteristics? The applications section addresses how personality characteristics affect people's mental and physical health.

THE SOCIALIZATION PROCESS

It is safe to assume that the subjects in the chapter experiment differed considerably in the personality characteristic, sociability. Theories and research concerned with the socialization process address the causes of such differences as well as the causes of similarities in the characteristics of a group of people.

This first section describes three theories of how humans become socialized. It also discusses the role of the socialization process in the development of people's self-concept and the development of gender differences in social behavior.

Because this is a textbook on social psychology, it places more emphasis on theories concerned with the social experiences of individuals than on theories concerned with the physical and intellectual changes in people. Be aware, however, that these other factors must be considered for an understanding of the socialization process. For example, puberty has dramatic effects on the way a person interacts with others. A ten-year-old boy normally treats girls with bemused disinterest. However, his social behavior will change considerably when his hormones go into action in two or three years.

Psychoanalytic Theories

Probably the first person to propose a formal theory on the origins of individual differences in social behavior was Sigmund Freud (1856–1939). According to Lamb (1984), Freud made two very significant contributions to theory and research on the socialization process: (1) He was one of the

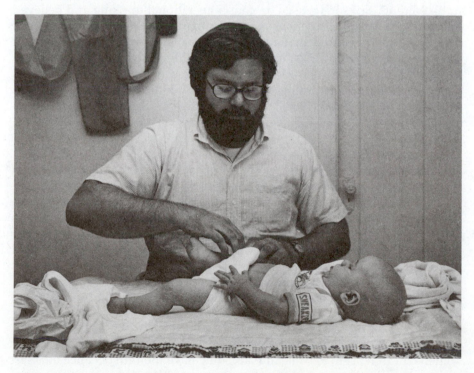

Parents do more than just take care of their children; they teach them social behaviors and help shape their personalities.

first people to propose that an understanding of an adult's emotions and personality characteristics depended in large part on an understanding of the adult's experiences as a child. (2) He argued that social experiences, such as the manner in which parents feed or toilet train a child, play an important role in personality and social development. Before Freud, these social experiences were considered relatively unimportant. But Lamb also points out that Freud was primarily interested in adults; he did not turn his attention to infant's and children's behavior until the last few years of his life. Freud's followers, particularly Erik Erikson, ultimately attempted to develop comprehensive theories of personality and social development among children.

Erikson studied under Freud's daughter, Anna, in the 1930s and was psychoanalyzed by her. Unlike many of Freud's followers, Erikson did not altogether reject Freud's ideas. Instead, he attempted to revise them so that they reflected the realities of the socialization process. Erikson believed, like Freud, that social development occurred in stages and that what happened in one stage was quantitatively and qualitatively different from what happened in another. Also, in Erikson's view each stage was marked by a crisis caused by the new demands the environment placed on people, and that this crisis had to be resolved before they moved into a new stage. In addition, he believed that the manner in which people resolved a crisis at one stage would affect how they resolved the crises that occurred during later stages. This idea was also borrowed from Freud. But unlike Freud, Erikson focused on conscious rational thinking and believed that the crises people experienced were primarily due to social factors. And whereas Freud believed that all the major stages in human development occurred by puberty, Erikson proposed that developmental stages occur throughout a person's entire life. He identified eight such stages and labeled each of them according to the crisis or conflict that occurs during it (Erikson, 1968; Erikson, 1969; Hall and Lindzey, 1978; Shaffer, 1979; Thomas, 1979).

Trust versus Mistrust

The first stage occurs during the first year of life. The conflict is between trusting others and mistrusting others. The primary determinant of whether people develop a trustful or distrustful view of the world around them is the manner in which their parents, especially their mother, respond to their physiological and emotional needs. If the mother is warm, nurturant, efficient, and consistent in the way she treats an infant, it will tend to develop trust in others and trust in itself. If the mother is cold, neglectful, and inefficient, the infant will develop an attitude of mistrust. This attitude will influence the individual's resolution of conflicts in later stages.

Autonomy versus Shame and Doubt

When children begin to walk and talk, they have their first chance to assert themselves. This can be seen in the two year old's discovery of the word "no." Most two year olds respond to this newfound power the way a dictator would respond to acquiring the atomic bomb. They view it as the ultimate weapon. Erikson believed that the manner in which the parents respond to the child at this stage has a strong influence on the child's future development. If they respond in a restrictive, punitive fashion, the child is unlikely to become an independent, autonomous adult.

Initiative versus Guilt

This stage takes place between ages three and six, when children are able to make plans to accomplish tasks and achieve goals. Their behavior has a purpose. Erikson believed that parents must, within limits, encourage these activities because they lead to feelings of independence. Note the phrase "within limits." The parents must teach the child what kinds of activities are appropriate (such as saving Christmas money to buy a new toy) and what kinds of activities are inappropriate (such as planning to steal a younger sister's money to buy a new toy).

Industry versus Inferiority

During this stage, children begin school and they begin to be influenced by people other than their parents. This precipitates a new crisis. Children compare their abilities to those of their classmates and they have demands placed on them by their teachers. If these experiences are positive, children will come to see themselves as competent and capable. If the experiences are negative, children will lack self-confidence as they move toward adulthood.

Identity versus Role Confusion

When children enter adolescence they confront, in Erikson's view, the most important stage in their development (Hall and Lindzey, 1978). During this stage they experience several changes that result in an **identity** crisis. Their bodies change in dramatic ways; for example, secondary sex characteristics begin to develop. People begin to treat them differently because they expect them to start acting and thinking like adults—to start making plans for their future and taking adult responsibilities. But adolescents are not adults. Who and what are they?

Identity crisis: a conflict people experience over who and what they are.

Erikson believed that adolescence was a time of searching for an identity. Teenagers who have not successfully resolved earlier crises may experience role confusion at this time—they may not know who they are or where they are going. Some may attempt to resolve this by identifying with a particular group, such as the hippies in the 1960s or the punk rockers in the 1980s. Others may attempt to establish their identity by clearly showing what they are not, which may lead to rebellion against their parents. A colleague once described his own adolescent rebellion in the following way: "I was unable to talk to my father for more than three minutes without having an overwhelming urge to pound the living crap out of him."

Successful resolution of the identity crisis is difficult. People who have resolved this issue have a good sense of who they are and where they are going. People who have not achieved this resolution have also failed to develop a sense of purpose or direction in their lives—a failure that continues to plague them as they go through the later stages of development.

Intimacy versus Isolation

During young adulthood, people must begin to consider marriage and other long-term relationships. If such relationships are to be successful, they must be willing to give of themselves, to be intimate with another person. Intimacy involves more than sexual relations: it involves the ability to trust another person and to care about and be concerned about that person without fearing the loss of individual identity. Thus, the extent to which people are capable of intimacy depends a great deal on how they have resolved their identity crisis; if they are still unsure of their own identity, they will be incapable of true intimacy.

Generativity versus Stagnation

People who are incapable of intimacy "stagnate" during the next stage. They are completely self-centered. When I think of this type of person, the image of Frank Burns on the old television series "M.A.S.H." comes to mind. The character Hawkeye Pierce represents the other extreme during this stage—a *generative* individual, who cares deeply about other people and desires to help them.

Ego Integrity versus Ego Despair

The last of Erikson's eight stages occurs during old age, the time of life when the proverbial chickens come home to roost. If people can look back on their life and say "I Did It My Way," they are experiencing ego integrity; if they ask "Why Me, Lord," they are experiencing ego despair.

Erikson's theory is a popular and interesting one. It has influenced the thinking of educators and psychologists. Erikson has used it to explain the behavior of notable historical figures such as Martin Luther, Adolph Hitler, and Mahatma Gandhi. For example, Erikson (1969) proposed that many of Gandhi's actions as an adult could be traced to the way he resolved his identity crisis when he was an adolescent. Unfortunately, it is quite difficult to empirically test Erikson's theory. Thus, acceptance of his ideas depends more on how good they sound than on objective facts. As a result, Erikson's theory has had somewhat less of an impact on contemporary views of the socialization process among social psychologists than have later theories. Despite this, it presents an insightful and thoughtful analysis of the socialization process and of personality development.

Cognitive Developmental Theories

The *cognitive developmental* approach to socialization is also a stage theory, but it defines the stages in terms of changes in a person's cognitive or intellectual abilities rather than in terms of the conflicts a person encounters. According to Jean Piaget (1965), the originator of this theoretical orientation, human development is marked by qualitative differences in the way people think. That is, the difference between a 12 year old and a five year old is not simply that the 12 year old has learned more but that the children think about themselves and the world around them in different ways. This approach proposes that the intellectual stages are the result of maturation and that all humans go through these stages in the same order, although at different ages.

Lawrence Kohlberg, an American follower of Piaget, applied Piaget's ideas on cognitive development to the socialization process. Kohlberg (1969) proposed that social and personality development proceeds through an ordered sequence of qualitatively different stages. The social behavior that occurs at each stage is the result of two factors: the level of the child's intellectual development and the kinds of social experiences the child encounters. In other words, social development parallels intellectual development. This relationship can be seen by examining developmental changes in children's **social cognitions** (Schantz, 1975). Kohlberg (1969) believed that changes in social cognitions parallel changes in intellectual reasoning. Thus, just as children are incapable of certain intellectual processes before a certain age, so are they incapable of certain social cognitions before a certain age.

Social cognitions: thoughts or ideas about another person or group of people.

A large amount of research has been done on the kinds of social cognitions children display at different ages. Before the age of five, children appear to have a very egocentric view of the world (Shantz, 1975). They are unable to put themselves in the place of others. When asked to describe another child, they will respond in terms of how that child treats them. For example, a four or five year old will probably use phrases such as "She gives me toys" or "He takes my candy" rather than "She is nice" or "He is mean" to describe another child. Preschoolers' social behavior reflects these social cognitions. For example, at this age they are not likely to help another child unless they are told to do so or are promised a clear-cut reward for helping.

As children move into the school years, two related changes in social cognitions can be seen. First, they have some understanding of how other people feel and they see that other people possess personal attributes, such as goodness or badness. They describe other people's personality characteristics in less egocentric terms, but their descriptions are still rather simplistic. Second, children begin to consider another person's intentions in their evaluations of his actions (Costanzo, Coie, Grumet, and Farnill, 1973). For example, before age four or five, children do not really distinguish between a little boy who breaks a glass while he is setting the table for dinner and a little boy who breaks a glass while stealing a cookie. To preschoolers, both have done something bad. By the time children are six or seven, they evaluate the actions of the helpful-but-clumsy child as less bad than the actions of the cookie thief. They are able to consider the reasons a person does something and are able to take another person's perspective. According to Kohlberg (1969), this is a vital part of the socialization process.

During middle childhood (ages 10 to 13), another important change occurs in social cognitions: Children see the behavior of others as being caused by their personalities. A study by Ruble, Feldman, Higgins, and Karlovac (1979) illustrated this. Preschoolers and 10 year olds were shown a videotape of a child choosing an object with which to play. Both groups were then asked to explain why the child on the videotape had chosen the object. The younger children tended to attribute the behavior to a characteristic of the object ("It is pretty"); the older children tended to attribute the behavior to some characteristic of the child ("He likes to play with blocks"). Adults also tend to make the second kind of attributions. (See chapter four.)

By the time adolescence occurs, children are quite sophisticated in their social cognitions. They can put themselves in another person's place and are capable of seeing themselves as others do. Further, they can recognize that other people's behaviors can be influenced by temporary circumstances. For example, adolescents can understand why their mother, who is usually quite warm and loving toward them, is cold and distant after she has had a fight with their father.

Kohlberg believes that the key to social development is a restructuring of the way children think about themselves and the people around them. Children develop from incredibly egocentric infants to adults who can see the world as other people do. Kohlberg's ideas on social development are considered quite important by social psychologists, and they appear frequently in this book.

Social Learning Theories

Social learning theory is based on the assumption that social behavior is almost entirely learned. This theory assumes that biological factors may play an indirect role in the socialization process, but that the experiences humans have as they grow up are crucial in the shaping of their personality and social behavior. Social learning theorists focus on the mechanisms whereby humans learn social behavior.

Although there are several different social learning theories, the most popular one among social psychologists is probably the theory proposed by Albert Bandura (1969, 1977). Bandura agreed with other social learning theorists that classical conditioning, operant conditioning, and drive reduction all play a part in the socialization process. But he felt that **observational learning** is the major mechanism responsible for social and personality development.

Observational learning: the process whereby people acquire new behaviors by imitating or modeling other people's behavior.

Bandura's theory began with the simple and noncontroversial premise that humans learn from observing other people's behavior. He proposed that three things are needed for observational learning of social behavior to occur. First, the children must attend to the person who is performing the behavior; this person is called a *model*. Second, the children must be able to remember what the model has done. And third, the children must engage in *motoric reproduction*. This means that the children must be able to practice the behavior they have seen. Through motoric reproduction the children get the "feel" of the behavior. Children's initial attempts to reproduce the original behavior are usually rather inept approximations of the real thing, but as they practice their actions become closer and closer to the original.

If Bandura's theory stopped here, it would be inadequate. It would not explain why some of the things we observe as children have an impact on our adult behavior and others do not. It would also fail to account for the differences in people's personality characteristics that result from the socialization process. To explain these, Bandura used the concept of reinforcement. Bandura disagreed with the proponents of other learning

Proponents of social learning theory believe that children learn a great deal simply by observing the behavior of adults.

theories who believed that reinforcement and drive reduction are necessary for learning to take place. He proposed that observational learning can occur in the absence of reinforcement, but that reinforcement is a crucial determinant of whether a person will actually perform a behavior. In other words, people learn a multitude of behaviors, but they perform and incorporate only those that are reinforced.

According to Bandura, there are three kinds of **reinforcement:** direct, vicarious, and self. *Direct reinforcement* is the consequence children experience when they perform a behavior. These consequences are usually determined by someone else. For example, a child has seen a model (his father) swear. When he performs this behavior, his mother spanks him. This should reduce the incidence of swearing in the future (at least in front of his mother). In *vicarious reinforcement*, the reinforcement is delivered not to the child, but to the model. For example, a child sees a parent swear and the parent's friends laughing in apparent approval. The laughter provides vicarious reinforcement by showing the child what will happen if he performs the same behavior.

Self reinforcement is the individual's own reaction to his own behavior. As the product of social experiences, children and adults develop internal standards of what is "good" or "bad" behavior. If a behavior meets a person's internal standards, it is a rewarding experience and the individual is likely to perform that behavior in the future. If the behavior does not meet these standards, the individual will try to improve the behavior. Failing this, they will abandon it. Once internal standards are developed,

Reinforcement: positive or negative consequences of a behavior which affect the probability that the behavior will occur again.

they influence the individual's behavior more or less independently of the actions of other people.

A personal example will illustrate Bandura's theory. I play racquetball. Unfortunately, I play it badly, and when I miss a shot I have a charming habit of slamming my racquet against the wall and swearing. For about two years my son watched me play with my friends, but because the game is somewhat dangerous he did not play with us. When he became old enough, I started playing racquetball with him. The first time we played, he missed a shot, slammed the wall with his racquet, and swore. As far as I know, he had never engaged in this behavior before; he learned simply from observing my (infantile) behavior. No reinforcement was needed for the learning to occur. Although he knew the behavior, he did not perform it until the appropriate situation arose. But why was he so upset with his performance? Because, based on his observations of adults playing the game, he had developed an internal standard of what was an acceptable level of racquetball skill. When he failed to reach this standard, he punished himself. While I find it "all right" for me to swear and hit things, I do not like my son to do this; therefore, I stopped behaving this way in front of him and punished him when he did. Despite this, he continued the behavior. As noted earlier, once people develop internal standards, those standards exert a tremendous influence on their behavior.

Bandura's theory has been influential among social psychologists primarily because, unlike some other theories, it can be experimentally tested. Note how it provides a mechanism to explain the two basic elements of the socialization process: the development of a common core of social behaviors among humans and the development of individual differences in social behavior.

Development of Self-concept

A person's *self-concept* is "a theory which the individual has unwittingly constructed about himself as an experiencing functioning individual" (Epstein, 1973, pp. 3–4). It is generally agreed that the development of a self-concept is a crucial aspect of the socialization process.

One major theoretical explanation of how social experiences influence a person's self-concept is proposed by the **symbolic interactionist** orientation. (See chapter one.) Symbolic interactionsts place great emphasis on the role society and other people play in the determination of social behavior. They also believe that individuals must interact with others to develop a self-concept (Schlenker, 1985).

Reflected appraisal: a self-appraisal that is based on other people's reactions to a person.

Other people appear to serve two functions in the development of a self-concept. The first is to provide a **reflected appraisal.** Consider one aspect of the self-concept, people's beliefs about their physical appearance. Other people's reactions to them influence whether people view themselves as attractive or unattractive. For example, a male college student has had three blind dates in the last month. In all three instances, 15 seconds after his date saw him she said she was sick and returned to her room. This man probably sees this behavior as an appraisal of his physical appearance and this, in turn, affects his self-concept.

Research Highlight

Self-concept in Chimpanzees

A fascinating series of studies by Gordon Gallup (1970, 1977) has provided information on exactly what self-concept is and how social experiences affect its development.

For a long time, biologists and anthropologists argued that only humans are capable of developing a self-concept. When humans look at themselves in a mirror, they know they are seeing a reflection, not another person. But most animals react to their mirror image as if it were another animal because they lack that ability of *self-recognition*, a vital component of self-concept. But Gallup claimed that chimpanzees and certain other great apes appear to have a self-concept. In saying this, he did not mean that chimpanzees think of themselves as smart or handsome, but that they recognize themselves as a distinct entity. He based this conclusion on observations of chimps' reactions to their mirror image.

Gallup let chimps look at themselves in a mirror for several days. Then he anesthetized them and used an odorless, nonirritating chemical to make a bright red mark on their faces. When the animals awoke, he placed them in front of a mirror again. Although the chimps had never seen this animal with the red-marked face before, they almost immediately recognized it as themselves. They repeatedly touched the red mark on their faces, apparently trying to figure out where the mark had come from. When Gallup later removed the mark, the self-touching stopped. When this same experiment is conducted with lower animals or other primates, they show no signs of self-recognition. They react to their mirror image as if it were another animal with a red mark on its face. Only humans and great apes have demonstrated the ability of self-recognition (Gallup, 1977).

Next Gallup examined the symbolic interactionists' argument that people develop their self-concept through interactions with others. He observed two groups of chimpanzees. Members of the first group had been reared with other chimps; members of the second group had been reared in social isolation. Again he let the chimps look at themselves in a mirror for a few days and then anesthetized them and marked their faces. When the animals in both groups awoke, he placed them in front of a mirror. Among the socially isolated chimps, there was virtually no touching of the red mark on their faces. The socially experienced chimps touched the mark repeatedly; they recognized themselves. The different reactions of members of each group are presented in the following figure.

In a similar study, Hill, Bundy, Gallup, and McClure (1970) gave some isolated chimps "remedial social experience"—they put them together in the same cage after initial testing. When these chimps were retested, they showed self-recognition. These findings suggest that "to conceive of yourself, you may need to see yourself as you are seen by others" (Gallup, 1977, p. 335). This conclusion is exactly what the symbolic interactionists argued.

Of course, chimps are not the same as humans. But observations have found that before the age of two, human infants react to their mirror image as if it were another playmate. After this age, they recognize themselves in the mirror. This suggests that self-recognition is an ability learned through social interactions with others.

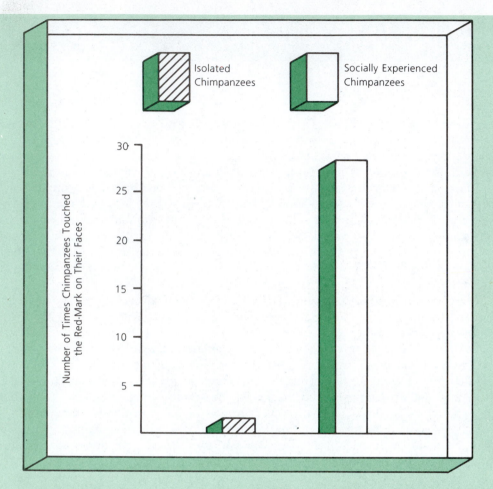

The animals raised in social isolation did not recognize themselves when placed in front of a mirror.
Source: Gallup (1977).

A study conducted with second graders illustrates how reflected appraisals can influence children's self-concepts and their behavior. The children were randomly assigned to one of two groups. In the first group, the children were told by their teacher that their performance in class indicated that they were quite good at and interested in mathematics. Children in the second group received a lecture from their teacher on the value of being good at and interested in math. Two weeks later the children in both groups were given tests that measured their self-confidence in mathematics and their ability to solve math problems. The children in group one, who received a positive reflected appraisal, displayed significantly more self-confidence about their math skills and performed significantly better on the math test than did the children in group two. (See figure 3-1.) In other

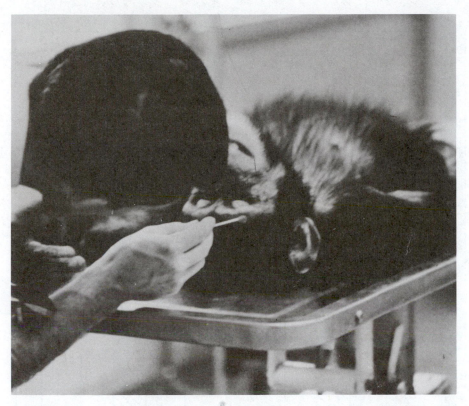

This is one of the chimpanzees being prepared for Gallup's self-concept experiments. If the animal touches the mark on its face when it sees itself in a mirror, this suggests it has a self-concept.

words, both groups of children saw themselves and acted in a way that was consistent with the judgments of other people (Miller, Brickman, and Bolen, 1975).

A second function other people serve is to provide **comparative appraisals.** This is also illustrated by my racquetball experiences. For several months, I played with other psychology professors and came to the conclusion that I was a pretty good racquetball player. Unfortunately for my self-concept, I decided that I was good enough to play with some friends who teach physical education. After 15 minutes of running into walls and chasing the ball, my opinion of my ability dropped dramatically; in comparison to my new partners, I was not a very competent player. The people against whom we compare ourselves are called a *reference group*. As our reference groups change, so do our self-evaluations (Schlenker, 1980).

Comparative appraisals: self-appraisals that are based on a comparison of a person's abilities and other characteristics to those of other people.

Sex Differences in Social Behavior

Close your eyes and imagine how a typical male subject in the earlier experiment would have acted toward the attractive female confederate. Form a mental image of his nonverbal behavior, his posture, and his verbal expression. Now imagine that the subject in the experiment is female and

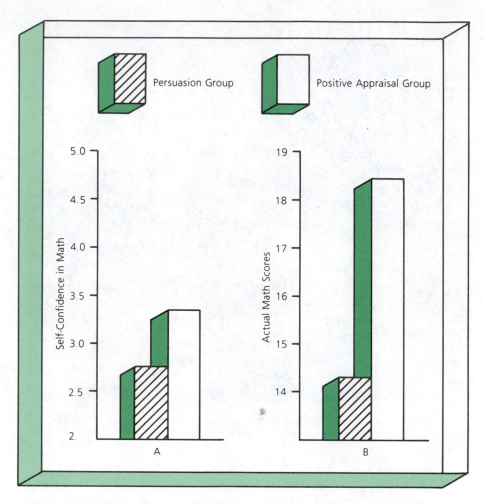

Figure 3-1. *Children who were told they already had mathematical ability did better than those who were told they should try to do well at math.*
Source: Miller et al. (1975).

the confederate is an attractive male. What would be a typical female subject's verbal and nonverbal social behavior?

It does not take much effort to conjure up two very different images. To be sure, many social behaviors are common to both males and females, but many others are quite different. Behaviors that are more characteristic of one sex, or gender, than another are called **sex role behaviors.** Recall the definition of a *role:* The behavior typically displayed by a person who occupies a certain position. Thus, a person who displays behavior typical of those who occupy the male position in a society is displaying masculine sex role behaviors, and vice versa.

Biological Explanations

As you have probably noticed, men and women are biologically different. They have different hormones, reproductive systems, external genitalia, and chromosomes (males have XY chromosomes, females have XX chromosomes). They also behave differently. In lower organisms, hormonal differences produce behavioral differences between the males and females of the species, but in humans the picture is less clear. The chromosomal sex of an individual can be determined through certain procedures, but other physical or social attributes may affect that individual's sex role behavior.

John Money and his associates (Money, Hampson, and Hampson, 1957; Money, 1965; Money and Ehrhardt, 1972) have extensively investigated biological causes of sex role behaviors. Money focused his attention on children with *hermaphroditism*, a rare biological anomaly in which a person possesses the reproductive organs of both sexes. One group of children studied by Money had a female (XX-chromosome) biological sex but had both female internal reproductive organs and a penis. At birth these children were labeled boys, even though they could have been labeled boys or girls. Money was interested in how these hermaphrodites would behave as they grew up: If biological sex was the sole cause of sex roles and sexual identity, they should display typical female behaviors as adults. However, Money found that less than five percent of the hermaphrodites displayed any deviance from typical male behaviors. In other words, the sex these people were labeled at birth—not their biological sex—determined their sex roles.

In some instances, the parents of hermaphrodites discover that they are raising their children as the "wrong" sex and wish to change and raise them according to their chromosomal sex. Studies disclose that until children are about three years old, their assigned sex can be changed and few if any problems will result. After this age, however, changes will cause problems in sex roles and sexual identity (Money and Ehrhardt, 1972).

The results of Money's research suggest that biological differences between males and females are not the primary reason males and females act differently. Sex differences in social behavior appear to be caused by how children are socialized.

Social Learning Theory Explanations

The basic premise of the social learning theory explanation of sex differences is that males and females have different learning experiences. From infancy, they are perceived to have different characteristics and, thus, they are treated differently by their parents. For example, Will, Self, and Datan (1976) gave mothers both male and female infants with which to play. They found that when a male infant was identified as a girl, the mothers smiled at it more and were more likely to give it a doll to play with than when it was identified as a boy. Female infants that were identified as boys were more likely to be given a train than were those identified as a girl. Two of the women were sure that the boy they had been given was a girl because "she" was sweet and cried softer than boys do!

Children receive continual reinforcement and encouragement for engaging in behaviors typical of their sex (Ruble, 1984). Male and female children are given different kinds of toys with which to play and are treated differently by their parents. Boys, for example, are more likely to receive physical punishment than are girls, and fathers play rougher with boys than with girls (Fagot, 1974; Jacklin and Maccoby, 1983).

Observational learning also appears to play a role in sex role socialization. Lamb and Urberg (1978) reported that children tend to observe and imitate same-sex parents more than they do opposite-sex parents. Given that the models boys and girls imitate display male and female sex roles, it is quite reasonable that boys adopt male sex roles and females adopt female sex roles. Further, it appears that the more strongly parents display stereotypical sex role behaviors, the more they reinforce stereotypical sex roles in their children. Thus, children have plenty of opportunities to learn sex role behaviors and receive plenty of reinforcement for displaying those behaviors.

Cognitive Developmental Explanations

Recall that the cognitive developmental view of socialization proposes that changes in children's social behavior are due to changes in their cognitions about themselves and the world around them. In turn, these changes in

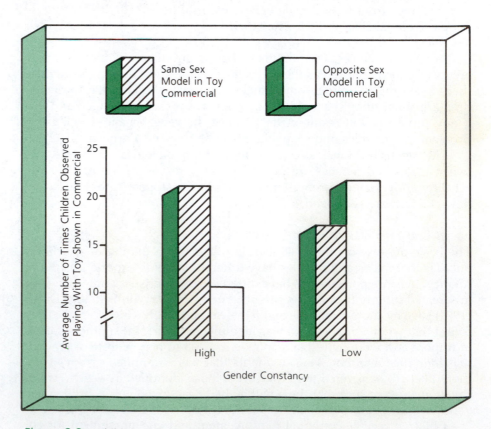

Figure 3-2. *Children who had reached the stage of gender constancy were more influenced by same sex than opposite sex models. Children who had not reached this stage were equally influenced by both models.*
Source: Ruble et al. (1981).

cognitions result from children's experiences and their intellectual maturation.

Children are aware of sex roles and have **sex role stereotypes** by the time they are three or four years old (Ruble, 1984). But according to the cognitive developmentalists, sex role behaviors are acquired primarily through the emergence of **gender constancy** (Ruble, 1984). Once children grasp the concept of gender constancy, they realize that despite changes in their appearance, interests, and so on, they will remain the same sex. They then show an increased tendency to engage in behaviors that are "appropriate" for their sex.

Some evidence suggests that gender constancy interacts with observational learning to affect the development of sex differences. Ruble, Balaban, and Cooper (1981) found that among children who had not yet developed the cognition of gender constancy, the actions of a same-sex model in a toy commercial were no more influential than were those of an opposite-sex model. But among children who had developed gender constancy, the same-sex model was much more effective. (See figure 3-2.)

This discussion of sex differences in social behavior must be placed in the proper context. Although men and women exhibit different behaviors, these behaviors occasionally overlap. Also, not all men and not all women act in the same way. And some individuals display both masculine and feminine behaviors; these are called **androgynous** individuals. In short, there are no hard and fast behavioral differences between the sexes. In addition, the fact that some differences do exist in the ways men and women act does not justify prejudicial attitudes and discriminatory behavior toward any person. (See the section on prejudice in chapter nine.)

Sex role stereotypes: beliefs that certain activities, behaviors, interests, and occupations are appropriate for and typical of each sex.

Gender constancy: people's consistent labeling of themselves and others as male or female.

SUMMARY

The socialization process produces both a common core of shared social behaviors and differences between people's personalities. A number of theories of how the socialization process affects people have been proposed. Erikson's theory is primarily concerned with personality development. He saw humans as progressing through a series of stages, each marked by a conflict or crisis. He believed that the manner in which people resolve these developmental crises shapes their adult personalities.

The cognitive developmental approach to socialization proposes that social development parallels intellectual development. The social behavior children display is the result of their level of intellectual development and the specific social experiences they have had. One of the changes that children go through is in the way they think about the behavior of other people; they move from an egocentric view of the world to being able to see the world from another person's perspective.

The social learning theory proposes that children are socialized through several learning mechanisms. One of the most important of these is observational learning, wherein children learn social behaviors by observing the actions of others.

Most male and female children are taught to act in a manner "appropriate" for their sex.

Another aspect of the socialization process is the development of a self-concept, or a person's "theory" of what kind of individual he or she is. The symbolic interactionists theorize that the self-concept is largely shaped by a person's experiences with other people. People learn who they are by seeing how others react to them and how they "stack up" against others.

Theories of the socialization process also consider the development of sex, or gender, differences in social behavior. The biological differences between males and females do not seem to be as important in the shaping of the adult personality as do the socialization experiences of boys and girls. Almost from birth, boys and girls are treated differently and are expected to act differently. They develop a sense that they are male or female and then appear to model the actions of members of their own sex. These experiences result in some of the differences between the social behaviors of men and women.

PERSONALITY CHARACTERISTICS AND SOCIAL BEHAVIOR

Like many of the constructs in which social psychologists are interested, personality has a number of different meanings. When *People* magazine talks about a "personality," it means some well-known public figure, such as Eddie Murphy or Brooke Shields. Freud used the term to describe the combination of the id, the ego, and the superego. A few years ago, the newspapers contained extensive analyses of the "personality" of John Hinckly, Jr., who expressed his love for actress Jody Foster by attempting to assassinate President Reagan. And there has been a best-selling book based on the sixteen "personalities" of a woman named Sybil.

Although all of these usages are reasonable, they are not what social psychologists mean when they talk about personality. Social psychologists define **personality** as the collection of characteristics possessed by a person that guides that person's thoughts and actions and makes him or her different from others. Rather than study the entire personality and how it affects people's social behavior, researchers usually study only individual characteristics, or **personality traits.** In the chapter experiment, Pryor and his associates investigated how the personality trait called sociability affected the social behavior of males when they interacted with a female confederate.

Personality traits: specific, enduring aspects of a person's personality which produce certain thoughts and actions.

This section presents three positions on the relationship between personality characteristics and social behavior: the trait approach, the situationist approach, and the interactionist approach.

Trait Approach

As explained in the chapter experiment, some researchers believe that personality traits explain consistencies in a person's thoughts and actions across time and situations as well as differences in the behaviors of two people in the same situation.

Consider Peter the Great, "Tsar of All the Russias," who ruled Russia from the late 17th through the early 18th century. His biographer, Robert Massie (1980), has detailed Peter's remarkable trait of personal courage and his consistent courageous behavior.

When Peter was 22, he found himself on a ship being battered by a storm. The other passengers hid in their cabins, sure they were going to die, and the priest gave them last rites. Peter, however, braced at the helm in the wind and spray [and] did not give up hope. Each time the ship rose . . . and fell . . ., Peter struggled with the rudder, trying to keep the bow into the wind. (Massie, 1980, p. 130)

Several years later, Russia was involved in a 20-year war with Sweden. Peter led his soldiers into combat. One of his advisors wrote:

[I had to remind him] that he was also mortal like all men and that the bullet of a musketeer could upset the whole army and place the country in serious danger. (Massie, 1980, p. 357)

Peter again showed courage in another battle:

Throughout this part of the battle, the tall figure of Peter was conspicuous among the Russian troops. Although his height made him an obvious target, he ignored the danger and spent his energies directing and encouraging his men. (Massie, 1980, p. 504)

The trait approach also proposes that all people possess the same basic traits but in different amounts, and that people behave differently depending on how much of a trait they possess. For example, Augustus, King of Poland, a contemporary of Peter's, was a royal wimp whose major lifetime achievement was fathering 354 illegitimate children. Rather than courageously leading his country, Augustus spent most of his time out of bed trying to figure out how to please anyone more powerful than he. He was installed as a puppet king of Poland by at least three different countries. Augustus was not a courageous man. He possessed less of the personality trait courage and behaved less courageously than did Peter the Great.

How do we measure such differences in the amount of a personality trait? The trait courage does not physically exist. It is a construct, inferred from the two kings' actions and used to explain the differences in their behavior. Since personality traits do not physically exist, social psychologists translate them into observable, measurable entities by using personality scales.

Personality Scales

Social psychologists translate personality traits into something concrete by creating a personality scale. A *scale* provides a numerical representation of how people differ on some variable. To be useful, the scale must be both reliable and valid.

Reliability In the chapter experiment, Pryor and his associates devised a 16-item scale to measure the trait, or construct, of sociability. Readers unfamiliar with the development of scales might wonder why they used so many items to measure a single trait. The reason is that for a scale to be reliable, or produce consistent measurements, it usually must contain several items. To understand why, imagine that you are interested in how much your dog weighs. You take the dog in your arms and get on the bathroom scale—200 pounds. Then you get on the scale alone—165 pounds. The dog weighs 35 pounds. Or does it? The scale is old and rusty and may be slightly off. You use another scale and it tells you that the dog weighs 36 pounds. You repeat this procedure with several other scales and you get weights of 34, 35, 36, and 35 pounds. You now can be pretty sure that the dog weighs 35 pounds. In this case, as in the case of personality scales, a single item gives a slightly inaccurate measure of the trait. But when a single item is put together with a number of other items, the total scale provides an accurate, or reliable, estimate of the trait of interest.

Validity   Personality scales must also be *construct valid*; they must measure the construct they are supposed to measure. In personality research, several techniques can be used to determine the construct validity of a scale. In the simplest, the *extreme group technique*, people are given a personality scale. On the basis of their scores, they are divided into high and low groups. Then behaviors that should differ between the two groups are examined.

This technique is illustrated by a study I recently completed. I was interested in the construct validity of a scale developed by Spielberger, O'Hagen, and Kling (1978) to measure sociopathy—the tendency to act in an egocentric, selfish, and uncaring manner. I gave the subjects the scale and classified them as high or low scorers. I then placed the subjects in the helping experiment described in the previous chapter to look at a behavior that should be related to this trait: willingness to help someone at some cost to the helper. (Sociopathic people should be less likely to do this than nonsociopathic ones.) I found that high scorers helped the confederate significantly less than did low scorers. This suggests that the scale is construct valid, although researchers would need to conduct many more similar studies before they could be sure that the scale really measured sociopathy.

Topic Background

Predicting Behavior the Easy Way

Psychologists use scales to measure people's personality characteristics and predict their behavior. Many people, however, believe that there is a much simpler way to do this: look to the stars. Although no scientific evidence supporting astrological predictions has yet been found, people continue to believe in them. Snyder and Shenkel (1975) have proposed an explanation for this phenomenon. They suggest that astrological predictions and descriptions are so generally worded that they apply to everyone. Thus, all readers will find something that applies to them. This is called the P. T. Barnum effect. (Barnum was a great showman and promoter of the 19th century. When asked the secret of the success of his circus, he replied that it contained something for everybody.)

Several studies support Snyder and Shenkel's explanation. In one, a general, flattering description of a person was given to a large number of people. Even though all the people received the same description, most strongly believed that it had been written expressly for them. In another study, a psychologist in France advertised himself as an astrologer and invited people to write in for their horoscopes. Although he sent the same description to everyone, more than 200 people wrote to tell him how accurate his description had been. Finally, Snyder and Shenkel gave the same horoscope to a large number of people. Some were told that it was a general description of people, while others were told that it was based on the year, month, and day they were born. People who believed that this description was written especially for them saw it as much more accurate than did those who believed it was a general description.

Another, more recent approach to the prediction of behavior is based on *biorhythms*. According to Gittleson (1975), from the moment of birth, humans are influenced by three biologically based cycles: physical, lasting 23 days; emotional, lasting 28 days; and intellectual, lasting 33 days. Within each cycle are positive and negative phases. One can determine which cycle and phase a person is in at a certain time by knowing the time and date of that person's birth. Advocates of biorhythms believe that the kinds of behaviors people engage in and the effectiveness of these behaviors are influenced by their cycles and phases. They propose, for example, that if you take a final examination on the day when your intellectual cycle is in a negative phase, you will perform poorly.

The validity of biorhythms is widely accepted. Biorhythm charts are found in the daily newspaper; they are computed by electronic calculators; they are used to predict the performance of professional athletes; and they are consulted by many large companies in Japan before their executives engage in a business transaction. But how accurate are these predictions?

David Holmes, Chris Curtright, Kevin McCaul, and David Thissen (1980) used hospital records and information found in the newspaper to determine how biorhythms affected three different aspects of people's lives: how long it took a person to recover from surgery, the date on which a person died, and the performance of professional golfers. They computed the cycle and phase a person was in on the day each event took place and then correlated this with what happened to the person. In all three instances, biorhythms predicted no better than a coin toss.

It is unlikely that findings such as those of Holmes and his colleagues will affect the public's acceptance of biorhythms. Like horoscopes, biorhythm charts make predictions that are so general there is some truth in them for everybody. As long as biorhythms take advantage of the P. T. Barnum effect, many people will continue to believe in them.

Situationist Approach

Standing in almost direct opposition to the trait theorists are researchers who take a *situational approach* to social behavior. The situationists acknowledge that people differ in their traits as the result of different socialization experiences. They contend, however, that human social behavior is not primarily caused by people's traits, but by the characteristics of the situations people encounter (Mischel, 1968). Although Mischel has tempered his position in recent years (Cf. Mischel, 1968, 1979, 1984), other situationists have not. For example, Richard Nisbett (1980) argued that personality traits are useless in predicting or understanding human social behavior and recommended that social psychologists abandon their interest in personality traits and instead concentrate on situational factors. Strong words. Why are the situationists so "down" on considering personality traits as causes of social behavior?

There are two interrelated reasons for the situationists' position. First, as discussed in the chapter experiment, reviews of research literature have disclosed that the correlation between personality traits and actual behavior is typically .30 or less. If you square a correlation, you find how much of the differences between people on one variable can be explained or predicted by differences on another variable. So, a correlation of .30 indicatesthat less than 10 percent of the differences between people's actual behavior can be predicted by differences in their personality traits. The situationists believe that this figure is low because the situation people are in determines what they will do. When examining the differences between Peter the Great and King Augustus, for example, they might point out that Poland's army was much weaker than Russia's and that Russia had never been successfully invaded while Poland was invaded almost annually during this period of time. Thus, Augustus could not afford to be as brave as Peter. In other words, situationists would look at the characteristics of the situations the two men were in to explain the differences in their behavior.

The second reason that situationists discount personality traits is also based on research findings. Recall that the trait position proposes that personality traits manifest themselves in consistency in people's behavior across time and situations. But the situationists point out that empirical studies of consistency in people's behavior do not support this claim (Mischel, 1968). Typically, it has been found that the correlation between people's behavior in one situation and their behavior in another is .30 or less. (Mischel, 1969). The situationists would note inconsistencies in Peter the Great's "courageous" behavior. For example, they might point out that on one occasion Peter fled a battle and left his troops to suffer a murderous defeat at the hands of the Swedish army. They would explain the consistency in his behavior in other battles as being due to similarities in the circumstances surrounding the battles, not as being due to consistency in Peter's personality traits. In sum, situationists feel that behavior is consistent across situations only if these situations place similar demands on the person (Mischel, 1979).

But if there really is no consistency in behavior, why do most people believe that there is? For example, Peter's biographer saw a consistent pattern of courageous behavior throughout Peter's life. And most people see a good deal of consistency in the behavior of others (Bem and Allen, 1974). In response to this argument, the situationists would point to research showing that people tend to see much more stability and consistency in the behavior of others than is really there (Jones and Nisbett, 1971; Nisbett, 1980; Shweder, 1975), and are thus not very accurate observers of others' behavior; or at least, that they do not really understand why other people act as they do.

Trait Rebuttal

Trait theorists agree that people are influenced by situational pressures. Certainly dramatically different situations produce dramatically different behaviors. But underlying these situationally induced differences are stable, consistent patterns of behavior due to personality traits. Trait theorists offer two ways of overcoming the troublesome .30 correlation: Better measurements of behavior and use of moderator variables.

Measurements of Behavior

The trait theorists criticize the procedures used in studies of the effects of personality traits on social behavior. Seymour Epstein (1979, 1980) points out that in the typical study only a single measure of behavior is obtained. He argues that it is unreasonable to expect a person's traits to manifest themselves in the same way in every single situation. Traits are manifested in consistent patterns of behavior across a variety of situations and over extended periods of time. Therefore, to obtain an accurate indication of the role traits play in social behavior, people must be observed in several social situations, just as they must be tested on several items in a personality scale to determine trait levels.

The following example may clarify Epstein's point. Imagine you are seeking a sales job, in which sociability is required. You have done quite well on a paper-and-pencil "test" of sociability, but your potential employer also wants to observe your actual behavior in a meeting with an attractive female. On your way to the meeting, you stop for a candy bar; while eating it, you lose a filling from a front tooth. You are angry, in pain, and feel embarassed over the gap in your mouth, but because you really want the job you go to the meeting and say nothing about your dental problems. You are about as sociable and friendly as an angry rock. Is your behavior an accurate indication of how sociable you normally are? Probably not; you are having a very bad day. A much better indication of how sociable you are would be obtained by observing your behavior over the course of several days.

In a 1979 article, Epstein reported on several studies in which he obtained multiple measures of people's behavior. In the first study, he addressed the question of consistency in people's behavior across time and situations. Subjects kept records of the behaviors they engaged in each day over the course of one month. Then Epstein looked at the consistency in these behaviors. When he computed a correlation between behaviors displayed on the first and the second day of the month or on the last two days of the month, he found it to be less than .30. But when he divided the month into odd-numbered and even-numbered days and computed the correlation between the behaviors displayed on these sets of 14 or 15 days, he obtained a correlation of .74. In other words, when he had a reliable measure, he found clear evidence of consistency in people's behavior. (See figure 3-3.)

In another study, Epstein addressed the issue of predicting behavior from scores on personality scales. Remember that the situationists say this correlation will be about .30. When Epstein used an estimate of behavior based on 14 consecutive days and correlated this with scores on a person-

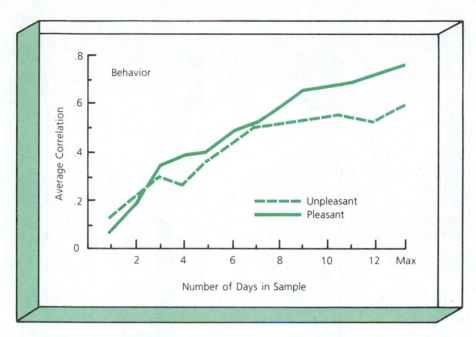

Figure 3-3. *As the number of days observed increased so did the consistency in the subjects' behavior. Copyright 1979 by the American Psychological Association. Adapted by permission of the author.*
Source: Epstein (1979).

ality scale, he obtained a correlation of .61. Epstein's research suggests that by using multiple measures of behavior, the correlations obtained between traits and behavior can be greatly improved.

Moderator Variables

A *moderator variable* influences or changes the relationship between two other variables. Many trait theorists now propose that certain moderator variables increase or decrease the relationship between traits and behavior. The moderator variables discussed here are self-awareness, individual differences in self-awareness, and self-monitoring.

   Self-awareness   In the prologue, Pryor and his associates believed that if people became more introspective and self-focused they would provide more valid and reliable data in their self-reports of personality traits and would thus exhibit increased correlations between scores on personality scales and actual behavior. The phenomenon they studied is called **self-awareness** (Buss, 1980).*

   Simply asking people to think about themselves and the kind of people they are will increase self-awareness, but several studies, including the

Self-awareness: a temporary increase in people's tendency to pay attention to and be aware of the private, internal aspects (attitudes, traits, motives) of themselves.

*Wicklund and Duval (1971) used the term *objective self-awareness* to describe basically the same phenomenon studied by Pryor and his associates. Buss used the term *private self-awareness*. There are differences between the two conceptualizations, but these are not of importance in this discussion.

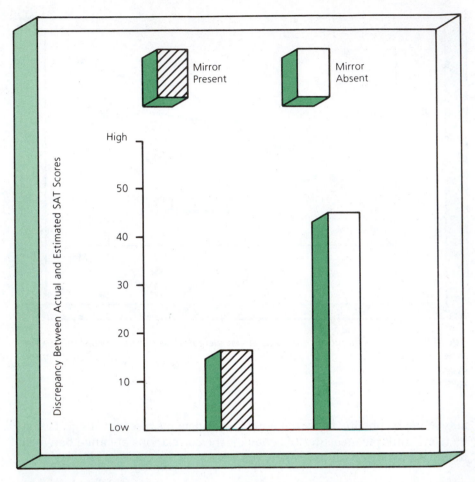

Figure 3-4. *Subjects were much more accurate in estimating their S.A.T. scores in the presence of a mirror.*
Source: Pryor et al. (1977).

one presented in the prologue, show that mirrors increase self-awareness and, thus, the accuracy of self-reports. In another experiment conducted by Pryor and his colleagues (1977), college students were asked to recall their scores on their college entrance examination. Half the subjects did this while seated in front of a small mirror and half did this without a mirror present. Their estimates were then compared to the actual scores obtained on the examination. Recollections of the subjects in the mirror condition were significantly more accurate than were recollections of subjects in the no-mirror condition. (See figure 3-4.)

Individual Differences in Self-awareness The results of several studies suggest that the manipulation of self-awareness can increase the accuracy of self-reports and, thus, the correspondence between scores on self-reports and actual behavior. But since people may show stable individual differences in the extent to which they are self-aware, self-awareness may itself be a personality trait that moderates the relationship between other traits and actual behavior.

The first thing that needed to be done to test this idea was to construct a scale that measured individual differences on the self-awareness characteristic. Fenigstein, Scheier, and Buss (1975) developed such a scale. It measures a construct they called **Private Self-Consciousness**. People who score high on this scale should know themselves quite well and, as a result, the correspondence between their traits and their actual behavior should be good. (See table 3-1 for some items from this scale.)

Private self-consciousness: a personality trait concerned with the extent to which people pay attention to and are aware of the private, internal aspects of themselves.

Table 3-1.   Some items from the scale which measures Private Self-Consciousness. Someone with this tendency would answer true to all the items.

1. I reflect about myself a lot.
2. I'm always trying to figure myself out.
3. I tend to scrutinize myself.
4. I sometimes have the feeling that I'm off somewhere watching myself.

Source: Fenigstein et al. (1975).

Scheier, Buss, and Buss (1978) conducted a study to test this concept. Subjects were classified as high or low on private self-consciousness and then they filled out a self-report scale that measured how aggressive they were. Several weeks later both high and low scorers took part in a laboratory experiment supposedly concerned with the effects of punishment on learning. Their task was to administer shocks to another person (a confederate) while he was learning to solve a problem. The experiment was carefully constructed so that the learner did nothing to provoke the subject. The dependent variable was the correlation between self-reports of aggressiveness and the amount of shock the subjects gave the confederate. Among the people who were rated low in private self-consciousness, the correlation was .09. This indicated that their self-report of how aggressive they were bore little relation to their actual behavior. Among the people who were rated high in private self-consciousness the correlation was .66, indicating that their self-report fairly accurately predicted their behavior.

Self-monitoring   Another personality trait that has been proposed as a moderator of the relationship between traits and behavior is **self-monitoring** (Snyder, 1974, 1979). Self-monitoring can be best explained by describing good self-monitors and poor self-monitors. Good self-monitors are concerned with how they present themselves to others. They are sensitive to the characteristics of the situation they are in and to the actions of other people they encounter in that situation. They use the cues they get from these sources as guidelines for controlling or monitoring their own behavior. As a result, their verbal and nonverbal behaviors fit the situation. In a phrase, they are socially skilled. Poor self-monitors are insensitive to the situation they are in and more or less oblivious of the actions of other people they encounter in that situation; their behavior is controlled by internal dispositions such as attitudes, moods, or traits. As a result, their

Self-monitoring: a personality trait concerned with people's tendency to monitor or control their behavior in social situations.

verbal and nonverbal behaviors are often inappropriate for the situation they are in. They are not very socially skilled.

Everyone can think of people who exemplify both high and low self-monitors. I have a friend whose social skills are awesome. He is at ease and his behavior is appropriate irrespective of the situation he encounters. I have seen him charm both police officers and "coke" freaks. He can converse with college professors and welfare mothers. He sticks to his ideas, but he changes his style of speech and nonverbal mannerisms enough to make his behavior fit the situation. He is a good self-monitor. By contrast, I have another friend who may be the world's worst self-monitor. His ways of speaking and acting are the same irrespective of the situation. For example, we both once attended a Christmas party where half the guests were little old gray-haired ladies wearing Christmas corsages and drinking nonalcoholic punch. My friend sat down in front of these women and proceeded to get very drunk. An hour later, he was lying on the floor when an attractive young woman entered the room. He looked at her, propped himself up on one arms, and in a very loud voice, propositioned her. He is a nice man, but a social disaster.

Snyder proposed that because the behavior of good self-monitors is controlled or guided by situational factors, it varies considerably from situation to situation. As a result, the personality traits and other internal dispositions of good self-monitors do not correlate very well with their actual behavior. In contrast, the behavior of poor self-monitors is consistent across situations because it is primarily guided or controlled by internal dispositions. As a result, their traits and other internal dispositions correlate rather well with their actual behavior.

Several studies have investigated these predictions. In one, Snyder and Monson (1975) looked at the consistency in behavior of good and poor self-monitors. High self-monitors reported significantly less consistency in their behavior across situations than did low self-monitors. At least three other studies have found a stronger relationship between internal dispositions and actual behavior among low self-monitors than among high self-monitors (Snyder and Swann, 1976; Snyder and Tanke, 1976; Zanna, Olson, and Fazio, 1980).

Snyder and Swann classified subjects as high or low self-monitors on the basis of a scale that measured this trait and then measured their attitudes toward affirmative action hiring practices. About two weeks later, the subjects read about a lawsuit in which a woman was suing a university for alleged sex discrimination. The subjects were asked to play the role of the judge in the case and present a verdict. Among the high self-monitors, there was little agreement between the self-reports of their attitudes and the decisions they reached. Among low self-monitors, the agreement was quite good. Evidently, the tendency to self-monitor moderates the relationship between internal dispositions and actual behavior.

Thus, it appears that people differ in the extent to which their internal dispositions determine their actual behavior; some people's behavior can be predicted from their personality traits and other people's cannot (Bem and Allen, 1974). A knowledge of the characteristics of the situation they are in provides the basis for explaining and predicting the behavior of people in the second group. Thus, while personality traits are probably much more accurate determinants of social behavior than the situationists believed, the pure trait position must be qualified somewhat. Traits do not equally impact the behavior of all people all of the time.

Interactionist Approach

Interactionism proposes that behavior is the result of the continuous interplay between people and the situations they encounter (Endler and Magnusson, 1976).* This approach, which has come to be accepted by most social psychologists, suggests that it is pointless to argue whether personality traits or situational characteristics are the more important determinants of social behavior because behavior is influenced by both. Interactionists argue that situational factors exert a strong influence on people's behavior, but they also point out that personality characteristics influence people's choices of the situations they enter.

A short example illustrates this point. If you regularly attend a church or a synagogue, you will notice a great deal of similarity between people's behavior during the services. They follow along with the prayer book; they read aloud when the minister, priest, or rabbi tells them to; they sing only when instructed to do so. Their behavior is clearly under the control of situational variables. But why are they in the church or synagogue in the first place? It seems quite reasonable to propose that internal dispositions such as personality traits influenced their decision to enter this situation. Most people do not lead a life of debauchery Monday through Saturday and regularly attend church on Sunday. People's internal dispositions produce consistency in the type of situations they choose.

Studies by Gormly (1983) and Monson (1985) provide empirical support for this proposal. Gormly found that subjects who rated themselves as energetic preferred to be in situations where energetic activities would take place, and subjects who rated themselves as sociable preferred to be in situations where they would interact with other people.

Internal dispositions also influence people's perceptions of situational characteristics and the actions of other people in a situation. This was demonstrated in a study conducted by David Rosenhan (1973). Rosenhan trained eight normal people to act as if they were suffering from schizophrenia and sent them to different mental hospitals. During their initial interviews they displayed the classic symptoms of schizophrenia. After they were admitted, however, they began to act normally. Did the hospitals' staffs notice? After a few days one of the actors was reclassified as a "schizophrenic in remission," which meant that he was still schizophrenic but he was not showing it. The diagnoses of the seven remaining people never changed! The hospitals' staffs never noticed that these actors were behaving normally. However, other patients did notice and reported to the staff that

---

*Although the names are similar, this position is unrelated to the symbolic interactionist orientation discussed earlier.

these people were not mentally ill. They thought the actors were newspaper reporters doing a story on the hospital. How could the staffs have missed this? Rosenhan attributed their oversight to the following: The staff members believed that anyone who was a patient at their hospital was mentally ill. This set, or expectation, colored their perceptions of the behavior they saw. Their internal dispositions determined how they reacted to the characteristics of the situation.

The final piece of information in support of the interactionist position is simple and straightforward. Knowing both the characteristics of the person and the characteristics of the situation yields a better prediction and explanation of social behavior than does knowing just one of these classes of variables (Epstein, 1979). As Kurt Lewin proposed some 50 years ago in his *field theory*, social behavior is caused by people's traits, by situational factors, and by the interaction between both kinds of variables. (See chapter one.) This is what Lewin meant in his famous formula $B = f (p,e)$.

A Concluding Comment

Some social psychologists differentiate between the study of social behavior and the study of personality traits. Myers (1983), for example, argued that social psychologists study overt social behavior and the reasons why large numbers of people display similar behavior, while personality psychologists study private, internal processes and why people differ in their social behavior. This is an accurate characterization of the differences in emphasis between these two types of psychologists. However, this book takes the position that if one's goal is to understand social behavior, then one must consider both overt behavior and private, internal processes. Further, one must be able to understand the causes of both similarities and differences in social behavior. Therefore, in the discussions of the causes of social behavior in the following chapters, you will find a consideration of both personality variables and situational variables.

SUMMARY

A personality trait is a construct proposed to explain consistency in a person's thoughts and actions across time and situations as well as differences between the thoughts and actions of two people in the same situation. Since traits are constructs, they must be translated into observable, measurable entities before they can be studied. This is done by creating a reliable, construct-valid scale that measures the traits of interest.

Although most psychologists agree that traits can be measured and that people differ in how much of a certain trait they possess, they disagree about how much these differences affect social behavior. The trait theorists see them as major causes of social behavior. The situationists propose that situations people are in determine social behavior.

Typically, the relationship between traits and actual behavior has been weak, but recent research suggests that using multiple measurements of the behavior of interest and considering moderator variables will strengthen the relationship. Two variables that have been found to moderate the relationship are self-awareness—the tendency to attend to and be aware of the private, internal aspects of the self, such as traits, and self-monitoring—the tendency to be sensitive to the characteristics of the situation one is in and to the behavior of other people. High self-awareness leads to a good correspondence between traits and behavior; high self-monitoring leads to poor correspondence.

Despite these findings, a pure trait-based explanation of social behavior seems no more valid than one based solely on situational factors. Social behavior is caused by both people's personal characteristics and the situations they encounter.

Applications

Personality Characteristics and Heart Disease: A Modern Problem

In this year alone, coronary heart disease will claim the lives of over one million Americans. It is the leading cause of death among American males. In 1900, less than 25 percent of all deaths in the United States were from strokes or heart disease; today these illnesses are responsible for 60 percent of the deaths in that country. Further, the incidence of heart failure among American men is twice as great as it is among Scandinavian men and five times as great as it is among Japanese men (Spielberger and London, 1982).

The immediate question raised by these statistics is What has caused these recent dramatic increases in the United States? Traditionally, risk factors such as a family history of heart problems, high blood pressure, lack of exercise, poor dietary habits, and excessive smoking were thought to be the primary reasons people had heart problems. However, systematic studies of these factors disclosed they were not good predictors of who would develop coronary heart disease (Jenkins, 1976). In the early 1970s, two cardiologists, Myer Friedman and David Rosenman, proposed an additional factor that might be related to coronary heart disease. They had observed that people who developed this illness often acted differently from people who did not. They called the former group of people Type As and the latter Type Bs. While Friedman and Rosenman did not discount the importance of the risk factors presented earlier, they did suggest that the personality characteristics they had observed in their patients may also contribute to the development of coronary heart disease.

Friedman and Rosenman described the *Type A* individual as a "person who is aggressively involved in a chronic incessant struggle to achieve more and more in less and less time, and if required to do so against the opposing efforts of other things or other people" (1974, p. 67). The major elements of a Type A's behavior are extreme aggressiveness, easily aroused hostility, a sense of time urgency, and competitive achievement striving (Rosenman, 1978). The *Type B* individual is someone who displays these characteristics to a lesser extent.

In 1976, Rosenman and his associates reported the results of a study that compared the incidence of coronary heart disease in Type A and Type B individuals. The subjects were 3,000 healthy men with no heart problems when the study began. They were given a complete physical examination and a 20-minute interview which assessed Type A characteristics. On the basis of this interview, the subjects were classified as Type A or Type B. For eight and a half years, Rosenman and his colleagues kept track of their subjects' medical conditions. Type As and Type Bs were matched on the basis of risk factors such as diet, amount of exercise, and smoking; then the incidence of heart attacks among the two groups was examined. Even

Hard driving, Type A individuals may have an increased risk of coronary heart disease.

when the two groups had equal risk factors, Type As had more than twice as many heart attacks as Type Bs.

Researchers who study the Type A phenomenon do not call it a personality trait; instead, they call it a "coronary prone behavior pattern." But it does not require too much stretching to view Type A as a collection, or pattern, of personality traits as defined in this chapter. Type As display consistent ways of acting and thinking across time and situations which are different from Type Bs.

As noted earlier, the terms Type A and Type B refer to the relative amount of the Type A characteristics a person possesses. This personality trait, or behavior pattern, is most commonly assessed by a fifty-item self-report scale (The Jenkins Activity Survey, Jenkins, Rosenman, and Zyzanski, 1974). (See table 3-2 for a few items from this scale.)

Table 3-2. *Items from a scale designed to distinguish Type A from Type B individuals. Type A answers are asterisked.*

For each of the following items, please circle the number of the *one* best answer:

1. Is your everyday life filled mostly by
    1. Problems needing solution.*
    2. Challenges needing to be met.
    3. A rather predictable routine of events.
    4. Not enough things to keep me interested or busy.

Table 3-2, cont'd. *Items from a scale designed to distinguish Type A from Type B individuals. Type A answers are asterisked.*

2. When you are under pressure or stress, do you usually:
    1. Do something about it immediately.*
    2. Plan carefully before taking any action.

3. How often are there deadlines on your job? (If job deadlines occur irregularly, please circle the closest answer below.)
    1. Daily or more often.*
    2. Weekly.
    3. Monthly.
    4. Never.

4. How often do you bring your work home with you at night or study materials related to your job?
    1. Rarely or never.
    2. Once a week or less often.
    3. More than once a week.*

Source: Jenkins, et al., (1974).

TYPE A BEHAVIOR

The following discussion considers first the manifestations of the Type A pattern, or trait, among adults. It then presents a theory of the origins of this characteristic. This theory incorporates many of the principles discussed in the section on the socialization process.

Physiological Responses

Why are Type As more likely to suffer from coronary heart disease than are Type Bs? One theory is that they are more likely to produce a group of chemicals called *catecholamines*. Catecholamines are present in everyone's blood, and it is believed that in high levels they may block the flow of blood and dramatically increase the chances of a heart attack (Frankenhauser, 1980). Why would Type As produce more of these chemicals? One possibility is that when Type As are exposed to certain kinds of stress, their catecholamine levels go up. This idea was tested by Goldband (1980).

Goldband administered the Jenkins Activity Survey to college students. On the basis of their scores, he classified each student as Type A or B. Then the subjects were randomly assigned to one of two conditions. The first condition was designed to contain the types of stressors that are believed to affect Type As: a feeling that they are in competition with other people; a lack of time to complete a task; and a lack of control over the situation. The second condition did not contain these stressors. In both conditions, subjects worked on a task while their level of catecholamine secretions was measured. The Type B subjects had the same catecholamine levels in both the stressful and the nonstressful conditions. But Type A subjects showed a much greater level of catecholamine secretions in the stress condition than in the nonstress condition.

In a second experiment, Goldband exposed Type As and Type Bs to physical rather than psychological stress. No differences were found between the two groups. Thus, it appears that Type A individuals are not more affected by stress in general; only certain types of stress cause the physiological responses in Type As that increase their risk of heart disease.

These findings illustrate the interaction of personality characteristics and situational factors. The physiological responses of the Type A subjects are the result of both their personality characteristics and the situations they encounter.

Interpersonal Style

The informal descriptions of classic Type A people suggest that they may not be terribly pleasant individuals with whom to interact. Experimental investigations of Type As support this. For example, it appears that Type As speak more quickly, more loudly, and more explosively than do Type Bs (Matthews, 1982). They have a greater sense of time urgency, as shown by the fact that they judge time to pass more quickly than do Type Bs (Burnam, Pennebaker, and Glass, 1974). They also tend to be less patient than are Type Bs. Two findings illustrate this. First, when Type As are given tasks in which success requires that they delay responding to some stimulus, they do quite poorly (Glass, Snyder, and Hollis, 1974). Second, Type As out-perform Type Bs on simple tasks that require speed and persistence, but Type Bs do better than Type As on tasks that require a slow, methodical approach (Glass et al., 1974). Putting these findings together, it appears that it would be difficult to work with a Type A person, or even to have a relaxed conversation with him or her.

Responses to Failure

As noted earlier, Type A people want to succeed at whatever they do. What happens when they fail? Brunson and Matthews (1981) investigated this question. In the first part of their experiment, Type As and Type Bs (again classified on the basis of responses to a scale) worked on four difficult but solvable problems. The quality of the strategies they used to solve these problems and the comments the subjects made about their performance were recorded. Type As and Bs did not differ. In the next part of the experiment, subjects were given unsolvable problems *and* were made quite aware that they were failing. In this condition, 80 percent of the Type As showed a deterioration in the quality of the strategies they used. Type Bs did not show this. Further, Type As attributed their failure to a lack of ability and effort. It seems that when people with Type A tendencies are confronted with failure, they do not "rise to the occasion"; rather, they become helpless and self-denigrating.

Aggressiveness

Carver and Glass (1978) investigated the tendency of Type As to aggress against another person. Subjects took part in a study they believed was concerned with the effects of punishment on learning. They were classified

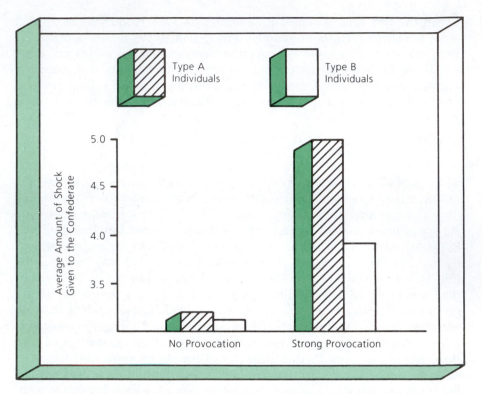

Figure 3-5. *In the absence of provocation, Type A and Type B individuals were equally aggressive, but when provoked, Type As were much more aggressive than Type Bs.*
Source: Carver and Glass (1977).

as Type A or B and then randomly assigned to one of two conditions. In both conditions, the subject's job was to monitor the performance of another subject (really a confederate) on a simple task and to give the other person an electric shock every time he made a mistake. The amount of shock given was left up to the subject. In the first condition, before beginning the monitoring session, the confederate mocked and ridiculed the subjects while they worked on this task. In the other condition (a control condition), subjects went immediately to the shock experiment. The dependent measure was the amount of shock the subjects gave the confederate. (See figure 3-5 for the results.)

In this experiment, the responses of Type As and Type Bs did not differ in the control condition. But in the provocation condition, Type As shocked the confederately significantly more often than did Type Bs. This finding provides another illustration that behavior is often the result of an interaction between traits and situational factors. Note that Type As were more aggressive than Type Bs only when they were provoked.

In addition to being more aggressive than Type Bs in certain situations, Type As have a style of interacting that appears to evoke anger in other people. For example, Van Egeren (1979) found that in a simple game, people who played against Type As became significantly more angry and more competitive than did people who played against Type Bs.

ORIGINS OF TYPE A CHARACTERISTICS

Karen Matthews (1981) has provided an interesting discussion of why some people become Type As and others do not. The following material is based primarily on her ideas.

Genetic Causes

One possible cause of differences is that the behavior patterns are inherited from parents. If Type A is an inherited characteristic, then identical twins, who have the same genetic structure, should show more similarity in their Type A behaviors than should fraternal twins or nonidentical siblings. However, studies have not provided any consistent support for this explanation. (Matthews, 1981).

Observational Learning

Observational learning may play a role in the development of Type A characteristics. Studies designed to investigate the relationship between the characteristics of parents and their children have found a small but significant correlation. Type A parents tend to have Type A children. Further, it appears that children may imitate, or model, the behavior type of the same-sex parent, as the correlation between males and their fathers is greater than the correlation between males and their mothers. This finding is consistent with the social learning theory that children model the same-sex parent more than they do the opposite-sex parent.

Parent-Child Interactions

Another possibility Matthews considered was that the parents of Type A children might treat their children differently than do parents of Type B children. Glass (1977) classified preadolescent boys as Type A or Type B (on the basis of a scale that measures this trait in children) and then observed how they interacted with their mothers. The boys were asked to work on tasks such as stacking blocks with one hand while blindfolded or throwing bean bags at a target. Their mothers were present and could assist them in any way except by actually doing the task for them.

Observers noted two major differences between the behaviors of mothers of Type A and Type B boys. First, the mothers of Type A boys gave significantly fewer positive evaluations than did the mothers of the Type B boys. Second, the mothers of the Type A boys (especially mothers who were Type Bs) pushed their sons to try harder than did the mothers of the Type B boys. They said things such as "You're doing fine, but next time let's do a little better."

These findings do not conclusively prove that mothers of Type A boys, especially mothers who are Type Bs, cause Type A behavior in their sons. Although parents do influence how their children act, children also influence how their parents act; thus, the sons' behavior could itself cause the mothers to respond as they did. Matthews (1977) investigated which of these explanations was correct. She had Type A and Type B boys work on the same tasks Glass used. But Matthews arranged for the boys to be assisted by a Type A or Type B woman who did not know them, instead of by their mothers. The question of interest was whether a stranger would react in the same way to the performance of Type A boys as did their mothers. If the stranger reacted the same, then it could be concluded that the boys were doing something to cause this behavior in adults.

Matthews's findings are quite interesting—and complex. Unlike the natural mothers, the strangers praised the Type A boys more than they praised the Type B boys. This indicates that the Type A boys were not causing the critical behavior in their mothers. But now consider the standards the strangers set for the boys' performance: Type B strangers acted in exactly the same way as did the Type A boys' actual mothers. They pushed the Type A boys harder and kept telling them they should improve their performance, but they did not do this with the Type B boys. This suggests that something in the Type A boys' behavior caused Type B women, whether strangers or mothers, to respond in a similar manner. Matthews believes that the continual changing of standards found in this study provides children with an ambiguous standard for evaluating their subsequent performance—"doing better than previously. They are not told precisely how much better is desirable" (1982, p. 246).

Thus, two aspects of the parent-child interaction may combine to produce a Type A adult. The first is that failing to praise children causes them to try even harder for excellence and productivity. The second is that setting ambiguous standards for what constitutes achievement of these goals forces children to continuously strive for something they can never reach. These findings may explain the struggling to achieve more and more in less and less time, the impatience, the concern with failure, and the competitiveness that is observed in Type A adults.

Matthews proposed that Type A patterns probably begin in about second or third grade. She based this statement on findings from cognitive developmental studies of children. Before age seven or eight, children appear not to use the opinions of others or the performance of their peers in their self-evaluations. Older children, however, use these opinions as standards against which to judge the quality of their own performance.

Matthews's theories on the origins of Type A characteristics provide a good illustration of how research on socialization is related to research on individual differences in social behavior. It shows how social experiences during childhood can leave their mark on the behavior of an adult. More generally, her research on the Type A behavior pattern provides an example of how the concepts discussed in this chapter have been used to understand and explain a modern problem.

Chapter Four

Social Cognition

Prologue

Solomon E. Asch. (1946). Forming Impressions of Personality.
The Journal of Abnormal and Social Psychology, **41,**
258–290.

Background

This chapter is concerned with the study of social cognitions, which are ideas or thoughts about other people. One of the first psychologists to experimentally study the processes involved in developing social cognitions was Solomon Asch. Asch was heavily influenced by the gestalt approach to psychology, which proposed that people process and organize the stimuli they receive into something meaningful and often quite different from the original stimuli. (See chapter one.) Asch believed that the same thing happens in impression formation: People combine bits of information they receive about someone into an overall impression that is quite different from the simple sum of reactions to individual items of information about that person. In this article, Asch reported on several experiments to test his idea, the first of which is described here.

Hypotheses

Asch did not formally propose a hypothesis, but his expectations about the results of the experiment were quite clear. Drawing on the gestaltists' finding that the context in which stimuli were presented could dramatically affect perceptions of the stimuli, Asch proposed that certain items of information in the description of a person are central to the overall impression because they influence people's reactions to other items. He also suggested that changing these central items would produce quite different overall impressions.

Subjects

The subjects were 166 students from colleges and universities in the New York City area. Because this study was conducted during the Second World War, most of the subjects were female.

Procedure

The experiment was conducted in the subjects' classroom. They heard a brief description of a man, which differed depending on the condition of the experiment in which the subjects had been placed. Subjects in one condition heard the man described as intelligent, skillful, industrious, *warm*, determined, practical, and cautious. Subjects in the other condition heard the man described as intelligent, skillful, industrious, *cold*, determined, practical, and cautious. The independent variable was whether the man was described as warm or cold.

After hearing the descriptions, the subjects wrote a short paragraph on their impressions of the person and then were given a list of 18 pairs of opposing terms (for example, unhappy-happy). Subjects indicated which term in a pair best described the man. These were the dependent variables.

Results

Changing a single term produced dramatic differences in the short descriptions written by subjects in the two groups. For example, one subject in the warm condition described the man as "a scientist . . . driven by the desire to accomplish something that would be of benefit." A subject in the cold condition described the man as "a rather snobbish person . . . calculating and unsympathetic." The opposing terms selected by subjects in the two groups also differed greatly. Most subjects in the warm condition saw the person as generous, wise, and humorous, but few subjects in the cold condition had the same impression. (See table 4-1 for summary of the differences between the subjects in the two conditions.)

Table 4-1.   *Subjects' impressions of a person differing greatly depending on whether he was described as warm or cold*

	Warm	Cold
Generous	91%	8%
Good-natured	94%	17%
Happy	90%	34%
Wise	65%	25%

Source: Asch (1946).

Implications

Before Asch's article, researchers had focused on how people's emotions can distort social cognitions, but had more or less ignored social cognitions themselves. Asch demonstrated that social cognitions were worthy of study; his findings generated considerable interest in impression formation in particular, and in social cognitions in general. Most of the material in the first part of this chapter is the direct or indirect result of Asch's research on impression formation.

Social cognitions: thoughts or ideas about another person or group of people.

The topic of this chapter is **social cognitions.** Currently, social psychologists devote more of their time and effort to the study of social cognitions than to any other area of social psychology because they believe that to understand people's social behavior they must understand how people receive, process, and organize information about others. This idea comes directly from the cognitive orientation to social behavior. (See chapter one.) The cognitive theorists did not view humans as creatures who automatically, without thinking, react to the stimuli in their environment, but as active processors and organizers of the information they receive. According to Fritz Heider (1958), humans are "naive psychologists": they collect data about other people, mentally analyze these data, and then reach conclusions about the character and actions of the people they have observed. Their behavior toward these people is largely based on their conclusions.

The first section of this chapter is concerned with forming impressions of people—the phenomenon studied by Asch in the prologue. The second section addresses a related aspect of social cognition, the manner in which people attempt to explain the behavior of others. This is followed by a section that examines the question of the accuracy of people's social cognitions. Finally, an applications section considers the role of social cognitions in the legal system.

FORMING IMPRESSIONS OF OTHER PEOPLE

People form impressions of others on the basis of information they receive about them. This information can be provided in a number of different ways. It can be presented in a written or verbal description of someone, as in the experiment presented in the prologue, or it can result from a direct encounter with another person. Still another way information can be provided is through physical appearance.

This section examines how people form impressions of others. It describes how physical appearance influences first impressions. It then describes several different models of how people form impressions. Finally, it explores how social schemata can influence the impressions people form.

Physical Appearance

A commercial for a breath mint goes something like this: An attractive young woman is seated in a theater, waiting for the play to begin. She unwraps a breath mint and slips it into her mouth. An equally attractive young man approaches and tells her that she is in his seat. A quick check of their tickets discloses that she has made the mistake. But as he is about to take his seat, he looks into her eyes—and evidently smells her breath—and decides that he is not interested in the play. They leave the theater together and go off into the night.

The makers of the breath mint would like you to believe that the woman's sweet-smelling breath was responsible for the man's action, but one suspects that her physical appearance played more than a minor role. It may be unfortunate, but people are judged on the basis of the way they look and dress. We assume that in almost every respect attractive people are better than unattractive people (Berscheid and Walster, 1974b).

The effects of physical appearance begin early in people's lives. Clifford and Walster (1973) randomly assigned fifth-grade teachers to one of two groups. Teachers in the first group received a picture of an attractive child and a supposed copy of the child's report card. Teachers in the second group received a picture of an unattractive child and a supposed copy of the child's report card. The report cards shown to the two groups were

People's physical appearance and mannerisms strongly influence our initial impressions of them.

identical. However, teachers rated the attractive children as brighter, more popular, higher achieving, and more likely to have parents who were interested in their education. In another study, Dion (1973) found that preschool children evaluated attractive age-mates more positively than unattractive ones.

The bias in favor of physically attractive people has also been found in a large number of studies with adults. In one study, attractive adults were seen as being kinder, more sensitive, more interesting, stronger, more poised, more modest, more sociable, sexually warmer, and as having better character (Dion, Berscheid, and Walster, 1972). In another study, Ungar, Hilderbrand, and Madar (1982) found that college students were more likely to identify unattractive women than attractive women as homosexuals. A study by Hobfoll and Penner (1978) illustrated how information about physical attractiveness can change perceptions of a person's emotional well-being.

In Hobfoll and Penner's study, undergraduate females who differed in their physical attractiveness spent 10 minutes talking to an interviewer. The interview was both audiotaped and videotaped and played back to graduate students in clinical psychology. After either listening to or watching an interview, the students rated the woman's self-concept. When the woman was unattractive, the ratings did not change from the audiotape to the videotape condition. But if the woman was attractive, the graduate

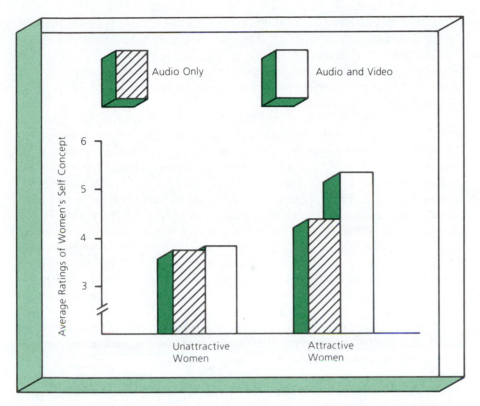

Figure 4-1. *Unattractive women received comparable ratings in the audio and video conditions; self-concepts ratings of the attractive women increased from the audio to the video condition.*
Source: Hobfoll and Penner (1978).

students saw her as having a significantly better self-concept in the video-tape condition than in the audiotape condition. (See figure 4-1.) In other words, they viewed her as better adjusted when they learned she was attractive. These results were not obtained for attractive and unattractive males. In general, physical attractiveness affects perceptions of women more than perceptions of men.

The subjects in these studies did more than react to another person's beauty; they extrapolated other characteristics from it to form an overall impression of that person. This supports Asch's proposal that humans actively process, organize, and modify the information they receive from the world around them.

In a few circumstances, attractive people fare worse than do unattractive people. Cash, Gillen, and Burns (1977) found that attractive women who applied for a job traditionally held by men were less likely to be hired than were unattractive women. Sigall and Ostrove (1975) looked at how physical attractiveness might affect jurors' reactions to a defendant. In general, they found that jurors treated attractive defendants more leniently than unattractive ones. But when attractive defendants had committed a crime that might have been aided by their physical appearance (for example, a swindle or a con game), they received more severe sentences than did unattractive defendants. These studies do not refute the impact of physical appearance on people's perceptions. They simply show that in some instances physicial appearance can work against attractive people, especially if they are female.

A study by Snyder, Tanke, and Berscheid (1977) illustrates how physical attractiveness (or at least the belief that a person is physically attractive) can influence social behavior. Male subjects talked over a telephone with female subjects, but did not actually see the women. Half of the men were told that the woman they spoke with was attractive and half were told she was unattractive. The conversations were taped and each woman's conversational behavior was rated on a number of different dimensions. Women who talked with men who had been told they were attractive were rated as more animated, more confident, and more enjoyable than women who talked with men who had been told they were unattractive. These results suggest that the men's perceptions affected the women's behavior. In the real world, where we usually see people before we call them, these effects would probably be much stronger.

Before leaving the topic of physical attractiveness, a few summary points are needed. First, physical appearance has its greatest impact on first impressions. As we get to know people, their physical appearance becomes a less important determinant of our perceptions of them. Second, while there is a bias in favor of both physically attractive males and physically attractive females, the available data suggest physical attractiveness has much more of an impact on people's perceptions of women than men. Indeed, among children there may be a bias against attractive boys (Langlois and Stephan, 1981). Third, initial judgments of people's character, interests, backgrounds, and so on are strongly influenced by their physical appearances. For example, blond women are seen as more sociable but less intelligent than brunettes; bearded men are seen as psychologically stronger than nonbearded men; and light-skinned people are evaluated more positively than dark-skinned people (Schneider, Hastorf, and Ellsworth, 1979).

You can see this for yourself with a simple experiment using the pictures on pages 128 and 129. Show a few friends the picture of subject A and show a few other friends the picture of subject B. Ask each person to give you a brief description of the man, and then compare these with the true descriptions that follow.

Subject A and Subject B were both arrested by the police. Subject A is Edward Lawson. When this picture was taken, Mr. Lawson was the head of his own consulting firm. He is now a law student at the University of California at Berkeley. Mr. Lawson was arrested by the San Diego police and convicted of failing to provide proper identification. He argued his own case before the Supreme Court and won. Subject B is Theodore Bundy. Mr. Bundy also argued his own case before a judge, but he lost. He is now awaiting execution for the brutal murders of three co-eds at Florida State University. According to some accounts, Mr. Bundy is the greatest mass murderer of women in the history of the United States.

Impression Formation

Impression formation is the formal name for the process people use to combine information about another person into an overall impression of that person.

Gestalt Position

The gestalt position on impression formation is that predictions of an overall impression that will be formed must be based on the entire set of characteristics used to describe a person. Asch proposed this in the prologue. He argued that a person's overall impression cannot be predicted by considering only the individual items provided in a description. This is because the context in which an item is presented influences the meaning a person assigns to it. For example, if the trait *happy* is presented along with the traits *silly* and *stupid*, it will be interpreted very differently than if it is presented along with the traits *warm* and *relaxed* (Schneider et al., 1979). In the first context, happy conveys to me the image of Bozo the Clown. In the second, I get the image of a contented, "laid-back" kind of person.

Linear Combination Position

Those who advocate a *linear combination position* argue that the meanings of individual items in a description of a person do not change when they are put together, and that an overall impression of a person is simply the result of combining reactions to the individual items. (The result is called a linear combination because linear refers to an equation in which terms are combined by addition or subtraction.) Note how the gestalt and linear combination positions differ. Asch says that overall impressions cannot be predicted from individual items; linear combination theorists say they can.

Most linear combinationists agree in their basic views of impression formation. However, they disagree to a certain extent on exactly how people combine the information. As a result, three different models have been used to describe how the individual items are combined. The *summation model* proposes that the total impression of someone is simply the sum of the reactions to all the individual items in a description. The *averaging model* argues that the total impression is the average reaction to the individual items. The *weighted averaging model* proposes that impression formation involves two things: people react to an individual item and then they assign importance to that item, just as an instructor may "weight" a final examination as being twice as important as a mid-term. In this model, the total impression is the average of the weighted evaluations. All three models and the differences between them may be made clearer by the following example.

At many universities, the only information students have about a potential instructor is evaluations from former students. Assume you are in this situation and you gather the following information about a potential instructor. She is well-groomed, entertaining, prompt, and concerned about students, but her tests are very difficult. You evaluate each of these characteristics in terms of how good or bad you think it is by assigning it a number from one to seven (one = a negative evaluation; seven = a positive evaluation). (See table 4-2 for one possible set of ratings.)

Subject A

Look at the second column in table 4-2. The summation model predicts that your overall evaluation will be 15; the averaging model predicts that it will be three ($15 \div 5 = 3$). Since one number is just a simple transformation of the other, these two models really do not differ in their predictions at this point. They do, however, differ in their predictions about the effects of additional information on the total impression. Imagine you later

Subject B

learn that this instructor gives extra-credit assignments to allow students to improve their grades, and you evaluate this as a three. According to the summation model, this would increase your overall evaluation to 18. But according to the averaging model, your overall evaluation of the instructor would stay the same (18 ÷ 6 = 3). The summation model stresses quantity and the averaging model stresses quality.

Table 4-2. *The Weighted Averaging Model Impression Formation*

Characteristic	Evaluation	Weight	Weight × Evaluation
Well-groomed	2	1	2
Entertaining	3	3	9
Concerned about students	6	2	12
Prompt	3	1	3
Gives hard tests	1	10	10
Sum:	15	17	36
Average:	3		

The third column in table 4-2 contains numbers that represent the relative importance a person places on each characteristic, from one, (not at all important) to ten, (very important). In the weighted averaging model, each evaluation is multiplied by the importance a person assigns to it. (See column four in table 4-2.) The products are then added up and divided by the sum of the weights. In this case, the result would be $36 \div 17 = 2.1$, a lower overall impression than is predicted by either of the two other models.

To determine which of the three models best predicts how people actually arrive at an overall impression, researchers present subjects with a set of individual items, obtain ratings of each item, and combine these ratings using one of the models. The product is then correlated with the subjects' overall impressions and the correlations produced by the different models are compared; the higher the correlation the more accurate the model. Although all three models appear to be valid, the weighted averaging model usually provides the most accurate prediction of people's overall impressions (Kaplan and Kemmerick, 1974). To make this model more accurate, Anderson (1965) suggests adding one more thing—a person's general tendencies in evaluating people. If an individual is an optimist, this would yield a positive bias; if she is a pessimist, this will yield a negative bias. Since most people begin with a neutral attitude toward others, overall impressions are usually less extreme than the original weighted averaging model would predict (Schneider et al., 1979).

Gestalt Position versus
Linear Combination Position
Does the gestalt position or the linear combination position provide a better description of the process of impression formation? Apparently the answer depends to a certain extent on the aspect of impression formation in which you are interested. Rokeach and Rothman (1965) have shown that the context in which an item is presented can affect its meaning. Consider the trait *dishonest*; a negative, but not damning, characteristic. Now combine it with *president*. As a former chief executive learned, people react much more negatively to the term *dishonest president* than to either of the terms presented by themselves. This supports the gestalt approach.

On the other hand, the linear combination theories seem to better explain a phenomenon in impression formation known as **order effects.** There are two types of order effects. One is called a *primacy effect,* which occurs when the first items presented about a person are the most influential in determining the overall impression. The other, *recency effects,* occur when the later items presented about a person are the most influential in determining the overall impression. Recency effects are somewhat less common than primacy effects (Jones and Goethals, 1972).

Order effects: a phenomenon wherein the order in which items are presented affects the impact they have on an overall impression.

Social Schemata

The task Asch presented to his subjects in the prologue was relatively simple. They listened to a list of terms describing a person, thought about it for awhile, and then wrote a short description of the person and chose from a list of traits that reflected their impressions of the person. Asch used this task because he was interested in the basic processes of impression formation, but he recognized that the task of forming impressions is often much more difficult in the real world. Often a wealth of information is presented, some of which is inconsistent or contradictory. There is little time to reflect on the information. How do individuals process a complex array of information?

Researchers propose that people use **social schemata** to help them quickly organize and make sense out of complex, inconsistent, or incomplete information about individuals in their environment (Fiske and Taylor, 1984). You have already been exposed to one example of social schemata. Think back to the descriptions of Mr. Lawson your friends provided. "Knowing" something about people who look like Mr. Lawson enabled your friends to form an overall impression of him without any further information. Sometimes—as in the case of Mr. Lawson—a social schema can be wrong. The crucial aspect of social schemata is not whether they are correct or incorrect, but that people believe they are correct. Thus, social schemata strongly influence people's views of others. Four social schemata that may influence people's impressions are discussed here: central traits, implicit personality theories, prototypes, and stereotypes.

Social schemata: a set of beliefs or ideas about the characteristics of a person or group of people.

Central Traits

Asch found that simply changing one word, *warm,* to another, *cold,* had a dramatic impact on his subjects' impressions of a person. Asch believed this happened because warm-cold is a **central trait.** He proposed that a central trait provides an organizational framework for other traits, irrespective of the particular situation. Subsequent research (Wishner, 1960) has shown that while certain traits in a description exert a disproportionate influence on the total impression, the specific trait that does this varies from situation to situation. The influence of an item depends on how well it correlates with the other traits in the description. If the correlation is high, the item is a central trait, but a trait that is central in one situation may not be central in another.

Wishner's research clarified the issue of central traits. It also demonstrated that people assume certain traits or characteristics are correlated.

Central traits: items in the description of a person which exert a disproportionate influence on the overall impression of that person.

This gave rise to research on another social schema people use, implicit personality theories.

Implicit Personality Theories

People have personal theories of what other people are like and of what personality characteristics go together; these are called **implicit personality theories.** Rosenberg and Sedlak (1972) found that people assume that someone who is persistent is also scientific and determined, and that someone who is clumsy is also unintelligent and naive. Implicit personality theories enable people to go from limited information about a person to an overall judgment of the person without taking time to seek out additional information. For instance, I don't need to find out if a person is unhappy if I know she is unpopular; I assume the two traits go together.

Some researchers claim that implicit personality theories are accurate reflections of what traits actually go together, and others claim that they are not (Schneider et al., 1979). This question is not yet resolved, but it is clear that people agree on what traits they believe go together (Gara and Rosenberg, 1981). In addition, we know that these theories influence people's social cognitions and behavior.

Prototypes

Prototypes: a person's conceptions of the set of characteristics that applies to the typical member of some group or category.

Another type of social schemata is **prototypes,** which influence social perceptions in two ways. First, impressions of a person who is a member of some group may be strongly influenced by conceptions of what the typical member of that group is like. For example, if you have never met Frank but someone tells you he sells used cars, you have a pretty clear picture of him based on your conception of a used-car salesperson. Second, people use information about others to place them in a group or category. If someone tells you that Frank loves parties, is always telling jokes, and works as a salesperson, you will probably classify him as an extrovert. In either case, using prototypes allows you to go beyond the immediate information you have about a person by giving you a plan or system for organizing and categorizing that person.

Cantor and Mischel (1979) have studied the factors that lead people to believe a person belongs to a particular category or group—that she fits the prototype. A person who consistently displays the central characteristics of some group is perceived as a member of that group. Others then go beyond the specific information they have about that person and assign her all the characteristics of the typical group member.

Stereotypes

Stereotypes: generalized beliefs about the characteristics of some group of people.

Another way of looking at prototypes is that they are the basis of **stereotypes,** which assume that if a person is a member of a group, that person possesses the same characteristics as do other group members. Historically, stereotypes have been viewed as the result of racial and ethnic prejudice. While not denying the role prejudice plays in the development of stereotypes, David Hamilton and his associates (Hamilton, 1979; Hamilton, Dugan, and Trolier, 1985) have proposed that some stereotypes may be

Research Highlight

And She Bakes Cookies at Christmas Time . . .

The constructs of prototypes and stereotypes are both based on the assumption that people have fairly detailed conceptions about the characteristics of members of certain groups and that people usually agree about what these characteristics are. Brewer, Dull, and Lui (1981) tested this assumption. The particular group of interest was grandmothers. Can people agree on what grandmothers look like and how they act?

To answer this question, Brewer and her associates obtained 16 photographs of elderly women. On the basis of their own ideas of what grandmothers look like, the researchers classified nine of the pictures as looking like grandmothers and seven as looking like nongrandmotherly senior citizens. Then they mixed the pictures up and showed them to a group of college students. The students' task was to look at a picture and decide if it was that of a grandmother or a female senior citizen. The students had little trouble doing this. Statistical tests showed significant agreement on which pictures were those of grandmothers and which were not. Further, the students' classifications were significantly correlated with the initial classifications made by Brewer and her colleagues.

In the second phase of this study, Brewer's group investigated the relationship between protoypes about how grandmothers look and prototypes about how they act. A new group of students was shown one of two sets of pictures. The first set consisted of three pictures of grandmothers. The other set consisted of pictures of grandmothers and pictures of female senior citizens. The students were given a list of traits and asked to check those all three people in the set probably had in common. Students who received the mixed set of pictures were unable to agree on what characteristics the three women had in common. Students who received the set of grandmother photographs were able to agree on the characteristics of these women. Over 50 percent of the students checked the following nine traits. Close your eyes, think of a grandmother, and then look at the list. I predict you will agree that these are the traits of a stereotypical grandmother.

Accepting	Helpful	Optimistic
Calm	Kindly	Serene
Cheerful	Old-fashioned	Trustworthy

simply due to the way people process and organize information about other people.

Hamilton suggested three related mechanisms that can lead to stereotypes in the absence of prejudice. The first mechanism is that when people become members of a group, they seek out information that shows they are similar to members of their own group and different from members of another group. This leads to stereotypes about the members of the other

Research suggests that college students have similar conceptions of what certain people look like. Does this woman fit your conception of a grandmother?

group. This occurs even when the person is a subject who has been randomly assigned to a short-term group in an experiment.

The second mechanism is that people usually interact with others who are racially or ethnically similar to them—blacks interact with blacks, whites interact with whites, and so on. And when individuals interact with a member of a different group, they are usually the only member of their own group present—the only black student in a class, for example. Laboratory experiments have shown that in such situations, whites see the behavior of the lone black person as much more distinctive than the behavior of other whites. As a result, the behavior is better remembered and is used to stereotype other blacks.

The third mechanism is called an *illusory correlation*, which is the false assumption that some characteristic correlates with, or goes along with, membership in a group. A study by Hamilton and Gifford (1976) demonstrated the development of an illusory correlation. Subjects read descriptions of two groups. The majority group (group A) was twice as large as the minority group (group B). Each description contained statements indicating that one-third of the members of the group had engaged in an undesirable behavior. After reading these descriptions, the subjects were given a list of negative behaviors and asked to guess which group the person who had engaged in these behaviors came from. If subjects had made their decisions on the basis of objective information, they should have assigned twice as many negative behaviors to members of group A.

Why? Because group A was twice as large as group B and an equal percentage of people in each group had engaged in negative behaviors. But the subjects estimated that over half of the undesirable behaviors were committed by members of the smaller group. The researchers concluded that when a small percentage of a small group engages in a behavior (whether positive or negative), people tend to assume that the behavior is representative of the entire group. However, when the same percentage of people from a large group engages in the same behavior, people do not make this assumption.

Once a stereotype is established, it can affect subsequent perceptions of the stereotyped individuals. Hamilton and Rose (1978) presented subjects with information about certain groups that was either consistent or inconsistent with stereotypes about those groups. Then they asked the subjects to recall both kinds of information. Information that was consistent with the stereotypes was recalled much more readily than information that was inconsistent with the stereotypes. Indeed, subjects overestimated the number of times they had heard the stereotype-consistent information.

Finally, there is reason to believe that people will sometimes unwittingly act in accord with the stereotypes others have of them. In a 1975 study, Zanna and Pack asked women to have a short conversation with a man who was presented as someone they might be interested in dating. Before they actually met the man, the women learned that he held a very traditional view of women and their role in society. When the women met the man, they acted in accord with this stereotyped view of women.

In many instances, ethnic and racial stereotypes are simply the product of an almost mindless dislike for some ethnic or racial group. (See chapter nine.) The point of Hamilton's proposals is not to excuse or condone racist stereotypes, but to suggest that stereotyping may be a complex process caused by things other than prejudice.

SUMMARY

Social cognitions are thoughts about other people. One kind of social cognition is impressions of another person's personal characteristics. People's physical appearance exerts a powerful influence on initial impressions of them. In general, first impressions of physically attractive people are more positive than first impressions of physically unattractive people. This bias in favor of attractive people begins in childhood and extends through the adult years.

Another influence on people's initial impressions is the information they receive about a person's psychological characteristics and behavior. Impression formation is the formal term for how people process this information and form an overall impression. Two general approaches are used to explain impression formation. The gestalt approach says that when all the information is put together it forms a unique configuration that cannot be generated by simply combining the individual items in a description. The linear combination approach proposes that an overall impression is the result of an algebraic combination of the individual items. Within this linear combination orientation, three specific models of how people form impressions have been proposed: summation, averaging, and weighted averaging.

When people are presented with limited or complex information about a person, they often process this information on the basis of their social schemata; their beliefs about the character of a person or a group of people. Four social schemata that people use are central traits—personality traits that provide an organizational framework for the other traits; implicit personality theories—a person's private ideas about what personality characteristics typically correlate, or go together; prototypes—conceptions of what the typical member of some group or category is like; and stereotypes—beliefs about the characteristics of the members of some group. While stereotypes often result from social and ethnic prejudice, they can also result from the way people process and organize information about individuals who belong to a certain group.

ATTRIBUTION PROCESSES

Very few readers of this text will go on to earn a Ph.D. in social psychology and conduct experiments on social behavior. But like social psychological researchers, most will spend a considerable portion of their time attempting to understand and explain human social behavior. The attempt to understand and explain the behavior of other people is called the *attribution process.*

The work of Asch led to much of the theory and research presented in the first section of this chapter. The work of Fritz Heider, a person with an almost identical background, led to much of the theory and research in this section. Heider (1958) said that humans are "naive psychologists" who, like researchers, believe that events have specifiable causes; they do not "just happen." Further, Heider proposed that naive psychologists believe they need to understand the causes of the behavior they observe—not to prove or disprove a theory, but to make their social world more orderly and predictable.

Most major theories of the attribution process are extensions and elaborations of Heider's basic ideas about how people explain the actions of others. Heider believed that when people, or *observers*, watch the behavior of others, or *actors*, they attempt to identify the causes of the behavior. Observers can make an **internal attribution** or they can make an **external attribution.**

Imagine you are an officer on the San Diego police force in the following situation.

It is about 2:00 A.M. and you are patrolling a quiet residential neighborhood. The residents of this area are upper middle class and most are white. You spot a black man walking down the street. You have seen him

Internal attribution: the belief that a behavior is caused by some characteristic of an actor, such as the actor's mood, personality, or interests.

External attribution: the belief that a behavior is caused by some aspect of the actor's environment.

walking the streets for the last three nights and decide to stop him for questioning. First you call the station for advice and learn that several other officers have also seen this man, that he has been stopped a number of times, and that he was arrested once for failing to identify himself. You then stop him, and he refuses to produce any identification.

What attributions would you make about this man's behavior? Was it internally or externally caused? If it was internally caused, what characteristic did it reflect?

This is a true story. The officer did stop the man and arrest him, and the man was convicted of failing to provide "credible and reliable" identification. The man's name was Edward Lawson; his picture and a short description of him appeared earlier in the chapter. Mr. Lawson sued the city of San Diego, and his case went all the way to the Supreme Court, where he plead his own case and won. Mr. Lawson argued that the police stopped him only because they considered him suspicious, not because he was breaking any law. In other words, Mr. Lawson claimed that the officers' attributions about the causes of his behavior were wrong and that they led to a violation of his constitutional rights. The major attribution models provide some explanations of why the police officers made these particular attributions.

This section presents three models concerned with the attribution process: the covariation model, the correspondent inferences model, and the causal schemata model. Finally, it discusses how observers make attributions about successes and failures.

Covariation Model

Harold Kelley's (1972a, 1973, 1978) **covariation model** of attributions was intended to explain how observers arrive at explanations of an actor's behavior after they have seen the behavior on several different occasions. Kelley proposed that observers examine the possible causes of an actor's behavior. They then explain the behavior on the basis of which of those causes *covary* with the behavior—that is, which causes are present when the behavior occurs and absent when it does not occur. A nonsocial example illustrates the principle of covariation. How do you know that turning the ignition key starts your car's engine? When you turn the key to On, the engine starts; if you do not turn the key, the engine does not start. So you reason that turning the ignition key to On covaries with, or goes along with, the engine starting.

According to Kelley, observers use three types of information to tell them how causes covary with a behavior. The first type is **consensus.** If all or most people engage in a behavior, the behavior does not vary, or differ, between people and consensus is high; if only the actor engages in the behavior, the behavior does vary between people and consensus is low. For example, Mr. Lawson's habit of walking alone in the middle of the night is a low-consensus behavior.

The second type of information about a behavior is its **consistency.** If an actor behaves the same way in all situations, the behavior does not vary depending on the situation and consistency is high; if the actor exhibits

Consensus: information about whether a behavior varies as a function of who the actor is.

Consistency: information about whether a behavior varies as a function of the situations an actor encounters.

Distinctiveness: information about whether a behavior varies as a function of the particular stimuli an actor encounters.

the same behavior only in a particular situation, the behavior does depend on the situation and consistency is low. For example, Mr. Lawson walks alone at night all the time. This is a high-consistency behavior.

The third type of information about a behavior is its **distinctiveness.** If an actor behaves the same way in response to an entire class of similar stimuli, the behavior does not vary depending on the stimuli and distinctiveness is low; if the actor responds the same way only to specific stimuli, the behavior does vary depending on the stimuli and distinctiveness is high. For example, Mr. Lawson's refusal to identify himself to any of the officers who stopped him is a behavior low in distinctiveness.

Kelley said that observers put these three types of information together and base their attributions of the causes of a behavior on the total pattern of covariation. If consensus is high (everybody exhibits the behavior), consistency is low (the behavior occurs only in a specific situation), and distinctiveness is high (only a particular stimulus causes the behavior), an observer will attribute the behavior to an external cause.

If, on the other hand, consensus is low, consistency is high, and distinctiveness is low, an observer will attribute the behavior to an internal cause. For example, Mr. Lawson's behavior was low in consensus, high in consistency, and low in distinctiveness. Thus, it was quite reasonable for the officer to arrest him because he attributed Mr. Lawson's behavior to an internal cause—to the personal characteristics of a criminal. The only thing wrong with the officer's decision was that he incorrectly identified the nature of the internal cause. (It is also reasonable to propose that social schemata about black people, especially blacks who look like Edward Lawson, may have increased the officers' tendency to believe he was up to no good.)

Correspondent Inferences Model

The covariation model is primarily concerned with how observers identify the causes of an actor's behavior. The **correspondent inferences model** (Jones and Davis, 1965; Jones and McGillis, 1976) goes beyond this. It considers the conditions under which observers conclude, or infer, that behavior corresponds to an enduring characteristic of the actor. The model proposes that three aspects of a behavior affect this attribution: social desirability, choice, and effects of an action.

Social Desirability

Social desirability: whether the actor's behavior deviates from what people like the actor should or would do in a certain circumstance.

The first factor Jones and his colleagues believed affected attributions was the **social desirability** of the behavior. This is conceptually the same as consensus. The correspondent inferences model proposes that the more an action deviates from what the average or typical person will do, the more information it provides about an actor and the more likely an observer is to make correspondent inferences. For instance, suppose Mr. Lawson liked to take walks in the park on Sundays. This would not provide you with much information about him, since most people like to do this; thus, you would be reluctant to make inferences from his actions. But since Mr.

Lawson likes to take walks in the middle of the night, his actions clearly set him apart from others.

Jones and McGillis (1976) proposed that two types of expectations influence judgments about social desirability. One is called a *target-based expectation*, which comes from what you know about a particular actor. For example, if a person is training for a marathon, then exercising—even in the middle of the night—would not strike you as unusual or socially undersirable. The other is a *category-based expectation*, which comes from what you know about particular classes or kinds of people. For example, if you know someone is a businessperson, you would not expect him to wear his hair in the style that Mr. Lawson did.

Choice

The second factor that affects attributions is **choice.** A behavior that is freely chosen is more likely to result in a correspondent inference than one that is forced on an actor. For example, if an observer had seen Mr. Lawson handcuffed in the back of a police car, the observer would probably not have attributed Mr. Lawson's impending trip to the police station to an interest in the day-to-day operations of the San Diego police force.

Choice: whether a person has freely chosen to engage in a behavior.

Effects of an Action

Jones and Davis (1965) proposed that observers look at the effects of an actor's actions to gain information about the actor. For example, imagine a friend has graduated and has been offered two jobs. In situation A, each job offers the same opportunity. (See table 4-3.) In this case, your friend's choice of a particular job would not tell you anything about her.

Table 4-3. *Situation A*

	Job 1	Job 2
Salary	$22,000	$22,000
Location	Boston	Boston
Position	Accountant	Accountant

Now consider the decision your friend would make in situation B. (See table 4-4.) At first glance, it would seem easier to infer something about your friend from the effects of a decision in this case, but it really isn't because the effects share so little in common. The salary or the location or the type of job may determine her choice.

Table 4-4. *Situation B*

	Job 1	Job 2
Salary	$23,000	$22,000
Location	Boston	Hawaii
Position	Salesperson	Accountant

Table 4-5.   Situation C

	Job 1	Job 2
Salary	$22,000	$22,000
Location	Boston	Boston
Position	Salesperson	Accountant

Finally, consider situation C, which provides some clear-cut information about the actor. Again your friend must choose between one of two jobs. (See table 4-5.) Assume she chooses job 1. Why? Based on the available information, the only possible explanation is that she prefers sales to accounting.

In this example, situation C had only one **noncommon effect.** The fewer noncommon effects produced by a behavior, the more information an observer receives about the actor and the more likely the observer is to make correspondent inferences.

Noncommon effect: a unique consequence of a behavior, one that cannot be produced by an alternative behavior.

Causal Schemata Model

Kelley's covariation model applies to attributions based on multiple observations of an actor. When observers have only limited observations of an actor, Kelley (1972b) proposed that they use **causal schemata** to make attributions. Causal schemata come from what people have experienced themselves and what they have been taught by others. They serve the same purpose as do social schemata; when people confront a situation that is complex or ambiguous, they use their preexisting beliefs about the causes of events to make sense out of the situation.

Causal schemata: beliefs about the nature of reality which people use when making attributions.

People use causal schemata to identify which of a number of possible causes produced a certain behavior. For example, imagine it is 15 minutes before the final examination in Dr. Smith's course and you see a classmate cleaning Dr. Smith's office. What is the cause of her behavior? It could be that the student is (a) fond of Dr. Smith, (b) playing up to Dr. Smith, or (c) complying with a demand from Dr. Smith. To identify the most likely cause in a case like this, you first determine which causes can be discounted or eliminated as an explanation. If you know that Dr. Smith bases her grades entirely on machine-scored examinations and has a strict rule against speaking to students outside of class, you can eliminate or discount causes b and c. This leaves you with cause a as the explanation for the student's behavior. But if Dr. Smith gives essays and often asks "favors" of her students, all causes are equally likely. If you cannot discount any causes for a particular behavior, you cannot make an attribution about the *student's* behavior. This process is known as the *discounting principle*.

Accuracy of the Models

The ultimate test of any model or theory is whether it accurately describes or predicts the phenomenon with which it is concerned. In this respect, the three models do fairly well. In general, people do make attributions in the manners they propose. There is, however, some dispute about the extent to which observers compare the behavior of an actor to the behavior of other people (the concept of consensus in the covariation model; the concept of social desirability in the correspondent inferences model). Some studies have found that observer's attributions are not influenced much by comparisons with other actors (McArthur, 1972; Nisbett and Borgida, 1975); others have found that they are (Wells and Harvey, 1977). Further, it appears that people do not compare an actor's behavior to the behavior of just any other person (Pruitt and Insko, 1980). Rather, they look for people who are similar to themselves. For example, if one of my students believed that the way I dress when I teach is unusual, she would base this on a comparison with the style of dress among other college professors. She would not compare my dress to that of Wall Street business executives.

Attributions About Success and Failure

Another popular model of attribution processes concerns observers' explanations of an actor's success or failure (Weiner, Frieze, Kukla, Reed, Rest, and Rosenbaum, 1972a). Weiner and his associates proposed that observers ask two interrelated questions about a success or failure: Was it due to an internal or external cause? and Was the cause stable and long term or unstable and transitory? Observers obtain their answers to these questions by using the types of information described in Kelley's covariation model—consensus, consistency, and distinctiveness. An example may explain.

Observers use the types of information identified in Kelley's covariation model to make attributions about success and failure.

Suppose the classmate who was cleaning Dr. Smith's office received 27 out of a possible 100 on Dr. Smith's final exam. Observers would use consensus to determine if this dismal performance was due to internal or external factors. First assume that everyone else in the class did poorly. Observers would attribute the actor's performance to an external factor because the performance did not vary with the person. Next observers would be concerned with whether the behavior was stable or unstable. Unstable performance can be due to luck, but luck is an unreasonable explanation here because the odds against so many unlucky people being in the same classroom are very high. Observers might also look at the scores on previous tests given by Dr. Smith and at the performances of her students in other classes (consistency and distinctiveness information). If the scores on previous tests were low and the scores in the other classes were much higher, then the observers would attribute the actor's performance to an external, stable factor—the difficulty of Dr. Smith's tests.

Now imagine that this student was the only student to do so poorly on Dr. Smith's examination. Observers would attribute her performance to an internal factor because it varied with the person. If an internal attribution is made, then the observer uses information about consistency and distinctiveness to determine whether the performance is stable or unstable. If the student has done well on all of Dr. Smith's other exams (consistency) and is earning As in all her other courses (distinctiveness), observers would attribute her performance on this test to an unstable factor, such as bad luck or lack of effort. But if the student's performance was terrible on all of Dr. Smith's previous exams and she is about to flunk out, observers would attribute her behavior on this test to a stable factor, such as lack of ability. (See table 4-6 for a summary of these possible attributions.)

Table 4-6. *Observers make attributions about the reasons for success and failure on the basis of their perceptions of the location of the cause and the stability of the cause. Observers use the kinds of information described in Kelley's covariation stability model to make judgments about location and stability*

	Stability of cause	
Location of cause	Stable	Unstable
Internal	Ability	Effort
External	Task difficulty	Luck

Source: Weiner et al. (1972a).

SUMMARY

The attribution process involves people's attempts to explain or understand the behavior of people around them. People make attributions because they believe that if they can explain the behavior of others, their social world will be more orderly and predictable.

Kelley's covariation model of the attribution process proposes that if observers have repeated opportunities to see the behavior of an actor, they will base their attributions on the causes that covary with, or go along with, the actor's behavior. Observers use three types of information about the behavior to make this determination: consensus, consistency, and distinctiveness.

The theory of correspondent inferences attempts to identify what leads an observer to infer that a behavior corresponds to an enduring characteristic of the actor. The theory proposes that three things provide information about the character of the actor and influence the inferences an observer makes: how socially desirable the behavior is, whether the behavior is freely chosen, and the effects produced by the behavior. The more information observers have, the more likely they are to make a correspondent inference.

When people make attributions after a single observation, they use causal schemata, which are general rules about causal relationships. People use causal schemata to explain someone's behavior when information about that person is limited.

Another theory of attributions attempts to explain how people make attributions about a person's success or failure at some endeavor. It proposes that observers first decide if the outcome has an internal or an external cause. Having done this, the observers use information about consensus, consistency, and distinctiveness to determine if the behavior is stable or unstable.

ACCURACY OF SOCIAL COGNITIONS

Thus far the discussion of social cognitions has focused on what they are and how they develop; the question of their accuracy has been more or less ignored. But as you might suspect, people's social cognitions are not always perfect reflections of reality. If distortions in social cognitions were small or inconsistent, few social psychologists would be interested in them. But this is not the case, as is seen in a classic study of Hastorf and Cantrill (1954). In 1951, Dartmouth played Princeton in a football game described as one of the dirtiest and roughest ever played by either school. Several players suffered broken bones and there were a number of fistfights. The researchers obtained a film of the game and showed it to students from each school. Students were to write down any rule violations they saw. Students from Princeton saw Dartmouth commit more than twice as many violations as they saw their own school commit. Students from Dartmouth saw the Princeton players as guilty of more violations than their own players.

The differences in the students' views of the game reflect a perceptual bias. A perception is *biased* if it does not reflect a rational, logical way of processing information about human behavior. Two types of bias in social cognitions are motivational and information processing.

Motivational Bias

When people's needs cause them to have biased social cognitions, this is called **motivational bias.** Freud identified one cause of motivational bias

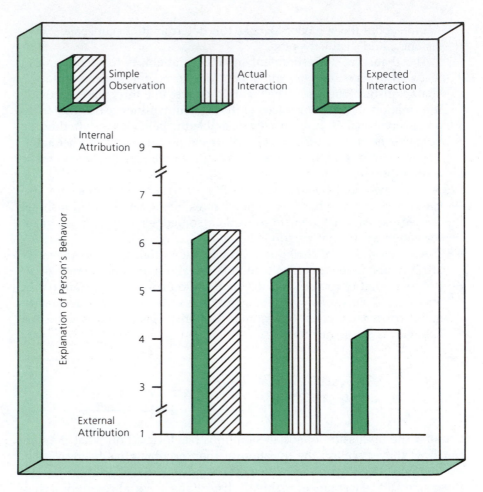

Figure 4-2. *When subjects thought they would be interacting with an unpleasant person, they attributed the person's behavior to external causes.*
Source: Knight and Vallacher (1981).

when he proposed the concept of *projection:* In an attempt to defend themselves against the recognition of their own undesirable traits, people may unconsciously assign these traits to others. Empirical research suggests that projection does occur, but not as the result of unconscious motivations. It appears that people are most likely to project an undesirable trait onto others when they are aware that they possess this trait and find it inconsistent with their self-concept (Bramel, 1962; Holmes, 1978).

Motivatonal Bias and Attributions
A recent study by Knight and Vallacher (1981) demonstrated how motivational biases can influence an observer's attribution of a behavior to an internal or an external cause. Subjects watched a videotape of a male confederate who acted in a negative, unpleasant manner. The subjects were randomly assigned to one of three conditions. Subjects in the first condition merely watched a videotape of the confederate answering questions. Sub-

jects in the second condition saw the same videotape, but as the result of a clever deception believed that the confederate was answering questions they had asked. In the third condition, subjects viewed the same tape, but were told that they would interact with the confederate after watching it. After the tape had been shown to all three groups, subjects rated the extent to which they thought the behavior of the confederate was internally caused (due to his traits) or externally caused (due to the situation). (See figure 4-2 for the results.)

Subjects in the observation and interaction conditions were more inclined to attribute the confederate's unpleasant behavior to an internal cause. But subjects who believed they would be interacting with the confederate in the future attributed his behavior to the situation. Knight and Vallacher said that these subjects' hopes that the future interaction would be pleasant biased their attributions. The researchers also found that when the videotape was of a pleasant actor, the subjects in the future-interaction condition attributed the confederate's behavior to his personality to a much greater extent than did subjects in the other two conditions. (See figure 4-2.) Again, their hopes influenced, or biased, their attributions.

Motivational Bias and Correspondent Inferences

In the original version of the correspondent inferences model of the attribution process, Jones and Davis (1965) proposed two motivational biases that might affect the type of inferences an observer makes—hedonic relevance and personalism.

Hedonic Relevance **Hedonic relevance** refers to the impact an actor's behavior has on the observer. This effect can be either direct (the actor does something to the observer) or indirect (the observer engages in an action that is important to the observer). The more an act affects the observer, the more hedonically relevant it is—and hedonic relevance increases the chances of a correspondent inference.

Personalism If the behavior is high in hedonic relevance, then **personalism** comes into play. The greater the perceived personalism, the greater the tendency to make a correspondent inference.

Personalism: the belief that an action is specifically directed at the observer.

Edward Lawson's troubles with the San Diego police department may illustrate these concepts. If Mr. Lawson was walking in an officer's own neighborhood when he was stopped, his behavior would have hedonic relevance for the officer. If, in searching Mr. Lawson, the officer found a piece of paper with the officer's home address on it, Mr. Lawson's behavior would have high personalism for the officer. Under such circumstances, the officer would be quite likely to make a correspondent inference—this man is out at night because he is a criminal who robs the homes of law-abiding citizens.

Information-Processing Bias

The second type of bias is the result of shortcomings in the way people process information about others. It is called a cognitive bias, or an **infor-**

mation-processing bias (Ross, 1977). This kind of bias can be illustrated by asking a couple of your friends the following question:

Of all the school children in the United States, what percentage are bused to achieve racial integration in the classroom?
a. Less than 5 percent
b. 5 to 25 percent
c. 25 to 50 percent
d. 50 to 75 percent
e. over 75 percent

According to a recent study, the correct answer is a; only 4 percent of all school children are bused to achieve racial integration (Daniels, 1983). But probably most of your friends (and you) made a much higher estimate. This section examines some of the possible kinds of information processing biases.

Implicit Decision Rules

Tversky and Kahneman (1973, 1974) would argue that the reason for the dramatic overestimation is not bigotry or opposition to busing, but the way information about busing is presented in the media and how people process this information. They believe that people use implicit decision rules called *heuristics*, to guide their estimates of the incidence of some phenomenon or their predictions of people's behavior. Heuristics provide the perceiver with a way of simplifying complex data. Unfortunately, using them can result in perceptual biases.

With regard to estimates about busing, two types of heuristics seem especially relevant. The first is the *availability heuristic*. According to this concept, people base their estimates of the frequency of some phenomenon not on objective incidence data, but on the vividness of the phenomenon. People readily remember vivid or dramatic events; thus, they often overestimate the incidence of such events. News reports of children being bused, accompanied by pictures of protesting parents and screaming kids, cause the public to overestimate the number of children who are being bused.

A second and related factor is the *representativeness heuristic*; people assume that what they have seen is representative of all incidences of the phenomenon. So people assume that busing in Chicago, Boston, or Miami is merely the "tip of the iceberg"; they do not consider whether these are representative of the total picture.

Even when people are given information about the true incidence of some event, they tend to ignore this information. For example, Kahneman and Tversky told subjects that the following person came from a group comprised of 70 lawyers and 30 engineers.

Jack is a 45 year old man. He is married and has four children. He is generally conservative, careful and ambitious. He shows no interest in political and social issues and spends most of his free time on his many hobbies, which include home carpentry, sailing and mathematical puzzles (1973, 241).

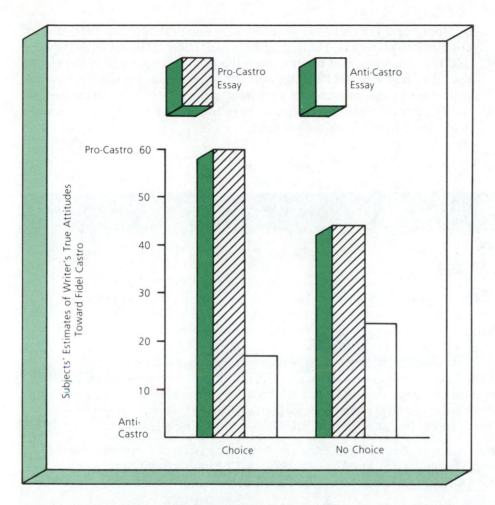

Figure 4-3. *Even when subjects were told the writers had no choice in the kind of essay they wrote, the subjects still made inferences about the writers from the essays.*
Source: Jones and Harris (1967).

Statistically, the odds are much greater that Jack is a lawyer than an engineer because 70 percent of the people in the group were lawyers. But when asked whether he was a lawyer or an engineer, the subjects chose engineer. They based their guess on the information about Jack, not on the statistical composition of the group.

Fundamental Attribution "Error"
Some researchers claim attributions contain a bias that is so basic and widespread it deserves to be called a fundamental error. This can be illustrated by a study originally intended to examine the effects of choice on the types of attributions observers make. Recall that according to the correspondent inferences model, observers will not make internal attributions if they believe the actor was forced to perform a behavior.

Jones and Harris (1967) gave subjects essays that either defended or criticized an unpopular political figure, Fidel Castro. Half the subjects were told that the writer had freely chosen the position expressed in the essay; the other half were told that the writer had been told to take the position expressed in the essay. After they read an essay, subjects estimated its writer's attitudes toward Castro; these estimates were the dependent variable. (See figure 4-3 for the results.)

Research Highlight

Reconstructing the Past

The research on stereotypes suggests that beliefs about people can influence perceptions of their actions. But can memories be biased in the same manner? Can new information about a person cause people to reconstruct their memories of her? In a 1978 study, Snyder and Uranowitz investigated this question.

Subjects read a detailed story about the life of a fictional woman, Betty K. The story began at Betty's birth and ended when she entered the medical profession. It provided information on things such as Betty's relationship with her parents and her social life in high school and college. Then the independent variable was administered. For about half the subjects, the story concluded with the following passage:

During her senior year, Betty met a lesbian who introduced her to homosexual activity. Betty felt exhilarated and that she had finally found herself, and went on to a successful medical career living with her lesbian mate.

For the other half, the story concluded with a different passage:

During her senior year Betty met a man who introduced her to sexual activity. Betty felt exhilarated and that she had finally found herself, and went on to a successful medical career living with her husband.

One week after the subjects had read the story, they returned and were asked a series of multiple-choice questions about factual events in Betty's life. Some of the questions were neutral, such as the name of Betty's high school guidance counselor, but others concerned the subjects' memories of Betty's sexual preferences. For example, one question read:

In high school, Betty
   a. occasionally dated men
   b. never went out with men
   c. went steady
   d. no information provided

The questions concerned with Betty's sexual preferences constituted the dependent measure. Would learning that Betty was a lesbian affect the subjects' memories of what they had read about her?

Labeling Betty as a homosexual or hetereosexual had no effect on the subjects' memories of neutral events, such as the name of her guidance counselor, but it did affect their memories of events concerned with her sexual preference. The answers to questions about these events indicated that the subjects' "memories" of Betty's life had changed as the result of the label placed on her. Subjects in the lesbian-label condition "remembered" events in her life that indicated she was homosexual. Subjects in the hetereosexual-label condition "remembered" events in her life that indicated she was straight. For example, subjects in the first condition were more likely than subjects in the second condition to choose the alternative "Betty never went out in high school." The subjects, according to Snyder and Uranowitz, unknowingly reconstructed their memories to fit their new beliefs.

Bellezza and Bower (1981) proposed an alternative explanation of these findings. They suggested that labeling does not cause people to reconstruct their memories; it simply produces a bias in the way they answer questions about the events they are trying to remember. Bellezza and Bower replicated Snyder and Uranowitz's original study with one change: In each of the questions concerned with sexual preference, they included an answer that was consistent with people's stereotypes about gay or straight individuals but described an event the subjects had not read about. Bellezza and Bower found that subjects in the lesbian-label condition were more likely than subjects in the hetereosexual-label condition to choose a lesbian-life-style answer even when this was the wrong one! Thus, it appears that people may not reconstruct their memories to fit their social cognitions. Until it can be determined which of these two explanations is more valid, the proposal that people reconstruct their memories on the basis of new information remains in doubt.

In the choice condition, the writer who wrote the pro-Castro essay was seen as being much more pro-Castro than the writer who wrote the anti-Castro essay. This writer was also seen as more pro-Castro than the person who wrote the same essay in the no-choice condition. These results support the correspondent inferences theory's prediction that people are more likely to make correspondent inferences when an actor has chosen to engage in the behavior.

But now look at the no-choice condition. Even when the observers were explicitly told that the writers had no choice in what they wrote, they still made inferences about the writers' attitudes from their assays. They believed that the no-choice pro-Castro writers had more favorable attitudes toward Castro than did the no-choice anti-Castro writers. There was a tendency to attribute the actors' behavior to a characteristic of the actors even when they did not choose to engage in the behavior. Ross (1977) and others call this the **fundamental attribution error.**

This tendency can be seen most clearly when one compares the attributions of actors and observers. Observers are much more likely to attribute an actor's behavior to an internal cause than are actors.*

Fundamental attribution error: the tendency of people to overestimate the role that internal dispositions (traits, attitudes) play in human behavior and to underestimate the role of external, situational factors.

---

*A word of explanation: Although observers are more prone to give internal explanations than are actors, both are more likely to explain behavior in terms of internal dispositions than in terms of external causes. Thus, the actor-observer difference is relative.

Saulnier and Perlman (1981) interviewed staff members (observers) who provided counseling to inmates (actors) at a prison. The counselors were asked to explain why certain inmates had committed the crimes that put them in prison and whether those crimes reflected enduring characteristics of the inmates. Then the inmates were asked the same question about their behavior. The counselors attributed the crime to a stable, internal cause; the inmates attributed it to an unstable, external cause. The difference was probably not due to a motivational bias on the part of the prisoners but rather reflects the fundamental attribution error. This type of actor-observer difference in attributions has been found in a wide variety of circumstances. It occurs even when the observer has engaged in exactly the same behavior as the actor (Watson, 1982). A good deal of research has addressed why observers are biased in favor of internal attributions for actors' behavior.

Salience of People and Situations

Salient stimuli: things that are especially vivid or prominent, or that catch people's attention.

Taylor and Fiske (1978) proposed that people tend to see **salient stimuli** as the cause of things, whether they are or not. Since actors are typically much more salient stimuli than the situations they are in, observers attribute the behavior they see to actors' personal characteristics rather than to situational factors. One way to test this explanation is to compare the kinds of attributions observers make about salient and nonsalient actors. McArthur and Post (1977) showed subjects videotapes of two actors. The actors' behaviors were identical in every respect, but a bright light was shone on one of them and a dim light was shone on the other. This created a difference in salience. After watching the tape, subjects made attributions about the causes of the actors' behaviors. These attributions were significantly more internal in the bright-light, or salient, condition. In another study, Quattrone (1983) systematically manipulated the salience of an actor and the situation in which her actions took place. When the situational factors were made more salient than the actions of the actor, people attributed the actions to situational pressures on the actor. These studies suggest that observers attribute a behavior to whatever is most salient.

Prediction and Control

Another explanation for attribution errors goes back to why people make attributions in the first place. Heider proposed that people make attributions because they believe attributions bring a measure of order and predictability to their social world. An internal attribution may serve this need better than an external one (Watson, 1982). The belief that an actor's behavior is stable and enduring gives observers more of a sense of being able to predict the actor's future behavior than does the belief that the behavior is unstable and transitory. There is some degree of support for this explanation. When observers expect to interact with an actor in the future, they tend to give an internal explanation of the actor's behavior. However, when observers do not anticipate future interaction, they tend to give an external explanation (Miller, Norman, and Wright, 1978; Miller and Porter, 1980). This explanation complements the explanation that when an actor's behav-

Research suggests that the more salient a stimulus an actor is, the more internal an attribution observers make. This street performer is a very salient stimulus.

ior is salient and important to observers, observers tend to give it an internal attribution.

Is It Human to Err? (A Digression)

Before concluding the discussion of accuracy in social cognitions, I wish to briefly discuss a controversy among social psychologists. In this review, I shifted from the word *bias* to the word *error*. This change was quite intentional since proponents of the fundamental attribution error argue that observers do not simply bias their perceptions, but commit basic perceptual errors. Although this position was and is widely accepted among social psychologists, in recent years several researchers have questioned whether this phenomenon is either fundamental or an error.

The proposal that observers make attributional errors is based, at least in part, on the situationist view of the causes of human behavior. The situationists propose that situational factors are stronger determinants of social behavior than are internal factors. Thus, an observer who attributes a behavior to an internal cause must be in error.

Harvey, Town, and Yarkin (1981) pointed out, however, that traits may be much more important determinants of social behavior than either situationists or proponents of the fundamental attribution error (often the same people) have proposed. Studies by Epstein (1979) showed that people do display consistency in their behavior across situations and that traits do accurately predict behavior. Given these and other findings, it seems premature to call the typical attribution of observers an error. Such a characterization should await a resolution of the person-versus-situation controversy in favor of a situational explanation.

Hamilton (1980) criticized the labeling of this tendency as an "error" on the grounds that the law differentiates between explaining a behavior and sanctioning it. For example, imagine a man is on trial for murdering his wife. The man does not deny the murder, but points out that his wife was frequently and flagrantly unfaithful. Outraged by her behavior, he lost control and murdered her. Anyone who had been subjected to this, he argues, would have done the same thing. The jury is aware of and understands the situational factors that brought about the man's action, but it refuses to sanction what he did—he was not forced to murder her; he could have left her or done something less violent. Thus, the jury convicts him. Has the jury made a perceptual error? If we define an error as a departure from a "scientific information-processing rule," then it has. But as Hamilton observes, few legal scholars or lay people would consider it so. He suggests that observers may feel that situational factors cannot absolve actors of responsibility for their behavior. Thus, the behavior is attributed to the actor's personality. This is an error only in terms of the rather narrow definition put forth by social psychologists.

SUMMARY

Humans exhibit consistent and significant biases in their social cognitions. In general, these biases are due to either motivational factors or the ways people process information about the world around them. With regard to motivational bias, it has been found that behaviors that have a direct or indirect effect on observers are usually attributed to stable characteristics of actors, and that observers bias their attributions to provide a more optimistic picture of the future.

One source of nonmotivational (information-processing) bias is certain implicit rules people use to help them make predictions about events or other people's behavior. These rules, called heuristics, provide people with a quick, easy way to draw conclusions about what they see, but they may sometimes yield conclusions that are not in accord with reality.

A well-documented bias on the part of observers is the tendency to overestimate the importance of personality traits as causes of behavior.

This bias has been found so consistently that some researchers have called it the fundamental attribution error. Several different explanations of this error have been proposed. One explanation is based on the fact that observers tend to attribute causes to salient stimuli. Since actors are typically much more salient stimuli than are the characteristics of the situation they are in, observers attribute the behavior to the actors rather than to the situation. A second explanation is based on people's need for order and predictability in their social world. Because behavior that has an internal cause is seen as more stable and predictable than behavior that has an external cause, observers are biased in favor of internal explanations—especially if they will encounter the actor again in the future.

Most researchers agree that these biases exist, but some question the appropriateness of calling them an error. They argue that the biases are errors only if it can be objectively demonstrated that they are wrong. The fact that attributions often differ from both psychologists' beliefs about the true causes of behavior and a logical, scientific decision rule does not automatically make them wrong.

Applications

Social Cognitions and the Legal System

The United States Constitution guarantees its citizens the right to a trial by a jury of their peers. This right is expanded and reinforced by the Fifth, Sixth, and Seventh amendments to the Constitution. A jury trial is believed to provide a fair and objective way of determining the guilt or innocence of a person accused of a crime. People assume that jurors will be presented with the true facts in a case and that they will base their decision on these facts and nothing else.

Another way to think of a jury trial is as an experiment with an independent and a dependent variable. The independent variable is the evidence in the case—the physical evidence and the testimony of witnesses. In an experiment, one of a researcher's chief concerns is the construct validity of the independent variable. In a trial, construct-valid evidence should be a faithful representation of all the facts in the case. The dependent variable is the jury's decision. In an experiment, researchers want the dependent variable to be due to the independent variable, or to have *internal validity*. Similarly, in a trial, the jury's decision should be based on the evidence and nothing else. Indeed, in 48 of the 50 states, jurors are either explicitly or implicitly told that their task is to determine the facts, not to interpret the law (Nemeth, 1981).

This way of looking at a trial provides a framework for examining the role of social cognitions in the legal system. If something causes the testimony of witnesses to be biased or inaccurate, the evidence is not construct valid and the trial is not fair and objective. If the jurors process and organize the information they receive at a trial in such a way that their decision is not based solely on the facts in the case, the trial is not internally valid and is thus unfair and nonobjective.

This section looks at both the construct validity of the testimony of witnesses and the internal validity of jury decisions.

Before turning to these issues, however, a few points merit mention. First, although all people accused of a crime or sued in a civil case (for example, a lawsuit over injuries suffered in an accident) are guaranteed the right to a jury trial, relatively few criminal or civil cases ever go to trial. Ellison and Buckhout (1981) estimated that no more than 10 percent of all criminal defendants seek a jury trial. Second, this review focuses on factors that could bias jury decisions. But studies suggest that in most instances jury decisions are unbiased and valid. Kalven and Zeisel (1966) examined the results of about 3,600 trials. They used as their measure of validity the agreement between the jurors' decision and the independent decision offered by the judge in each case. They found that judges and jurors agreed 78 percent of the time. So, while the emphasis is on the invalidity of jury trials, it must be remembered that by most criteria, the majority of jury trials produce valid results. Finally, an important aspect of jury trials is not covered here. This is the dynamics of jury deliberations, which include how many jurors are selected, whether decisions require a majority or a unanimous vote, and who the foreperson is. These dynamics influence the decisions juries make (see Kessler, 1977; Penrod and Hastie, 1979). (See chapter thirteen for more about these variables.)

TESTIMONY OF WITNESSES

This section discusses the construct validity of one kind of common trial evidence, the testimony of witnesses. Witnesses provide types of testimony. They can identify the person who committed a crime and thus provide evidence that the person on trial is or is not the guilty party. They can also provide information on an event, such as an automobile accident, that the jury needs to make a decision.

Jurors place great faith in *eyewitnesses*. In a study conducted by Elizabeth Loftus (1979), college students played the role of jurors. Half of them read a synopsis of a trial in which there was no eyewitness. The other half read exactly the same synopsis, plus testimony from a person who claimed to have seen the defendant commit the crime. The defendant was found guilty by 18 percent of the jurors in the first group and by 72 percent of the jurors in the second group. A study of actual trials in England (Devlin, 1976) supported Loftus' findings. When the only evidence against a defendant was an eyewitness identification, the conviction rate was 74 percent. As Loftus said, "When no other evidence is available, the testimony of one or more eyewitnesses can be overwhelmingly influential" (1979, p. 9).

Before eyewitnesses testify in court, they must be able to pick out the defendant from a group of people. Police departments use two techniques to obtain these identifications: a *photospread*, which is simply a set of photographs, and a lineup. If witnesses cannot make a positive identification, they are not asked to testify. If they do testify, the information they give may contain inaccuracies.

Accuracy of Eyewitness Identifications

John Brigham and his associates (Brigham, Maass, Snyder, and Spaulding, 1982) conducted a field experiment on photospreads. Confederates entered convenience stores and engaged clerks in a four- to five-minute transaction. To ensure that the clerks looked at the confederates' faces, they requested directions to the local airport. Twenty-four hours later, the clerks were asked to pick the confederates out of a six-person photospread. Less than 8 percent of the identifications were correct. In another part of the same study, the time interval between the encounter with the confederate and the identification was shortened to two hours. The accuracy rate increased to 34 percent. In this study no crime was committed; perhaps witnesses of a crime would be more accurate.

Several studies have investigated the accuracy of identifications made by witnesses of a crime, and the results are much more encouraging. Lindsey, Wells, and Rumpel (1981) staged a crime in which a confederate, standing a few feet from a subject, stole a calculator. The confederate spoke with the subject for about 20 seconds before he committed the theft. About a minute after the "thief" left, subjects were asked to identify him from a photospread. The accuracy rate was 64 percent. If the thief wore a knit cap that covered his hair and part of his ears, the accuracy rate dropped to about 29 percent. In another study, Buckhout (1980) obtained permission from a television station to show a simulated crime on an evening news program. Shortly after the crime was aired, viewers were shown a lineup of possible suspects and asked to phone in their identifications. Less than 15 percent of the 2,100 viewers who called in were able to correctly identify the criminal.

Lindsay et al. also found that irrespective of an eyewitnesses' actual ability to identify someone, jurors were more likely to believe a confident than a nonconfident eyewitness. (See figure 4-4.) The accuracy of eyewitness reports is influenced by the way identifications are obtained and by cultural factors, stress, and memory.

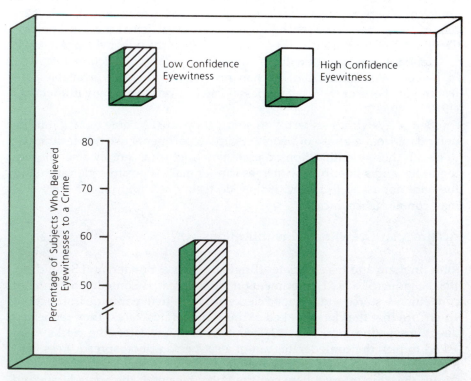

Figure 4-4. *Although confident eyewitnesses were only slightly more likely than nonconfident eyewitnesses to be accurate, subjects were much more likely to believe their testimony.*
Source: Lindsay et al. (1981).

Obtaining Identifications: Will the Real Criminal Please Stand Up?

A few years ago a store owner was murdered in the course of a robbery. Several witnesses told the police that the robber was a black man. A short time later, the police arrested a suspect and arranged a lineup for the witnesses. All of them positively identified the suspect as the murderer. Was this good police work? Maybe not—the suspect was the only black person in the lineup! While this true incident illustrates a rather gross error in an identification procedure, more subtle biases in obtaining identifications can also influence witnesses.

Several researchers have staged crimes and then examined how the identifications by eyewitnesses could be influenced. One study showed that if one picture in a photospread is presented differently from the others, eyewitnesses will identify that person as the guilty person (Ellison and Buckhout, 1981). In another study, eyewitnesses to an actual crime were shown a photospread of six innocent men. The person conducting the experiment smiled and nonverbally reinforced the selection of one of the pictures. Thirty-eight percent of the witnesses said the man in that picture was the criminal (Fanselow and Buckhout, 1976). Finally, Malpass and Devine (1981) investigated the way people are asked to make identifications. Subjects who had seen an actual act of vandalism were asked to look at a lineup of five possible suspects. The real vandal was not among the five. Some of the witnesses were given biased instructions: "We believe the [vandal] is present in the lineup." Others were given unbiased instructions: "The [vandal] may be one of the five [but] . . . is also possible he is not in the lineup." Seventy-eight percent of the witnesses who received biased instructions chose one of the people in the lineup; only 33 percent of the witnesses who received unbiased instructions did this. Further, witnesses in the biased condition had significantly more confidence in their choices than had witnesses in the unbiased condition.

Cultural Factors

Evidence suggests that cultural factors may influence the accuracy of eyewitness identifications. Malpass and Kravitz (1969) reported that people are better at identifying faces of members of their own racial or ethnic group than faces of members of a different group. Further, the more contact whites have had with blacks, the better they are at identifying black individuals. Blacks, probably because they have more contact with whites than whites have with blacks, may be better at cross-racial identifications than whites (Brigham et al., 1982).

Racial prejudice does not appear to affect the accuracy of eyewitness identifications, but it may affect how a witness remembers an incident and describes it. This was illustrated in a famous social psychological experiment by Allport and Postman (1947). Subjects saw a drawing of a black man and a white man speaking to one another; the white man held a straight-edged razor in his hand. Then the subjects described the scene to another person. The second person told a third, and so on. As the story went from one person to another, the razor moved from the hand of the white man to the hand of the black man.

The training manual for the International Association of Chiefs of Police provides a real-life example of this phenomenon. A middle-aged woman of European extraction lived in a neighborhood into which a large number of Hispanics were moving. She was quite bothered by this. One day the woman was robbed of several thousand dollars. She described the robber as an Hispanic with a dark complexion. When the robber was caught, he had blue eyes and a very light complexion (International Association of Chiefs of Police, 1967).

Stress

The amount of stress people are under influences their ability to recall and identify the person who victimized them. Up to a point, stress or arousal will improve people's memories for the face of a criminal. But if victims are too stressed, the completeness and accuracy of their memories are impaired. Kuehn (1974) examined the descriptions victims gave of a criminal and found that the more violent the crime, the less complete a description of the perpetrator the victim gave the police. A closely related phenomenon, *weapon focus*, causes people to focus on a weapon rather than the features of the person holding it. As a result, they provide a poor description of the criminal.

Memory

Loftus and her associates have shown that the manner in which people are asked about an event they have seen can influence their memory of it. For example, Loftus and Palmer (1974) showed subjects a film of a traffic accident. After seeing the film, half of the subjects were asked how fast the cars were going when they *smashed* into one another; the other half were asked how fast the cars were going when they *hit* one another. A week later, the subjects returned and were asked additional questions about the accident, including "Did you see any broken glass?" Although there was no broken glass, 32 percent of the subjects in the smashed condition reported seeing it; by contrast, 14 percent of the people in the hit condition reported seeing it.

In another study, Hastie, Landsman, and Loftus (1978) showed subjects a film of an accident in which an automobile hit a pedestrian. Shortly thereafter, the subjects were asked a series of questions about the accident, including one about the color of a station wagon that had supposedly passed the accident. Two days later, the subjects returned and were asked other questions about the accident, including "Did you see the station wagon which passed the accident?" Most subjects reported seeing it and were quite confident in their recollections. In fact, no station wagon was shown in the film.

In still another study illustrating this phenomenon, a film of a car accident was shown to subjects. Half the subjects were asked questions like "Did you see *a* broken headlight?"; the other half were asked questions like "Did you see *the* broken headlight?" (In the second question, there is an implicit assumption that there was a broken headlight. In fact, there was no broken headlight in the film.) Subjects in the the condition were two or three times more likely to report having seen the broken headlight than were subjects in the a condition. (Loftus and Zanni, 1975).

In other studies, Loftus was able to get subjects to remember people, stop signs, and even a large red barn when these did not appear in the films they saw. Loftus did not think that her subjects were trying to please the people who asked questions. Rather, she proposed that the manner in which the questions were asked caused the subject to alter their memories of the events; they really remembered the objects or events as they were described in the questions. In the same way, witnesses who are asked leading or biased questions may fail to tell the truth without lying.

As citizens, how concerned should we be about these findings? In terms of absolute numbers, inaccuracies in identifications or reconstructed memories probably influence very few legal proceedings. Remember, only 10 percent of all people accused of a crime ever have a trial. But, as Loftus has pointed out, there is another reason to be concerned:

> Every time an innocent person is convicted of a crime that she or he did not commit, a guilty person is still free, possibly committing other crimes. (1983, p. 577)

Research on juries suggests that social cognitions about the testimony of witnesses and the character of the defendant may influence the decisions a jury reaches.

Social Cognitions and the Jury

This section discusses the internal validity of a jury trial; it examines some factors which might cause a jury to base its decision on something other than the evidence that is presented at a trial.

Pretrial Publicity

Over the years, the legal system has developed an extensive set of rules for what constitutes a fair trial. At the core of these rules is an attempt to ensure that the jury will base its decision only on the facts or evidence the presiding judge feels presents a fair and unbiased picture of the matter at hand. But if the case concerns a well-publicized crime, prospective jurors might be exposed to a considerable amount of information about the crime or the person accused of it. Lawyers disagree as to the effects of pretrial publicity. Some argue that jurors' decisions are not influenced by it; others argue that jurors' decisions are dramatically affected by it.

The issue of pretrial publicity has been addressed by several researchers. Padawer-Singer and Burton (1975) conducted a fairly elaborate study. They selected subjects from a list of people eligible for jury duty in areas near New York City and told them they were to hear a murder trial. Half of the prospective jurors read newspaper articles that were biased against the defendant. The articles reported that he had a prior criminal record and had confessed to the crime but had later retracted the confession. These items were deleted from the article the other half of the jurors read. Then both groups heard an audiotaped re-creation of the actual trial this study was based on. After hearing all the evidence, the jurors deliberated for four to six hours. Among the jurors who had read the biased article, 78 percent voted to convict the defendant; among the jurors who had read the unbiased article, 55 percent voted for conviction.

In a real trial, defense lawyers have a chance to question prospective jurors and challenge those they believe are prejudiced against the defendant. Padawer-Singer and Burton used this procedure in the second part of their study. Volunteer lawyers interviewed prospective jurors, while other volunteer lawyers acted as the judge and ruled on objections to the inclusion of certain jurors. (In law, this process is called the *voir dire*). Despite this procedure, 83 percent of the jurors who read the biased article voted for conviction, but only 55 percent of the jurors who read the unbiased article favored conviction.

Inadmissible Evidence

Inadmissible evidence consists of physical evidence or testimony that a judge rules cannot be presented at a trial. Some examples of this are hearsay testimony or physical evidence that has been obtained illegally. Although judges try to screen the evidence presented at a trial, evidence is often presented to the jury and then ruled inadmissible. When this happens, the judge instructs the jury to disregard the information. Is this instruction effective?

In one study that investigated the effects of inadmissible evidence, mock jurors heard proacquittal inadmissible evidence, proconviction inadmissible evidence, or no inadmissible evidence. Immediately after the evidence had been ruled inadmissible, the judge told the jurors, "It is your legal duty to ignore testimony ruled inadmissible when considering your verdict." Despite this, jurors who heard evidence that favored acquittal were significantly less likely to find the defendant guilty than were jurors in the other two groups (Thompson, Fong, and Rosenhan, 1981).

An alternative procedure for reducing the effects of juror biases was proposed by Kaplan and Schersching (1980). They argued that the importance, or weight, jurors place on their initial impressions of the defendant or on inadmissible evidence should be decreased and that the weight jurors place on admissible evidence should be increased. This proposal for reducing juror bias was derived directly from the *weighted averaging model* of impression formation.

Kaplan and Miller (1978) investigated the effects both juror bias and the evidence presented at a trial had on a juror's decision. Juror bias was operationally defined as the juror's general attitude toward the treatment of criminals. Half the jurors had harsh attitudes; half had lenient attitudes. Equal numbers from each group were randomly assigned to one of two conditions. In the first condition, jurors were led to believe that the evidence was accurate and reliable; in the second, the evidence was presented as inaccurate and unreliable. After hearing the evidence, jurors rated how guilty they thought the defendant was. (See figure 4-5 for these ratings.)

The jurors' general attitudes affected their guilt ratings in the unreliable-evidence condition, but did not when the jurors believed the evidence was accurate and reliable. This was true whether the evidence favored the prosecution or favored the defense.

In the United States, each side presents its version of the facts and challenges the accuracy of the other side's evidence. According to Kaplan and Schersching (1980), this adversary system may convince jurors that they cannot believe either side. As a result, the jurors may decide the case on the basis of their biases. Kaplan and Schersching suggested that the United States reduce the effects of juror bias by adopting a practice that is common in Europe—having an independent fact finder present the evidence to the jury.

Testimony of Witnesses

In the adversary trial system, each side presents witnesses who support its position. Vidmar and Laird (1983) studied how motivational biases on the part of witnesses can affect their testimony. Subjects who had witnessed a fight were told that they would have to testify in court as to what they had seen. The subjects received subpoenas, which were issued by the court either on behalf of the plaintiff in the case or on behalf of the defendant.

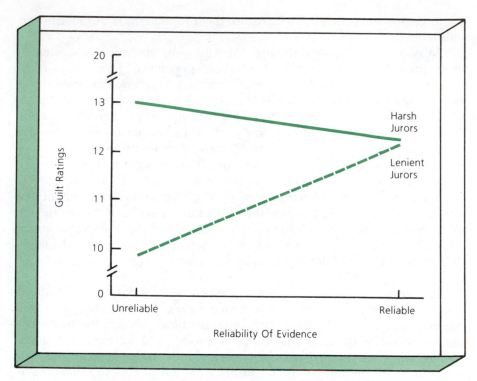

Figure 4-5. *When the evidence presented was seen as unreliable, jurors' attitudes greatly affected their opinion of the defendant's guilt. Copyright 1978 the American Psychological Association. Reprinted by permission of the authors.*
Source: Kaplan and Miller (1978).

Mock jurors rated which side these witnesses' testimonies favored. Witnesses called by the plaintiff were seen as giving testimony that favored him and those called by the defendant showed a bias in favor of him. But the witnesses saw their testimony as objective and unbiased. Subsequent analyses of the witnesses' testimonies suggest that the witnesses did not show bias by giving different information about the fight; they simply described the fight in words and phrases that favored whichever side had subpoenaed them.

One of the most important witnesses at a trial is the person on trial. However, defendants have the right not to testify at their trial. Further, if they take the stand, the Fifth Amendment to the Constitution gives them the right to refuse to give evidence that would incriminate them in the crime they are accused of or in any other crime. Many people see the exercise of either right as an admission of guilt. Shaffer and Case (1982) presented mock jurors with one of two transcripts of a trial. In one transcript, the defendant invoked his Fifth Amendment rights and refused to answer any questions. In the other, the defendant answered all the questions asked of him. Jurors were significantly more likely to find the defendant who refused to testify guilty. Evidently, they assumed that an innocent man would not "take the Fifth."*

Attribution Processes

The models of attribution processes may also be used to explain how people view crimes and criminals. Kelley's covariation model has been used to explain how differences in consensus and consistency affect such attributions. It was found that crimes that are relatively infrequent or are committed by one person (are low in consensus) are viewed as being more serious and are judged more harshly than are crimes that are frequent or committed by several people (are relatively high in consensus) (Perlman, 1980). In addition, defendants with a history of criminal offenses (with high-consistency behavior) are more likely than defendants without such a history to receive high bail fees, convictions, and long jail sentences (Perlman, 1980). These findings are consistent with Kelley's theory that behaviors low in consensus and high in consistency lead to an internal attribution and, thus, harsher treatment of the person accused of the crime.

Other researchers have applied the theory of correspondent inferences to people's attributions about crimes. West, Gunn, and Chernicky (1975) presented subjects with a description of someone who either refused or agreed to take part in a Watergate-style burglary. Consistent with the theory's prediction about the effects of social desirability, observers tended to attribute the socially desirable decision (refusal) to an external cause, but tended to attribute the socially undesirable decision (agreement) to some enduring characteristic of the actor.

The construct of hedonic relevance also affects the type of attributions a person makes. For example, the more observers feared that they might be the victim of a crime, the more internal an attribution they made about the person who had committed it (Carroll and Payne, 1977).

What conclusions can be drawn from this review? It would be quite incorrect to conclude that jury decisions are usually based on invalid evidence or biased social cognitions. No systematic study of actual juries has ever found this. In fact, most evaluations of the jury system find that it works quite well. But the studies presented here do suggest that social cognitions can influence the testimony people give and the manner in which jurors make decisions. These findings strengthen some of the theories of social cognitive processes and suggest that the study of social cognitions can contribute to the understanding and improvement of the legal system.

---

*You may wonder why an innocent person would refuse to testify. An example: One person accused of being involved in a plot to assassinate President Kennedy refused to testify in an open hearing not because he was guilty, but because he was afraid his testimony would reveal that he was a homosexual.

Chapter Five

Self-Perception and Presentation

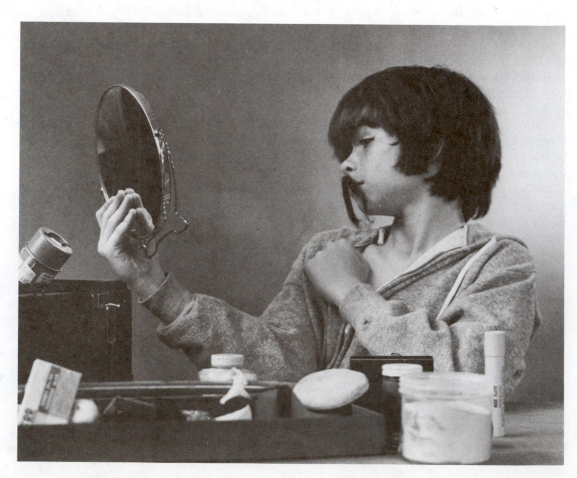

Prologue

Stanley Schachter and Jerome Singer (1962). Cognitive,
Social, and Emotional Determinants of Emotional State.
Psychological Review, **69,** 379–399.

Background

Research on the self has focused on how people perceive themselves and
present themselves to others. In the area of self-perception, one of the
oldest questions asked by psychologists concerns the processes people use
to label or identify the emotions they experience. In the late 1800s, William
James proposed that the emotions people experience correspond directly
to some internal physiological state (heart pounding, for instance) and that
changes in this physiological state produce changes in the emotions. In
the 1920s, however, Walter Cannon conducted a series of experiments and
found that different emotions were often accompanied by exactly the same
physiological response and that people had difficulty noticing differences
between physiological responses. These findings led Cannon to dismiss
the importance of physiological changes in the identification of emotions.
The issue was argued back and forth through the 1930s, 1940s, and 1950s.
In the late 1950s, Stanley Schachter proposed that both physiological responses and social factors play a role in labeling emotions. This experiment
was designed to objectively test Schachter's ideas.

Hypothesis

It was hypothesized that when people experience arousal but are unable
to fully explain its cause, they will label the arousal as a certain emotion
on the basis of information from their environment, such as the reactions
of other people in the same situation. If, however, people experience exactly
the same arousal and are able to fully explain its cause, they will not label
it on the basis of information from the environment. In other words, two
people with exactly the same kind of physiological arousal may label it
quite differently.

Subjects

The subjects were 185 males enrolled in introductory psychology at the
University of Minnesota.

Procedure

The subjects were told the study concerned the effects of a vitamin compound on their vision and were then randomly assigned to one of three
conditions. Subjects in two conditions received an injection of epinephrine,
a stimulant that produces increases in the heart rate and blood pressure
as well as other physiological responses. Subjects in the first condition

were told that the vitamin compound (really epinephrine) would have certain side effects and were given accurate information about how it would affect them. Subjects in the second condition also received epinephrine, but were given no information about how it would affect them. And subjects in the third (control) condition received a placebo injection (a saltwater solution) and no information about possible side effects. The differences between the three conditions constituted the first independent variable.

Immediately after they received the injections, the subjects were placed with another person (a confederate). They were told this other person had also received the vitamin compound, and that the two would wait together for the injection to take effect. The confederate's behavior during the time he was with the subject was the second variable manipulated in the experiment.

For about half the subjects, the confederate acted in a giddy, euphoric manner; he made paper airplanes, used a hula hoop that was lying in the room, and devised a game of "basketball" using crumpled paper. For the remainder of the subjects, the confederate's behavior was quite different. He and the subjects were asked to fill out some questionnaires while they waited for the injection to take effect. The confederate pretended that he was offended by the personal nature of some of the questions. He became so "angry" that after several minutes, he tore up the questionnaire and left the room.

The behavior of the subjects while they were with the confederate was observed and the amount of euphoria or anger they displayed was rated. At the end of the confederate's performance, subjects indicated how angry they felt and how happy they felt. The ratings and the self-reports were the dependent variables.

Results

If the hypotheses about how people identify their emotions were correct, then subjects who did not know why they were aroused should have labeled the arousal quite differently from those who knew why they were aroused. This was found to be true. (See figure 5-1.) Subjects with the euphoric confederate who received the epinephrine injection but were not told about the true effects of the drug reported feeling significantly happier than did those who were told about the drug's effects. Similarly, subjects with the angry confederate who did not know how the epinephrine would affect them displayed much more anger than did subjects who knew how the epinephrine would affect them. In other words, subjects who had no ready explanation for the arousal they felt labeled, or identified, it on the basis of their observations of the confederate's reactions to the injection.

Implications

This experiment led to the development of a formal, widely accepted theory of how people label their emotions that has been used to explain social phenomena ranging from aggression to helping to love. However, researchers have recently raised some questions about Schachter and Singer's

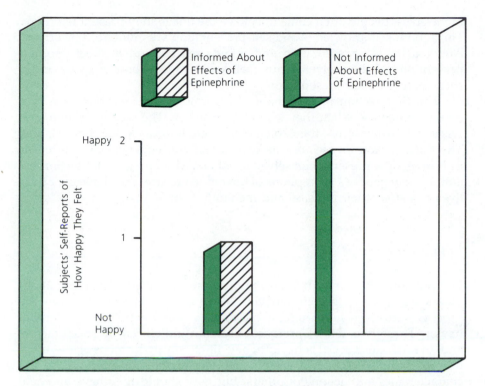

Figure 5-1. *Subjects who were not informed of the effects of epinephrine were more influenced by the mood of the euphoric confederate than were subjects who were informed of the drug's effect.*
Source: Schachter and Singer (1962).

original experiment and the conclusions they drew from it. The first part of this chapter presents their criticisms and alternative theories of how people come to know themselves.

This chapter is about the self. The **self** can be defined as "the individual as perceived by the individual" (Stang and Wrightsman, 1980); people's private personal views of who they are and what they think and feel. According to Schlenker (1985), theory and research on the self has focused on two concepts: **self-knowledge**—the processes that enable people to gain knowledge about who they are and what causes their behavior (the issue addressed by Schachter and Singer in the prologue) and **self-presentation**— the factors that influence how people present themselves to others. Self-knowledge and self-presentation are related in several ways. First, the images people project to others and the manner in which they do this are influenced by their self-knowledge, or the perceptions they have of themselves. Second, the act of self-presentation changes the way people perceive themselves; people often come to believe the image they present to others. Third, both self-knowledge and self-presentation are influenced by others. And fourth, self-presentation and other's reactions to it affect people's perceptions of themselves. Thus, self-knowledge is both a cause and a consequence of self-presentation.

The first section in this chapter concerns self-perceptions—the processes people use when they look at themselves. The second section concerns self-attributions—the explanations people provide for their actions. The third section focuses on the causes and consequences of differences in how people present themselves to others. The applications section examines how people's perceptions of how much control they have over their lives can affect their physical and mental health.

SELF-PERCEPTIONS

The previous chapter addressed the processes involved in learning about others and explaining their behavior. Much of this chapter addresses the processes involved in learning about ourselves and explains our own behavior. These two sets of processes are both influenced by social factors and, in turn, affect social behavior. They differ only in the focus of interest—others versus the self. It is easy to see why people are interested in the characteristics and actions of others, but why should they have an equal if not greater interest in themselves? Because if people understand (or believe they understand) what they are feeling or why they are acting in a certain way or why something is happening to them, they have a better picture of what kind of people they are, guidelines for their future actions, and a sense of control over their social world. This section examines three theories concerned with people's attempts to understand their actions and their feelings: Bem's theory of how people make inferences about their attitudes and traits, Schachter's two-factor theory of labeling emotions, and self-awareness theory.

Bem's Self-perception Theory

You are alone in your room and your phone rings. You answer it and the person on the other end tells you that he is conducting a national survey. It will take only a few minutes and no personal or embarrassing questions will be asked. You agree to take part in the survey. After asking a few questions about your age, race, sex, and so on, the interviewer turns to your attitudes. "Do you prefer the Republicans or Democrats?" "Do you favor or oppose school busing?" "Are you positive, negative, or neutral toward nuclear disarmament?" "Do you think the government should ban or allow abortions?" You answer all these questions quite easily. But then the interviewer throws you a curve. "How do you know that you prefer the Republicans?" he asks. "What?!" you reply. "Look," he says, "I get a lot of people who claim they prefer the Republicans and I'm not so sure that all of them are telling me the truth. I want some proof, dammit!"

If you do not hang up on this emotionally unstable interviewer, you might find yourself stuttering and stammering for awhile and then saying, "Well, I'm registered as a Republican; I voted for the Republican candidates in the last elections; uh, I once donated ten dollars to Ronald Reagan's campaign fund and . . . "

You have provided the interviewer with a number of behavioral incidents that should convince him that you do indeed prefer the Republicans. But you have also provided information that should convince *you* that you prefer the Republicans. In his **self-perception theory,** Daryl Bem (1967, 1972) proposed that people often observe their own behavior and draw inferences about their beliefs, attitudes, and values from it.

Self-perception theory originates in a behavioristic approach to human behavior, which proposes that social behavior is primarily determined by external stimuli, or the situations people encounter. (See chapter one and chapter three.) There is, however, a serious problem with this position: Most people believe that their internal dispositions (traits, attitudes) play an important role in their behavior. Just as observers are biased in favor of internal causes as explanations of other people's behavior, so are actors—to a lesser extent—biased in favor of internal causes as explanations of their own behavior (Watson, 1982).

Bem's theory of self-perception represents an attempt to reconcile this bias with the behavioristic point of view. The theory contains three basic ideas. First, people use the same processes in explaining their own behavior as they use in explaining the behavior of other people. Second, people do not really possess enduring, salient attitudes or traits; instead, people infer their internal dispositions from observations of their own behavior. And third, the primary cause of people's behavior is not internal dispositions, but external stimuli such as rewards or social pressure. Thus, people's beliefs in the importance of attitudes and other internal characteristics are based on a faulty attribution.

Most of the research that has attempted to test Bem's theory has focused on the second idea—that people infer their internal dispositions from their overt behavior. In an early test of self-perception theory, Bandler, Madaras, and Bem (1968) examined people's perceptions of pain. Subjects were randomly assigned to three different conditions. In all three conditions, subjects received shocks of exactly the same intensity. (Remember this; it is important). In the first two conditions, subjects were told that they were free to decide how much shock they would receive and that they could terminate the shock by pressing a button in front of them. However, in the first of these conditions, they were told they *should* press the button if the shock became uncomfortable; in the second condition, they were told they *should not* press the button unless necessary. In the final condition (the control condition,) subjects could press the button, but doing so would not terminate the shock. After all three groups of subjects had received several shocks, they were asked to rate how painful the shock was.

Self-perception theory would predict that subjects in the first condition would perceive the shock as more painful than would subjects in the other conditions, and that subjects in the second condition would perceive the shock as less painful than would subjects in the other conditions. The results supported self-perception theory. In Bem's terms, the subjects inferred their pain from their actual behavior. Those who pushed the button frequently (subjects in the first condition) felt they had experienced more pain than those who had pushed the button infrequently (subjects in the second condition). And remember, the shock was of equal intensity in all three conditions. The differences in perceptions were after-the-fact explanations of their own behavior.

A study by Fazio, Effrein, and Falender (1981) provides another illustration of this process. Subjects were asked a series of questions by an interviewer. For half of the subjects, these questions were designed to elicit answers an extroverted person would give. For example, these subjects were asked, "What would you do if you wanted to liven up things at a party?" The other half were given questions that would elicit answers an introverted person would give: "What things do you dislike about loud parties?" Following this questioning, subjects filled out a self-report questionnaire about their traits and engaged in a ten-minute conversation with a confederate.

Although the two groups of subjects did not differ in introversion-extroversion before the interview, they did afterward. Subjects who received the extrovert questions described themselves as significantly more extroverted than did those who received the introvert questions. The self-perception theory explanation of this difference is that subjects inferred their traits from their answers to the questions in the interview. Perhaps more impressive is the fact that the two groups also acted differently after the questioning. The confederate (who did not know which set of questions the subjects had received) rated those who received the extrovert questions as significantly more extroverted than those who received the introvert questions. Thus, people not only infer their internal dispositions from their actions, they also change their behavior to fit these inferences. (See figure 5-2).

As noted earlier, Bem's original position was that attitudes and traits do not really exist; they are after-the-fact explanations of one's behavior. Subsequent research, however, caused him to revise his ideas. In later writings, Bem acknowledged that people infer their internal dispositions from their overt behavior only when internal cues "are weak, ambiguous, or uninterpretable" (1972, p. 2). People are more aware of their traits than was originally proposed. For example, suppose it is 8:00 A.M. and you have to catch a bus. As you near the bus stop, you see the last few passengers boarding the bus. You run, but despite you best effort the bus pulls away without you. You do not stand at the bus stop, panting and sweating, and say, "I ran because I really love jogging." You know you ran because you were trying to catch the bus. The process described by Bem occurs only when there is no ready explanation for the behavior.

Another qualification to Bem's theory concerns the consequences of self-perception. In general, the more important the consequences of a self-perception, the less likely people are to infer their internal dispositions

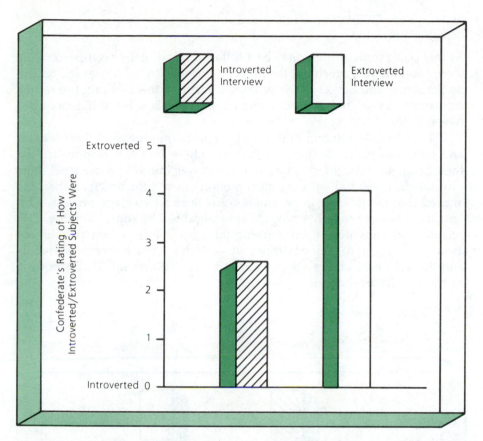

Figure 5-2. *Subjects who had undergone the introvert interview were rated as more introverted than those who had undergone the extrovert interview.*
Source: Fazio et al. (1981).

from some overt or external stimulus. This can be shown by reviewing two studies. In one study, Valins (1966) gave male subjects *Playboy* centerfolds to look at. The subjects heard what they thought was their own heartbeat as they looked at the pictures. (In fact, the subjects heard recordings of heartbeats). Valins found that the subjects rated pictures accompanied by (false) changes in their heartbeat as more attractive than pictures accompanied by (false) unchanged heartbeats. In a replication of this study, Taylor (1975) told subjects that they would meet and go out with people they rated as attractive. Under these conditions, the false-heartbeat information had little effect on attractiveness ratings. The subjects viewed their ratings as having important personal consequences, so they did not infer the ratings from overt or external stimuli.

Thus, Bem's theory is valid and useful, but limited. People infer their internal dispositions from overt stimuli only when there is no ready explanation for their behavior and the consequences of the self-perception are relatively unimportant.

Schachter's Two-Factor Theory of Emotion

At this point some readers may be a little confused. Bem's self-perception theory sounds very much like the theory developed by Schachter and tested by Schachter and Singer in the prologue. The two theories propose rather similar processes, but a closer examination reveals some differences between them.

Bem was interested in how people identify the causes of their actions and why they conclude that a certain attitude or trait was responsible for their behavior. Schachter's primary interest was in how people label their physiological arousal as a certain emotion. In a 1964 article, Schachter argued that the labeling of an emotion involves a two-stage process. The first stage is a general physiological arousal caused by some stimulus. The second stage involves cognitions or thinking. Thus, when people are aroused they turn to their environment—the characteristics of the situation and the actions of others—to explain and label the arousal. This is known as the **two-factor theory of emotion.**

Two-factor theory of emotion: a theory that emotions are the product of both people's physiological responses and their thoughts about the reasons for those responses.

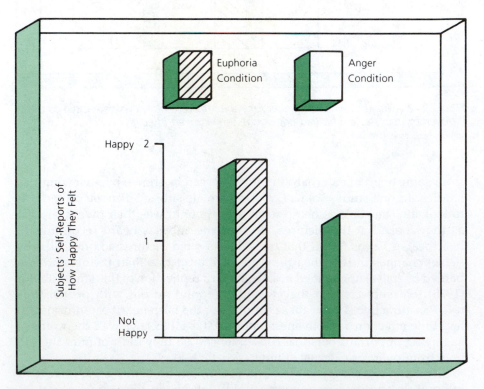

Figure 5-3. *Although subjects in the euphoria condition reported feeling happier than subjects in the anger condition, this difference was not statistically significant.*
Source: Schachter and Singer (1962).

Schachter's two-factor theory leads to the conclusion that emotions can be totally determined by external stimuli. If Schachter is correct, then it should be possible to "fool" people into mislabeling their emotions. This was demonstrated in the experiment in the prologue, where subjects who experienced identical levels of physiological arousal were fooled into reporting different levels of emotion. However, subsequent research and other data from Schachter and Singer's original experiment suggest this is not the case (Reisenzein, 1983).

In this experiment, the subjects in the euphoric condition who did not know the effects of epinephrine said they were happier than subjects in the euphoric condition who knew how epinephrine would affect them; this suggests that people's thoughts entirely determine the emotions they feel. However, a comparison of the ignorant subjects in the euphoric condition with the ignorant subjects in the angry condition suggests something quite different. (See figure 5-3.) If the subjects' emotions were totally determined by their thoughts and external events, then subjects in the euphoric and angry conditions should have reported very different feelings. They did not; the feelings of the ignorant subjects in the two conditions were not significantly different. External cues do influence how people identify their emotions, but their primary function is to intensify the experience of an emotion. In other words, they affect the quantity but not the quality of an emotion.

This does not mean that Schachter's theory is worthless. As noted in the background section of the prologue, it has been used to explain a wide variety of social phenomena. And as the research highlight illustrates, people do mislabel their physiological arousal when the situation they are in provides them with a reasonable explanation of why they feel a certain way.

Research Highlight

Don't Be So Shy

Chronic shyness is a problem for approximately 85 million Americans (Zimbardo, 1977). Carol Burnett, Johnny Carson, Phyllis Diller, and Barbara Walters are among the public figures who say they are uncomfortable in the presence of others. Shyness is probably a learned response to social stimuli, but it has some clear physiological symptoms, including an accelerated pulse and heart rate, perspiring, and "butterflies in the stomach."

In a 1981 study, Brodt and Zimbardo investigated whether the principles contained in Schachter's two-factor theory of emotion could be used to change, at least temporarily, the social behavior of shy people. They reasoned that if people who normally have these physiological responses in the presence of others could be led to believe that the responses were not due to shyness, they would no longer act in a shy manner.

The subjects in this experiment were three groups of women. Two groups were composed of women who had indicated on a survey that they had problems with shyness, especially when they talked to a member of the other sex. The third group was made up of "not-shy" women and was used as a comparison group. Members of all three groups were told that the purposes of the study was to investigate the effects of noise pollution on physiological responses. They were told they would hear three minutes of excessive noise, have a five-minute recovery period, and then hear a second three minutes of noise. In the room with all three groups was an attractive male confederate, who was supposedly another subject. The dependent measure was a woman's behavior toward the male confederate while she was left alone with him during the five-minute recovery period.

The first group of shy women was told that common effects of excessive noise are an increased pulse and an increased heart rate for several minutes after the noise

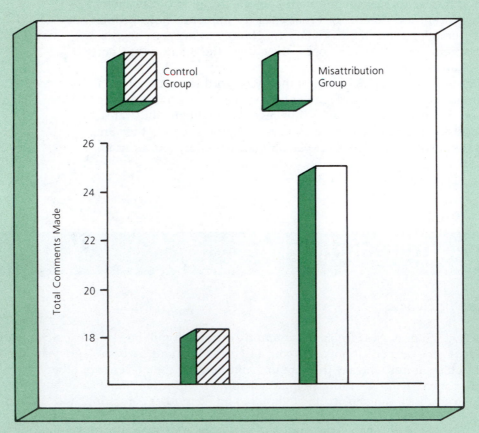

When shy women misattributed the symptoms of shyness, they became more extro-verted.
Source: Brodt and Zimbardo (1981).

has stopped; these physiological responses are, of course, common symptoms of shyness. The second group of shy women was told that the noise would cause a dry mouth and slight tremors; these are symptoms rarely associated with shyness. The not-shy women were given the same expectations as the first group.

After each woman heard the three minutes of noise, she was reminded of the carry-over effects of the noise and then left alone with the confederate. While the two conversed, Brodt and Zimbardo secretly recorded how much the woman talked, how often she changed the topic of conversation, whether she broke silences, and other similar things. Some of their results are presented in the figure.

Note the difference between the two groups of shy women. Those who were led to attribute the physiological symptoms of shyness to the noise talked significantly more than did those who were not given this explanation of their symptoms. Their behavior was virtually indistinguishable from that of the not-shy women. Not only was their behavior more sociable and extroverted, but they seemed to like talking to their male partner—something not characteristic of a shy person. When asked if they would have preferred to be in the experiment by themselves or with the confederate, 66 percent of the women who had an alternative explanation for their symptoms said they preferred being with the confederate. By contrast, only 14 percent of the other group of shy women said that they would have preferred being with the confederate.

Self-awareness Theory.

People sometimes engage in behaviors with little awareness of what they are doing; their attention is elsewhere. For example, until about a year ago I was a heavy smoker. When I worked on this book, I would retire to a room where my students and my colleagues could not find me, review my notes from the reading I had done, take a sip of coffee, light up a cigarette, and begin to write. Barring interruptions, I worked for about two hours straight. In this time I would write about five pages *and* smoke ten cigarettes; or one cigarette every 12 minutes.

If you are reading this book in a library or a study hall, you can probably see other examples of the same phenomenon. Stop for a moment and look at the nonverbal behavior of the people around you. Some touch their face every few seconds, others twist their hair, those who wear glasses probably adjust them several times, and you may even find a few people placing their fingers inside their noses!

Excessive smoking and potentially embarrassing nonverbal behaviors are both performed with little conscious awareness; I did not attend to how much I smoked and people in study halls do not attend to what they are doing with their hands. **Self-awareness theory** concerns what happens when people do become aware of their own behavior (Wicklund, 1975, 1978; Wicklund and Frey, 1980). One aspect of self-awareness theory is that people who are made self-aware provide more accurate descriptions

Self-awareness theory: a theory concerned with the effects of focusing attention on oneself and one's behavior.

Self-awareness: a temporary increase in the tendency to pay attention to and be aware of the private, internal aspects (attitudes, traits, motives) of oneself.

of themselves and that this serves to increase the relationship between self-reports and actual behavior. (See chapter three.) Another effect of **self-awareness** is its influences on people's behaviors and self-perceptions.

As explained earlier, looking at oneself in a mirror increases self-awareness or self-focus. For example, Carver and Scheier (1978) had subjects complete a sentence in the presence or absence of a mirror. The responses of the subjects were scored for focus on the self or focus on the external world. Subjects in the mirror condition gave significantly more self-oriented responses than subjects in the no-mirror condition. Similarly, people's awareness of their own behaviors can be increased. I could have rigged my ashtray with a heat-sensitive alarm that made a loud buzzing noise every time I put out a cigarette. This would have made me aware of the amount I had smoked.

When people become self-aware, they compare their actual behavior (or whatever they have become aware of) to some internal standard. For example, if the alarm had made me aware of my smoking, I would have compared my actual behavior to my internal standard of how much I should smoke. Self-awareness theory proposes that I then would have done one of two things. I may have attempted to bring my behavior in line with my standard by reducing the amount I smoked. If I had been unable to change my behavior, I may have attempted to reduce my awareness of it by physically removing myself from the situation causing the self-focus (the buzzing ashtray).

A study by Duval and Wicklund (1972) illustrates this second possible behavior. Two groups of subjects were given a test that supposedly measured creativity. A discrepancy with a self-standard was created by telling half the subjects that they had done very poorly on the test. Half of the subjects were then placed in a room with a mirror; the other half were placed in another room without a mirror. All of the subjects were asked to wait for a second experimenter. They were told he might not show up and that if he did not arrive in five minutes they could leave. The dependent measure was how long subjects waited for the experimenter. As figure 5-4 shows, among the subjects who had not experienced any discrepancy, the presence or absence of a mirror had no effect. But among the subjects who had experienced a discrepancy, the presense or absence of the mirror influenced how long they waited for the experimenter. When there was a mirror in the room, subjects waited a significantly shorter period of time. In other words, they removed themselves from a situation that increased their self-awareness.

The next section considers how self-awareness can affect people's self-perceptions.

Self-awareness and Self-perceptions
The manner in which increased self-awareness affects people's perceptions of their own actions and feelings depends on where people's attention is focused. When it is focused on their own behavior, it increases their propensity to infer their attitudes from that behavior. In a study by Pryor and several associates (1977), subjects were presented with a series of unfamiliar

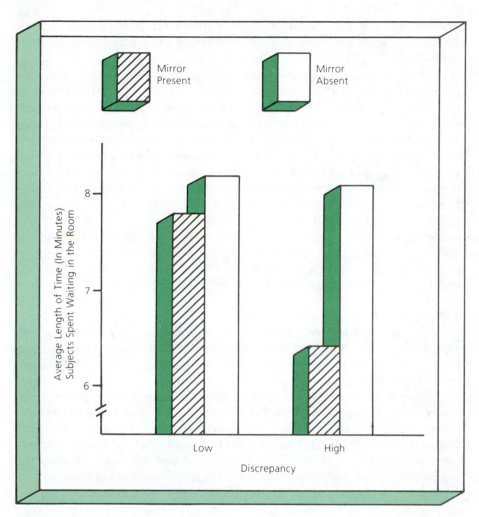

Figure 5-4. *When subjects experienced a high discrepancy with their self-standard, those in the mirror condition left the room sooner. This did not occur among subjects who experienced a low discrepancy.*
Source: Duval and Wicklund (1972).

mental games, such as unscrambling the letters in words (anagrams) or finding figures hidden in a picture. The subjects tried the games out in a random fashion. Then the subjects were asked to rate how attractive they found each game. Since the subjects held no strong attitudes toward any of the games, self-perception theory would predict that their attractiveness ratings would be correlated with the amount of time they spent playing a game (that they would infer their attitudes from their behavior). This did not occur when the subjects tried the games in the absence of a mirror. But when a mirror was placed in the room and the subjects could watch their own behavior, the correlation between the time they spent playing a game and the rating they gave it was .74. These subjects' attitudes went along with their behavior because they were made aware of what they were doing, and the subjects used this knowledge to infer their attitudes.

Now consider what happens when people are caused to focus on their internal feelings. In a 1979 study, Gibbons, Carver, Scheier, and Hormuth had subjects swallow a small capsule containing a dose of baking soda. Although baking soda has no physiological effects on people, the subjects were led to believe that the substance they ingested would make them physiologically aroused—their heart rates would increase, their palms would sweat, and so on. A few minutes later, subjects filled out a self-report scale on how they actually felt. Half the subjects filled this out in front of a mirror, half did not. Among the subjects in the no-mirror condition, the placebo had its suggested effect. They indicated they were aroused. But when a mirror was present, the placebo failed miserably. Gibbons and associates reported that subjects in the mirror condition specifically examined themselves for the supposed symptoms of the drug they had taken and concluded that they were not experiencing any.

Individual Differences in Self-awareness
As discussed earlier, people display stable individual differences in self-awareness. (See chapter three.) This characteristic, called **private self-consciousness** (Fenigstein et al., 1975), seems to affect people's behavior in the same way as does self-awareness. In another experiment conducted by Gibbons and his associates (1979), subjects were given a peppermint-flavored drink and asked to rate how strong it was. Then the subjects were given a second drink and were told that it was stronger than the first (it was actually weaker). This suggestion influenced the subsequent ratings of people low in private self-consciousness. It had no effect, however, on people who were high in private self-consciousness. Most of these people shifted their ratings away from the experimenter's suggestion and toward the actual taste of the drink. This study indicates that people who are high in private self-consciousness are aware of what they are experiencing and resistant to external cues about what they feel. Thus, their self-perceptions often differ from those who are low in private self-consciousness.

SUMMARY

Self-perception concerns how people come to ''know'' their emotions, feelings, attitudes, and so on. It is influenced by social factors and has consequences for social behavior.

Three theories have been proposed to explain the acquisition of knowledge about the self. Bem's self-perception theory proposes that people infer their attitudes and feelings from observations of their own behavior. In addition, it suggests these inferences are not the cause of people's behavior, but are after-the-fact explanations of their actions.

The predictions made by self-perception theory are most likely to be supported in situations where there is no clear-cut explanation for a behavior and the consequences of drawing conclusions about how one feels are relatively minor.

Schachter's two-factor theory concerns the labeling of emotions. It proposes that people first experience a physiological arousal caused by some stimulus and then label that arousal as some emotion. It further suggests that if the stimulus causing the arousal is not obvious to people, they will turn to their environment for an explanation.

Self-awareness theory concerns how people become aware of certain aspects of themselves and how they react to this awareness. Self-awareness can be induced by any stimulus that causes people to focus on themselves. When people become aware of some characteristic or behavior, they compare it to an internal standard of how they would like to be and then attempt to meet this standard. If this is impossible, they try to reduce their self-focus.

SELF-ATTRIBUTIONS

I recently watched a championship prizefight on television. Five seconds after the opening bell rang, the champion was pummeling his opponent. Two minutes into the first round, the challenger's left eye was swollen and bruised. By the fourth round, the challenger's eye was completely closed, his nose was bloody, and there was blood coming from his ear. The challenger had managed to get this way without landing more than five punches in the fight. About midway through the fifth round, the champion hit the challenger with a thunderous right hook and the challenger went down. He managed to stagger to his feet, then was hit two or three more times. Mercifully, the fight was stopped. The postfight interview with the challenger went something like this:

INTERVIEWER: When did you first know you were in trouble?
CHALLENGER: I was never in trouble, I had him right where I wanted him.
INTERVIEWER: (mouth open in disbelief): Then how come you lost?
CHALLENGER: Because he poked me in the eye with his thumb in the fifth round.
INTERVIEWER: You know, you'd be champ if you could fight as well as you explain things.

Consider this exchange from the perspective of **self-attributions.** Just as people try to identify the causes of other people's behavior, they also try to identify the causes of their own behavior. And just as the observer's explanation involves either an internal or external cause, so the actor's explanation involves either an internal or external cause. The challenger explained that he lost the fight not because he was less skilled or less able

Self-attributions: the explanations people offer for their own behaviors.

than the champion, but because the champion cheated. Is this type of attribution typical?

One of the more consistent phenomena in social psychological research is that people tend to attribute their successes to stable, internal factors and their failures to unstable, external factors. Lau and Russell (1980) collected newspaper interviews with baseball and football players after their teams had won or lost a game. The content of these interviews was analyzed to find the explanations given for the victory or defeat. Over 80 percent of the winners attributed their success to internal causes such as ability, effort, and skill. Internal explanations were given by only 50 percent of the losers. The most widely accepted explanation for these attributions is that they are self-serving; they serve to enhance or maintain people's self-images and the images they present to others.

An alternative explanation, presented by Miller and Ross (1975), is that these kinds of self-attributions reflect the way people, in general, view the causes of successes and failures. Specifically, Miller and Ross proposed two explanations of this phenomenon. One is that people tend to attribute expected outcomes to internal causes and unexpected outcomes to external causes. Since most people expect to succeed on a task, they attribute the unexpected outcome (failure) to external causes. The other explanation is that people see a stronger relationship between a behavior and an outcome when the outcome is a success than when it is a failure.

Miller and Ross argued that these attributions for success and failure are not self-serving because both the people performing the behavior and those observing will make the same type of attributional "error." Since the observers have nothing to gain from these kinds of attributions, they are considered to reflect a general way of perceiving people's behavior.

Like many theoretical arguments in social psychology, this one has generated a fair amount of research and data to support both points of view. Most of the evidence supports the explanation that these attributions are self-serving. One indication of this is that the more important success is to people the more likely they are to attribute their success to an internal cause. Another indication is that actors are more likely to attribute their successes to internal causes and their failures to external causes than are observers (Lau and Russell, 1980; Miller, 1976; Stephan, Rosenfield, and Stephan, 1976).

Lau and Russell examined this indication by analyzing sportswriters' descriptions of football and baseball games. The sportswriters were not as likely as the players to attribute the team's victories to internal factors and losses to external factors. Lau and Russell also found no support for the idea that expectancies about success and failure affect self-attributions. Members of teams that unexpectedly won or lost a game were no more likely to make an external attribution than were members of teams that performed as they had expected. This finding casts some doubt on Miller and Ross' explanation of why self-attributions after a success are more internal than are self-attributions after a failure.

Belief in Self-attributions

Do people really believe that they are more responsible for their successes than for their failures, or do people use these attributions to enhance their images in the eyes of other people? The answer to this question is yes! People do both.

Evidence that people do believe their self-attributions can be found in a study by Reiss, Rosenfeld, Melburg, and Tedeschi (1981). Subjects were led to believe that they had done well or poorly on a test and then asked to make self-attributions under one of two conditions. In the first condition, the subjects were hooked up to a lie detector and told that the machine could detect whether or not they were telling the truth. In the second condition, no lie detector was used.

Reiss and his associates reasoned that if people really believe they are more responsible for their successes than for their failures, they will make the same kinds of self-attributions whether or not they think they could be caught lying. But if people use these self-attributions to improve the impression they make on others, they will make them only when they know they cannot be caught lying. However, the researchers discovered that the presence or absence of a lie detector had no effect in this experiment. Whether or not the subjects thought they could be caught lying, they attributed their successes to internal causes and their failures to external causes.

But other studies have shown that people's self-attributions are also used to enhance their images in other people's eyes. Weary (1980) manipulated whether subjects believed they had failed or succeeded by giving them false feedback on their performance. She then asked them to explain this outcome in one of two conditions. In the first condition, subjects were observed by someone else; in the second condition they were alone. Subjects were more likely to attribute failure to external factors in the public condition than in the private condition.

Reactions to Self-attributions

Not surprisingly, people feel better about their successes than their failures, and this appears to affect their self-attributions about why they succeed or fail as well as their self-attributions about the outcomes of their actions. McFarland and Ross (1982) systematically manipulated subjects' beliefs about whether they had passed or failed a test. They then led half the successful subjects to believe that their performances were due to their ability (an internal cause). The other half were led to believe that their performances were due to an easy test (an external cause). The same procedure was used to create two groups of "failures." That is, subjects were told they failed because of a lack of ability or they were told they failed because of test difficulty. Then all the subjects' reactions to their performances were measured. (See figure 5-5 for some of the study's findings.)

Subjects who attributed their failure to a difficult test reported feeling better than did subjects who attributed their failure to their lack of ability.

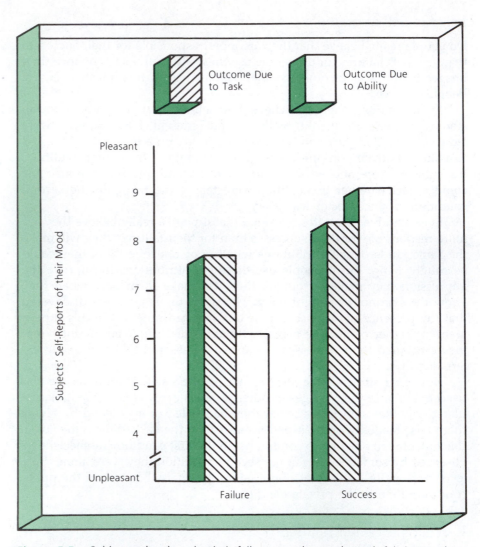

Figure 5-5. *Subjects who thought their failure was due to the task felt better than those who thought it was due to their ability. The opposite was true for subjects who had been successful.*
Source: McFarland and Ross (1982).

Subjects who attributed their success to their ability reported feeling better than those who attributed their success to an easy test—although this difference was not significant. Thus, self-attributions of success and failure do more than simply enhance or maintain people's self-images and the images they present to others. They also influence how people feel.

Feelings of success should, in turn, affect people's subsequent behaviors. That is, if people are successful and believe they are responsible for a success, then they should continue to engage in similar behaviors. But if they attribute a success to external factors or, worse, attribute a failure to internal factors, then they will probably give up the task. Weiner and his associates (1972b) used this idea to explain differences in people's de-

People differ in the extent to which they believe they are controlled by forces beyond their control. Some see themselves as puppets; others see themselves as the puppeteer.

sires to achieve certain goals. People who are high achievers attribute their successes to stable, internal factors and their failures to unstable, external factors. People who do not strive to achieve attribute their successes to unstable, external factors and their failures to stable, internal factors.

Effects of Individual Differences in Locus of Control on Self-attributions

Thus far, self-attributions have been treated as if they are totally determined by situational factors. But there are individual differences in self-attributions. Consider this true description of Karl S. (Phares, 1976).

Karl was a young man who sought psychotherapy because he was extremely unhappy and distressed. After several sessions, his therapist decided that the source of Karl's problem was an almost total lack of social skills. He didn't know how to talk to people and as a result had no job, no friends, and no female companions. The therapist adhered to a learning theory orientation, so he decided that rather than explore the roots of Karl's problems he would teach him the skills he lacked. The therapist's reasoning was that if Karl could learn these skills, he would have successful social experiences and be a happier person. The therapist was very successful in teaching Karl how to talk to a potential employer, and Karl eventually got a job. He taught Karl how to talk with women, and Karl met and dated several different women. There was only one problem: Karl was still miserable.

Perplexed, the therapist sought to find out why Karl wasn't feeling any better. The reason soon became apparent. Karl did not believe he was responsible for any of his successes. He believed that he got his job because the employer was partial to veterans (Karl was a vet). He believed women dated him because they had no one else to date. In contrast to the usual patterns of self-attributions, Karl attributed his successes to external rather than internal causes! One explanation of Karl's behavior lies in the personality trait locus of control.

The concept of locus of control was originally introduced as part of a criticism of the radical behaviorists' explanation of human behavior. The behaviorists proposed that the primary determinant of whether people will engage in a behavior is whether they have been previously reinforced for doing so. Julian Rotter (1966) and other theorists pointed out that people often do not act in accord with this proposal. Rotter believed that to understand people's behavior researchers must consider additional factors, including people's beliefs about whether their actions will produce a reinforcer. If they believe that what they do will not determine whether they are reinforced, they will either not engage in the behavior or, like Karl S., not derive any satisfaction from its consequences.

In his early research, Rotter was most interested in the situational factors that influence people's beliefs about the relationship between their behaviors and the outcomes they receive. However, people like Karl S. and the results of several experiments led Rotter and his associates to propose a general personality characteristic called **locus of control.** (See table 5-1 for a portion of a scale used to measure this characteristic.)

Locus of control: the general tendency to attribute what happens to oneself either to one's own actions or to factors beyond one's control.

Table 5-1.   *Some items from the original Locus of Control scale. Subjects choose one from each pair. The orientation of each item is presented in the parentheses.*

1a. I am the master of my fate. (Internal)

1b. A great deal that happens to me is probably a matter of chance. (External)

2a. Promotions are earned through hard work and persistence. (Internal)

2b. Making a lot of money is largely a matter of getting the right breaks. (External)

3a. It is only wishful thinking to believe that one can really influence what happens in society at large. (External)

3b. People like me can change the course of world affairs if we make ourselves heard. (Internal)

4a. In my case, the grades I make are the results of my own efforts, luck has little or nothing to do with it. (Internal)

4b. Sometimes I feel that I have little or nothing to do with the grades I get. (External)

Source: Rotter (1966).

On the basis of their answers to the questions on this scale, people were classified as having either an internal or an external locus-of-control orientation. People with an *internal* orientation tend to see what happens to them as due to their own actions; people with an *external* orientation tend to see what happens to them as being unrelated to their own actions. Note the word *tend;* the differences between people with internal and external locus-of-control orientations is one of degree. Also, people's self-attributions are influenced by both their locuses of control and the situation. In situations where there is no clear information about the causes of reinforcement, people's locus-of-control orientations influence their behavior and their self-attributions. For example, if a four-foot ten-inch person fails to make a basketball team, he knows why and his locus of control orientation has little impact on his self-attributions. But if an aspiring basketball player is over six feet and fails to make the team his explanation of this failure would be much more influenced by his locus-of-control orientation.

Like other personality traits, locus of control is present to different degrees in different people. It also affects the social behavior of people and it can change during a person's lifetime.

Origins of Differences in Locus of Control

It is generally agreed that the socialization process is a major influence in the development of a person's locus-of-control orientation. There is much less agreement on what specific experiences lead to these differences. Some studies have found that the parents of internally oriented children are warmer, more accepting, more supportive of attempts at independence, and more consistent in administering discipline and setting standards than are parents of externally oriented children (Chance, 1972; Davis and Phares, 1969; MacDonald, 1971; Phares, 1976). But other studies have found that mothers of internally oriented children may be more critical and less accepting than mothers of externally oriented children (Strickland, 1977).

There is somewhat more agreement on the effects race and sex have on locus of control. Most racial studies have focused on comparisons between blacks and whites. These studies have found that, in general, blacks have a more external orientation than do whites (Phares, 1976). The most common explanation of these differences is that because of economic and social conditions, blacks have less real control over what happens to them than do whites. Thus, an external orientation on the part of blacks reflects a realistic perception of the world around them.

It is generally agreed that women are more externally oriented than men (Cooper, Burger, and Good, 1981), but it is not clear why this is the case. Crandall (1969) proposed that this finding was due to differences in the way boys and girls are socialized, but recent studies (Cooper et al., 1981) have failed to find substantial differences between the locus-of-control orientations of school-age males and females. This study instead provided data suggesting that, at least in activities related to school, girls may be more internally oriented than boys. Another study (O'Leary, 1974) suggested that differences between locus-of-control orientations of adult males and females may be due to the experiences women have later in their lives. Specifically, because of occupational and social barriers to achievement, women may come to hold a more external locus-of-control orientation.

Locus of Control and Social Behavior
Entire books have been written on how individual differences in people's
locus-of-control orientations affect their social behavior (for example,
Phares, 1976; Lefcourt, 1976). Two commonly studied effects are attributional style and achievement.

Attributional Style   As already suggested, internally oriented people
are more likely to attribute their successes to ability than are externally
oriented people (Sobel, 1974). Internally and externally oriented people
also differ in the ways they explain other people's behavior. For example,
Sosis (1974) classified subjects as internal, external, or moderate on the
basis of their scores on Rotter's (1966) Locus of Control Scale. Then all
three groups were asked to read a detailed description of an automobile
accident and the person driving the car. Internally oriented people saw the
driver as more personally responsible than did either moderately or externally oriented people. In another study (Hochreich, 1972), subjects were
asked to assign responsibility for a massacre during the Vietnam War (the
infamous My Lai incident). Internally oriented female subjects tended to
place the blame on the lieutenant in charge of the soldiers, but externally
oriented females blamed the United States government and the military
establishment.

Achievement   The rationale behind research on the relationship between locus-of-control and achievement-oriented activities is that since
internally oriented people believe that they control what happens to them,
they will go out and "make things happen." They try harder than externally
oriented people because they believe their efforts will be rewarded.

Over 275 studies have been conducted on the relationship between
locus-of-control orientation and academic achievement. Most have found
that internally oriented people do better in school than do externally oriented people (Findley and Cooper, 1983), even when students were equated on intelligence. The reason for this difference between the academic
performance of internally and externally oriented people appears to be that
internally oriented people work harder at intellectual and achievement
tasks and that these efforts produce better grades.

School performance is not the only area in which internally and externally oriented people differ. Wright, Holman, Steele, and Silverstein
(1980) looked at the performance of prison inmates who had been classified
as internal or external. The prison had an incentive program allowing
inmates who acted responsibly and obeyed prison rules to earn better living
situations and be treated less like prisoners. (For example, they were not
required to wear prison clothes and could have weekend furloughs.) Internally oriented individuals were more likely to expect that they would
succeed at the incentive program than were externally oriented individuals—and their expectancies were confirmed. Fifty percent of the externally
oriented inmates failed at some point in the program, while only 30 percent
of the internally oriented inmates failed. When asked to explain their success, internally oriented inmates were more likely to attribute it to ability
than were those who were externally oriented. Externally oriented inmates,

on the other hand, were more likely than internally oriented inmates to attribute their success to luck.

It must be remembered that people's locus-of-control orientation is not the only factor that determines their self-attributions and related social behaviors. Other personal characteristics such as intelligence, ability, and motivation are also strong determinants, as are situational variables. In addition, particular circumstances may change a person's locus-of-control orientation (Strickland, 1977), and people's locus-of-control orientations may change over their lifetimes.

Changes in Locus of Control

In general, people become more internal as they grow older (Nowicki and Strickland, 1973), but this may not be a steady increase. Some evidence suggests that during adolescence people become temporarily more external. This is because the teen years are a time of uncertainty, which may lessen people's beliefs in personal control over their own environments. Life events can also affect a person's locus-of-control orientation. For example, Doherty (1983) found that women became significantly more external in the three-year period after their divorce.* In general, any life event that creates uncertainty will cause a person to become, at least temporarily, more external.

Some researchers have reported success in changing children's locus-of-control orientations. In a 1972 study, de Charms reported on a program that taught teachers exercises they could use to move their students' locus-of-control orientations in an internal direction. After the training, the teachers tried these exercises with economically disadvantaged sixth and seventh graders. Not only did the children become more internal, but their academic performance improved as well. Thus, people's locus-of-control orientations are not fixed throughout their lifetimes. They can and do change as the result of formal or informal experiences that change people's beliefs about the extent to which they are responsible for the things that happen to them.

SUMMARY

Self-attributions are the explanations people offer for their own behavior. They provide people with an explanation of their past behaviors and a prediction about future behaviors. They also enhance people's self-images as well as the images others have of them.

Most of the research on self-attributions has focused on how people explain their successes and their failures. In general, people attribute successes to personal, internal causes—such as ability or effort and their failures to external, situational causes—such as bad luck or a

---

*This change was not permanent. After about three years, the women's locus of control orientations were no more external than those of married women.

difficult task. Research also indicates that people vary in the extent to which they believe self-attributions, and that people react to self-attributions in different ways.

Self-attributions are also influenced by personality characteristics such as locus of control. People can have either an internal locus-of-control orientation or an external orientation. Differences in these orientations are probably due to differences in life experiences, and they manifest themselves in self-attributions, attributions about other people's behavior, and various types of social and nonsocial behavior.

IMPRESSION MANAGEMENT

Impression management: the conscious or unconscious attempts of people to control images of themselves in social situations.

The focus now turns from the manner in which people perceive themselves to the manner in which people present themselves to others. This phenomenon is usually called **impression management** (Schlenker, 1980).

There are a number of ways of conceptualizing impression management, but the one that has gained most popularity was proposed by Erving Goffman (1959, 1963, 1971). Goffman said that people manage the impressions they create in a manner akin to the way an actor behaves on stage. Both put on a *performance* that influences the thoughts and actions of other people.

JOHN DARLING   ARMSTRONG & BATIUK

JOHN DARLING by Armstrong & Batiuk. © by and permission of News America Syndicate.

In the ancient Greek theater, actors used masks to convey a certain image. Goffman argued that in a social interaction people assume a *face*, which is the image they want to project. Sometimes it is an accurate reflection of what people really feel and sometimes it is not. Imagine, for example, a child who is being threatened by the neighborhood bully. On one occasion, his face may be what he really feels—unbridled fear. The child shows this face in the hope that either the bully will take pity on him or other children will come to his rescue. On another occasion, his face may be one of courage and bravado because he hopes to frighten off the bully or at least impress others while he is being beaten up.

It is difficult to specifically predict what kind of face someone will put on, but people usually project a face that they think will gain social approval and support. Once a face is assumed, people are under some obligation to keep it because others generally do not like "two-faced" people. Someone who is constantly changing his or her face is unreliable and untrustworthy (Schlenker, 1980).

When actors play a part, they dress and carry themselves in a certain way. Goffman believed that in everyday life people use their appearance and manner to let others know how they expect to be treated. Further, if people have control over the situation in which an interaction takes place, they will use a "prop" (the physical environment) for the same purpose.

Both professional actors and ordinary people put on a face and give a performance when they appear before others.

Dramatized performance: a behavior that reflects exactly how a person views a situation.

Idealized performance: a behavior that reflects other people's expectations about how a person should behave.

For example, business executives who want to be in charge of a conversation sometimes arrange the chairs in their office so that the one they sit in is a little higher than those available to visitors. They do this to communicate who is in charge—and who is not!

Schlenker (1980) has identified two types of performances common in impression management. One is called a **dramatized performance.** A professor who impatiently taps his fingers on his chair, yawns, and looks away while you are talking is giving a dramatized performance. The other is called an **idealized performance.** A story told by a successful black attorney illustrates this concept. He purchased a home in a neighborhood that had previously been all white. One morning he put on a pair of jeans and a sweat shirt to take out the garbage. As he carried the cans to the curb, he heard someone calling, "Boy, come here please."

He turned and saw the visiting mother of his next-door neighbor. The attorney decided to give the woman an idealized performance. He lowered his head and slowly walked over to her. Politely he answered, "Yes ma'am?"

"You're not the boy who usually picks up the garbage. What are you doing here?" she asked.

In the heaviest black dialect the attorney could muster, he slowly replied, "No ma'am, I'm not the 'boy' who picks up the garbage. I'm the 'boy' who lives next door to your daughter," and walked back to his home.

People engage in impression formation for three interrelated reasons: to gain social approval from others; to enhance their own views of themselves (their self-images); and to control the outcome of an interaction (Schlenker, 1980). They do not merely play parts when they interact with others. Sometimes a performance is a faithful reflection of how people really feel and how they expect to be treated. In addition, people often come to believe they are the people they portray. Bem's self-perception theory may explain this effect. Recall that this theory proposed that in certain circumstances people infer their attitudes from their behavior.

A study by Jones, Rhodewalt, Berglas, and Skelton (1981) examined this idea. The subjects were two groups of male college students who initially did not differ in their levels of self-esteem. The men in one group were persuaded that it was a good idea to emphasize their positive attributes and present themselves in a very favorable light during an interview; the men in the other group were persuaded that it was a good idea to emphasize their negative attributes and present themselves in a very unfavorable light. After the interview, the self-esteem of both groups was measured. (See figure 5-6 for the results.) The group that had engaged in a positive self-presentation had significantly higher self-esteem scores than did the group that had engaged in a negative self-presentation. Evidently the manner in which subjects presented themselves influenced their self-perceptions.

Another reason for not dismissing performances as mere playacting is that in some instances people are not even aware of their behavior. For example, in almost every one of my classes, I have a student who nods in agreement with everything I say. One day I "called" a student on this.

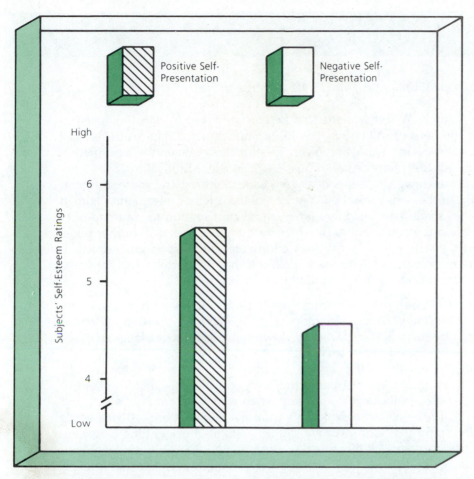

Figure 5-6. *When subjects had presented themselves in a positive manner, their sub-sequent self-esteem was higher than the self-esteem of subjects who had presented themselves in a negative manner.*
Source: Jones et al. (1981).

The look of embarrassment and despair on the student's face made it clear to me that he was, until my comment, totally unaware of what he had been doing.

If people do not merely play parts, why did Goffman and others compare people to actors? The major reason is that both playacting and impression management are responses to the presence of an audience. Our behavior when we are in front of other people (or even when we imagine ourselves to be in front of other people) is different from our behavior when we are alone (Schlenker, 1980). This public behavior affects our self-image, the image others have of us, and the character of our interactions with others.

This section examines several tactics people use in the process of impression management. It also discusses in personality characteristics that affect impression management.

Topic Background

Impression Management among Airline Pilots: The Right Stuff

General Charles (Chuck) Yeager was the first person to fly faster than the speed of sound, and he is the personification of "The Right Stuff." "The Right Stuff" is hard to define, but basically it is the ability to confront life-threatening events in a competent and calm manner. All test pilots aspire to possess "The Right Stuff."

Most Americans are aware of General Yeager's contribution to the space program, but Tom Wolfe, the author of a book about Yaeger and the original astronauts, claimed that the general has made another, more far-reaching contribution to contemporary society: He has influenced the manner in which airline pilots speak. Whether pilots are from the north, south, east or west, they all imitate the West Virginia drawl of Chuck Yaeger in an attempt to create the impression that no matter what happens, they have the situation under control. Wolfe gives an example:

Anyone who travels very much on airlines in the United States soon gets to know the voice of the airline pilot . . . coming over the intercom . . . with a particular drawl, a particular folksiness, a particular down-home calmness that is so exaggerated it begins to parody itself [nevertheless!—it's reassuring].

"Now, folks, uh . . . this is the captain . . . ummmm . . . We've got a little ol' red light up here on the control panel that's tryin' to tell us that the landin' gears're not . . . uh . . . lockin' into position when we lower 'em . . . Now . . . I don't believe that little ol' red light knows what it's talkin' about—I believe it's that little ol' red light that iddn' workin' right . . . [faint chuckle, long pause, as if to say, I'm not even sure all this is really worth going into—still, it may amuse you] . . . "But . . . I guess to play it by the rules, we oughta humor that little ol' light . . . so we're gonna take her down to about, oh, two or three hundred feet over the runway at Kennedy, and the folks down there on the ground are gonna see if they caint give us a vis-ual inspection of those ol' landin' gears . . . if I'm right . . . they're gonna tell us everything is copa-cet-ic all the way aroun' an' we'll jes take her on in . . . "

"Well, folks, those folks down there on the ground—it must be too early for 'em or somethin'—I 'spect they still got the sleepers in their eyes . . . 'cause they say they caint tell if those ol' landin' gears are all the way down or not . . . But, you know, up here in the cockpit we're convinced they're all the way down, so we're jes gonna take her on in . . . And oh" . . . [I almost forgot] . . . "while we take a little swing out over the ocean an empty some of that surplus fuel we're not gonna be needin' anymore—that's what you might be seein' comin' out of the wings—our lovely little ladies . . . if they'll be so kind . . . they're gonna go up and down the aisles and show you how we do what we call 'assumin' the position' . . . . another faint chuckle. Even though in your pounding heart and your sweating palms and your broiling brainpan you know this is a critical moment in your life, you still can't quite bring yourself to believe it, because if it were . . . how could *the captain*, the man who knows the actual situation most

General Charles E. (Chuck) Yeager was the first man to fly faster than the speed of sound. He also is the person imitated by many airline pilots to convince others that they possess the "right stuff."

intimately . . . . how could he keep on drawlin' and chucklin' and driftin' and lollygaggin' in that particular voice of his—

Well!—who doesn't know that voice! And who can forget it!—even after he is proved right and the emergency is over. (Wolfe, 1979, pp. 44–46)

Tactics of Impression Management

You have already read about some of the tactics people use in impression management, but you may not be aware of it. The experiment presented in the prologue to chapter two found that students are likely to wear clothing with school emblems on it after their school teams had won. This is a tactic of impression management known as *association*, which means that people improve their images by establishing a relationship between themselves and some positive person or event. Several attribution processes may also be considered tactics of impression management, including the tendency of observers to attribute an actor's behavior to internal causes. Jellison and Green (1981) have proposed that this attribution may be due in part to observers' attempts to manage the impressions they create. They suggest that people who make internal attributions about an actor's behavior receive more social approval than do people who make external attributions. They also suggest that people asked to make a positive impression on others are more likely to make internal attributions about an actor's behavior than are people asked to make a negative impression. Other studies have shown that self-attributions of successes and failures can also be seen as tactics of impression management. People who engage in any of these tactics may not be fully aware of what they are doing, but people who use the tactic of ingratiation are quite aware of what they are doing and why.

Ingratiation

Ingratiation: a tactic used by people to increase another person's liking for them.

Jones and Wortman (1973) proposed that people sometimes use the tactic of **ingratiation** in social interactions. Jones (1964) identified four techniques of ingratiation: (1) using compliments or flattery; (2) agreeing with the attitudes, beliefs, and values of another person; (3) doing favors for another person; and (4) describing oneself in an extremely positive fashion. People engage in ingratiation to make another person like them so they can control that person—control they will use to their own ends. In Jones's view, ingratiation is a deceitful act. Ingratiators present themselves dishonestly to trick another person into doing something for them.

Jones, Gergen, and Jones (1963) observed attempts at ingratiation among naval cadets who were engaged in conversation. The conversation was arranged so that one participant was of low status (a freshman) and one was of high status (an upperclassman). Jones and his associates analyzed the content of the conversation for ingratiation tactics. They found that low-status cadets were much more likely to flatter high-status cadets than vice versa. They were also likely to agree with the opinions of their high-status partners. The self-descriptions of the low-status cadets were quite interesting; the cadets described themselves favorably, but only on characteristics that were not related to performance at the naval academy. In other words, they presented a positive image, but did so in a way that would not threaten their high-status partners. The high-status cadets did not show these behaviors. But were the behaviors of the low-status cadets ingratiation tactics or were they true reflections of how the cadets felt? In another condition of the study, the low-status cadets were told to be as honest and accurate as they could be, and the flattery and agreement disappeared! The low-status cadets had used these tactics to ingratiate themselves with the high-status cadets.

Self-handicapping Strategies

Self-handicapping is a tactic people use to increase the reasonableness of attributing their failures to an external cause (Berglas and Jones, 1978). Berglas and Jones proposed that if people have reason to expect they will fail on a task, they may arrange things before they perform the task so that it looks like they are not responsible for the anticipated failure. For example, suppose your roommate has an examination in theoretical physics at 9:00 A.M. tomorrow. He understands theoretical physics about as well as he understands the *Tibetan Book of the Dead*—he is going to fail the examination, and badly. So he engages in self-handicapping behaviors to provide an external explanation for his expected performance. He calls his parents to inquire about his cousin, who is ill. His parents casually mention that he should visit his cousin. Your roommate decides now is the time. He drives 100 miles to see his cousin, and by the time he gets back to campus it's 5:00 A.M. He gets a few hours sleep and takes the exam. A few days later you ask how he did. He replies, "Well, I flunked it, but you've got to remember I didn't get any sleep and I couldn't study because of poor, sick Harold."

This example illustrates the concept of self-handicapping, but it does not speak to the question of whether people use this tactic to manage the impression they make on others. A recent study (Kolditz and Arkin, 1982) investigated this question. Subjects were led to believe that they were part of an experiment concerned with the effects of certain drugs on intellectual performance. They were asked to take the same intelligence test twice, the second time under the influence of a drug that would help or a drug that would hurt their performance. (The drugs were actually harmless substances that would have no effect on their performance.) The subjects could choose which drug they took. After completing the test the first time, half the subjects were led to believe that they would do poorly on the test the second time. The other half believed they would do well. Before taking the test the second time, half the subjects in each group were asked to choose a drug while the experimenter was present; the other half (supposedly) made a private, hidden choice. The dependent measure was which drug the subjects chose and how much of it they took. (See figure 5-7 for the results of this experiment.)

Among the subjects who expected to be successful, the presence of the experimenter had no effect on drug choice. But the subjects who expected failure acted quite differently. When the experimenter was unaware of which drug they chose, subjects tended to pick the drug that would improve their performance. But when they were watched, they picked the drug that would hurt their performance. Indeed, almost all of the subjects who chose the debilitating drug did so when the experimenter was watching. In other words, subjects used a self-handicapping strategy only when there was a witness. This suggests that self-handicapping is most likely to occur when people expect to fail and someone else can corroborate their explanations of why they failed. Then they can say to anyone who challenges their explanation, "Well, if you don't believe me, you can go ask Joe. He knows that it wasn't my fault." In legal circles, this is called having an "alibi witness."

The results of this and other studies (Berglas and Jones 1978; Jones and Berglas, 1978) suggest that people do use self-handicapping in impression management, but this does not mean that the tactic is used solely for the benefit of others. Like other behaviors discussed in this chapter, self-

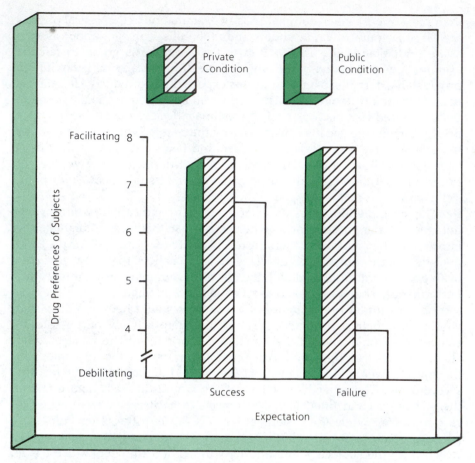

Figure 5-7. *Subjects who expected to succeed chose the same drug in the public and private conditions, but subjects who expected failure chose the debilitating drug in the public condition.*
Source: Kolditz and Arkin (1982).

handicapping may have an impact on people's views of themselves. To paraphrase Darley and Goethals (1980), we may often get taken in by our own face-saving explanations of our performance.

Individual Differences in Impression Management

While it appears that all people either consciously or unconsciously attempt to manage the images they present to others, some people are more willing and more able to do this than others. People vary in the degree to which they possess some of the personality characteristics associated with individual differences in impression management, including the characteristics of self-monitoring, public self-consciousness, and need for approval.

Self-monitoring

Self monitoring refers to individual differences in the way people present themselves to others. High self-monitors are concerned about the situational and social appropriateness of their behavior, and are thus especially sensitive to the characteristics of situations they encounter and the actions of people in those situations. They use this information to guide their own behavior. Low self-monitors are insensitive to these sources of information.

Another way of looking at high self-monitors is that they are "skilled impression managers" (Snyder, 1981). Good impression managers should be able to effectively communicate their emotions to other people through the "face" they present. In a 1974 study, Snyder asked high and low self-monitors (classified on the basis of their scores on his Self-monitoring Scale) to express various emotions, and he had other people guess each emotion. The judges were much more accurate in identifying the emotions shown by high self-monitors than those shown by low self-monitors.

Good impression managers should also be effective in changing their demeanors to fit the situation. Lippa (1976) asked subjects to act shy and withdrawn in one situation and extroverted and outgoing in another. High self-monitors were much better at changing the way they acted in the two situations.

A study by Snyder and Monson (1975) showed how high self-monitors change their behavior to fit the demands of the situation. Subjects participated in a group discussion under one of two conditions. In the first condition, they were told that the discussion would be videotaped and shown to their classmates. In the second condition, subjects were told that only the other group members would know what they did. Snyder and Monson measured the degree to which high and low self-monitors conformed to the opinions of other group members in each condition. The researchers predicted that the behavior of the low self-monitors would not change across conditions. They also predicted that high self-monitors would not conform to the opinions of others in the videotape condition but would conform in the private condition. Snyder and Monson reasoned that high self-monitors would present different images to the two audiences because they would not want their classmates to see them as spineless and wishy-washy, but they also would not want other group members to see them as deviant. The researchers were right. (See figure 5-8.)

The amount of conformity displayed by low self-monitors did not differ between the two conditions. But high self-monitors conformed very little in the public condition and a great deal in the private condition. They used their behavior to manage the impressions they made on others so that they would look good in either situation.

Public Self-consciousness

Private self-consciousness is the tendency to be aware of and attentive to the private, internal aspects of the self (Fenigstein et al., 1975). (See chapter three.) Fenigstein and his associates also proposed a trait they called **public self-consciousness.** Buss (1980) proposed that people high in public self-

Public self-consciousness: the tendency to be aware of and attentive to the public, external aspects of the self.

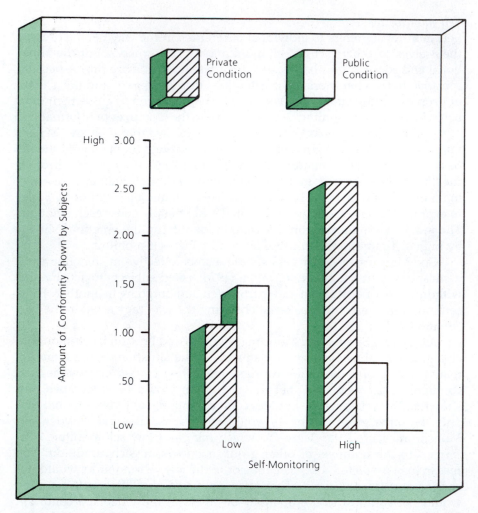

Figure 5-8. *Although low self-monitors conformed about an equal amount in both the public and private conditions, high self-monitors conformed much more in the private than the public condition.*
Source: Snyder and Monson (1975).

consciousness are more concerned about the impression they make on others than are people low in that trait. Although only a few studies have tested this prediction, their results tend to support it. Fenigstein (1979b) found that people who were high on this trait were bothered more by rejection than were people who were low. Miller and Cox (1982) found that the more aware of the public aspects of the self a woman was, the more makeup she wore. It appears that women high in public self-consciousness are quite concerned with the impressions they make on others. More recently, Fenigstein (1984) found that people high in public self-consciousness overestimated the extent to which other people were interested in their behavior.

Need for Approval

Crowne and Marlowe (1964) proposed that there may be stable individual differences in the **need for approval**. The manner in which Crowne and Marlowe measured this characteristic was extremely clever. (See table 5-2 for some items from their Social Desirability Scale.)

Need for approval: a personality trait concerned with the tendency to seek the approval of others for one's actions.

Table 5-2.   Some items from the Social Desirability Scale. A person with a high need for approval would give the answers indicated in the parentheses.

1. Before voting I thoroughly investigate the qualifications of all the candidates. (True)
2. I have never intensely disliked anyone. (True)
3. I'm always willing to admit it when I make a mistake. (True)
4. There have been occasions when I took advantage of someone. (False)
5. I like to gossip at times. (False)
6. I can remember playing sick to get out of something. (False)

The first three items contain statements that most people would like to be true about themselves, but that are false of almost everyone. The second three contain statements that most people would like to be false about themselves, but that are true of almost everyone. Someone who consistently answers true to the first three items and false to the second three has a high need for social approval, which is manifested in attempts at impression management. People who score high on this scale are likely to use ingratiation tactics (Strickland, 1977) and to describe themselves positively after they have failed on a task. The problem with these people is that, unlike the high self-monitor, they are not very successful in their attempts to be socially accepted. They have difficulty making their behavior fit the situation and are unable to effectively communicate what they are feeling (Schlenker, 1980). As a result, they are seen as unfriendly and they tend to be rejected by others.

SUMMARY

When people are in the presence of others, they attempt to present themselves in a favorable manner through their speech, demeanor, and appearance—just as actors attempt to convey an image to an audience.

Many social behaviors can be viewed as tactics of impression management. Among these are associating with successful people or groups, ingratiating oneself, and denying responsibility for one's failure. Ingratiation involves flattering people, agreeing with their opinions, and doing favors for them in order to gain some degree of control over them. If people expect to fail at a task, they sometimes arrange the situation so that they handicap themselves before they begin the task; this provides them with an excuse for their failure and thus preserves their image.

Three personality characteristics have been found to be associated with impression management: self-monitoring—the tendency to monitor and control one's behavior in social situations; public self-consciousness—the tendency to be aware of and attentive to the public, external aspects of the self; and need for approval—the tendency to seek the approval of others.

The particular manner in which people present themselves is determined by the characteristics of the situation they encounter, their personality characteristics , and the manner in which they see themselves.

Applications

Self-perceptions and Health

In the last few years, theories developed by social psychologists have been used by their colleagues in clinical psychology to help understand the origins of various health problems. For example, an increasing number of researchers have turned their attention to the question of how self-attributions can affect a person's emotional and physical well-being. This section reviews three aspects of this research: attributional style and depression, perceptions of self-control among the elderly, and locus-of-control retraining in the elderly.

ATTRIBUTIONAL STYLE AND DEPRESSION

It is estimated that over 2 million Americans suffer from profound depression and that over 25 million Americans will have an episode of severe depression at some time in their lives (Brown, 1974; President's Commission on Mental Health, 1978). We all get depressed from time to time; it is normal to feel sad or depressed after you have failed a test or lost a loved one. Indeed, it would be abnormal not to feel depressed after one of these events. But in *neurotic depression,* "the individual reacts to some distressing situation with more than the usual amount of sadness and dejection and often fails to return to normal after a reasonable period of time" (Coleman, Butcher, and Carson, 1980). Some types of depression result from biochemical, neurological, or hereditary factors, but it is believed that neurotic depression is primarily caused by certain experiences the depressed person has. One theory of what experiences cause neurotic depression is based on Martin Seligman's (1975) model of learned helplessness.

Learned Helplessness Theory

Seligman's model had its origins in laboratory studies of learning in animals. The animals were placed in a box with a low barrier in the middle of it and a signal was presented for a few seconds. If the animal jumped the barrier during this time period it could avoid getting shocked, but if the animal did not jump the barrier it would receive an electric shock. Animals can easily learn to do this; however, if an animal has been exposed to uncontrollable shocks (shocks it can neither escape or avoid) before it is placed in the box, it will not learn to jump the barrier. Instead, it will passively take the shock, a response that is called **learned helplessness.** Similar results have been obtained with humans (Hiroto, 1979).

Seligman (1975) proposed that learned helplessness has three primary consequences—reduced motivation to control the outcome of an event,

Learned helplessness: a theory that experience with uncontrollable events leads an organism to "learn" that it cannot control what happens to it.

Depression is a problem which afflicts a large number of people. Some theories of depression focus on the manner in which depressed people make attributions about their successes and failures.

interference with learning the response that will control the outcome, and feelings of fear and (later) depression. He also observed that these consequences are very similar to the characteristics of depression in humans, which led him to suggest that learned helplessness may be a causal factor in the development of depression. This suggestion spawned a good deal of research on the similarities between learned helplessness and neurotic depression. The research produced some good news and some bad news for Seligman's theory.

On the positive side, it was found that depressed people and people who had experienced learned helplessness did display similar behaviors (Klein, Fencil-Morse, and Seligman, 1976). But it was also found that when depressives failed at a task they tended to make *internal* attributions about their failure (Kuiper, 1978). This result refuted the learned helplessness model of depression, which proposed that depressives should attribute the outcome of some event to external causes because they consider outcomes to be beyond their control. These findings led Abramson, Seligman, and Teasdale (1978) to offer a reformulated version of the learned helplessness explanation of depression. Their version is largely based on the principles of the attribution process (see chapter four) and the principles of self-attributions (see the section on self-attributions in this chapter).

According to the reformulated version, the person first learns that certain outcomes do not depend on (or are not controlled by) what he does. Following this, the person makes a self-attribution regarding the lack of a relationship between his response and the outcome. These self-attributions vary along three dimensions. The first is an internal or an external cause.

The outcome can be due to some characteristic of the person (such as ability or effort) or some characteristic of the situation in which the outcome occurs (such as bad luck or the difficulty of the task the person is working on). The second dimension is stable versus unstable. That is, the cause can be long-term and constant (such as the person's ability or the difficulty of the task he is working on) or short-term and variable (effort or luck). The final dimension is global versus specific. Global causes occur across a wide variety of situations; specific ones occur only in the one which the person has encountered.

Depressed and nondepressed people differ in their attributional styles. When depressed people experience a success, they tend to attribute it to external, unstable, and specific causes; when they experience a failure, they tend to attribute it to internal, stable, and global factors. In other words, depressives take the blame for their failures, but they do not take credit for their successes. (Note how different this is from the self-attributional styles described earlier this chapter.) The consequences of the depressive's attributional style, according to Abramson and her colleagues, are that it leads to the typical symptoms of neurotic depression—deficits in motivation and performance, lowered self-esteem, and depression.

Few studies have tested Abramson and her associates' predictions about the attributional style of depressives, but those that have tend to support it. Sweeney, Shaeffer, and Golin (1982), for example, classified subjects as depressed or nondepressed and then presented them with descriptions of some situations with positive outcomes and some with negative outcomes. The subjects were asked to place themselves in a situation and make self-attributions. Depressed subjects were more likely to accept responsibility for negative outcomes and deny responsibility for positive outcomes than were nondepressed subjects. In another part of the same study, the researchers investigated whether depressives make these kinds of attributions about other people as well. They found that depressed and nondepressed people did not differ in the attributions they made about another person. Thus, the researchers concluded that the differences between depressed and nondepressed people appear to be confined to self-attributions.

Other studies (for example, Barthe and Hammen, 1981; Seligman, 1981) have looked at how depressed and nondepressed college students react to success or failure on an examination. Students were classified as depressed or nondepressed before they found out how they had done on the exam. The depressed students were less likely to attribute their success to ability and more likely to attribute their failure to a lack of ability than were the nondepressed students.

Treatment of Depression

Seligman (1981) described three major techniques that can be used by a psychotherapist to treat depression. All of these are derived from the learned helplessness model of depression. Two techniques involve giving depressed people a more positive, controllable environment. The third technique involves attribution retraining; that is, teaching depressed people new ways to explain their successes and failures. Seligman described a study (Layden, 1978) in which this third technique was tried. Each week a group of women who were depressed and low in self-esteem were required to write down several bad things that had happened to them (for example, fighting with a lover, not being hired for a desired job). They were then asked to give an external attribution for these negative events. For example, rather than attributing a fight with her boyfriend to her own stupidity, a woman would attribute the fight to the boyfriend's bad mood. According to Layden, this retraining increased the women's self-esteem and decreased their depression. While more research is needed on the effects of attribution retraining, it seems to hold some promise for the treatment of neurotic depression.

Perceptions of Self-control among the Elderly

As noted in the discussion of locus of control, life events can influence how internally or externally oriented a person is. A number of social psychologists have come to view the aging process as a significant determinant of a person's perceptions of control. They have argued that one of the major problems for elderly people is that they believe they have lost personal control over their environment (Rodin and Langer, 1980; Schulz and Hanusa, 1980).

An elderly person might feel this way for several reasons. For some people, old age is a time when they do lose control. If they are retired, they have less control over their finances; if they have medical problems, they are more dependent on others to meet their day-to-day needs. In addition, stereotypes influence the self-perceptions of elderly people. Although less than 5 percent of all people over 65 in the United States require custodial care (Brotman, 1974), elderly citizens are seen by others as less competent, more helpless, and more infirm than younger people (Rodin and Langer, 1980). Many elderly people (especially those with reduced abilities) may come to believe that this stereotype is accurate. This produces a loss of self-esteem, which contributes to a sense of loss of control, which further lowers self-esteem—and the two self-perceptions continue to feed off one another.

The need to feel that you control what happens to you cannot be overestimated. Theorists from Alfred Adler and Bruno Bettelheim to contemporary experimental social psychologists have argued that a sense of competence and control is vital to a human's well-being. To quote Lefcourt:

> The sense of control, the illusion that one can exercise personal choice, has a definite and positive role in sustaining life. (1973, p. 424)

Langer and Rodin (1976) suggested that elderly people's belief that they have lost control over their environment can lead to mental illness, psychological withdrawal, and even physical deterioration. The physical consequences of a loss of control are suggested by a study by Ferrare (1962,

For some people old age is accompanied by a sense of loss of control over their lives. This can have negative physical and psychological consequences.

cited in Seligman, 1975). The subjects were two groups of elderly people, both facing a move to a new residence. Members of the first group reported that their only alternative was to move into an old-age home. Members of the second group felt they had a choice in where they lived. Within ten weeks, 94 percent (16 out of 17) of the people in the first group were dead! While this was not a carefully controlled study, its implications are dramatic. If the deaths of these elderly people were even in part due to a sense of loss of control over where they lived, then there is a need to determine if this self-perception can be changed in elderly people.

Locus-of-Control Retraining in the Elderly

In the last ten years, two major studies have investigated means to restructure elderly people's locus-of-control orientations from external to internal. The first was conducted by Richard Schulz (1976). The subjects were residents of an institution for elderly individuals. They were randomly assigned to three experimental groups and one control group. In all three experimental groups the subjects received visits from a college student over an extended period of time. Subjects in the first group could decide when they were visited and for how long. Subjects in the second group were told when the visits would occur, but had no say in when they took place. Members of the third group were visited on a random schedule. No visits were made to members of the control group.

Schulz's initial results were encouraging. The elderly subjects in groups one and two, who could either control or predict when the visits would occur, showed much greater improvement in both their physical and mental health than did members of the other two groups. But this improvement was short-lived. Within a few months after the visits stopped, people in the first two groups had declined to a point below that of the people in the random or no-visit conditions. Schulz used the reformulated learned helplessness model of self-attributions to explain this decline. He argued that the elderly people in the first two groups did not really change their self-attributions about control over their environment; they saw the visits as external, unstable, and specific. They believed that someone else (the institution staff) was allowing them to control a short-term event (the visits), and that they still had little control over other aspects of their lives. Once the visits stopped, these self-attributions were confirmed and the feeling of a loss of control accelerated.

The second study, conducted by Ellen Langer and Judith Rodin (1976, 1977), produced much more positive results. The subjects were residents on two different floors of a nursing home. Subjects in the first group (the experimental group) were given a talk by the nursing home staff on their rights and responsibilities. The major thrust of the talk was that if they decided to, they could control what happened to them. They could decide how the furniture in their room was arranged, who they visited, when they engaged in social activities, what movies they saw, and in general how things were run at the home. The talk concluded with the statement, "It's your life and you can make of it whatever you want" (Langer and Rodin, 1976, 194). The control group received a similar lecture, but no mention was made of the subjects' rights and responsibilities.

For three weeks after the talk, the psychological and physical characteristics of subjects in the two groups were recorded. Subjects in the experimental group described themselves as happier and more active than those in the control group. They were also seen as more active, more sociable, and more healthy by the staff. Eighteen months later the researchers returned to the nursing home to examine the long-term effects of the intervention (Rodin and Langer, 1977). Subjects in the experimental group were still rated by their nurses as happier, more active, more sociable, and more independent than subjects in the control group. They were also rated as healthier. But the most striking data were the relative death rates of the two groups. Before the study began, subjective ratings of physical health had disclosed no difference between the two groups. But 18 months later the death rate among members of the control group was twice that among members of the experimental group. Thirty percent of the people in the control group had died; only 15 percent of the people in the experimental group had died.

I do not want to overstate the role of self-perceptions in people's physical and mental health. A host of other variables influence our health. But it does appear that the way in which we see ourselves can influence our psychological and physical well-being, as well as our social behavior.

Chapter Six

Interpersonal Attraction: Liking and Loving

Prologue

Donald G. Dutton and Arthur P. Aron (1974). Some evidence for heightened sexual attraction under conditions of high anxiety. *Journal of Personality and Social Psychology*, **30:** 510-517.

Background

Researchers interested in interpersonal attraction often study the development of positive and negative feelings between people. One feeling that has generated a good amount of research interest is romantic, or sexual, attraction. In earlier research by one of the authors of this study, males were asked to act either highly emotional or minimally emotional in the presence of an attractive female confederate. Then the men's feelings toward the woman were measured. The men in the highly emotional condition reported greater sexual attraction toward the woman than did men in the minimally emotional condition. Donald Dutton and Arthur Aron suggested that the effects of general arousal on sexual attraction may be at least partially explained by Schachter's two-factor theory of emotions. (See chapter four.) This study tested their proposal that if people are aroused by some nonsexual stimulus, but there is a reasonable object of sexual attraction present (an attractive member of the opposite sex, for example), people may label this arousal as romantic or sexual attraction.

Hypothesis

It was predicted that males who were experiencing fear would show more sexual attraction toward a female than would males who were not experiencing fear.

Subjects

The subjects were 90 males between the ages of 18 and 35 who were visiting a recreational area in Vancouver, British Columbia, Canada.

Procedure

The study had a high-fear and a low-fear condition. Subjects in the high-fear condition were alone when they crossed a suspension bridge 230 feet above a river in the recreational area. The bridge was five feet wide and 450 feet long. It was made of wooden boards and cables; it had low, wire-cable handrails; and it swayed, wobbled, and tilted when people used it, giving them the sensation they were about to fall off. The bridge could be easily reached by tourists to the area and, despite its characteristics, was a popular tourist attraction.

    Subjects in the low-fear condition were alone when they crossed another bridge in the recreational area. This bridge was about ten feet above a small stream. It was made of heavy wood, had high handrails, and did not sway, wobble, or tilt.

As subjects in the two conditions were crossing the bridges, they were approached by either a male or an attractive female interviewer. The interviewers told the subjects they were doing a psychology project on the effects of "scenic attractions on creative expression" and asked them to fill out a short questionnaire. If a subject agreed, he answered a few questions about his age, education, and so on, and then was asked to look at a drawing of a young woman and write a brief story based on this drawing.

After each subject had written his story, he was thanked for his help and told that if he was interested in more information about the study, he could call the interviewer. The interviewer tore off a piece of paper, wrote his or her name and phone number on it, and gave it to the subject.

The content of the stories written by the men was analyzed for sexual or romantic themes, and the percentage of men in each condition who later called the interviewer was recorded. These were the two dependent variables.

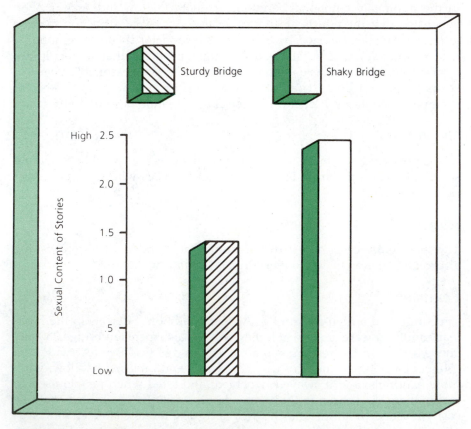

Figure 6-1. *Men who met the female confederate on the shaky bridge wrote stories with greater sexual content than did those who met her on the sturdy bridge.*
Source: Dutton and Aron (1974).

Results

The results supported Dutton and Aron's hypothesis. (See figure 6-1.) The sexual or romantic content of the stories written by men who met the attractive woman on the high, shaky suspension bridge was much greater than the sexual content of the stories written by the men who met the attractive woman on the low, sturdy bridge. Also, 50 percent of the men in the high-fear condition later called her, but only about 10 percent of the men in the low-fear condition called her. These differences were not found with subjects who encountered the male interviewer. In other words, emotional arousal that was not due to sexual stimuli produced an increase in sexual attraction only when there was an appropriate object for this attraction.

Implications

This study attracted considerable attention among social psychologists interested in interpersonal attraction—and not simply because of the dramatic way in which Dutton and Aron tested their hypothesis. As is explained in this chapter, interpersonal attraction concerns the development of both friendships and romantic relationships. Researchers interested in interpersonal attraction have disagreed about whether the factors that lead to liking also lead to love. Some have proposed that loving and liking are often quite different processes. They have used the results of this study to support their position that while arousal and fear do lead to sexual attraction, they do not lead to friendship. Others disagree with this position and its explanation of Dutton and Aron's findings. They believe that liking and loving are basically due to the same factors.

This chapter is concerned with **interpersonal attraction.** Researchers interested in interpersonal attraction focus most of their attention on why one person likes another and why one person loves another; this chapter reflects this emphasis.

There is another way of describing what this chapter is about. Consider the word *relationship*. Webster's Dictionary defines a relationship as "a joining or being joined; coupling, union; the relation between things that depend on (or) involve . . . each other" (1953, 311). This chapter examines the reasons why this "joining" or "union" occurs and the factors that lead a person to become dependent on or involved with another.

In the first section, the importance of relationships to humans and the manner in which relationships develop are discussed. This is followed by a section on friendship and a section on romantic attraction. The applications section examines sexual attitudes and behavior.

Interpersonal attraction: an individual's tendency to react positively or negatively to another person.

LONELINESS AND AFFILIATION

> [My] only affliction was that I seemed banished from human society . . . I was alone . . . condemned to what I called Silent life; . . . I was as one who Heaven thought not worthy to be numbered among the living, or to appear among the rest of His creatures; . . . to have seen one of my own species would have seemed to me a raising me from death to life, and the greatest blessing that Heaven itself, next to the supreme blessing of salvation could bestow. (Defoe, 1719)

When Daniel Defoe's character, Robinson Crusoe, spoke these words almost 300 years ago, he stood alone on the beach of a desert island. But physical isolation is not a prerequisite for loneliness; even someone who lives in the middle of a crowded city or attends a large university can feel lonely. In fact, it is estimated that over 50 million Americans experience feelings of loneliness (Perlman and Peplau, 1982). This section examines the phenomenon of loneliness and people's need for affiliation.

Loneliness

Loneliness occurs when people feel that they do not have enough social relationships or are dissatisfied by the quality of those they have (Peplau and Perlman, 1979). Thus, one cannot simply look at the number of friends someone has and determine whether or not that person is lonely. As Perlman and Peplau (1982) pointed out, loneliness is not the same thing as social isolation, solitude, or being alone. People feel lonely for many different reasons, they react to this feeling in different ways, and they find different ways to overcome loneliness.

Causes of Loneliness

Certain groups of people are more likely to experience loneliness than are others. For example, women are more likely to report that they are lonely than men, people who are divorced or widowed are more likely to experience loneliness than people who are married or people who are single and have never been married, and loneliness is more prevalent among low-income individuals (Perlman and Peplau, 1982). Feelings of loneliness also vary with age (Rubenstein and Shaver, 1982; Parlee, 1979). The highest incidence of loneliness is found among adolescents: In one study, 79 percent of the adolescents interviewed said they were sometimes or often lonely. There are two possible explanations for this somewhat surprising finding. One explanation is that contemporary teenagers may have been taught it is all right to acknowledge this kind of feeling. Thus, the data may simply reflect a willingness to report one's feelings among younger people. (This may also explain why women report more loneliness than men.) An alternative explanation is based on the social expectations of adolescents. Adolescence is usually a time of extensive social encounters, and teenagers may have unrealistically high expectations about what the quantity and quality of these will be. When their expectations are not met, they experience loneliness.

Like many other social phenomena, loneliness is caused by personality variables, situational variables, and the interaction between the two. Perlman and Peplau (1981) identified several personality characteristics associated with loneliness, including an external locus-of-control orientation, introversion, shyness, low self-esteem, and—most important—few social skills. Social relationships do not just happen; the development of a friendship requires a certain number of social skills. Horowitz, French, and Anderson (1982) found that lonely people are less able to make friends, to actively participate in group activities, and to make phone calls to initiate social activities. When conversing with others, lonely people tend to talk about themselves, ask few questions of their partners, and change the topic frequently (Jones, 1982). These behaviors seldom lead to the development of close friendships.

No one is immune to loneliness. Just as Crusoe, through no fault of his own, became shipwrecked on a desert island, many people find themselves in situations that can cause loneliness. If you attend a university away from your home town, remember back to your first few days on campus. You probably felt excited, scared, and lonely. Separation from friends and family increases the chances of experiencing loneliness (Peplau

Feelings of loneliness can occur even when a person is around other people.

and Perlman, 1979). The loss of a loved one through death or divorce or the end of a dating relationship often results in loneliness. A change in status that reduces the level of an individual's social contacts can also result in loneliness; thus, lonely people can be found among those who have recently retired or been fired. It is even possible for a job promotion to cause loneliness if the promoted worker must leave friends behind (Peplau and Perlman, 1979). And finally, a simple decline in the quality of a person's social relationships can engender loneliness. Loneliness is relative. It is not being alone that causes loneliness, but rather a decrease in the quantity and quality of a person's social relationships.

Reactions to Loneliness

Rubenstein, Shaver, and Peplau (1979) asked a large number of people to describe their feelings when they were lonely. The most common reaction was one of desperation. Lonely people experience depression, panic, fear, helplessness, hopelessness, and a sense of being abandoned. This is almost exactly what Crusoe felt. Milder forms of loneliness are accompanied by *impatient boredom* (Rubenstein et al., 1979). Lonely people do not want to be where they are, they are bored with the situation and angry that they are in it. And lonely people put themselves down (self-deprecation), describing themselves as stupid, ashamed, and insecure.

Although loneliness is a subjectve feeling, there are scales that can reliably and validly measure it, such as the UCLA (University of California at Los Angeles) Loneliness Scale (Russell, Peplau, and Cutrona, 1980). (See table 6-1 for some items from this scale.)

People who score high on this and similar scales report that they feel depressed, empty, hopeless, isolated, and unsociable. They also report a less active and less satisfying social life. They are more likely to do things by themselves and have fewer friends (Russell et al., 1980). Jones (1982) found that while lonely and nonlonely people have the same total number of social interactions, lonely people have more contacts with strangers and casual acquaintances and fewer with family and friends. Again, loneliness is not simply a reaction to the quantity of social interactions, but to their quality as well.

Overcoming Loneliness

Given that loneliness is an unpleasant state, it is not surprising that people try to overcome it. Peplau and Perlman (1979) proposed three ways in

---

Table 6-1. *Some items from the UCLA Loneliness Scale. Lonely people would* not *endorse the asterisked item, but would endorse the other items.*

1. I lack companionship.
2. I do not feel alone.*
3. I am no longer close to anyone.
4. No one really knows me well.

Source: Russell et al. (1980).

which people try to do this. First, they may change their standards of what is an acceptable level of social contact and whom they would find a satisfying companion. A study by Pennebaker, Dyer, Caulkins, Litowitz, Ackerman, Anderson, and McGraw (1979) illustrates how standards can change. The subjects were patrons in a college bar. Pennebaker and his associates interviewed the same people at three different times during the same evening: 9:00 P.M., 10:30 P.M., and 12:00 P.M. Each time, the subjects were asked to rate the attractiveness of one opposite-sex person and one same-sex person in the bar. The attractiveness ratings of the same-sex person did not change over the course of the evening. The ratings of the opposite-sex person did. As the evening wore on, the opposite-sex person was rated as more attractive by the subjects. This was true whether the rater was a male or female.

Second, people may attempt to rationalize away the disparity between their actual level of social relations and what they desire. They do this by denying that the disparity exists, by diminishing its importance, or by engaging in behaviors that reduce its negative impact. For example, it is believed that alcohol and drug use may often be responses to loneliness (Rouse and Ewing, 1973). Third, people may attempt to increase either the number of their social contacts or the quality of their existing ones to bring their network of social relationships to an acceptable level.

Affiliation

As mentioned before, humans are incredibly social creatures who desire the company of others and dread being alone. Some theorists have argued that the desire to affiliate, or be with others, is an innate response that has its origins in human evolution. The human infant is a helpless creature; it needs adults to care for it over an extended period of time. According to Ainsworth (1969), Bowlby (1973), and others, infants who could elicit caretaking behaviors from others were most likely to survive and pass this tendency on to their descendants. Thus, the desire to be with others has been cultivated through the process of natural selection. This desire can be observed in very young infants. They attempt to be near other humans and if they find themselves alone, they engage in behaviors that bring people to them, such as crying.

Other explanations of the need for affiliation are based on learning theory. Some learning theorists (for example, Harlow, 1961) believe that the desire to affiliate with others is learned through the process of classical conditioning. Each time a parent feeds a child or gives it comfort, human contact is associated with the reduction of a negative drive or with a pleasurable experience. After a number of these pairings, an infant becomes conditioned to its parent. Affiliation, according to these theorists, is a conditioned response to the stimulus that provides for the infant's basic needs.

Another learning theory explanation of the desire to affiliate with others is based on instrumental conditioning, which states that the consequences of a behavior determine the probability that it will occur again. Affiliating with others, it is argued, usually produces valuable resources and positive reinforcement; thus, this behavior is learned through instrumental conditioning (Weiss, 1974). The story of Crusoe provides an illustration. Crusoe had been alone on the island for three years when he discovered human footprints on the beach. Although he desperately desired human companionship, he feared his first meeting with another inhabitant of the island. His fears became even greater when he found that the other human was not a "proper Englishman" but a "savage." Crusoe initially treated Friday with a good deal of caution, but after some time had passed his feelings changed considerably.

> I needed none of all this precaution; for never had man a more faithful, loving, sincere servant than Friday was to me; without passions, sullenness, or designs, perfectly obliged and engaged; his very affections were tied to me, like those of a child to a father; and I dare say he would have sacrificed his life for the saving of mine upon any occasion whatsoever; the many testimonies he gave me of this put it out of doubt and soon convinced me that I needed to use no precautions as to my safety on his account. (Defoe, 1719)

The reinforcers Friday provided caused Crusoe to change his view of him. Similarly, people may desire the company of others because of the rewards and resources they provide. This does not mean that people always desire the company of others and choose associates indiscriminantly. Unlike the forelorn Crusoe, we live in densely populated environments where we can decide when we interact with other people and with whom. Our choices will be influenced by the characteristics of a particular situation.

Situational Influences on Affiliation

The prologue experiment used Stanley Schachter's *two-factor theory* of emotion to explain the effect of arousal on sexual attraction. Schachter's work on emotions grew out of his earlier research on fear and the desire to affiliate with others (Evans, 1980). In 1959, Schachter reported on the results of an experiment concerned with this issue. A group of women were recruited to take part in an experiment on the effects of electric shock. For half the women, the experiment was quite frightening. They were greeted by a serious-looking character named Dr. Gregor Zilstein. Standing in front of an array of electrical equipment, Dr. Zilstein told them that in a few minutes they would undergo a series of extremely painful electric shocks. The doctor then told them that the experiment would begin in about 10 minutes. The other half of the women were treated quite differently by Dr. Zilstein. They were told they would receive a mild electric shock that would produce a very slight tingling sensation. As with the first group of women, there was a ten-minute delay before the study started. In both conditions of the experiment, the women were given a choice of spending the 10 minutes alone or in the company of other people. Sixty-three percent of the women in the high-fear condition desired to wait with other people; only 33 percent of the low-fear subjects chose to wait with others. Fear increased the desire to affiliate with others (Schachter, 1959).

Subsequent research by Schachter found that when people are frightened they do not want the company of just anybody. They want to be with people who are in the same circumstance—"misery loves miserable company." Apparently, frightened people use the reactions of others to evaluate the reasonableness of their own reactions. If the situation confronting them is novel and arousing, people are not sure how they should react. The reactions of others in the same situation enable them to label and identify their own reactions. This, in turn, reduces their anxiety. This explanation is consistent with Schachter's theory of emotion that when people are not sure of their feelings they turn to others to help them identify or understand what they are experiencing.

While fear may lead to the desire to be with other people, other emotions can lead to a desire to be alone. Sarnoff and Zimbardo (1961) found that people waiting to engage in an embarrassing activity (for example, sucking on a baby bottle) prefer to wait alone. Also, if people become extremely emotional, they prefer to be alone. In such situations, people do not need to evaluate their own emotions; they know how they feel. They also want to avoid the embarrassment of showing their extreme reaction to others. And finally, they are afraid that the reactions of others

Fear can cause people to seek the company of others.

in the same situation might heighten their own emotional response (Wheeler, 1974).

We do not want to be with others only when we are frightened. Usually, when we interact with other people we are feeling fine. Further, most social interactions do not involve people huddling together with strangers who are also awaiting the return of someone like the dreaded Dr. Zilstein. Most social interactions involve close friends and loved ones.

Development of Social Relationships

Think about a close friend. The relationship between the two of you probably did not develop overnight. Friends and lovers delight in telling stories about the first time they met, what they thought about one another then, and how their feelings have changed. The relatedness and social penetration models describe how relationships between people develop and change.

Relatedness Model

Relatedness model: the theory that as a social relationship develops, the people in it become interrelated and dependent on one another.

Levinger and Snoek (1972) proposed a **relatedness model.** This model states that people start out being totally unrelated and independent but, over time and through a series of stages, they become more and more related and interdependent. (See figure 6-2 for a diagram of Levinger and Snoek's model.) For example, Quentin and Elaine live in the same city and have many friends in common, but they do not know one another. They are at the first stage, called *zero contact*. One night, at a party, a friend points Elaine out to Quentin. He finds her quite attractive, bright, and pleasant. The couple has now entered the second stage, *unilateral awareness*—one is aware of the other and has some initial impressions of what kind of person she is, but there really is no interaction between them. A few months later, Quentin finds himself working at the same place as Elaine. One day he is out of cigarettes and remembers that Elaine smokes. He goes to Elaine's office and borrows a cigarette. As time passes, he sees her more often and they begin to have short conversations; they even have coffee every few weeks. The relationship is now at the third stage, *surface contact*—the two people interact on a very limited basis and their behaviors are quite independent. Finally, Quentin decides to ask Elaine out. For the first few months they see one another once or twice a week, but as time passes they begin to see one another every day. Quentin gives up his racquetball game on Tuesday to be with Elaine; Elaine rearranges her tennis game for the same reason. Her actions affect his life, and vice versa. The relationship has progressed to the fourth stage, *mutuality*—there is some degree of interrelatedness between the people.

If the give and take that exists during the mutuality stage of a relationship is satisfactory to both people, their relationship will lead to marriage or some other type of commitment. From this time on, they are highly interrelated and interdependent. The long-term success of a relationship depends on the extent to which this level of interdependence provides positive outcomes for both people.

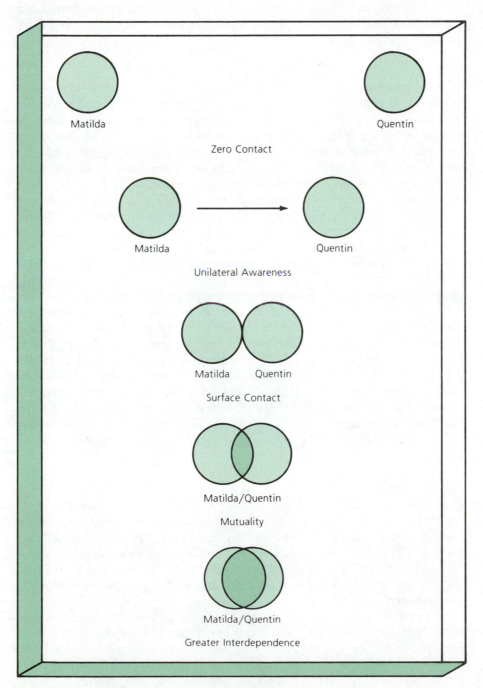

Figure 6-2. *Levinger and Snoek's Relatedness Model of Social Relationships.*
Source: Levinger and Snoek (1972).

Note how well the relatedness model fits the definition of the word *relationship*. A relationship is a connection. Quentin and Elaine started out totally unconnected, but by the advanced stages of mutuality they were strongly connected.

Social Penetration Model

Social penetration model: the theory that as a social relationship develops, the people in it become more open, more self-disclosing, and more emotionally intimate with one another.

A somewhat different view of the development of a relationship is proposed in the **social penetration model** (Altman and Taylor, 1973; Altman, Vinsel, and Brown, 1981). It suggests that when two people first meet, they do not let one another know a great deal about themselves. In essence, they erect barriers between themselves. Altman and Taylor (1973) called this the *orientation stage*—the point when Quentin and Elaine first spoke and their conversation was very superficial. But as a relationship develops, each person allows the other to penetrate these barriers and they enter the *exploratory affective exchange stage*—the point when Quentin and Elaine started talking over a cigarette or coffee. The level of self-disclosure then becomes somewhat broader and deeper as the two people move into the *true affective exchange stage*—when Quentin and Elaine began to date and the relationship became "serious" (Altman and Taylor, 1973). At this point, people are willing to be open with each other. Quentin expresses his positive and negative feelings to Elaine and his behavior becomes more personal and intimate. Elaine does the same. In the final stage of Altman and Taylor's model, the *stable exchange state*, both people are totally open with one another and have no misunderstandings or miscommunication. While we could hope this for Quentin and Elaine, couples rarely achieve this stage (Altman and Taylor, 1973). In fact, in a later version of this model, Altman and his associates (1981) proposed that even stable, long-term relationships fluctuate between superficial and intimate levels of communication. Even among happily married couples, there is some need for privacy.

Self-disclosure

Self-disclosure: the process of providing honest and frank information about oneself to another person.

One aspect of communication between people is **self-disclosure** (Jourard, 1964). Perhaps the clearest example of self-disclosure can be found in the comedy routines of Joan Rivers. She begins her act with the question "Can we talk?" and then proceeds to tell her audience how she feels about the size of her breasts and to describe her first sexual experience, how often she has intercourse with her husband (very rarely), and the quality of his performance (very poor).

Of course, people are not always as willing as Joan Rivers to self-disclose. Self-disclosure, like most social phenomena, is influenced by both personality factors and situational factors. Some of the personality traits related to self-disclosure are need for social approval—people high in need for approval engage in relatively little self-disclosure (Brundage, Derlega, and Cash, 1977); locus-of-control orientation—people with an external locus-of-control orientation are also less self-disclosing (Rychman, Sherman, and Burgess, 1973); and extroversion—social, outgoing people are more self-disclosing (Archer, 1979).

One situational variable that influences self-disclosure is how well people know one another. Joan Rivers gets laughs (and lots of money) by telling her most intimate secrets to total strangers, but most people are reluctant to be so open in normal situations. Why? Imagine that you met Joan Rivers at a party. In the first 30 seconds of your conversation, she describes in detail her sex life. You would probably feel uncomfortable and find her rather strange. Chaikin and Derlega (1974) found that subjects perceive people who give intimate information to strangers to be less well adjusted than those who reveal such information to friends.

Self-disclosure is also influenced by the number of people present in a social situation. In a laboratory experiment, Taylor, Desoto, and Lieb (1979) measured the levels of self-disclosure in two-person and three-person groups. The conversations between two people were significantly more intimate and revealing. Evidently, subjects in the dyads were more likely to feel that personal information was safe with the person who received it.

Another variable that has consistently been found to increase self-disclosure is reciprocity—people are more likely to self-disclose if their partner does so also (Taylor, 1979; Worthy, Gary, and Kuhn, 1969). Reciprocity increases self-disclosure even when it leads people to dislike the discloser (Derlega, Harris, and Chaikin, 1973). The most widely accepted explanation for this effect is that when people receive intimate information from others, they feel obligated to reciprocate by self-disclosing. If they do not, the relationship will be unequal or unfair, and people do not like such relationships.

SUMMARY

Research on interpersonal attraction concerns friendships, romantic attraction and social relationships in general. When people feel that the quantity or quality of their social relationships is less than they desire, they experience loneliness. Some people are more likely to be lonely than others; for example, people who are deficient in the skills that would enable them to improve the quantity and quality of their social relationships are likely to be lonely. Situational factors such as the death of a loved one, separation from one's family, or a job change can also cause loneliness. When loneliness occurs, people feel desperate, bored, depressed, and inferior. They attempt to alleviate these feelings by either changing their standards about their social relationships or physically increasing the quantity or quality of their relationships.

The desire to affiliate is so pervasive among humans that some theorists have proposed that it is innate. Others, however, have argued that it is a behavior learned through classical and instrumental conditioning. The need for affiliation is reinforced by the fact that the presence of others often reduces the level of fear associated with a particular situation.

Relationships between people develop and change over time. The relatedness model sees relationships as developing along a continuum of relatedness; over time, people go from a stage in which they are totally unrelated and independent to a stage in which their lives are intertwined. The social penetration model proposes that relationships develop along a continuum of openness and intimacy; in the early stages of a relationship, people erect barriers that hide their "true" personalities and behaviors from one another, but as the relationships develop, these barriers are penetrated.

For a relationship to progress, the people in it must be willing to engage in self-disclosure, providing another person with honest and frank information about themselves. Many factors affect people's willingness to self-disclose, including reciprocity; people tend to reciprocate another person's self-disclosure.

FRIENDSHIP FORMATION

The development of a friendship between two people is not a chance happening. Certain specifiable variables influence whether one person likes or dislikes another. This section presents the variables of propinquity, similarity, and reciprocity. It also examines several theories of how friendships develop.

Propinquity

Propinquity means physical closeness. All other things being equal (and this is an important qualifier), the closer two people are the more likely they are to like one another. A study by Segal (1974) illustrates this. She found a police academy where propinquity was determined by a random process, the "accident" of family name. New recruits were assigned roommates and seats in their classes on the basis of alphabetical order. Thus, recruits named Abrams and Abramson would spend more time together than would recruits Adams and Zephron. After the recruits had been there for a while, they were asked to name their closest friends at the academy. It was found that the closer two recruits' names were in the alphabet, the more likely they were to become friends. (See figure 6-3.)

Mere Exposure and Attraction

Zajonc (1968) proposed that mere repeated exposure to another person is sufficient to produce positive feelings toward that person. Saegert, Swap, and Zajonc (1973) demonstrated this in a clever experiment. Female subjects were recruited to take part in a series of taste tests. Different liquids were placed in different cubicles and pairs of subjects were asked to sample each. Each subject shared a cubicle with the same person zero, one, two, five, or ten times. While they were together in the cubicles, subjects were asked not to speak with one another and not to make any faces or gestures

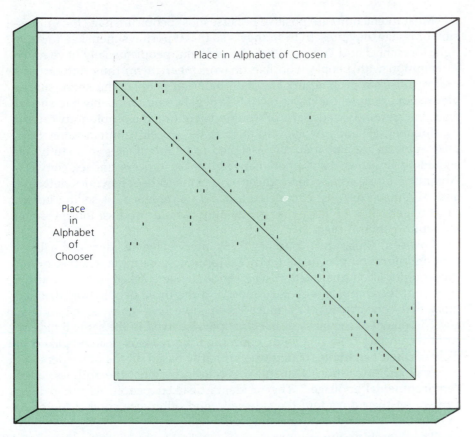

Figure 6-3. *The closer together the cadets sat (because of the alphabetical order of their names), the more likely they were to choose one another as a friend. Copyright 1974 American Psychological Association. Reprinted by permission of the author.*
Source: Segal (1974).

that might influence the other person. After the tasting was over, the women filled out a number of questionnaires, including one that measured how much they liked one another. The more frequently the women had shared cubicles, the more they liked one another. In another study on mere exposure, Grush (1980) found that the more political candidates were exposed to voters, the more popular and successful they became.

Limitations on the Effects of Propinquity

At this point, you may be saying to yourself, "If propinquity makes people so attracted to each other, why do I want to strangle the person who lives next door?" Questions like this lead to qualifications about the effects of propinquity on interpersonal attraction. It is generally agreed that physical closeness interacts with other factors to affect liking. Propinquity provides the opportunity for people to interact, but the nature of the interaction determines the level of interpersonal attraction. If an interaction is positive, we like the other person; if it is negative, we dislike the person.

Most interactions are positive because most people manage the impression or image they present to strangers so that it portrays them in a positive light (Berscheid and Walster, 1969). In addition, people usually have much in common with people who live or work near them; thus, interactions that result from propinquity are often between people who share similar views. For example, the police recruits in Segal's study probably had similar ages, backgrounds, and views of society. Therefore, the propinquity caused by alphabetical similarity allowed them to have positive interactions. Suppose subjects are alphabetically assigned to be roommates in a study designed to improve the rapport between police officers and ex-convicts. Abrams is an aspiring police officer who plans to be a narcotics detective and Abramson has just completed a five-year sentence for selling heroin to teenagers. It is unlikely that propinquity would produce interpersonal attraction between them.

Ebbesen, Kjos, and Konecni (1976) interviewed residents of a large condominium complex in southern California to determine whether or not propinquity leads to attraction. The residents were asked to list the three people in the complex they liked most and the three people they disliked most. Sixty-one percent of the most-liked people lived in the same building, and 55 percent of the most-disliked people also lived in the same building. Another finding from this study concerned the reasons residents liked or disliked their neighbors. Liking was primarily based on the other person's personal characteristics. Disliking was caused by what the authors called "environmental spoilage." The residents disliked people who had loud parties, let their dogs foul the sidewalk, and otherwise spoiled the environment at the condominium complex.

Thus, propinquity provides people with the opportunity to interact with one another. If this interaction is positive or even neutral, physical closeness will produce liking. But if this interaction is negative, it will produce disliking.

Similarity

One of the most reliable findings in all of social psychology is that friends are more similar to one another than are strangers (Newcomb, 1978). But it is also true that friends see more similarity between them than actually exists (Newcomb, 1978). These two results suggest that similarity causes liking, and that liking causes perceived similarity.

Similarity as a Cause of Liking
If we believe that someone holds beliefs, attitudes, and values similar to our own, we tend to like that person. This is true whether the person is a stranger we have met for a few minutes (Byrne, 1971) or someone assigned as our roommate in a dormitory (Newcomb, 1961, 1978). The relationship between attitudinal similarity and interpersonal attraction is so reliable that Byrne and Nelson (1965) developed a mathematical formula to describe it. A study by Gonzales, Davis, Loney, Lu Kens, and Junghans (1983) showed that Byrne and Nelson's formula yields an accurate prediction of

interpersonal attraction even when the person in question is someone we have never met. In this study, a large number of college students filled out an attitude survey. A few weeks later, each student was given one of three copies of the same survey—supposedly filled out by another student—in which 0, 50, or 100 percent of the answers agreed with those they had given. After examining the other person's answers, the students rated how much they liked that person. The prediction made by Byrne and Nelson's formula and the student's ratings of liking were then compared. (See figure 6-4.)

Note three things about these findings. One, the formula predicted the greater the amount of attitudinal agreement, the greater the liking.

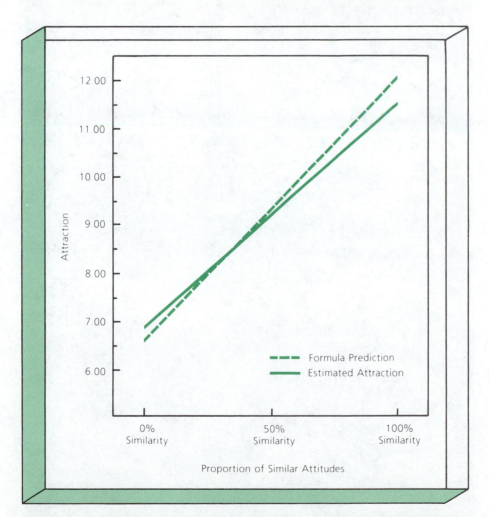

Figure 6-4. As Byrne and Nelson's model would predict, the more similarity between people's attitudes, the more they like one another. Copyright 1983 American Psychological Association. Reprinted by permission of the authors.
Source: Gonzales et al. (1983).

Two, the actual ratings matched the prediction almost exactly. And three, the ratings matched the predictions even though the students had never met the people they rated. Perceived similarity, even in the absence of an actual interaction, produced liking.

Similarity of attitudes and values is not the only kind of similarity that leads to liking. It has been found that similarity in economic background, personality characteristics, physical attractiveness, and self-concept also lead to interpersonal attraction.

Similarity of interests, attitudes, and values often leads to friendships.

In certain instances, however, similarity does not lead to liking. One of these is when a similar other is much more successful than you are (Nadler, Jazwinski, and Lair, 1975, cited by Berscheid and Walster, 1978). People may be more threatened by the success of a similar other than by the success of a dissimilar other; as a result, they may like the former more than the latter. For example, when I was in high school I had the "misfortune" to have an older brother who was an honor student and a National Merit Test finalist. I, on the other hand, did a fair impression of a juvenile delinquent. The comparisons of my academic performance with his did not fill me with brotherly love.* However, I was not bothered by his friends' academic performance because I shared less in common with them than with my brother.

We also may not like similar others if the similarity involves some characteristic we view as undesirable. As Heider pointed out: A person with a disability who wishes to deny it may dislike and even feel hostile toward another person similarly afflicted (1958).

In a 1968 study, Novak and Lerner systematically manipulated the similarity between subjects and a stranger. Subjects were asked whether they would prefer to interact with a similar or a dissimilar stranger. The similar stranger was preferred. But when subjects were told that both strangers had a history of mental illness, they preferred the dissimilar stranger. Evidently, subjects felt threatened by their similarity to a person with a history of mental illness and wanted to keep their distance from that person.

We may also prefer a dissimilar other if he or she possesses certain attributes that we find desirable. Hendrick and Brown (1971) presented introverted subjects with two strangers; a similar introvert and a dissimilar extrovert. Subjects rated each stranger in terms of liking, interesting at a party, and preference as a leader. The introverts rated the dissimilar extroverts higher on all three of these measures. The dissimilar extroverts' social skills made them more desirable companions than the subjects' fellow introverts.

Liking as a Cause of Perceived Similarity

Newcomb (1961) studied the development of friendships among college students. He found that as people became friends, they came to see their attitudes and values as more similar than they actually were. Newcomb called this the *strain toward symmetry*. Other studies have also shown the effects of liking on perceived similarity. Byrne and Wong (1962) asked subjects who differed in prejudice toward blacks to estimate the attitudes of a black stranger or a white stranger. Unprejudiced whites saw the attitudes of blacks and whites as equally similar to their own; prejudiced whites saw the white stranger's attitudes as much more similar to their own than the black stranger's attitudes.

---

*As the dedication in this book suggests, my feelings toward my brother have changed considerably.

Reciprocity

Reciprocity: responding to a person's feelings or behavior with identical or comparable feelings or behavior.

Another factor that influences liking is **reciprocity.** If people reciprocate our positive actions toward them, we will like them; if people do not reciprocate, we will dislike them.

We expect other people to reciprocate a number of specific types of actions. Liking is one. If people indicate that they like us, usually we will like them (Backman and Secord, 1958). Reciprocity of liking is most important in early states of a friendship. As a relationship develops, other factors such as the personal characteristics and similarity in the attitudes of the people involved become more important. This makes sense. Initially, it makes us feel good to know someone else likes us. But if we come to view this person as obnoxious or as sharing little in common with us, our liking will decrease.

Norms: standards or guides for people's behavior and beliefs.

Much of people's behavior with their friends and acquaintances is governed by **norms** about reciprocity (Gouldner, 1960). The norm of reciprocity says that people should help others who help them and that people should not hurt others who help them. In other words, "Do unto others as you would have them do unto you."

Reciprocity affects not only what people do to others but the nature of what they say to them. People are more intimate and self-revealing when the other person reciprocates this self-disclosure. Reciprocity of self-disclosure leads to interpersonal attraction (Derlega, Wilson, and Chaikin, 1976). As people become closer, this kind of reciprocity becomes less important, probably because they come to feel more comfortable with each other. Also, as a relationship develops, there may be other reasons for exchanges between the parties; for instance, the discloser in an intimate, long-term friendship may be looking for sympathy or support rather than evidence that a friend is willing to engage in reciprocal self-disclosure.

Theories of Friendship Formation

Social psychologists usually agree that propinquity, similarity, and reciprocity influence the formation of friendships—or at least an initial liking for someone. They have developed two major theoretical explanations of why these variables lead to interpersonal attractions: They are based on balance theory and learning theory.

Balance Theory

Imagine a circus performer on a high wire. The performer is using a balance bar, a long pole that enables her to walk across the wire. If you watch her carefully, you will see that she adjusts the pole until she has achieved a balance point; a position in which she doesn't sway to one side or the other. If she begins to fall, she shifts the pole to regain her balance. She desires balance.

According to balance theorists, the same principle applies to social relationships, such as friendships. People desire a balance or equilibrium between the various parts of their social world because they believe balance will make their social encounters more controllable, more predictable, and more successful. This idea comes from the cognitive orientation to social behavior. (See chapters one and four.) One way people attempt to obtain and maintain balance in their social relationships is by changing the way they see themselves and other people.

This is not the first time you have come across the idea that people may modify their perceptions of the world to achieve predictable and controllable social encounters. This is the basic premise of why people make attributions about other people's and their own behavior. These ideas are similar because they were all first proposed by the noted Gestalt psychologist Fritz Heider (1958). Heider was probably the first person to argue that people attempt to balance their interpersonal relationships. A relationship is *balanced* when the elements contained in it fit together harmoniously and there is no disequilibrium between them. Imagine you know two people who are always together and you ask one of them why she spends so much time with the other person. If she replies, "Because I can't stand her; she makes me sick," you would think she is mentally unbalanced—her reason doesn't fit with her behavior. Heider said most people would not hold such contradictory thoughts; instead, they would say to themselves, "If I spend a lot of time with a person, I must like her." Heider proposed that people attempt to create balance between **unit relationships** and **sentiment relationships.** A balanced relationship exists when both the unit and the sentiment relationships are positive, when they fit together with no strain or disharmony, or in the terms of the high-wire walker, when the two sides of the pole are balanced.

Unit relationships: the perception that two things belong together.

Sentiment relationships: the perception that a person likes or dislikes another person or thing.

Just as these circus performers desire balance when they cross the high wire, people desire balance in their social relationships.

Heider and other balance theorists (for example, Newcomb, 1961, 1978) used a simple model to explain why similarity leads to liking. It is composed of three elements: the perceiver (p), another person (o), and some object in their environment (x). The object could be a political issue, another person, or anything about which people have positive or negative feelings. In the following example, p is Matilda, o is Josie, and x is nuclear disarmament. Remember, the model is concerned with Matilda's perspective. A number of relationships between these elements are possible. (See figure 6-5.)

The top two triads in figure 6-5 are balanced relationships. Look at triad A: Matilda likes Josie; Matilda and Josie both favor nuclear disarmament. Triad B is also a balanced relationship: Matilda dislikes Josie and favors nuclear disarmament; Josie opposes nuclear disarmament. The bottom two relationships are unbalanced. In triad C, Matilda likes Josie and favors nuclear disarmament, but Josie opposes it. And in triad D, Matilda dislikes Josie, but both she and Josie favor nuclear disarmament. (A simple way to determine if a triad is balanced is to multiply the signs. If the product is positive, the triad is in balance.)

According to balance theory, if Matilda finds herself in triad C or D, she will change her feelings about Josie or about nuclear disarmament to reestablish balance. In triad C, she could convince herself that Josie favors nuclear disarmament. In triad D, she could decide that she likes Josie after all. Balance theory explains why people see their friends' values as more similar to their own than they actually are. They try to maximize the balance in their relationship.

Balance theory can also be used to predict how we will feel about another person. For example, how would you feel about someone who dislikes an enemy of yours? Balance theory would predict that if you dislike your enemy and another person also dislikes your enemy, you should like this other person. When Aronson and Cope (1968) tested this prediction, they found it was accurate. To quote the title of their study, "My Enemy's Enemy Is My Friend."

There may be a very simple reason people desire balance in their social relationships. Their lives may be more pleasant and less stressful if these relationships are balanced. For example, the conversations between Matilda and Josie may be full of strife and conflict if Matilda feels that someone who opposes nuclear disarmament is a mindless warmonger and Josie feels that someone who supports nuclear disarmament is a foolish dupe of the Communists. To eliminate this conflict, Matilda would need to change her feelings about Josie or about the issue that divides them.

Admittedly, the p-o-x model provides a simplistic view of interpersonal attraction. It cannot deal with situations in which a person holds similar attitudes to someone with undesirable traits. Nor does it allow for degrees of liking and disliking—although more sophisticated versions of the theory do (for example, Cartwright and Harary, 1956). Further, in some circumstances its predictions would be wrong. For instance, two women who are attracted to the same man probably will not like one another. Balance theory can, however, explain the effects of propinquity, similarity, and even rec-

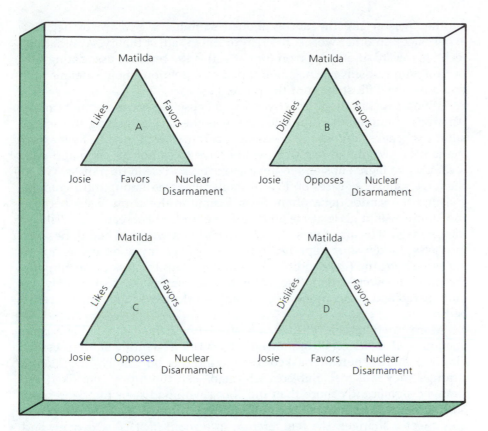

Figure 6-5. The top two triads are balanced; the bottom two triads are unbalanced.

iprocity on interpersonal attraction. People are motivated by a desire for balance in their social relationships and will order these relationships, or at least their perceptions of them, in accord with the principles of balance theory.

Learning Theory
Another widely accepted explanation of the formation of friendships is provided by learning theory. Its basic premise is that liking is determined by the reinforcers others provide. The most popular learning theory of interpersonal attraction is the **reinforcement affect theory** (Clore and Byrne, 1974; Lott and Lott, 1974). Clore and Byrne (1971) turned to the principles of classical conditioning to explain how other people become associated with positive and negative feelings.

Classical conditioning involves the association of a neutral stimulus (a conditioned stimulus) with a stimulus that produces a response in the person (an unconditioned stimulus). If the two stimuli are presented together enough times, people will react to the conditioned stimulus in the same manner as they react to the unconditioned stimulus. In the case of interpersonal attraction, the conditioned, or orginally neutral, stimulus is

Reinforcement affect theory: the theory that liking is caused by changes in people's feelings; people like individuals they associate with positive feelings and dislike individuals they associate with negative feelings.

another person and the unconditioned stimulus is positive or negative experiences. In other words, the reinforcement affect theory says that our feelings toward another person (our affect) is the result of associating that person with a positive or negative experience (reinforcement). Let me give you a personal illustration of the process at work.

When I was in the third grade, I was chosen as a classroom monitor. Among my numerous responsibilities was the task of getting the school janitor whenever one of my classmates became physically ill. Every time the janitor saw me he knew he would have to gather his mop and pail, walk up two flights of stairs to my classroom, and clean up a mess. Given the large number of cases of flu and similar illnesses among third graders, I visited the janitor quite often. Soon I came to dread my visits because the janitor would glare at me and curse me under his breath. He disliked me intensely. His affect was not in response to anything I had done—my mother's chicken soup kept the flu bug away from my door. It was due to his associating me (the conditioned stimulus) with the task of cleaning up the mess in my classroom (the unconditioned stimulus). (Fortunately, he only glared and swore at me; the ancient Greeks used to kill the bearer of bad news.)

More carefully controlled demonstrations of this process have been documented. Gouaux (1972) showed subjects either a funny or a depressing film and shortly thereafter asked them to indicate how much they liked a stranger they had met. Subjects who had seen the funny film liked the stranger significantly more than did those who had seen the depressing film. Other studies have shown that the type of music people hear when they meet a stranger, the temperature in a room (if it is excessive), and similar stimuli can influence how much they like someone (see Griffitt, 1970; May and Hamilton, 1977).

The reinforcement affect theory has been used to explain why we tend to like people who are similar to us. Byrne and his associates (Byrne, 1971; Byrne and Clore, 1970; Golightly and Byrne, 1964) have shown that attitudinal similarity has the properties of a positive reinforcer. In a 1978 article, Huston and Levinger proposed several reasons for this. First, attitudinal similarity confirms or supports one's view of the world. When a judgment concerns social reality (such as whether a Subaru is a better car than a Toyota), people turn to other people for confirmation of their views. This is known as the **social comparison process** (Festinger, 1954). If someone else expresses the same attitudes as you do, this person is, in essence, saying, "Your view of the world is correct. Your are competent." This is reinforcing (White, 1959). Second, agreement with your attitudes implicitly communicates a positive evaluation of you; the person likes you and your ideas (Gonzales et al., 1983). Third, similarity of attitudes suggests that future interactions will be quite positive; that you and the other person would enjoy the same activities and not have any conflicts when you get together again. For example, if both you and your new roommate like the "Tonight Show," then you can expect that she will not object to the television being on at 11:30 P.M. And fourth, Huston and Levinger suggest

Social comparison process: the process of comparing one's own attitudes, beliefs, and personal characteristics to those of other people.

that because of past experiences, similarity had acquired the properties of a reinforcer and that similarity is directly reinforcing. It does not have to be associated with anything else—people simply feel good when others agree with them.

SUMMARY

Social psychological research has identified several variables that seem to influence how much one person likes another person. One variable is propinquity; all other things being equal, people are more likely to like someone who lives or works close to them. Another variable is similarity between people. As a rule, the more similar two people are, the more they will like one another. In addition, people tend to see their friend's attitudes as being more similar to their own than they actually are. Reciprocity is also a determinant of liking. People expect that if they act positively toward someone else, that person will respond in kind, whether the action concerns the expression of positive feelings, self-disclosure, or simply doing a favor. If there is reciprocity, liking will occur.

   Two general theories explain why these and other variables lead to liking. The balance theory explanation proposes that people have a basic need to keep their social relationships, or at least their ideas about their social relationships, in balance or consistent. A learning theory explanation of liking proposes that people like others who are associated with positive feelings. These other people become associated with positive or negative feelings through the process of classical conditioning.

ROMANTIC ATTRACTION

The character of a romantic relationship differs from that of a friendship in three ways: a romantic relationship is usually more intense and involving than a friendship; romantic relationships either currently involve or could reasonably lead to sexual relations between the two people; and, while social conventions have changed dramatically in the last 10 to 15 years, it is still true that most romances are between a man and a woman and that friendships are usually between members of the same sex. It is difficult to overestimate the importance of romance in our social lives. Without romance, many philosophers, poets, songwriters, and novelists would not have written some of their best material. The public's fascination with romance, made the Friedman twins from Sioux City, Iowa rich and famous. You know them as Ann Landers and Dear Abby. Social psychologists are also interested in romance. This section discusses their research on dating, love, and marriage.

Dating: Choosing a Romantic Partner

Some romantic relationships are intense and passionate from the beginning, but most evolve slowly over a period of time. They evolve in the manner described by the relatedness and social penetration models of interpersonal relationships. This discussion assumes that a relationship has made it through the stage of unilateral awareness and is somewhere between surface contact and mutuality. The two people have at least a passing knowledge of one another and have interacted on a few occasions.*

The principle of *matching* proposes that people date individuals whose personal characteristics match their own. There are two kinds of matching. One is on the basis of personal, physical, and demographic (age, race, religion) attributes. Another is based on people's assets.

Matching Based on Personal, Physical, and Demographic Attributes

A good deal of evidence suggests that people with similar attributes choose to date each other. Burgess and Wallin (1953) investigated the degree of similarity among engaged couples and found remarkable similarity on the following characteristics: physical attractiveness, physical health, mental health, social popularity, race, religion, parents' educational levels, parents' incomes, and the quality of parents' marriages.

At first glance, the finding of similarity between physical attractiveness appears to conflict with the findings that people's initial impressions of an attractive person are usually positive and that attractive people are usually seen as desirable romantic partners (Tesser and Brodie, 1971; Walster, Aronson, Abrahams, and Rotterman, 1966). (See chapter four.) Since not all of Burgess and Wallin's subjects could have looked like movie stars, we would expect that many of them were engaged to people who were appreciably more or less attractive than they were. These two conflicting findings can be reconciled by the fact that while people may desire physically attractive people as dates, they choose to date people who are similar in attractiveness to themselves (Berscheid, Dion, Walster, and Walster, 1971). In studies by these researchers, subjects either met or saw pictures of a number of potential dates. They chose people whose physical attractiveness was comparable to their own. Observations of dating, engaged, or married couples also show that there is a strong tendency for couples to be similar in physical attractiveness (Murstein, 1972; Murstein and Christy, 1976; Price and Vandenberg, 1979). Berscheid and her associates offered the following explanation of these findings. Although they may prefer to date someone who is attractive, people recognize (or believe) that the more attractive a person is, the more selective he or she can be in choosing dates. Therefore, people choose to date those they feel would be interested in them. People match

---

*Heterosexual romantic attraction is discussed because most romantic relationships are between people of the opposite sex and most of the research has focused on this type of relationship. However, the material presented could also apply to homosexual relationships.

their own characteristics with those of their potential dates. After all, what's the point in being rejected by someone who looks like a movie star?

There is also reason to believe that the more similar a man's and a woman's behaviors and interests are, the better they will get along. Ickes and Barnes (1978) observed conversations between a male and a female who had just met. They studied three kinds of couples. In the first, the man engaged in stereotypically masculine behavior and had masculine interests; the woman's behavior and interests were stereotypically feminine. There was very little in common between their sex-typed behavior and interests. In the second kind of couple, one of the people was **androgynous.** The third kind of couple contained two androgynous people. At the conclusion of the conversation, the members of each couple indicated how much they liked one another. The couples with two sex-typed people spoke less often, looked at one another less often, and liked one another less than did either of the other two kinds of couples. (See figure 6-6.) To quote Ickes and Barnes:

> There was considerable evidence . . . of greater interpersonal incompatibility and stress in the dyads [couples] comprised of a masculine sex-typed male and a feminine sex-typed female than in dyads in which one or both members were androgynous. (1978, p. 680)

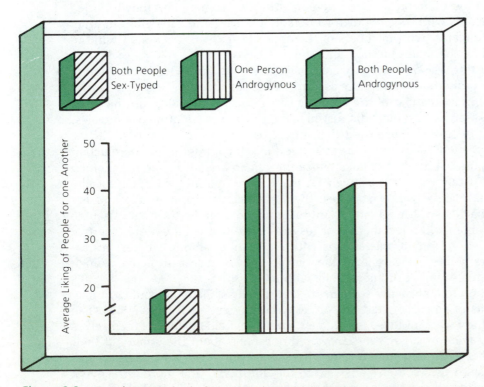

Figure 6-6.   *Couples comprised of two sex-typed people liked one another the least.*
Source: Ickes and Barnes (1978).

Research Highlight

The Social Lives of Attractive and Unattractive People

Many studies have found a positive bias toward physically attractive people. They are seen as brighter, as more competent, and as better dates. But most of these studies investigated only initial impressions of attractive and unattractive people. Are attractive people also favored in day-to-day interactions with others?

A recent study by Harry Reis and his associates (Reis, Wheeler, Spiegel, Kernis, Nezlk, and Perri, 1982) attempted to answer this question. Their subjects were 43 male and 53 female seniors at a northeastern university. Each subject was rated by a panel of judges on his or her physical attractiveness. The students kept a daily record of both the quantity and the quality of their social activities for about two weeks. They also filled out questionnaires concerned with things such as their self-esteem, assertiveness in social situations, and fear of rejection.

Reis and his colleagues' findings in the daily records of their subjects' social lives are interesting and, in some instances, a little surprising. Compared to unattractive males, attractive males spent more time with females and less time with males, interacted with a greater number of different females, had more interactions with females, and spent longer interacting with females. Attractive males were more likely to initiate an interaction with a woman and felt that there was a greater level of intimacy and self-disclosure during their interactions.

No such relationship was found between the women's physical attractiveness and the quantity or quality of their social interactions. Attractive women were less likely to initiate a social interaction than were unattractive women, and they reported that their interactions with other women were more pleasant and satisfying. In other words, social popularity with members of the opposite sex was associated with attractiveness among the males but not among the females.

Other interesting sex differences were obtained on the questionnaires. Among males, attractive individuals were more assertive in social situations and less fearful of being rejected by a member of the opposite sex. Attractive females, on the other hand, were less assertive and more distrustful of men than were unattractive females.

Reis and his colleagues suggested that attractive men are more socially active than less-attractive men because they are assertive and self-confident and not reluctant to meet women and ask them for dates. Since these men are attractive, the women they ask out are likely to react positively. Attractive women are not more socially active than less-attractive women because they are relatively unassertive and are unlikely to approach men. Men are reluctant to approach them because they assume that attractive women will reject them. The less-attractive women are more assertive and are more likely to initiate interactions with men. Thus, among women, attractiveness and assertiveness cancel one another out; attractive and less-attractive women have about an equal number of interactions with men.

The assumption that attractive women are less socially skilled and confident may explain the results of an earlier study reported by Berscheid and Walster (1972). The subjects in this study were middle-aged women. They provided pictures of themselves taken when they were in college and answered questions about the quality of their present lives. The pictures were rated for physical attractiveness and those ratings were correlated with the women's answers to the questions. The more attractive a woman had been in college, the less satisfied, happy, and well adjusted she was 25 years later. Reis and his associates suggested that these women may have problems because when they were younger, people reacted primarily to their physical appearance. With age, their beauty faded and they possessed few of the social skills that would make their lives enjoyable.

Matching Based on People's Assets

The second kind of matching is somewhat more complex. Specific assets vary from person to person, and sometimes people pick as dates individuals whose assets are different from their own but are of comparable value. The matching concept proposes that someone who is physically unattractive but wealthy, may well become involved with someone who is physically attractive but poor. While these people differ in certain specific attributes, there is a match, or equality, in the value of their overall assets. Berscheid, Walster, and Bohrnstadt (1973) conducted interviews with 2000 men and women who were involved in an ongoing romantic relationship. First the subjects were divided into three groups: those who thought they were much more attractive than their partners; those who thought they were equal to their partners; and those who thought they were less attractive than their partners. Then the researchers obtained information about the attributes of the partners. In accord with the matching concept, the more attractive people were relative to their partners, the wealthier, the more loving, and the more self-sacrificing the partners were. These data show that beauty is an asset used to attract other people with the same asset or to attract other people with different but equally desirable assets.

Passionate Love and Liking

Of all the emotions humans experience, probably none interests people more than love. If you go to the movies, listen to records, or read novels, you are constantly exposed to people's views of love. Some successful publishing companies put out nothing but romance novels. If it weren't for love (especially unrequited love), country and western singers would have little to sing about. But what is love? What causes us to fall in love with someone? Or as Frankie Lymon and the Teenagers put it some 30 years ago: "Hey, dum whap ah, dum whap ah, dum whap ah. Ooh wah, ooh wah, oo-h wah, ooh wah. Why do fools fa-ll in love?" These are not easy questions to answer.

There are essentially two positions on the nature of love. One is that love is merely an intense form of liking. Although friends and lovers act quite differently, the causes of love are the same as the causes of liking (Kenrick, Cialdini, and Linder, 1979; Rubin, 1973). The other position is that there are different kinds of love and that one kind is both qualitatively and quantitatively different from liking. Walster and Walster (1978) called this romantic, or passionate, love.

Companionate love: a friendly affection for and deep attachment to someone.

Rubin (1970) developed a scale that measures *passionate love*, but it is quite difficult to give a precise and concise definition of the concept. Walster and Walster distinguished it from **companionate love,** which is similar to liking. They defined passionate love as

> a wildly emotional state, a confusion of feelings: tenderness and sexuality, elation and pain, anxiety and relief, altruism and jealousy. (1978, p. 2)

Think back to how you felt the first time you were in love. Compare how you acted and what you felt to the actions and feeling of your grandparents. Unless you have very unusual grandparents, their love is of the companionate variety, while yours was passionate and romantic. This does not mean that your grandparents do not love one another. It means that your first love was not at all like a friendship, but their love is.

Berscheid and Walster (1974) proposed several differences between passionate love and friendship. Liking, or friendship, depends on actual rewards, but passionate love often depends on rewards that are the product of fantasy and imagination. Friendships increase over time, passionate love decreases. A number of researchers (for example, Huston, 1983) have reported that as the number of years a couple is married increases, their level of passionate love decreases. Also, friendships are consistently associated with positive feelings, while passionate love is associated with both positive and negative feelings. In fact, research suggests that negative feelings might increase a person's passion. One example of this is provided by research on how parental interference can affect love.

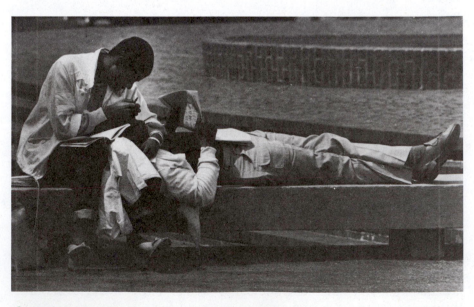

Some theorists argue that love relationships, such as this one, are quantitatively and qualitatively different from liking relationships.

Parental Interference

One long-running play on Broadway was *Fantastiks*. It is a musical fantasy about two friends' desire that their son and daughter marry. To facilitate this romance, the friends pretend they detest one another, and go so far as to build a wall between their homes. They believe that making their children think they disapprove will drive them into one another's arms. Their plan ultimately works. But what about real life? Driscoll, Davis, and Lipitz (1972) found that the more parents disapproved, the more intense was the love a couple felt for one another and that as parental disapproval decreased, so did the love. Driscoll and his associates used the concept of reactance to explain this. According to Brehm (1966), people value their freedom of choice. If someone attempts to restrict their freedom, they will react negatively and desire the person or object they have chosen even more. So, if your parents tell you that Mr. or Ms. Right looks like a junkie and you must never see him or her again, you may desire that person all the more.

Arousal and Sexual Attraction

Another source of support for the argument that passionate love and liking are different phenomena comes from research on arousal and sexual attraction. An integral part of passionate love is sexual attraction. Unlike liking, sexual attraction seems to be increased by arousal. The experiment presented in the prologue was not the only study to find this.

White, Fishbein, and Rutstein (1981) looked at how **excitation transfer** (Zillman, 1971) might affect sexual attraction. The theory of excitation transfer is quite similar to Schachter's two-factor theory of emotion. It proposes that if people are physiologically aroused by some stimulus, their arousal continues after the stimulus stops. It also suggests that people are not generally aware that they are still aroused. If a new stimulus is presented and it could be a reasonable source of their arousal, they may attribute their feelings to the second stimulus. Thus, they may transfer the cause of their excitement from the first to the second stimulus. If this second stimulus is a reasonable love object, people might label their feelings as love. Note the qualifier—is a reasonable love object. The theory does not propose that the arousal will be attributed to just anyone.

To test this proposal, White and his associates randomly assigned male subjects to two groups. Subjects in the first group were aroused by two minutes of running in place. Subjects in the second group ran in place for 15 seconds. Then both groups rested for 15 minutes. (Fifteen minutes after strenuous exercise, people feel unaroused, but in fact still are.) Half the subjects in each group were then shown a videotape of an attractive woman, while the other half were shown a videotape of an unattractive woman. Finally, all the men filled out a scale that measured their romantic attraction toward the women. (See figure 6-7 for the results.)

The continuing arousal from strenuous exercise increased romantic attraction toward the attractive woman, but decreased romantic attraction toward the unattractive woman. The subjects labeled their arousal as romantic attraction only when this was a reasonable self-attribution.

Excitation transfer: the process by which the arousal caused by one stimulus is attributed to or transferred to another subsequent stimulus.

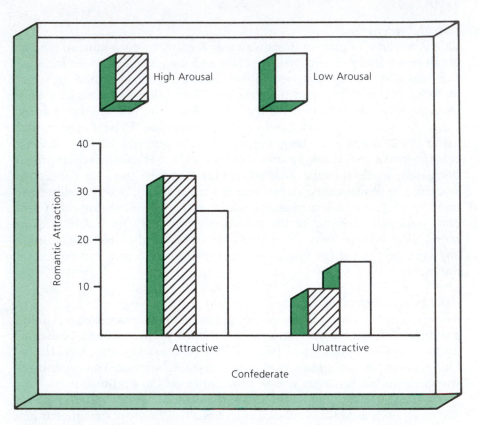

Figure 6-7. *When subjects were confronted with an attractive confederate, arousal increased romantic attraction; when subjects were confronted with an unattractive confederate, arousal decreased romantic attraction.*
Source: White et al. (1981).

The results of the experiment in the prologue, Dutton and Aron's study, indicated that arousal with a much less ambiguous origin can increase sexual attraction. The arousal of the men on the suspension bridge was clearly due to a negative experience, and it occurred simultaneously with the meeting of an attractive woman. Despite this, the men showed increased sexual arousal. In a subsequent laboratory study, Dutton and Aron showed the same effect for males who expected to receive an electric shock.

The finding that arousal—even arousal caused by fear—often increases romantic or sexual attraction led many researchers to agree with Berscheid and Walster's proposal that passionate love is a unique process. Negative experiences and arousal do not lead to liking.

Although many researchers accepted this argument, many did not. Among the dissenters were Douglas Kenrick and Robert Cialdini (1977). They proposed an alternative explanation of Dutton and Aron's results, based on Schachter's (1959) two-factor theory of emotions and on the reinforcement affect model of interpersonal attraction (Clore and Byrne, 1974). According to Schachter, frightened people desire the company of others because other people reduce their fear. According to Clore and Byrne, we like people who are associated with either positive reinforcers or reduced levels of negative reinforcers. Thus, the men in the high-fear condition may have been more attracted to the woman not because they mislabeled their arousal, but because they associated her with the reduction of their fear.

Subsequent research tended to support the fear-reduction explanation (Kenrick, Cialdini, and Linder, 1979; Kenrick and Johnson, 1979; Riordan and Tedeschi, 1983). Riordan and Tedeschi created arousal by threatening men with electric shock. While the men were still aroused they met a confederate's posing as another subject. The subjects' level of arousal, explanations for the arousal, and attraction to the confederate were measured. The men did not attribute their arousal to the confederate. Rather, the confederate's presence had the effect of reducing the perceived unpleasantness of the threatened shock and calming the men down. Also, the men were most attracted to the confederate who was most effective in reducing their fear—even if that confederate was a man!

The following conclusions about passionate love seem appropriate. It is probably true, as Berscheid and Walster (1974) have proposed, that arousal plays an important role in passionate love. When a person is aroused by some pleasant event that can be associated with a love object, romantic feelings are likely to occur. Also, if it is reasonable to do so, unexplained arousal will be labeled as romantic attraction. But (and this is a big but), people do not totally ignore the sources of their arousal. The men on the shaky bridge in Dutton and Aron's study were probably attracted to the woman because she served to reduce their fear. Finally, the reinforcement affect model may apply to passionate as well as companionate love and liking. While this suggests that passionate love and liking have much in common, it would be wrong to conclude they are the same. Anyone who has ever fallen in love knows that they are not. The point is that many of the same things that lead to liking lead to love, and perhaps love is not so mysterious after all.

Topic Background

Love and Marriage: The Latest Fad?

In this last part of the twentieth century, most of us would disapprove of two people getting married without loving one another. It may come as a surprise to learn that love as the basis for marriage is a relatively recent invention of western society. It is no more than 200 years old (Murstein, 1974b). What follows is a brief history of love and marriage. If you are interested in a more detailed discussion of this topic, you can find it in Murstein's book, *Love, Sex and Marriage through the Ages.*

In ancient Greece, love in marriage was virtually unknown, and any man who proclaimed that he loved his wife would probably have been seen as somewhat of a fool. Women were uneducated and considered inferior to men. Since love usually begins with friendship and the only reasonable friend for an educated Greek male was another male, love often bloomed between men. The only reason for taking a wife, the Greeks thought, was to have someone who would do the household chores and bear children.

Until the late Middle Ages, most marriages were arranged by the couple's parents. Indeed, children were often not even consulted about an impending marriage. Epton (1959) tells the story of a French nobleman, who was asked by his son if it was true that he (the son) was going to marry a certain woman. The father replied, "Son, mind your own business." In the sixteenth century, the Catholic Church ruled that marriages must be between mutually consenting adults, but it was still believed that these adults' parents should decide whom they should marry. Martin Luther believed that while parents should not compel their children to marry someone, they certainly had the right to forbid their children to marry anyone the parents did not like (Murstein, 1974b). Since the parents controlled the children's finances, their will was easily enforced.

During the seventeenth and eighteenth centuries, the role of parents in marital choice diminished somewhat, but the role of love did not increase appreciably. Marriage was to be based on cold, hard reason, and love as a basis for marriage was frowned upon. In an early eighteenth-century book on marriage, Mary Astell wrote that a marriage based on love was "govern'd by irregular appetites" (cited by Murstein, 1974b). In *Gulliver's Travels*, Jonathan Swift praised a race visited by Gulliver because its people married purely for rational reasons—and the major (perhaps only) rational reason was procreation. Daniel Defoe, the author of *Robinson Crusoe*, believed that if a woman who was unable to bear children married, she was a lecher (Epton, 1959). John Locke, a noted eighteenth-century social philosopher, believed that once children had been born and raised, there was little reason to continue a marriage.

Our ancestors did fall in love, but the nature of most love relationships was quite different than it is today. Between 1000 and 1300 A.D., something called courtly love emerged. "Courtly love had little to do with marriage and probably not much to do with overt sexual behavior" (Hendrick and Hendrick, 1983, p. 94). A young man would be smitten by a fair lady, who was usually already married. He would then engage in a prolonged courtship to win the lady's favor. This favor might be a caress or a smile, and only infrequently did it involve actual intercourse. Consider a German nobleman, Ulrich von Lichtenstein. For many years he courted a married princess. To win her favor, he cut off one of his fingers and sent it to her in a velvet case, had his harelip corrected, let her pull out a handful of his hair, and participated in several hundred jousting tournaments in her honor. After 15 years, the princess finally relented and spent a few minutes alone with Ulrich. They parted company soon thereafter. Ulrich's goal was not a life-long relationship—he was married and had several children—but to demonstrate his love for the princess.

According to Murstein, courtly love was the precursor to romantic love. By the early nineteenth century, novels and plays about romantic love were quite popular. This led young people to begin to associate love with sexual relations and marriage. Parents attempted to maintain control over whom their children married by changing their own views dramatically. Where they had once argued that love was a poor reason for sex and an even worse reason for marriage, they now argued that love and sex were only appropriate between a married couple. As time passed, young adults became freer to choose their mates, and usually chose someone they loved. Today, sex without marriage is condoned and most people believe that love is the only reason for marriage.

One last bit of history about marriage. Giovanni Vigliotto holds the world's record for marriages. In the past 33 years, he has married 105 different women. Unfortunately, he only divorced two or three of them. Mr. Vigliotto was tried for bigamy and fraud (*Newsweek*, 1983). One wonders what Ulrich von Lichtenstein would have thought of him.

Marriage

In most instances, people who have a long-term romantic relationship will marry. Despite what you might have read, marriage is still a thriving institution. While the number of unmarried couples living together has tripled in the last decade, this arrangement is chosen by less than 5 percent of all cohabiting couples in the United States (Spanier, 1983).

The questions of how and why humans select a mate have long intrigued social scientists. Emile Durkheim proposed a theory of mate selection over 100 years ago, and the early Freudian theorists gave considerable attention to this phenomenon. Some Freudians (for example, Hamilton and MacGowan, 1929) proposed that marital choice is often due to an unresolved Oedipus complex; men marry women who physically resemble their mothers. There is, however, no evidence to support this idea. The contemporary theories of marital choice presented below tend to focus on the same kind of variables presented in the discussion of friendship and romantic attraction.

Homogamy

Durkeim (1893) proposed the concept of **homogamy** to explain marital choice. The idea that we marry people similar to us is quite old and still widely accepted. Assuming that people who live in the same area share a good deal in common, some findings support homogamy as a major influence on marital choice. Koller (1962) found that among unskilled American workers, the median distance between the premarital residences of married couples was five blocks. In a more recent study, Ineichen (1979) looked at the characteristics of 232 couples who had married over a two-year period. Almost 65 percent of these couples lived in the same city before their marriage, and most of these lived in the same area or in adjacent areas of the city.

Other studies suggest that there may be more to choosing a spouse than just homogamy. These studies have looked at the correlations between the attitudes, interests, and personality characteristics of married couples. Typically, these correlations are positive (indicating homogamy) but small

Homogamy: the proposal that people will marry someone who is quite similar to them.

According to Winch's theory of mate selection, people choose mates whose characteristics complement their own.

(Nias, 1979). Nias administered scales that measured personality characteristics and interests to 586 couples. He found an average correlation of .12 between a couple's personality characteristics and a correlation of .10 between their interests. Thus, homogamy can only partially explain why we select a certain mate.

Complementarity

Complementarity theory: the theory that people are attracted to and marry individuals whose needs complement their own.

In 1958, Robert Winch proposed the **complementarity theory** of mate selection. This theory differs dramatically from the theories of interpersonal attraction, which stated that attraction is based on similarity. Winch suggested that attraction is based on need satisfaction; thus, we do not desire people who possess the same needs as we do, but people whose needs complement ours. Complementarity can be achieved in two ways. First, a couple's needs can vary in degree. Someone who is dominant, for example, would be attracted to someone who has little need to dominate others. Second, a couple's needs may differ in kind. For example, someone who has a need to care for people would be attracted to someone who has a need to be cared for. In a more extreme example, a masochist would be attracted to a sadist. If Winch was correct, then research should find a negative correlation between the personality characteristics of married couples. Further, these negative correlations should be found most often among happily married couples. Note that this correlation should be negative, not merely small, it should show that people select opposites as mates.

Winch (1954) claimed to have found results that supported his theory. However, subsequent, independent studies have not (for example, Levinger, Senn, and Jorgenson, 1970). Cattell and Nesselroade (1967) examined the correlations between the personality characteristics of couples who were happily married and of couples who were unhappily married. It was only among the unhappily married couples that negative correlations were found. Thus, need complementarity may lead to marital distress rather than marital harmony.

Stimulus-Value-Role Theory

The *stimulus-value-role theory* of mate selection (Murstein, 1976) proposes that there are three stages in the development of an intimate relationship such as marriage. The first is the *stimulus stage,* which is almost equivalent to the stage of *unilateral awareness* discussed earlier. For example, Quentin sees Elaine at a party. His reaction to her is based on her physical appearance, her demeanor, and what he can learn about her from others. If he does not like Elaine's looks or he learns she is a snob, the relationship will end there. But if Quentin likes what he sees and hears, the relationship moves into the *value stage.* The couple begins to date, assuming that Elaine likes what she sees and learns about Quentin. During the value stage, the couple learns about one another's attitudes and values. If these are similar, the relationship will progress. If they are dissimilar, the relationship is in trouble. Finally, if the relationship has survived the first two stages, it moves into the *role stage.* (Recall that a role is a behavior displayed by someone who occupies a certain position.) At this stage, the question is whether the role behaviors of the two people are compatible. Quentin must decide if the behavior displayed by Elaine is the type he desires in a mate. If Quentin wants a woman who doesn't work outside the home, has a child every ten months, and is only slightly more assertive than the family cat, but Elaine has a career, practices birth control, and demands to be treated as an equal, he will not marry Elaine. Elaine will probably not be thrilled with Quentin either, and would probably not desire him as a mate.

Although Murstein (1974a) has shown that couples do display role compatibility, no data show that intimate relationships develop in the manner his theory proposes. We simply do not know if couples go through the stages in the sequence proposed by Murstein. Murstein's theory may well be valid, but at this point it has not been fully tested.

Exchange Theory

The final explanation of marital choice is based on an **exchange theory** view of social behavior. This theory proposes that even an intimate relationship like marriage can be conceptualized as a business transaction in which the people involved make an investment and expect a reasonable return (Hatfield, Utne, and Traupmann, 1979; Levinger, 1979). This leads to the prediction that people choose a mate they believe will provide them with something in return. The "investment" can be something on which you cannot put a price tag, such as a sense of humor, love, devotion, or comfort giving.

One specific exchange theory used to explain mate selection is **equity theory** (Berscheid and Walster, 1978; Hatfield et al., 1979). (See also chapter twelve.) People desire to be in a relationship where the ratio of what each person puts in to it to what each person gets out is the same for both parties. If these ratios are not equal, the couple will experience distress. This is true whether they are getting too much or too little.

No study has ever specifically shown that people choose their mates on the basis of equity considerations, but considerable evidence suggests that equity (or the lack thereof) affects the stability of a romantic relationship and people's satisfaction with it. Berscheid and Walster (1978) interviewed over 500 people who were dating one person regularly. These people estimated what they and their partners contributed to the relationship (their inputs) and what each got out of it (their outputs). This provided a measure of perceived equity. Three months later the subjects were again interviewed. People who had seen their relationship as an equitable one were much more likely to still be together and had more optimistic estimates for the future of the relationship. Another study (Hatfield et al., 1979) investigated the effects of equity among newlyweds (couples married eight months or less). Subjects who thought the relationship was equitable felt more positive about it, were happier, and were more satisfied with their marriage than were those who felt the relationship was inequitable. This was true whether the inequity was due to the person getting too much or too little from the marriage.

And finally, some studies (for example, Hill, Rubin, and Peplau, 1976; Levinger, 1979) have found that the primary reason long-term relationships end is that the partners feel they are not getting a sufficient "return" on the investments they have made in the relationship. Since people are unlikely to marry someone with whom they have an unstable, unhappy, and "unprofitable" relationship, it would seem that exchange theory may offer a reasonable explanation of marital choice. However, marital choice is a very complex social phenomenon, and it may defy any one simple, concise explanation. The romantic in me thinks that maybe this is not so bad.

Equity theory: the theory that people expect to receive outcomes from interactions with others which are in keeping with their contributions.

SUMMARY

In contemporary western society, romantic attraction most commonly begins with a dating relationship. People usually choose to date individuals whose personal attributes match their own or whose attributes, while perhaps different from theirs, are of equal value. For example, a woman who has the asset of wealth will date a man who has the asset of physical attractiveness.

Another aspect of romantic attraction is love. Some theorists believe there are two major kinds of love, passionate and companionate. Companionate love is seen as an intense form of liking that is directed at a single person; passionate love is seen as differing in degree and kind from liking. The argument that passionate love and liking are different phenomena is based on findings showing that negative experiences and general arousal can lead to sexual attraction, a major component of passionate love. Other theorists argue that liking and loving are not all that different; that liking and sexual attraction can both be the result of someone providing a person with relief from negative stimuli. The most recent research suggests that both views of love have some merit.

The final stage of many romantic relationships is marriage. There are several different theories of mate selection. One is homogamy, which suggests that similar people are attracted to one another. Another is complementarity, which suggests that people marry individuals whose needs complement their own. Still another, the stimulus-value-role theory, proposes that before people marry, their relationship must survive a series of stages. The first stage involves their initial impressions of one another; the second stage involves the similarity of their values; and the final stage involves the compatibility of their behaviors or roles. And finally, the exchange theory proposes that marriage is akin to a business transaction. Thus, mate selection and marital success depend upon each person obtaining a fair and satisfactory amount of rewards from the relationship.

Applications

Sexual Attitudes and Behavior

According to most observers of contemporary society, there has been a "sexual revolution" in the last 15 to 20 years. Dramatic changes have occurred in people's attitudes about sex and sexual behavior. Perhaps the clearest evidence of this revolution can be found in college classrooms. Twenty years ago, the only courses that dealt with sexual behavior were in departments of biology or zoology, and these courses usually concerned such wildly erotic topics as the sex life of swamp frogs. With the exception of the landmark work of Alfred Kinsey and his associates (Kinsey, Pomeroy, and Martin, 1948; Kinsey, Pomeroy, Martin, and Gebhard, 1953), little research had been done on human sexuality and no textbooks had been written on the topic. How different things are today. A large number of human sexuality courses are taught, many researchers focus on this topic, and at least 15 textbooks have the term *human sexuality* in their titles. It is—no pun intended—a hot topic. While some might argue that the academics brought human sexuality "out of the closet," it is more likely that the explosion in research and books on sexual behavior is largely a response to changes in societal norms and mores.

This section first examines the changes in attitudes that brought about the sexual revolution. It then discusses sexual attraction and arousal. Finally, it focuses on sex in romantic relationships.

THE SEXUAL REVOLUTION

For various reasons, Americans' attitudes about sexual behavior became decidedly more liberal in the 1970s, and this trend has continued in the 1980s. Masturbation had long been viewed as an unnatural and unhealthy act. But by the early 1970s, only 8 percent of the men and women interviewed in a national survey thought it was wrong (Hunt, 1974). As late as 1959, only 22 percent of people in the United States approved of premarital sex. By 1972, 80 percent of males and 70 percent of females interviewed in a national survey believed that it was all right for someone who was in love to engage in sexual intercourse before marriage. Between 1964 and 1974, the percentage of people who disapproved of premarital sexual relations dropped by 20 percent (Hunt, 1974).

Attitudes about different kinds of sexual activities also appear to have changed. Until the 1960s, oral sex was rarely even discussed in marriage manuals and other "legitimate" books about sex. By 1972, over 75 percent of the people interviewed by Hunt saw nothing wrong with either a man or a woman engaging in oral sex. Less than 30 percent of the people Hunt interviewed believed that anal intercourse was wrong (Hunt, 1974). Exchanging mates was viewed as an acceptable practice by approximately 30 percent of the men and 20 percent of the women interviewed in Hunt's survey.

With such a dramatic change in attitudes, we would expect that people's behavior has changed as well—and the evidence suggests that it has. In 1950, less than 70 percent of unmarried males and 30 percent of unmarried females had experienced intercourse by the age of 25 (Kinsey et al. 1953). In 1972, 97 percent of unmarried males and 81 percent of unmarried females reported that they had had intercourse by the time they were 25 (Hunt, 1974). Mahoney (1983) estimated that today there is virtually no difference between the sexes in the incidence of premarital intercourse. People's preferences for various forms of sexual activities have changed as well. The number of married couples who engaged in oral sex increased by a third between 1950 and 1970 (Hunt, 1974). Mahoney (1983) reported that oral sex among college students was virtually nonexistent in 1950, but a 1978 survey of sexually experienced college students disclosed that almost 65 percent of them had engaged in oral sex. This was true of both men and women.

These data might suggest to some that our society is headed into a pit of sexual degeneracy. But many of the values your parents and grandparents held about sex are still in force today. There has been no increase in the incidence of bestiality (intercourse with animals) or of sadomasochistic relationships (Hunt, 1974). Although a great deal has been written about "spouse swapping," less than 4 percent of couples have engaged in this practice. Most college students still disapprove of casual sex (Mahoney, 1983). And, for better or for worse, the double standard about virginity in males and females still holds. Janda, O'Grady, and Barnhart (1981) reported that both males and females view sexually liberated females (women who have sex with anyone they really like) very negatively. Also, virgin males prefer a virgin female as a marriage partner (Istvan and Griffitt, 1980).

So, the sexual revolution must be placed in context. There have been similar revolutions in the past (Smith and Hindus, 1975). Americans in the 1980s are more "enlightened" and liberal in their sexual attitudes and behavior than Americans in past eras, but the United States has not become a nation of libertines. The current revolution seems to be limited to what is considered appropriate behavior in a hetereosexual romantic relationship. Attitudes about premarital sex and what is "natural" or "normal" sexual activity have certainly changed, but even the liberated college students of today believe that love and caring are important components of a sexual relationship. At the same time, it does appear that societal norms about the role of sex in a relationship have changed dramatically.

THE SOCIAL PSYCHOLOGY OF SEXUAL ATTRACTION AND AROUSAL

When humans engage in sexual intercourse, their physiological responses are not very different from those of animals. But unlike most animals, humans' choices of with whom they will have sex and their feelings during the sex act are strongly influenced by social psychological variables, including attraction and arousal.

Sexual Attraction

Among animals, sexual attraction is more or less determined by who is available and interested. Male dogs, for example, are not terribly selective about which females they have as sex partners. Humans, however, are more selective—what turns one person on may turn another off. Different cultural and individual learning experiences may result in these different tastes. For example, in American culture most men do not find obese women sexually arousing, but in the old Hawaiian culture obese women were considered quite erotic (Mahoney, 1983). The classical conditioning, instrumental conditioning, and observational learning that are part of the socialization experience play a role in sexual attraction. At the same time, there are certain constants across members of the same culture.

One constant is physical attractiveness. In general, we are more sexually aroused by a physically attractive person than by a physically unattractive person (Mathes and Edwards, 1978). Thus, just as we would prefer to date attractive people, we find them sexually appealing. People also find different parts of the body sexually arousing. For example, American women find a man's chest more sexually stimulating than his buttocks, legs, or penis. Men are most stimulated by the size of a woman's breasts (Wildman, Wildman, Brown, and Trice, 1976). However, a large bust size is not an unmitigated blessing for a woman. While men are aroused by large breasts, they also believe that a woman who possesses this characteristic is less competent, less intelligent, and less moral than a woman with small breasts (Collins, 1981). Another physical attribute that affects sexual attraction is the manner in which a person dresses. Women, especially, are aware of this. In a study by Tavris and Sadd (1977), 66 percent of the women interviewed said they wore sexy or suggestive clothing as a means of sexually arousing men.

These findings can be contrasted to the findings on forming friendships and choosing dates. It is quite reasonable that we should like people who hold similar attitudes to our own or who reciprocate our actions toward them. This makes for a smoother, more positive relationship. The matching process that influences dating choices also appears to be a rather logical decision rule. But why should we find people with well-developed chests (both male and female) more sexually appealing than people without this characteristic? It is hard to see why sex with someone who is built like Arnold Schwarzenegger would be any more physiologically satisfying than someone with the physique of, say, Woody Allen. These preferences probably reflect cultural stereotypes about what is sexy. This would suggest that it may be more difficult to rationally explain sexual attraction than friendship or mate selection.

Sexual Arousal

There is little question that the sex act itself is physiologically arousing. Masters and Johnson (1966) have clearly identified the kinds of physiological arousal that occur during sexual intercourse (coitus). But now consider another possibility. Perhaps physiological arousal is a cause, as well as a consequence, of sexual activity. This idea should sound familiar because it is based in part on the results of the experiment in the prologue. Recall that in some instances, feelings of passion may result from the mislabeling of general arousal. Since sex is usually an integral part of a passionate relationship, it would seem reasonable to investigate whether sexual arousal can be induced in the same manner as passionate love (Rook and Hammen, 1977).

The logic behind this proposal is as follows. In the early stages of the sexual response cycle, people's physiological responses are nonspecific and similar to those found in other emotions. Physiological arousal, which is due to nonerotic stimuli, may in certain instances be labeled as sexual arousal. A study by Cantor, Zillman, and Bryant (1975) demonstrated this. One group of males engaged in five minutes of strenuous exercise, while another did not. After several minutes had passed, both groups of men were shown photographs from magazines such as *Playboy* or *Penthouse*, and their levels of sexual arousal were measured. The exercise group displayed significantly more sexual arousal. The explanation of this finding is the same as that proposed in the studies of a romantic attraction. The men who had exercised were still aroused but were not aware of this. They labeled some of their arousal as sexual arousal in response to the erotic stimuli. Other studies (for example, Rovario and Holmes, 1980; Wolchik, Beggs, Wincze, Sakheim, Barlow, and Mavissakalian, 1980) have found that even arousal caused by distressing or frightening stimuli can be labeled as sexual arousal.

A more recent study (McCarty, Diamond, and Kaye, 1982) provides another illustration of how Schachter's two-factor theory of emotion may apply to sexual arousal. Subjects were given vodka to drink, but told that it was tonic water. Then they were shown erotic photographs. These subjects reported significantly more sexual arousal than did those who actually drank tonic water or those who were aware they were drinking vodka. The explanation of this was that the subjects who were misinformed as to what they were drinking labeled the effects of the vodka as sexual arousal in reponse to the erotic stimuli.

One interesting implication of these findings concerns the effects of aphrodisiacs—substances that are supposed to increase a person's sexual power and pleasure. Many people believe that some illegal "recreational" drugs such as amyl nitrate, cocaine, and marijuana enhance lovemaking. In fact, none of these drugs have any effect on responsiveness of the genital organs or sex centers in the brain (Hollister, 1975). Indeed, no true aphrodisiacs have been found, but people continue to believe that certain chemical substances enhance their sexual pleasure. Rook and Hammen (1977) suggested that these drugs may create physiological changes which people label as sexual arousal. Thus, aphrodisiacs may increase sexual pleasure, but only because of how people label their effects.

SEX IN ROMANTIC RELATIONSHIPS

Sexual activities are a necessary component of any romantic relationship. One comprehensive study of sexual practices among people involved in a romantic relationship was carried out by Peplau, Rubin, and Hill (1977). They conducted a two-year-long study of over 200 dating couples in the Boston area. The research addressed two major questions: Is it the man or the woman who determines the nature of a couple's sexual activities? and What is the relationship among dating couples between emotional and sexual intimacy?

To answer the first question, the couples were divided into three groups—those who had abstained from coitus, those who had engaged in coitus within the first month of their relationship, and those who had engaged in coitus after one month. Then the characteristics of the men and women in the three groups were compared. There were virtually no differences between the men in the abstaining group and the men in the coitus groups. However, women who abstained from coitus with their partner differed from those who did not in the following ways: (1) they were more likely to be Catholic than to be Jewish or Protestant; (2) they more strongly endorsed traditional sex roles for men and women; (3) they were more likely to pursue traditionally feminine careers, such as nursing or education; and (4) they were more likely to prefer a traditional lifestyle over an "alternative" one.

When the couples who had engaged in early intercourse were compared to those who had engaged in late intercourse, the men in the two groups again did not differ, but the women did. Early-and late-coitus women differed in the same four ways as those who had abstained differed from those who had not. In addition, the early-coitus women were more likely to be nonvirgins when they entered the relationship, and they rated themselves as more creative, more desirable as a date, more intelligent, and more self-confident. In summary, the woman decided if a couple was going to have coitus and when in the relationship this would occur.

Both the relatedness and the social penetration models of relationship development presented in the chapter would predict that emotional intimacy should precede sexual intimacy. Peplau and her associates' data do not totally support this, since over 40 percent of the couples reported having coitus within 30 days of the time they started dating. Is it possible that these couples were able to achieve emotional intimacy very quickly? Probably not. According to Peplau and her colleagues, the early-coitus couples comprised people who believed that "while sex with love is desirable, sex without love is also acceptable" (1977, p. 98).

Early-and late-coitus couples appeared to have differed in their feelings about the relationship between emotional and sexual intimacy. (See table 6-2 for some of these differences.) The late-coitus couples were more likely

Table 6-2. *All ratings were made on nine-point scale.*

	Early Coitus	Late Coitus
How much they loved one another	6.80	7.35
How well they knew one another	7.30	7.75
How close they felt to one another	7.55	8.10
Likelihood they would marry	4.10	6.10

Source: Peplau et al. (1977).

to report they loved their partner, felt close to one another, and knew their partner well. Evidently, among the late-coitus couples, emotional intimacy preceded sexual intimacy.

Do men and women differ in the importance they place on emotional intimacy as a precursor to sex? Given the traditional differences in the ways males and females are socialized about sex, we would expect they do, and the available data support this expectation. Simon and Gagnon (1977) found that men reported having intercourse one to three times with their first sexual partner; women reported on average of ten or more times. This suggests that a man's first sexual experience may be part of a casual relationship, but a woman's still will be part of a stable, ongoing relationship. Mahoney (1979) provided data that show this more clearly. Male and female college students were asked to describe the nature of their relationship with their most recent sexual partner. Almost 30 percent of the men said that she was at most a casual friend; less than 15 percent of the women had had a comparable sexual partner. By far the most common lover for the women was a man with whom they were in love or engaged to be married. Finally, Houston (1981) found that 55 percent of the men he interviewed identified a good sexual relationship as the most desirable thing in a date, but only 11 percent of the women felt this way. Almost 80 percent of the women, but only 14 percent of the men, thought that a good intellectual relationship was the most important part of a date. Perhaps the male view of the relationship between emotional and sexual intimacy was best summarized by Woody Allen. An interviewer once asked him what a woman had to do to have sex with him. "Show up," Allen replied.

Equity and Sex in Relationships

Another approach to the study of sex in relationships has been to investigate how feelings of equity affect a couple's sexual activities. Elaine Hatfield and her associates (Hatfield, Traupmann, and Walster, 1979; Hatfield, Walster, and Traupmann, 1979) investigated the effects of perceived fairness on couples' sexual activities. One of their studies looked at equity and the sexual activities of unmarried couples. The subjects were over 500 college students who were currently dating someone. The researchers first assessed how equitable the subjects saw their relationship as being and then asked the subjects questions about their sexual relationship with their dating partner.

The results indicated that people who saw their relationship as being basically equitable had a more active and more enjoyable sexual relationship. Couples in a relatively equitable relationship were more likely to engage in intercourse, had experienced intercourse more frequently, and had engaged in more sexual activities than those who felt they were being greatly overrewarded or underrewarded in their relationship. Also, among couples who were engaging in coitus, this was likely to be a mutual decision if equity existed. These findings are not terribly surprising. As Hatfield and her associates pointed out, inequitable love relationships are full of strife and turmoil. One partner feels cheated, the other feels guilty. As discussed in the previous section, the quality of a couple's overall relationship strongly influences their sex life.

In another study, Hatfield and her associates examined inequity as a cause of extramarital sexual affairs. The subjects were about 1,000 individuals who took part in a national survey conducted by *Psychology Today*. The results of this study were simple and straightforward.

The underbenefited people engaged in extramarital affairs sooner and more often, whether the couple had been together for a short or long period of time. One must consider the possibility that the subjects used inequity to justify their extramarital affairs. But it at least seems reasonable to conclude that perhaps these people were using extramarital sex to achieve equity in their relationships. Thus, while sex is clearly a physiological response to biological needs, it does appear that it is influenced by social psychological variables.

Chapter Seven

Aggression

Prologue

Jack E. Hokanson and Michael Burgess (1962). Effects of Three Types of Aggression on Vascular Processes. *Journal of Abnormal and Social Psychology*, **64,** 446–449.

Background

This chapter concerns why humans aggress and how aggression might be controlled or eliminated. One theory used to answer these questions is the catharsis hypothesis. First formally suggested by Freud, the catharsis hypothesis proposes that when there is a buildup of aggressive energy in a person, aggression is likely to occur; when this aggression occurs, it lowers the level of aggressive energy and, thus, reduces the likelihood of further aggression. In other words, if aggressive energy can be purged or "catharted" from people's systems, they are less likely to be aggressive. In the late 1950s, Jack Hokanson and his colleagues carried out a comprehensive research program to test certain aspects of the catharsis hypothesis in situations where people are angry or frustrated. This experiment with Michael Burgess was part of that research program.

Hypotheses

Hokanson and Burgess did not make any formal hypotheses, but they did ask two research questions: What effect would frustration have on aggressive energy? and Would aggression by frustrated people serve to lower their level of aggressive energy? The construct of aggressive energy was operationalized as physiological arousal.

Subjects

The subjects were 56 female and 24 male students at Florida State University.

Procedure

The subjects were told that the experiment concerned physiological responses during an intellectual task. Equipment that measured blood pressure and heart rate was attached to each subject, and the subjects were asked to count backward from 100 to 0 by twos (100, 98, and so on) as rapidly as they could. Half the subjects were assigned to a high-frustration condition. Following a written script, the experimenter interrupted these subjects repeatedly, criticized them for counting too slowly, made them start over three times, and finally, told the subjects that they were uncooperative and that their data were worthless. In a no-frustration condition, the experimenter did not interrupt or criticize the subjects and said "Good" when they reached 0. In the next phase of the study, both frustrated and nonfrustrated subjects were randomly assigned to one of three different conditions.* Subjects in the first condition had the chance to verbally aggress against the experimenter; they filled out a questionnaire on his ability, competence, and manner of treating the subjects. Subjects in the second condition had the chance to physically aggress against the experimenter. They thought of a number between one and ten; if the experimenter could not correctly guess it, the subjects depressed a plunger which supposedly delivered electric shock to the experimenter. (In fact, no shock was delivered; the experimenter merely behaved as if he had been shocked. This procedure is used in almost all aggression experiments.) The experimenter made ten guesses and received an average of eight shocks. Subjects in the third condition could not aggress against the experimenter. They too played the guessing game, but when they depressed the plunger it merely turned on a small light.

The dependent measures were the subject's blood pressure, measured before the counting task and every two minutes thereafter, and heart rate, measured continuously throughout the experiment.

Results

To address the first research question—What effects would frustration have on aggressive energy?—Hokanson and Burgess examined the subjects' blood pressure and heart rate at the conclusion of the counting task. Among the subjects in the high-frustration condition, there were significant increases in blood pressure and heart rate after the counting task. As predicted by the catharsis hypothesis, frustration caused physiological arousal.

To answer the second question—Would aggression by frustrated people serve to lower their aggressive energy?—Hokanson and Burgess examined the subjects' blood pressure and heart rate after the second phase of the experiment. (See figure 7-1 for blood pressure changes.) When highly frustrated subjects were able to aggress (either physically or verbally) against the source of their frustration, the experimenter, their blood pressure returned to the level it had been at the beginning of the experiment. When, however, frustrated subjects were not able to aggress, their blood pressure remained considerably higher than it had been at the beginning of the experiment. The same findings were obtained for heart rate. As predicted by the catharsis hypothesis, aggression reduced physiological arousal, or aggressive energy.

Implications

This study provides an example of how social psychologists study aggression in a laboratory. It also provides a clear-cut demonstration of how frustration, a variable studied extensively by aggression researchers, affects

---

*A fourth condition was used in this phase of the experiment. However, it is not relevant to the main purpose of this experiment; thus, it is not discussed here.

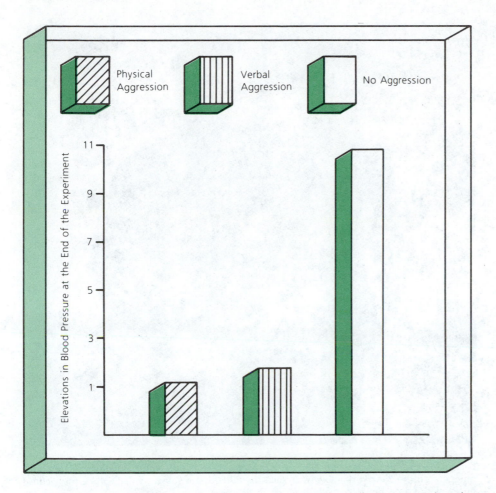

Figure 7-1. *When subjects were allowed to verbally or physically aggress against the cause of their frustration, their blood pressure returned to normal levels.*
Source: Hokanson and Burgess (1962).

people. In addition, this study was one of the first to provide what appeared to be an empirical confirmation of the catharsis hypothesis. Hokanson and his colleagues conducted further research on the catharsis hypothesis and came to the conclusion that it may not be correct. In this chapter, the theories based on the catharsis hypothesis and the evidence that led Hokanson and others to challenge it are presented.

It is impossible to avoid being aware of **aggression**; it is a fact of modern life. According to police records, in 1980, one out of every 180 Americans was the victim of a violent crime—murder, rape, robbery, or assault (United States Department of Justice 1983)—and over three million incidents of

Aggression: a behavior that is intended to cause harm or injury to another living thing.

Bernard Goetz, pictured above, became a hero to many people when he shot four alleged muggers on the New York subway. In fact, the odds that a subway rider will be the victim of a violent crime are very small.

aggravated and simple assault* were reported. While the number of other kinds of crime in the United States has declined somewhat in recent years, the incidence of violent crimes has not. For example, the number of homicides has doubled in the last ten years (United States Department of Justice, 1983).

Popular belief would attribute this violence to hardened professional criminals, but only 16 percent of all homicides are committed by someone who is unknown to the victim. Almost half of all violent assaults are committed by an acquaintance or relative of the victim (United States Department of Justice, 1983). A survey conducted by Straus, Gelles, and Steinmetz (1980) showed how pervasive violence is within the American family. Almost 30 percent of the married couples interviewed had had at least one

*An aggravated assault is a physical attack with a weapon or an attack that results in serious bodily injury. Simple assault is a physical attack that produces minor injury.

violent confrontation in the course of their marriage, and one out of 25 people reported having used a gun or a knife on their spouse! If we add the figures on domestic violence to the numbers of incidents of parents assaulting their children (or vice versa), then we can see that people have much to fear from members of their immediate families. By contrast, in the "dangerous" New York subway system, less than one in a million riders is the victim of a violent crime (Rangel, 1985). Humans are not the only species to kill one another, but they do engage in a great deal of aggression.

Aggression is not limited to physical assaults. One can be verbally aggressive. For example, telling someone that he is homely, stupid, or foul-smelling can inflict considerable harm on him. One can even display aggression by failing to do something. For example, if your roommate keeps "forgetting" to throw out the pizza that has been rotting in the corner of your room for three weeks, and you also refuse to throw it out, you both may be engaging in *passive aggression*. You are harming one another by doing nothing.

This chapter presents what social psychologists have learned about the causes of and cures for human aggression. The first section addresses the question of why human beings are predisposed to be generally aggressive. The second section examines some of the variables that produce specific acts of aggression. The third section discusses what can be done to control or reduce human aggression. The applications section applies these concepts to a specific social problem—sexual violence against women.

THEORIES OF HUMAN AGGRESSION

Given the pervasiveness of human aggression and its negative consequences, it is not surprising that many social scientists have studied aggressive behavior and attempted to explain it. The major theories explaining general aggressive tendencies in humans range from proposals that aggression is an innate, inherited aspect of human behavior to proposals that aggression is almost entirely a learned social behavior. This section presents two instinctual theories of aggression as well as social learning explanations of aggressive behaviors.

Instinctual Theories

The instinctual theories use humans' biological characteristics and genetic heritage to explain aggression. In essence, they propose that humans are "programmed" to act aggressively (Baron 1977). The best-known and most influential instinctual theories were put forth by a psychoanalyst, Sigmund Freud, and an ethologist, Konrad Lorenz.

Freud's Theory
In 1932, Albert Einstein wrote a letter to Sigmund Freud. In it he asked Freud, "Is there any way of delivering mankind from the menace of war?"

In his response to Einstein's question, Freud outlined his theory of human aggression.

The ideas expressed by Freud represented his second formal attempt to explain human aggression. The basic elements of Freud's original theory of aggression were introduced in the prologue to this chapter. Freud (1920) believed that people had an instinctive need to seek pleasure and avoid pain; anything that interfered with this need caused tension, or aggressive energy, to build up in people, and aggression represented an attempt to reduce this tension. While other theorists accepted Freud's original ideas about the causes of aggression, two things caused him to propose another explanation of it. The first was the self-destructive behaviors he and others had observed in their patients. If people were motivated only to prolong and enhance their lives (in other words, were motivated only by the life instinct), how could self-destructive behaviors such as suicide and masochism be explained? The second was the incredible destruction and carnage that characterized the First World War. The killing of 50,000 people in a single battle was not simply a response to interference with the seeking of pleasure.

Eros: Freud's life instinct; the desire to seek pleasure and avoid pain.

Thanatos: Freud's death instinct; the desire to end one's life and, thus, eliminate all stimulation.

These observations led Freud to propose that human aggression is the result of conflicts within a person. He proposed that humans are motivated by two basic instincts: **eros** and **thanatos.** In some people, thanatos manifests itself in suicidal or self-destructive behaviors; in other people, eros and thanatos are in conflict. The result of this conflict is a redirection of the death instinct away from the person and toward other people. Aggression, thus, is the result of a conflict within a person; the stronger this conflict, the more aggressive the person.

This is a pessimistic view of human aggression. Thanatos is part and parcel of the human character, resulting in either self-destruction of the person or harm and injury of those around the person. Freud felt that the manner in which people express their aggression can be modified somewhat, but that "there is no likelihood of our being able to suppress humanity's aggressive tendencies." Freud concluded his letter to Einstein with "sincere regrets . . . [that]this exposé should prove a disappointment to you" (1933; reprinted in Bramson and Goethals, 1968, pp. 77, 80).

Lorenz's Ethological Theory
Ethology is the scientific study of animal behavior in its natural environment (Stang and Wrightsman, 1981). Ethologists believe that most behaviors have their origins in instincts. Most ethologists have focused their interest on the behavior of nonhuman organisms, but one noted ethologist, Konrad Lorenz (1966), has considered human behavior as well and has sought to provide an instinctual explanation of human aggression.

Lorenz's theory, like Freud's, is based on the notion of a buildup of aggressive energy. Unlike Freud, Lorenz did not believe that aggressive energy is solely the result of interference with certain activities. Instead, he proposed that a fighting instinct has evolved in all animals and that this instinct causes aggressive energy to build up within organisms. Lorenz believed that the fighting instinct may benefit a species. For example, in many species, only male animals who possess the strongest fighting instincts are allowed to mate with fertile females. Thus, these males are the most likely to reproduce, and they pass strong fighting instincts on to their offspring. The aggressive offspring use these instincts to defeat their enemies and, thus, preserve the species. Basically, the fighting instinct produces the "survival of the fittest."

However, the fighting instinct may also present a danger to a species, especially if its members possess attributes that make them efficient killers, such as teeth and claws. If an animal directs its aggression against its own kind, a species may fight itself into extinction. Lorenz (1966) said that because of this, mechanisms have also evolved that inhibit intraspecies aggression. Baboons, for example, usually bare their teeth, make loud sounds, and assume threatening postures before they fight. In intraspecies fights, these behaviors often cause one of the baboons to back off, and the fight is avoided. If there is a fight, baboons have ways of preventing the loser from being killed. When a baboon is losing a fight, it often turns and presents its rear end to the other baboon; the stronger baboon responds by breaking off the fight and mounting the loser. (Washburn and DeVore, 1962). Similarly, a dog or wolf who is losing a fight stops and bares its neck to the stronger opponent; this submissive gesture appears to mean "I quit, you are the victor and you can kill me if you desire." The stronger opponent usually breaks off the fight and lets the loser live. Other animals engage in ritualized fighting. The combatants go through all the motions of a real fight, but no one is seriously injured or killed. The winner is usually the animal who persists longest in the ritual.

Lorenz viewed humans as the most dangerous creatures on earth. He said that humans, like all other animals, have a fighting instinct which causes a buildup of aggressive energy. Humans, however, are basically harmless creatures, they lack the natural weapons (claws, fangs, venom) that could be used to kill other members of their species. Thus, automatic aggression-inhibiting mechanisms were not needed to ensure the survival of the human species. Humans are also much more intelligent than other animals. They have used this intelligence to develop highly sophisticated weapons for killing one another and the skills to use them. A lion, for example, who weighs 130 pounds, has one bad eye, and rotting fangs will not be able to kill a 450-pound leader of the lion pride. But a 130-pound human who has one bad eye and rotting teeth would have little difficulty killing a 280-pound defensive tackle of a professional football team—if he used a .357 Magnum.

According to Lorenz, specific acts of human aggression are the result of an interaction between the amount of aggressive energy present in a person's system at a given time and certain stimuli in that person's environment. If a person has little aggressive energy, it will take a good deal of provocation to get that person to aggress. But if an individual has a great deal of aggressive energy, even the weakest provocation will result in aggression.

Lorenz made many significant contributions to ethology and received a Nobel Prize for some of his ethological research. However, his theory of aggression is not accepted by most social scientists. Many researchers have seriously questioned the wisdom of generalizing from the behaviors of lower-order animals to the behaviors of humans. In general, research shows that as we go up the evolutionary ladder, the role of innate, or biological, factors in the control of behavior decreases (Beach, 1969; Bandura, 1973). For example, among lower-order animals, the propensity to aggress is strongly related to the level of androgen in their systems. The more of this male hormone present in an animal's system, the more aggressive the animal. Among humans, an increase in androgen may make a person hairier and more muscular, but it has little if any effect on aggressiveness (Beach, 1969; Ehrhardt, Epstein, and Money, 1968).

Studies of human and animal physiology point out another major problem in Lorenz's theory. There is little question that certain structures in the brain exert an influence on aggression (Goldstein, 1974). Delgado (1967), for example, has shown that the electric stimulation of the hypothalmus can produce aggression in the absence of an external stimuli. But careful studies of the human nervous system (Lehrman, 1953; Scott, 1972) have found no evidence of any mechanism that could cause the buildup of aggressive energy in the manner Lorenz proposed, nor any mechanism that could "bottle up" this energy.

Finally, Lorenz's belief that aggression can be genetically transmitted is based on an unusual view of how genes influence human behavior. As Corning and Corning (1972) have pointed out, genes do not produce specific behaviors; they produce the capacity to perform specific behaviors. For example, our genetic heritage gives us the ability to manipulate things with our fingers and the ability to remember the face of someone who insulted us three months ago. It does not preprogram us to stalk that person for three months and then murder him by pulling the trigger of a gun.

Sex Differences

Biological and instinctual theories of aggression in general have not been well received by social psychologists. However, many social psychologists have used biology to explain sex differences in aggression. Among most—but not all—animals, males are more aggressive than females (Scott, 1958). The source of this difference appears to be in the hormones that males and females secrete. For example, increases in the level of androgen, a male hormone, produce increases in aggression, but increases in estrogen, a female hormone, produce decreases in aggression (Floody and Pfaff, 1974).

This fact has led some researchers to propose that biological factors might be responsible for sex differences in human aggression, and they have provided data to support this argument. Studies of children under the age of two have usually found that male infants are more aggressive than female infants (Rohner, 1971; White, 1983). It is argued that since children this young are probably displaying unlearned behaviors, these data support a biological explanation of the sex differences in adult aggression. Indeed, earlier reviews of sex differences in social behavior (for example, Maccoby and Jacklin, 1974) often concluded that biological factors were responsible for men being more aggressive than women.

But more recent examinations of this topic have led many researchers to question whether sex differences are innate. Some researchers argue that the manner in which boys and girls are socialized may be responsible for these differences (Bandura, 1973; White, 1983). They point to several findings that support this position. In certain instances it has been medically necessary to increase the level of the male hormone androgen in female infants. Systematic observations of these females' behaviors fail to show that they are any more aggressive than females with normal androgen levels (Ehrhardt et al., 1968).

Topic Background

The XYY Syndrome

The possibility that males may be inherently more aggressive than females led some researchers to further explore genetic causes of aggression. Findings obtained in the 1960s and 1970s indicated that a relatively rare genetic disorder, or anomaly, may cause some extreme acts of aggression in men (Jacobs, Brunton, and Melville, 1965; Jarvik, Klodin, and Matsuyama, 1973).

Normal human cells contain 23 pairs of chromosomes, and one pair plays a major role in the determination of a person's biological sex. In females, this pair comprises two X chromosomes; in males it comprises an X and a Y chromosome. The Y is considered a "male" chromosome. However, in a relatively rare genetic anomaly, the XYY syndrome, a man has an extra Y chromosome. This syndrome is normally found in about one out of every 1,000 males, but among male prisoners, the incidence of the XYY syndrome is about 15 times as great (Jarvik et al., 1973).

Findings such as these led Jarvik and his associates to suggest that the extra Y chromosome may cause people to be aggressive. It is possible, they proposed, that "the single Y chromosome in which every normal male is endowed may itself be the genetic root of normal aggression" (1973, 80). This and similar conclusions received considerable public attention. Indeed, the XYY syndrome was used as a defense in a murder trial. The lawyer of Richard Speck, a man accused of brutally murdering eight student nurses, argued that his client should not be found guilty because Speck suffered from the XYY syndrome and, thus, was not responsible for his actions. (This defense failed, at least in part, because Speck did not have the XYY syndrome.)

While the XYY syndrome was receiving much media attention, researchers were quietly attempting to determine if Jarvik and his colleagues' conclusions were correct. The most comprehensive study was conducted by Witkin and his colleagues (1976). They tested over 4,000 Danish men for the XYY syndrome and then obtained complete data on their physical characteristics, intelligence, and criminal records. (This study was conducted in Denmark because the Danish government keeps such records for every citizen. It would have been impossible to collect such data in the United States.) Witkin's group failed to find any evidence supporting a link between the XYY syndrome and violence. Twelve of the men tested had this genetic anomaly, and they were more likely to have been convicted of a crime than the XY men. But when they were compared to other criminals who did not possess the anomaly, the XYY criminals were *less* likely to have committed a crime of violence than the XY criminals.

If the XYY syndrome is not related to aggression, why are criminals more likely to have this anomaly than noncriminals? It was found that while the XYY males were not any more violent than normal males, they were less bright. The researchers speculated that because of their lower intelligence, XYY males are more likely to be caught when they commit a crime, which would account for their overrepresentation in prison populations.

Even if hormones do play a role in aggression, one cannot discount the even stronger role that social experiences may play. Eron (1982) has found that things such as exposure to aggressive models and parental reinforcement of masculine behaviors and interests result in greater aggressiveness in both males and females. Further, changes in societal norms and mores about how boys and girls should act seem to have reduced the magnitude of sex differences in aggression. As the tendency to teach girls to be passive and submissive has declined in our society, so have the number of studies that find sex differences in aggression.

Men are somewhat more likely to aggress than women, but whether this is due to biology or to social experiences is not known. When women are provoked, they are just as capable of displaying aggression as are men. A study by Richardson, Vandenburg, and Humphries (1983) showed this. A male or a female played a game against an opponent. Both players tried to respond to a stimulus as quickly as possible. The person who lost would receive an electric shock, its intensity determined by the winner. The first few times a subject lost, he or she received a very mild shock from the other player. (The experimenter rigged the game so subjects would lose half the time and controlled how much shock they received.) But as the game progressed, the subjects received more intense shocks from their opponent. Did male's and female's behaviors differ? When the opponent did not provoke them, males gave more intense shocks than did women. But when the opponent provoked them, women acted just as aggressively as did men. (See figure 7-2.)

Frustration-Aggression Hypothesis

Frustration-aggression hypothesis: originally, a theory that proposed that frustration always causes aggression and is the only cause of aggression.

In the 1930s, two learning theorists, John Dollard and Neil Miller, began an ambitious project: to recast Freud's ideas about human behavior in a learning theory framework. The particular learning theory they used was drive reduction theory. (See chapter one.) As part of this effort, Dollard, Miller, and some of their colleagues (Dollard, Doob, Miller, and Mowrer, 1939) proposed a modified version of Freud's original theory of aggression. They called it the **frustration-aggression hypothesis.** This hypothesis pro-

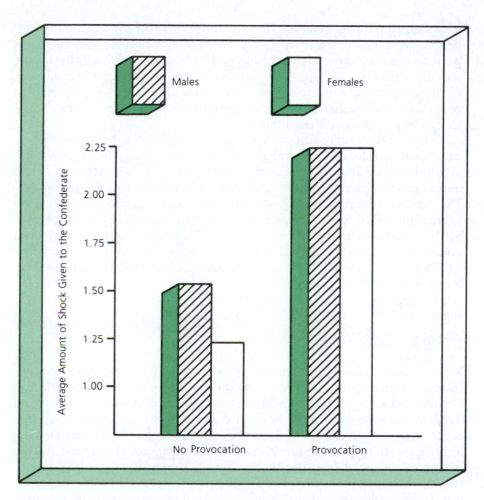

Figure 7-2.   *In the absence of provocation, males were more aggressive than females, but when provoked, females were as aggressive as males.*
Source: Richardson et al. (1983).

posed that human aggression is partly due to learning and partly due to innate responses.

The theory proposed that interference with goal-oriented activities (thwarting) produces frustration, and that this frustration creates a specific aggressive drive in a person which, in turn, causes the person to aggress. For example, imagine you have a test on this chapter tomorrow. Studying this chapter is a goal-oriented activity. If your roommate turns off all the lights or takes the book away from you, you will be frustrated and you will develop an aggressive drive. According to the theory, you will reduce this drive by hurting your roommate.

The frustration-aggression hypothesis has influenced contemporary social psychological theories of human aggression more than have Freud's or Lorenz's theories. Originally, it was used to explain both specific acts of aggression and general aggressive tendencies. It proposed that some people are generally more aggressive than others because they have experienced more frustrations in their lives. It is now used primarily to explain specific acts of aggression, such as why people in situations like the one in the chapter experiment aggress more than nonfrustrated people. Few contemporary researchers use it to explain why one person may be chronically more aggressive than another.

Some of the proposals contained in the original version of the theory have been abandoned or modified. Dollard and his associates initially proposed that frustration always produces aggression. This is incorrect. Frustration produces a number of responses, only one of which is aggression. The original theory also proposed that frustration is the only cause of aggression. More recent research suggests that aggression can be caused by things other than frustration (Baron, 1977). Finally, contemporary proponents of the frustration-aggression hypothesis (for example, Berkowitz, 1965, 1969) have argued that frustration does not lead directly to aggression, but produces the emotion of anger, which creates the readiness to aggress. Actual aggression depends upon the stimuli present in a person's environment when he or she is frustrated.

Social Learning Theory

Most contemporary researchers interested in general aggressive tendencies take a position quite different from the positions of Freud, Lorenz, or Dollard and associates—that aggression is a learned behavior. This explanation of aggression is more hopeful than an instinctual explanation because if aggression is learned, it can be unlearned or at least controlled by applying learning theory principles. This view of aggression is most clearly expressed in **social learning theory,** which proposes that aggression is neither the result of instincts nor an automatic response to some stimulus; it is a social behavior learned through classical conditioning, instrumental conditioning, and observational learning, and it is maintained by the reinforcers people receive for engaging in aggression (Bandura, 1973, 1983). Most of the research conducted by advocates of this position has focused on the learning of aggression through instrumental conditioning and observational learning.

Instrumental Conditioning

In its simplest form, **instrumental conditioning** maintains that the reinforcements people receive after they have engaged in a behavior determine whether they will learn the behavior. Rats will learn to press a bar if this behavior is reinforced (with food); they will not learn to do this if the behavior is not reinforced.

Many studies have demonstrated that positive reinforcers such as money, toys, candy, social approval, and increased status can be used to teach people aggressive behavior (Baron, 1977). In addition, several studies have shown that when people are angry, inflicting pain on the source of their anger can serve as a reinforcer (Baron, 1974; Feshbach, Stiles, and Bitter, 1967; Hartman, 1969). When angry people learn that the person they are angry at is in pain, their level of aggression may increase, and the reinforced aggressive behavior is likely to recur. This can be illustrated by an episode from the life of Rubin Carter.

Rubin "Hurricane" Carter, once the leading contender for the middleweight boxing championship of the world, served 20 years of a life sentence for the murders of six people—crimes he claims he did not commit. In the following passage, Carter describes an incident that occurred when he was five years old and his brother had been severely beaten by a boy named Bully. Rubin decided to retaliate:

> I hurled my body into him with all my might, and with a vengeance that shocked even me. I hadn't known I was capable of such feelings.
>
> Bully tripped and went down. I crouched over him, whaling like mad, until he finally managed to fight his way back to his feet. We stood toe to toe, slugging it out, swinging for all we were worth. Then I landed a sizzling haymaker against his bullet head, and he started backing up, with me crowding him, firing on him. The fighting became easier then, and I found I liked it. The more we fought, the better I seemed to get.
>
> A shiver of fierce pleasure ran through me. It was not spiritual, this thing that I felt, but a physical sensation in the pit of my stomach that kept shooting upward through every nerve until I could clamp my teeth on it. Every time Bully made a wrong turn, I was right there to plant my fist in his mouth. After a few minutes of this treatment, the cellar became too hot for Bully to handle, and he made it out the door, smoking.
>
> This was my first experience in fist fighting, and the fruits of my victory were sweet indeed. I could feel the pull of the little muscles interlinked and interchained from my fingertips to the small of my back. I felt the muscles in my legs too, from hip to toe, supporting me as I swayed, tired now. But dammit, I felt *good*. Even though I had come out with a busted lip, I had beaten the big bad block bully—and man, I was hot-to-trot to fight some more. (Carter, 1975, pp. 21–22)

Observational Learning

Observational learning is based on the idea that humans acquire many behaviors by watching other people, or models. Many social behaviors are the result of attending to the actions of a model, remembering what the model has done, and being able to reproduce what has been seen. Albert Bandura (1973, 1983) has argued that aggressive behaviors are acquired through observational learning. Models can teach observers specific acts of aggression that they previously did not know; models can teach observers that actions of aggression they already know are acceptable ways of acting; and models can lower observers' inhibitions against acting aggressively.

Many studies support this proposal (Bandura, 1973; Bandura and Walters, 1963). Bandura, Ross, and Ross (1963) looked at how aggressive models can affect the behavior of nursery school children. These children were randomly assigned to one of five conditions. In the first three conditions,

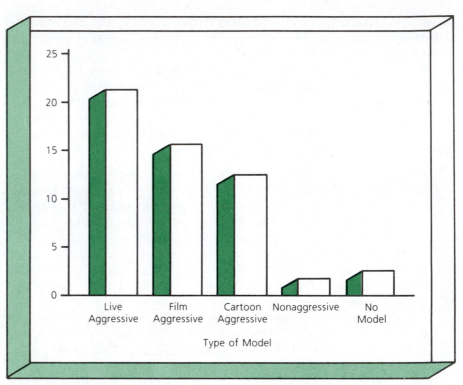

Figure 7-3.   *Children who observed aggressive models engaged in more imitative and general aggression.*
Source: Bandura et al. (1963).

children saw either a live model, a filmed model, or a cartoon character act in an aggressive way toward a large toy doll. Children in the remaining two conditions were either exposed to a nonaggressive model or exposed to no model. Then all five groups of children were placed in a playroom and their behaviors toward the doll were observed.

The greatest imitation of aggression was found among the children who saw a live aggressive model, but even the children who saw filmed and cartoon models imitated what they had seen. Like the models, they hit, kicked, and sat on the doll. Not only did the children imitate specific acts of aggression, but they also engaged in more general aggression than did the children who saw a nonagressive model or no model. (See figure 7-3 for the results of this study.)

Studies of children in their natural environment also suggest that instrumental conditioning and observational learning play an important role in the development of aggressive tendencies. Bandura (1960) and Bandura and Walters (1959) compared the behaviors of parents of boys who had been classified as aggressive or nonaggressive. In both studies, it was found that the parents of aggressive boys discouraged aggression directed toward themselves, but encouraged aggressive behaviors toward others. The mother of one of the aggressive boys described an interaction between her husband and their son after the son had been bothered by two other children:

> So [my husband] went up, took off his belt, and he said, "Glen, I'm going to tell you something. You're going to whip these boys or else I'm going to whip you." So he made him stand up and fight both of them. (Bandura, 1973, p. 95)

Further, the parents of the aggressive boys were much more likely to use physical punishment on their children. This type of "training" provides a child with a vivid example of how aggression can be used to control the behavior of others, even if it occurs in a relatively nonviolent situation. For example, a friend came home one evening and found that the needle on his turntable had been destroyed by someone playing a record backward. He called his two children and asked which one had done it. Both denied responsibility. He proceeded to spank both of them. When I heard this story, I asked why he had punished both children. "Well," he explained, "one of them was punished for breaking the needle and the other learned what would happen to him if he ever did this." I would also add that he provided both sons with a good model of aggression.

There is validity to all of these theories of the origins of aggressive tendencies. However, most social psychologists view the social learning theory as the most comprehensive and valid explanation of human aggression.

SUMMARY

Aggression is defined as an action that is intended to harm or injure another living thing. A number of theories attempt to explain the pervasive tendency of humans to aggress.

Freud and Lorenz proposed instinctual theories of aggressive tendencies in humans. Freud believed that aggression results from a person's internal conflicts between the life and death instincts. Lorenz proposed that all animals, including humans, have an inherited fighting instinct, which produces aggressive energy; as the aggressive energy increases, so does the likelihood of aggression. Humans are the most dangerous of all creatures, according to Lorenz, because they do not have innate mechanisms to control their aggressive energy. Instinctual, or biological, theories have been used to explain sex differences in aggression. Some biological differences do explain why men are often more aggressive than women, but recent research suggests that the manner in which men and women are socialized plays a greater role than do biological differences.

Another theory of aggressive tendencies, the frustration-aggression hypothesis, proposes that when a person's attempts to reach some goal are blocked, or thwarted, frustration occurs. Frustration, in turn, produces an aggressive drive that makes the person ready to aggress.

Today, the most widely accepted explanation of general aggressive tendencies is based on social learning theory, which acknowledges that biological factors play a role in human aggression, but proposes that aggression can be primarily explained by learning experiences. This theory contends that classical conditioning, instrumental conditioning, and observational learning are the mechanisms whereby people learn aggressive behaviors and when to use them. Some researchers question specific aspects of the social learning explanations, but most agree that human aggression is a learned social behavior.

SPECIFIC ACTS OF AGGRESSION

Probably few readers have been in an experiment on aggression, but most have probably engaged in a number of aggressive actions. In most cases, these will have occurred in circumstances similar to those created in the experiment presented in the prologue; you aggressed because somebody did something to you that you did not like. Most researchers believe that the key to understanding aggression in such situations lies in a careful analysis of the stimuli in the situation, rather than in general theories of aggressive tendencies.

Aggression motivated by people's desires to achieve some goal for themselves is called *interpersonal aggression*. Aggression motivated by people's desires to achieve some goal for an institution they represent—such as a government, a religious sect, or a political party—is *institutional aggression*. Thus, a citizen of an occupied country who kills a foreign soldier because that soldier raped his sister is engaging in interpersonal aggression; another citizen who kills a soldier in order to drive the "foreign devils" from his homeland is engaging in institutional aggression.

The most common form of institutional aggression is war. In the 5,000 or so years that humans have been recording their history, there have been more than 14,600 wars (Montague, 1976). This averages out to almost three wars per year. Between 1815 and 1965, over 70 million people died in wars (Singer and Small, 1970). Institutional aggression is a common and devastating human activity, but because social psychology studies the behavior of individuals in response to social stimuli, the focus in this chapter is on interpersonal aggression.

Angry versus Instrumental Aggression

Angry aggression: aggression that results from some internal state, such as anger or frustration.

Instrumental aggression: aggression that results from the desire to reach some goal; it is not preceded by anger or frustration.

Most researchers believe there are two general kinds of interpersonal aggression, caused by different variables and having different goals. Buss (1971) has labeled these **angry aggression** and **instrumental aggression.** Angry aggression is a response to some sort of provocation; one person provokes another, who becomes angry and aggresses. The goal of the aggressor is very simple: To cause pain and suffering in the other person. Instrumental aggression is a little more complex. The cause is not provocation, but the possibility of receiving some reward. Aggression is an activity that is instrumental in obtaining the reward. Vincent Teresa, a man who retired from the Mafia and lived to tell about his experiences, provides a dramatic example of instrumental aggression:

> Today, every mob has its own assassination squads made up of men who get a regular weekly salary just to be ready for the day a hit is needed. The members of the squad are hand-picked by a boss. Their talents always include three things. They are experts with a variety of guns and other weapons. They are cool under pressure. They also have no emotion.
>
> I remember there was one guy I heard about who worked for Anastasia's old Murder, Inc., who is typical of what I mean. They called him Ice Pick Barney. His technique was as cold and as calculating as they come. He and other men assigned on a hit would force their victim into a men's room. Then Ice Pick Barney would pull out his ice pick and, while the others held the guy, he'd put the ice pick through the guy's eardrum into his brain. The pick left a tiny hole and would cause very little bleeding. They'd wipe away the blood that trickled from the ear, but the bleeding in the brain would cause the guy to die. When a doctor examined him, he'd rule the guy died from a cerebral hemorrhage. They're a special breed, the assassins. (Teresa, 1973, p. 185)

Ice Pick Barney engaged in aggressive behavior simply because this was what he was paid to do. This is not to suggest that angry aggression is never rewarding. As pointed out earlier, hurting someone who has attacked you is often a positive reinforcer (Baron, 1977). However, in angry aggression, pain or suffering is the ultimate goal of the act; in instrumental aggression, the ultimate goal is the achievement of some external reward.

The same act of aggression can have both angry and instumental motivations (Bandura, 1973). In a school yard fight, for example, the immediate goal of the combatants is to hurt each other, but the winner gets some rewards, such as increased status and respect in the school yard.

The statistics presented at the beginning of this chapter suggest that most acts of interpersonal aggression are motivated by anger—almost half the assaults and most of the murders in the United States are between friends, lovers, or relatives. If the statistics do not convince you, think back to your own experiences. How many times have you engaged in instrumental aggression, aggression in which the primary goal was something other than the injury of another person? Unless you are someone like Ice Pick Barney, the answer is probably never. This section presents the precursors to angry aggression and examines how situational and environmental variables affect the manner in which angry aggression is displayed.

Instigators of Angry Aggression

On rare occasions, humans engage in "blood feuds" which go for years, but most acts of aggression are of a relatively short duration. All incidents of aggression begin with some sort of instigation. Most people behave

aggressively because they feel they have a "good" reason for doing so.*
Angry aggression occurs when one person mistreats another (or at least is
believed to mistreat another) person. Bandura (1983) proposed four major
instigators of aggression: physical assaults, verbal insults or threats, blocking
the completion of some activity (thwarting), and depriving a person of
some reward. Without one or more of these, angry aggression will not
occur. However, these instigators do not themselves cause aggressive behavior. They produce physiological arousal, which people may label as
anger and which may lead to aggressive behavior.

Physiological Arousal
Most, if not all, aggression researchers believe that instigators do not directly lead to aggression. A person's first reaction is an internal physiological response, such as the increases in heart rate and blood pressure
Hokanson and Burgess found in the prologue.

This can be illustrated by describing an aggressive incident I was involved in when I was a graduate student. I had spent a year collecting data
for a professor. After I had analyzed the data, I brought the results to him.
They were, to say the very least, discouraging. He looked over the tables
and statistical tests and then stared at me.

"Have I made a mistake?" I asked.

"No," he replied. "I'm the one who made the mistake. I should've
never hired someone as lazy and incompetent as you."

"I don't understand. Did I leave something out of the analysis? Did I
screw up the statistics?"

"No, no," he replied. "They're okay, I guess. But you didn't collect
enough data. And you know why? Because you are a lazy, incompetent
sonofabitch."

"Don't call me that!"

"It's true. You're lazy, incompetent, and a liar, as well."

"Please! That isn't true."

As I said this, I could feel my stomach churn, my face become warm,
and my fingers begin to tingle. Sound familiar? The situation was unusual
(professors do not usually insult graduate students), but my initial reaction
was typical—the first response to an aggression instigator is physiological
arousal (Bandura, 1983; Berkowitz, 1983). Eventually, I also engaged in
some rather colorful verbal aggression. But for physiological arousal to be
translated into aggression, it must first be identified by the person experiencing it as anger or frustration.

Labeling Arousal as Angry Aggression
For many years, researchers used Schachter's (1964) **two-factor theory of
emotion** to explain how arousal came to be labeled as anger or frustration.

**Two-factor theory of emo-
tion:** the theory that the
identification of emotions is
the product of both physiological responses and people's thoughts about the reasons for those physiological
responses.

_____

*These are, of course, instances in which physical problems (such as a
brain tumor) or mental problems (such as delusions of persecution)
cause people to act aggressively. These will not be considered here.

It was proposed that the physiological reactions to attacks, insults, and other instigators are quite general and not easily identifiable as one specific emotion. Aroused people look to their environment to tell them what emotion they are experiencing. If the environmental cues reasonably suggest that the arousal is due to anger or frustration, they will label it as such. So there are two factors: general arousal and thoughts about the arousal.

More recent research suggests that people's emotions are not as maleable as Schachter's theory implies, and that arousal following an instigator is often more or less automatically labeled as anger or frustration (see Berkowitz, 1983; Zillman, 1983). However, in some instances, a general, nonspecific arousal can affect aggression.

This is explained by Zillman's theory of **excitation transfer.** Zillman proposed that if people are generally aroused by an activity like exercise or watching an exciting movie and are then provoked by someone, the residual arousal from the initial stimulus may increase their response to the provocation. They may transfer the excitation caused by the first stimulus to the second stimulus. This will not occur, however, if people are aware that part of the arousal they feel is due to the first stimulus. A study by Zillman, Johnson, and Day (1974) illustrates this process.

Excitation transfer: the process by which arousal caused by one stimulus is attributed to or transferred to another, subsequent stimulus.

Subjects were provoked by a confederate and then allowed to retaliate by giving electric shocks. Between the provocation and the retaliation, the subjects had different experiences. Two groups did exactly the same things, but in a different order. One group of subjects sat quietly for six minutes, then spent 90 seconds pedaling a stationary bicycle. Immediately after they finished the strenuous exercise, they were allowed to retaliate against the person who had provoked them. A second group of subjects pedaled for 90 seconds, then rested for six minutes. Immediately after they finished the rest period, they were allowed to retaliate. (Unless people are in very good shape, six minutes after they have exercised they are still aroused but are usually not fully aware that they are.)

The researchers predicted that when the subjects in the first group retaliated, they would be quite aroused, but they would know the source of this arousal—the 90 seconds of exercise that had immediately preceded the retaliation. The situation would be quite different for the subjects in the second condition. They would still have residual arousal from the exercise, but would be less likely to attribute it to the exercise because of the six-minutes wait. Instead, they might label the arousal as anger caused by the original provocation. If they did this, they should aggress more than the subjects in the first group. (See figure 7-4 for the results of the experiment.)

Zillman and his associates found subjects who could reasonably attribute the residual arousal to the original provocation aggressed much more than did subjects who could attribute their arousal to the exercise. Other research has found that arousal created by such diverse stimuli as noise, music, speeches, and erotic pictures can increase a person's propensity to aggress (Zillman, 1983).

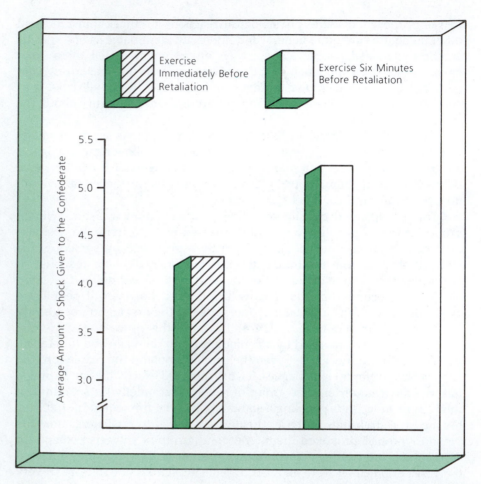

Figure 7-4. *Subjects who exercised immediately before retaliation experienced less excitation transfer and, thus, aggressed less.*
Source: Zillman et al. (1974).

Don't worry if you are supposed to meet your roommate five minutes after he has jogged three miles. The effects of transferred arousal on aggression are limited by many variables, especially by the context in which the arousal occurs. A study by Zillman, Katcher, and Milavsky (1972) showed that arousal (due to exercise) in the absence of any provocation will not increase aggression. In other words, people do not aggress just because they are aroused. They must have a reason to label this arousal as anger. And people are usually fairly aware of why they are experiencing physiological arousal.

Situational and Environmental Influences on Angry Aggression

Environmental and situational variables play a role in the early stages of an aggressive episode, but their strongest influence occurs after people have experienced physiological arousal and identified it as anger or frustration. Some situational factors that influence people's actual behavior are fairly obvious. For example, the more ability their target of aggression has to retaliate, the less likely people are to aggress (Baron, 1973). Also, the attributions people make as to why they were attacked effect their propensity to aggress. If they can identify causes that might explain, justify, or mitigate the treatment they have received, they aggress less. For example, Kremer and Stephens (1983) exposed subjects to two people who treated them rudely. One person's behavior was explained by the fact that "he's really worried about a midterm." Subjects aggressed significantly less against this person than against the person whose behavior was not explained.

Aggression-Eliciting Stimuli

Leonard Berkowitz (1969, 1974) has proposed that the tendency to aggress is strongly influenced by something called *aggression-eliciting stimuli* (also called aggressive cues). These are stimuli which, through classical conditioning, have come to be associated with anger or aggression. Because of this association, they can increase an angry person's propensity to aggress.

In their movies, Abbott and Costello often used the concept of aggression eliciting stimuli. Lou Costello would send people into a rage by saying things such as Niagara Falls. An explanation of Costello's problem follows.

The stimuli can be things people generally associate with aggression—such as weapons—or they can be things a specific person associates with aggression because of some experience in that person's life (Berkowitz and Geen, 1968; Geen and O'Neal, 1969; Berkowitz and Knarek, 1969).

The concept of aggression-eliciting stimuli can be illustrated with an old vaudeville routine popularized by the comedy team of Abbott and Costello. Costello is in a prison cell with a mentally deranged man. This man has killed his wife and her lover at Niagara Falls. Costello is told that the man is harmless unless someone says "Niagara Falls"; if he hears these words, he will fly into a frenzy and attack whoever is nearby. If you have ever seen an old Abbott and Costello movie, you know what happens next. The words *Niagara Falls* keep coming up in Costello's conversation with the man. Every time this happens, Costello's cell mate loses control. With vacant eyes, he approaches Costello and says: "Slowly I turned, step by step, inch by inch, ever closer. Until . . . I grabbed them and hit them and knocked them down and crushed the life out of their bodies." Having said that, he grabs poor, pudgy little Costello and tosses him around the cell. The assault continues until he almost re-creates the original crime.

Topic Background

Are Guns a Menace? Ask Harry

Leonard Berkowitz (1968) has argued that guns, because of their association with aggression in general, have become aggression-eliciting stimuli. To quote Berkowitz: "Guns not only permit violence, they can stimulate it as well" (1968, 22). In a 1968 study, Berkowitz and Le Page found that angry subjects who were in the presence of a gun aggressed significantly more than did angry subjects who were not exposed to a gun. Similar results have been obtained by Frodi (1975) and Leyens and Parke (1975). Other aggression researchers, however, questioned Berkowitz's claim about the effects of guns (Baron, 1977; Buss, Booker, and Buss, 1972). Even Berkowitz (1971, 1983) acknowledged that the aggression-eliciting effects of weapons are not very strong and that other factors in a situation can override their impact.

While the question of whether or not guns stimulate aggression remains open, there is no question that humans can do some incredible things when they get a gun in their hands. Consider the case of Harry, the winner of columnist Mike Royko's annual, tongue-in-cheek Gun Owner of the Year award. In his column, Royko described the event that earned Harry the 1982 award:

Harry had been feuding with some of his relatives, so he slept with his pistol on the bedstand in case any of his relatives showed up in his bedroom.

One night, he awoke and thought he saw somebody standing at the foot of his bed.

He grabbed his pistol and fired one shot.

He didn't hit the person at the foot of the bed because there wasn't anybody there.

But the bullet did hit his penis and his leg.

Harry, our Gun Owner of the Year, was undaunted by the experience, and was even philosophical about it. As he said after the nurses patched him up:

"Heck, it was only a .22 caliber pistol. It could have been a lot worse if I had a .45" (Royko, 1982)

According to Berkowitz, Costello's misfortune was due to the following process. His cell mate was mentally deranged and ready to aggress—aggression-eliciting stimuli will affect aggression only when a person is ready to aggress. Given this state, the words *Niagara Falls,* which were associated with an earlier act of aggression, served as a cue which sent the man into a frenzy.

A study by Swart and Berkowitz (1976) demonstrated how initially neutral stimuli can become associated with aggression. The subjects believed that the purpose of the study was to investigate the effects of stress on learning. In the first part of the experiment, each subject engaged in a task and was evaluated by another subject (a confederate) who used electric shock. Half of the subjects received a large number of high-intensity shocks, which made them quite angry. The other half received only one shock.

In the second part of the experiment, the confederate (the subject's evaluator) engaged in a task while the experimenter gave him shocks. The subject's job during this part of the experiment was to record how often the confederate was in pain. A white light on a panel in front of the subject would go on every time the confederate was in pain. This white light was the conditioned stimulus. It was paired with the unconditioned stimulus, pain in the confederate (who had made some of the subjects very angry earlier). Thus, the originally neutral white light became associated with pain in the confederate.

The effect of the association could be seen in the third part of the experiment, where the subject was to administer 40 shocks to still another person in the experiment (not the confederate) in order to distract this person while he worked on a task. The subject could decide the intensity and duration of each shock. Shortly before 20 shocks were given, the white light went on; shortly before 20 other shocks were given, a blue light went on. The dependent measure was the amount of shock subjects gave after the white light and after the blue light.

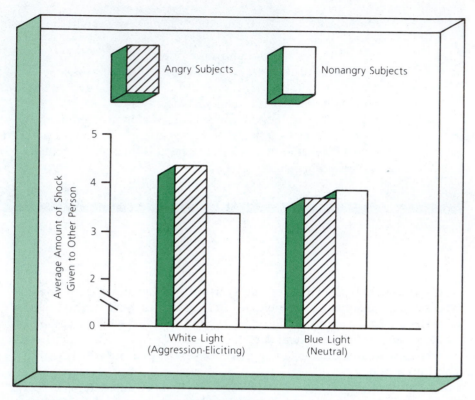

Figure 7-5. *The white light, which was associated with pain in the confederate, served as an aggression eliciting stimuli for angry subjects.*
Source: Swart and Berkowitz (1976).

If the white light had become, through classical conditioning, an aggression-eliciting stimuli, angry subjects should have given more shock when it was on than when the blue light was on. The white light had been paired with pain in someone who had angered them; the blue light had not. The white light should have had little or no effect on the nonangry subjects, however. It had been paired with pain in someone who had not angered them. (See figure 7-5 for Swart and Berkowitz's results.)

The white light produced more aggression only among the angry subjects. It had become, for the angry subjects, an aggression-eliciting stimulus. And note, this was nonangry aggression toward an innocent bystander!

Environmental Stressors

Environmental stressors: negative or unpleasant aspects of the environment— such as air pollution, high temperatures, and noise— which produce stress in people.

One inevitable byproduct of living in a modern, industrialized society is increased exposure to **environmental stressors.** These stressors present some danger to our physical and mental health, and they may also affect aggression. Aggression researchers have studied how one particular environmental stressor, excessive ambient temperature, might affect aggression. (See chapter fourteen for a more general discussion of how environmental factors affect social behavior.)

Mueller (1983) proposed three reasons why environmental stressors, such as high temperatures, may increase the likelihood of aggression. First, stressful environments put people in a bad mood. Naturally, someone who is in a bad mood is more likely to aggress than someone who is in a good mood (Bandura, 1973). Second, environmental stressors can often cause people to feel that they are unable to control their environment. This can engender frustration, a precursor to aggression. Third, environmental stressors can generate physiological arousal, which can be labeled as anger or frustration (through processes such as excitation transfer), and make aggression more probable or more intense.

Mueller's analysis leads to the prediction that the higher the temperature, the more likely people are to aggress. But laboratory experiments have not fully supported this prediction. Baron and Bell (1975) found that angry subjects in a very hot room aggressed less than did angry subjects in a comfortable room. Bell and Baron (1976) also found that increases in temperature were associated with increased aggression only up to a point; beyond that point, aggression decreased. (This is called a *curvilinear relationship*.) Baron and Bell suggested that the combination of being angry and experiencing very high temperatures made their subjects feel extremely unpleasant. If they had engaged in high levels of aggression, they might have felt even worse because they may have also been afraid of retaliation or felt guilty about what they had done; therefore, they displayed less aggression than did angry subjects in a comfortable environment.

This explanation leads to the prediction that if one could reduce the level of discomfort among angry subjects, one might increase their level of aggression. Baron and Bell (1976) also tested this prediction. Subjects were made angry and then placed in a very hot room. Half of these subjects were given a drink of cool water before they were given a chance to aggress; the other half were not given a drink. Subjects in the first group aggressed significantly more than did subjects in the second group.

Effects of Alcohol and Other Drugs on Angry Aggression

Recently, an interracial murder occurred in the city where I live. The tragic events began at about 2:00 A.M. Two black men were having a cup of coffee in a restaurant with two white women. Two young white males entered the restaurant and saw the interracial couples. Enraged, the white men made racial slurs and threatened the black men. The black men finished their coffee and left. As they drove home, a pickup truck carrying the two whites pulled alongside of them. One of the white men drew a pistol, shot, and killed one of the black men. The killer was arrested and charged with first-degree murder. At the trial, it was disclosed that the defendant was an alcoholic, had been drinking for several hours before the murder, and was drunk at the time he pulled the trigger. His lawyer attributed his actions to the alcohol in his system. (The jury was unable to reach a verdict.) Was there any validity to the lawyer's argument?

Research Highlight

Temperature and Aggression: Beyond the Laboratory

In the late 1960s, violent riots occurred in the ghettos of many major American cities. In the aftermath, government commissions studied what caused the riots. The major cause was found to be the living conditions in the ghetto areas. A contributing factor seemed to be ambient temperature. Most of the riots took place in the summer, usually on days when the temperature was higher than normal (Goranson and King, 1970). This finding led to the laboratory research on temperature and aggression discussed in this chapter. A number of laboratory experiments found, however, that under extremely high ambient temperatures there was less aggression than under normal temperatures. This discrepancy between laboratory and field findings caused Baron and Ransberger (1978) to reexamine the data on the relation between ambient temperature and the outbreak of riots. Baron and Bell's findings led them to predict that up to a certain temperature, as temperature increased, so would the likelihood of a riot. But beyond that temperature, the likelihood of a riot would decrease. (This is called a curvilinear relationship; graphed it looks like an inverted U.) Baron and Ransberger found that there were more riots on days when the temperature was in the 80s than on days when the temperature was in the 70s. But there were fewer riots on days when the temperature was in the 90s than when the temperature was in the 80s. This pattern was consistent with the pattern obtained in the laboratory experiments on temperature and aggression.

However, Baron and Ransberger's reasoning contained a serious error. One likely explanation of why there were fewer riots on days in the 90s than on days in the 80s is that there were fewer 90-degree days than 80-degree days (Carlsmith and Anderson, 1979). To illustrate this error, Carlsmith and Anderson demonstrated that not only were riots less likely to occur on 90-degree days than on 80-degree days, but so were baseball games.

In a more recent study, Anderson and Anderson (1984) examined the relationship between ambient temperature and aggression. As their measure of aggression, they used daily reports of the number of murders, rapes, and other violent crimes that occurred in a large southern city. To overcome the weakness in Baron and Ransberger's analysis, they collected data for an equal number of 70-, 80-, and 90-degree days. Crimes in general did not increase with increases in temperature, but violent crimes did. (See the figure below.)

The Andersons' study does not conclusively prove that temperature increases make people more aggressive. To show this, they would have needed to manipulate the daily temperatures in the city they studied; this, of course, was impossible. Their findings, however, do suggest that one should be very careful when generalizing from laboratory results.

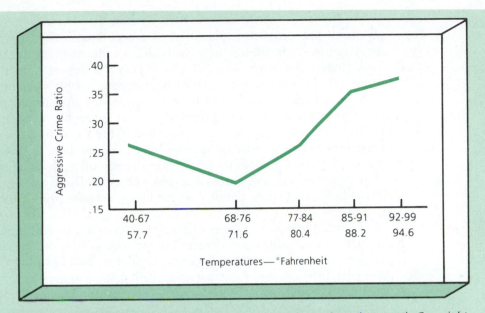

As the temperature increased the percentage of violent crimes increased. Copyright 1984 American Psychological Association. Reprinted by permission of the authors.
Source: Anderson and Anderson (1984).

Research provides only partial support for the lawyer's position. Alcohol consumption cannot explain the man's hatred for blacks or his rage at the sight of an interracial couple, and people do not aggress just because they are drunk. Research does suggest that alcohol may facilitate angry aggression. Wolfgang and Strohm (1954) examined police reports on approximately 600 homicides. In 64 percent of the cases, either the attacker or the victim had been drinking. Shupe (1954) obtained urine samples from 882 people who had been arrested either while committing a felony or immediately thereafter. Seventy-five percent of those arrested for assaults, stabbings, shootings, or murders were legally intoxicated at the time of the crime. More recent studies (for example, Haberman and Baden, 1978) have reported that alcohol was a contributing factor in over 80 percent of the homicides studied.

Laboratory experiments also show that alcohol increases aggression (Taylor and Leonard, 1983). Taylor and Gammon (1975) angered subjects and then administered either large or small amounts of alcohol to them. When the subjects were given the chance to shock their attackers, those who received large amounts of alcohol aggressed significantly more. (For some reason, drinking vodka produced more aggression than did drinking bourbon.)

While it seems clear that alcohol serves to increase aggression, the reason for this has not yet been determined. Taylor and Leonard (1983) proposed one possible explanation that begins with the premise that in most aggressive incidents there are both cues that facilitate aggression and cues that inhibit aggression. Actual aggression depends on the relative influence of the two sets of cues. Alcohol impairs people's abilities to attend to different cues in their environment. Thus, the intoxicated person will focus on cues that are most prominent; in an aggressive incident these are likely to be the instigators of aggression. This focus increases both the probability and intensity of aggression. In this context, it should also be noted that when people focus on external stimuli such as aggression instigators, their **self-awareness** decreases. Prentice-Dunn and Rogers (1983) have shown that when people become less self-aware, they are more likely to aggress.

Given the legal problems of obtaining so-called recreational drugs for research, few studies have been done of their effects on aggression. But Taylor, Vardaris, Rarvitch, Gammon, Cranston, and Labetkin (1976) have compared the effects of alcohol and marijuana on aggression. Alcohol increased the subjects' levels of aggressiveness; the psychoactive agent in marijuana—tetrahydrocannabinol (THC)—inhibited aggression.

SUMMARY

Aggression researchers have identified two general kinds of aggression, which differ in their causes and their goals: angry aggression—a response to a provocation which has as its ultimate goal the harm or injury of the person responsible for the provocation, and instrumental aggression—aggression used to achieve some goal.

The most common instigators of angry aggression are physical attacks, verbal threats or insults, thwarting some activity, and depriving a person of a reward. These instigators do not lead directly to aggression, but cause physiological arousal, which may be labeled as anger. Although this is often an automatic, nonconscious process, in certain instances people's thoughts may affect how they label the arousal.

Anger or frustration is necessary before angry aggression will occur, but neither automatically leads to actual aggression. The translation of these emotions into aggression is greatly influenced by situational and environmental factors such as aggression-eliciting stimuli and environmental stressors.

Alcohol may also affect aggression. Studies have found a strong association between alcohol consumption and violent criminal behavior. Some people suggest that this relationship is due to the fact that violent people drink a great deal. Laboratory studies suggest that alcohol consumption causes an already angry person to act more aggressively.

CONTROL OF AGGRESSION _____

This section is based on a simple premise: Aggression is an undesirable social behavior. Thus, it is in a society's best interest to control or prevent displays of aggression by its members. The following material presents what social psychologists have learned thus far about the control of general aggression and of specific aggressive acts. They are a long way from solving the problem, for aggression is a very complex social behavior. There are no simple answers to the question "How can we prevent it?"

Reducing General Aggressive Tendencies

Humans have been trying for a long time to devise a way to control aggression. When Moses came down from Mount Sinai, the sixth commandment he brought with him was "thou shall not kill" (Exod. 20:13). Moses offered no suggestions on how murder and other forms of aggression might be controlled or prevented. However, social scientists have proposed two methods of reducing general aggressive tendencies: social learning theory and the catharsis hypothesis.

Social Learning Theory
The social learning theory position on the control of aggression follows directly from its position on the causes of aggression. Since aggression is a learned social behavior, principles of learning can be used to control it. Some research has concentrated on the use of punishment to teach control.

   Most societies have laws that threaten punishment for acts of aggression. Do such laws deter aggression? Traditionally, aggression researchers have believed that the threat of punishment will cause people to inhibit their aggression. In the original version of the frustration-aggression hypothesis, Dollard and his associates (1939) proposed that the more punishment people believed they would receive if they aggressed, the less likely they were to aggress. Similar views have been expressed by Walters (1969) and Berkowitz (1962). But more recent laboratory research suggests that it is not quite this simple.

   Baron (1977) has summarized the conditions under which the threat of punishment will affect actual aggression. First, such threats will only affect the behavior of someone who is not very angry. Second, the punishment must be quite severe and quite likely to be administered. And third, the punishment must outweigh any gains achieved by aggression. These findings come from laboratory experiments, and one must be careful about generalizing from them. But they would at least suggest that punishments that are threatened but rarely used (such as capital punishment) may have little effect on a person's propensity to commit murder.

   Punishment can deter aggression, but it must be very carefully used. The use of punishment to inhibit aggression involves four potential dangers. First, as suggested earlier, the administration of punishment may provide the people who receive it with an aggressive model. Thus, while the immediate effects of the punishment might be to inhibit aggression, the long-term effects may be to teach people how to act aggressively when someone does something they do not like (Baron, 1977). Second, the punishment may be intended as a legitimate and appropriate action, but may be labeled by the recipient as an act of aggression and, thus, may elicit rather than inhibit overt aggression (Zillman, 1978). Third, if the punishment inhibits aggression but does not address the source of a person's anger, subsequent aggression is likely to occur. People usually have a reason to aggress, and interventions that do not eliminate the reason will probably not be effective. Fourth, punishment will only produce long-term changes in aggression when it is administered regularly and predictably, whenever people aggress (Fantino, 1973). Although this can be done in laboratory experiments, it is often difficult to achieve a high level of consistency in the real world. Parents are often inconsistent in their punishment of their children, and the law is even more inconsistent in the punishment of aggressive acts.

This is not to say that learning theory principles are worthless when it comes to the control of aggression. Bandura (1973) pointed out that many of the procedures learning theorists have used to modify other kinds of social behavior can be used to control aggression. For example, rewarding nonaggressive acts and withholding rewards when aggression occurs have been found to be effective in changing the behaviors of hyperaggressive boys (Levin and Simmons, 1962). Also, extinction (failing to reinforce a behavior) has been found to reduce aggressiveness among boys in a nursery school (Brown and Elliott, 1966). Contrary to what the instinctual and drive theories of aggression would predict, aggression can be unlearned—but only through a very difficult and time-consuming process.

Catharsis Hypothesis

One widely accepted position on the control of aggression has applied the **catharsis hypothesis** to general aggressive tendencies. This approach to the control of aggression is derived, at least in part, from Lorenz's ethological theory. Lorenz believed that nothing can be done about the fighting instinct and resultant aggressive energy. He also believed that the manner in which this energy is manifested can be controlled and modified. The most obvious way to purge energy from people's systems is through actual aggression, but catharsis theorists believe that other activities will also rid a person's system of aggressive energy. Feshbach and Singer (1972) proposed that people can express their aggressive tendencies vicariously; through the actions of other people. The observation of aggressive actions in others can serve to reduce or control aggressive impulses and behavior among people with such tendencies. Note that this proposal is exactly opposite to the position of the social learning theorists, who argue that the observation of aggressive models increases aggression in the observer. The research on the effects of media violence on aggression in those who watch it speaks to the validity of these two positions.

Media Violence and Aggression

The media, especially the medium of television, are rife with aggressive models. Violence occurs 50 times more often on television than it does in real life (Comstock, Chafee, Katzman, McCombs, and Roberts, 1978). Prime-time television dramas show about eight acts of violence per episode, and children's cartoons average at least twice as many acts of violence per episode (Slaby, Quarforth, and McConnachie, 1976). Although violence on television declined somewhat during the late 1970s, recent surveys of television show an increase in the level of violence presented on network television (Gerbner, 1982).*

Early research on the effects of media violence employed the procedures described in the discussion of observational learning and aggression (for example, Bandura et al., 1963; Bandura, 1965). Children were shown a model who aggressed against an inflatable doll, and then the children were allowed to aggress against the doll themselves. The findings indicated that observing aggressive models increased the children's levels of aggression. Critics argued that one could not generalize from these findings to media violence. They pointed out several shortcomings in the research. First, the target of aggression was a doll, not a real human; children might act quite differently if the target of their actions were another human. Second, the aggressive episode the children saw was quite different from what they would see on a television program; the aggression was not justified and it was not placed within the context of a plot (Baron, 1977). Third, these experiments demonstrated only the short-term effects of observing aggression; the argument against violence in the media is that it will produce long-term increases in aggression.

Subsequent laboratory experiments (for example, Berkowitz and Alioto, 1973; Liebert and Baron, 1972) used films similar to those shown on television and used human targets of aggression, but these studies were still deficient in one respect. Typically, they measured aggression almost immediately after the subjects had seen the film. This showed the effects of observed violence on specific acts of aggression, but again said little about long-term effects in the real world.

In recent years, several researchers have investigated the long-term effects of media violence in natural settings. Eron (1982) obtained measurements of how much violent television primary school children watched and measurements of their aggressive tendencies based on classmates' ratings. He found that the more violent television the children watched, the more aggressive they were. This result was obtained in the United States, as well as in Finland and Poland.

Other studies have provided even stronger evidence for the causal relationship between violent television and aggression. Lefkowitz, Eron, Walder, and Huesmann (1977) found that the amount of violent television male children watched when they were 8 years old was significantly correlated with how aggressive they were at age 18. However, aggressiveness at age eight was not related to how much violent television the subjects

---

*Contrary to what some defenders of television have argued, there is no correlation between the amount of violence contained in a program and its standings in the ratings of how much people enjoy it (Diener and DeFour, 1978; Himmelweit, Swift, and Jaeger, 1980). In other words, violence is not necessary to make a show popular.

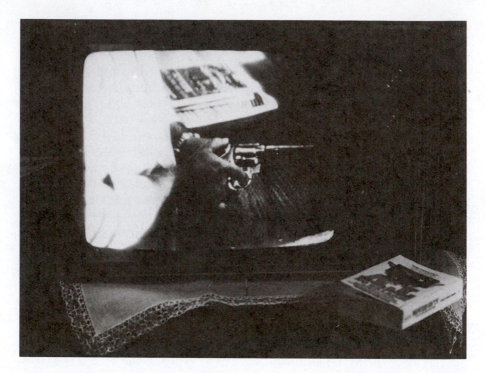

Advocates of the catharsis hypothesis and advocates of social learning theory disagree about the effects of violent television on the viewer.

watched at age 18. Singer and Singer (1982) obtained similar results. Williams (1978) conducted a **quasi-experiment** on the effects of television on aggressiveness in children. The subjects were school children in rural parts of Canada where television had just been introduced. It was found that these children became more aggressive after television was introduced. No comparable increase was found among other Canadian school children during the same time period. Together, the results of these and many other studies make it clear that watching violent television increases aggression in children.

Other data suggest that the relationship between media violence and aggression is much more complex than these findings indicate. For example, aggressive children prefer violent television (Fenigstein, 1979a; Singer and Singer, 1982). This does not contradict the earlier conclusion, but it does point out that violent television can be an effect as well as a cause of aggressiveness. In addition, the correlation between watching violent television and aggressiveness is typically less than .30, and it is often nonexistent for females (Eron, Huesmann, Lefkowitz, and Walder, 1972). This means that less than 9 percent of the difference between people's levels of aggression can be explained by how much violent television they watch. Thus, it would be inappropriate to blame only television for an aggressive child. Children do spend more time watching television than doing any other activity except sleeping, but other factors exert an equal if not greater influence on their aggressiveness.

Eron (1982) has identified some of these other variables. Children who are socialized into a masculine sex role are more aggressive than those who are socialized into a neutral sex role. This is true whether the child is male or female. This finding reflects a societal bias: In American society, males are much more likely to be reinforced for aggressive activities than are females. It may also explain why the long-term effects of watching violent television are much more likely to be found among males than among females. It is reasonable to assume that the manner in which girls have been traditionally socialized (girls should not be aggressive) may serve to counteract the effects of what they see on television.

Also, the parents of aggressive children may serve as aggressive models. Eron and others have found that the more aggressive a child, the more likely his or her parents are to use physical punishments. Finally, Eron's data suggest that frustration may play some role in childhood aggression. He found that the best single predictor of children's aggressiveness was social popularity; the least socially popular children were also the most aggressive. Further, the more children were rejected by their parents, the more aggressive they were. (See figure 7-6.)

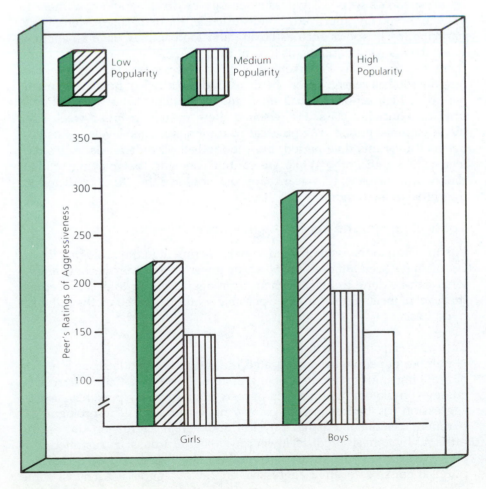

Figure 7-6. *The more aggressive children were less popular with their peers.*
Source: Eron (1982).

It is quite possible that these children were unpopular and rejected because they were so aggressive. It is also possible that social and parental rejection created considerable frustration, which in turn caused aggression. A recent study by Parker and Rogers (1982) suggested that frustration and media violence may work together to increase aggressiveness. Parker and Rogers frustrated children and then gave them the choice of watching an aggressive or a nonagressive model. Frustrated children preferred to watch the aggressive model. Thus, frustration may increase "the probability that an individual will observe, remember and hence perform more acts of violence" (Parker and Rogers, 1982, 302).

In summary, watching violent television does make the observer more aggressive. But this relationship is not very strong (Freedman, 1984). Many other variables affect aggression. Even if all violence were removed from television, the levels of aggression in our society would not drop appreciably.

Participation in Sports and Aggression

Another prediction made by the advocates of catharsis is that one can reduce people's level of aggressive energy or drive by allowing them to engage in socially approved, nondestructive, forms of aggression. Thus, participating in sports such as boxing and football may have a beneficial effect, by allowing participants to vent their aggressive energy and making them less aggressive. Patterson (1974b) tested this prediction. A week before the football season began, he measured the levels of hostility in members of a high school football team and in students who were taking a physical education class. He repeated these measurements a week after the season had ended. The physical education students' levels of hostility declined over this time period, but the football player's levels of hostility increased significantly. While we cannot conclude that playing football caused this increase, it is clear that it did not have the effect predicted by the catharsis hypothesis.

Controlling Specific Acts of Aggression

We now turn to the issue that led to the experiment in the prologue. When people have been attacked, insulted, or thwarted and they become angry, what can be done to prevent them from aggressing or to at least reduce the level of their aggression? One possible solution is based on the catharsis hypothesis.

Catharsis Hypothesis Revisited

Catharsis hypothesis: the theory that aggression is caused by a buildup of aggressive energy; if this energy is purged from people's systems, they are unlikely to aggress.

A number of people have advocated the **catharsis hypothesis** as a means of reducing angry interpersonal aggression. They argue that if aggressive energy (physiological arousal) is purged from an angry person's system, aggression will be less intense or may not occur at all. The prologue experiment demonstrated that physical and verbal aggression do, as the catharsis hypothesis predicts, lower physiological arousal in frustrated people. Advocates of the catharsis hypothesis believe that people can also purge themselves of their aggressive energy by aggressing against some inanimate object, engaging in rigorous physical activity, or observing aggression in others (Perls, 1969, cited in Berkowitz, 1973). Thus, while the arousal can only be reduced by aggressive activities, these activities do not have to involve physical aggression against another person (Geen and Quantz, 1977).

This view of the control of aggression has gained considerable support among the general public. Parents are advised to buy their children inflatable dolls, which the children can beat up instead of an irritating younger brother or sister. Couples are often told to yell at one another to prevent physical assaults. And a few years ago, workers in Japan were given dolls that looked like their bosses and told to hit them (rather than the bosses). Despite the widespread acceptance of the catharsis hypothesis, a large number of social scientists, including the authors of the experiment in the prologue, have come to doubt its validity. The weaknesses of the catharsis hypothesis have been exposed by empirical tests of its basic premises.

Effects of Aggression on Arousal   When people are attacked or insulted, they become physiologically aroused. Research evidence suggests that when angry people aggress, their physiological arousal decreases (Hokanson, 1970). However, in many instances aggression does not result in decreased arousal. Hokanson and Burgess (1962) repeated the prologue experiment with a major modification: In some conditions, the person who frustrated the subjects was introduced as a high-status individual (a new faculty member); in other conditions, the person was introduced as a low-status individual (an undergraduate doing a class project). Verbal aggression did reduce arousal when the target was the low-status person, but it did not reduce arousal when the target was the high-status person.

Further research by Hokanson and his colleagues has cast more doubt on this aspect of the catharsis hypothesis. Hokanson, Willers, and Koropsak (1968) conducted an experiment in which subjects were shocked by a confederate and then could choose one of three responses: aggressive—they could push a button that delivered a shock to the confederate; friendly—they could push a button that delivered a reward to the confederate; or neutral—they could push a button that produced neither a shock nor a reward. Female subjects showed no decline in arousal when they chose shock, but did show a decline when they chose reward. Subsequent research (Sosa, 1968) found that males also showed a decline in arousal when they acted in a friendly manner. It appears that any activity that alleviates unpleasant stimuli can reduce arousal. This finding creates some serious problems for the proposal that only aggressive activities will reduce arousal.

Effects of Verbal Aggression   Catharsis theorists believe that angry people should be allowed to express their anger; if people verbally aggress, this will reduce the chances that they will engage in further aggression. The results of several studies suggest that this proposal is incorrect. Ebbesen, Duncan, and Konecni (1975) studied workers who had recently been laid off. Some of these workers were allowed to verbally express their anger toward their former employer, while others were prevented from doing so. Subsequently, both groups were asked to describe their former employer. In direct contradiction to the catharsis hypothesis, workers who had been allowed to freely express their feelings were much more punitive in their descriptions than were workers who had been prevented from expressing their feelings. Straus and his associates (1980) asked over 2,000 married couples to provide anonymous reports of how much verbal and physical aggression occurred between them. Among those that engaged in little or no verbal aggression, there was little or no physical aggression. But among couples who engaged in a great deal of verbal aggression, the majority (83 percent) engaged in physical aggression. These and similar studies have not conclusively proven that verbal aggression causes physical aggression, but they clearly show that it does nothing to reduce physical aggression.

Effects of Substitute Aggression   Catharsis theorists also believe that activities such as the observation of aggression, strenuous exercise, and aggressive play will reduce people's aggressive drives. Several studies show that when people are angry, exposure to aggressive models increases rather than decreases their aggression (see Baron, 1977; Geen, 1983). Similarly, it has been shown that strenuous exercise and aggressive play increase angry people's propensities to aggress (Geen and Quantz, 1977). Social learning theory explains why the exposure to violence increases aggression, but why do the other forms of substitute aggression have this effect? Think back to the theory of excitation transfer (Zillman, 1978). Physical activity generates arousal, which can be mislabeled as anger and, thus, may increase a person's willingness to aggress.

Effects of Physical Aggression   The crux of the catharsis hypothesis is that when angry people aggress, their physiological arousal is lowered and, thus, subsequent aggression is less likely. Geen, Stonner, and Shope (1975) tested this proposal using a procedure similar to the one used in the prologue. The subjects were hooked up to equipment which measured their blood pressures and then were attacked by a confederate. Some of the subjects were allowed to immediately retaliate against their attackers; others were not allowed to immediately retaliate. Then Geen and his associates did something not done in the earlier experiment: They allowed *both* groups of subjects to aggress against the confederate. The dependent measure was how much shock the confederate was (supposedly) given.

As in the prologue, the subjects' blood pressure increased after they were attacked; the subjects who were allowed to retaliate immediately had lower blood pressure after retaliation; and the blood pressure of the subjects who were prevented from retaliating remained the same. So far, so good for the catharsis hypothesis, but the final measure of aggression indicated something quite different. Subjects who had already retaliated once shocked the confederate significantly *more* than did subjects who were initially prevented from retaliating. In other words, retaliatory aggression *decreased* physiological arousal but *increased* actual aggression. Aggression begat aggression.

   The studies just reviewed are fairly devastating to the catharsis hypothesis. Geen and Quantz (1977) proposed several reasons why engaging in aggressive activities increases aggression. The first was based on the premise that most people have learned inhibitions against aggression. An act of aggression, if it does not produce any negative consequences for the aggressor, may lower these inhibitions. To illustrate this, Geen and Quantz gave the example of a man who murdered four people. According to the arresting officer, the man told him that the first murder was difficult, but the next three were "easy." The second explanation was based on Berkowitz's concept of aggression-eliciting stimuli. It proposed that the aggressor's own behavior may serve as a cue that increases subsequent aggression. For their third explanation, Geen and Quantz turned to the principles of reinforcement. As discussed earlier, hurting someone who has angered us can often be positively reinforcing (Baron, 1979), and behavior that is reinforced is likely to recur. Thus, rather than reduce subsequent aggression, retaliatory aggression may produce reinforcers which increase the likelihood and intensity of aggression. Catharsis does not reduce aggression.

Baron's research suggests that humorous material may induce responses that are incompatible with anger and this may reduce a person's tendency to aggress.

Inducing Incompatible Responses

In a recent article, Baron (1983) proposed another means by which aggression in response to some stimulus can be controlled or reduced. He began with the following fact: Humans are incapable of simultaneously engaging in two incompatible responses or simultaneously experiencing two incompatible emotions. For example, we cannot be anxious and relaxed at the same time. Applying this to aggression, Baron proposed that any stimulus that produces behavior or feelings that are incompatible with anger or overt aggression may prevent such responses.

A number of stimuli could produce such incompatible responses, but most research has looked at the effects of humorous and erotic materials. Baron and Ball (1974) angered subjects and then exposed half of them to humorous cartoons. Then both groups and subjects were allowed to aggress against the person who had angered them. Subjects who had been exposed to the cartoons aggressed significantly less. Similar results were obtained by Landy and Mettee (1969) and Mueller and Donnerstein (1977). Baron and others (for example, Baron, 1974; Frodi, 1977; White, 1979) found that exposure to mildly erotic material reduced aggression among angry subjects. This was true whether the subjects were male or female (Baron, 1979).

Baron (1976) conducted a field experiment on incompatible responses. The subjects were motorists stopped behind a car blocking their way at a busy intersection. Prior research had shown that when motorists are in this situation they honk their horns to express their annoyance, and that the targets of horn honking find this rather unpleasant. Therefore, the primary dependent measures in this study were the number of motorists who honked their horns and the amount of time it took before they began to honk their horns. A confederate placed his car at a red light and waited for the light to turn green. When it did, he delayed moving for 15 seconds. Incompatible responses were created by a female confederate, who dressed in different costumes and crossed the street while the light was still red. Some subjects saw her hobble across the street on crutches: others saw her wearing an outlandish clown mask; and still other subjects saw her dressed in a brief and revealing outfit. Motorists' responses in these three conditions were compared to their responses when the confederate was absent or simply walked across the street while dressed in a normal fashion. (See figure 7-7 for Baron's findings.) The crippled, humorous, or sexy confederate had a dramatic effect on the motorists. Compared to the control condition, fewer motorists honked and those who did waited much longer before doing so.

Baron believed that his findings could have great promise for the control of aggression. However, it is quite possible that attempts to create incompatible responses may increase another person's anger and aggression. Baron and Ball (1974) have found that humor in which someone is harmed or made to look foolish can increase aggression. One must be sure that what is intended to generate an incompatible response actually has this effect. This approach to controlling aggression also requires a "cool

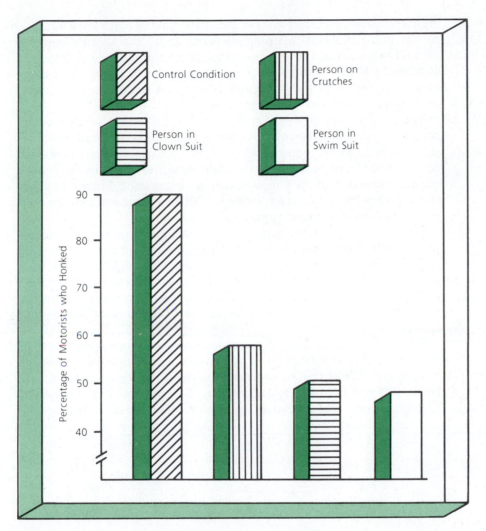

Figure 7-7. *When the confederate elicited incompatible responses, the subjects showed less aggression toward the stopped car.*
Source: Baron (1983).

head." In many aggressive incidents, people are not capable of such calm and rational thinking. This does not mean that Baron was wrong or that his suggestions were without merit—only that aggression is not easy to control.

SUMMARY

It is generally agreed that aggression is an undesirable social behavior and that society must attempt to reduce or control it. Two broad theoretical approaches suggest ways to reduce general aggressive tendencies in humans. Social learning theorists argue that aggression is a learned behavior and, thus, can be modified through the application of learning theory principles. Some of these applications have been successful, but to be truly effective they must also address the source of a person's aggressive tendencies.

The catharsis hypothesis proposes an alternative view on the control of aggression: General aggressive tendencies can be reduced by allowing people to purge aggressive energy from their systems. One way in which this can be done is through the observation of aggressive models. Research on the effects of media violence and of sports refutes this aspect of the catharsis hypothesis. Media violence and participation in sports tend to increase aggression in people.

With regard to specific acts of aggression, the catharsis hypothesis proposes that once people have been angered, they become aroused and they must purge their aggressive energy through activities such as verbal aggression, substitute forms of aggression, or physical aggression. Contrary to the catharsis hypothesis, however, these actions appear to increase rather than decrease the probability of subsequent aggression.

Some researchers have proposed that specific acts of aggression can be prevented or at least reduced by generating incompatible responses in a person. While the available data suggest that this technique will work, it is not a cure-all for aggression. It is unlikely that a behavior as complex and widespread as aggression will be easily controlled.

Applications

Sexual Assaults and Violence against Women

Aggression can take a variety of different forms. This section concerns a kind of behavior that until recently many people did not see as aggression—sexual assault. Sexual assaults are acts of aggression, not acts of love gone astray; the only thing these acts of aggression and acts of love have in common is that in both someone may experience an orgasm. Rape illustrates this point. In addition to the extensive pain a forced vaginal penetration can cause a woman, it is likely that she will receive other injuries. McDermott (1979) obtained data from victims of completed rapes in 26 different cities and found that over 90 percent of the women involved received some sort of physical injury. The psychological damage of a rape can persist long after the bruises have healed. Kilpatrick, Resick, and Veronen (1981) found that adult rape victims experienced increases in anxiety, fear, and confusion for at least one year after the rape. As Francoeur said, "Rape is an act of violence; sex is the weapon" (1984, 413).

The first part of this section discusses the frequency of sexual assaults, the motives behind rape, people's attitudes toward rape and other kinds of sexual assault, and the characteristics of people inclined to engage in such actions. The second part discusses the effects of one situational variable—pornography—on sexual violence against women. (Both men and women can be the victims of a sexual assault, but typically the target is a woman and the perpetrator is a man.)

RAPE AND SEXUAL ASSAULTS

Most crime reports provide data only on rape, although there are other kinds of sexual assault. Rape has been defined by the United States Department of Justice as "unlawful sexual intercourse with a female by force or without legal or factual consent" (1983). In 1980, there were approximately 170,000 reported rapes (United States Department of Justice, 1983). Given that there are over 100 million women in the United States, these statistics would suggest that rape is a relatively rare occurrence. The number of rapes reported to the police is, however, a poor indicator of the extent of the problem. Estimates vary, but most researchers agree that only between 25 and 50 percent of the rapes and other sexual assaults that occur are reported. A study by Burt (1980) may give a more accurate view of how widespread rape and other forms of sexual assault really are. Burt interviewed a randomly selected group of adults from a large midwestern city and found that 27 percent of the women interviewed had had an experience in which a man unsuccessfully attempted to force them into a sexual activity. Another 18 percent of the women interviewed had been forced to engage in some sexual act because of actual or threatened violence. Mahoney (1983) used data such as these to estimate that over 3 million women are raped every year in the United States.

Even more disturbing is the context in which rapes and other sexual assaults occur. In most instances, the rapist knows his victim (Francoeur, 1984) and he may even be involved in a long-term relationship with her. Recent surveys of female college students disclosed that 60 percent had experienced at least one sexual assault in the course of a dating relationship (Joseph, 1981). Twenty-five percent of the male college students interviewed by Kanin (1967) reported that on at least one occasion they had attempted to force a woman into having intercourse with them. In a follow-up study, Kanin and Parcell (1977) found that 24 percent of female college students had been forced into intercourse by a man at least once.

Motives for Rape

Acts of aggression do not just happen; they have a specifiable cause and a specifiable goal. The same is true of rape. Groth, Burgess, and Hohlstrom (1977) and Mahoney (1983) have proposed that there are three kinds of rape. The first is rape motivated by *sexual gratification*. The rapist uses force or violence to achieve this goal. The second is called a *power rape*. The attacker's behavior is somewhat motivated by a desire for sexual gratification, but his primary goal is to show that he has power over his victim and can control her. The third is called *angry rape*. It can be illustrated by the following story told to me by an ex-convict who took my social psychology course. He had been part of a gang that carried out burglaries and armed robberies. The female member of the gang was caught by the police and, to avoid going to prison, she became a police informant. The men in the gang learned this and four of them raped her. This act was not motivated by a desire for sexual gratification; instead, it was motivated by the desire to vent anger, rage, and hatred on the victim. Thus, the rape was an act of angry aggression. Among convicted rapists, power and angry rapes are far more common than sexual-gratification rapes (Mahoney, 1983).

Attitudes toward Sexual Assault

Given the brutal and destructive nature of most sexual assaults, one would expect most people to view such acts with disgust and to have little sympathy for the people who commit them. But this is not the case. For example, a judge in Wisconsin dismissed charges against a 15-year-old male who had raped a 16-year-old female. The judge acknowledged that the boy had raped the girl, but attributed his behavior to a "reasonable" cause: On the day of the rape, the victim wore a skirt that was too short. She had so

A scene from the trial of the men accused of the gang rape of a woman in a bar in New Bedford, Massachusetts. The lawyer is pointing to a model of the bar. For many people, this trial became symbolic of sexual violence against women.

inflamed the boy's passions that he could not help but rape her. To quote this sage jurist: "Whether you like it or not a woman's a sex object and they're the ones who turn the man on, generally" (cited in McCagny, 1980, 118). A few months after this decision, a judge in Los Angeles stated that if a female hitchhiker is raped, it is *her* fault (McCagny, 1980).

These are extreme examples, but the public is more accepting of rape than one might expect. In 46 of the 50 states, a husband who rapes his wife will not be charged with a crime; legally, rape cannot occur within a marriage. Mahoney (1983) asked male college students if it was acceptable for a husband to hold his wife down and force her to have intercourse with him, and over 40 percent said yes. Nearly 40 percent of the male high school students surveyed by Giarrusso, Johnson, Goodchilds, and Zellman (1979) said that forced intercourse with a woman is acceptable if she is under the influence of alcohol or some other drug.

Burt (1980) has studied some of the variables associated with attitudes toward rape. She gave about 600 randomly selected men and women a scale that measured the extent to which people accept certain myths about rape. (See table 7-1 for part of this scale.)

Burt's results showed the extent to which certain rape myths are accepted by the general public. For example, she found that over half the sample agreed with statements such as "In the majority of rapes, the victim was promiscuous or had a bad reputation." She also found that certain characteristics were associated with acceptance of rape myths. Older and less educated people were more accepting of the myths. In addition, people

Table 7-1. Some items from the Acceptance of Rape Myths Scale. Someone who accepts these myths would give the answers indicated in the parentheses.

1. A woman should be a virgin when she marries. (True)
2. A woman will only respect a man who will lay down the law to her. (True)
3. A woman who initiates a sexual encounter will probably have sex with anyone. (True)
4. Being roughed up is sexually stimulating to many women. (True)

Source: Burt (1980).

Sex role stereotypes: beliefs that certain activities, behaviors, interests, and occupations are appropriate for and typical of each sex.

who accepted the myths differed from those who did not in three sets of attitudes. First, they were more likely to hold **sex role stereotypes.** Second, these people believed that sexual relationships are usually mutually exploitative and involve dishonesty, cheating, and manipulation. Third, they felt interpersonal violence is a necessary and legitimate means for one person to gain control over another, especially in a sexual relationship. Remember these findings; they are associated with more than just attitudes about rape.

Characteristics of the Rapist

Contrary to popular belief, the potential rapist is not one of a small number of violent, sexual deviants who share little in common with normal healthy males. In several different studies, Neil Malamuth and his associates (for example, Malamuth, 1981; Malamuth and Check, 1980a; Malamuth, Heim, and Feshbach, 1980) asked young men if they would commit a rape if they were sure that they would not be caught or punished. The men chose from answers ranging from "not at all likely" to "very likely." About 35 percent of the men answered that there was at least some likelihood they would commit a rape under such circumstances and 20 percent answered that there was at least a fair likelihood they would. Malamuth and his associates compared the attitudes and behaviors of these men—possible rapists—to those of men who had actually committed a rape—actual rapists—and to those of men who had answered that they were not at all likely to commit a rape—nonrapists.

The three groups differed in their attitudes toward sex and sexual violence. The actual rapists and the possible rapists were much more likely than the nonrapists to hold callous attitudes about the purpose of sex, to hold strong sex role stereotypes, and to accept myths about rape (Wolfe and Barker, 1980; Check and Malamuth, 1983; Malamuth, 1981). These two groups also appeared to be more accepting of using interpersonal violence to gain control over one's sexual partner. These attitudes were the same as those found by Burt in her study of rape myths.

The three groups also differed in their reactions to various kinds of sexually explicit material. In several studies, the men were exposed to a scene that depicted sex between two consenting people or to a scene that depicted a rape. Then self-reports and physiological measures of sexual arousal were obtained. Actual and possible rapists were just as aroused by the rape scene as by the consenting-sex scene. Nonrapists showed significantly more arousal to the consenting-sex scene than to the rape scene (Abel, Becker, and Skinner, 1980; Malamuth and Check, 1980b).

These results suggest that sexual assaults are due, at least in part, to a man's general attitudes about women and to the way he relates to women. They further suggest that tendencies to commit rape are not confined to a deviant few. This does not mean that the men labeled possible rapists are going to commit a rape, but it does indicate that such tendencies exist among a sizable segment of the general male population.

One other characteristic of the rapist deserves mention. If rape is an act of aggression, then it is reasonable to propose that people who are inclined toward rape will also be inclined toward other forms of violence. In a 1983 study, Malamuth investigated this issue. His subjects were men who had responded to the question about the likelihood they would commit a rape. Several days later, they worked on a task with a female confederate. In the early stages of the experiment, she insulted the men and mildly rejected them. Malamuth measured how much this angered the men, how much they wanted to hurt her, and how much they aggressed against her when they were given the chance. On all three measures, men classified as possible rapists scored significantly higher than those classified as non-rapists, strongly suggesting that the tendency to commit rape is associated with the tendency to commit other forms of aggression against women.

PORNOGRAPHY AND SEXUAL VIOLENCE

The discussion of the causes of aggression presented evidence that certain stimuli in people's environment can affect how much they aggress. This also appears to be true of sexual violence. One stimulus that has received considerable attention is pornography.

Since the late 1960s, there has been an explosion in the amount of pornographic material produced and sold; magazines that primarily present soft-core pornography (for example, *Penthouse* and *Playboy*) earn profits in excess of $500 million per year (Serrin, 1981) and theaters that show hard-core pornographic films take in over $10 million per week (Serrin, 1981). The famous (or infamous) pornographic film *Deep Throat*, which cost $25,000 to make, has earned over $50 million (Mahoney, 1983). And most recently, "x-rated" video cassettes have become a multi-million dollar industry.

Paralleling the growth in the availability of pornographic material to the general public has been an increase in the concern over its effects on people. In the late 1960s, a national commission on pornography was established by the president. In its report, the National Commission on Obscenity and Pornography (1970) concluded that there was no evidence to suggest that exposure to such material increased a person's propensity to engage in antisocial behavior. Critics of this report argued that the commission did not pay sufficient attention to the relationship between aggressive pornography and violence against women.

Today, most people distinguish between (1) *soft-core pornography*, which presents nude or seminude individuals and scenes that suggest but do not

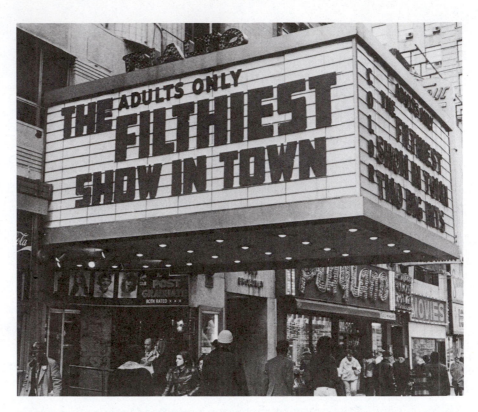

As this theater marquee suggests, pornography has become a very open and very lucrative business.

Aggressive pornography: material that contains portrayals in which one person is blatantly coerced into sexual activities by another or of violent episodes in which one person is beaten, tortured, or humiliated by another person.

explicitly show sexual intercourse or comparable acts and (2) *hard-core pornography*, which usually explicitly depicts sexual activities and things like group sex and sexual relations between animals and humans. A specific kind of hard-core pornography is **aggressive pornography** (Malamuth and Donnerstein, 1983; Steinem, 1980).

The critics claimed that while soft-core pornography and even certain forms of hard-core pornography may not affect people's behavior, aggressive pornography may affect their propensity to engage in sexual violence. It may convey the impression that victims enjoy being beaten and coerced into sex; thus, it may influence people's general views of how women react to a sexual assault. Also, the repeated pairing of sex and aggression may result "in conditioning processes whereby aggressive acts become associated with sexual arousal, a powerful unconditioned stimulus and reinforcer" (Malamuth and Donnerstein, 1983, p. 106).

No long-term field studies have been conducted to investigate the effects of aggressive pornography on those who watch it, but some laboratory experiments have examined such effects. These studies are subject to all the limitations of any laboratory experiment, but their results give some reason for concern.

Aggressive Pornography and Attitudes
toward Sexual Assaults

If aggressive pornography affects a man's view of sexual violence, then exposure to such material should increase the incidence of the kinds of attitudes and perceptions held by men who are inclined toward sexual assaults; aggressive pornography should produce more callous attitudes about sex, greater acceptance of myths about rape, and greater acceptance of interpersonal violence as a means of controlling one's sexual partner. Malamuth and his associates (Malamuth et al., 1980; Malamuth and Check, 1980b; Malamuth and Check, 1981) have investigated this. In all of their studies, male subjects were presented with depictions of sexual activities, including a rape in which the woman became sexually aroused, a rape in which the woman became disgusted, and a relationship between two consenting adults. Subjects who were exposed to the sexually aroused rape scene were significantly more likely than those exposed to the other sex scenes to believe that women enjoy being forced into sex, to see the consequences of a rape as less serious, and to accept interpersonal violence against women (Donnerstein, 1983; Malamuth and Check, 1981b). Given these effects, it is not surprising that Malamuth, Haber, and Feshbach (1980) found the sexually aroused rape scene also produced an increase in the subjects' estimates of the likelihood that they would commit a rape. These results do not mean that aggressive pornography will turn an otherwise normal man into a rapist, but they do suggest that aggressive pornography increases the acceptance of attitudes and perceptions associated with the propensity to rape.

Aggressive Pornography and Aggression
against Women

A study by Donnerstein (1980) examined whether aggressive pornography affects a man's willingness to engage in nonsexual aggression against a woman. Donnerstein randomly divided male subjects into two groups. Subjects in one group were attacked by a male confederate; subjects in the other group were attacked by a female confederate. Before they were allowed to retaliate, subjects in each group saw one of three films: one was neutral, another contained erotic material, and the other contained aggressive pornography. The dependent measure was the amount of shock subjects gave the confederate when they were allowed to retaliate. (See figure 7-8 for the results.)

Among the subjects who retaliated against the male confederate, both the erotic and aggressive pornographic films produced more aggression than did the neutral film (perhaps because of excitation transfer). Among the subjects who retaliated against the female confederate, however, those who saw the aggressive pornography aggressed significantly more than did subjects who saw either of the other two films. Subsequent research has shown that aggressive pornography produces more aggression against

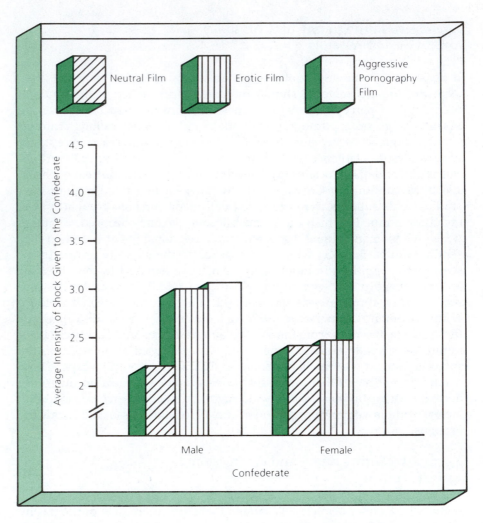

Figure 7-8. *Erotic and aggressive pornographic films produced equal amounts of aggression against a male confederate; the aggressive pornographic film produced high levels of aggression against a female confederate.*
Source: Donnerstein (1980).

a woman than does a film that is only pornographic or only aggressive (Donnerstein, 1983). However, this does not occur when the target of the aggression is a man.

So, it appears that aggressive pornography's effect on aggression is highly dependent on the sex of the target of the aggression. When the target is a man, it does not seem to appreciably increase the propensity to aggress, but when the target is a woman, it significantly increases aggression. This effect is further heightened if the aggressive pornography depicts an episode in which the woman appears to enjoy being raped (Donnerstein and Berkowitz, 1981).

Malamuth and Donnerstein (1983) suggested that aggressive pornography may affect men's propensities toward nonsexual aggression against women in two ways. First, most men have relatively strong learned inhibitions against harming a woman, but exposure to a scene that suggests women enjoy being abused may serve to lower such inhibitions. The second explanation is based on Berkowitz's concept of aggression-eliciting stimuli. Recall that Berkowitz believed stimuli associated with either a person's anger or a person's act of aggression may increase the probability that a person who is ready to aggress will actually do so. Malamuth and Donnerstein proposed that aggressive pornography may be one such stimulus. In support of this proposal is the fact that aggressive pornography affects aggression only against a woman, a target who could be reasonably associated with the aggression a man has just seen. There is, however, a problem with this explanation. While aggressive cues are only supposed to impact the behavior of a person who is angry, Donnerstein and Berkowitz (1981) found that when the aggressive pornography depicted a positive outcome (the woman became sexually aroused), aggression increased even among nonangry men. Thus, the effects of this kind of pornography cannot be totally explained by aggressive cues. As Malamuth and Donnerstein (1983) have proposed, aggressive pornography probably has a number of effects, all of which contribute in some way to increased aggression against women.

These findings do not conclusively prove that long-term exposure to aggressive pornography will produce sexual violence, but they do suggest that these effects should be investigated. What does seem clear is that aggressive pornography degrades women and demeans sexual relations. It also fosters attitudes that may at best interfere with positive relations between the sexes and that may at worst contribute to violence against women.

Chapter Eight

Prosocial Behavior

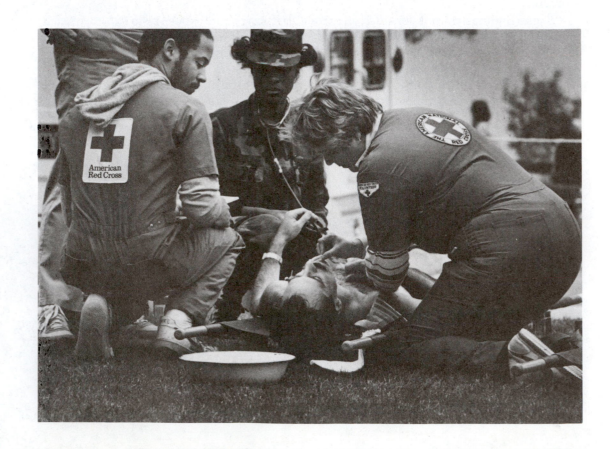

Prologue

Robert F. Weiss, Jenny L. Boyer, John P. Lombardo, and
Mark H. Stitch (1973). Altruistic Drive and Altruistic
Reinforcement. *Journal of Personality and Social Psychology,*
25, 390–400.

Background

This chapter concerns helping; one person doing something that benefits
another. One major question asked by researchers interested in this aspect
of social behavior is: What motivates people to provide help? Some theorists
have argued that helping is not likely to occur unless the potential helper
expects an external reward such as money or praise. Other theorists, including Robert Weiss and his associates, have argued that in many instances
people help because this behavior is intrinsically reinforcing. They have
proposed that helping others achieve positive outcomes is a positive reinforcer, and helping others avoid or escape negative outcomes is a negative
reinforcer; thus, people help others to achieve positive reinforcement or
to avoid negative reinforcement.

   About two years before this study was published, Weiss, Buchanan,
Alstalt, and Lombardo (1971) conducted an experiment to test their proposal. The results of the experiment generally supported the notion that
helping is intrinsically reinforcing, but the procedure used in that experiment did not allow the researchers to definitely conclude that the subjects
were helping because of the intrinsically reinforcing properties of helping
behavior. In this study, Weiss, Boyer, Lombardo, and Stitch improved on
the earlier procedure and conducted three separate experiments concerned
with the same issue. The first of these experiments is described here.

Hypothesis

Weiss and his colleagues predicted that if helping others was intrinsically
reinforcing, then subjects would change their behavior to achieve this reinforcer.

Subjects

The subjects were 48 male and female students enrolled in psychology
classes at the University of Oklahoma.

Procedure

The procedure used by Weiss's group was heavily influenced by theory
and research on instrumental conditioning; it may be valuable, therefore,
to digress and briefly describe how researchers interested in instrumental
conditioning determine that something is a reinforcer. Typically, they see
if an organism will perform a behavior more often or more rapidly because

of the reinforcer. For example, researchers know that food is a positive reinforcer for rats because rats will increase the number of times they press a bar if the bar pressing produces food. Similarly, researchers know that electric shock is a negative reinforcer for humans because humans will increase the speed with which they press a lever if this enables them to avoid or escape shock.

In this study, Weiss and his associates wanted to determine if humans would increase the speed with which they pressed a button when this enabled another person to temporarily escape electric shock: Would the subjects acquire a behavior that was reinforced by the alleviation of suffering in another person?

The subjects were led to believe that their job was to observe and then evaluate the performance of other people while these people attempted to track a moving object. The subjects were told that because the researchers were interested in the effects of stress, the people they would observe would receive painful, continuous electric shock. The people were, in fact, confederates and received no shock.

The experiment was divided into 15 trials. Each trial began with shock being given to a confederate and lasted about 30 seconds. Approximately 15 seconds into a trial, subjects received a signal to evaluate the confederate's performance on the task. They did this by setting three dials, which corresponded to three aspects of the confederate's performance. After the dials were set, a "report signal" came on and the subjects were to transfer their evaluations to a magnetic tape by pushing six buttons, one after the other. When the subjects had pushed all the buttons, the trial was over and a new trial began.

In fact, the researchers had no interest in the evaluations; the dependent measure was how quickly the subjects pushed the buttons after the report signal was lit. This was measured in hundredths of a second by a clock which started when the report signal went on and stopped when the first button was pushed.

Half the subjects were assigned to a reinforcement condition; as soon as they pushed the sixth button, the shock stopped and confederates breathed a sigh of relief as they received a ten-second break from the shock. The other half of the subjects were assigned to a no-reinforcement, or control, condition; the shock continued after the final button was pushed and the confederates continued to behave as if they were receiving electric shock.

Results

If the hypothesis that people will change their behavior to achieve the reinforcer of helping another person were correct, then the behavior of the subjects in the reinforcement condition should have differed from the behavior of the subjects in the no-reinforcement, or control, condition. Over the trials, they should have become faster in responding to the report signal because the faster they responded, the sooner shock to the confederate was stopped. Control subjects, who were not reinforced for fast responses, should not have become faster over the trials. This is exactly what happened. (See figure 8-1.)

Implications

Weiss and the others had demonstrated that people respond to a negative reinforcer (shock) directed at another person as if the negative reinforcer were directed at them; they change their behavior to escape it. No one told the subjects that it was their job to help the confederate escape the shock, and no external rewards were given for this behavior. It appears that subjects in the reinforcement condition became faster because it was intrinsically reinforcing "to deliver another human being from suffering" (Weiss et al., 1973, 390). This chapter presents several theories of why helping someone else may be reinforcing and addresses the question of why, despite this, people often fail to offer help to someone in distress.

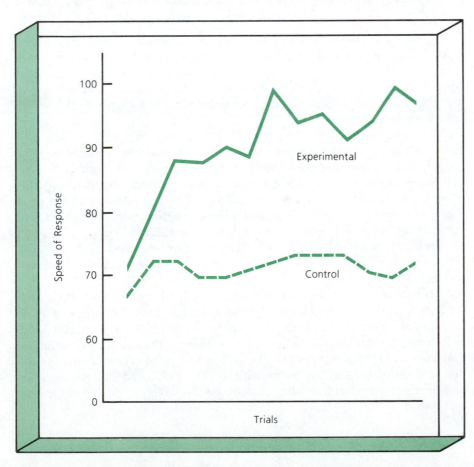

Figure 8-1. *Subjects who could help another person by responding quickly learned to increase the speed of their response. Copyright 1973 American Psychological Association. Reprinted by permission of the authors.*
Source: Weiss et al. (1973).

Why do humans help one another? This is a question of considerable interest to social psychologists, members of related sciences, and the general public. Part of the reason for their interest is the fact that humans are capable of both callous indifference to other people in need and acts of selfless sacrifice. Consider these two true incidents:

> An 18-year-old woman is raped and beaten. She momentarily escapes and runs naked and bleeding into the street. As 40 people stand and watch, in broad daylight, the rapist tries to drag her away; no one interferes (Latan'e and Darley, 1970).

> A man is attacked by an unknown assailant. He is stabbed several times and lies helpless on the ground. As the assailant is about to deliver the fatal blow, a friend dives between the man and the assailant. He saves the man's life, but is severely wounded (*Tampa Tribune*, 1984).

In the literature on helping behavior, two terms are often used interchangeably: helping and altruism. In fact, these terms have quite different meanings. *Helping* is a voluntary act "performed with the intent to provide some benefit to another person" (Dovidio, 1984). This definition says nothing about the person's motivation for helping; it is a broad definition of behaviors ranging from helping with the expectation of payment to helping without anticipation of a reward. *Altruism* is a specific kind of helping; voluntary acts, which produce no external or tangible rewards for the helper, but instead are performed to benefit another person. Altruistic behaviors are divided into two classes. One is **strong altruism** and the other is **weak altruism.** You saw an example of weak altruism in the prologue. According to Weiss and his colleagues, the subjects helped the confederate because it was intrinsically reinforcing to do so.

Helping, the broader term, is used in this chapter unless the theoretical position being reviewed clearly identifies the phenomenon of interest as strong or weak altruism.

This chapter examines the variables responsible for both selfish and selfless actions. The first section presents some general theories of why humans are motivated to help. The second section looks at a specific kind of helping, bystander intervention, and examines the situational variables that appear to influence people's behavior. The third section concerns individual differences in the propensity to offer help, and the applications section discusses characteristics of people who have provided help in the real world.

Strong altruism: behavior that provides no reinforcement of any kind for the helper and is motivated solely by the desire to increase another's welfare.

Weak altruism: behavior that provides some internal reinforcement for the helper and increases another's welfare.

WHY DO PEOPLE HELP?

The experiment presented in the prologue demonstrated that people will help even when there are no external rewards for doing so. It did not explain the origins of this behavior. This section presents two general theoretical answers to this question based on a biological and a social learning viewpoint.

Biological Viewpoint

The biological position is that just as humans have innate tendencies to satisfy their need for food and water, so they have innate tendencies to satisfy their need to help others. This explanation of helping is primarily the product of a branch of biology called **sociobiology.** Sociobiologists approach human social behavior with a perspective quite different from that of most social psychologists. (See chapter one.) They view many social behaviors as being caused by human genetic heritage. The sociobiologists believe there is such a thing as strong altruism. Strong altruism occurs in the absence of any benefit for the altruist; thus, sociobiologists argue that something other than rewards or punishments is reponsible for it. That "something," they believe, is genes. The following true examples of helping behavior are the kinds sociobiologists find interesting.

Sociobiology: a branch of biology that proposes that a substantial portion of human social behavior is genetically determined.

> While walking through an African jungle, a group of travelers was attacked by a hungry leopard. Several members of the group fled, but a few young males stood their ground. They ripped small trees from the ground and used these as whips to ward off the leopard. As a result, the other members of the group escaped unharmed (Wilson, 1975).

> A swimmer was stunned by an accidental underwater explosion. Several individuals saw the injured swimmer lying helpless in the water. They swam to her and held her head above water until she recovered from the explosion (Sienbenalar and Caldwell, 1956).

> A small child, Margaret, and her friend, Red, were seated in the backseat of Margaret's parents' car. Suddenly, the car burst into flames. Red jumped from the car, but realized Margaret was still inside. He jumped back into the burning automobile, grabbed Margaret by her jacket, and pulled her to safety (Batson, 1983).

Sociobiologists would argue that these incidents reflect strong altruism, that they were caused by certain genetic characteristics. But could there be other explanations? Could the males have fought off the leopard simply to prove how "macho" they were? Might Red have saved Margaret because he was afraid that he would be punished if he abandoned her? Should we view these actions as caused by an altruistic impulse inherited from their ancestors? Well, maybe—because the heroes of these three stories were animals, not humans. The act of courage in the jungle was displayed by a group of chimpanzees; the swimmer and her rescuers were dolphins; and Red was an Irish Setter.

Sociobiologists point out that such acts of altruism are commonly observed in a variety of animals. These behaviors, they argue, are not learned, but are part of an animal's genetic heritage—whether the animal walks on four feet or two.

Evolution of Altruism

Charles Darwin (1859) argued that the evolution of certain characteristics in a species is the result of natural selection. An organism's environment determines to a great extent who will survive and who will not. If an organism possesses characteristics that enable it to survive, it will be able to reproduce and pass this characteristic on to its descendants. Consequently, natural selection often produces changes in the dominant characteristics of a species.

Darwin's (1859) original theory cannot fully explain how a tendency that might result in people sacrificing their own lives for others would have survival value. Death would greatly reduce the number of offspring the altruist could produce and would thus reduce the frequency of this genetic tendency in the next generation. Recent revisions of Darwin's theory (for example, Dawkins, 1976; Hamilton, 1972; Wilson, 1975) propose a mechanism that would explain the survival value of altruism—**kin selection.** Kin selection proposes that certain characteristics will survive if groups of related individuals who possess them are able to avoid genetic extermination.

Kin selection: the concept that the genetic survival of a species depends on the survival of characteristics that related members of the species share.

Strong altruism can serve this end. For example, imagine that a group of our ancestors is attacked by a dangerous animal. One of the group fights the animal and, in the process of saving the other group members, is killed. This reduces the chances that the rescuer will be able to pass her own genes on to offspring, but because of her altruism, her brother survives. He shares 50 percent of her genes. He lives to father eight children, each of whom shares 25 percent of their dear, departed aunt's genes. In this way, the rescuer contributed to the survival of a common gene pool. Groups with members like the heroine of this story are more likely to survive than those without. To quote Edward Wilson:

> So long as the beneficiaries of . . . altruism themselves carry some of the altruistic genes and so long as the benefit they receive permits them to multiply those genes to a more than compensating degree, the genes will increase in the population as a whole, and the altruistic behavior will spread. (1978, pp. 11, 12)

According to the theory of kin selection, species that are genetically programmed help their relatives (organisms with common genes) are likely to survive. However, in many incidents, the recipient of an altruistic act is not a relative of the altruist, but a biological stranger. Trivers (1971) has proposed the concept of *reciprocal altruism* to explain why humans would help strangers. According to Trivers, any of our ancestors who were willing to help a nonrelative were likely to have the favor reciprocated. Thus, if acts of altruism did not cost altruists their lives, they may have resulted in the altruists surviving longer because they got help when they needed it. As a result, these ancestors were able to transmit the altruism characteristic to their offspring.

In general, social psychologists have not been very accepting of biological explanations of human social behavior. The sociobiological explanation of helping has had a somewhat more favorable reception among social psychologists, but it also has critics. The major criticisms are that no good studies with humans have supported the biological explanation of helping and that the sociobiologists have ignored the social learning theorists' extensive research on the causes of helping in humans.

Social Learning Viewpoint

Advocates of social learning theory reject the notion that helping is due to innate drives. They believe that this social behavior originates in the socialization process. They propose that classical conditioning, instrumental conditioning, and observational learning all play a role in the development of helpful tendencies and can eventually produce the kinds of behavior displayed by the subjects in the prologue.

Classical Conditioning and Empathic Responses

It is generally agreed that most acts of helping are preceded by an **empathic response** (Hoffman, 1981). The following examples illustrate the difference between a true empathic and pseudo-empathic response. In the first, your uncle Percy dies and this causes both you and your sister to feel sad. Your sadness, even though it is the same feeling as your sister's, is a pseudo- rather than a true empathic response. While you have the same feelings as someone else, the feelings are the result of something which directly affected you and represent a pseudo-empathic response. But if instead your roommate's uncle Percy whom you have never met dies and you experience the same sad feeling as your roommate, this is a true empathic response. Your feelings are essentially the same as those of someone whose uncle has just died, but they are caused by something that happened to another person.

> **Empathic response:** emotions or feelings that are caused by something that has happened to another person.

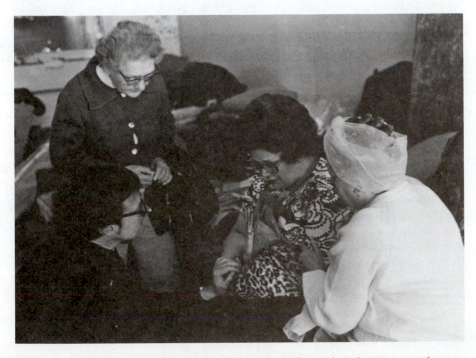

A group of neighbors console a victim of a fire. The looks on their faces suggest they are experiencing empathic responses to the woman's plight.

Research suggests that from a very early age, people experience empathic reactions to others' distress (Hoffman, 1981; Piliavin, Dovidio, Gaertner, and Clark, 1981). Some researchers (for example, Hoffman, 1981) believe that humans are biologically preprogrammed to respond empathically, and some evidence supports this belief. For example, one- to two-day-old infants cry or show similar reactions when they hear other infants cry (Martin and Clark, 1982; Sagi and Hoffman, 1976; Simmer, 1971). They appear genuinely distressed, and they are not simply reacting to unpleasant stimuli. Loud noises made by machines or the cries of nonhuman animals do not produce comparable reactions. Since two-day-old infants have not had much of a chance to learn that society approves of empathic responses, some theorists attribute this response to human's genetic heritage.

Learning theorists would argue that the babies' cries were not a true empathic response. They propose that true empathic responses are acquired through classical conditioning. Studies by Aronfreed and Paskal (1965, 1966) and Midlarsky and Bryan (1967) have shown that children can learn empathic responses through classical conditioning and that once they have learned empathic responses, they perform helping behaviors in the absence of external rewards.

Instrumental Conditioning and Helping
If you directly reward a child for helping another person, the child's willingness to help will increase. Among younger children, material rewards (such as money or candy) are more effective than social rewards (such as praising the child). By the time children are ten to 12 years old, both types of rewards are equally effective (Fisher, 1963; Midlarsky, Bryan, and Brickman, 1973; Rushton and Teachman, 1978). But children do not respond indiscriminately to social rewards. If the rewards come from someone a child dislikes or distrusts, the rewards have an effect opposite to that intended. Consider this study by Midlarsky and her associates (1973). Twelve-year-old girls watched one of two adults play a game in which the adult won prizes. The first adult gave a sizable portion of her winnings to a fund for needy children. The other adult refused to donate any of her winnings and kept them for herself. Then, as the adults watched, the children played the game; each time the children won a prize they had the choice of keeping it for themselves or donating it to the needy children. The adults either praised them for their charity or said nothing. When the charitable model praised the children, the children gave more. But when the selfish adult praised them, they gave less. (See figure 8-2.) Evidently, the children were aware of the selfish adult's hypocrisy and did not view her praise as a positive reinforcer. If parents want helpful children, they better practice what they preach!

Observational Learning and Helping
Recall that in observational learning, an observer watches a model and, as a result, learns something from the model's actions. Studies have consistently shown that helpful models produce long-term increases in children's willingness to help (Midlarsky and Bryan, 1972; Rice and Grusec, 1975;

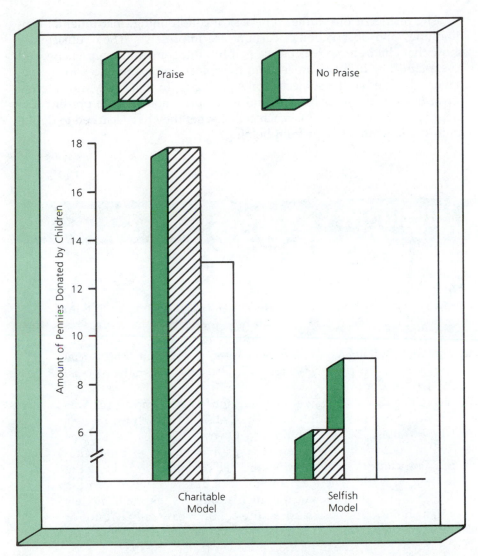

Figure 8-2. *Praise from a charitable model increased children's giving; praise from a selfish model decreased children's giving.*
Source: Midlarsky et al. (1973).

Rushton, 1975; Rushton and Littlefield, 1979). It also appears that these effects are strongest when the model has some degree of control over the child and has a warm, nurturant relationship with her (Grusec, 1981; Rutherford and Mussen, 1968; Yarrow, Scott, and Waxler, 1973). However, children are discriminating in their reactions to a model; what a model does appears to have more impact on a child than what the model says. Midlarsky and Bryan (1972) exposed children to either an adult who acted charitably but preached greed or an adult who acted greedily but preached charity. Watching the first model produced 50 percent more helping behaviors than did watching the second model.

The results of the studies on classical conditioning, instrumental conditioning, and observational learning are impressive. They consistently show that children can learn to be helpful. But something more is needed to explain how humans move from these learning experiences to the behavior observed in the subjects in the prologue. In that study, no external rewards were given for helping and no helpful models were present. Evidently, by the time humans reach college age, they have learned to derive an intrinsic reinforcement from helping.

Research Highlight

Something Good about Television

Because televison shows are rife with violent episodes, most research concerned with television's effects on social behavior has focused on how it affects aggression. This research has shown a weak but positive relationship between media violence and antisocial aggressive behavior among viewers. (See chapter seven.) But if antisocial models on television can affect people's behavior, is it also possible that prosocial models can affect people's behavior?

Two approaches have been used to answer this question. The first approach was conducting experiments on the effects of televised presentations of helpful models (for example, Bryan and Walbek, 1970; Rushton and Owen, 1977). These studies indicated that televised models are nearly as effective as live models in producing helping behaviors. But one can question whether this tells us anything about the effects of television in the real world. There are a number of differences between the televised models children watched in these experiments and the televised models they would watch in their homes. In these studies, the children saw only helpful or nonhelpful models; on "real" television, such models would be embedded in a program and their actions might have little impact on a viewer (Rushton, 1982).

This fact led to the second approach. Children were shown actual television shows that contained prosocial models, and then the effects of the models were examined. In a study by Murray and Ahammer (1977), five year olds watched either neutral or prosocial programs for one-half hour a day for four weeks. At the conclusion of the four weeks, the incidence of prosocial behavior among members of both groups were examined. Boys who watched the prosocial shows were more willing than boys who watched the neutral shows to forego playing with an attractive toy in order to help another child. This effect was not found for girls, although both boys and girls who watched the prosocial shows were more cooperative than boys and girls who watched the neutral shows.

Field experiments have produced similar results. Moriarity and McCabe (1977) selected children who played in sports leagues (baseball, ice hockey, lacrosse) as their subjects. Over several weeks, the children watched television shows that presented antisocial, prosocial, or neutral aspects of the sports they played. Then the behavior of the children as they played a game was recorded. Baseball players were not affected by the content of the programs, but players in the rougher contact sports were affected. Hockey and lacrosse players who were exposed to prosocial portrayals of their sport played the game in a more helpful, prosocial manner. In an experiment conducted with adults, Loye, Gorney, and Steele (1977) found that couples who watched five days of prosocial programs were less likely to engage in "hurtful" actions toward one another than were couples who watched violent or neutral programs.

These findings suggest that television has at least the *potential* of promoting helpfulness and cooperation among its viewers. The question remains as to whether there could ever be enough prosocial models on television to influence the behavior of those who watch it.

Research suggests that television has the potential for teaching prosocial behavior to children.

Changes in the Motivation to Help

Robert Cialdini and his associates (Cialdini, Baumann, and Kenrick, 1981; Cialdini, et al. 1982) have proposed a three-stage model of how changes occur in human's motivations for helping others. In the first stage, called the *presocialization stage,* children do not want to help others because helping does not benefit them and may punish them (they may have to sacrifice something of value). Among young children, even acts of weak altruism are rare. In the second state, *awareness of norms*, children learn two inter-related things. First, they learn that a societal norm, or standard, says that people should help. Second, through social learning experiences, they learn that they will be rewarded for adhering to the norm and sometimes punished for failing to do so. At this stage, children help others in order to achieve rewards and avoid punishments. The repeated pairings of positive consequences with helping and negative consequences with not helping lead to the third stage, *internalization*. Conditioning causes helping to become a positive reinforcer in and of itself; it makes the person feel good. At this stage, helping can occur in the absence of external reinforcers.

A 1976 study by Cialdini and Kenrick tested the proposal that children's motivations for helping change as they mature. These researchers reasoned that if helping (weak altruism) were a positive, self-reinforcing behavior, then people who feel bad would, if given the chance, engage in helping because helping would provide relief from their negative state. This is called the **negative state relief hypothesis** (Cialdini, Darby, and Vincent, 1973).

The subjects were drawn from three different age groups: 6 to 8 year olds, 10 to 12 year olds, and 16 to 18 year olds. Within each age group, half the subjects were instructed to think about sad experiences from their

Negative state relief hypothesis: the hypothesis that people may help when they feel bad because helping in certain circumstances makes them feel good and, thus, provides relief from a negative state.

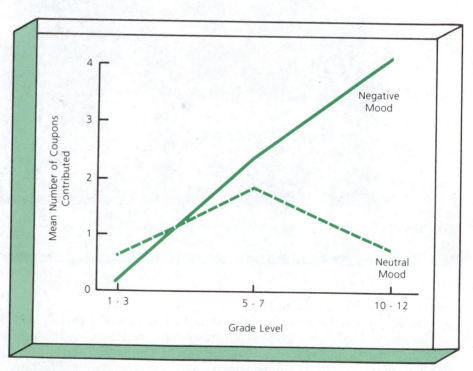

Figure 8-3. *Negative moods caused less helping among the younger subjects but more helping among the older subjects. Copyright 1976 American Psychological Association. Reprinted by permission of the authors.*
Source: Cialdini and Kenrick (1976).

pasts and half were instructed to think about something neutral. Following this, all subjects were given the chance to help by making an anonymous donation to charity. (See figure 8-3 for the amounts donated by the subjects.)

The results were consistent with the hypothesis about developmental changes in the nature of helping. Among the youngest subjects, more was donated by subjects in a neutral than in a bad mood. Among the oldest group, this pattern was reversed; subjects in a bad mood donated significantly more than those in a neutral mood. The older subjects used helping to relieve their negative moods. It appears that helping, like a good wine, becomes more pleasurable with age. Do not, however, conclude that negative moods invariably produce an increase in helping. Under some circumstances, bad moods will produce a decrease in helping. (See section on individual differences in helping in this chapter.) This study merely demonstrated that the motivations for helping may change as the result of socialization.

Reconciling the Biological and Social Learning Viewpoints

The biological and social learning explanations of helping are quite different; however, it may be possible to reconcile them. Perhaps humans are not genetically programmed to help, but have an inherited tendency to respond empathically to the distress of others, making it easier for them to learn that helping is a reinforcing experience. And perhaps learning this depends on the socialization experiences a person has. If so, it may be true that humans are predisposed to be helpful, but that helpfulness is not an innate, automatic, or universal behavior.

SUMMARY

The study of helping concerns the reasons people engage in actions that are intended to provide some benefit to another person. Helping may be caused by desires to achieve tangible, external reinforcers or internal, intrinsic reinforcers, or they may be caused by an innate drive to help others.

Sociobiologists—biologists who are interested in the biological causes of social behavior—have argued that helping is the result of certain genetic predispositions among humans which had survival value for their ancestors. Thus, helping was genetically transmitted from generation to generation. This argument is based on the concept of kin selection, which proposes that genetic survival depends not only on the survival of individuals' genes but also on the survival of the gene pool of a group of related individuals.

Social learning theorists believe that through the socialization process, people learn to help in exchange for both external and internal reinforcers. As the result of classical conditioning, people learn to be empathic; through instrumental conditioning and observational learning, people learn that helping is often rewarding. Young children help because they associate helping with tangible reinforcers. As children grow up, they discover that helping is reinforcing in its own right. By mid- to late adolescence, most people feel better after they have helped someone, even if helping provides no tangible rewards.

WHEN WILL PEOPLE HELP?

The results of the experiment in the prologue and the material presented thus far might reasonably lead one to conclude that because of innate characteristics or socialization experiences, humans will invariably rush to the aid of someone in distress. Unfortunately, this is not true.

On March 13, 1964, 28-year-old Catherine ("Kitty") Genovese was walking from her car to her apartment across the street. Ms. Genovese managed a bar, and she was returning home quite late—it was 3:20 A.M. Suddenly, she saw a man holding a knife. She ran down the street, but he caught and stabbed her. "Oh, my god, he stabbed me!" she screamed. "Please help me!"

Across the street, windows opened and lights went on. "Let that girl alone!" a man yelled. Her assailant, Winston Moseley, walked back toward his car. But as he later told the police, "I had a feeling this man would close his window and go back to sleep and then I could return." Mr. Moseley was right. As Ms. Genovese's neighbors watched from behind closed curtains—one couple turned out the light to see better, and pulled chairs up to their apartment window—Moseley returned. Ms. Genovese had staggered into the lobby of a building in an attempt to hide from him. But he found her, stabbed her eight more times, and then sexually molested her. Approximately 30 minutes after the attack began, the local police received a phone call from an anonymous witness. He reported the attack, but declined to give his name because he did not want to "get involved" (Dowd, 1984).

Before this attack took place, the topics of helping and people's responses to emergencies attracted little attention from social scientists—less than 100 scholarly articles had been written on it. Since the death of Ms. Genovese, over 1,000 research articles have been written about the behavior of people who observe emergencies (Dovidio, 1984).

Bystander intervention: the process wherein observers see a person in distress, and they must decide whether or not to intervene and help the person.

Most of this research has focused on the phenomenon of **bystander intervention.** This can occur in response to an emergency that requires immediate action, or it can occur in circumstances where the need for immediate help is less pressing. Some bystander intervention studies have looked at behaviors such as helping a stranded motorist (for example, Penner, Dertke, and Achenbach, 1974) or returning a lost item of value (for example, Hornstein, 1970).

When John Darley and Bibb Latan'e began their pioneering work on bystander intervention in emergencies (Darley and Latan'e, 1968; Latan'e and Darley, 1970) they focused on the reasons bystanders, such as the

A paramedic risks his life to save one of the survivors of the 1982 crash of an Air Florida jet liner. Unlike some other instances, bystanders were willing to help the victims of the crash.

witnesses to Kitty Genovese's murder, often fail to intervene. Their orientation to this question led many people to believe that nonintervention is the typical response in emergencies. This is incorrect; bystanders often attempt to help people in distress. For example, when Air Florida Flight 90 crashed into the Potomac River in January 1982, witnesses to the disaster offered help. One man swam out to the wreckage and yelled encouragement to the survivors of the crash. Another jumped into the freezing water and pulled a survivor to shore.

Maybe people who live in Washington, D.C., are more helpful than those who live in New York. Individual differences in people's personalities play a role in helping, but most research suggests that differences in the behavior of the bystanders are due to differences in the situations that confront them. In laboratory studies of bystander intervention, it has been found that under one set of circumstances no one will help a stricken person, but when certain situational factors are changed, 90 to 100 percent of the subjects will come to the aid of the same person within five to ten seconds of the onset of the emergency (Hoffman, 1981). This section examines some of the variables responsible for these differences in bystanders' behavior.

A number of general models attempt to explain situational influences on bystander intervention (for example, Latan'e and Darley, 1970; Schwartz, 1977), but perhaps the most comprehensive model was put forth by Jane Piliavin and her colleagues (Piliavin et al., 1981). This section uses their model to present the research on bystander intervention. The model proposes that when bystanders observe someone in trouble, they go through three stages before they respond to the person. In the first stage, they become physiologically aroused by the sight of another's distress. In the second stage, bystanders label this arousal as some emotion or feeling. And in the third stage, bystanders evaluate the consequences of offering or not offering help.

Stage 1: Physiological Arousal

When people witness distress in another person, their first reaction is a physiological one. This is, of course, a true empathic response. It is not caused by something that has directly impacted them, but by something that has happened to the distressed person. Surprisingly, bystanders often show a decline in their heart rates and other similar physiological responses when they first see an emergency (Piliavin et al., 1981). This does not mean that another's distress has a calming influence on observers; instead, it reflects the *orienting reaction* (Piliavin et al., 1981). When humans first encounter a novel or unexpected stimulus, they attend to it and try to figure out what is going on. Their physiology "quiets down" so they can efficiently process the available information. But very soon, there is a dramatic increase in physiological arousal. This is called the *defense reaction.* The observer is getting prepared to do something. This type of arousal is typical of what happens when people directly encounter a strong stimulus. But in the case of bystanders, it is an empathic response, caused by something that happened to someone else.

It is generally agreed that in emergency situations, the magnitude of a person's defense reaction is strongly correlated with helping. The greater the arousal, the greater the chances that a bystander will help (Piliavin et al., 1981). When Gaertner and Dovidio (1977) measured how quickly subjects came to the aid of a woman who had been hurt by falling chairs, they found a strong positive correlation between the speed of the subjects' responses and their heart rate. Similar correlations have been obtained in several other studies (for example, Gaertner, Dovidio, and Johnson, 1979a, 1979b; Sterling, 1977).

The strength of a bystander's empathic physiological reaction is influenced by both social and nonsocial factors. Researchers have found that as the severity and clarity of the victim's problem increases, so does the strength of a bystander's physiological arousal (Geer and Jarmecky, 1973; Sterling, 1977). In Sterling's study, it was found that subjects were more aroused by an emergency they could see and hear than by one they could only hear. In a study of social factors, Krebs (1975) gave some subjects information about another person (a confederate) that led them to believe their attitudes and interests were quite similar to those of the other person.

He gave other subjects information that led them to believe their attitudes and interests were different from those of the other person. Then both groups of subjects observed as the confederate (supposedly) received electric shock. Bystanders who thought they were similar to the other person experienced more empathic physiological arousal than did bystanders who thought they were dissimilar.

Stage 2: Labeling the Arousal

In general, physiological arousal does not automatically produce certain specific emotions; people's cognitions or thoughts about the arousal determine what emotions they feel. This is also true of empathic physiological arousal. Mueller, Donnerstein, and Hallam (1983) and Piliavin, Piliavin, and Truddell (1974) have shown that **excitation transfer** can influence the actions of potential helpers. In Piliavin and her associates' 1974 study, subjects saw either an exciting (arousing) or neutral movie and then were witnesses to a staged emergency. Subjects who had watched the exciting movie were significantly more likely to help than were subjects who had watched the neutral movie. Evidently, the subjects who had seen the exciting movie transferred some of the arousal from the first stimulus, the movie, to the second stimulus, the emergency, and this transfer significantly increased their willingness to help.

In most instances, physiological arousal produces two distinct emotions: **personal distress** and **empathic concern** (Batson and Coke, 1981; Davis, 1980; Piliavin et al., 1981). Another's distress produces both kinds of emotions, and situational factors determine which kind will be a stronger motivator. Thus, a bystander's motivation for helping may differ considerably as a function of which kind of emotion predominates.

Personal Distress
Piliavin and her colleagues believed that empathic physiological arousal is often labeled by a bystander as personal distress. This is most likely to occur if the bystander does not have a close personal relationship with the victim or if the situation involves a highly arousing emergency. Studies that have investigated bystanders' reactions to distress in others support this proposal. Marks, Penner, and Stone (1982) found that subjects who observed a confederate supposedly receive painful electric shock experienced significant increases in the amount of anxiety they felt. Gaertner and Dovidio (1977) found the same kind of reaction when subjects believed that a confederate had been injured by falling chairs.

Piliavin and associates proposed that helping others serves to reduce the bystander's personal distress. They suggested that helping is usually motivated by hedonistic, self-serving concerns; bystanders help because it serves their needs, not because it serves the needs of the victim. A purely hedonistic view of helping is disputed by many researchers (Batson and Coke, 1981; Krebs, 1975; Weiss et al., 1973), but some data show that personal distress often does lead to helping. Marks and his associates (1982) found that anxiety in response to another's distress caused an increase in

Personal distress: a response to another person in distress in which the bystander feels anxious, distressed, or upset.

Empathic concern: a response to another person in distress in which the bystander feels compassion and concern for that person.

subjects' willingness to help the the other person avoid shock. And Gaertner and Dovidio (1977) found that the more upset subjects were, the faster they came to an injured woman's aid.

Empathic Concern
C. Daniel Batson and his associates (Batson and Coke, 1981; Batson, Duncan, Ackerman, Buckley, and Birch, 1981; Coke, Batson, and McDavis, 1978; Toi and Batson, 1982) have conducted a large number of studies on the circumstances that produce empathic concern and the ways in which this feeling affects bystanders' motivations to help. According to Batson and associates, when bystanders believe that they are similar to a person in distress or identify with that person, a condition of "we-ness" is created and the bystanders are likely to experience empathic concern. When bystanders experience empathic concern, their motivations to help are quite different than when they experience personal distress. Their primary goal is to increase the other person's welfare, and their helping is an altruistic act. This proposal was tested in a study by Batson, Duncan, Ackerman, Buckley, and Berch (1981).

Batson and his associates led half their subjects to believe they were similar to another person (a confederate); they led the other half to believe they were dissimilar to her. The subjects then watched as the confederate engaged in a task that was supposed to continue for 10 trials. On each trial, she received painful electric shock. Half the subjects in the similar condition and half the subjects in the dissimilar condition were told that they would be required to watch only two of the 10 shock trials; the other half of the subjects in the two conditions were told that they would be required to watch all 10 shock trials. For reasons which will become apparent, these were called the easy-escape condition and the difficult-escape condition, respectively.

Then the subjects watched a videotape of the confederate receiving shock. Things did not go well for the confederate. During the first shock trial, she gave every indication that she found the shocks very unpleasant. Midway through the second trial, the confederate looked so upset that the experimenter stopped the study and asked if she were all right. The confederate requested a glass of water. When the experimenter returned with the water, she and the confederate talked about how the confederate felt. When the confederate explained that she had had a traumatic experience with shock when she was a child, the experimenter asked if she wanted to continue the experiment. The confederate said she wanted to continue, but the experimenter suggested that maybe the observer might be willing to take her place. The experimenter then asked the subjects if they would take the confederate's place, making it clear that they were under no obligation to do so. In the easy-escape condition, the subjects were told that if they did not take the confederate's place, they could leave. In the difficult-escape condition, the subjects were told that if they did not take the confederate's place, they would observe her for the next eight trials and then leave. The dependent measure was whether a subject would take the confederate's place.

Batson and his associates reasoned that if perceived similarity engenders empathic concern, and if empathic concern, in turn, produces altruistic helping, then subjects in the similar condition should be unaffected by the ease or difficulty with which they could escape. They would help in both conditions. Subjects in the dissimilar condition would not experience empathic concern, so their decisions would be influenced by the ease or difficulty of escape; they would be much less likely to help in the easy-escape condition than in the difficult-escape condition. (See figure 8-4 for the percentage of subjects who helped in each of the four conditions.)

The results were exactly what the researchers had predicted, and similar results have been obtained in several other studies (for example, Batson et al., 1983; Toi and Batson, 1982). It appears as if empathic concern engenders altruistic behavior.

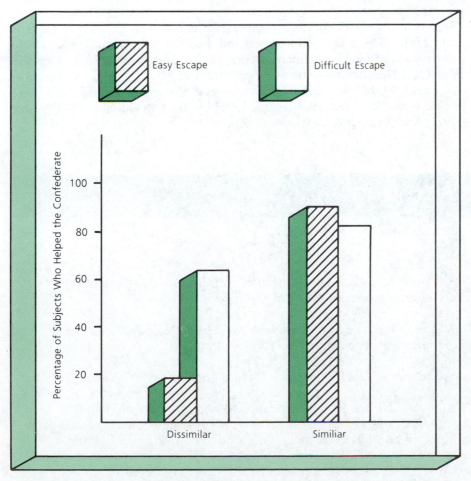

Figure 8-4. *If the subjects believed they were similar to the confederate, they helped equally in the easy and difficult escape conditions.*
Source: Batson et al. (1981).

Batson and his colleagues acknowledged, however, that a special set of circumstances is required for bystanders to ignore costs and to help solely because of empathic concern. In many arousing emergencies, the bystanders' predominant reaction is personal distress, and they must evaluate the situation before taking any action (Batson, O'Quin, Fultz, Vanderplas, and Isen, 1983; Piliavin et al., 1981).

Stage 3: Evaluating the Consequences of Helping

Piliavin and her colleagues proposed that before bystanders engage in any actions, they will evaluate the consequences of those actions. Specifically, bystanders weigh the costs of offering direct help to the victim against the costs of not offering direct help. They then choose the course of action that will reduce their personal distress at the lowest cost.

Costs of Helping

Two common costs of offering direct help to a person in distress are time and effort. The greater these costs, the less likely a bystander is to help (Batson, Cochran, Biederman, Blosser, Ryan, and Vogt, 1978; Darley and Batson, 1978). In situations like the murder of Ms. Genovese or the crash of Flight 90, helping might produce physical harm or injury, and these costs also will reduce the likelihood that bystanders will help (McGovern, 1976; Midlarsky and Midlarsky, 1973).

Topic Background

One Man's Best Friend

The following incident provides a dramatic illustration of how empathic concern can lead to helping, even when the costs of providing help are very high.

Robert "Shorty" Henderson lay in a hospital bed Monday with a punctured lung and a slashed liver, suffered when he stepped in front of a knife that was being thrust at his friend Daniel Evans.

"Danny is a friend of mine," said Henderson. "Is he a good enough friend to die for? Yes he is."

Henderson, a 23-year-old black man, was stabbed Sunday by an unidentified attacker to save the life of Evans, his 22-year-old friend, who is white. He was listed in good condition Monday at a Miami hospital with a punctured lung and slashed liver.

Both construction workers and Miami residents, the pair have been friends for more than three years. Henderson said when he saw the knife coming at Evans, all he could think of was Evans' 4-month-old son.

Speaking from Henderson's hospital room, the men said they just finished a roof repair job and were standing in the back of Evans' truck when a black woman and a baby came down the street. The trouble started when Evans spoke to the woman and her infant.

"The next thing you know, I walk in the yard and some guy comes up and says I was talking to a black woman," Evans said. " . . . His face looked like he just wanted to kill me."

The unidentified attacker, described as tall and brawny, stabbed Evans in the shoulder several times. Evans started to fall and the man struck him in the throat.

"I heard Danny sayin, 'Shorty Shorty. He got a knife.' I went around the corner and I seen he'd stabbed Danny in the arm.

"I ran over to get in it, too, and I saw the knife coming but I couldn't grab his arm. I just dove between him and Danny," Henderson said.

"If he'd of stabbed Danny he would have killed him."

Emergency room surgeons had to massage Henderson's lungs and heart to bring him back to life. Henderson said he has no medical insurance.

Evans required 250 stitches for wounds to his neck, shoulder and chest.

"When (Henderson) saw that guy stabbing me and knew I was going to die, he told me all he could see was my four-month-old son," said Evans, his voice cracking. "He said he couldn't let it happen. Not as much as he loved me." (*Tampa Tribune*, April 3, 1984)

Piliavin and her associates focused primarily on the costs of helping. However, they also acknowledged that helping can bring financial rewards, social praise, and even an enhanced view of oneself. Consider Lenny Skutnick, a bystander who jumped into the Potomac River and saved the life of one survivor of the crash of Flight 90. When interviewed the next day, Skutnick spoke of his high school track coach who many years earlier had called him a quitter. He compared his feelings about himself then to his feelings after his heroic act: "When I got out of the water, I was satisfied. I did what I set out to do" (*Washington Post*, 1982).

Costs of Not Helping

Piliavin and her associates proposed two classes of costs that can result from not helping: empathy costs and personal costs. They and other researchers also proposed that the characteristics of the victim and the relationship between the bystander and the victim affect the costs of not helping.

Empathy Costs   **Empathy costs** are affected by the same variables that affect empathic arousal in response to another's distress. Thus, the clarity of the emergency, its severity, and the closeness of the bystander to the victim will increase the empathy costs of not helping. In addition, since similarity between the bystander and the victim increases empathic arousal (Krebs, 1975), it will also increase the empathic costs bystanders would

Empathy costs: continued unpleasant empathic arousal in response to another person's distress.

pay if they did not help. In other words, anything that increases the impact of the victim's distress on bystanders will make it more costly for them not to help (Piliavin et al., 1981).

Personal costs: negative consequences, such as public censure or self-blame, which bystanders would experience if they did not help.

Personal Costs   **Personal costs** are, in essence, punishments for not helping. The personal costs of helping are usually determined by such straightforward factors as the time, effort, or danger involved in helping. The costs of not helping are influenced by somewhat less obvious variables.

For example, shortly after I learned about the "Kitty Genovese Incident," I found myself in a situation quite similar to the one that confronted her neighbors. It was about 2:00 A.M., and I was awakened by a woman screaming, "Help me, please help me!" My first response was that of any normal red-blooded American male: I pulled the covers over my head. But then I thought, I'm not going to be like those people who let Kitty Genovese be murdered. The thought of the public censure I might experience if I did not help caused me to leave my cozy apartment and venture into the night. (Fortunately for me—and perhaps for the woman——the police arrived before I did.)

Darley and Latan'e (Darley and Latan'e, 1968; Latan'e and Darley, 1970) looked at whether helping was influenced by how many people witnessed the emergency. In their 1968 study, subjects were asked to engage in a group discussion about problems adjusting to college life. The subjects were told that because the topic might be embarrassing to some people, they would not see one another, but would communicate over an intercom. Subjects were randomly assigned to one of three experimental conditions: (1) a discussion between the subject and one other person, (2) a discussion between the subject and two other people, and (3) a discussion between the subject and five other people. A few minutes into the discussion, disaster struck. One of the participants supposedly had an epileptic seizure (actually subjects heard a prerecorded tape). Darley and Latan'e recorded the number of subjects who intervened and the length of time that elapsed before they did so. Subjects intervened more often and more quickly when they believed they were the only witnesses to the emergency. (See figure 8-5.)

Latan'e and Nida (1981) reviewed over 50 studies that had investigated the effects of group size on helping. These studies had been conducted in a variety of settings, had involved a number of different types of emergencies, had used both male and female subjects, and had differed in a number of other ways, yet they all produced the same finding: The more people to observe a person in trouble, the less likely they are to intervene. It is believed that the major cause of this effect is that the presence of others reduces the cost of not helping.

One reason for this is that people experience less physiological arousal in response to distress when they are with others than when they are alone (Gaertner and Dovidio, 1977). A more significant effect of the presence of others is **diffusion of responsibility.** Latan'e and Darley (1970) proposed that if a bystander is the lone witness to an emergency and does nothing, that person may feel that she bears all the responsibility for not helping.

Diffusion of responsibility: the belief that another person or persons has the responsibility to provide help.

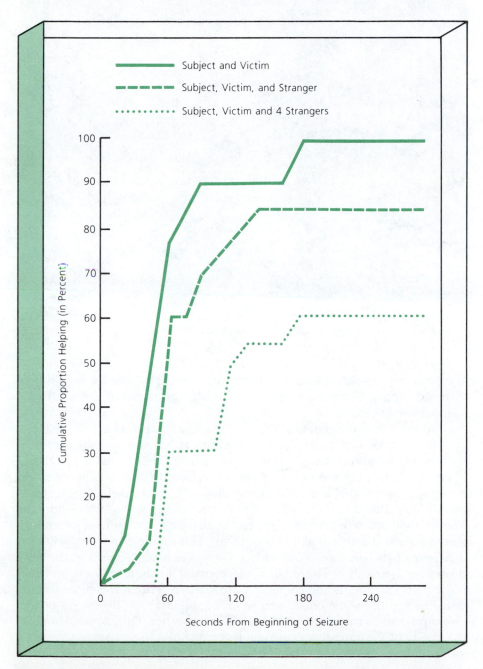

Figure 8-5. *Subjects responded to an emergency more often and more quickly when they thought they were the only bystander than when they thought that others were present. Reprinted by permission of the authors.*
Source: Latan'e and Darley (1970).

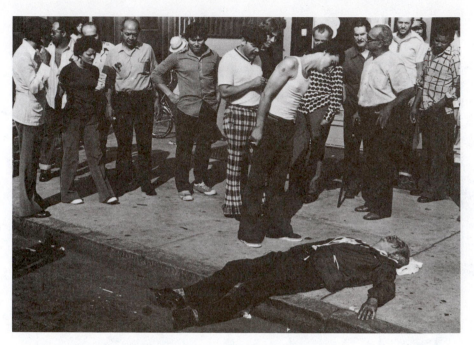

Latane and Darley's research on bystander intervention indicated that the more people who witness an emergency, the less likely any one person is to help.

If others are present, the responsibility for not helping (or for helping) is diffused among the bystanders. As a result, the personal costs for not helping are lowered.

Others can also influence how a bystander interprets an emergency. A good deal of ambiguity often surrounds an emergency situation. In ambiguous situations, people look to others to tell them what is going on. If no one is helping the victim, a bystander could conclude that there is no emergency. If this is a valid explanation of the group-size effect, then researchers should find that allowing bystanders to communicate with one another will increase helping. This has been found in a number of studies (for example, Latan'e and Darley, 1976). This finding may explain the difference between the actions of Ms. Genovese's neighbors and the witnesses to the crash of Flight 90. Ms. Genovese's neighbors were in their individual apartments and communication between them was difficult; the witnesses to the plane crash were standing together on the banks of the river and could easily communicate with one another. This, combined with the clarity of the emergency, made it less likely that the presence of others would inhibit bystander intervention in the crash situation.

Characteristics of the Victim   Certain victim characteristics also affect the costs of not helping. The greater the victim's need for help, the greater the costs of not helping (Piliavin et al., 1981). Several studies have found that a victim's need affects helping. Baker and Reitz (1978) found that subjects were more willing to help a blind person who had called the wrong number than a sighted person. Two other studies have manipulated the legitimacy of the victim's need (Bickman and Kamzan, 1973; Field, 1974). In both experiments, the confederates asked bystanders for a small amount of money to help them purchase an item in a grocery store. Bystanders were less likely to help when the item was a bag of cookies or beer than when the item was milk or ointment for a burned infant. According to Piliavin and her colleagues, the legitimate requests for help increased the empathic costs of not helping because they made bystanders more likely to identify with the victim and to experience empathic arousal. The legitimate requests also increased the personal costs of not helping because they made it more difficult for bystanders to view the victim as someone they were not obligated to help.

Relationship between the Victim and the Bystander All other things being equal, the more similar the victim is to the bystander, the more likely the bystander is to help (Gross, Wallston, and Piliavin, 1975; Krebs, 1975; Pandey and Griffitt, 1974). The major reason for this appears to be that similarity engenders greater physiological arousal in bystanders and, therefore, a greater empathic cost. Also, the personal costs for not helping a similar victim may be greater than those for not helping a dissimilar victim. Others may be more likely to censure someone who does not help a friend than someone who does not help a stranger (Piliavin et al., 1981).

Reward/Cost Matrix
Piliavin and her colleagues used the reward/cost matrix shown in figure 8-6 to describe how the costs just discussed will affect bystanders' responses in an emergency.*

The lower right-hand corner of the matrix describes a situation in which the costs of helping are high and the costs of not helping are low. To demonstrate this, imagine you are one of 50 witnesses to a knife fight between two drunken men. The high costs of helping are obvious. The costs of not helping are low because (a) you can diffuse responsibility for not helping and (b) the victims are not deserving of help (they brought their troubles on themselves). In such a circumstance, bystanders will leave the scene or ignore the victim's plight; they will not help. The lower left-hand cell describes a situation in which both types of costs are low. In such a situation, the offering of help will, according to the researchers, depend on personal norms.

Now to the upper left-hand cell. Here the cost of helping is low and the cost of not helping is high. For example, imagine a parent who sees her child drowning in the shallow end of a swimming pool. In such a situation, the parent would directly intervene. Finally, in the upper right-hand cell, both types of costs are high. Piliavin and her colleagues said that bystanders may engage in *indirect intervention* in such situations. For

---

*This matrix does not apply to emergencies where bystanders must act so quickly they do not have time to evaluate the costs of their actions (Piliavin et al., 1981).

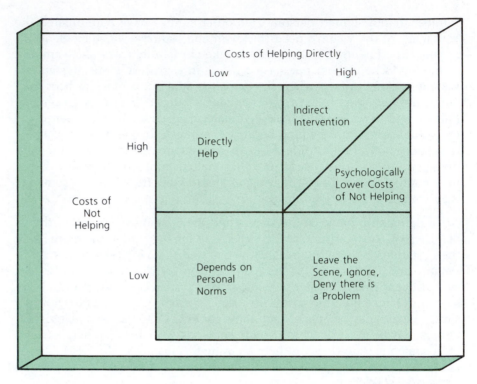

Figure 8-6. *Piliavin and her colleagues' model of how costs affect bystanders' reactions to a victim's problems.*
Source: Piliavin et al. (1981).

example, a neighbor of Ms. Genovese might have called the police. This action would help the victim, but would incur a low cost. If indirect intervention is not possible, then bystanders may resolve their dilemma by psychologically lowering the costs of not helping. If the situation is ambiguous, they may reinterpret it as one in which the victim does not, in fact, need help. Or bystanders may resolve their problem by derogating the victim. If bystanders can convince themselves that a victim is a bad person or is personally responsible for her or his plight, they can reduce the costs of not helping.

Diffusion of responsibility provides another means to reduce the costs of not helping. A study by Piliavin, Piliavin, and Rodin (1975) illustrated how diffusion of responsibility can affect a bystander's behavior when the costs of helping are high. Riders in a New York City subway car saw a man (a confederate), carrying a cane, fall to the floor of the subway car. He appeared to be unconscious. In the high-cost-of-helping condition, stage makeup had been used to create a large, ugly birthmark on the man's face. In the low-cost-of-helping condition, the man did not have the ugly birthmark on his face. (Prior research had shown that people find physical disfigurement unpleasant and are motivated to avoid contact with physically disfigured individuals. [Piliavin and Piliavin, 1972; Piliavin et al., 1975].)

For half the subjects in each condition, another confederate, dressed as a medical intern, was present when the man fell. For the other half, another confederate dressed in ordinary street clothes was present. In the low-cost condition (no birthmark), people helped an equal amount whether the intern was present or absent. But in the high-cost condition (birthmark), 72 percent of the bystanders helped when there was no intern present and only 48 percent of the bystanders helped when there was an intern present. It appears that in the high-cost-of-helping condition, bystanders diffused responsibility for helping onto the intern, thereby lowering the costs of not helping.

SUMMARY

Most of the research on situational influences on helping among adults has focused on a phenomenon known as bystander intervention—whether or not someone who sees another person in need of help will intervene on that person's behalf.

One comprehensive model of why bystanders do or do not offer help proposes that before bystanders make a response to the person, three interrelated stages occur. The first stage is physiological arousal in response to another's distress; this arousal is not due to anything that happens directly to the bystanders, thus it is an empathic response. The stronger the bystanders' physiological arousal, the more likely they are to intervene. In the second stage, this arousal is labeled as some emotion or feeling. Sometimes bystanders label this arousal as personal distress and sometimes as empathic concern for the person in trouble. If the latter emotion predominates, helpers are relatively unconcerned with the possible costs of helping someone; if the former emotion predominates, bystanders must evaluate the possible costs of helping. In the third stage, potential helpers evaluate the costs of helping and not helping before they act. The costs of helping include time and effort; the costs of not helping include public censure and self-blame. Estimates of the costs of not helping are influenced by the bystander's relationship with the victim, the deservingness of the victim, and the presence of other possible helpers.

Whether or not bystanders offer help depends on their evaluations of the two kinds of costs. As estimates of the costs of helping increase and estimates of the cost of not helping decrease, direct helping becomes less likely. If both kinds of costs are high, people will often psychologically lower the costs of not helping by doing things such as diffusing responsibility for not helping onto others.

INDIVIDUAL DIFFERENCES IN HELPING

Until this point, the discussion has focused almost exclusively on the characteristics of the situation a bystander encounters and has virtually ignored the question of how the characteristics of bystanders might affect their willingness to offer help. To a certain extent, this omission reflects the current emphasis in the literature on situational causes of helping behavior, but even diehard situationists acknowledge that there are individual differences in helping. This section first considers how temporary states of potential helpers may affect their decisions to help. It then discusses some personal characteristics that may influence helping.

Temporary States and Helping

From the material presented thus far, one might get the image of the bystander as a peculiar kind of robot, standing in a corner motionless and inactive, waiting for a specific signal—another person's distress. When this signal is received, the bystander springs into action, responding in a robotlike fashion to the characteristics of the situation encountered. While it might be nice to have such a robot around, this does not describe reality. Bystanders have complex and active life outside of the situation in which the help is needed and it may affect their willingness to help.

Positive Moods

It appears that people help when they are in a positive mood (Rosenhan, Salovey, Karylowski, and Hargis, 1981). For example, helping is more likely on mild, sunny days than on cold, overcast days (Cunningham, 1979); people who find money help more than people who do not find money (Isen and Levin, 1972); and people who have succeeded on a task help more than people who have failed on a task (Isen, 1970).

Alice Isen and her colleagues (for example, Isen, Shalker, Clark, and Karp, 1979; Isen and Simonds, 1978) proposed one explanation of why positive moods have this effect on helping. They suggested that positive moods influence the way people think about their lives and the actions they take. Someone who is in a good mood is more likely to focus on the rewards for helping than on the costs. But are people in a good mood simply more willing to comply with requests from others, or does a positive mood specifically impact helping? A study by Isen and Levin (1972) seems to answer this question. Isen and Levin created a good mood in their subjects by letting them find a small amount of money. Then half of the subjects were asked to volunteer to help someone, and half were asked to volunteer to harass someone. Good moods increased the subjects' willingness to help someone, but not their willingness to harass someone. People who feel good are likely to engage in actions that are consistent with that feeling.

Guilt

Another temporary state that appears to affect helping is feeling guilty. A large number of studies have found that subjects who have committed a transgression (such as breaking equipment, cheating, hurting another person) are more willing to engage in helping than subjects who have not committed a transgression (Dovidio, 1984). It would not be surprising to find that people often try to make amends to someone they have harmed by helping that person. But is is surprising that research has found that people who have committed a transgression are more willing to help even when the recipient of their help is not the victim of their transgression (for example Cunningham, Steinberg, and Grev, 1980; Harris and Samorette, 1976). One explanation of why guilt may increase helping is based on Cialdini and his associates' (1982) **negative state relief hypothesis.** This explanation of the effect of guilt on helping suggests that transgressors help because it relieves their negative mood. The negative state relief hypothesis also explains why people are more likely to help even when they are only a witness to a transgression (Konečni, 1972; Rawlings, 1968). Presumably, witnessing a transgression puts people in a bad mood, and helping serves to alleviate this mood.

Negative Moods

From what you have read so far, you would expect that people who are in a negative mood should be more willing to help than people who are not. This is a reasonable expectation, but research results do not always support it. Some researchers (for example, Cialdini et al., 1982) have found that negative moods increase helping, but others (for example, Moore, Underwood, and Rosenhan, 1973; Underwood, Froming, and Moore, 1977) have found that negative moods decrease helping.

Rogers, Miller, Mayer, and Duval (1982) demonstrated how other factors can affect the relationship between a negative mood and helping. In the first phase of their study, all the subjects experienced a negative mood as the result of reading a very depressing series of statements. Half the subjects were then told they were personally responsible for how they felt, and the other half were told that the statements they had read were responsible for their feelings. This was the first independent variable: responsibility for the negative mood. Next, half the subjects in each condition were presented with a salient, clear-cut request for help, and half the subjects in each condition were presented with a less salient, less clear-cut request for the same kind of help. (The request was to make phone calls to raise money for a campus radio station.) This was the second independent variable: salience of the request for help. The dependent measure was the number of phone calls subjects were willing to make. (See figure 8-7 for the results.)

First consider subjects' responses to the salient request for help. Subjects who felt responsible for their mood volunteered to make twice as many calls as did those who did not feel responsible. According to Rogers and her associates, this difference was due to the fact that responsible subjects had a greater need than nonresponsible subjects to reduce their negative feelings, and the salient request provided an obvious way to do this.

Now consider the nonsalient-request condition. The pattern of helping was reversed; responsible people helped less than did nonresponsible people. Rogers and her colleagues suggested that when people feel responsible for their negative moods, they become preoccupied with their own feelings

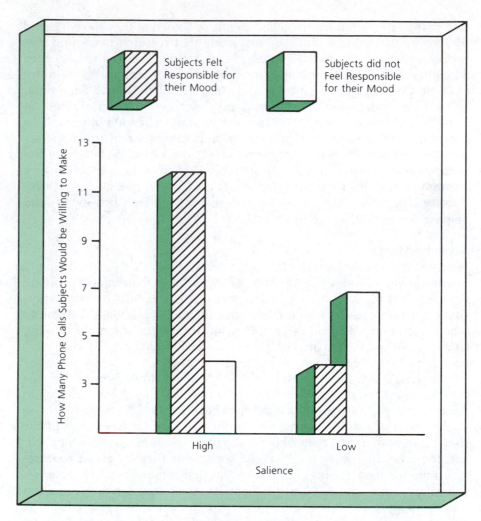

Figure 8-7. *When the request for help was salient, subjects who felt responsible for their mood offered more help than did subjects who did not feel responsible. The opposite was true when the request was nonsalient.*
Source: Rogers et al. (1982).

and are less attentive to things around them. Thus, the nonsalient request had less of an impact on the responsible subjects than on the nonresponsible subjects, and the responsible subjects were less likely to help. Unlike the effect of positive moods, which invariably seems to be an increase in helping, the effect of negative moods on helping depends on the context in which the negative mood occurs.

Personality Characteristics and Helping

Most researchers acknowledge that personality characteristics play a significant role in the determination of this behavior. However, their attempts to identify a "generalized helping personality" have not been successful (Piliavin et al., 1981) for several reasons. One is that helping can take different shapes and can occur under different circumstances. For example, helpers may anonymously donate money to a needy person or they may personally lend money to a boss in the hope that this will bring a promotion. They may engage in low-cost helping, such as picking up a bag of groceries for someone, or they may engage in high-cost helping, such as intervening in an emergency. It is unlikely that the same personality variable or set of personality variables would be equally related to all these different kinds of behavior. A study by Gergen, Gergen, and Meter (1972) supports this conjecture. They administered a battery of personality tests to their subjects and then presented them with five different requests for help. Gergen and his associates found that certain personality characteristics correlated with each type of helping, but they were unable to find any one personality characteristic that consistently correlated with all five types of helping. In other words, the characteristics of people who offered one type of help were not the same as the characteristics of people who offered another type of help.

Topic Background

A Full-time Helper

Individual differences in helping have received much less research attention than have situational differences. The following description suggests that a full understanding of helping may require a consideration of personality, as well as situational, variables.

John Fling is a 62-year-old delivery person for an automobile dealership in Columbia, South Carolina. He does not own a telephone, a television, or an automobile. He and his wife live in a small apartment. Mr. Fling has an unusual hobby: helping people. He does not represent a church or a civic organization; on his own, Mr. Fling spends 40 hours a week helping the poor, the sick, and the disabled in his city (Pressley, 1984).

A typical day for Mr. Fling begins with his giving an elderly blind woman 50 pounds of food to feed her cats and a hot chicken for her dinner. He leaves her home and drives to the home of a family that has recently immigrated to the United States from Vietnam. He gives the children money for their school supplies. He asks one of the children to tell him what time it is. Proudly, 10-year-old Oanh Dao looks at her new watch, which John Fling gave her last week. His next stop is the home of Edith Lewis and her 16 dogs. John raised the money that Mrs. Lewis used to purchase her home. Today, he unloads 125 pounds of dog food and gets a shopping list from Mrs. Lewis. A half hour later, John returns with the groceries, most of which he has paid for. Later, he takes a group of blind people for an excursion in the park. His last visit is to a two-room shack that houses 14 people. He checks on the health of an eight-year-old child who is deaf and mute. He gives her mother his last four dollars to buy food for the child and leaves toys for one of the other children.

Mr. Fling has been doing things like these for the last 25 years. In the last 10 years, he has signed over three cars to people who had no transportation. Why does he do this? His answer: "Early in life, I learned you share everything in this world." Mr. Fling is a full-time helper.

Another reason researchers have not been able to find a general personality characteristic associated with helping is that in many instances—such as emergencies—situational variables are so powerful that they overcome individual differences in helping (Staub, 1978). For example, it is unlikely that people would differ greatly in their reactions to a small child who had fallen and was badly in need of help. Since most studies of helping have used very powerful manipulations of situational variables, it is not surprising that the effect of these has been much greater than the effect of personality variables (Staub, 1978).

Personality characteristics cannot explain helping in general. Nor can personality characteristics, by themselves, explain why a person does or does not help. But certain personality characteristics—including empathy, denial of responsibility, and sociopathy—in combination with situational variables, may determine whether or not a person helps.

Empathy
Earlier in this chapter, you read that humans often have empathic reactions when they see another person in trouble. The stronger these reactions, the greater the likelihood that help will be given. Two questions interest researchers: Are there enduring individual differences in the tendency to respond empathically to the plight of others? And if there is such a trait as empathy, is it related to helping? The answers to these questions are, respectively, yes and maybe.

Many personality scales produce reliable and valid measurements of the construct of empathy, but research that has investigated the relationship between scores on these scales and helping has yielded mixed results (Eisenberg, 1983; Underwood and Moore, 1981). A few studies have found a positive relationship between scales that measure empathy and behaviors such as volunteering time to help another person or making donations to a charity (Mehrabian and Epstein, 1972; Davis, 1983). Other studies have found no relationship between empathy and helping. A study by Archer, Diaz-Loving, Gollwitzer, Davis, and Foushee (1981) may explain why.

Subjects filled out a scale that measured the trait of empathy. Several weeks later, the subjects took part in a study in which they heard about a graduate student who needed help to complete her master's thesis. Then subjects were presented with the opportunity to help. It was found that subjects who had scored high on the empathy scale were significantly more likely to offer help than were subjects who had scored low. But Archer and his associates also found that the relationship between empathy and helping may be greatly affected by situational variables. They systematically manipulated the subjects' beliefs about how much physiological arousal the request for help had produced (by providing false information about their arousal) and their beliefs about whether others would know if they had helped. These situational variables had no effect on low-empathy subjects. But among high-empathy subjects, the greatest helping was found when they believed that (a) they were greatly aroused by the woman's request for help and (b) others would know whether or not they had helped. In this study, the personality variable of empathy and certain situational variables interacted to determine how much subjects would help.

Denial of Responsibility

Shalom Schwartz (Schwartz, 1977; Schwartz and Howard, 1982) has proposed another personality trait that may influence helping. Schwartz's theory of helping was based on his belief that social and personal **norms** influence people's behavior. He suggested that people are expected to adhere to *social norms,* which are established by the society in which they live and which provide general guidelines for their behavior. For example, the norm of aiding (Karylowski, 1982) says that society expects people to help those who are dependent on them. A *personal norm* is more specific than a social norm. It is a feeling of personal obligation brought on by certain situational factors. Different consequences result from violating these two types of norms. If people violate a social norm, they might expect punishment from society or from an agent of society (such as a partner or a teacher). But if people violate a personal norm, they punish themselves; no external agent is needed.

Norms: standards or guidelines for people's behavior and beliefs.

Schwartz argued that because social norms are broad and general, they exert relatively little influence on specific acts of helping. He felt that personal norms are stronger determinants of whether or not people will help. According to Schwartz, people show stable individual differences in the extent to which they deny or accept responsibility for the consequences of their actions. He believed that this trait moderates the relationship between personal norms and helping. Recall that a moderator variable is a variable that affects the relationship between two other variables. In the case of helping, Schwartz proposed that among people who deny responsibility, personal norms will have little impact on helping, but among people who accept responsibility, personal norms will have considerable influence on helping. This was demonstrated in a study by Schwartz and Fleischman (1982).

Married women living in a midwestern city were sent two questionnaires. The first assessed whether the women felt they were personally obligated to take certain actions that would help people on welfare. On the basis of their responses, the subjects were classified as having a positive personal norm to engage in these actions or no personal norm to do so. The second questionnaire was Schwartz's (1973) Responsibility Denial

Scale. It measured their general tendencies to deny responsibility for the consequences of their actions. Several weeks later, the women were asked to volunteer their time in a campaign to increase the welfare payments received by the elderly. The dependent measure was the amount of time the women were willing to give.

Among the women who denied responsibility for their actions, there was no differences between those who had a positive personal norm and those who did not—both helped a small amount. Among women who accepted responsibility for their actions, however, those with a positive personal norm volunteered twice as much of their time as did those who had no such norm. Denial of responsibility moderated the relationship between personal norms and helping.

Sociopathy

Sociopathy: the tendency to engage in callous, selfish, and irresponsible behaviors; sociopathic individuals have difficulty feeling guilt when they hurt someone.

Historically, **sociopathy** has been a personality characteristic of more interest to clinical than social psychologists because researchers have believed that only a small segment of the population have such characteristics. More recent research (for example, Hare, 1970) has found that sociopathy is a personality trait present to a greater or lesser degree in all people, and that it may affect empathic reactions and helping behavior.

Sociopathy and Empathic Reactions   The first reaction of people to distress is an empathic one, and the greater this empathic response, the more likely people are to help (Piliavin et al., 1981). The description of sociopathic individuals would suggest that they may, relative to nonsociopathic individuals, experience less of an empathic reaction when they see another person in distress. The research supports this proposal. Dengerink and Bertilson (1975) and House and Milligan (1976) exposed people who scored high and people who scored low on a scale that measured sociopathy to the sight of another person in distress. Both studies found that sociopathic individuals displayed less physiological arousal than did nonsociopathic individuals. In a later study, Marks and his associates (1982) classified subjects as high or low in sociopathy. Several weeks later, they exposed the subjects to a confederate who was supposedly receiving electric shock. Subjects indicated how much anxiety they felt as they watched this. Marks and his colleagues found that high-sociopathy subjects experienced significantly less empathic anxiety than did low-sociopathy subjects.

Sociopathy and Helping   If high-sociopathy subjects experience less of an empathic reaction than low-sociopathy subjects, it follows that they should also help less. This idea was directly tested in an experiment by Marks and his colleagues (1982). They used almost exactly the same procedure as was described in the prologue. Recall that in this study subjects thought their job was to evaluate the performance of confederates who received electric shock while they performed a simple task. In fact, the variable of interest was how quickly subjects pressed the button that supposedly recorded their evaluations. Half of the subjects were in a reinforcement condition; the faster they pressed the button, the less shock the confederate received. The other half were in a no-reinforcement, control, condition; the speed with which they pressed the button was unrelated to how much shock the confederate received. Marks and his associates recorded the time it took high- and low-sociopathy subjects to press the button in these two conditions. (See figure 8-8 for their results.)

First consider the low-sociopathy subjects. They responded significantly faster in the reinforcement than in the no-reinforcement condition. In other words, they responded to the opportunity to help the confederate by helping him. But now consider the high-sociopathy subjects. When high-sociopathy subjects could help the confederate by responding quickly (as in the reinforcement condition), they slowed down. Not only did they fail to help the confederate, they showed a tendency to increase his discomfort.

Like the other personality variables discussed, sociopathy's relationship to helping is moderated by situational variables. Penner, Summers,

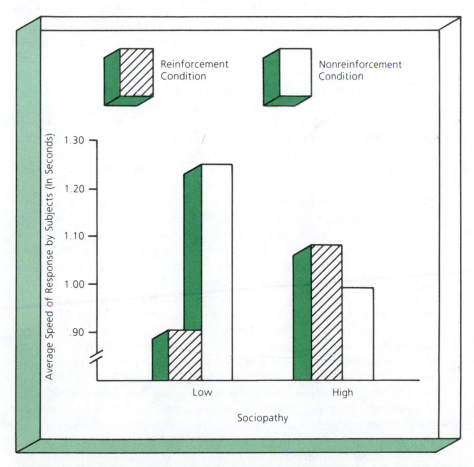

Figure 8-8. *Low sociopathic subjects responded more rapidly in the reinforcement than the nonreinforcement condition; the opposite was true of high sociopathic subjects.*
Source: Marks et al. (1982)

Brookmire, and Dertke (1976) conducted a study in which helping involved returning a lost item of value. They found that sociopathy was related to helping only when there were no strong situational influences on the subjects' behavior. This finding reinforces the point made at the beginning of this discussion. While personality variables are related to helping, the strength of this relationship will depend on the nature of the situation encountered by the potential helper.

SUMMARY

Individuals can differ from one another in their willingness to offer help because of the temporary states they experience and because of relatively permanent differences in their personality characteristics.

Researchers interested in the effects of temporary states and moods on helping have investigated how both good and bad moods affect helping. Good moods generally increase people's willingness to help because people in a good mood are more likely to focus on the potential rewards for helping others. Negative moods are most likely to increase helping when people feel personally responsible for their mood and when the request for help is salient and obvious. When the request is not salient, people who are in a bad mood will help less than people who are a neutral mood. The temporary state of feeling guilty also increases helping because it can help restore the person's self-concept and provide relief from the negative state that guilty individuals often feel.

No single personality characteristic or set of characteristics is consistently related to all kinds of helping, and the effects of personality characteristics can be overridden by strong situational variables. However, some personality variables have been found to affect helping. Among these are traits concerned with empathy, denial or responsibility for one's actions, and sociopathy. Although it appears that some people are more empathic than others, studies have not found a consistent relationship between empathy and helping. The reason for this seems to be that there are only certain circumstances in which empathic people are more likely to help than are nonempathic people. The personality characteristic of denial of responsibility may moderate the relationship between personal norms and helping; people who feel that they have an obligation to engage in a specific kind of helping and who accept responsibility for their actions are more likely to help than are people who feel the personal obligation but deny responsibility for their actions. People who are inclined to be sociopathic show less physiological and emotional arousal when they see a person in distress than do people who are not inclined to be sociopathic. Sociopathic people are less likely to offer help, and there is some reason to believe that they enjoy seeing distress in others.

Applications

Heroes and Helpers

This section is concerned with two very different kinds of helping in the real world. One involves acts of heroism that benefit another person at the risk of the helper's life. The other kind of helping is considered less dramatic and involves helping people with emotional and personal problems.

HEROES

Humans are capable of callous indifference to others, but some people perform heroic, self-sacrificing actions to help another person.

Rescuers

From the early 1930s through the mid-1940s, Adolf Hitler conducted a systematic campaign to exterminate Jews and other groups of people considered undesirable by the Third Reich. During this period of time, approximately six million Jews were killed. Often this campaign of genocide was aided by Christian residents of the countries occupied by Germany, but there were also a large number of Christians who risked their lives to help Jews escape from Hitler's concentration camps. When the Nazis ordered all the Jews in Denmark to wear arm bands carrying the Star of David, the Christian king of Denmark also donned an arm band and many Christian citizens followed his lead. In addition, hundreds of Danes organized an effort to help Danish Jews escape arrest by the Nazis; in a single night, approximately 8,000 Jews were secretly transported by boat from Denmark to Sweden, a country not occupied by the Nazis (Arnold, 1975).

In the years following the Second World War, social scientists became interested in what motivated these activities. In the early 1960s, Perry London (1970) was able to interview a number of people who had helped the Jews. The interviews disclosed that these people shared three characteristics. The first was that they were *socially marginal*. This does not mean that they were social deviants or oddballs, but that they were not part of the dominant culture in the area where they lived. For example, one of the rescuers interviewed was a Seventh-Day Adventist in Holland, where this was not the dominant religion and where there was some prejudice toward Seventh-Day Adventists. Another was a German whose family spoke a different German dialect from its neighbors and whose mother, unlike her neighbors, refused to attend church. The constructs of similarity and empathy may, at least in part, explain why socially marginal people risked their lives to save Jews. As explained in this chapter, the more similar potential helpers are to a victim, the more likely they are to offer help. Socially marginal individuals probably perceived themselves as more similar to the Jews (who in many countries were not even allowed to be citizens) than did people who were well integrated into the dominant culture. Also, having themselves been rejected and isolated from their neighbors, these people were probably better able to empathize with what the Jews were experiencing.

A second characteristic found in this research was that most of the rescuers were adventurous people. They seemed to almost enjoy dangerous, exciting activities. One person enjoyed racing motorcycles over narrow boards on top of deep ditches. Another put sugar in the gas tanks of German trucks "for fun." And one man engaged in his own private campaign of anti-Nazi sabotage, blowing up the property of organizations that supported the Nazis. In one daring exploit, he pretended that he had secret verbal orders from Hitler and talked guards into releasing a resistance leader from a prison.

In the model of bystander intervention proposed by Piliavin and her associates (1981), one major determinant of whether people will offer help is their estimates of how much this help will cost them. The rescuers probably estimated the costs of their actions, in terms of physical danger, to be low.

The third characteristic found by London was that almost all of the rescuers strongly identified with a parent who held "very firm opinions on moral issues and [served] as a model of moral conduct" (1970, p. 247). One consequence of identifying with such a parent may be the development of personal norms (Schwartz, 1977) about one's obligations to help others. For example, one Dutch minister organized a large and very effective operation for rescuing Jews, although he described himself as moderately anti-Semitic. He explained his behavior by saying that it was a Christian's duty to help others. Failure to adhere to this personal norm may have produced costs for the minister (guilt, shame, remorse, for instance) which outweighed the costs of offering help.

Civil Rights Supporters

In the mid-1980s, overt, active support of civil rights for blacks and other minority groups is socially acceptable and, for the most part, not terribly dangerous. But 25 years ago, things were quite different—especially in the southern United States. Attempts to integrate restaurants and other public facilities or to register blacks to vote often encountered violent resistance from racist whites. In 1964, three young civil rights workers on their way to help blacks register in Mississippi were pulled from their car and murdered. Among the culprits was the sheriff of the county in which the murder occurred. A year or so later, a white housewife from Detroit, Michigan, was shot and killed as she drove back from a civil rights march in Selma, Alabama. Many other people who participated in the movement for black civil rights were beaten and jailed. In this text, the people who engaged in these activities are considered heroes, but during the civil rights movement, many were seen as radicals or kooks (Rosenhan, 1970). Participation in the fight for civil rights was often a dangerous activity which provided few if any external rewards for the people involved.

David Rosenhan (1970) conducted in-depth interviews with people who had actively participated in the civil rights movement during the 1960s. He classified these people as belonging to one of two groups: partially committed and fully committed. Members of the partially committed group had engaged in one or two civil rights activities; members of the fully committed group had spent at least a year, more or less, continuously engaged in civil rights activities. Rosenhan found two characteristics that differentiated between the members of these groups. One, the fully committed individuals were much more likely to have positive, warm feelings toward their parents than were the partially committed individuals. Two, the parents of the fully committed were likely to have a long-term commitment to an altruistic cause and to have manifested this commitment in both their words and their deeds. According to Rosenhan, the fully committed had "positive training for prosocial action" (1970, p. 263). But what about the partially committed? Their parents also preached support for altruistic causes, but their deeds were often quite different from their words. Many of the partially committed saw their parents as hypocrites, saying one thing and doing another. Rosenhan suggested that these differences were at least in part responsible for the differences in the extent of commitment between the two groups. His interpretation is consistent with the research on the effects of models (for example, Midlarsky et al., 1973). Models who practice what they preach are much more likely to produce prosocial behaviors in the children who observe them than are models who do not practice what they preach.

Further evidence of the relationship between parental actions and the behavior of their offspring was provided in a study by Hoffman (1975). He obtained classmates' ratings of how helpful and altruistic a group of fifth graders were. He found three major differences between the parents of children classified as helpful and the parents of children classified as non-helpful. First, parents of the helpful children had warmer and more affectionate relationships with their children. Second, they were more likely to hold altruistic values. And third, they were more likely to directly reinforce their children's prosocial actions. Whether one is talking about rescuers in Europe in the 1940s, civil rights activists in the 1960s, or primary school children in the 1970s, parental behaviors play a significant role in their children's willingness to help others.

Crime Stoppers

The final group of real-life heroes were individuals who had attempted to stop a crime in progress and had been injured as a result. Under a law passed by the state of California, these people were designated Good Samaritans and were compensated for their injuries. Huston, Geis, and Wright (1976) interviewed several of these people. The results of their interviews were not what one might expect.

While humans often ignore the plight of others, they are also capable of great acts of courage.

These individuals had not been socialized to be altruistic and helpful. A large percentage of them liked to take risks, were emotionally volatile, were quick to anger, and had a history of assaultive behavior. They were "on familiar and rather amiable terms with violence" (Huston et al., 1976, p. 2). Their motivation for intervening seemed to be desire to hurt the criminal rather than a desire to help the victim. Under other circumstances, they might have acted in a very antisocial manner.

These people were confronted by situations that were quite different from the situations confronting the people who rescued Jews or supported civil rights. The rescuers and supporters were engaged in long-term activities that required a long-term commitment. These helpers probably spent some time thinking about what they were doing. On the other hand, stopping a thief or mugger is a spur-of-the-moment activity. The crime stoppers were probably impulsive individuals and were probably unaware of or unconcerned about the costs of their actions.

The specific situation that confronts a potential helper can greatly influence the type of person who offers help. Social behavior is the result of an interaction between situational variables and personality variables. The person who offers help in one situation may be quite different from the one who offers help in another. Perhaps this is why the search for the "generalized helping personality" has not been successful.

HELPERS

The kinds of helping just presented are exciting and interesting. They are also quite rare. Think of the last time you rescued someone from an impending disaster, risked your life in support of some cause, or stopped a criminal from committing a crime. Most of us go through our entire lives without either needing or providing these kinds of help. But there is a kind of help needed by many people. It is aid in solving personal and emotional problems.

People who provide this type of help come from one of two groups. The first group is mental health professionals. These people are trained in psychology, psychiatry, or allied professions and earn their livings by providing mental health services. The second group is difficult to label and characterize. These people lack any formal training in mental health and do not earn their livings by providing mental health services. But because of their jobs or their positions in the community, others often seek their help in solving personal and emotional problems. The first group can be labeled professional helpers, and the second group, nonprofessional helpers. These labels do not reflect a judgment about the quality of the help the two groups provide; rather, they reflect differences between the two groups in the training they have received and how they earn their livings.

Professional Helpers

The people who earn their living as mental health professionals are unlike bystanders. Bystanders who see someone in trouble help through short-term physical action. Therapists provide help through a series of face-to-face conversations. Bystanders are under no formal obligation to help, but therapists are ethically obligated to offer help to anyone who requests it. Most therapists are both intrinsically and extrinsically motivated to help their clients, but their professional success may depend on the quantity and quality of the help they provide. Therapists are paid professional helpers.

Given this, you might think that the quality of the help therapists provide is not affected by the same things that affect the quality of help unpaid, nonprofessional helpers provide. Research suggests, however, that the effectiveness of therapists in helping their clients may be affected by the same things that influence bystanders' decisions to help people in trouble.

Similarity and Attraction

The review of the bystander intervention literature pointed out that the more similar potential helpers believe they are to a person in distress, the more likely they are to want to help. This may also be true of mental health professionals. Therapists are obligated to help anyone who requests their services, but they prefer to have clients they perceive as similar to themselves (Lorion, 1974; Wills, 1978). Further, the effectiveness of psychotherapy is influenced by the degree of similarity between the therapist and his or her client and by how much a therapist likes a client. The more similar a client is to the therapist, the less likely the client is to drop out before the therapy is completed (Baekeland and Lundwald, 1975). Smith and Glass (1977) found that the more similar clients were to their therapists, the greater the improvement they experienced. Luborsky, Chandler, Auerbach, Cohen, and Bachrach (1971) reported that the more a therapist likes a client, the greater the improvement in the client at the completion of psychotherapy.

The helping literature can at least partially explain these findings. Perceived similarity leads to greater empathy with the person in distress (Krebs, 1975). The greater the empathic response, the more motivated a bystander is to help (Batson and Coke, 1981). Also, most research on psychotherapy suggests that a therapist's empathy can determine the success of psychotherapy.

Common sense suggests another explanation of why similarity and liking are positively associated with the outcome of psychotherapy. Therapists may find interacting with a liked, similar client pleasant; as a result, they will expend more time and effort in trying to help the client. So, just as bystanders' feelings about a victim affect the quantity and quality of the help they give the victim, therapists' feelings about a client affect to some extent the quantity and quality of help they give the client.

Social Cognitions about the Client

In Piliavin and her associates' (1981) model of bystander intervention, great emphasis was placed on what the bystander thought about the victim and the cause of the victim's problems. If the victim is perceived as a less-than-admirable person or the problem is attributed to a personal, internal cause (such as drinking too much), help is less likely to be offered.

Some researchers (for example, Wills, 1978) have argued that therapists are biased by social cognitions involving perceptions of the client and of the client's problem. Therapists may focus more on a client's weaknesses than on her strengths. Hill (1974) studied the amount of time therapists spent pointing out their clients' weaknesses and their clients' strengths. Neither activity was very common in a therapy session, but therapists pointed out weaknesses approximately five times more often than they pointed out strengths.

Therapists are also more likely to attribute their clients' problems to an enduring personal characteristic of the client than to a situational variable over which the client has no control (Batson, O'Quin, and Pych, 1982; Wills, 1978). One illustration of this was provided by Valins and Nisbet (1972). A newly married woman sought the services of a psychotherapist because she was experiencing abdominal pains at bedtime. The therapist attributed her pains to sexual fears. Over time, her conditon and anxiety increased and the woman sought the help of a physician. He discovered that her pains were not due to fears about sex, but to a simple allergic reaction to tomatoes.

Some researchers (for example, Wills, 1978) have argued that professionals are more subject to this kind of attributional error than are lay people. Batson and his associates (1982), however, failed to find any greater bias among professionals than among lay people. At this point, it is not clear how frequently attributional errors occur among professionals, or even why they occur. But it is generally agreed that when a therapist inappropriately focuses on the negative aspects of a client and overestimates the extent to which clients are the cause of their problems, the outcome of therapy is less positive (Batson et al., 1982; Wills, 1978). Even paid professional helping is affected by the helper's view of the person in distress.

Nonprofessional Helpers

Imagine that you have an emotional problem and you decide to seek help. To whom would you turn? If you are like most other Americans, you would not go to a mental health professional. Several national surveys of people who sought help for emotional problems have found that no more than 20 percent approached mental health professionals (Cowen, 1982). Instead, they talked to people they already knew, trusted, and had access to almost immediately. The two occupations most often called upon to provide nonprofessional mental health services are physicians and members of the clergy (Gurin, Veroff, and Feld, 1960). People in other, less obvious, occupations also regularly provide help for emotional and personal problems.

Emory Cowen and his associates (for example Cowen, 1982; Cowen, Gesten, Boike, Norton, Wilson, and DeStefano, 1979; Cowen, Gesten, Davidson, and Wilson, 1981a; Cowen, McKim, and Weissberg, 1981b) investigated nonprofessional helping among members of some less obvious occupations.* Two of the groups they studied were bartenders and hairdressers. People with these two very different jobs often find themselves listening to the problems of their customers. The amount of time they spend helping, the types of problems presented to them, and their reactions to the problems tell something about helping in general.

Amount of Time Spent Helping
Overall, bartenders spend about half as much time listening to their customers' problems as do hairdressers. Bartenders interviewed by Cowen and his associates (1981b) reported that 16 percent of their clientele presented moderate to serious personal problems. Hairdressers reported that 33 percent of their clientele raised similar problems (Cowen et al., 1979, 1981a). However, bartenders served almost ten times as many customers per week as did hairdressers. So, while the percentage of customers that asked bartenders for help was much smaller than the percentage that asked

---

*I am grateful to Ellis Gesten for bringing this research to my attention.

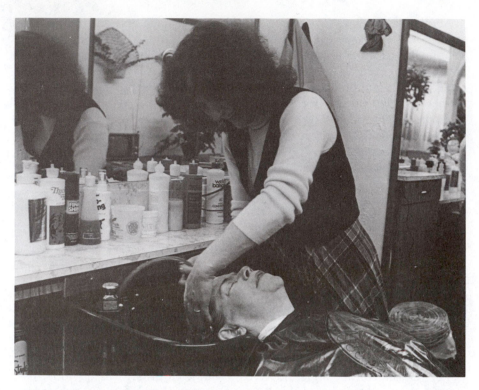

This hairdresser may give her customer more than a shampoo and a new hair style; she may listen to and offer advice on the woman's problems.

hairdressers, the absolute number of troubled people with whom bartenders spoke (over a 100 per week) was much greater.

The conversations about problems were much shorter among bartenders than among hairdressers (Cowen, 1982). But this difference was probably not due to less compassion or concern among the bartenders. The typical bartender had from eight to ten customers at the same time, while the typical hairdresser had only one or two. The bartenders simply could not afford to spend too long conversing with a single customer, but the hairdressers had fairly long periods of time when nothing interfered with their conversation.

Types of Problems Presented
Customers in a bar were most likely to present problems that concerned their jobs, marriages, and finances. Customers in a beauty salon presented problems that concerned their children, physical health, and marriages. Bar customers were much less likely than beauty salon customers to discuss emotional problems such as depression and anxiety (Cowen, 1982). There are two explanations for these differences: sex differences and differences in the physical environments of bars and beauty salons. Most of the bartenders' customers were male, and most of the hairdressers' customers were female. Men and women have different kinds of problems, and wom-

en tend to be much more self-disclosing than men. The booth or stalls in a beauty salon are more private and secure than is an open bar and, thus, the probability that another customer would overhear a conversation in the beauty salon was much smaller than the probability that another person would overhear a conversation in the bar.

Reactions to the Problems

The predominant response of the bartenders when a customer presented a problem was to just listen, but the hairdressers offered support and encouragement. This difference may be due, in part, to differences between the job responsibilities of the two groups. A large part of bartenders' incomes depends on their ability to serve a number of people at the same time. A long conversation with one customer may prevent them from serving other customers; as a result, their tips would suffer. By contrast, the tips and return business for the hairdressers may have, in part, depended on their ability to offer support for their customers. As one hairdresser put it:

> [I'm a] "B−" hairdresser. But my business is booming. Mostly that's because I listen to people and care about their personal concerns, and try to be helpful. The guy down the street is really an A+ hairdresser . . . But he's going out of business because he can't stand anyone and is incapable of listening sympathetically to anyone's problems. (Cowen, 1982, p. 390)

Hairdressers and bartenders both reacted positively to requests for help, but hairdressers felt they were more effective in dealing with their customers and that helping was a more integral part of their jobs than did bartenders. Cowen suggested that this difference was largely due to the fact that the majority of hairdressers were female and the majority of bartenders were males. In his view, women are more likely than men to have been socialized into the role of providing help for other people with problems.

The findings from these studies are interesting, but as Cowen (1982) acknowledged, they do not tell us much about why people seek help from nonprofessionals and what will influence the quantity and quality of help provided. It may be worthwhile to explore the extent to which the models of bystander intervention could be used to explain this type of helping.

Chapter Nine

Attitudes and Behavior

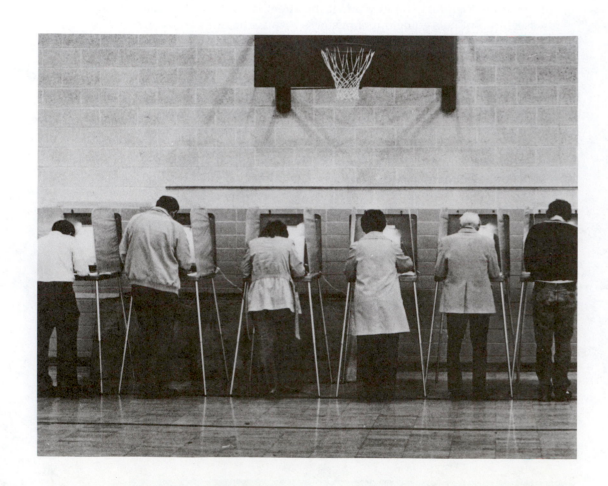

Prologue

Richard T. La Piere (1934). Attitudes versus Actions. *Social Forces*, **13**, 230–37.

Background

During the early 1930s, Richard La Piere spent two years traveling throughout the United States with a young Chinese couple. Because of the prejudice that existed toward Chinese at that time, La Piere expected they would often encounter difficulties at hotels and restaurants. Very early in the trip, they stopped at the best hotel in a "small town noted for its narrow and bigoted 'attitude' towards Orientals" (La Piere, 1934). With some fear, the travelers asked for rooms and were given them without a moment's hesitation. Surprised by this, La Piere decided to try another test of this town's attitudes toward Chinese. Several weeks later, he called the hotel and asked if it would accept a "Chinese gentleman" as a guest. Without a moment's hesitation, the hotel representative said no. This disparity between a verbal statement about and actual behavior toward Chinese aroused La Piere's interest and led to the following study. It was not an experiment—it had no independent variable or experimental and control groups—but it did provide some important data on the relationship between attitudes and behavior.

Hypothesis

The basic hypothesis was that in many instances there is a weak relationship between attitudes and behavior.

Subjects

The subjects were the owners or managers of 251 hotels, inns, campgrounds, and restaurants located in different parts of the United States.

Procedure

During the two years that La Piere and the Chinese couple spent traveling, they visited 184 restaurants and 67 different hotels, inns, and campgrounds. The first measure taken at each place was whether or not the Chinese couple were served. If they were, La Piere rated the quality of the service they received.

Six months after their visit, La Piere mailed each establishment a questionnaire with the following question: "Will you accept members of the Chinese race (sic) as guests in your establishment?" To control for the possibility that the responses of the establishments would be influenced by the couple's earlier visit, La Piere sent the same questionnaire to other establishments in the same area that had not been visited by the couple.

Results

The Chinese couple were refused service at one of the 251 places they visited. This happened when they arrived late at night at a campground and the manager refused them service because "I don't take Japs." La Piere's ratings of the quality of the service the couple received indicated that most of the time they were treated with more than typical courtesy. In only one hotel and one restaurant were they treated rudely.

The response to the question about accepting Chinese as guests was not influenced by whether the establishment had been visited by the couple, and the response was also totally unrelated to the treatment the couple actually received. Ninety-two percent of the places that had accepted the couple as guests said they would refuse service to people of Chinese ancestry, and 91 percent of the restaurants that had served meals to the couple said they would refuse service to people of Chinese ancestry.

Implications

La Piere was among the first social psychologists to raise some serious questions about the value of studying attitudes to understand human social behavior. Although his study is now over 50 years old and contains some methodological weaknesses, it addressed an issue that is still the subject of considerable debate among social psychologists. If, as La Piere and many others have found, attitudes are unrelated to behavior, why study them? This question is addressed directly in this chapter, and some reasons for La Piere's findings as well as current thoughts on the true relationship between attitudes and behavior are discussed.

From almost the beginning of social psychology as a formal discipline, social psychologists have studied attitudes. Indeed, some early writers defined social psychology solely as the study of attitudes (Thomas and Znaniecki, 1918; Watson, 1925). When Gordon Allport wrote about attitudes 50 years ago, he said that they were "the most distinctive and indispensable concept in social psychology" (1935, p. 798).

Research on attitudes has primarily focused on three questions: What is an attitude? How does it develop? and What role does it play in social behavior? The first section of this chapter addresses the first question, discussing the structure of attitudes and techniques for measuring them. The second section presents research on the acquisition of attitudes and examines how attitudes affect social behavior. The third section also addresses the role of attitudes in social behavior; it considers the issue raised in the prologue—whether or not attitudes are related to behavior. The applications section focuses on negative attitudes toward people because of their appearance or beliefs—prejudice.

NATURE OF ATTITUDES _____

The word *attitude* is derived from the Latin word *aptus*, which means fit or ready for action. The Latin word refers to something that is directly observable, such as a runner getting in position for a race. Today, the word attitude refers to something unobservable which precedes people's actions.

An **attitude** is a consistent predisposition to respond to some object in a favorable or unfavorable manner. Attitudes affect the likelihood that people will act in a certain way, but they cannot be equated with behavior. As you saw in the prologue, in some instances attitudes are not at all related to a person's behavior. Also, the object of an attitude can be another person, a place, a thing, or even an activity. For example, you have attitudes toward the president, a local restaurant, nuclear disarmament, and mowing the lawn. When you think about or confront an object, your attitude toward it predisposes you to react favorably or unfavorably.

This section presents two models of the structure of attitudes. It then discusses several scales used to measure attitudes.

Structure of Attitudes

You cannot see, touch, or physically examine an attitude; it does not exist in the physical sense. An attitude is a **hypothetical construct.** Social psychologists have proposed theoretical models of the structure of attitudes to show how they can be conceptualized and how they should affect people's behavior.

Hypothetical construct: a concept used to explain why some observable event occurs.

The use of theoretical models to describe unobservable or nonexistent entities is quite common in science. The equation $E = MC^2$—energy equals mass times the speed of light, squared—is probably the most famous equation in modern science. Einstein based this formula on a theoretical model of how energy, light speed, and mass are related.

Theoretical models of attitude structure serve the same purpose as Einstein's formula. Two such models are the three-component model and the expectancy-value model. The relative validity of these two models can be determined by the extent to which they enable us to understand the causes of social behavior toward an object and to predict this behavior.

Three-Component Model

The most widely accepted model of attitude structure proposes that an attitude is made up of three separate, yet related, components (Krech, Crutchfield, and Ballachey, 1962; Rosenberg and Hovland, 1960; Rokeach, 1968). Each of these components concerns a person's attitude toward an object. The first is called the **affective component.** If we wanted to determine the affective component of people's attitudes toward lawyers, for instance, we would ask them to respond to statements concerned with positive or negative feelings toward the attitude object "lawyers." (See part A of table 9-1.)

Affective component: how much a person likes or dislikes an attitude object.

Table 9-1. *Three Components of Attitude toward Lawyers*

Part A: Affective Component

I like and respect lawyers.

It would make me proud if my child became a lawyer.

The ethical standards of lawyers sicken me.

I feel positively about the legal profession.

Part B: Cognitive Component

All lawyers have gone to law school.

Lawyers are motivated by a sense of justice.

Lawyers are motivated by greed and avarice.

Lawyers make a very good income.

Part C: Behavioral Component

I would not follow a lawyer's advice under any circumstances.

I would vote for a candidate who was a lawyer.

I would support laws which gave lawyers more control over the legal system.

I would let my child marry a lawyer.

Cognitive component: information about the attitude object and beliefs about its attributes.

The second part of an attitude is the **cognitive component.** To determine the cognitive component of people's attitudes toward lawyers, we would ask them to respond to questions that reflect beliefs about lawyers. (See part B of table 9-1.) If you examine the statements in table 9-1, you will notice that some are fairly neutral and could be objectively proven or disproven. For example, one could easily determine whether "All lawyers have gone to law school." Other statements, however, describe positive or negative characteristics and are much more difficult to prove or disprove. For example, "Lawyers are motivated by a sense of justice" is a positive but subjective statement; "Lawyers are motivated by greed and avarice" is a negative but subjective statement.

Behavioral component: feelings about how one would act toward an attitude object.

The third part of an attitude, according to this model, is the **behavioral component.** (See part C of table 9-1 for statements that represent the behavioral component of an attitude).

To determine the validity of this model, studies must examine its two proposals: (1) that the three components are related and (2) that the three components are consistent with one another. One could test the first proposal by asking people questions that reflect each of the three components and then computing correlations between the three scores. Campbell (1947) conducted such a test by examining white high school students' attitudes toward black people. Using separate scales, Campbell measured how much the students liked blacks (affective component), their beliefs about the characteristics of blacks (cognitive component), and their willingness to interact with blacks (behavioral component). On the average, scores on the three scales had a .50 correlation, suggesting that the three components are related but not the same thing.

Studies by Rosenberg (1960) and Brehm (1960) examined the validity of the second proposal in this model. These studies indicated that, as the model predicts, changes in one component cause changes in another. Rosenberg (1960) used hypnosis to change the affective component of subjects' attitudes toward the United States policy of giving economic aid to other countries. No hypnotic suggestions were made about the cognitive component, yet Rosenberg found that subjects' beliefs about economic aid changed to match the affective changes. Brehm (1960) changed the behavioral component of adolescents' attitudes toward disliked foods by getting them to eat the disliked food. He found that if the adolescents agreed to eat the food, they also changed their beliefs about its vitamin content.

Expectancy-Value Model

There are several different versions of the **expectancy-value model** of attitude structure. All assume that people's feelings (affect) toward an attitude object are determined by (a) their *expectancies* about what characteristics or attributes are possessed by an attitude object and (b) the *value* they place on these attributes. Martin Fishbein's (Fishbein, 1963; Fishbein and Ajzen, 1975) expectancy-value model makes a very specific proposal about how these two things determine people's feelings toward an attitude object. If one wants to know a person's attitude toward an attitude object, Fishbein said that one needs to learn three things: the person's beliefs about the characteristics of this attitude object; the person's estimate of how likely it is that the attitude object possesses these characteristics; and, how the person evaluates the characteristics.

Again suppose that the attitude object is lawyers. According to Fishbein's model, a person's attitude toward lawyers is determined by his expectancies about the characteristics lawyers possess and the value he places on these characteristics. (See table 9-2). Imagine that the four statements presented in the left-hand column of table 9-2 represent someone's attitude toward lawyers. In the next column is a set of numbers preceded by a decimal point. The numbers represent the person's subjective estimate, or expectancy, that each statement is true of lawyers or that lawyers possess each characteristic. This person's expectancy is .99 for the statement "Lawyers go to law school." And .10 for the statement "Lawyers are motivated by greed and avarice." The person is 99 percent sure the former statement is true of lawyers, but only 10 percent sure the latter statement is true of lawyers. The third column contains the person's evaluation of each attribute; a plus 3 indicates a positive evaluation and a minus 3 indicates a negative evaluation. This column represents the *value* the person places on each attribute. To determine the person's affect toward lawyers—how favorably or unfavorably he feels toward lawyers—multiply the expectancy (column two) by the value (column three) for each statement, and add the products. (See column four in table 9-2.)

To test this model, Fishbein and his associates (for example, Fishbein and Feldman, 1963; Fishbein and Coombs, 1974) presented subjects with a series of statements about the attributes of various attitude objects (political candidates, for instance). They then obtained the subjects' estimates

Expectancy-value model: a model that proposes that an attitude toward some object is determined by beliefs about the object's characteristics and by the value placed on those characteristics.

Table 9-2. An Expectancy-Value Model conceptualization of an attitude toward lawyers. E = expectancy, the likelihood that the attitude object possesses this characteristic; V = value, the value the person places on this characteristic; E × V = the product of these two. The sum of E × V is the person's attitude.

Statement	E	V	E × V
All lawyers have gone to law school.	.99	0	0
Lawyers are motivated by greed and avarice.	.10	−2	−.20
Lawyers are motivated by a sense of justice.	.25	+3	+.75
Lawyers make a very good income.	.50	+1	+.50
Attitude toward lawyers			1.05

of how likely it was that the object possessed those attributes and recorded the value the subjects placed on them. Next they combined the expectancies and values in the manner specified by the model. The resultant scores were used to predict the subjects' feelings toward the attitude object, which were assessed by asking the subjects how much they liked or disliked the attitude object. The correlation between the scores and the subjects' feelings was very high, showing that the model is viable.

There is a major difference between this model and the three-component model. The three-component model proposes that part of people's attitudes is the behavioral component—how they intend to act toward the attitude object. Fishbein's model says nothing about the behavioral component because Fishbein believed that intentions to behave in a certain way toward an attitude object are quite separate from feelings toward the object. (See figure 9-1.) He proposed that our intentions to behave are not directly determined by how much we like or dislike the attitude object. This difference provides the first clue as to why attitudes and behavior were unrelated in the prologue, and it is discussed again when the relationship between attitudes and behavior is considered.

Measurement of Attitudes

To move from the stage of theorizing to empirical tests of a theory's validity, the researcher must translate the constructs in it into things that are directly observable and measurable. This is true whether the researcher is a physicist interested in subatomic particles or a social psychologist interested in attitudes. La Piere translated the construct "attitude toward Chinese" into the subjects' responses to the question "Would you accept members of the Chinese race as guests in your establishment?" The subjects' answers became his operational definition of the construct. There are other ways to operationalize attitudes.

Direct Measures
Direct measures of attitudes all share one basic assumption: If you want to know people's attitudes toward an object, just ask them. This could be done by presenting people with a single question about their attitudes, but

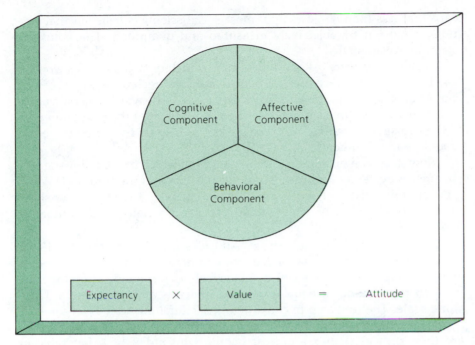

Figure 9-1. *The three-component model of attitude structure (top) and the expectancy-value model of attitude structure (bottom).*

typically researchers use **attitude scales.** Scales are preferred over single-item measures for two reasons. First, they provide a more reliable estimate of people's attitudes. Reliability concerns the consistency of a measure. (See chapter two.) If researchers want to compare the attitudes of two different groups or want to use attitudes to predict behavior, they must have estimates of the attitudes which are reasonably consistent. In general, the more items contained in a scale, the more reliable it will be (Kidder, 1981).

The second reason researchers use scales is that they must be concerned with the construct validity of their measure of an attitude. Recall that a measure is **construct valid** if it provides a faithful and accurate representation of the construct of interest. Attitudes are complex entities, and in most instances, a scale provides a more construct valid measure of a complex entity than does a single item. To illustrate, imagine two tests of mathematical ability. The first contains one item: What is the formula for computing the circumference of a circle. The second contains items on geometry, algebra, and calculus. Which test is more valid? Clearly, the answer is the second one. Three scales researchers have used to measure attitudes are Thurstone scales, summative scales, and semantic differential scales.

Thurstone Scales Public opinion polling and other forms of attitude measurement are a fact of modern life. Millions of dollars are spent each year to measure people's attitudes. Thus, it may come as a surprise to

Attitude scales: measurements of attitudes obtained by asking several questions about the attitude object and combining the responses to those questions to form a scale.

learn that less than 60 years ago, most social scientists believed that attitudes could not be objectively measured and quantified. The following example explains why.

Imagine you were asked to determine which of two pieces of wood is heavier. You could place each piece on a scale and record its weight or you could get people's judgments of which piece is heavier. Several people could hold a piece in each hand, and you could record their judgments as to their relative weights. The piece judged as heavier by the most people would be the "winner."

Now imagine you were asked to determine which of the following two statements expresses a more negative attitude toward gun control: (1) When guns are outlawed, only outlaws will have guns. (2) They'll have to shoot me first to take my gun. How would you judge whether one is more or less negative than the other?

Louis Thurstone, in his article "Attitudes Can Be Measured" (1928), showed that the relative favorableness or unfavorableness of statements about feelings or attitudes can be objectively determined. Thurstone developed the method of equal-appearing intervals and produced a **Thurstone scale.** The first step in constructing a Thurstone scale is to generate a large number of statements about some attitude object. These statements are then presented to a group of people who judge how favorable or unfavorable a sentiment each statement expresses toward the object. They do this by rating the statement on an eleven-point scale, 1 equals a very favorable sentiment toward the attitude object and 11 equals a very negative sentiment. The average rating given an item by the judges is called its **scale value.** For example, the statement "When guns are outlawed, only outlaws will have guns" might receive an average rating from the judges of 10.5, indicating that it expresses a very unfavorable sentiment toward gun control. The statement "Private citizens should not be allowed to own handguns" might receive an average rating of 1.5, indicating that it expresses a very unfavorable sentiment toward gun control. This average, or scale value, is conceptually the same as the numbers that would appear on a scale used to measure the relative weights of two pieces of wood.

Scale value: a number that indicates how favorable or unfavorable a statement is toward an attitude object.

Finally, subjects who are asked to complete the Thurstone Scale check all the statements with which they agree. Their attitudes toward the object being measured are then operationally defined as the average scale value of the items they checked. (See table 9-3 for an example of a Thurstone scale.)

Summative Scales   The Thurstone scale represented an important advance in attitude research, but it had certain drawbacks. Chief among these were the time and effort involved in obtaining the scale values for each statement. A somewhat easier means of measuring attitudes is the **summative scale** developed by Rensis Likert (1932). Likert's method begins in the same way as Thurstone's. A large number of statements that clearly express positive or negative sentiments toward the attitude object are obtained. Instead of being rated by judges, the statements are presented to a group of subjects and the subjects indicate how they feel about each

Table 9-3. *Some items from Thurstone and Chave's original scale of attitudes toward the church, the first Thurstone scale. The scale values represent the judges' ratings and do not appear on the actual scale. The subjects' attitudes are operationally defined as the average of scale values of the items they have circled. The higher the scale value the more negative the sentiment toward the church.*

Instructions: Circle the items with which you agree

Scale Value

11.0	1.	I think the church is a parasite on society.
0.8	2.	I feel the church perpetuates the values which humans put highest in their philosophy of life.
5.6	3.	Sometimes I feel that the church and religion are necessary and sometimes I doubt it.
0.2	4.	I believe the church is the greatest institution in America today.

Source: Thurstone and Chave (1929).

statement. For example, in a summative scale concerned with attitudes toward gun control, one of the items might be as follows:

When guns are outlawed, only outlaws will have guns.

1. Strongly disagree

2. Disagree

3. Neutral

4. Agree

5. Strongly agree

Subjects would circle the answer that comes closest to their feelings about the statement. Their responses to this statement and other statements concerned with gun control would be added together, and each subject's attitude toward this object would be operationally defined as the *sum* of the responses to the items. (See table 9-4 for an example of a summative scale.)

Semantic Differential Scales   In the mid-1950s, Charles Osgood and his associates (Osgood, Suci, and Tannenbaum, 1957) developed an instrument to measure the connotative meaning of words. The connotative meaning of a word can differ from its denotative, or dictionary, definition. For example, the dictionary definition of the word *boy* is "a male child from birth to puberty." The connotative meaning of *boy* might be quite different to an adult black male, who sees it as a racial "put-down." The instrument was called the **semantic differential** because it was used to differentiate between the connotative meanings people place on different words. Osgood and his associates found that three factors determined the connotative meanings of most words: an evaluative factor—how good or bad, valuable or worthless something is; a potency factor—how strong or weak something is; and an activity factor—how active or passive something is.

What does all this have to do with attitude measurement? Osgood (1965) proposed that the evaluative factor in the semantic differential scale

Semantic differential:
a technique for determining the connotative meaning of a word.

Table 9-4. *An example of a summated scale which measures people's attitudes toward their job. The people's attitudes are operationally defined as the sum of the numbers they place in the blanks. (Note: The first item is reversed when this scale is scored.)*

Instructions: Write a number in the blank before each statement based on this scale:

1. Disagree Strongly   2. Disagree   3. Agree   4. Agree Strongly

_____ 1. I frequently think of quitting this job.

_____ 2. I am generally satisfied with the kind of work I do in this job.

_____ 3. My opinion of myself goes up when I do this job well.

_____ 4. The work I do on this job is very meaningful to me.

Source: Smith et al. (1969).

could be used to assess people's attitudes toward an object. He believed that attitudes were evaluative responses to objects and that one can measure people's attitudes toward some object by presenting them with that object and asking them to indicate how good or bad they think it is. For example, a researcher could present the concept of gun control to subjects and ask them to rate it on the following pairs of adjectives:

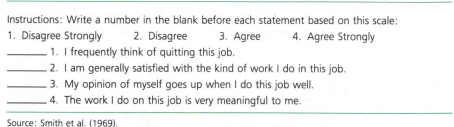

Gun Control

Good	1 2 3 4 5 6 7	Bad
Positive	1 2 3 4 5 6 7	Negative
Pleasant	1 2 3 4 5 6 7	Unpleasant

Subjects would respond by circling one of the seven numbers between each pair of adjectives. For example, if gun control meant something bad to them, they would circle number 7 in the good-bad pair. If gun control meant something good to the subjects, they would circle number 1. The subjects' attitudes toward the object would be operationally defined as the sum of the numbers they had circled.

This technique can be used to determine more than whether a person reacts favorably or unfavorably toward an attitude object. Adjectives concerned with activity and potency could be used to determine how active or passive and strong or weak the attitude object is in the eyes of the person filling out the scale. For example, in the 1968 presidential election, Richard Nixon's advisors used the semantic differential scale to determine whether people liked or disliked him and to determine their perceptions of how active and powerful a person he was (McGinness, 1971).

Indirect Measures

Direct measurement techniques yield reliable and valid measures of an attitude, but they are subject to a potential weakness: They can be reactive measures. A reactive measure may cause a change in the thing being measured. (See chapter two.) When people fill out a Thurstone scale, a summative scale, or to a lesser extent, a semantic differential scale, they know almost immediately which of their attitudes are being measured. If these attitudes concern a sensitive topic (attitudes toward homosexuals, for example), people may not give their true attitudes. Because of this potential problem, social psychologists sometimes use other techniques to measure attitudes, such as the bogus pipeline or unobtrusive measures.

Bogus Pipeline   The **bogus pipeline** is used to increase subjects' willingness to give honest and frank responses to attitude scales (Jones and Sigall, 1971). Before subjects fill out a scale or respond to any other direct measure of attitudes, they are hooked up to a piece of equipment which they believe records their physiological responses to the attitude object of interest. The equipment is bogus, or phony, but the subjects are told that it can detect whether or not they are giving honest answers.

The logic behind the bogus pipeline is that people do not want to be identified as liars by the machine, so they will give more honest answers to sensitive questions. Studies support this logic. Faranda, Kaminski, and Giza (1979) divided males and females into two groups. One group filled out a questionnaire concerned with their attitudes toward women's rights. The other group filled out the same questionnaire, but were attached to a bogus pipeline. Among subjects in the first group, there were no differences between the attitudes expressed by men and women. Among subjects in the second group, men expressed more negative attitudes than did women. Similar findings have been obtained when attitudes toward blacks have been measured (Sigall and Page, 1971).

The bogus pipeline seems to increase the validity of measurements of people's attitudes, but it is often not very practical. For example, if you wanted to measure the attitudes of two hundred students toward cheating on examinations, it would be very time-consuming to collect data from them one at a time while the were attached to a bogus pipeline. Unless your research were being supported by someone named Rockefeller, you would not have the funds to buy two hundred bogus lie detectors. More economical means are available, including unobtrusive measures.

Unobtrusive Measures   An *unobtrusive measure* of attitudes attempts to solve the problem of reactivity by not letting people know that their attitudes are being measured. A behavior believed to be related to the attitude of interest is observed and recorded. Naturally occurring behaviors are often observed to determine the attitudes of a large group of people. For example, Jorgenson and Lange (1975) used graffiti on a college campus to assess students' attitudes before an upcoming election. Milgram (1969) used people's willingness to mail supposedly lost letters as a measure of their attitudes toward the recipients of those letters. Even some very natural behaviors can be used to estimate people's likes and dislikes. For example, when commercials interrupt a television program, people usually get themselves something to eat or drink or they get rid of something they have eaten or drunk. Thus, commercial time during a popular television show should be accompanied by a dramatic decline in water pressure (Webb et al., 1981). This hypothesis was tested during a recent super bowl game. Records of water usage in a large midwestern city showed that water pressure declined by 30 million gallons during halftime.

Bogus pipeline: a procedure used to increase the honesty of people's answers by convincing them that the researcher will know if they lie.

Topic Background

Randomized Response Technique

The randomized response technique is another means for increasing people's willingness to give honest and frank answers to sensitive questions. A researcher can use this technique to get an estimate of how many people in a group have answered a question in a certain way, while at the same time guaranteeing individual members of the group that no one will ever be able to determine how they answered the question. Here is how it works.

Suppose the question of interest is "Have you ever cheated on any examination?" A group of 200 students is asked this question. Before they answer, they flip a coin. If the coin lands on heads they are to answer yes whether or not they have ever cheated on an examination. If the coin lands on tails, they are to answer truthfully. If someone looked at an individual student's answer sheet and saw the answer yes, there would be no way to determine if the student answered yes because the coin had landed on heads or because yes was a truthful statement.

So the students' anonymity on this question is guaranteed. But how can the researcher get a valid estimate of how many students have ever cheated? The answer requires some simple mathematics. If the coins are unbiased, 50 percent of the students should answer yes because the coin landed on heads and 50 percent should answer honestly. (In fact, the percentages would probably not be exactly fifty-fifty, but small deviations would not invalidate this technique.)

Suppose that 180 students answered yes to the question and 20 students answered no. About 100 of the yes answers were due to the coin landing on heads. But about 80 of the yes answers were due to the coin landing on tails and the students answering honestly. That is, of the 100 students who answered honestly (the coin landed on tails), 80 percent said they had cheated on an examination. What differentiates these students from the 100 who answered yes because of the coin landing on heads? Absolutely nothing other than a chance, or random, event—the flip of a coin. Therefore, it is quite reasonable to assume that had they been required to answer honestly, a comparable percentage would have answered yes. Thus, the researcher can *estimate* that, overall, 80 percent of the students in this group had cheated on an examination, while not knowing how any individual member of the group had answered the question.

Does this technique increase people's willingness to answer honestly? Two recent studies speak to this question. In this first, Himmelfarb and Lickteig (1982) developed a set of questions with different probabilities that people would answer them honestly. Some questions were neutral (Did you vote in the last election?), while others addressed sensitive issues (Have you ever had more than one sexual partner?). These questions were given to two groups of students. In both groups, the students answered the questions anonymously, but students in the first group used the randomized response technique and students in the other group answered the questions directly.

The more likely a question was to elicit an untruthful answer, the greater was the difference between the answers given by the two groups. For example, 3 percent of the students admitted to cheating on their taxes in the direct-answer group, while in the randomized-response group 13 percent indicated they had cheated on their taxes. In the direct-answer group, 60 percent admitted they read soft-core pornography, but in the randomized-response group, 76 percent of the students reported reading soft-core pornography.

Shotland and Yankowski (1982) tested the value of the randomized response technique more directly. They had a confederate tell subjects the correct answers to a test before the subjects took it. After the test was completed, subjects answered a question about whether they had prior information about the correct answers on the test. Eighty percent of the subjects who used the randomized response technique to answer this question answered yes; only 10 percent of the subjects who answered the question directly anawered yes.

As Shotland and Yankowski concluded, the randomized response technique is a valid and ethical means of obtaining sensitive information from subjects.

Unobtrusive measures can also be used to estimate the attitude of an individual. For example, a person's nonverbal behavior, or body language, can sometimes provide a measure of that person's attitude. Something that happened during my doctoral dissertation research illustrates this—and explains why people do not always provide their true attitudes.

I was interested in the relationship between white college students' attitudes toward civil rights for blacks and their reactions to an individual black person. I hired two black students to act as confederates and conducted a number of training sessions in which I instructed them to respond neutrally no matter what the white subjects said or did during the experiment. I then placed a white subject in a room with a black confederate and observed the subject's eye contact, posture, and distance from the confederate during a ten-minute conversation. During one of these conversations, a white student told the confederate that he planned to become a police officer when he graduated from college. Despite my instructions to respond neutrally, the black confederate berated the student, calling him a racist and a fool. During the ten-minute conversation, eye contact, posture, and distance from the confederate were recorded. At the end of the conversation, the student was sitting turned in his chair so that his side faced the confederate, with his head down and his arms and legs tightly crossed. When I entered the room to stop the experiment, he looked at me the way settlers besieged by Indians looked at the cavalry in the old cowboy movies.

After separating the two, I had the student fill out a questionnaire on his reactions to the confederate. In response to the question "How much did you like you partner?" he answered "very much." Why did he lie? Probably because he did not want to appear to be antiblack. On a college

People's nonverbal behavior can sometimes reflect a person's true feelings or attitudes. While the losers in this body-building contest are applauding the winner, their faces suggest they are less than overjoyed with her victory.

campus in the late 1960s, it was not socially desirable to indicate that you disliked blacks. Thus, despite an extremely unpleasant ten minutes, the student evaluated the black confederate very favorably. The student's nonverbal behavior, of which he was much less conscious, suggested a different (and negative) reaction.

Unobtrusive techniques of attitude measurement are widely used and are valuable tools in a social scientist's research "arsenal." There are, however, some potential problems with them. First, the usefulness of an unobtrusive measure depends on whether the behavior observed is a valid indicator of a person's attitude. Since researchers do not usually directly determine a person's attitude, they may make an incorrect leap from the behavior to the attitude that supposedly caused it. In other words, the construct validity of many unobtrusive measures is open to question (Webb et al., 1981). The second problem concerns the ethics of unobtrusive techniques. The examples presented here concern fairly innocuous attitudes and behaviors. However, there is a real question as to whether social psychologists have the right to invade the privacy of their subjects by using unobtrusive measures. This is not to say that this technique is unethical, but to suggest that it could be used in an unethical manner. Researchers must be extremely sensitive to their subjects' rights.

©, Meyer—San Francisco Chronicle. Distributed by Special Features.

The various techniques of attitude measurement have their pluses and their minuses. The ideal strategy is to use more than one technique to measure the same attitude. If the different measures agree with one another, then researchers can be fairly confident that they have reliably and validly measured the attitude of interest.

SUMMARY

An attitude is a hypothetical construct used to explain why people are predisposed to act favorably or unfavorably toward a person, place, or thing in their environment. Two major models of the structure of attitudes have been proposed.

The three-component model proposes that an attitude is comprised of an affective component—positive or negative feelings about the attitude object; a cognitive component—beliefs about the characteristics of the attitude object; and a behavioral component—beliefs about how the person will act toward the attitude object. These components are separate but highly related; typically, they are consistent with one another.

The expectancy-value model proposes that an attitude is composed of people's beliefs (expectancies) about how likely it is that the object possesses certain characteristics and people's evaluations (value) of whether these characteristics are positive or negative. The degree of liking or disliking a person has for an attitude object is the product of both expectancies and values. One major difference between the two models is that the former includes a behavioral component, while the latter proposes that behavioral intentions are quite separate from people's feelings about an attitude object.

The most common way to measure attitudes is to construct an attitude scale. The three most widely used scales are Thurstone scales, summative scales, and semantic differential scales. These scales assess attitudes by determining how positive or negative people feel toward an attitude object.

All three types of scales provide reliable and valid measurements of many attitudes, but researchers may encounter some problems when using them to assess an attitude of interest that concerns a topic about which people are reluctant to openly express their attitudes. One solution to this problem is to use the bogus pipeline, in which people are led to believe that the researcher has means to determine if they are answering an attitude scale in an honest and frank manner. Another is to use unobtrusive measures to observe, without people's awareness or knowledge, behaviors that are thought to reflect the attitude of interest.

FORMATION AND FUNCTION OF ATTITUDES

The study in the prologue only concerned one aspect of attitude research—how people's present attitudes are related to their behavior. Among social psychologists who study attitudes there is also considerable interest in the origins of people's attitudes and why people hold certain attitudes. These issues are addressed by considering the formation of attitudes and their functions.

Formation of Attitudes

Most researchers agree that genetic or biological factors play little if any role in the formation of people's attitudes. Attitudes are thought to be learned as part of the socialization process (Fishbein and Ajzen, 1975; McGuire, 1969; Oskamp, 1977). They may be learned through direct experiences or through interactions with others.

Direct Experiences
Many of the attitudes people hold are the products of direct experiences with attitude objects. People encounter an attitude object and have a positive or negative experience which, at least in part, shapes their attitudes toward that object. A number of researchers have stressed the importance of traumatic or frightening experiences in the formation of attitudes (for

example, Oskamp, 1977; Sargant, 1957). For example, I don't like dentists. My present dentist is a pleasant, competent professional, who typically causes me little pain. But I dread seeing him; I do not even want to speak to him when I see him on the street. My brother and sister share my dislike of dentists. We agree that our attitude stems from our experiences with the first dentist who treated us. He was a remarkably incompetent person, who believed that novocaine was a needless expense. He began using a high-speed drill (which causes considerably less pain) about six to eight years after other members of his profession. Visits to him produced terror and pain.

Several processes have been proposed to explain the effects of personal experiences on attitude formation. Among these are classical conditioning, information gain, mere exposure, and self-perception.

Classical Conditioning   In classical conditioning, the attitude object (for example, dentists) is a conditioned stimulus which is repeatedly paired

Direct experiences with an object can shape people's attitudes toward it.

with an unconditioned stimulus (for example, pain). Soon, a conditioned response develops (for example, a fear of and dislike for dentists). A number of studies have demonstrated that people's liking or disliking for an attitude object can be classically conditioned. Staats, Staats, and Crawford (1962) presented subjects with a series of neutral words. Some of the words were accompanied by painful electric shock; others were not. After several presentations of the words, the subjects' affective reactions to the words were measured. As predicted, subjects liked the words associated with shock significantly less than they liked the other words. A few years later, Zanna, Kiesler, and Pilkonis (1970) paired the word *dark* with shock and the word *light* with termination of the shock. The subjects' affective reactions to light were much more positive than were their affective reactions to dark.

Fishbein and Ajzen (1975) have proposed that direct experiences can affect attitudes toward an object in another way—by providing people with information about the attributes of the attitude object. According to the expectancy-value model of attitude structure, this information leads to beliefs that will influence how much people like or dislike the attitude object. Direct experiences that are especially negative or traumatic make certain beliefs about the object more salient than others. For example, my experiences with my first dentist made the belief "Dentists hurt their patients" especially salient for me and this influenced my attitude toward dentists.

Direct experiences do not always produce negative attitudes toward an object. (See Zajonc's work on the effect of mere exposure in chapter six.) Zajonc found that merely exposing a person to another person increased liking. The same effect has been obtained for mere exposure to inanimate attitude objects. For example, Zajonc (1968) systematically varied how many times subjects were exposed to a set of meaningless words. Even though these words were not associated with positive reinforcers, the more times subjects were exposed to the words, the more they liked them. However, Perlman and Oskamp (1971) found that the effect holds only for positive or neutral stimuli; repeated exposure to negative stimuli will not produce increased liking. In fact, it may produce the opposite effect.

Self-perception Theory Daryl Bem's (1972) **self-perception theory** proposes that people may acquire "knowledge" about what kind of person they are by looking at their own behavior and asking, "Why did I do that?" (See chapter five.) Bem believed that many attitudes are acquired in this fashion. A person engages in a behavior toward an object for no particular reason. After the behavior has occurred, the person makes an attribution about its causes which leads the person to believe that he has a certain attitude toward that object. For example, if you asked Bem if he likes brown bread, he would answer, "I suppose so; I'm always eating it." This is Bem's favorite illustration of how an attitude is an after-the-fact explanation of behavior.

Research Highlight

Democracy for Sale

Many people have become concerned about the continuing trend of high campaign spending in American politics. Candidates for president are prohibited by law from spending more than a certain amount in their election campaigns, but no such restrictions apply to candidates for other offices. The amounts spent in some election campaigns boggle the mind. In 1984, over $1.8 billion was spent on political campaigns. In *one* contest for a seat in the United States Senate, the candidates spent over $20 million. Most of this money was used to conduct advertising campaigns on television and radio. These figures lead some to question whether an election can be bought.

The research on frequency of exposure and attitude formation suggests that money used to publicize a candidate may affect the outcome of an election. Grush (1980) tested the proposal that the better known a candidate is, the more likely he is to win an election. Grush examined the results of presidential primary elections in twenty-four states. Grush believed that three things would effect how well known a candidate was and, thus, the candidate's chances of winning: the amount of money the candidate spent, the distance from the candidate's home state to the state where the primary election was being held, and the candidate's performance in prior primaries (the better the performance, the more publicity received). He found that the best predictor of how a candidate would do in a primary was how much money the candidate had spent on the election. When Grush used information on all three variables to predict the outcome of elections, he found that he could predict the winner in nineteen out of the twenty-four contests.

As Grush pointed out, these results have both theoretical and practical implications. They indicate that frequent exposure to positive or neutral stimuli increases liking for those stimuli, and they raise some questions about the election process in America. Do we desire a political system where people's chances of being elected depend more on their wealth than on their abilities?

Bem's theory suggests that people act and form attitudes without thinking. Some attitudes may be formed in this fashion, but most are probably developed through learning processes like classical conditioning, and people usually know at some level why they act a certain way or hold a particular attitude.

Interactions with Others

It almost goes without saying that direct experiences are not the only source of attitudes. An equally important, if not more important, source of attitudes is the actions of other people. In the early years of people's lives, the most influential "other people" are their parents.

Parents   Parents, either knowingly or unknowingly, use the processes of classical conditioning, instrumental conditioning, and observational learning to shape their children's attitudes.

In the examples of classical conditioning presented earlier, the unconditioned stimulus was a physical event such as electric shock. Concepts or words can also be used to condition a person's attitudes through a process known as *higher-order conditioning*, which involves two stages. In the first stage, people learn to associate certain meanings with certain words. For example, a parent who says the word *bad* before slapping a child's hand is teaching the child the meaning of that word. In the second stage, the word *bad* becomes an unconditioned stimulus for other words. A story told by the comedian Gabriel Kaplan illustrates this process:

Kaplan's parents were worried about blacks moving into their building in Brooklyn. At dinner, they constantly talked about the *schwartzes*—a negative Yiddish term for black people—moving in and how bad this would be. As a child, Kaplan shared their concern. There was one small problem, however: He had no idea what a schwartze was. He did know that whatever it was, it was bad, since his parents always paired it with words that had negative connotations. One day, while playing in the yard, Kaplan saw a black child whose family had just moved in. Kaplan approached him and told him that his (the black child's) parents had picked a bad place to live. "Why?" asked the black child. "Because," Kaplan replied, "schwartzes are moving in." (Also see chapter one.)

The theory of observational learning suggests another way in which parents shape their children's attitudes: Parents provide models for their children to imitate. An example can also be used to illustrate this process.

On December 28, 1979, two American businessmen working in Iran were arrested. Although they were not charged with any crime, their bail was set at $12 million. Ross Perot was the president of the company that employed the men. When he realized that the men would not be released even if the bail were paid, he decided to rescue them from the Iranian prison. His advisors told him that if the plan failed, Perot's multimillion dollar company would be destroyed, and the United States government refused to help him. But Perot persisted. In the course of the rescue effort, Perot spent close to a million dollars and placed his own well-being at risk several times. But in February 1980, the two men were rescued and escaped from Iran.

What drove Perot to risk all he had built for two employees? Ken Follett (1984), the author of a book on the rescue operation, attributed Perot's behavior to his attitude about the responsibility of an employer to those who work for him. Follett described the possible origins of this attitude:

Another of [Perot's] father's principles had been: take care of the people who work for you. Perot could remember the whole family driving 12 miles on Sundays to visit an old black man who had used to mow their lawn, just to make sure that he was well and had enough to eat. Perot's father would employ people he did not need, just because they had no jobs. Every year the Perot family car would go to the County Fair crammed with black employees, each of whom was given a little money to spend and a Perot business card to show if anyone tried to give him a hard time. Perot could remember one who had ridden a freight train to California and, on being arrested for vagrancy, had shown Perot's father's business card. The sheriff had said: "We don't care whose nigger you are, we're throwing you in jail." But he had called Perot Senior, who had wired the train fare for the man to come back. "I been to California, and I'se back," the man said when he reached Texarkana; and Perot Senior gave him back his job.

Perot's father did not know what civil rights were; this was how you treated other human beings. Perot had not known his parents were unusual until he grew up.

His father would not leave his employees in jail. Nor would Perot. (1984, p. 188)

Perot's mother also shared this attitude. At the time of the men's arrest, she was dying of cancer. She insisted Perot leave her bedside and rescue the men. She told Perot: "You don't have a choice . . . You are responsible for them."

These examples illustrate some of the mechanisms by which parents *could* influence their children's attitudes. In fact, the correspondence between parents' and children's specific attitudes toward a particular issue or group is positive but weak (Connell, 1972). For attitudes toward broad issues, however, the relation is very strong. Jennings and Niemi (1968) interviewed over 1,600 high school seniors and their parents. The correlation between parents' preferences for a political party and their children's preferences was .60. The correlation between the parents' preferences for a particular religious denomination and their children's preferences was .88.

School and Peers   When children enter school, other people begin to exert an influence on their attitudes. Schools do more than teach children to read and write; they intentionally and unintentionally teach children certain attitudes. For example, teachers leading their students in the Pledge of Allegiance are influencing the students' attitudes toward their government (Oskamp, 1977).

In the later school years, children's peers may supplant their teachers and even their parents as shapers of their attitudes. Peers serve as a **reference group.** A study done over forty years ago illustrates the influence of reference groups on people's attitudes. Theodore Newcomb (1943) measured changes in political attitudes among female college students from their first term until graduation. When they began school, most of the women held the same conservative attitudes as did their parents. Over the next four years, their attitudes became more like those of their peers— more liberal—and these new attitudes persisted for many years (Newcomb, Koenig, Flacks, and Warwick, 1967).

Reference group: a group people identify with, compare their attitudes to, and use as a means to evaluate those attitudes.

Television and Other Media   If this book had been written 35 or 40 years ago, the media's role in attitude formation would not have been mentioned because people were not exposed to much media communication other than the news on the radio, which was primarily taken from newspapers (Kendrick, 1969). Few families had a television. Today, the average American household has a television turned on for nearly seven hours a day (Oskamp, 1984).

The impact of television on adults' attitudes is not as great as people have proposed (Oskamp, 1984), but there is little question that television plays an important role in attitude formation among children. There are two major reasons for this: First, mass communication is most influential when attitudes are not strongly held, as is usually the case with a young child (Goldberg and Gorn, 1974). Second, before the age of seven, children get most of their political information from television (Chaffee, Jackson-Beeck, Durall, and Wilson, 1977). This information was found to influence children's attitudes toward political institutions and politicians (Atkin, 1977; Rubin, 1978).

One also cannot ignore the impact of commercials on children's attitudes. Children who are heavy television watchers were found to be twice as likely as light television watchers to believe that sugar-coated candies and cereals are nutritious (Atkin, 1980). In the same study, it was also found that two-thirds of a group of children who saw a circus strong man eat a certain cereal believed it would make them strong.

The preceding discussion should not lead you to conclude that all important attitudes are formed before adulthood and remain fixed thereafter. New attitudes can be formed throughout people's lifetimes, but it is probably safe to say that a large percentage of people's attitudes are formed before adulthood. The emergence of new attitudes and the changing of old ones is probably greatly influenced by the attitudes formed when a person was young.

Functions of Attitudes

It is generally agreed that attitudes do more than simply predispose people to act favorably or unfavorably toward objects in their environment. Smith, Bruner, and White (1956) and Katz (1960) proposed that attitudes serve four other functions. They lead to understanding and knowledge, meet certain needs, protect people's egos, and help people express values.

Understanding and Knowledge
People use schemata to help them organize and understand complex information that they receive. (See chapter four.) Katz (1960) argued that attitudes provide a sort of schema that people use when they receive information from the world around them. Attitudes can provide a clarity and consistency in people's explanations and interpretations of events (Oskamp 1977). For example, you may have known nothing about the reasons Iran and Iraq waged war against one another in the early 1980s. However, your attitudes toward objects such as Arabs, the Ayatollah Khomeni, and the price of oil may have given you a framework in which to interpret news about the war. Laboratory studies of this function of attitudes have focused on how they affect people's perceptions of the world and how people process information they receive.

Judd and Johnson (1981) studied two groups of women—one was comprised of feminist women and the other was comprised of nonfeminist women. Both groups were asked to estimate the attitudes of adult Americans toward the feminist movement. The feminist women's estimate was considerably greater than the estimate of the nonfeminist women. The feminists were also more likely than the nonfeminists to believe that people's attitudes toward women's rights provided information about their basic personality structures.

People's attitudes toward a political figure can also influence their perceptions of where that politician stands on certain issues. Judd, Kenny, and Krosnick (1983) found that voters who favored the Republican candidate in a presidential election saw the candidate's position on the issues as closer to their own than it actually was, and saw the position of the unfavored Democratic candidate as further from their own than it actually was. Voters who favored the Democratic candidate showed the same pattern of **assimilation** and **contrast**.

People's attitudes affect the manner in which they process information they receive. Information that is relevant to people's attitudes is processed more quickly and remembered better than information that is irrelevant to people's attitudes (Judd and Kulik, 1980). A study by Ross, McFarland, and Fletcher (1981) suggests that attitudes may also affect how people remember their own behavior. Ross and his associates manipulated subject's attitudes toward brushing their teeth after every meal. Some of the subjects received a persuasive message that was positive toward this activity; other subjects received a message that was negative toward this activity. The procedure reliably produced more positive attitudes toward tooth brushing in the former group than in the latter group.

Immediately after the subjects heard the two messages, they were asked to take part in another study. The second study was supposedly a survey of college students' health care practices. Embedded among the survey questions was one that asked how often the person had brushed his teeth in the last two weeks. This question concerned the subjects' behaviors *before* they had received the persuasive messages; its purpose was to determine if the subjects' changed attitudes affected their recall of their own behaviors. If attitudes serve as schema, the group whose attitudes toward tooth brushing were positive should have estimated the frequency of this behavior to be greater than the group whose attitudes were negative. And they did. Subjects in the positive-message condition gave an estimate about 25 percent higher than the estimate given by subjects in the negative-message condition. A later study by Ross, McFarland, Conway, and Zanna (1983) showed the same effects for people's recall of how much they exercised.

Meeting Needs

Katz (1960) and Smith and his associates (1956) proposed that another reason people may hold a specific attitude toward some object is that they believe the object will benefit them in some way. For example, workers may hold positive attitudes toward labor unions because they believe the

Assimilation: seeing someone's position on some issue as closer to one's own than it actually is.

Contrast: seeing someone's position on some issue as further from one's own than it really is.

unions will provide them with better working conditions. The owners of the company they work for may hold negative attitudes toward labor unions because they believe unions will reduce worker productivity and profits.

Research Highlight

Hearing What You Want to Hear

There is an old joke about a farmer who, before he gave a command to a very stubborn and uncooperative mule, would bash the mule over the head with a two-by-four. When asked why, the farmer replied, ''Well, if you want him to listen to you, first you gotta get his attention.'' Sometimes it seems to be just as difficult to get another person to listen.

We do not know why the mule would not listen to the farmer, but we do understand some reasons humans fail to listen to others. People often engage in selective exposure; they seek out information that is consistent with their attitudes and avoid information that is inconsistent. A recent study of voters in the 1972 presidential election by Sweeney and Gruber (1984) illustrates how selective exposure operates. In 1972, Richard Nixon was reelected by one of the largest majorities in American history. His Democratic opponent, George McGovern, tried to raise the issue of Watergate during the election. However, it was several months after the election before the public became interested in the scandal and the Senate began to investigate it.

The subjects in Sweeney and Gruber's study were people who were first interviewed after the 1972 presidential election but before the Senate hearings on Watergate had begun. During the first interview, the subjects were asked how they had voted in the election. On the basis of their responses, they were classified as McGovern supporters, Nixon supporters, or neutrals (those who had either not voted or could not recall for whom they had voted). During the course of the Senate hearings, the three groups were reinterviewed. Sweeney and Gruber investigated how the Nixon supporters, McGovern supporters, and neutrals dealt with information about Watergate.

As the nationally televised hearings progressed, it became clear that Mr. Nixon and his staff were deeply involved in an attempt to cover up their misdeeds. This disclosure had different effects on the members of the three groups. The neutrals' interests in politics and Watergate stayed about the same, but Nixon supporters reported less interest and McGovern supporters reported more interest. Nixon supporters became less likely to discuss the scandal than McGovern supporters. One consequence of these differences in interest was differences in knowledge. At the first interview, the three groups did not differ in their abilities to name the people involved in the scandal. By the final interview, McGovern supporters were significantly better at this than were either the neutrals or the Nixon supporters. At the final interview, Nixon supporters also knew less about the hearings than did either the neutrals or the McGovern supporters. McGovern supporters acquired information because it was consistent with their attitudes; Nixon supporters avoided information because it was inconsistent with their attitudes.

As a result of selective exposure, the Senate hearings had relatively little impact on the views of Mr. Nixon's supporters. The hearings made them no less likely to vote for a Republican and no more likely to believe that Mr. Nixon should resign. Perhaps what Paul Simon and Art Garfunkel said in the song "The Boxer" is true: "A man hears what he wants to hear, and disregards the rest."

Protecting One's Ego

This aspect of attitude functions is based on the premise that one's personality structure significantly influences the development and maintenance of one's attitudes. It has been proposed that certain attitudes will enable people to enhance their self-images and to protect themselves from "assaults" on their egos. For example, very poor and insecure white people may hold very negative attitudes toward blacks because these attitudes make them feel superior to at least somebody. The use of attitudes as defense mechanisms was the core of Adorno, Frenkel-Brunswik, Levinson, and Sanford's (1950) theory of racial and ethnic prejudice. They believed that many people are prejudiced because of deficiencies in their own personality needs.

Expressing Values

The final proposed function of attitudes is to provide people with a means of expressing their values. This view of attitudes is an integral part of Milton Rokeach's theory of values (Rokeach, 1968, 1973, 1979). Rokeach argued that a person's psychological being can be conceptualized as a series of concentric circles. At the center of this structure is the self-concept—who and what the person believes he is. The next circle comprises a person's values; their primary function is to "help maintain and enhance one's total conception of oneself" (1973, 216). A value is a belief about what goals one should strive for and how one should behave. Rokeach conceptualized values as being organized into two separate, but related systems. The first he called **terminal values.** The second he called **instrumental values.** (See table 9-5 for lists of the values Rokeach believed made up each system.)

Terminal values: beliefs about final goals or end states of existence.

Instrumental values: beliefs about modes of conduct.

Note two things about these lists. First, they each contain only eighteen values. Rokeach acknowledged that there may be more terminal values and more instrumental values than he identified, but not many more. He thought that humans may have hundreds, if not thousands, of attitudes, but very few values. Second, the values in the lists are general; they are

Table 9-5. *Rokeach's list of Terminal and Instrumental Values. Subjects rank order each list in order of importance to themselves. Reprinted by permission of the author.*

Terminal values	Instrumental values
A Comfortable Life	Ambitious
An Exciting Life	Broadminded
A Sense of Accomplishment	Capable
A World at Peace	Cheerful
A World of Beauty	Clean
Equality	Courageous
Family Security	Forgiving
Freedom	Helpful
Happiness	Honest
Inner Harmony	Imaginative
Mature Love	Independent
National Security	Intellectual
Pleasure	Logical
Salvation	Loving
Self-Respect	Obedient
Social Recognition	Polite
True Friendship	Responsible
Wisdom	Self-Controlled

Source: Rokeach (1967)

According to some theorists, attitudes provide people with a means of expressing their values.

not concerned with specific objects or situations. Rokeach speculated that responses to specific objects are determined by people's attitudes, which are in turn determined by the importance people assign to certain values.

Rokeach and his colleagues have shown that specific attitudes are related to the importance people assign to certain values. For example, Rokeach (1973) found that the importance assigned to the value of equality was correlated with such specific attitudes as reactions to the assassination of Dr. Martin Luther King, Jr., intermarriage between blacks and whites, the student protest movement, and communism. (In all instances, the more important people considered equality, the more positive were their attitudes toward these objects.) These findings alone do not show that attitudes are in the service of values. To show this, Rokeach would need to change a person's values and then determine if the person's attitudes also changed. Such studies have been done and are discussed in chapter ten.

SUMMARY

Attitude formation is the process wherein a person goes from having no attitude toward an object to having some attitude toward it. Direct experience can shape attitudes. If, for example, an attitude object is repeatedly associated with some unconditioned stimulus, classical conditioning will cause a person to develop feelings toward that attitude object.

Many attitudes are learned from others. People's parents play a vital role in the formation of attitudes. Parents can shape their children's attitudes toward objects their offspring have never seen, and parents provide models from which their children learn attitudes toward objects in their environment.

As children mature, they learn many attitudes from school experiences and their peers. Peers provide a reference group, with which people identify, to which they compare their attitudes, and through which they evaluate the quality of their attitudes. Finally, mass media, especially television, play a part in attitude formation among children.

It appears that attitudes serve four major functions. First, they help people understand and organize the information they receive from the world around them. Second, they help people meet their needs. Third, they can help people protect and defend their egos. And fourth, they are an expression of the values people consider important.

ATTITUDES AND BEHAVIOR

The study which began this chapter illustrates the problem considered in this section: Attitudes and behavior should be strongly related, but often they are not. La Piere's study contained several weaknesses—the measure of attitudes toward Chinese was of questionable validity and reliability, and there was no way of knowing whether the person who served the Chinese couple was the same person who answered the question about serving Chinese. Other, less flawed studies have typically found a weak relationship between attitudes and behavior. In a 1969 article, Wicker reviewed the findings of over 30 studies of the relationship between attitudes and behavior. Based on the data from these studies, Wicker concluded that "it is considerably more likely that attitudes will be unrelated or only slightly related to [actual] behaviors than that attitudes will be closely related to actions" (1969, p. 65).

One might say that attitude researchers have a bit of a problem. All of the material presented thus far has been explicitly or implicitly based on the assumption that attitudes cause behavior. If they do not, then there is little point in learning about them. While most attitude theorists acknowledge that the empirical evidence is not encouraging, they reject the notion that attitudes are unrelated to social behavior. This section presents the explanations that have been offered for the weak relationship between attitudes and behavior and discusses ways in which the relationship can be strengthened.

Theoretical Explanations

Theoretical explanations differ considerably in the approaches they take to the problem, but they all share one characteristic: They propose that the failure of attitudes to correlate strongly with behavior is primarily due to inadequate conceptualizations of the nature of attitudes or the relationship between attitudes and behavior. One such theory is the **theory of reasoned action.**

This theory was first presented by Martin Fishbein in 1967 and more fully described and developed by him and Icek Ajzen (Fishbein and Ajzen, 1975; Ajzen and Fishbein, 1980). It has its origins in Fishbein's expectancy-value model of an attitude's structure, which did not have a behavioral component. The model assumed that feelings about how they would behave toward an attitude object are separate from how much they like or dislike the attitude object. In the theory of reasoned action, it is further argued that attitudes toward an object are not directly related to behavior toward that object.

Behavioral intentions: a subjective estimate of the probability that one will act in a certain way in response to an attitude object.

The theory proposes that the direct cause of people's behavior is **behavioral intentions** (Ajzen and Fishbein 1980). As the name of the theory suggests, the intention to behave in a certain way (for instance, to serve Chinese guests) is the result of a careful and thoughtful consideration of the implications and consequences of this action—the action is reasoned.

Fishbein and Ajzen set forth a conceptual model of the factors that influence a person's behavioral intentions. (See figure 9-2.) Two things have a direct impact on behavioral intentions. The first is the **attitude toward the behavior.** This is an attitude just like any other attitude; it is the result of beliefs about the characteristics of some object and the evaluations of those characteristics—but in this instance, the object is a behavior, not a person or thing.

Attitude toward the behavior: how favorable or unfavorable a person feels toward some behavior.

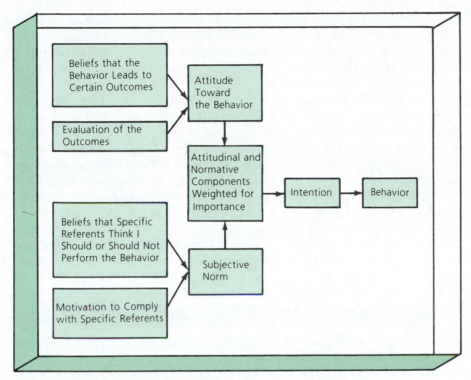

Figure 9-2. *Fishbein and Ajzen's model of the factors that determine a person's behavior toward an attitude object.*
Source: Fishbein and Ajzen (1975).

To understand the model, apply it to the task of predicting attendance at religious services. The first step in predicting whether or not people will attend religious services is to determine how favorable or unfavorable they feel toward this activity. To do this, you could present your subjects with the following question:

My attitude toward attending religious services is:
favorable $\frac{\quad}{1}$ $\frac{\quad}{2}$ $\frac{\quad}{3}$ $\frac{\quad}{4}$ $\frac{\quad}{5}$ $\frac{\quad}{6}$ $\frac{\quad}{7}$ unfavorable
(Place a check above the number which comes closest to your attitude.)

The second factor that determines people's behavioral intentions is the **subjective norm** (Ajzen and Fishbein 1980). A person's subjective norm toward attending church could be assessed by the following item:

Most people who are important to me think:
I should $\frac{\quad}{1}$ $\frac{\quad}{2}$ $\frac{\quad}{3}$ $\frac{\quad}{4}$ $\frac{\quad}{5}$ $\frac{\quad}{6}$ $\frac{\quad}{7}$ I should not
attend religious services.
(Place a check above the number which comes closest to your estimate.)

According to the theory of reasoned action, the behavioral intention, which is directly related to behavior, is determined by the relative impor-

Subjective norm: the perception of the social pressures to perform or not perform a certain behavior.

tance a person places on his attitude toward the behavior and on the subjective norm. So even a person with a negative attitude toward attending religious services may go to church if (a) the subjective norm supports such an action and (b) this norm is given more importance than the attitude toward the behavior.

The theory of reasoned action is a theoretical model. Like other theoretical models, it can be used to generate predictions about observable entities. One prediction generated by the model is that attitudes toward the object, attitudes toward the behavior, and subjective norms do not directly influence behavior, but they do exert an indirect influence through their effect on behavioral intentions. This prediction has been supported in studies of behaviors ranging from family planning practices to toothpaste purchases (Fishbein and Ajzen, 1975; Ajzen and Fishbein 1980; Fredricks and Dorsett, 1983).

Another, more important prediction is that behavioral intentions predict behavior more accurately than do attitudes toward an object. Davidson and Jaccard (1979) studied this issue. Their subjects were 244 women of childbearing age. The women answered two questions concerning birth control pills and later indicated whether they had used oral contraceptives as a means of birth control. The first question assessed their attitudes toward birth control pills. Their answers correlated .32 with their actual behavior. This correlation is typical of the correlations that have been found in attitude research and that led to questions about the relationship between attitudes and behavior. The second question concerned behavioral intentions; the subjects answers correlated .57 with actual behavior.

Other studies of the relationship between behavioral intentions and actual behavior have obtained even stronger correlations. Fishbein, Ajzen, and Hinkel (1980) found that voting intentions correlated .80 with how people actually voted in the 1976 presidential election, and Fishbein, Bowman, Thomas, Jaccard, and Ajzen (1980) found a correlation of .89 between voting intentions and how people voted in a referendum on nuclear power.

The theory of reasoned action proposes that if we want to predict people's behavior, we must assess more than just their feelings toward an attitude object. When we obtain information on a person's attitudes toward the behavior, the person's perceptions of the subjective norm, and the person's behavioral intention, our ability to predict that person's behavior increases greatly.

Other-Variables Explanation

The other-variables explanation can, in some ways, be viewed as providing a reason behavioral intentions predict behavior so much better than do attitudes. Basically, it argues that an attitude is only one determinant of people's behavior and that a researcher must consider how other variables affect people's behavior.

Situational factors may cause people to act in a manner inconsistent with their true attitudes (Calder and Ross, 1973). For example, a motorist who feels that the fifty-five mile-per-hour speed limit is stupid and un-

Situational factors may produce an inconsistency between people's attitudes and behavior. It is unlikely this man will express his true feelings to the police officer approaching his car.

necessary would probably not express this attitude to a police officer who has just pulled him over for speeding.

Campbell (1963) argued that the disparity between attitudes and behavior is often due to differences in situational characteristics. La Piere's study illustrates Campbell's point. La Piere measured attitudes toward Chinese by having the subjects (the managers of hotels and restaurants the couple had visited) respond to a question, but he measured behavior by recording how the subjects treated a Chinese couple who entered their places of business. It was much easier for the subjects to express anti-Chinese sentiments in response to the question than in the presence of a Chinese couple. Campbell would argue that the inconsistency La Piere reported was a **pseudo-inconsistency.** A true inconsistency between attitudes and behavior would have existed if the subjects had performed a hard action (refused to serve the Chinese couple) but not an easy action (expressed negative attitudes toward Chinese). A study by Warner and DeFleur (1969) supported Campbell's position. Warner and DeFleur found that when there were situational pressures on antiblack subjects not to act in a prejudiced manner, the correspondence between attitudes and behavior was low. When these pressures were removed, the correspondence was much greater.

Rokeach and Kliejunas (1972) approached the influence of the situation on the relationship between attitudes and behavior from a somewhat different perspective. They pointed out that people do not encounter attitude

Pseudo-inconsistency: an apparent, but not actual, inconsistency between attitudes and behavior.

objects in a vacuum, but in the context of a situation. If we want to predict people's behavior toward an object within a situation, we must assess both their attitudes toward the situation and the relative importance they place on each kind of attitude.

To test this proposal, Rokeach and Kliejunas (1972) attempted to predict class attendance among college students. They obtained the students' attitude toward the object (how much they liked the class instructor), attitude toward the situation (how much they liked attending classes in general), and estimates of the relative importance of these two attitudes. The attitude toward the object did not predict class attendance very well. The attitude toward the situation predicted attendance slightly better. The best prediction was obtained when both attitudes were combined and weighted for their relative importance to the person.

Finally, it has been proposed that other variables, such as people's habits and their degree of control over the behavior of interest, must be considered (Petty and Cacioppo, 1981; Triandis, 1980). Habits are behaviors that are automatic in certain situations and occur with little if any thought. Smoking, for example, is for many people an unthinking habitual response, due at least in part to a physiological addiction. Thus, their behavior—smoking—may bear little relation to their attitudes about cigarettes. An illustration of this is the fact that 72 percent of smokers interviewed in a national survey agreed that smoking was one of the causes of lung cancer, and 71 percent agreed that "cigarette smoking causes disease and death" (Oskamp, 1984).

Moderator-Variable Explanation

Moderator variables are variables that affect the relationship between two other variables. (See chapter three.) It has been proposed that certain variables may moderate the relationship between attitudes and behavior. One of these is the personality trait, **self-monitoring.** (See chapter three.) People high on this trait will essentially modify their behavior to fit the situations they encounter; people low on this trait will not (Snyder, 1979). It has been found that attitudes predict behavior much better among low self-monitors than among high self-monitors (Snyder and Monson, 1975; Snyder and Tanke, 1976; Zanna, Olson, and Fazio, 1980).

Personality characteristics are only one of the variables that have been found to moderate attitude behavior consistency. Fazio and Zanna (1981) focused on direct experience, with the attitude object as a moderator of this relationship. They hypothesized that attitudes based on direct experience with the attitude object are more predictive of actual behavior than are attitudes not based on direct experience. Several studies support this hypothesis. Regan and Fazio (1977) investigated students' willingness to work to solve a campus housing shortage. Half the students had learned about the shortage from the campus newspaper or conversations with friends. The other half were victims of the housing shortage themselves, and most were sleeping on cots in a dormitory lounge. Regan and Fazio assessed both groups' attitudes and behaviors toward the issue of a housing shortage. They found a much greater correlation between attitudes and behavior among students who had direct experience with the housing shortage than among students who had heard about it but not experienced it. Sherman and his associates (Sherman, Presson, Chassin, Bensenberg, Corty, and Olshavsky, 1982) found that attitudes were more predictive of the intention to smoke among teenagers who had direct experience with smoking than among teenagers who had no direct experience with smoking. Sherman and his colleagues proposed that direct experience with an object makes attitudes about it more vivid and salient for people. As a result, these attitudes have a greater impact on behavior than do attitudes based on information from others.

Methodological Explanations

The basic premise underlying methodological explanations of the low correlation is that the failure to find a strong relation between attitudes and behavior is largely due to problems in the way attitudes and behavior have been measured.

Attitude Measurement

Attitude researchers often measure the attitudes of interest in a very general way and then attempt to predict a very specific behavior. For example, according to La Piere, the Chinese couple with whom he traveled was "personable, charming, and quick to win the admiration and respect of those they had the opportunity to become intimate with." But La Piere attempted to predict behavior toward them by asking about "members of the Chinese race," that is, Chinese in general. It has been argued that it is an error to attempt to predict a specific behavior from a measure of general attitudes (Fishbein and Ajzen, 1975; Petty and Cacioppo, 1981). If one wants to predict specific behaviors, one must assess specific attitudes.

Ajzen and Fishbein (1977) noted that a behavior comprises four elements: the behavior itself, the target toward which the behavior is directed, the context in which the behavior takes place, and the time frame in which the behavior occurs. Failure to include these elements in the measurement of attitudes will produce low correspondence between attitudes and behavior because the attitude measurement is not specific enough. Again, La Piere's study illustrates the point. His attitudinal measure concerned general policies toward "members of the Chinese race"; his behavioral measure was whether a particular Chinese couple (the target) was or was not served (the behavior) at a given establishment (the situation) at a given point in time. Failure to include these elements in the question may have lowered the correlation between attitudes and behavior. A number of studies have shown that as the measurement of attitudes becomes more specific, the correlation between attitudes and behavior increases (for example, Davidson and Jaccard, 1979; Fishbein, 1966; Weigel, Vernon, and Tognaci, 1974).

Behavior Measurement

Fishbein and Ajzen (1975) proposed that general attitudes will not predict single, specific behaviors very well, but that they will predict general patterns of behavior. For example, it is unlikely that your general attitudes toward the United States government's policies in Central America would provide a good prediction of how you would respond to a request to sign a petition in opposition to United States troops in El Salvador. Your general attitudes would, however, predict a general pattern of behavior in response to this attitude object, such as the books you read or the candidates you support.

Unfortunately, many studies use only a single act as their measure of behavior. This, Fishbein and Ajzen argued, is too specific a measure. They recommend using two strategies to assess general patterns of behavior. The first is to make repeated observations of the same specific behavior in response to different yet related targets, or in different situations, or at different times. Return to La Piere's study. If the behavior of interest were being hospitable to Chinese and other people of Asian ancestry, La Piere could have measured the subjects' behavior in response to other people from the same ethnic group, or in situations other than the subjects' places of business.

Multiple-act criterion: a measurement of behavior obtained by observing different, yet related, behaviors.

Second, Fishbein and Ajzen recommended using a **multiple-act criterion.** A study by Rokeach (1964) provides an illustration of this procedure. As part of his work on the origins and modifications of beliefs, Rokeach brought together three schizophrenic patients in a mental hospital, all of whom believed they were Jesus Christ. He was interested in whether a confrontation would produce changes in these men's delusional belief systems.

After several weeks of meeting with the other two ''Christs,'' one of the men announced that he was no longer Jesus Christ of Nazareth; he was now Dr. R. J. Dung, and had taken a new wife, Madame Yeti Woman. Rokeach decided to determine if the man really believed that he was married to this woman.

''Dr. Dung'' began to receive letters (written by Rokeach's assistants) from his wife. In the first few letters, it was suggested that he go to places in the mental hospital he had never visited before, such as the hospital store and library. The man did this. Later his ''wife'' sent him some money. Although previously the man had refused all money, he accepted his wife's gift. Subsequent letters also contained money, with instructions on how to spend it; the man followed the instructions. And finally, in the past the man had opened the meetings between himself and the other ''Christs'' by singing ''America.'' Following one of his ''wife's'' suggestions, he changed the song to ''Onward Christian Soldiers'' and continued to open meetings with this song long after the suggestion had been made. By using the multiple-act criterion, Rokeach was able to determine that the man really believed what he was saying.

Findings from other studies also suggest that when general patterns of behavior rather than a single, specific behavior are measured, the correlation between attitudes and behavior increases markedly. Weigel and Newman (1976) assessed subjects' general attitudes about the environment. After the assessment, the subjects were given the chance to sign several different petitions concerned with the environment, to participate in a campaign to pick up litter, and to take part in an eight-week recycling program. The correlation between the subjects' general attitudes and the specific behaviors rarely, if ever, surpassed .30. But when these specific behaviors were combined into an overall measure of behavior, the correlation rose to .62. General attitudes predicted a pattern of behavior quite well.

The solutions to the problem of low correlations between attitudes and behavior are not easily implemented. Attitudes are not the only causes of a person's behavior, but they are more strongly related than the typical .30 correlation indicates. Thus, it is reasonable for someone interested in the causes of social behavior to study attitudes.

SUMMARY

Social psychologists study attitudes primarily because they assume that attitudes cause social behavior toward an attitude object, but research studies find only a weak to moderate relationship between attitudes and behavior. One explanation of this finding is based on the premise that the weak relationship is often the result of inadequate conceptualizations of the nature of an attitude or of the relationship between the attitudes and the behavior. The theory of reasoned action proposes that behavior toward an object is not directly determined by people's likes or dislikes for an attitude object, but by people's intentions to behave in a certain way. Attitudes and social pressures determine these intentions. It has also been proposed that an attitude is only one determinant of people's behavior and that other factors must be considered when attempting to predict behavior. Among these are situational pressures which may inhibit attitude-consistent behavior, strongly ingrained habits which may override people's attitudes, and people's attitudes toward the situation in which they encounter the object.

Other researchers have focused on the personality and situational variables that might moderate the relationship between attitudes and behavior. One moderator variable is the amount of direct experience people have had with an attitude object. People who have had direct experience with the object will show much greater attitude-behavior correspondence than will people who have not had direct experience with the object.

Another set of explanations is based on weaknesses in the methods used to measure people's attitudes or behavior. Often, very general attitudes are measured and used to predict very specific behaviors. This difference in level of specificity may be partly responsible for the low correlation. Some researchers have argued that if one is interested in general attitudes, one must measure general patterns of behavior by measuring the same behavior in a number of different contexts or by measuring different related behaviors in the same context.

Applications

Prejudice: The Problem and a Remedy

This section concerns a social problem that directly or indirectly affects all of us—prejudice. It first defines prejudice and examines its causes. It then discusses a concerted attempt to reduce prejudice and discrimination in the United States.

THE PROBLEM

It is the Fourth of July. A crowd has assembled to hear a black activist speak on racism in America.

> What to the American slave is your Fourth of July? I answer, a day that reveals to him more than all other days of the year, the gross injustice and cruelty to which he is the constant victim. To him your celebration is a sham; your boasted liberty an unholy license; your national greatness, swelling vanity; your sounds of rejoicing are empty and heartless; your denunciation of tyrants, brass-fronted impudence; your shouts of liberty and equality, hollow mockery; your prayers and hymns, your sermons and thanksgivings, with all your religious parade and solemnity, are to him mere bombast, fraud, deception, impiety, and hypocrisy—a thin veil to cover up crimes which would disgrace a nation of savages. There is not a nation of the earth guilty of practices more shocking and bloody than are the people of these United States at this very hour.
>
> Go where you may, search where you will, roam through all the monarchies and despotisms of the Old World, travel through South America, search out every abuse and when you have found the last, lay your facts by the side of the everyday practices of this nation, and you will say with me that, for revolting barbarity and shameless hypocrisy, America reigns without a rival.

Four years earlier, a group of feminists had held a convention on women's rights. In their closing statement, they had described how American males treat females.

> He has monopolized nearly all the profitable employments and from those she is permitted to follow, she received by scanty remuneration. He closes . . . all avenues to wealth and distinction which he considers most honorable to himself. As a teacher of theology, medicine, and law, she is not known. He has endeavored in every way possible to

Susan B. Anthony, one of the founders of the women's rights movement in America. Some of the issues which confronted Ms. Anthony 130 years ago still confront women today.

destroy her confidence in her own powers, to lessen her self-respect and to make her willing to lead an abject and dependent life.

Do these two quotations sound a little strange? Is the wording a little stilted? Both were written more than 125 years ago. The condemnation of racism was made by Frederick Douglas in 1852; the declaration on sexism was issued by the Seneca Falls Convention in 1848. Despite their ages, these quotations describe a phenomenon that still exists—prejudice in the United States.

The problem of prejudice is not confined to the United States. People of different religions wage campaigns of terror against one another in India, Lebanon, and Northern Ireland. People who are the targets of prejudice in one country may be the purveyors of hatred and bigotry in another. For example until quite recently the Argentinian government often persecuted and tortured Jewish Argentinian citizens because Jews were considered "a threat to the country" (Timmerman, 1980). In Israel, some Jews preach racial hatred against Arabs. In Sudan, the Arab majority oppresses the black minority, and on, and on. One characteristic which, unfortunately, all humans seem to have in common is the ability to hate others because of their appearance or their beliefs. Prejudice, its results and its causes, is widespread and pervasive.

Prejudice Defined

Prejudice: a negative attitude toward a group of people who share some characteristic.

The word prejudice is derived from the Latin word *praejudicum,* which means to prejudge. But when social scientists talk about **prejudice,** they mean a negative attitude toward a group and members of that group. If the group is defined by the sex of its members, the prejudice is called *sexism.* Prejudice due to a group's religion, race, nationality, language, or culture is called *ethnic prejudice* (Harding, Proshansky, Kutner, and Chein, 1969). *Racism* is one kind of ethnic prejudice.

If prejudice is an attitude, then it has a structure, just as any other attitude. The three-component model of attitude structure proposes that attitudes have affective, cognitive, and behavioral components. For example, a person who dislikes Japanese (the affective component) would hold negative beliefs about Japanese (the cognitive component), and would act negatively toward Japanese (the behavioral component).

Stereotype: a generalized belief about the characteristics of a group of people.

In the case of prejudice, the cognitive component of an attitude is usually based on a **stereotype.** Initially, there may be some factual basis for a stereotype. Consider the stereotype of Jews as "money hungry." This belief probably had its origins in the Middle Ages, when the Catholic Church prohibited its members from earning money by lending it to others and charging interest. Jews were not prohibited by their religion from doing this; thus, many of the money lenders in Europe were Jewish. Out of necessity, Christians dealt with Jewish money lenders, but they saw the practice of charging interest as a basically unethical and sinful action, motivated by greed. This led people to perceive the average money-lender as money hungry. This perception, in combination with the absence of interactions with Jews in other contexts, caused many Christians to assume that all Jews, irrespective of their occupations, were interested only in making money. This stereotype was passed on to others.

The problem with stereotypes is that they continue in the absence of any factual basis and are applied in an indiscriminate, unthinking manner. A person is believed to possess certain characteristics simply because he or she belongs to a certain group, and his or her characteristics are assumed to be shared by every other member of the group.

Discrimination

Just as attitudes, in general, are believed to cause behavior, so specific prejudicial attitudes are believed to cause behavior. This behavior is usually called *discrimination.* Discrimination can range from relatively minor actions, such as sneering at members of an ethnic group, to actions with more serious consequences. A few years ago, two unemployed auto workers were drinking and discussing why they had been laid off. Aided by the alcohol, they came to the conclusions that their plight was due solely to the Japanese auto industry and that they would punish the Japanese for their situation. On their way home, the two men saw Vincent Chin, a Chinese-American. Mistaking him for a Japanese, they beat him to death (*Newsweek,* 1984).

This case of discrimination was carried out by individuals. **Institutional discrimination** is carried out by groups. Some examples of institutional discrimination are South Africa's apartheid policy, club policies against accepting people from certain ethnic groups as members, and company policies against hiring women for certain positions or of paying women less than men for the same work.

Individual discrimination usually follows and is caused by prejudice. This may be less true for institutional discrimination. Blalock (1967) has argued that often governments and other institutions discriminate against an ethnic group because they expect an economic gain for doing so. In such cases, prejudicial feelings and beliefs about members of a group may be after-the-fact justifications of the discriminatory behavior.

Causes of Prejudice

Theories of the causes of prejudice have focused primarily on ethnic prejudice, such as racism. The variables that lead to racism also lead to sexism; thus, both forms of prejudice are discussed here. A few theorists (Freedman, 1974; Wilson, 1975) believe there may be an innate component to prejudice, but the most widely accepted position is that prejudice is an acquired attitude. The next section discusses some theoretical explanations of the origins of prejudice.

Learning Theory

The basic premise of the learning theory view of prejudice is that as humans are socialized, they may be taught negative attitudes toward certain groups or they may receive information that leads them to believe certain groups possess undesirable characteristics. The processes by which prejudicial attitudes are learned are the same as the processes by which other attitudes are learned: classical conditioning, instrumental conditioning, and observational learning. Just as people can be taught to react positively or negatively to some inanimate object, so they can be taught to react positively or negatively to members of a group.

The formation of a particular attitude among children may be greatly influenced by the media, especially television because television is such an integral part of most children's lives. The manner in which a particular group is portrayed in the media can similarly greatly influence people's beliefs about that group. For years, blacks, women, and other groups have claimed that mass media have done little to reduce prejudice against them and may have contributed to it. These claims seem to have merit. Weigel, Loomis, and Soja (1980) analyzed race relations on prime-time television and found that blacks are underrepresented. Blacks comprise 10 to 15 percent of the United States' population, yet in 96 percent of the scenes involving only one person, that person is white. Television also presents few models of interracial interactions. In 98 percent of the scenes where two or more people are interacting, the people are of the same race.

Research on the manner in which women are presented on television provides similar data (Courtney and Whipple, 1983). Fifty-one percent of

Institutional discrimination: negative behavior toward members of a group due to an institution's official policies.

© 1983 Jim Borgman—Cincinnati Enquirer. By permission of King Features Syndicate.

the United States' population is female, yet one study found that only 32 percent of the characters on the top 40 television shows were female. Further, while women comprised approximately 40 percent of the work force, they comprised only 22 percent of the work force on television (United Methodist Church Television Monitoring Project, 1976).

More recent studies of the content of television commercials suggest that women continue to be underrepresented and stereotyped. Pesch (1981) reported that less than 10 percent of the announcers in television commercials are female. Females who appear in commercials are most likely shown at home doing something for their families (82 percent), while males are most likely shown working outside the home (67 percent).

Such portrayals may influence the development of children's perceptions of and attitudes toward the roles of men and women in society. Freuh and McGhee (1975) found that the more time children spent watching television, the more sex typed was their behavior. Beuf (1974) looked at how television affected children's ideas about careers. Heavy television watching was associated with choosing traditionally sex-typed careers. Also, when girls who watched a lot of television were asked what careers they would choose if they were boys, many could not imagine any occupation where sex would not be a barrier. When boys were asked what careers they would choose if they were girls, one boy replied, "Oh, if I were a girl, I'd have to grow up to be nothing."

Ethnocentrism

Another view of prejudice is that it may be due to **ethnocentrism** (Brewer, 1979; Levine and Campbell, 1972). Two general theories of the causes of ethnocentrism have been proposed. One is that certain individuals have a *need* to glorify their own group and disdain members of other groups. The other general theory is that ethnocentrism is a natural consequence of group membership.

Authoritarian Personality Research on the **authoritarian personality** was largely motivated by the Nazi holocaust of the Jews. In the years immediately following World War II, the American Jewish Congress commissioned a group of researchers to investigate the following question. If a fascist political movement were to emerge in the United States, what kind of people would be attracted to it? The fear of a nazilike movement in the United States may seem paranoid in the mid-1980s, but in the late 1940s there were good reasons for Jewish leaders to worry. Six million of their brothers and sisters had been slaughtered only a few years before, many businesses and professions were still closed to American Jews, and

Ethnocentrism: the belief that one's own ethnic group is better than any other group and the tendency to dislike members of other groups.

Authoritarian personality: personality characteristics that lead a person to uncritically submit to and identify with authority figures.

Some of the survivors of the Buchenwald concentration camp. The Nazi's campaign of genocide against the Jews lead to research in the United States on the authoritarian personality.

the level of public anti-Semitism in postwar America was greater than the level of anti-Semitism in prewar Germany (Adorno, Frenkel-Brunswik, Levinson, and Sanford, 1950).

Adorno developed a scale to measure the authoritarian personality. Among the characteristics of such an individual are conventionalism—rigid adherence to middle-class conventional values; authoritarian submission—submissive, uncritical attitudes toward the leaders of the individual's group and obedience to that group; authoritarian aggression—the tendency to reject and punish people who violate middle-class values; and power and toughness—identification with power figures perceived as strong and tough. The prototypical authoritarian personality is Archie Bunker.

Adorno and his associates found that people with high scores on their scale were, as predicted, more ethnocentric than those with low scores. Authoritarianism has also been found to be associated with specific kinds of prejudice, such as anti-Semitism and racism (Klein, 1963). (See chapter eleven for more on this personality characteristic.)

Group Membership   The other major explanation of ethnocentrism is that favoring one's own group over others is a consequence of identifying oneself as the member of a group. It is remarkably easy to create this bias. Tajfel, Billig, Bundy, and Flament (1971) created in-groups and out-groups among their subjects by dividing them on the basis of such things as preferences for different kinds of art. They then placed subjects in a situation where they could distribute rewards to members of their own group (the in-group) and to members of the out-group. When they distributed the rewards, subjects treated members of the out-group unfairly and members of their own group fairly.

In a more recent experiment, Park and Rothbart (1982) looked at the effects of group membership on beliefs about the characteristics of members of an out-group. The in-group/out-group distinction was based on sex. They found that male's and female's estimates of the percentage of members of their own sex who acted in accord with sex role stereotypes were significantly lower than their estimates of the percentage of members of the opposite sex who acted in accord with sex role stereotypes. In other words, both males and females saw members of their own sex as "variegated and complex," but they saw members of the other sex as homogeneous.

Race and Shared Beliefs

Rokeach and his colleagues (Rokeach 1960; Rokeach and Mezei, 1966, Rokeach, Smith, and Evans, 1960) have proposed that people assume if someone belongs to a group different from theirs, that person must have beliefs, attitudes, and values different from theirs. Thus, they may dislike the person, not because of some ethnic characteristic, but because of perceived dissimilarity. If this proposal is valid, then information that someone from a different ethnic group holds similar beliefs and views should override the effects of ethnic difference. In a 1966 study, Rokeach and Mezei tested this idea. They presented white subjects with other whites whose beliefs differed from theirs and with blacks whose beliefs were similar to theirs; they "pitted" shared race against shared belief. Subjects indicated a greater preference for members of a different race who held similar beliefs than for members of their own race who held different beliefs.

Rokeach's claim that perceived differences in beliefs are a major cause of racial prejudice has been strongly disputed by Triandis (Triandis, 1961; Triandis and Davis, 1965). Using procedures different from those used by Rokeach, Triandis found that people's preferences for an individual were more strongly influenced by the other person's race than by his beliefs.

Like many controversies in science, this one went on for quite a while and often produced more heat than light. Recent research, however, has suggested a resolution. Moe, Nacoste, and Insko (1981) found that the relative effects of shared race and shared beliefs depend on a person's perceptions of how others would react to their interacting with someone of a different race. If they think others would approve of interracial contact, then preferences are made on the basis of shared belief rather than shared race. But if they think that others would disapprove of interracial contact, then preferences are made on the basis of shared race rather than shared belief.

Realistic Group Conflict

Another explanation of prejudice proposes that the basis of prejudice is the belief that a group threatens one's well-being. Levine and Campbell (1972) called this the theory of **realistic group conflict.** This kind of prejudice is realistic in the sense that a person *believes* members of another group constitute an actual threat; this belief may or may not be based on correct information. Prejudice that results from realistic group conflict has three key characteristics. One, two groups are in competition for a valued resource. Two, the objective competition is usually accompanied by one group's subjective perception that the other group constitutes a threat to its well-being. And three, members of each group strongly identify with their group and see its interests as their own (Ashmore and Del Boca, 1976; Bobo, 1983). For example, a black construction worker may dislike whites not solely because he has been taught antiwhite attitudes, but because he fears that whites may get the construction jobs he and other blacks want.

Muzafer and Carolyn Sherif and their associates conducted some classic studies on how competition between groups can lead to prejudice and discrimination (Sherif, Harvey, White, Hood, and Sherif, 1961; Sherif and Sherif, 1969). These studies were conducted at summer camps for boys. After letting the boys spend a few days getting acquainted, the Sherifs and their associates divided them into two groups. The more friendly two boys were, the less likely they were to be assigned to the same group. Initially, the boys felt little attraction toward other group members, but certain experiences quickly made them ethnocentric and devoted to members of their own group. Then the Sherifs and their associates created a number of situations in which the two groups had to compete for prizes and valuable resources. They heightened the effects of the competition by introducing events in which one group apparently frustrated the other. For

Realistic group conflict: a negative attitude toward some group due to the perception that it is a serious threat to one's well-being.

example, on one occasion both groups were invited to share some cake, but one group was told to arrive several minutes before the other. By the time the second group had arrived, only unappetizing crumbs were left.

The boys in both groups were from the same racial and ethnic group, yet they developed a dislike for one another that rivaled most ethnic and racial prejudices. They began calling one another names and committing acts of vandalism against one another. Soon there were acts of physical violence between the groups.

If competition created this prejudice and discrimination, then a need for cooperation should reduce it. And this is what these researchers found. They created a number of situations in which either group had to cooperate with the other to achieve a goal. The camp's water system "broke down" and could only be fixed if the two groups worked together. A truck also "broke down" and could only be started if both groups pulled it. Cooperative efforts such as these produced dramatic changes in the boys' attitudes and behaviors. Intergroup friendships developed and the name calling and violence decreased dramatically.

The Sherifs' work suggests that prejudice due to realistic conflict may be easily eliminated. However, as Tajfel (1982) pointed out, once the researchers eliminated the competitive conflict, there was no reason for members of the two groups to dislike one another. They all came from the same racial and ethnic group, and the things that had divided them had been short-term creations of the experimenters. In the world outside a summer camp, a conflict may be difficult to eliminate; past histories may cause groups to dislike one another even if they occasionally cooperate. For example, it is unlikely that a single act of cooperation between the Protestants and Catholics in Northern Ireland would so easily override the years of hatred that have existed between these two groups.

Stephen Worchel and his associates (for example, Worchel, Axsom, Ferris, Samaha, and Schweitzer, 1978; Norvell and Worchel, 1981) have conducted several investigations of how group identification can moderate the effects of cooperation. The results of these studies are fairly consistent. If there is reason for people to maintain an in-group/out-group distinction, then group divisions may persist after the two groups have cooperated.

Realistic Conflict versus Symbolic Racism

In recent years, some social psychologists have turned their attention to an interesting social phenomenon. Public opinion polls have indicated a decline in antiblack sentiments among whites, yet there has been increased resistance among whites to laws and public policies that might benefit blacks. Two explanations of this have been proposed. One is based on the concept of **symbolic racism;** people express racism in a symbolic way by opposing the things that members of certain racial groups desire (Kinder and Sears, 1981; Sears, Lau, Tyler, and Allen, 1980). Symbolic racism is the product of racist attitudes acquired during the socialization process. The other explanation is that racial opposition is based on realistic group conflict; people oppose some action because they perceive the action as posing a threat to them.

Symbolic racism: the manifestation of racist attitudes in negative attitudes toward actions that would benefit a racial group.

Bobo (1983) conducted an analysis to determine which of these two explanations can better account for whites' negative attitudes toward busing to achieve racial integration. He used data from two national surveys and found that antiblack attitudes and negative stereotypes about blacks were not related to antibusing sentiments. Antibusing sentiments were related to the belief that black civil rights activities constituted a threat to whites. Bobo's analysis suggests that opposition to busing can be better explained as the result of a perceived threat than as the result of symbolic racism.

Prejudice and discrimination that are caused by a perceived threat are no more defensible than are prejudice and discrimination that result from a dislike for some group. Recall the incident of the two unemployed auto workers who beat to death a man of Chinese ancestry they mistook for Japanese. The Japanese auto industry may threaten the American auto worker, but that threat cannot justify their action.

A Remedy

It is often difficult for people who were born in the 1960s, especially if they are white, to understand and appreciate the history of racial prejudice and discrimination in the United States. A little over 20 years ago, a black person could be legally refused service at a restaurant or hotel, and many states did not allow black people to vote. And a little over thirty years ago, over 10 million children were required by law to attend segregated schools (Cook, 1984). Since the 1950s, many attempts have been made to reduce racial prejudice in the United States. This section looks at perhaps the most ambitious one.

Desegregation of Schools

In 1954, the United States Supreme Court ruled on the constitutionality of segregated schools. Part of the evidence considered by the court was a statement prepared and signed by 32 social scientists. This statement addressed the psychological aspects of school segregation. It argued that continued school segregation was highly detrimental to black children and of no value to white children. It stated that if schools were integrated, three things were likely to occur: (1) self-esteem among black children should increase because black children would no longer feel they were inferior, second-class citizens; (2) integration would have no impact on the academic achievement of white students, but it should produce an improvement in academic achievement among black students; and (3) racial prejudice would be reduced.

What Were the Effects?
Historians have different views of the role that the social science statement played in the Court's decision to rule segregation unconstitutional. Rosen (1972) argued that the court relied heavily on the statement's conclusions, but Kluger (1976) believed that the justices cited the statement in their decision as part of an attempt to increase public support for their ruling.

Whatever the truth, this statement represented a major attempt to apply research findings to a social problem and to affect public policy.

Another way to look at the statement is as a set of hypotheses about the effects of an independent variable—integration—on three dependent variables—self-esteem, academic achievement, and racial prejudice. A number of studies have investigated the validity of these hypotheses.

Self-Esteem   Contrary to the first prediction made, desegregation has not resulted in increased self-esteem among minority group members (Stephan, 1978). In a fairly comprehensive study of the effects of desegregation on Mexican-American children, Gerard and Miller (1975) found increased levels of anxiety, greater self-criticism, and less favorable self-concepts.

Academic Achievement   The research on academic achievement provides a mixed picture. Several studies (for example, Gerard and Miller, 1975; Moskowitz and Wortman, 1981; St. John, 1975) have failed to find any improvement in academic achievement among minority group children as the result of desegregation. Cook (1979, 1984), however, has presented data that suggest that if black children enter desegregated schools early and their academic achievement is measured over the long run, their academic achievement does improve. Jones (1984) reported that during recent years there has been a decline in the difference between the reading and mathematics achievement scores of black and white high school students.

Racial Prejudice   The social science statement predicted a decline in racial prejudice as the result of desegregation. But Stephan found that desegregation "generally does not reduce the prejudices of whites toward blacks . . . [and] desegregation leads to increases in black prejudice toward whites about as frequently as it leads to decreases" (1978, p. 217). And St. John (1975) found that white racism is frequently aggravated by "mixed schooling."

What Went Wrong?
Some social scientists (for example, Gerard, 1983) have argued that the original social science statement was based more on rhetoric than on good research evidence, and that the formulators of the statement were naive and did not foresee the difficulties of school integration. But Stuart Cook (1979, 1984), one of the people who drafted the statement, defended its scientific merit. Part of Cook's defense was based on weaknesses in the studies that have examined the effects of desegregation, but his most persuasive arguments were based on the way in which school desegregation has been implemented in the United States. The social science statement's predictions were predicated on the assumption that schools would be integrated in a manner that would produce "equal status contact" (Allport, 1954). According to Allport, it is not enough to simply put blacks and whites together. Interracial contact will produce positive outcomes only if (1) the parties to the contact are of equal status, (2) the parties are encouraged to cooperate rather than to compete and (3) the contact is promoted and supported by the institutions in the community. Cook observed

that status differentials between majority and minority group students are often maintained in integrated classrooms and that the reward systems in most classrooms encourage competition rather than cooperation. And in many communities, especially in those that use busing to achieve integration, the officials actively resist integration. Cook proposed that if the conditions specified in the original statement had been met, integration would have had the predicted positive effects. One possible way to meet these conditions is discussed in the next section.

Jigsaw Technique

In response to interracial conflict in the Austin, Texas school system, Elliot Aronson and his colleagues (Aronson, Blaney, Stephan, Sikes, and Snapp, 1978; Aronson and Osherow, 1980) attempted to develop a teaching method that would promote harmony in the newly integrated schools. This method was called the **jigsaw technique.** It was largely based on the ideas proposed in Allport's equal status contact hypothesis. In the first stage of implementation, teachers attend a workshop on what the jigsaw technique is and how to use it. Then the children are introduced to the instructional method. At first they work at simple, nonacademic exercises which help them learn certain cooperative skills. Then they are divided into racially and ethnically heterogeneous groups of five or six students. Each group meets for several hours a day and works on some academic topic. The topic is divided into several sections, and each member of the group is given the responsibility of learning his or her own section and then teaching it to the other group members. Students from different groups who are responsible for the same sections are encouraged to help one another learn the material. Thus, the method fosters intergroup cooperation as well as intragroup cooperation and interdependence. The students are tested individually so one child is not penalized because others have not learned the material. If the jigsaw technique is to be used for a prolonged period of time, Aronson and his associates recommended changing the composition of the groups so students can interact with more of their classmates.

Only a limited amount of research has been done on the effectiveness of this method of instruction, but the results are encouraging. Blaney, Stephan, Rosenfield, Aronson, and Sikes (1977) created jigsaw groups composed of children from different racial and ethnic backgrounds and then compared their performances to those of children in more traditional classrooms. The children in the jigsaw classroom exhibited increases in self-esteem and liking for their jigsaw group partners. Lucker, Rosenfield, Sikes, and Aronson (1977) did a controlled study on the effects of the jigsaw technique on academic performance. Students in six classes that used the jigsaw method were compared to students in five classes that used traditional methods of teaching. The dependent measure was scores on a test of American history. The results showed little difference between majority group students in the jigsaw and traditional classrooms. But minority group students who participated in the jigsaw groups improved significantly

Jigsaw technique: a method of instruction in which children from different ethnic groups work cooperatively to learn new material.

more than did minority group members in the traditional classroom. (See figure 9-3.)

Geffner (1978) found that children who participated in the jigsaw technique showed a decline in negative ethnic stereotypes. Johnson and Johnson (1981) reviewed 13 studies that had used the jigsaw technique or other cooperative instructional methods in racially mixed classrooms. In 11 of the studies, significant improvement in interracial relations was found.

These findings suggest that it may be inappropriate to consider the attempt to integrate schools a failure. When the principles proposed by Allport in his equal status contact hypothesis are incorporated into the classroom, integration does appear to benefit minority group and majority group children and to reduce prejudice.

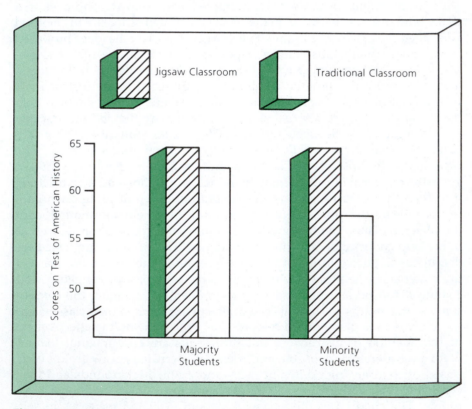

Figure 9-3. *The usage of the jigsaw technique greatly improved the performance of minority group students.*
Source: Lucker et al. (1977).

Chapter Ten

Attitude Change

Prologue

Leon Festinger and James M. Carlsmith (1959). Cognitive
Consequences of Forced Compliance. *Journal of Abnormal
and Social Psychology*, **58,** 203–210.

Background

Two general methods are used to change attitudes. In one, people are
presented with a speech or message intended to change their attitudes;
they are passive recipients of the message. In the other, people actively
participate in the change process; they are induced to engage in some
behavior that produces attitude change. Leon Festinger and James Carlsmith's experiment used a variant of the second technique to change subjects' attitudes. Subjects were influenced to behave in a way that was
discrepant from their present attitudes but was consistent with a new
attitude. This experiment produced results that directly or indirectly led
to hundreds of other experiments on attitude change.

Hypothesis

The major hypothesis was based on Festinger's (1957) theory of cognitive
dissonance. It was predicted that subjects who were given a small reward
or incentive to engage in behavior that differed from their attitudes would
show more attitude change than would subjects who were given a large
reward to engage in this attitude-discrepant behavior.

Subjects

The subjects were 60 male undergraduates at Stanford University.

Procedure

In the initial part of the study, all the subjects spent one hour performing
two boring tasks. One task consisted of placing thread spools in a tray,
emptying the tray, and repeating this over and over. The second consisted
of turning pegs of wood for a half hour.

   At the end of the hour, the subjects were given a false story about the
purpose of the experiment. The subjects were led to believe that the purpose of the experiment had been to investigate how people's expectations
affect their performances on the tasks and that there had been two groups
in the experiment. Members of one group had performed the tasks with
no prior expectations about them. Members of the other group had had a
positive expectation before they performed the tasks; a person who supposedly had been in the experiment had told them the tasks were enjoyable
or interesting. All the subjects were told that they had been in the first
group.

The true independent variable was a reward then offered to the subjects for saying something they really did not believe. One-third of the subjects were assigned to a small-reward group. The experimenter, with some embarrassment, told them that the person who usually talked to the other subjects was unable to do this today, and asked the subjects if they would be willing to take the other person's place. In exchange for doing this and for being on call for future experiments, they would receive one dollar. Another one-third of the subjects were assigned to a large-reward group. They were told the same story and offered twenty dollars to take the person's place and to be on call for future experiments. The remaining one-third of the subjects were assigned to a control group and were simply asked to complete the tasks.

Subjects in the small- and large-reward groups then spoke with a female confederate and told her how interesting and enjoyable the tasks had been. Then they and the subjects in the control group were interviewed by the

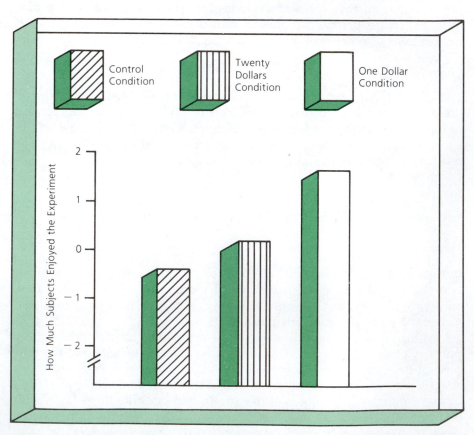

Figure 10-1. *Subjects who received one dollar to participate in a boring experiment enjoyed it more than did subjects who received twenty dollars or memebers of the control group.*
Source: Festinger and Carlsmith (1959).

person who was supposedly collecting data on students' perceptions of experiments.

The information collected in this interview provided the dependent variable—subjects' attitudes toward the task. Subjects rated how enjoyable the tasks were, how important the tasks were to science, and how willing they would be to take part in similar experiments in the future. Following this, the true purpose of the experiment was revealed to the subjects.

Results

Since all three groups of subjects were randomly assigned to the different conditions, there is no reason to suspect that their attitudes toward the tasks differed before the independent variable was administered. The size of the reward for the attitude-discrepant behavior did produce differences in their attitudes toward the task. (See figure 10-1.) As predicted, the subjects in the small-reward group rated the tasks as significantly more enjoyable than did subjects in the large-reward and control groups. The same kind of differences were also found on the questions concerned with scientific importance and willingness to participate in future experiments, but these differences were not statistically significant.

Implications

Many theories of social behavior propose that if you want people to change, you must give them a reward or incentive for doing so. The results of this experiment suggest that giving a people a large reward for an attitude-discrepant behavior may have just the opposite effect. This chapter presents Festinger and Carlsmith's explanation of their results and examines why their findings sparked much controversy and research.

Stop for a moment and think about your attitudes toward some of the objects in the world around you. What are your feelings about the major you have chosen? A certain fraternity or sorority on your campus? Abortion? The nuclear freeze? Raising the drinking age to 21? Now try to remember how you felt about these objects when you first started college. Your attitudes toward some of these objects may be relatively the same as they were a few years ago. Other attitudes have probably changed considerably since you started college. This chapter is concerned with how these changes occurred; it is about the processes whereby people's attitudes are changed.

As noted in the background of the prologue, one of two general ways to change people's attitudes is to present them with a **persuasive message.** The first section of this chapter addresses the variables that determine whether or not a persuasive message will be effective. In the other general technique of changing people's attitudes, called active participation, people engage in some activity that produces a change in their attitudes. The

Persuasive message: a communication or message that is intended to influence people's attitudes.

second section of this chapter addresses this approach to attitude change. Techniques like the one used in the prologue are discussed and explained. In the applications section, these concepts are applied to advertising effectiveness and public health campaigns.

PERSUASIVE MESSAGE

Using persuasive messages to change attitudes is an old and widespread technique. If we believe Eve's version of why she ate the forbidden fruit, the serpent used a persuasive message in the Garden of Eden. The Sermon on the Mount was a persuasive message, as were the Declaration of Independence, the Gettysburg Address, and each president's inaugural speech. It has been estimated that in the course of one day, the average American is exposed to more than 1,500 persuasive appeals from national advertisers alone (Will, 1982).

Despite the large role persuasive messages play in determining human social behavior, only in the last 30 to 40 years have social scientists extensively studied why a persuasive message is effective or ineffective. The event that provided the original impetus for this research was the Second World War (Eagly and Himmelfarb, 1973). The American military realized that soldiers' attitudes were creating problems that impeded the war effort. For example, the war against Germany ended long before the war against Japan. This led many of the soldiers fighting the Japanese to become demoralized because their part of the war was continuing or to believe that the fighting was all but over. As a result, they were less motivated to fight (Hovland, Lumsdaine, and Sheffield, 1949). In response to such problems, the army devoted considerable resources to the development of effective means to change the attitudes of American soldiers. Among the people involved in this effort was an experimental psychologist from Yale University, Carl Hovland. As the result of his work for the army, Hovland's research interest changed from experimental to social psychology. When the war ended, he returned to Yale, and with his colleagues, began to work on a comprehensive theory of attitude change (Hovland, Janis, and Kelley, 1953).

Hovland and his associates' theory of attitude change was greatly influenced by learning theory, particularly the drive reduction theory. These researchers proposed that attitude change occurs in a manner analogous to behavior change. First people are taught the behavior, and then they are motivated to perform it. In the case of a persuasive message, people first have to learn the contents of the message and then must be motivated to accept the contents.

Incentives: promised or expected rewards.

Learning requires that people attend to, comprehend, and remember the contents of the persuasive message. Acceptance, according to Hovland and his associates, depends on the **incentives** offered in the persuasive message. For this reason, their approach is often called an incentive theory of attitude change. The incentives can be tangible—for example, a television evangelist recently announced that if people supported his ministry by sending him one thousand dollars (his persuasive message), they would receive ten thousand dollars (a tangible incentive) from God. More commonly, incentives are intangible—for example, the promise of social approval.

Hovland and his associates believed that the key to understanding why people would attend to, understand, remember, and accept a persuasive message is to study "who says what to whom"—to study the characteristics of the person who presents the messsage, the contents of the message, and the characteristics of the person who receives the message. These three things are called the source, the message, and the recipient. Attitude researchers have focused most of their attention on how the source and the message affect attitude change.

Source Characteristics

The person who develops or originates a persuasive message is called the *source*. The person who presents the message is called the *communicator*. The source and the communicator of a message can be one and the same (see the following cartoon), or they can be two separate entities. For example, the television evangelist did not claim to be the source of the persuasive messages he delivered; he claimed to be communicating the message from God. The research literature on persuasive messages uses the terms source and communicator almost interchangeably. In the interest of clarity, only the term source will be used in the material that follows. One of the initial and continuing interests among attitude researchers is in how source credibility and other source characteristics influence the effectiveness of a persuasive message.

Credibility
In an early study by Hovland and Weiss (1951), subjects received a persuasive message concerned with the practicality of building a nuclear-

DOONESBURY   by Garry Trudeau

powered submarine. (This study was conducted several years before such a submarine was actually built.) For half the subjects, the message was attributed to a well-known and respected American nuclear scientist. For the other half, it was attributed to the official newspaper of the Soviet Communist party, *Pravda*. The message attributed to the scientist produced much more immediate attitude change than did the message attributed to *Pravda*.

Why were the subjects more accepting of the scientist's message? Two characteristics make him a more persuasive source. First, he has expertise in the matter at hand; he knows what he is talking about. Second, he is more trustworthy (at least in the subject's view) than is *Pravda*. He is less likely to have some ulterior motive for trying to change the subjects' minds. When sources possess both these characteristics, they are *credible*, or believable. All other things being equal, people are more likely to be persuaded by credible than by noncredible sources.

Expertise   *Expert sources* are those who are perceived as being knowledgeable about the issue at hand. The expertise of a source appears to be a potent variable in producing attitude change. A study by Maddux and Rogers (1980) illustrates this. Some theorists (for example, Kelman, 1961) have argued that experts do not persuade people just because they are experts; the messages they present must contain valid, cogent arguments in support of their position. Maddux and Rogers tested this proposal by systematically manipulating source expertise and the arguments presented by the source. The topic of the persuasive message was how much sleep a person needs. Half the subjects were exposed to a persuasive message from an expert source (an international authority on sleep); half the subjects were exposed to a persuasive message from a nonexpert source (an international authority on music). Both sources took exactly the same position— a person needs only four hours of sleep a night. For half of the subjects exposed to each source, this position was accompanied by several supporting arguments; for the other half, the position was presented without supporting arguments. The dependent measure was subjects' responses to questions about how much sleep a person needs.

Maddux and Rogers found that an expert source had more impact on the subjects than did a nonexpert source, even when no supporting arguments were present. It appears that people can be swayed by experts even when experts do nothing more than express a point of view.

Trustworthiness   *Trustworthy sources* are those who are perceived as presenting their true positions and having no ulterior motives for presenting them. Hovland and his associates reasoned that a trustworthy source would be more effective than an untrustworthy one. For example, an economist who argued, on the basis of her research, that interest rates on home mortgages should be increased would be seen as more trustworthy than the head of a mortgage company who argued the same position. Research on the effects of source trustworthiness has generally supported this prediction (Petty and Cacioppo, 1981).

Hovland and his associates' original explanation of the effects of source trustworthiness was based on the incentives offered by trustworthy and untrustworthy sources. They suggested that people discover through learning experiences that there are negative consequences when someone untrustworthy manipulates them, so they have little incentive to accept messages from untrustworthy individuals.

Recently, some researchers have argued that trustworthiness (and other source characteristics) may affect attitude change by influencing people's thoughts about a persuasive message (Eagly and Chaiken, 1984). Alice Eagly and her associates proposed that the recipient's attributions may explain why an untrustworthy source often produces less attitude change (Eagly, 1983; Eagly, Wood, and Chaiken, 1978; Eagly, Chaiken, and Wood, 1981). They argued that recipients of a persuasive message often ask themselves Is the content of the message accurate or is it biased in some way? There are two possible kinds of bias: **knowledge bias** and **reporting bias.** If recipients come to believe that either bias is present, they will discount the accuracy of the message and will not be influenced by it.

Eagly and her associates (1978) studied what leads recipients to attribute either type of bias to a source. They found that when a source presents a position that is consistent with her own attitudes, people are more likely to assume the position contains a knowledge bias than when the source presents a position that is inconsistent with her own attitudes. The assumption of a reporting bias is most likely to occur when there are situational pressures on the source to take a certain position. For example, when Eagly and her colleagues' subjects read a proenvironment speech and were told it had been delivered to an audience with proenvironment attitudes, they were more likely to believe that it contained a reporting bias than when they read the same speech and were told it had been delivered to an audience with antienvironment attitudes. If a source's behavior is attributed to either type of bias, subjects are less likely to believe that the content of her message is accurate. As a result, they are less likely to change their attitudes.

Expertise versus Trustworthiness   Source expertise and trustworthiness usually go hand in hand. But under certain circumstances, people encounter a source who is an untrustworthy expert. Consider former president Richard Nixon's attempts to change the American public's attitudes about himself after the disclosure of the Watergate scandal. Mr. Nixon was perceived as an expert on this situation in which several men had been caught breaking into the headquarters of the Democratic party. But in the final days of his presidency, he was also perceived as a person who had something to gain from changing people's attitudes about the scandal. Mr. Nixon's failure to persuade his audience that he was innocent can be largely explained by research that has focused on expertise or prestige versus trustworthiness.

Walster, Aronson, and Abrahams (1966) proposed that irrespective of sources' expertise or prestige, they will be more effective when they argue

Knowledge bias: a situation where sources believe they are giving unbiased information, but because of their own positions on the issues they give biased information.

Reporting bias: a situation where sources know the correct facts, but give biased versions of them.

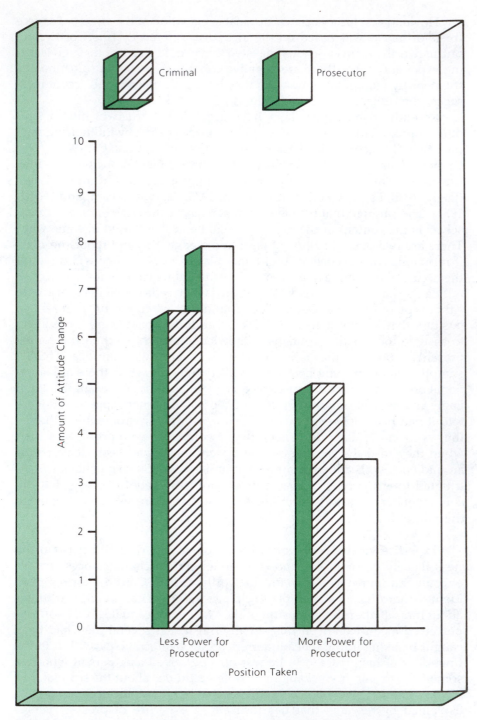

Figure 10-2. *When the sources argued for positions counter to their own interests, they were more effective than when they argued for positions which served their own interests.*
Source: Walster et al. (1966).

a position that is not in their self-interest than when they argue one that is in their own self-interest. High school students read interviews with either a low-prestige source (a convicted criminal) or a high-prestige source (a highly successful prosecutor). In half of the interviews, the source argued that the police and prosecutors should be given more power to convict criminals; in the other half, the source argued that the police and prosecutors should be given less power. Note that in two of the experimental conditions, a source was arguing against his own best interests. The crucial question was whether this would override the effects of the sources' prestige. (See figure 10-2 for the answer to this question.)

When both the prosecutor and the criminal argued for more power for the police, the criminal was more effective than was the prosecutor. But when both the sources argued for less power for the police, the prosecutor was more effective than was the criminal.

Other Characteristics
Because of the important role source credibility plays in the acceptance of persuasive messages, it has received a great deal of attention from attitude change researchers. Other source characteristics that affect whether recipients will accept or reject a persuasive message include attractiveness, likableness, and similarity.

Ronald Reagan embodies most of the characteristics that make the source of a persuasive message effective. This is perhaps why he has been called "the great communicator."

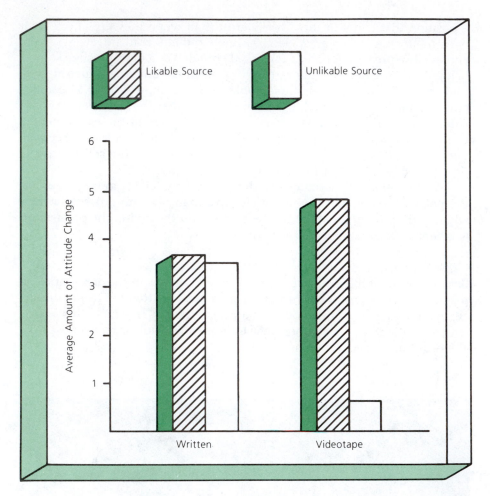

Figure 10-3. *When the message was written, the likable and unlikable sources were equally effective; but when the messages were videotaped, the likable source produced much more attitude change.*
Source: Chaiken and Eagly (1983).

Attractiveness and Likableness   In the early 1980s, it was almost impossible to spend an evening in front of the television without seeing the comedian Bill Cosby in a commercial. He simultaneously appeared in commercials for several products, including a home computer and a frozen pudding bar. Mr. Cosby had not been chosen to promote these products because he worked for little money or because he had special expertise. He had been chosen because advertising firms had determined that the public found him attractive and likable. The logic behind those advertising campaigns was that attractive, likable spokespeople are persuasive.

Attitude research generally supports this logic (Chaiken, 1979, 1983). It also appears that the more salient these characteristics are, the greater their impact will be. Chaiken and Eagly (1983) presented subjects with a message advocating that their university switch to a trimester system. Half the subjects heard this message from a likable source—he said positive things about the subjects' university. Half heard this message from an unlikable source—he said negative things about their university. Half the subjects in each condition saw a videotape of the source delivering the messages; the other half read a written transcript of the message. This constituted the manipulation of source salience; the videotaped source was more salient. The dependent message was attitude change. (See figure 10-3 for the results.)

When the subjects read a transcript, both sources were equally effective. But when the subjects saw a videotape, the likable source produced 10 times more change than did the unlikable source.

Similarity   Since people tend to like those who are similar to them, sources who are similar to a recipient should be more persuasive than sources who are dissimilar to a recipient. However, it is not quite this simple (Eagly, 1983; Petty and Cacioppo, 1981). When the issue concerns a matter of taste or judgment (for example, the question of which is the prettiest building in the United States), similar sources are more accepted than are dissimilar sources. But when the issue concerns a matter of fact (the question of which is the tallest building in the United States), dissimilar sources are more accepted (Goethals and Nelson, 1973). Eagly (1983) again used attribution theory to explain this finding. She reasoned that people may attribute their own and similar others' perceptions of facts to the same set of error-producing characteristics, but that people may not find it reasonable to make the same attribution when dissimilar others' perceptions agree with their own. As a result of their desire to be correct when the issue concerns a fact, people may be more influenced by the views of dissimilar others.

Research Highlight

The Illusive Sleeper Effect

In an early study of source credibility, Kelman and Hovland (1953) presented subjects with a persuasive message that was attributed to either a high-credibility or low-credibility source. Attitude change was measured once immediately after presentation of the message and then a second time, three weeks later. The researchers found a greater immediate attitude change for the high-credibility than for the low-credibility source. Three weeks later, they found that the amount of attitude change produced by the two sources was the same.

Kelman and Hovland called the delayed impact of the low-credibility source a sleeper effect. To explain why the effectiveness of the persuasive message increased over time, Kelman and Hovland proposed that source credibility affects recipients' decisions to accept or reject the position advocated in a message, but it does not affect how well recipients understand and remember the content of the message. Over time, people will dissociate the message from its source. In essence, they remember the content of the message but not who said it. When the effectiveness of the message is measured several weeks later, the content influences people's attitudes.

In the years following Kelman and Hovland's experiment, other researchers tried to determine if their explanation was correct and whether there is such a thing as the sleeper effect. Gillig and Greenwald (1974) pointed out that in the original experiment, the effectiveness of the low-credibility source stayed the same while the effectiveness of the high-credibility source decreased over time. Consequently, after three weeks, the two sources had an equivalent impact on the subjects' attitudes. This suggests that in the long run, a low-credibility source will sometimes be as effective as a high-credibility source, but it does not fit the definition of a true sleeper effect.

Subsequent research has found that under certain circumstances, a true sleeper effect will occur (Cook and Flay, 1978; Greenwald, Baumgardner, and Lippe, 1979). Imagine that you and a friend hear a speech from a local politician. You know that the speaker is about to serve a three- to five-year prison term for accepting bribes, so you do not pay very close attention to her speech and you do not accept the position she advocates. As a result, her message produces little immediate or delayed change in your attitudes. Now imagine you know nothing about the speaker, and you pay close attention to what she says. After the speech, your friend says, "You know about her, don't you? She's about to serve a three- to five-year prison term for accepting bribes."

This information does not affect how much attention you paid to the speech; you have already heard it. But it does affect your willingness to accept the position the speaker advocates. As a result, the message produces little immediate change in your attitudes. However, several weeks later, you find your attitudes have changed because you paid close attention to the content of the message.

This example shows that the sleeper effect depends on when a recipient learns that a source is noncredible. If this occurs before the message is presented, there will be no sleeper effect. If this occurs after the message is presented, there will be a sleeper effect.

The conditions that produce a true sleeper effect probably do not occur very often. Most of the time, we know something about the sources of messages we receive before the messages are delivered. If that knowledge leads us to pay little attention to a message, there is little immediate or delayed change in our attitudes.

Message Characteristics

As noted earlier, Hovland and his associates divided the study of persuasive messages into the examination of *who* says *what* to *whom*. Thus far, only the *who*—source characteristics—has been discussed. Now the focus moves to the *what*—the contents of a persuasive message, including how much change the message advocates, whether the message is one-sided or two-sided, and whether the message arouses fear.

Amount of Change Advocated

One way of looking at the goal of a persuasive message is that it attempts to move a recipient's position on some issue from point A (the recipient's present position) to point B (the position advocated in the message). Someone who is really interested in attitude change, not just in expressing an opinion must seriously consider what point B should be. For example, during the Vietnam War, I was actively involved in efforts to end America's military presence in Southeast Asia, and I gave speeches on this issue. On one occasion I was asked to speak to a group of students who strongly favored an *increase* in America's military efforts in Vietnam. I accepted the invitation because it gave me a chance to present a persuasive message to them and perhaps to change their attitudes. In preparing my speech, I had two options. I could take a position that differed greatly from that of my audience—the American involvement in Vietnam is morally and ethically indefensible and the troops should be withdrawn at once. Or I could take a position somewhat closer to that of my audience—the American involvement in Vietnam has not been effective, and the government should begin to reduce the number of troops stationed there. I chose to present the latter position because of the social psychological research on this topic.

Studies examining the effects of the position taken in a persuasive message have generally found a curvilinear relationship between the amount of change advocated in a persuasive message and the amount obtained (Aronson, Turner, and Carlsmith, 1963; Bochner and Insko, 1966; Insko, 1967). A curvilinear relationship looks like an upside-down U. (See figure 10-4.) Translating this figure into words, it says that up to a certain point, the more change advocated, the more obtained (the top of the upside-down U). Beyond that point, the more change advocated, the less obtained.

It is not enough to know the nature of this relationship; we also need to know why it exists. One possible explanation is provided by social judgment theory. Before this theory's explanation of the curvilinear relationship is presented, the manner in which it conceptualizes people's attitudes must be explained. Suppose someone is interested in your attitudes toward various foods. You are given a long list of foods and asked to place them in one of two categories: those you like and those you hate. Each category will contain several different foods. The like category will contain your most preferred food (perhaps fried chicken) plus foods you like somewhat less but that are still acceptable to you (perhaps broiled fish and beef Stroganoff). The same is true of the dislike category. You absolutely despise liver, but feel somewhat less strongly about corned beef and pickled pigs feet.

Social judgment theory (Sherif and Sherif, 1967; Sherif, Sherif, and Nebergall, 1965) claims that people's attitudes toward any issue or object can be conceptualized by using such categories. The first category is called the **latitude of acceptance;** the second category is called the **latitude of rejection.** The widths of a person's latitudes of acceptance and rejection are largely determined by how ego involving the issue is to that person.

Latitude of acceptance: a person's most preferred position on some issue, plus other positions the person would accept.

Latitude of rejection: a person's least preferred position on some issue, plus other positions the person would reject.

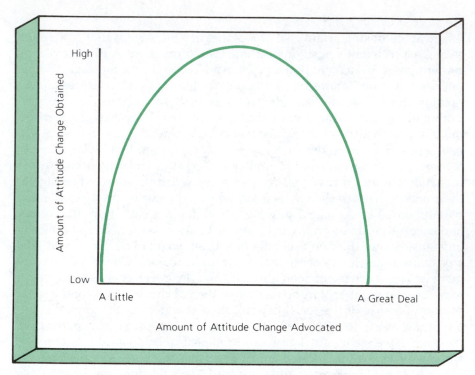

Figure 10-4. A model of the curvilinear relationship between amount of attitude change advocated and the amount obtained.

A person who is extremely ego involved will have a very narrow latitude of acceptance and a broad latitude of rejection (Sherif et al., 1965).

Attitudes serve certain functions, and one is to influence the way people process complex information from the world around them, to serve as schemata. (See chapter nine.) Recall, for example, the finding that people's attitudes toward a political candidate can influence their perceptions of where the candidate stands on certain issues (Judd et al., 1983). Social judgment theory proposes that when people receive persuasive messages, their perceptions of the messages are influenced by their own attitudes. If a position advocated is not exactly a person's most preferred one, but still falls within the latitude of acceptance, it will be **assimilated,** or seen as closer to the person's most preferred position than it actually is. If the position advocated falls in a person's latitude of rejection, it will be **contrasted,** or seen as further from the person's most preferred position than it actually is.

In summary, social judgment theory predicts increasing attitude change up to the point where the position advocated is beyond a recipient's latitude of acceptance. When the position falls within the latitude of rejection, the more it differs from the recipient's position, the less the attitude change. This prediction of a curvilinear relationship between the amount of change advocated and the amount obtained is basically what has been found.

One-sided versus Two-sided Messages

Many Americans turn on a television news program while they prepare for work. When there is some controversy of issue of concern to the public, these programs present government officials or politicians who express their views on the matter. These issues are often quite complex and subject to many different points of view, yet these people usually present a simplistic, one-sided position of the issue. For example, the secretary of defense is unlikely to acknowledge that there is any validity to the position of those who advocate nuclear disarmament, and those who advocate nuclear disarmament are unlikely to acknowledge that the secretary of defense's position might have some validity. Given that these people are supposed to represent certain groups or points of view, it is not surprising that their presentations are one-sided. But is it possible that they would better serve the groups they represent by presenting a more balanced position on an issue?

The answer is a qualified yes. Hovland and his associates (1949) and Lumsdaine and Janis (1953) found that if recipients are poorly informed about the topic of a message or are already in general agreement with the sentiments expressed by the source, a one-sided message is more effective than a **two-sided message.** But if recipients are well informed about or in general opposition to the sentiments expressed by the source, a two-sided message is more effective than a one-sided message.

Lumsdaine and Janis's study also suggested another benefit of presenting a two-sided message. Some time after their subjects were exposed to both types of persuasive message, the subjects heard arguments counter to those expressed in the original messages. Subjects who had received the two-sided message were less influenced by this counterpropaganda. A few years later, a colleague of these researchers proposed a theory to explain this finding.

William McGuire (1964) drew an analogy between protecting a person's body from disease and protecting a person's attitudes from counterpropaganda. Many diseases can be prevented by an inoculation. People receive a small dose of the germs that cause the disease and their bodies build up a natural resistance to those germs. Attitudes, McGuire proposed, can be like a body that has not been inoculated. To increase people's resistance to counterpropaganda, you need to give them weak doses of arguments that favor a different position and teach them how to build up their resistance.

McGuire and Papageorgis (1961) presented one group of subjects with a persuasive message and with arguments against the position advocated in that message. They gave another group of subjects only the persuasive message. When both groups of subjects were later presented with a persuasive message that took an opposite point of view, the former group was significantly less influenced than was the latter. This difference has been found even when the arguments presented in a subsequent message are different from the arguments presented in the original message (Papageorgis and McGuire, 1961). People can be inoculated against counterpropaganda.

Two-sided message: a message that contains arguments in support of the source's position and much weaker arguments against the source's position.

Fear-arousing Messages

A basic premise of Hovland and his colleagues' (1949, 1953) theory was that if you want to get people to change their attitudes, you must offer them incentives for doing so. The incentives discussed thus far have been positive, such as the expectation that accepting the persuasive message will lead to holding correct ideas or to gaining social approval. Another incentive could be the expectation that if people accept the persuasive message, they can avoid some negative consequence. This type of reasoning led one of Hovland's colleagues, Irving Janis, to investigate the effects of **fear-arousing messages** (Janis and Feshbach, 1953; Janis, 1968).

Fear-arousing messages: messages that first create fear in the recipient and then explicitly or implicitly suggest that if the recommendations contained in them are followed, the source of the fear can be reduced or eliminated.

This is a popular type of persuasive message. Pictures of bloodied and mutilated bodies are used by various groups to convince people not to drink and drive. Fear-arousing appeals have been used by groups who want more tax money spent on nuclear weapons and by groups who want less tax money spent on these weapons systems. But do such messages work?

Janis and Feshbach's (1953) original results suggested that they do not. Janis and Feshbach addressed the topic of oral hygiene habits and presented subjects with one of three types of fear-arousing message: high, moderate, and low. The high-fear message addressed the potentially life-threatening consequences of not brushing one's teeth regularly—the dangers of gum disease and secondary infections that could lead to paralysis or blindness. In the moderate-fear message, a more realistic and less emotional laden portrayal of the dangers of not brushing were presented. In the low-fear message, subjects heard emotionally neutral material about the growth and function of teeth. Janis and Feshbach found that the low-fear-arousing message was marginally more effective than were the other two, and they offered the following explanations of this finding.

The high-fear message was so upsetting to the subjects that it caused them to avoid thinking about the issue, as a result, it had little effect on the subjects' attitudes. Other researchers (for example, Leventhal, 1970; Mewborn and Rogers, 1979; Rogers, 1975) have questioned Janis and Feshbach's methodology and argued that under certain circumstances, high-fear-arousing messages can be quite effective.

Janis and Feshbach's high-fear message frightened the subjects, but it did not provide reasonable recommendations about what actions would enable the subjects to avoid the perils of poor oral hygiene habits. Rogers (1975) proposed that for a fear-arousing message to be effective, it must do three things. First, it must clearly specify how unpleasant the consequences will be if the recommended actions are not followed. Second, it must discuss the likelihood that these consequences *will* occur if the recommendations are not followed. Third, it must contrast the dire results of inaction with the likelihood that these consequences *will not* occur if the recommendations are followed. Research suggests that this type of fear-arousing message is effective in changing people's attitudes (Eagly and Himmelfarb, 1978).

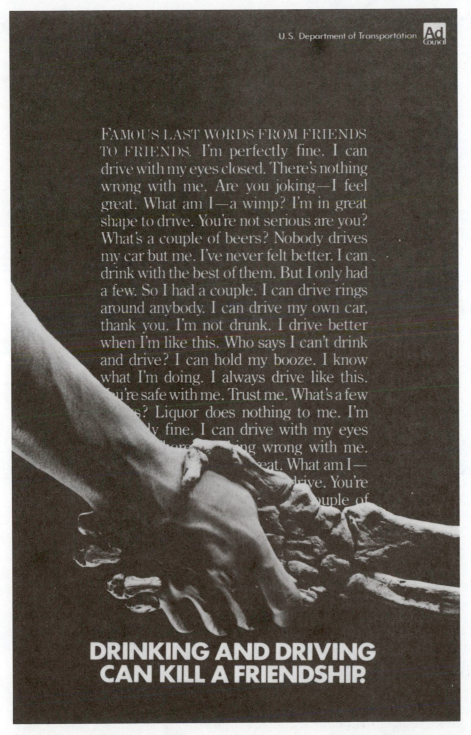

Fear arousing messages such as this one are intended to change people's attitudes toward drinking. Research suggests, however, they are not always effective.

Source versus Message

The previous sections contain two somewhat contradictory ideas. First it was implied that if a source is credible, attractive and similar to the recipient, the content of the source's message is irrelevant to attitude change. But then it was implied that if a message is well constructed, the characteristics of the message's source are irrelevant.

To a certain extent, this contradiction is the result of the way the material was presented here: first one aspect of persuasive messages was presented, then another. But it is still reasonable for someone interested in attitude change to ask, If I want to change people's attitudes, should I focus on the source or on the message? Some recent work by Petty and Cacioppo (1981, 1983, 1984) suggests an answer to this question. Petty and Cacioppo (1984) argued that attitude change can occur through a **central route** or through a **peripheral route.** They believed that the central route involves a thoughtful consideration of the issue at hand, while the peripheral route "is not a very thoughtful one" (Petty and Cacioppo, 1981, 256).

The relative importance of the source versus the message may depend upon whether attitude change occurs through the central route or through the peripheral route. When the central route is activated, message characteristics are more important; when the peripheral route is activated, source characteristics are more important.

When will each route be activated? Petty and Cacioppo claimed that one determinant is people's personal involvement with an issue. People will think carefully about the content of a persuasive message about involving issues—these issues will activate the central route. Issues that are not involving to people will activate the less thoughtful, peripheral route.

In a 1984 study, Petty and Cacioppo demonstrated this. Students were presented with a persuasive message that advocated an increase in tuition. To manipulate personal involvement, half the subjects were told that this increase would occur at their university; the other half were told that this increase would occur at another university. Subjects in both the high-involvement condition and the low-involvement condition received one of three persuasive messages. The first contained three well-thought-out, cogent arguments in favor of a tuition increase; the second contained three superficial, weak arguments in favor of an increase; the third contained six arguments, three cogent and three superficial. The dependent measure was how much the subjects changed their attitudes in response to the messages. (See figure 10-5 for Petty and Cacioppo's results.)

Among the low-involvement subjects, the simple quantity of the arguments affected attitude change; the message that contained six arguments (three strong, three weak) produced more attitude change than did the message that contained three strong messages. But among the high-involvement subjects, the quality of the arguments affected attitude change. The message that contained three strong arguments was more effective than the one that contained three weak arguments, and it was equally as effective as the message that contained six arguments.

Central route: the process of attitude change that results from a careful consideration of the contents of a persuasive message.

Peripheral route: the process of attitude change that results from the rewards or punishments associated with the message or the recipient's perceptions of the source.

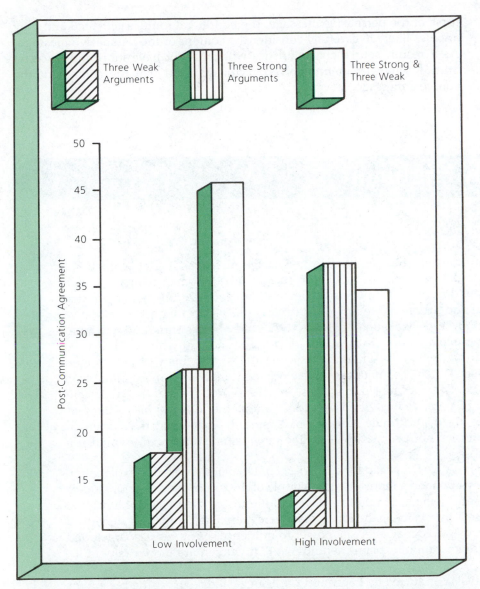

Figure 10-5. *When there was low involvement, the quantity of arguments affected attitude change; but when there was high involvement, it was the quality of the arguments that affected attitude change.*
Source: Petty and Cacioppo (1985).

Subsequent research by Petty and Cacioppo (1984) replicated this finding and showed that high-involvement subjects think more about persuasive messages than do low-involvement subjects. Apparently, when recipients are involved with the topic of a persuasive message, the central route to attitude change is activated and they carefully consider the content of the persuasive message. But when recipients are not involved with the topic of the persuasive message, the peripheral route is activated and they are less likely to carefully consider the content of the persuasive message. As a result, source characteristics will probably have more influence on attitude changes in uninvolved recipients than will the content of the source's message.

Research Highlight

The More Persuadable Sex?

One consistent finding in the literature on persuasive messages is that women are more persuadable than are men (Cooper, 1979; Eagly, 1978). Some researchers have proposed that this difference exists because females are socialized to be cooperative and nonassertive and are therefore less resistant than males to attempts to influence them (Eagly, Wood, and Fishbaugh, 1981). A 1971 study by Sistrunk and McDavid suggested another explanation. Sistrunk and McDavid found that women were more easily influenced than men only when the topic of interest was one with which men were more familiar. When the topic was female oriented, men were more influenced than were women. This finding led many researchers to propose that the consistent difference found in persuadability had been due to a methodological bias—the persuasive messages used in attitude research had typically concerned male-oriented topics. Had the topics not been sex biased, the male-female differences would not have been found.

In a 1981 article, Alice Eagly and Linda Carli set out to determine if this explanation were correct. They obtained a representative sample of the topics used in prior studies and asked males and females to rate their levels of interest in them. They found that females were no less interested in the topics than were men. Eagly and Carli suggested that the sex bias of a topic may affect its power to influence, but they also concluded that sex-bias in topics cannot explain the findings that women are more easily influenced than men.

Another analysis conducted by Eagly and Carli suggested a surprising reason for the consistent finding that women are easily influenced. These researchers looked at a large number of research articles and recorded the sex of the person who had published the article and whether or not sex differences in persuadability had been found. Male researchers had found significantly more persuadability among women than had female researchers. Eagly and Carli proposed that researchers of both sexes may have been unintentionally biased toward their own sex when they had designed their studies and reported their results. And since two-thirds of these researchers were male, this has produced a preponderance of findings which show that women are more easily persuaded than men.

SUMMARY _____

There are two general ways to change people's attitudes: present them with a persuasive message (a speech or an advertisement) intended to influence their attitudes, and get them to engage in behaviors that will produce changes in their attitudes. Two aspects of persuasive messages that have attracted research attention are the characteristics of the person who presents the message and the content of the messages.

One source characteristic is source credibility, which has two components: expertise or knowledge of the matter at hand, and trustworthiness or absence of ulterior motives for presenting a certain position on an issue. Attitude change is considerably more likely when either or both of these components are present. The original explanation of the effect of source credibility was based on learning theory. It has more recently been proposed that source characteristics may affect the manner in which recipients of a message process the information contained in it.

The attractiveness and likableness of sources and their similarity to the recipients of a persuasive message are also characteristics that affect attitude change. Attractive, likable sources are usually more effective than unattractive, dislikable sources, especially if this characteristic is made salient to recipients. The effects of source similarity appear to depend on the content of the persuasive message.

Attitude change also depends greatly on the content of a persuasive message and on the interaction between the content of the message and the characteristics of the recipients. One message characteristic is the amount of change it advocates. Research suggests that, up to a certain point, the more distant a message is from a recipient's own position, the more change will occur. Beyond that point, increases in the distance from the recipient's own position result in decreases in attitude change. According to social judgment theory, this occurs because persuasive messages advocating positions that are different from recipients' own positions but that are judged acceptable are seen as closer to recipients' own positions than they actually are. Messages advocating positions that are unacceptable to recipients are seen as more different than they actually are.

Sometimes one-sided messages are more effective than two-sided messages, and sometimes they are not. When recipients of a message are not in sympathy with the source's position or are well informed on the topic of the message, two-sided messages are usually more effective. Two-sided messages may also immunize the recipients against subsequent attempts to change these newly acquired attitudes.

Current research suggests that fear-arousing messages will be effective only if the consequences of following and not following the recommendations contained in the message are very clearly specified.

When the issue addressed in a message is not very important to recipients, they tend not to think about the message's content and instead attend to the characteristics of the source. When, however, the issue is important to recipients, they more carefully and thoughtfully evaluate a message's content and tend not to think about the source.

ACTIVE PARTICIPATION

At about the time that Carl Hovland and his associates were studying attitude change for the United States Army, another psychologist was studying attitude change for a civilian government agency. He was Kurt Lewin, the Gestalt psychologist and originator of field theory. The need to feed the thousands of soldiers involved in the war effort had created serious shortages of certain kinds of food for the civilian population. For example, it was difficult to find steak or roast beef. One solution to this problem was to persuade homemakers to serve other nutritious cuts of beef to their families. But there was a serious obstacle to overcome before this could be accomplished: other cuts of beef were not very appetizing. Homemakers were not thrilled at the prospect of serving beef hearts, kidneys, or sweetbreads (thymuses). Lewin's task was to change homemakers' attitudes toward these foods.

In the 1940s, Kurt Lewin studied the effects of active participation on attitude change by having homemakers engage in group discussions of how to get other homemakers to serve certain foods to their families.

Because of his theoretical orientation to social behavior, Lewin did not believe persuasive messages would be the most effective way to change attitudes. He believed that attitude change could be best achieved if the recipients were actively involved in the change process. To test this idea, Lewin (1943) gave one group of homemakers a persuasive lecture on the benefits of serving beef hearts and other meat specialties to their families. Another group of homemakers were asked to participate in a discussion of how people like themselves could be induced to serve such foods to their families. A week later, Lewin determined how many of his subjects had actually served these foods to their families. Only 3 percent of the people in the persuasive-message condition had served the new foods to their families, but 32 percent of the people in the discussion condition had done so.

Lewin's work in the 1940s provided much of the theoretical impetus for later research on active participation, but he was not the first person to propose that active participation is an effective means of producing change. Approximately 70 years earlier, Freud had argued that psychotherapy in which a patient is actively involved in the change process produces more positive results than psychotherapy in which a therapist lectures on the cause and cure of the patient's problems (McGuire, 1969).

The idea that actively involving people in the attitude change process might be more effective than presenting a persuasive communication did not bother learning or incentive theorists like Hovland and his associates. They had also found that in certain circumstances, active involvement produces more attitude change than a persuasive message. Irving Janis, one of Hovland's early collaborators (Janis and King, 1954), had conducted an experiment that examined the effects of **role playing.** In the role-playing condition of this experiment, subjects were asked to give speeches that advocated a position different from their own. In the persuasive-communication condition, the subjects listened to a speech that advocated a position different from their own. Giving the speech (playing a role) produced significantly more attitude change. In a later article, Janis (1968) proposed that role playing induces attitude change because people learn the position they are advocating in the role play. He also suggested that the more motivated people are to learn, the greater their attitude change. One way to increase people's motivations is to offer them an incentive for their active participation (Insko, 1967). It follows from this point of view that the larger the incentive, the greater the learning and, thus, the greater the attitude change.

In the prologue the subjects engaged in a form of role playing called **counterattitudinal advocacy.** Festinger and Carlsmith (1959) found more attitude change among subjects who received $1.00 for engaging in counterattitudinal advocacy than among subjects who received $20.00 for the same action. The less the incentive for the behavior, the greater the attitude change. This result would be surprising to a learning theorist, but it did not surprise Festinger and Carlsmith. To understand why, we must turn to Festinger's (1957) theory of **cognitive dissonance.**

Role playing: an activity in which a person assumes a particular position and acts in a manner consistent with that position.

Counterattitudinal advocacy: the public expression of an attitude that is counter to a person's true, private attitude.

Cognitive dissonance: a negative drive state which occurs whenever a person simultaneously holds two or more cognitions that are psychologically inconsistent.

Theory of Cognitive Dissonance

You may be better able to understand the theory of cognitive dissonance if you know a little about the person who proposed it and the ideas that influenced him. Leon Festinger was a student of Kurt Lewin and was influenced by the gestalt approach to psychology. Festinger believed that humans are active processors and organizers of the information they receive from the world around them and of the cognitions (attitudes, beliefs, ideas, opinions) they have about the world. He proposed that one principle that guides the organization of people's cognitions is **consistency.** Festinger argued that people prefer that their different cognitions fit together in a logical manner; that one cognition follow from or be logically consistent with another. Most people would be uncomfortable, for example, if the cognition "I don't believe in God" coexisted with the cognition "I believe I should attend church every week." This is not the first time you have encountered the proposal that humans strive to make their cognitions consistent. Heider's balance theory explanation of interpersonal attraction presented similar ideas. (See chapter six.)

According to Festinger (1980), the specific event that led him from these general ideas to the theory of cognitive dissonance was reading an article on the rumors that occurred after a devastating earthquake in India. Festinger was intrigued to learn that among the people who were *outside* the area of destruction there was a rash of rumors predicting catastrophic events in the future. Why, wondered Festinger, would people spread and believe stories that frightened them? He proposed that these people who had not been injured by the earthquake had been quite frightened by it, and that they needed some way to justify the fear they felt. The rumors provided this justification.

Festinger proposed that people will change their ideas to make them consistent with what they are feeling or with how they are acting (Festinger, 1980). This is the basic premise of the theory of cognitive dissonance.

Causes and Consequences of Cognitive Dissonance

People will experience cognitive dissonance if they simultaneously hold two or more cognitions (attitudes, beliefs, ideas, opinions, thoughts) that are psychologically inconsistent (Aronson, 1969). The amount of dissonance people experience increases as the importance and number of inconsistent cognitions increases. Dissonance may result when a person has made a choice between two desirable alternatives. In such a situation, cognition one (I have chosen alternative A) is psychologically inconsistent with cognition two (I find alternative B very desirable). If alternative A is a steak dinner and alternative B is a roast beef dinner, there will not be much dissonance. A decision about what food you have for dinner is not all that important. But if alternative A is attending law school and alternative B is attending medical school, there will be considerable dissonance.

According to Festinger (1957), the immediate consequence of cognitive dissonance is physiological arousal of the type people experience when

Consistency: the state which exists when a person's cognitions logically or psychologically fit together.

they are hungry or thirsty. Dissonance is like a negative drive; people are motivated to reduce or eliminate it. Although this is a very important aspect of this theory, empirical evidence that dissonance causes arousal has only recently emerged.

To explain how this evidence was obtained, it is necessary to describe a procedure for creating dissonance that is similar to the procedure used by Festinger and Carlsmith in the prologue. If a person *freely chooses* to engage in a public behavior that is inconsistent with her true attitude—to engage in counterattitudinal advocacy—dissonance is often engendered. In such situations, one cognition (I did X) is psychologically inconsistent with another cognition (I believe Y). However, if a person is *forced* to engage in counterattitudinal advocacy, there will be no dissonance. Why? Because a third cognition (I was forced to do X) explains why the behavior did not match the attitude.

Croyle and Cooper (1983) divided subjects into three groups. Subjects in the first group were asked to publicly present a position with which they did not agree—that alcohol should be banned from their college's campus. It was made clear to these subjects that they could refuse to do this if they so desired. Subjects in the second group were asked to present the same position, but were not given the choice of refusing. Subjects in the third group were asked to present a position with which they agreed— that alcohol should not be banned from their college's campus. Only members of the first group freely chose to engage in counterattitudinal advocacy, so only they should have experienced cognitive dissonance. While members of all three groups were presenting their positions, Croyle and Cooper measured their physiological arousal. (See figure 10-6.) The subjects in the first (dissonance) group showed significantly more physiological arousal than did members of the other two groups. When there is a psychological inconsistency between people's attitudes and their behavior (cognitive dissonance), they become physiologically aroused.

Reduction of Cognitive Dissonance

When people experience dissonance, they attempt to find a justification or rationalization for the psychological inconsistency between their cognitions. For example, the subjects in the experiment presented in the prologue who received $20.00 to say that a boring experiment was interesting had received a large amount of money for their inconsistent performance. This provided them with a ready explanation of why their attitudes toward the tasks were inconsistent with their behavior.

But consider the subjects who received $1.00 for the same behavior. This paltry sum did not provide sufficient justification for their actions. Theoretically, these subjects were left in dissonance. However, they could reduce the dissonance by changing their attitudes toward the experiment. If they could convince themselves that the experiment was in fact interesting, there would be no dissonance. This is what the subjects in the $1.00 condition appear to have done.

In general, if people can be induced to engage in a public behavior that is inconsistent with their private attitude *and* if they have insufficient

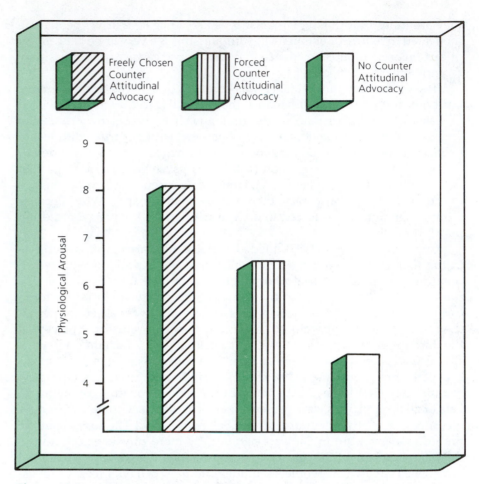

Figure 10-6. *Subjects who freely chose to express an attitude counter to their true feelings showed the most physiological arousal.*
Source: Croyle and Cooper (1983).

justification for the inconsistent behavior, dissonance will occur. People will resolve this dissonance by changing their attitudes to match the behavior.

Cognitive Dissonance and Attitude Change
Wait a minute. Humans are constantly bombarded with attempts to change their attitudes. Has anyone ever used the specific procedures just discussed to change your attitudes? Probably not. But the *principles* of cognitive dissonance probably have been responsible for many changes in your attitudes.

People need a reason for engaging in any specific behavior. If the behavior itself is adequately rewarding or if it produces adequate rewards, there is a reason for the behavior. As a result, there is no cognitive dissonance and no need to justify the behavior. If, on the other hand, the behavior itself is inadequately rewarding or it produces inadequate re-wards, there is no obvious reason for the behavior. As a result, there is cognitive dissonance and a need to justify the behavior. One way to justify the behavior is to change one's attitudes to match it.

The following true story illustrates this principle. Chris Boyce and Daulton Lee were two young men from a wealthy, conservative suburban area in California. Their fathers were wealthy businessmen. Boyce's father had been a Federal Bureau of Investigation agent and was director of se-curity for a large aircraft manufacturer; Lee's father was a successful phy-sician. Their families were devoutly religious, and both Boyce and Lee had been altar boys at a Catholic church. After high school graduation, Lee enrolled in a local junior college and Boyce, through his father's contacts, obtained a job with a company that did top secret work for the Central Intelligence Agency. To the outsider, their lives were a model of upper-middle-class America.

But there was a sinister side to Boyce's and Lee's lives in the late 1970s. For almost two years, Boyce stole top secret documents from the company he worked for and gave them to Lee, who sold them to Soviet agents. Lee was supposed to split the money he received with Boyce, but he kept most of it for himself. Eventually, Lee's greed and lack of judgment led to his and Boyce's arrests for espionage. The damage the two young men did to America's security may never be fully known. The documents they gave to the Soviets were so sensitive that even the jurors at their trial were not allowed to see them.

Both men engaged in essentially the same behavior; they betrayed their country. What impact did this have on their attitudes? Lee had been ad-equately compensated for his efforts. Thus, dissonance theory would pre-dict that he had no need to justify his behavior by changing his attitudes to fit his actions. This prediction is supported by the following passage from a letter Lee wrote to a friend while awaiting trial.

> The government we've got now—mealy mouthed . . . socialists are leading capitalism and free enterprise to the grave. Our country is beseiged by . . . politicians pushing socialistic measures to acquire votes . . . To hell with socialism, long live free enterprise and capital-ism. I will not equivocate. (Lindsey, 1979, p. 330)

Unlike Lee, Boyce had received little money for his efforts. Dissonance theory would predict that he must justify his behavior, and a reasonable way to do this would be through attitude change. Here is an excerpt from a letter Boyce wrote while he was in jail:

> When I was twenty-one and not so very wise, I considered American society and government degenerate . . . I would be misrepresenting myself were I not to state that my disillusionment now is greater than ever. (Lindsey, 1979, p. 446)

Thus far, dissonance theory has been used only to explain the effects of engaging in attitude-discrepant behavior. It can also be used to explain a more common phenomenon. In many instances, people engage in a behavior because they believe that this behavior will produce a reward for them. For example, if a college student goes through a strenuous initiation ceremony to join a sorority she thinks she likes, her behavior is consistent with her attitude. But what if, after she is admitted to membership, she discovers that most of the sorority's members are boring? (They were carefully hidden in closets until the initiation was over.) The student should be in dissonance; cognition one (I worked hard to join Alpha Beta Gamma) does not match cognition two (the members of Alpha Beta Gamma are boring). Since the student cannot retract her behavior, she must find another way to reduce her dissonance. One way to do this is to change her perceptions of the members of Alpha Beta Gamma. If she decides that the members of the sorority are really quite interesting, she can justify her initiation and reduce her dissonance.

A study by Gerard and Mathewson (1966) demonstrated that people do use this means of dissonance reduction. Gerard and Mathewson systematically manipulated the difficulty of an initiation into an informal discussion group. Objectively, the discussions the subjects were trying to participate in were quite boring. The more difficult the initiation, however, the more the subjects liked the group.

Research Highlight

Working Off the Pounds

Joel Cooper (1980) has proposed that the principle of justification of effort can be used to improve the effectiveness of certain kinds of treatment programs. Cooper and Axsom (1982) tested this proposal with subjects who were overweight females interested in losing weight. They were supposedly recruited to be part of a newly developed program for weight reduction, but the procedures used in this program had actually been designed to create cognitive dissonance.

The first variable studied was choice. Half the subjects were given the choice of refusing to participate in the program; the other half were not given this choice. The second variable was the amount of effort expended by the program participants. Subjects were told prior research had shown that increases in a person's perceptual sensitivity lead to weight loss; thus, they would engage in exercises that would increase their perceptual sensitivities. In fact, this had never been found, and the exercises were tasks in visual and auditory perception. Half the subjects in the choice group and half in the no-choice group were given tasks that required considerable effort. The other half of the subjects in each group were given tasks that required little effort. The dependent measure was the amount of weight subjects lost.

Cooper and Axsom predicted the greatest weight loss among subjects in the free-choice, high-effort group because they felt that these subjects would have the greatest need to justify their participation in the program. The following figure shows the average weight loss in each of the four conditions of the experiment six months after the program was completed. On the average, women in the free-choice, high-effort group had lost 9.75 pounds. In contrast, women in the groups that should have produced the least dissonance (the low-choice groups) had lost little weight.

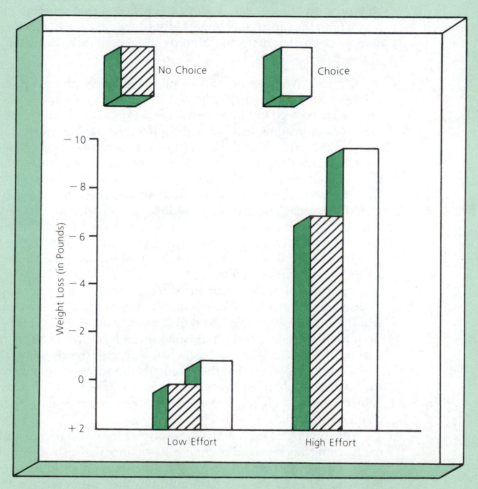

The women who freely chose to engage in the program and exerted high effort lost the most weight.
Source: Cooper and Axsom (1982).

Limitations of Cognitive Dissonance Theory

From what has been presented in the last few pages, one could get the impression that the theory of cognitive dissonance has enjoyed a privileged existence in social psychology—that unlike most other theories, it has never been questioned. Nothing could be further from the truth. From the time Festinger published his first book on cognitive dissonance theory in 1957 until today, it has been criticized and challenged. Much of the criticism has had merit and has produced changes and refinements in the theory. For example, in the original formulation of cognitive dissonance, it was implicitly assumed that a discrepancy between two cognitions would invariably produce dissonance. Today, it is believed that whether or not dissonance (and thus attitude change) occurs depends on other factors, including choice, commitment to the attitude-discrepant behavior, and impact on others.

Choice   Whether or not people have freely chosen to engage in a behavior influences whether they will experience cognitive dissonance. If people are coerced or forced into some action, they usually experience little dissonance. Imagine that you were a feminist, taking a speech class in the fall of 1984, when Geraldine Ferraro was a candidate for vice-president. Your instructor assigned you the task of presenting a speech proposing that women are physically unfit to be a president or vice-president of the United States. You strongly opposed this position, and said you would not give the speech. The instructor said that if you refused, you would fail the course. Not being a total fool, you gave the speech. Was any dissonance created? Probably not; the instructor's insistence that you give the speech provided an explanation, or justification, of the discrepancy between your attitude and your behavior.

In a study of when dissonance theory does and does not apply, Linder, Cooper, and Jones (1967) systematically manipulated two variables: (1) whether or not subjects could refuse to write an essay that was discrepant from their attitudes, and (2) the amount of incentive subjects received for writing this essay. When subjects had a choice, the results almost exactly matched those obtained in the prologue: the smaller the reward, the more their attitudes changed toward the position taken in the essay. But when subjects had no choice, the larger the reward, the more their attitudes changed. (See figure 10-7.)

This finding at least partially resolves a long-running dispute between the learning theorists and cognitive dissonance theorists. Learning theorists also believed that when people publicly state an attitude or engage in a behavior that reflects a certain attitude, they often change their private attitudes in the direction of that public action (Petty and Cacioppo, 1981). But learning theorists proposed that the larger the reward given for public behavior, the greater the attitude change. Linder and associates showed that both positions have merit. Under some conditions, people change their attitudes because of the incentives offered for adopting an attitude-discrepant behavior. Under other conditions, people change their attitudes because of a need to justify engaging in an attitude-discrepant behavior.

Commitment to Attitude-Discrepant Behavior   Initially, cognitive dissonance theory did not consider how committed a person was to the attitude-discrepant behavior. For example, it did not distinguish between a

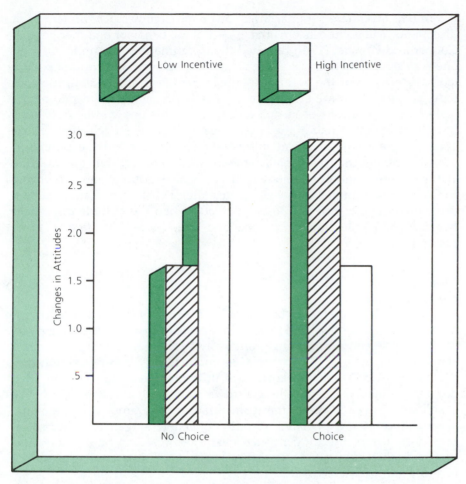

Figure 10-7. *In the no choice condition, the greater the reward the greater the attitude change; the opposite was true in the choice condition.*
Source: Linder et al. (1967).

feminist who agreed to give an antifemale speech and one who actually gave such a speech. If both had been given the choice of refusing, both would be in dissonance and both would change their attitudes to fit their behavior.

Subsequent research (for example, Brehm and Cohen, 1962; Davis and Jones, 1960) showed that only the woman who actually gave the speech would be likely to change her attitudes. If people merely think about or agree to perform an attitude-discrepant behavior, they can easily resolve any dissonance by simply saying to themselves, I didn't really intend to perform the behavior. Thus, they have no need to change their attitudes. But if they actually perform the behavior in front of others, they are committed to the behavior. Others have seen them and they cannot deny it. As a result, they must find another way to resolve their dissonance. The best way to do this is to change their attitudes.

Impact on Others   A final limitation on the circumstances under which dissonance will occur concerns the impact of the behavior on other people. Cooper and Worchel (1970) repeated the experiment in the prologue with one very significant addition. When half of the subjects told another person (a confederate) that the boring experiment had been interesting, the confederate said, "You are entitled to your opinion, but every experiment I have ever been in has been dull and I expect this one will be dull too." But when the other half of the subjects gave their sales pitch, the confederate became very excited and enthusiastic about being in the experiment. Dissonance effects (the smaller the reward, the greater the attitude change) were found only among subjects in the second group. According to Cooper and Worchel, this was because their behavior had an impact on someone else and thus had to be justified. When the attitude-discrepant behavior had little impact on someone else, there was little need to justify it.

Current Status of Cognitive Dissonance Theory

Cognitive dissonance theory has had a stormy history in social psychology. Festinger's original ideas had to be refined and sharpened. Dissonance was not as easy to create as Festinger originally believed, and in some circumstances other theories (for example, incentive theory, self-perception theory) may provide a better explanation of attitude change than does cognitive dissonance theory. Despite the controversy, cognitive dissonance theory is still strong over 30 years after it was first formally proposed. It remains a widely accepted explanation of attitude change and many other social behaviors. It has directly generated over 1,000 research publications and will probably continue to be an integral part of social psychological theory (Cooper and Croyle, 1984).

Alternative Explanations of Cognitive Dissonance Effects

Under certain conditions, people will show attitude change that is entirely consistent with the predictions made by the cognitive dissonance theory (Cooper and Croyle, 1984; Petty and Cacioppo, 1981). But some social psychologists have argued that this change is not due to the basic mechanism proposed by dissonance theory—a desire to reduce or eliminate psychological inconsistency. Two alternative explanations of the attitude change produced by insufficient justification are based on self-perception theory and impression management.

Self-perception Theory

In his **self-perception theory,** Daryl Bem basically proposed that people are often called upon to make attributions for their own behavior; they must explain why they acted in a certain way. (See chapter five.) When they do this, they use the same type of information and reach the same kind of conclusions as would any observer asked to make an attribution.

Imagine that you are the confederate in the prologue experiment and you hear a subject describe the experiment as interesting. You know that the subject only received one dollar to do this. As you are about to leave, the experimenter asks to speak with you for a moment. "I was wondering," he says, "if you would be willing to make a guess about the subject's true opinion of the experiment." In essence, he is asking you to make an attribution about why the subject acted as he did. Given that the subject received only one dollar to say the experiment was interesting, the money does not provide a very reasonable explanation of his behavior. A much more reasonable explanation is that the subject did in fact find the experiment interesting.

Bem (1965, 1972) proposed that the subjects in the chapter experiment made similar self-attributions. Bem did not question Festinger and Carlsmith's proposal that in certain circumstances, the smaller the reward for counterattitudinal advocacy, the greater the attitude change. He questioned the cognitive dissonance theory argument that an attempt to reestablish psychological consistency was responsible for such change. Bem's argument, based on self-perception theory, was that subjects looked at their own behavior and made the self-attribution that if they said they liked the experiment, they must have liked it.

Since both theories make the same predictions about the effects of incentives on attitude change through active participation, researchers have had a difficult time determining which of the two has more merit. Fazio, Zanna, and Cooper (1977) and Zanna and Cooper (1974) have proposed that different situations may activate the processes proposed by the self-perception and cognitive dissonance theories. If a behavior is not too unpleasant for people (such as advocating a position that is not their own but is acceptable to them), then an attitude change is due to self-attributions. But if a behavior is unpleasant for people (such as advocating a position that is not acceptable to them), they experience considerable psychological tension and an attitude change is due to cognitive dissonance reduction. Fazio, Zanna, and Cooper obtained data that supported their proposal, but other researchers (for example Bond, 1981) have not. At this point, it is not clear whether self-perception theory or cognitive dissonance theory provides a better explanation of why small rewards for role playing often produce attitude change.

Impression Management
Other researchers (for example, Tedeschi, 1981; Riess, Kalle, and Tedeschi, 1981) have proposed that the change obtained in studies such as the Festinger and Carlsmith study is not true attitude change. They suggest that the subjects in these studies merely reported that their attitudes had changed in order to create the impression that their attitudes were consistent with their behavior. This argument is based on the concept of impression management. (See chapter five.)

Research Highlight

Too Much of a Good Thing?

Self-perception theory may not provide a better explanation of the effects of small rewards on attitude change than does cognitive dissonance theory, but it does provide a good explanation of a related phenomenon—the overjustification effect. A study by Lepper, Greene, and Nisbett (1973) illustrates this effect.

The subjects were nursery school children who liked to draw pictures. They were randomly assigned to one of three groups. In the first group, the experimenter asked the children to draw some pictures and promised them a reward if they did so. In the second group, the children were also asked to draw pictures and were given an unexpected reward after they were done. Children in the third group received no reward for drawing pictures. A few weeks later, the children were placed in a situation where they could draw if they wanted to, and the amount of time they spent drawing was recorded. As the following figure shows, the children who had initially drawn pictures because they were offered a reward spent significantly less time drawing than did those who had received no reward or an unexpected reward. The reward appeared to have undermined their interest in the activity.

Bogart, Loeb, and Rittman (1968) offered psychiatric patients either $8.00 or $2.00 a month to attend therapy sessions. The effect of the $8.00 reward was to increase attendance over what it had been before the reward system was implemented. But when the reward was discontinued, attendance dropped below the prereward level. In the $2.00 reward condition, attendance also increased, but unlike the $8.00 condition it remained at this level even after the reward was withdrawn. Again, the large reward appeared to undermine interest in the activity.

Self-perception theory would propose that in both experiments, the effects were due to after-the-fact attributions made by subjects in the large-reward conditions. For example, when the large reward was discontinued, the psychiatric patients may have asked themselves, Should I continue to attend the sessions? and Why am I attending the sessions? They may have looked at their behavior and concluded that they were attending not because they enjoyed the sessions or were being helped by them, but because they wanted the reward. When the reward stopped, they had no reason to continue.

The overjustification effect has certain implications for educational practices. Teachers often use external reinforcers to motivate students to engage in certain learning activities. If these external reinforcers actually undermine the students' intrinsic interests in those activities, the reinforcers are, in the long run, counterproductive. Greene, Sternberg, and Lepper (1976) found that rewards increased students' willingness to work on math problems as long as the rewards were in effect. But when the rewards were discontinued, the students were less interested in math than were students who had never been rewarded.

More recent research (Boggiano and Ruble, 1979; Deci and Ryan, 1980) has suggested that rewards will not invariably reduce intrinsic interest in an activity. If a reward is administered in such a way that it is seen as a reward for competent

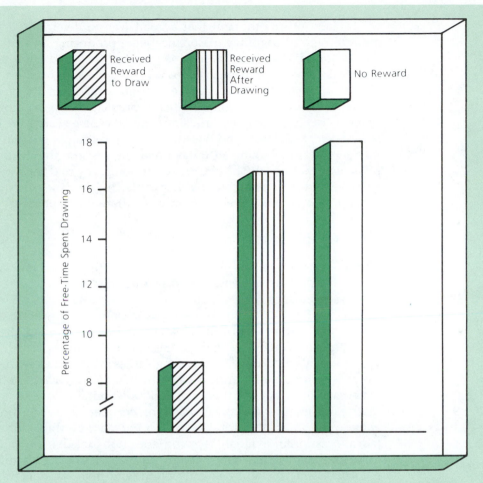

Children who were given a reward as an incentive to draw spent less time on this activity than did children who were later given a reward or received no reward.
Source: Lepper et al. (1973).

performance rather than as a means of controlling a student's behavior, rewards are an effective educational technique.

There is little question that people are concerned about the impressions they present to others, but most researchers doubt that impression management is the only reason attitude change is obtained in the typical study on counterattitudinal advocacy (Cialdini, Petty, and Cacioppo, 1981; Cooper and Croyle, 1984). Probably both cognitive dissonance reduction and impression management are at work when people receive a small incentive for advocating a position counter to their own.

Initially, it was thought that a good way to determine if impression management or cognitive dissonance were producing an attitude change was to measure subjects' arousal levels after they had engaged in an attitude-discrepant behavior. If there was no arousal but there was attitude change, then impression management probably was the cause of the change. (Remember, dissonance theory predicts that psychological inconsistency is physiologically arousing). But recent research on impression management (Tedeschi and Rosenfeld, 1981) has suggested that when people feel they are making an unfavorable impression, they will experience physiological arousal. The two explanations of why role playing sometimes produces attitude change differ very little. Indeed, they may merely describe the same phenomenon from two different perspectives.

Value Confrontation Procedure

Milton Rokeach's value confrontation procedure is based on his belief that people's values are closely related to their self-concept, since values are used as standards for evaluating oneself (Rokeach, 1973). The attitudes people hold are an expression of the importance they place on certain values. If people's values could be changed, Rokeach argued, their attitudes and behavior would also change. (See chapter nine.)

Rokeach's procedure for changing values incorporates elements of both the persuasive message and active participation approaches. People receive a message that suggests there is a contradiction or inconsistency between their self-concepts and their values or between their self-concept, their values, and their attitudes. Consider a person who thinks of herself as a fair and caring individual, but who does not consider the value equality to be important. If it is suggested to her that a lack of concern for equality is inconsistent with this self-conception, and if she accepts this message, then something must change. As dissonance theory proposes, she cannot tolerate inconsistencies between her cognitions. Since it is easier to change her values than to change her self-concept, she will probably decide that the value equality is, after all, important to her.

Rokeach's way of creating an inconsistency is quite different from that proposed by cognitive dissonance theorists, who induce an inconsistency by getting people to engage in a behavior that is not in accord with their cognitions. Rokeach created inconsistency by pointing out contradictions that already existed among central cognitions such as values.

In a 1971 study, Rokeach investigated whether (a) values could be changed in this way and (b) changes in values would affect people's attitudes and behavior. The subjects were university students divided into an experimental and a control group. Members of the control group ranked their values in order of importance to themselves and received a short lecture on the nature of values. Members of the experimental group received a procedure designed to change their values. After the subjects had ranked their values, the experimenter presented them with actual value rankings from other students at the same university. He drew attention to the fact that these students considered the value freedom to be much more important than the value equality. He suggested that these students "are much more concerned in their own freedom than they are in freedom for other people" (Rokeach, 1973, p. 237). He then invited the subjects to compare their own value rankings with these data. The purpose of this was to arouse a state of dissatisfaction about a contradiction between self-conceptions and values.

Then subjects were asked to indicate their attitudes toward civil rights for blacks and were shown actual data that indicated people with unfavorable attitudes toward civil rights considered freedom to be much more important than equality. The experimenter concluded this presentation by proposing that perhaps people who oppose civil rights are really saying "that they care a great deal about *their own* freedom but are indifferent to other people's freedom" (Rokeach, 1973, p. 238). The purpose of this was to arouse a state of dissatisfaction about a contradiction between self-conceptions, values, and attitudes.

Rokeach found that among members of the experimental group, the value equality received a significantly higher ranking three weeks, three months, and 15 months after the message had been presented. A similar change was found for the subjects' attitudes toward civil rights. When these were measured three and 15 months later, they had become significantly more positive. No such changes were found among the control subjects.

Rokeach's most impressive findings concerned long-term differences in the behavior of the two groups. Researchers often have difficulty finding behavior change as the result of attitude change (Calder and Ross, 1973). To determine if this procedure also produced behavior change, Rokeach devised the following procedure. Several months after the subjects had ranked their values, members of both the experimental group and the control group received a membership request from an organization that supported civil rights for black Americans. To join, the person would have to pay $1.00 and volunteer to work for the organization. About three times as many subjects in the experimental group as in the control group joined the organization.

In Rokeach's original study, the subjects were in the same room as the person who spoke about their values. Recently, Rokeach and his colleagues have investigated whether the value confrontation procedure can by presented effectively through the mass media (Ball-Rokeach, Rokeach, and Grube, 1984). Actor Ed Asner (he played Lou Grant in the television series of the same name) volunteered to make a half-hour television program which presented the value confrontation procedure. This program aired on television stations in three small communities in the state of Washington. Ball-Rokeach and her associates compared the values and behavior of people who watched the entire program to the values and behavior of those who did not. People who watched the entire show reported significant increases in the importance they placed on the value equality; people who did not watch the entire show did not. Some time later, subjects in both groups were given a chance to contribute to a black support group; people who watched the entire show contributed about five times as much money.

The effects of the value confrontation procedure do not appear limited to attitudes and behavior toward civil rights. Greenstein (1976) used discrepancies between values and self-concept to change the behavior of students training to be teachers. Conroy, Katkin, and Barnette (1973) attempted to reduce smoking by using the value confrontation procedure. Their subjects were smokers randomly assigned to an experimental group and a control group. Members of the control group received a fear-arousing message about the dangers of smoking. Members of the experimental group received this message plus a message that suggested continued smoking might be inconsistent with their values and self-concept. (See figure 10-8 for the effects of these messages on smoking.)

Initially, both the fear-arousing message and the value confrontation procedure reduced smoking. But after 16 days, members of the control group were smoking 14 cigarettes per day, while members of the experimental group were smoking less than two.

Rokeach's procedure has been questioned by some theorists (for example, Cook and Flay, 1978), but it remains an intriguing approach to attitude and behavior change. However, the procedure does not automatically produce value, attitude, and behavior change. Carl Hovland and his associates pointed out, a persuasive message will produce attitude change only if the recipients attend to, comprehend, and accept the contents of the message. Rokeach (1973, 1979) recognized this when he observed that the value confrontation procedure will be effective only for people who accept the message and feel dissatisfied with their values, and that many people reject messages about inconsistencies in their values. Thus, the procedure may work only with people who are receptive to new ideas and willing to change their values and behavior. It remains for future research to further explore the utility of Rokeach's value confrontation procedure.

Attitude Change and Behavior Change

An impressive amount of theoretical and empirical work has been done on attitude change. The logic underlying these efforts is that attitudes cause behavior and, thus, if we can change people's attitudes we can change their behavior. However, often attitudes do not accurately predict behavior; in most instances, no more than 9 to 10 percent of the differences in people's behavior can be predicted from differences in their attitudes. (See chapter nine.) As a result, it is often difficult to find a strong relationship between attitude change and behavior change. Part of the resolution of this problem lies in the application of the theoretical and methodological remedies for the low correlation between attitudes and behavior. (See chapter nine.) But even if researchers correctly conceptualized attitudes and behavior and committed no methodological errors in their measurements, they might still find a weak relationship between attitude change and behavior change. Calder and Ross (1973) suggested three reasons for this: the attitude change may not persist, the individual may be too committed to the existing behavior, or the individual may fear the consequences of the behavior change.

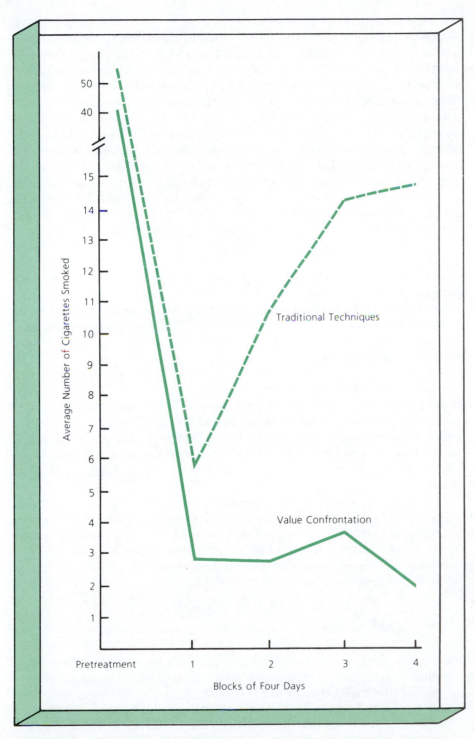

Figure 10-8. *The value confrontation procedure was more effective in reducing smoking than traditional techniques.*
Source: Conroy et al. (1973)

Attitude Change May Not Persist

A persuasive message delivered by a credible source may produce considerable short-term attitude change, but this attitude change may not last long (Cook and Flay, 1978). If a persons's attitudes quickly revert to what they were originally, there is little chance that there will be behavior change. Several ways to produce longer-lasting attitude change have been proposed. Rokeach believed that attitude change will persist if it is preceded by value change. Festinger (1964) has suggested that the key to long-term attitude change lies in providing recipients with environmental support for their new attitudes. For example, recipients must be brought into contact with people who will share and reinforce their new attitudes. Groups such as Alcoholics Anonymous (AA) recognize this fact. Part of AA's treatment program for alcoholics trying to quit drinking is to have them meet at least weekly with other people who have given up drinking.

Commitment to Existing Behavior

Greenwald (1966) has proposed that people may be so committed to their behavior that even though their attitudes change, their behavior does not. For example, as the product of persuasive appeals, someone who does not exercise may come to have positive feelings about exercise, but she may be unable or unwilling to engage in the behavior. Attitude change may simply be easier than behavior change.

Consequences of Behavior Change

If people so desire, they can change their attitudes and not let anyone know this change has occurred. Attitude change is a hidden, covert process, unless people desire to share it with others. Behavior change, on the other hand, is an overt process. If there are situational pressures to maintain old behavior, these pressures may result in attitude change without behavior change.

For example, when I was an adolescent, my attitudes toward organized religion and God became very negative. But I continued to attend religious services and to celebrate religious holidays. Why? Because my parents and most of my friends were quite religious. I feared that if I changed my behavior, my parents would punish me and my friends would reject me. My attitudes had changed, but not my behavior.

SUMMARY

People often change their attitudes to match their public actions. The theory of cognitive dissonance proposes that this is because people desire that their behavior and their attitudes be consistent unless there is some good reason for a discrepancy. Cognitive dissonance theorists have provided support for this proposal by showing that if a public behavior that is inconsistent with private attitudes is inadequately rewarded, people will change their attitudes to match the behavior. If such a behavior is adequately rewarded, people do not change their attitudes.

A large number of studies have found that inadequate rewards do produce attitude change. However, this effect will only occur when people freely choose to engage in the behavior, cannot retract the behavior or diminish the behavior's importance, and when the behavior affects others. If these conditions are not present, the greater the reward for the behavior, the greater the attitude change.

Some theorists have offered alternative explanations of why small rewards for active participation often lead to attitude change. Self-perception theory proposes that attitude change is not due to a desire to justify one's actions, but to self-attributions people make about the causes of their behavior. The impression management explanation of the effects of small rewards is that they do not produce true attitude change, but that people simply report their attitudes as consistent with their behavior in order to appear logical and consistent to others.

The value confrontation procedure contains elements of both the persuasive message and the active participation approaches to attitude change. A source presents a message that proposes there are inconsistencies between people's values and their self-concept or between their values, their self-concept, and their attitudes. Acceptance of this message can lead to value change and resultant attitude change and behavior change.

All of these procedures can produce behavior change as well as attitude change, but it is more common that attitude change is not accompanied by behavior change.

Applications

*Beyond the Laboratory: Influencing
Attitudes and Behaviors*

To some people, theory and research on attitude change may seem far removed from the everyday kinds of persuasion around them, but this view is not shared by professionals who are responsible for attempts to change attitudes. Many of the advertisements you read and commercials you see were developed on the basis of the principles presented in this chapter. The first part of this section examines how one theory of persuasive message effectiveness can be used in the design of advertising. The second part of this section considers applications of theory and research on attitude change from a somewhat different perspective. It examines the effectiveness of antismoking campaigns and considers why some of these campaigns work and some do not.

RESEARCH ON ADVERTISING EFFECTIVENESS

In the first section of this chapter, it was noted that, each day the typical American is exposed to at least 1500 persuasive messages in the form of advertisements. The amount of broadcast (radio or television) and print (newspaper or magazine) advertising is greater than it has ever been, although advertising is not an invention of the twentieth century. Five thousand years ago, Babylonian rulers advertised their civic accomplishments by having their names placed on the buildings they constructed. The Rosetta stone, found during the eighteenth century, is credited by archaeologists as providing the key to deciphering Egyptian hieroglyphics. This ancient tablet was, in fact, an advertisement for a ruler of Egypt (Ulanoff, 1977).

The first real explosion in advertising occurred shortly after Guttenberg invented the printing press to produce books. Within thirty years of its invention, the printing press was being used to produce advertisements for books that were not selling well. The first true newspaper, published in 1665, refused to accept advertisements because they were not "properly the business of a Paper of Intelligence" (cited in Ulanoff, 1977), but other newspapers were quite willing to do so, and the amount of advertising available to the public grew rapidly.

In the early 1920s, radio began to supplant newspapers as a mass conveyer of information. And in the mid-1950s, television became the primary broadcast medium. Accompanying the growth of these media was a growth in the amount of advertising presented to the public.

In the United States, people are constantly bombarded by advertisements. Over 26 billion dollars is spent on advertising each year.

It is difficult to obtain a precise estimate of the amount spent in the United States on all forms of advertising, but the Bureau of the Census has put the annual figure at 26 billion dollars, or two percent of the gross national product (Pope, 1983). Advertising can be used to educate, inform, or persuade. Theory and research on attitude change is most applicable to advertising that is intended to persuade people. The kind of persuasive advertising considered here is that which uses a persuasive message to convince people to purchase a product.

Persuasive Messages

When Hovland and his associates (Hovland et al., 1953) began their pioneering work on persuasive messages, they used principles of learning theory to explain why certain factors produced attitude change. The effectiveness of a persuasive message depended upon how well a recipient comprehended and learned its content. More recent theories of attitude change have taken a somewhat different approach. Theorists such as Eagly and Chaiken (1984) and others (for example, Greenwald, 1968; Petty and

Cacioppo (1985); Petty, Ostrom, and Brock, 1981; Weiss, 1968) have proposed that the learning of a message may be less important than the kind of thoughts it evokes in the recipient. The goal of a persuasive message, therefore, should be to get a recipient to develop thoughts that are conducive to attitude change. This point of view has gained acceptance among people interested in advertising effectiveness (Kassarjian, 1982; Wright, 1980, 1981).

Thinking about Advertisements

Woodside (1983) investigated how thinking about an advertisement might be related to its effectiveness. The subjects were 60 women with an interest in gardening. They were visited in their homes and presented with several magazine pages, including some articles and advertisements. The crucial advertisement was one for a flower seed. The ad discussed the benefits of this particular product and contained an offer of free samples.

The women were asked to read the material and to tell the interviewer any thoughts they had about it. No restrictions were placed on the kind of thoughts they had or when they reported them. The women's verbalizations were tape-recorded, and later judges counted the number of thoughts each woman had had about the advertisement for the flower seed.

Some of the women reported no thoughts about the ad (remember, it was embedded in other material), and some of the women reported a number of thoughts about the ad. Woodside compared these two groups of women on their attitudes toward the product and their intentions to respond to the free offer. Women who had reported thoughts about the ad had significantly more positive attitudes toward the product and were significantly more likely to send for the materials offered than were the women who had not thought about the ad. Also, at the end of the interview, the women were offered 10 dollars worth of products as compensation for their help. Among these were products from the seed company. Women in the thoughts group were more likely to select these products than were women in the no-thoughts group.

This finding suggests that advertisers may want to consider ways to get people to think about their advertisements. Several studies have examined different ways to achieve this end.

Central and Peripheral Routes

As discussed earlier, Petty and Cacioppo's theory of central and peripheral routes to attitude change proposes that under some circumstances, attitude change occurs through a central route; the person carefully considers and thinks about the content of the persuasive message. But under other circumstances, the change occurs through a peripheral route; the person thinks little about the message's content and instead is influenced by source characteristics or by the rewards offered for a change. Petty and Cacioppo believed the extent to which a person is personally involved with the topic of the message plays an important role in whether a central or peripheral route is activated. Attitude change through a central route is likely to occur if the person is involved; attitude change through a peripheral route is likely to occur if the person is uninvolved. In a 1983 article, Petty, Cacioppo, and Schumann addressed how this might affect the effectiveness of advertising.

The subjects were asked to look at a booklet that contained advertisements for 12 different products. Eleven of the ads were real, but one was developed especially for this study. It was for a fictitious product, the Adze Disposable Razor. Petty and his associates manipulated personal involvement with that ad by putting half of the subjects in a high-involvement condition. These subjects were told that as a reward for participation, they would later be able to select a free disposable razor from a group of razors. The other half of the subjects were in a low-involvement condition. They were told that as their reward, they would be able to select from a group of toothpastes.

For half the subjects in each condition, the ad began with the headline "Professional athletes agree," followed by a statement about the benefits of the Adze. Contained in the ad were pictures of two famous athletes. For the other half of the subjects, the ad began with the headline "Bakersfield California agrees," followed by the same statement about the benefits of the Adze. Contained in the ad were pictures of two ordinary people.

Petty and his associates used the semantic differential scale to measure how favorably or unfavorably the subjects reacted to the different versions of the ad. (See figure 10-9 for the ratings obtained from the semantic differential scale.)

In the low-involvement condition, the endorsement of athletes produced a much more favorable reaction than did the endorsement of ordinary citizens. But in the high-involvement condition, there was no difference. According to Petty and Cacioppo's theory, this is because subjects in the high-involvement condition were more careful and thoughtful in their consideration of the ad and thus were influenced less by such peripheral factors as endorsement of the product.

In another part of the same study, the researchers manipulated the quality of the arguments presented on behalf of the fictional razor. Half the subjects in each involvement condition read valid reasons for buying the Adze razor (such as the handle is built to prevent slipping) and half read invalid reasons for buying the Adze (such as it is designed with the bathroom in mind). Among low-involvement subjects, the valid and invalid reasons were equally effective; among high-involvement subjects, the valid reasons produced much more positive attitudes toward the product.

An advertisement must, however, do more than influence attitudes; it must also influence behavior. Petty and his colleagues addressed this issue. They asked their subjects to rate the likelihood they would purchase an Adze the next time they needed a razor. Attitudes toward the product were much more strongly related to intention to purchase in the high-involvement condition than in the low-involvement condition. Petty and Cacioppo (1983) suggested that this was because the attitude change in the high-

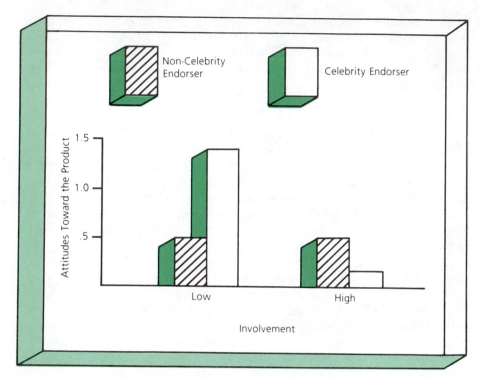

Figure 10-9. *The endorsements of celebrities was only effective in the low involvement condition.*
Source: Petty et al. (1983).

involvement condition occurred through the central route. This kind of thought-induced change is more permanent and, thus, more likely to lead to behavior change.

Repetition
It is not as easy to activate the central route in the real world as it was in Petty and his associates' experiment. Many ads concern products which, at least initially, are not personally involving. People are often exposed to ads in situations that distract them from the message—phones are ringing, other people are talking. And sometimes people simply tune out commercials.

One possible remedy is to repeatedly expose people to a commercial, in the hope that this will provide potential consumers with additional opportunities to think about and consider the product. While repetition may increase thoughts, this practice contains an element of risk; if the recipients become bored with the commercial or object to being bombarded with the same message, they may generate thoughts that are not conducive to acceptance of the message. Cacioppo and Petty (1980) called this process **wear-out.**

Wear-out: a reduction in a commercial's power to persuade consumers as the result of excessive repetition.

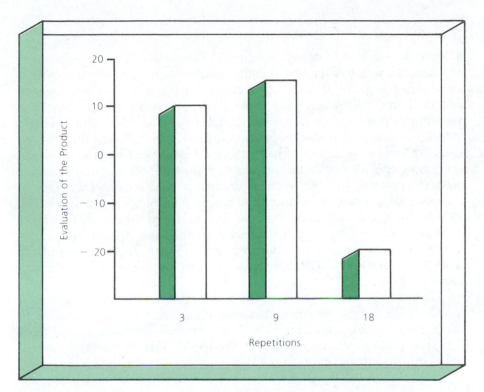

Figure 10-10. *As the number of times subjects saw the commercial increased, their evaluation of the product advertised decreased.*
Source: Calder and Sternthal (1980).

Cacioppo and Petty (1980) and Calder and Sternthal (1980) have investigated the effects of repetition on the effectiveness of commercials. In Calder and Sternthal's study, the subjects were college students who were paid to watch selected television shows over a three-week period. Embedded in these shows were commercials for certain products. Over the three weeks, subjects saw a given commercial 3, 9, or 18 times. After each viewing session, the subjects indicated their reactions to the commercials and the products they saw advertised by rating them on the semantic differential scale. Wear-out occurred very quickly for the commercials themselves. As the number of repetitions increased from three to nine, the subjects' reactions became less favorable. (See figure 10-10 for reactions to the product as a function of repetition.)

Evaluations of the product improved as repetitions increased from three to nine, but beyond nine repetitions, reactions to the product became dramatically less favorable. Simply repeating the commercial did not increase its effectiveness. Brock and Shavitt (1983) proposed that more attention should be given to how the content of a commercial might increase people's propensities to think about the message it is presenting. It remains for future research to determine how this might be done.

ANTISMOKING CAMPAIGNS

Most of the millions of reports produced by the United States government are read by one or two interested politicians and then filed away in a cabinet somewhere to gather dust. A significant exception to this general pattern was made for the 1964 surgeon general's report on the health hazards of smoking (United States Department of Health Education and Welfare, 1964). The surgeon general claimed that there was a direct link between smoking and cancer of the larynx and lungs. Subsequent reports have been even more critical of cigarette consumption. In 1979, the surgeon general's office claimed that smoking was a major cause of heart attacks, emphysema, complications during pregnancy, and many other medical problems. The 1984 report attributed the deaths of several hundred thousand Americans each year to smoking, and estimated that 40 billion dollars per year is lost in health expenses and reduced productivity among members of the work force who smoke (United States Department of Health and Human Services, 1984).

Claims such as these have sparked several different actions designed to reduce the number of Americans who smoke. Federal laws intended to make smoking less attractive have been passed. For example, in 1965, Congress passed a law requiring that all packs of cigarettes display a warning about the effects of smoking. This warning was changed in 1969 and again in 1984 in the hope of making it more effective. In 1971, Congress

Women are now as likely to start smoking as are men. Efforts to reduce the number of women and men who smoke have been only partially successful.

passed a law that banned all cigarette advertisements from radio and television and required that all print advertisements contain the statement "Warning: The Surgeon General has determined that cigarette smoking is hazardous to your health." However, cigarette companies still spend over half a billion dollars per year on advertising (Oskamp, 1984).

Since the first surgeon general's report, smoking has declined in the United States. The percentage of adult males who smoked decreased from 53 percent in 1954 to 37 percent in 1979. The number of males who start to smoke has declined by about a third (Oskamp, 1984). But the problem is far from solved. The decline in the percentage of adult women who smoked from 1959 to 1979 was only 5 percent, and whereas women used to be less likely to start smoking than men, women are now almost as likely as men to become smokers. About one-third of all adult Americans still smoke. Among smokers, daily consumption of cigarettes has increased over the years. In 1935, the average smoker consumed 12 cigarettes a day; in 1979, she or he consumed 33 cigarettes per day (United States Department of Health and Human Services, 1981).

In response to the continued danger presented by smoking, public and private agencies have decided that it is not enough to warn people and limit advertising—they must directly try to get people to stop smoking. Leventhal and Cleary (1980) identified two general approaches to this goal—therapy and public health.

Therapy Approach

The therapy approach attempts to treat smoking by using techniques developed to treat certain mild forms of mental illness. Sometimes the therapy involves a long-term one-to-one interaction between a professional and a "patient," and sometimes it involves a number of people who have enrolled in a packaged smoking cessation program. The techniques used in therapy can range from behavior modification to hypnosis to traditional forms of "talk" psychotherapy.

Research on the effectiveness of this approach indicates that smoking decreases dramatically during treatment, but that within 12 months after therapy has been completed, 75 to 90 percent of the patients are again smoking (Leventhal and Cleary, 1980). Even if the long-term effects of smoking cessation therapies were more positive, there would still be a serious drawback to them: They require extensive amounts of time and effort on the part of both the therapist and the patient, and they are usually quite expensive. If one is interested in the reduction of smoking on a broad scale, it is unlikely that the therapy approach provides a way to do this.

Public Health Approach

The public health approach uses the mass media to present persuasive messages and other techniques to change people's attitudes and behavior about smoking. Advocates of this approach believe that if advertising and mass media can be used to get people to start smoking, they can be used to get people to stop smoking. This approach is more cost effective than are the various kinds of smoking cessation therapies. The strengths and weaknesses of this approach can be illustrated by considering some studies that have addressed smoking in several communities and a study done with school children.

Community Interventions

Meyer, Nash, McAlister, Maccoby, and Farquhar (1980) carried out an extensive program to reduce the risk of cardiovascular disorders among residents of three small communities in northern California. Since smoking is believed to cause such illnesses, a large part of the effort was directed at this activity and data were collected on how the program affected smoking. Residents of one community were assigned to a control group, while residents of two other communities were assigned to one of two experimental groups. In the experimental group, residents were exposed to a two-year media campaign designed to decrease smoking and improve other health-related activities. Persuasive messages were presented on radio, television, billboards, posters on buses, and in literature mailed directly to the residents' homes. The second experimental group was composed of people who, in addition to the media campaign, received individualized treatment to help them quit smoking. Two years after the program began, Meyer and his associates obtained data on changes in the incidence of smoking among members of the three groups. In the control group (residents of a community that received neither the media campaign nor individualized treatment), there were 12 percent more smokers than there had been two years earlier. There were 5 percent fewer smokers in the media-campaign-only group, and 17 percent fewer smokers in the media-plus-individualized-treatment group.

At about the time that Meyer and colleagues were working in northern California, McAlister, Puska, Koskela, Pallonen, and Maccoby (1980) conducted a nationwide antismoking campaign in Finland. For seven weeks, a Finnish television station aired a program that instructed people on how to quit smoking. In addition, in some parts of the country, the researchers organized social support groups. Members of these groups watched the programs together and then helped one another to quit smoking. Since everyone in Finland who owned a television set could have seen the programs, there were no true control groups. But McAlister and his associates did conduct national surveys of smoking before and after the programs were shown and compared the viewers who were part of the social support groups to those who were not.

The surveys disclosed that about 250,000 people (7 percent of Finland's population) watched four or more of the programs, and that among these people were 80,000 to 100,000 smokers. Slightly less than half these people reduced their smoking to some degree as the result of the programs.

The programs in combination with the self-help social support groups were much more effective. McAlister and his colleagues compared smoking rates among residents of areas where these groups were organized with smoking rates in areas where they were not. The people in the social support areas were more likely to watch the program and twice as likely to try to quit smoking as were people in the non-social-support areas. They were also significantly more likely to abstain from cigarettes for six months than were people from the non-social-support areas. The researchers estimated that the program caused about 10,000 Finns (about 1 percent of the smokers in Finland) to abstain from smoking for at least six months. And this was achieved at the cost of less than one dollar per ex-smoker.

Some comments about the two studies are in order. First, they seem to illustrate a point made over 40 years ago by Lewin. Lewin argued that active involvement in the change process, such as the individualized treatment in the California study and the social support groups in the Finland study, will be more effective than a simple persuasive message. In both studies, it was only when the media compaign was combined with active involvement that significant effects were obtained. This does not mean that media campaigns are totally without merit. As Oskamp (1984) pointed out, mass media campaigns, even those used in politics and advertising, produce only small changes in people's attitudes. Continued publicity about the dangers of smoking, however, may have a stronger cumulative effect. Warner (1977) estimated that without the antismoking campaigns of the 1960s and the 1970s, the level of cigarette consumption in 1975 would have been 20 to 30 percent higher than it was.

Leventhal and Cleary (1980) pointed out that while it is possible for media campaigns to affect smoking, most of the campaigns actually conducted have been failures. They faulted researchers for taking too simplistic a view of how to change attitudes and behavior about smoking. These campaigns, Leventhal and Cleary argued, are based on the assumption that if an antismoking persuasive message is presented enough times, people will learn it, accept it, and stop smoking. But people smoke for different reasons, and these reasons must be addressed in the persuasive messages. People may accept the message but, because of other factors such as nicotine dependence, they may be unable to quit. Statistics show that most smokers have negative attitudes toward smoking. Leventhal and Cleary's point was that attitudes are only one cause of people's behavior.

School Interventions

Another approach to reducing the number of people who smoke is to persuade them to never start. This idea is predicated on the notion that it is easier to prevent than to change a behavior. To accomplish this, many schools have developed educational campaigns for students who have not yet begun to smoke. Unfortunately, few of these campaigns have been effective in reducing the number of young people who smoke (Oskamp, 1984).

Richard Evans (1980; Evans, Rozelle, Mittlemark, Hansen, Bane, and Havis, 1978) has proposed one possible reason for the lack of success in school interventions. He believed that when many teenagers first consider smoking, at about age 13, they already know about the long-term negative effects of smoking. However, at this age, children are probably more influenced by peer pressures and what they see on the media than they are by concerns about their health 20 years in the future. Therefore, anti-smoking campaigns aimed at children this age must address the "here and now" issues.

Evans and his associates (1978) tested this idea in a study with 750 junior high school students. These students were assigned to one of four groups. Members of the control group simply provided data on whether they smoked at the beginning of the study and again 10 weeks later. Two experimental groups were used to examine certain components of the treatment, and are not discussed here. Members of the third experimental group filled out the initial measures of smoking and then were exposed to the antismoking campaign. The campaign was based largely on McGuire's inoculation theory of resistance to persuasion. Children were shown videotapes that addressed the major sources of pressures to smoke (peers pressuring them to smoke, seeing their parents smoking) and explained how they could deal with such pressures. These videotapes lasted 10 minutes and were shown on four consecutive days during physical education classes. Because Evans and his colleagues believed that active participation plays a significant role in attitude change, these tapes were followed by a group discussion in which students exchanged ideas about how to cope with pressures to smoke.

Members of the third experimental group were tested one, five, and ten weeks after the pretest. Evans and his associates were concerned that the students, especially those in the experimental group, might be less than honest in their self-reports about how much they smoked. Therefore, they used a measurement technique based on the same logic as the bogus pipeline procedure. (See chapter nine.) Students in the experimental group were shown a film demonstrating how people's saliva could be analyzed to determine if they had been smoking. Then the students gave a saliva sample before they filled out their self-reports about smoking. Other research had shown that the belief that the saliva test (which, in fact, was never carried out) would identify people who were untruthful served to increase the honesty of the self-reports.

Ten weeks after the pretest, 8 percent of the control group and 10 percent of the experimental group had begun smoking. This difference, while small, was statistically significant. We have no way of knowing whether Evans's procedure only delayed the onset of smoking among the experimental subjects or actually reduced the likelihood they would smoke. A long-term longitudinal study is needed to determine this. Evans (1980) reported that he had begun such a study, and initial findings suggest that this campaign may decrease the likelihood of smoking. But, while Evans's results are encouraging, most school interventions have not been successful (Leventhal and Cleary, 1980).

Why haven't antismoking campaigns been more successful? Part of the answer to this question was supplied about twenty years ago by Carl Hovland, the man responsible for much of the current interest in attitudes and attitude change. Hovland (1959) believed that the theories of attitude change he and others had developed were applicable beyond the laboratory. But in the real world, attitudes and behavior are often deeply ingrained in a person or maintained by situational factors, and are thus more difficult to change than the results of laboratory experiments would suggest. Also, attitude change is often much easier to accomplish than behavior change, and most of the antismoking campaigns address attitudes. This was essentially the point made by Leventhal and Cleary (1980) in their criticism of the public health approach. As someone who quit smoking after 25 years, I can tell you that it was much easier to change my attitudes than to change my behavior.

Chapter Eleven

Social Influence

Prologue

Stanley Milgram (1965). Some conditions of obedience and disobedience to authority. *Human Relations*, **18,** 57–76.

Background

This chapter is about social influence, the ability to change a person's beliefs or behavior. One form of social influence is obedience to authority. The writer and philosopher C. P. Snow once observed that "when you think about the long and gloomy history of man, you will find more hideous crimes have been committed in the name of obedience than have ever been committed in the name of rebellion." The truth of this statement can be found in historical examples—the behavior of the guards in Hitler's concentration camps and the mass suicide among followers of the Reverend Jim Jones.

In the late 1950s, Stanley Milgram began a series of experiments on what would lead people to obey an unethical or immoral command from an authority. The following experiment was the first of several that Milgram conducted on this topic.

Hypothesis

Milgram did not propose a formal hypothesis. His purpose was to determine whether his subjects would obey commands to harm another human being. He suspected they would not.

Subjects

The subjects were 40 males recruited from the general community in New Haven, Connecticut. Their occupations ranged from unskilled worker to engineer. Subjects were paid $4.50 for their participation.

Procedure

When a subject arrived at Milgram's laboratory, he was told that the money was his for simply showing up, and he could keep it no matter what happened later. Then he was introduced to another man, a pleasant-looking individual in his late forties. The subject believed that this man was also a subject, but he was a paid confederate. The experimenter told the confederate and the subject that the study concerned the effects of punishment on learning. While one of them attempted to learn, the other would be the teacher and would administer punishment whenever a mistake was made. Then a rigged drawing was held which resulted in the subject always being the teacher and the confederate always being the learner.

The experimenter showed the subject and the confederate into an adjacent room. As the subject watched, the confederate was strapped into a chair and an electrode was attached to his wrist. After returning to the original room, the subject was seated in front of a large shock generator. On the generator were 30 levers, each clearly labeled with the amount of shock it would deliver, ranging from 15 volts for the extreme left-hand lever to 450 volts for the extreme right-hand lever.

The teacher (the subject) was given 45 volts of electric shock to let him know what shock felt like, and then the experiment began. The teacher read to the learner (the confederate) a list of word pairs—for example, blue-girl, nice-day. Following this, he read the first word from each pair and gave the learner four other words. The learner's task was to indicate which of these four words was originally paired with the first word by pressing a switch in front of him. The teacher was told that the learner must be shocked every time he chose the wrong word, and that this shock should be increased one level for each successive wrong answer.

The learner (who was never really shocked) gave the wrong answer about 75 percent of the time. He grunted from discomfort when the shock reached 75 volts; by 150 volts, he was pleading with the experimenter to let him out; at 270 volts, he screamed in response to the shock and again demanded he be let out of the experiment. At 300 volts, he announced that he would no longer choose any of the words, and he said nothing for the remainder of the experimental session. The subject was told that if the learner did not respond, his silence was to be considered a wrong answer and shock was to be given. When subjects were reluctant to administer the shock, the experimenter verbally urged them to continue.

The experimental session ended when a subject either refused to give any more shock or had reached the maximum shock level (450 volts). The dependent measure was the highest level of shock a subject gave the confederate. At the conclusion of an experimental session, the subject was told the true purpose of the experiment; it was made clear that he had not harmed the confederate and that the confederate bore him no ill will. The experimenter attempted to deal with any discomfort the subjects felt.

Results

Milgram had expected most of his subjects to either refuse to shock the confederate at all or to break off the shock as soon as the confederate indicated any discomfort. This view was shared by other social scientists Milgram consulted before he conducted the experiment. However, this is not what the subjects did. No subject disobeyed the experimenter's commands before 135 volts. Seventy-five percent of the subjects gave at least 300 volts, and 63 percent went all the way to the maximum voltage.

Implications

These findings illustrate the phenomenon of interest in this chapter. The subjects did not want to shock the other person, nor did they enjoy his (supposed) suffering; but they did engage in the behavior desired by the experimenter. This chapter examines why they did this, and more generally, what gives one person the ability to change the beliefs and behaviors of another.

━━━━━━━━━━━━━━━━━━━━━━━━━━━━━━━━━━

This chapter addresses the factors that give an individual or a group **social influence.** It attempts to answer the question asked by Robert Cialdini (1984) in his book *Influence:* "What are the factors that cause one person to say yes to another person?" No single factor enables an individual or a group to exert influence over someone else. Also, different types of influence produce different types of effects. Sometimes people say "yes" or acquiesce to another person not because they believe in what they are doing, but because something in the situation forces them to do so. The term for this is **compliance.** On other occasions, people acquiesce because they believe in what they are doing. The name for this is **private acceptance.**

The first section of this chapter concerns the attributes and tactics that give individuals influence over other people. The second section examines the methods used by groups to influence individuals. Many of the processes that result in people acquiescing to an individual also result in people acquiescing to a group. The applications section addresses the manner in which these processes and variables affect health care.

Social influence: the ability of an individual or group to change a person's beliefs or behaviors.

Compliance: a change in overt behavior, without a change in actual belief.

Private acceptance: a change in actual belief.

INDIVIDUAL INFLUENCE

In general, the abilities of individuals to control or change the behavior or beliefs of other people come from one of two things. The first of these is an attribute that some individuals have which enables them to "exert their will" over others. For example, school children may follow the recommendations of their teacher because the teacher has the ability to punish them; husbands may follow the recommendations of their wives because of their love for them; and a defendant in a court case may follow his lawyer's recommendations because of the lawyer's expertise. Secondly, the ability to control or change another person can come from the tactics an individual uses. A study by Langer, Blank, and Chanowitz (1978) illustrates how simple a tactic can be.

The subjects were people who were using a photocopier in a university library. A confederate approached them and asked if he could use the machine. The request was made in one of three ways: (1) "Excuse me. I have five pages. May I use the Xerox machine?" (2) "Excuse me. I have five pages. May I use the Xerox machine because I am in a rush?" (3) "Excuse me. I have five pages. May I use the Xerox machine because I have to make some copies?"

The percentages of people who agreed to the three requests were 60, 94, and 93 percent, respectively. (See figure 11-1.) Look at the second and third requests closely. The second request provides a justification; the third request *appears* to provide a justification, but in fact says nothing. Of course he needs "to make some copies"; why else would he be using the machine?

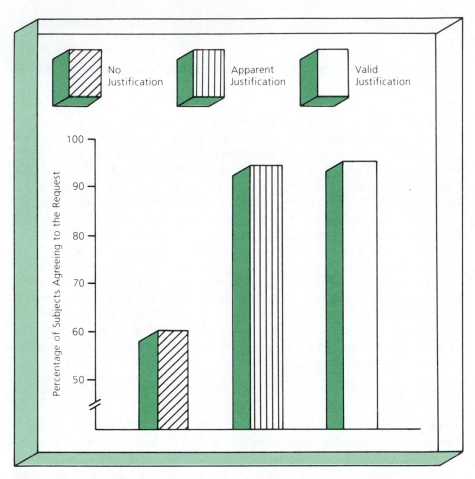

Figure 11-1. *Subjects agreed to a request without a valid justification as often as they agreed to one based on a valid justification.*
Source: Langer et al. (1978).

But the appearance of a justification enabled the person to exert control over another person.

Attributes

Every time I describe the prologue's experiment to a social psychology class, I ask my students, "Would you do what Milgram's subjects did? Would you obey the experimenter's orders?" Few students ever say they would. "Well, then," I continue. "Why do you think the subjects acted as they did?"

The first answer is almost always the same: The subjects had some sort of personality flaw that made them different from the typical person. Because of this flaw, they either felt no remorse at what they did or, worse, they enjoyed it. This explanation, while quite reasonable, is wrong. Milgram's subjects anguished over what they were doing, and many argued with the experimenter. This is illustrated in the first topic background presented in this chapter.

Few of us will ever encounter a situation as dramatic as the one Milgram created in his laboratory, but we almost daily act in ways that are quite similar. For example, have you ever acted deferentially toward an instructor you did not respect? Have you ever thanked your Aunt Charlotte for the cookies she sent you, even though they tasted like sand? A fact of social life is that often we do things that we would, at least initially, prefer not to do; we say "yes." French and Raven (1959) have proposed that often we do this because of the **social power** held by the person attempting to influence us.

Social power: the ability to influence the thoughts or actions of another person.

Topic Background

I'm Not Going to Kill That Man

The following exchange between a subject (the teacher) in Milgram's (1965) experiment and the experimenter began after the teacher had already administered 270 volts to the learner.

TEACHER: Aw, no. I'm not going to kill that man. You mean I've got to keep going up with the scale? No sir. He's hollering in there. I'm not going to give him 450 volts.

EXPERIMENTER: The experiment requires that you go on.

TEACHER: I know it does, but that man is hollering in there, sir.

EXPERIMENTER: As I said before, although the shocks may be painful . . .

TEACHER (interrupting): Awwww. He—he—he's yelling in there.

EXPERIMENTER: Start with blue, please, at the top of the page. Continue, please, Teacher. Just go ahead. [The learner's task is to indicate which word goes with blue.]

TEACHER: Blue—boy, girl, grass, hat. (Buzz indicates answer.) Correct. Night—day, sky, job, chair. (Buzz.) Wrong. The answer is day. Two hundred and eighty-five volts. (Zzumph!)

LEARNER: Ohhhuhhooohhh!

EXPERIMENTER: Continue, please.

TEACHER: Fat—man, lady, tub, neck. Answer, please. (Buzz.) Wrong. The answer is neck. Three hundred volts. (Zzumph!)

LEARNER: Ohhh. I absolutely refuse to answer any more. Let me out of here. You can't hold me here. Get me out. Get—me—out—of—here.

EXPERIMENTER: Continue. The next word is green, please.

TEACHER: Green—grass, hat, ink, apple.

TEACHER: I don't think he is going to answer.

EXPERIMENTER: If the learner doesn't answer in a reasonable time, about four or five seconds, consider the answer wrong. And follow the same procedures you have been doing for wrong answers. Say "wrong," tell him the number of volts, give him the punishment, and read him the correct answer. Continue, please.

TEACHER: Green—grass, hat, ink, apple. Answer, please.

EXPERIMENTER: Go on with the procedure, please, Teacher.

TEACHER: Three hundred and fifteen volts. The answer is ink.

LEARNER: Ohh. Oohh.

TEACHER: Next one . . .

LEARNER: I absolutely refuse to answer.

TEACHER: You got to. You get a shock if you don't answer.

TEACHER: I think something's happened to that fellow in there. I don't get no answer. He was hollering at less voltage. Can't you check in and see if he's all right, please?

From this excerpt, you might predict that this subject was one of the relatively few people who eventually disobeyed the experimenter. He was not; he went all the way to 450 volts and repeatedly gave the learner this level of shock. Despite his initial protest, had the situation been real, he may well have killed that man.

The basis of the social power possessed by the experimenter in the study presented in the prologue and the basis of someone's Aunt Charlotte's social power are quite different. French and Raven (1959) originally proposed five attributes, or characteristics, which give a person social power: having the ability to reward; having the ability to punish; being liked, respected, or admired; being an expert, and having the right to control.

Having the Ability to Reward

The first basis of social power is the ability to reward, or *reward social power*. A person who can control the rewards people receive for performing a behavior can exert control over them. You have been exposed to this basis of social power if you have ever mowed the lawn on a hot day because your parents offered to pay you, worked overtime on a job in exchange for extra pay, or written a term paper in exchange for extra credit in a class.

The ability to reward will produce social power, but it is not an efficient way of controlling other people's behavior. Two characteristics of reward social power make it inefficient. First, it requires that the person, usually called an *influencing agent*, keep an eye on the target of the influence attempt. For example, imagine a father who regularly goes on three- to four-week business trips. He asks his son to mow the lawn every week while he is gone, and offers the son $5.00 per mowing. The son is lazy but clever. He realizes that his father will never know whether he has mowed the lawn every week or only once the day before the father returns. Without some way of monitoring his son weekly, the father loses a good deal of control over his son's behavior.

Socially dependent: a change that depends solely on some characteristic of the influencing agent.

Second, according to Raven and Rubin (1983), this type of power produces a change that is **socially dependent.** If, for example, the father de-

Social power is the ability to influence a person's behavior and/or beliefs. This police officer posseses social power.

cides to stop paying the son or loses his job and cannot pay him, the desired behavior stops. The only motivation for the behavior is the reward offered for doing it.

Having the Ability to Punish

An influencing agent who can control the punishment people would receive for not performing a behavior can also exert control over them. This form of social power, called *coercive social power*, is sometimes used by governments to bring political dissidents back into line. For example, the Soviet government uses the threat of banishment to work camps in Siberia or involuntary institutionalization in so-called mental hospitals as a means of suppressing dissent.

Coercive social power may be effective in the short run, but it is not a very efficient form of social power. Like reward social power, it requires surveillance and produces a behavior that is socially dependent. Coercive social power has an additional drawback: People often react to an attempt to control their behaviors with punishment in a very negative manner. Punishment sometimes increases their resolve to resist the influencing agent. This is evidenced by an episode from the life of Lillian Hellman, the noted American screenwriter, playwright, and novelist. In the early 1950s, a wave of paranoia about the "Communist menace" swept the United States. During this period, a congressional committee decided to investigate Communist influence in the motion picture industry. Many actors, directors, and screenwriters testified before this committee. They used flimsy evidence and hearsay to identify their co-workers as Communists because they believed that failure to do so would mean the ends of their own careers. Ms. Hellman, however, would not cooperate. She did not simply refuse to appear before the committee—she appeared and publicly denounced the committee and its purposes. Her heroic words bear repeating:

> To hurt innocent people whom I knew years ago to save myself is, to me, inhuman. I cannot and will not cut my conscience to fit this year's fashion . . . (Hellman, 1953, cited in Navasky 1981, p. 34)

There is evidence from other types of social interactions that coercive social power often produces effects opposite to those that are desired. Birchler, Weiss, and Vincent (1975) examined the techniques married couples use to control one another's behavior. They hypothesized that couples who were experiencing marital difficulties would be more likely to use negative means (such as threats and complaints) to control each other's behavior than would couples without marital problems. To test this hypothesis, Birchler and his associates observed interactions between distressed couples and nondistressed couples. They found that people in distressed marriages were one and a half times more likely to use threats, complaints, and other negative means to control one another's behavior than were people in nondistressed marriages. This difference was not due to general unpleasantness among people who were in distressed marriages; when these people interacted with a stranger, they were no more likely to use negative means of control than were people in nondistressed marriages. One cannot conclude from this study that coercive social power caused the marital problems, but the findings do suggest that coercive social power is associated with negative reactions. One possible reason for this is provided by reactance theory.

Reactance Theory   According to Brehm (1966; Brehm and Brehm, 1981) people believe that they are free to choose how they will behave. If they perceive that someone is attempting to control their behaviors against their wishes, they will experience a state of **psychological reactance.** To eliminate this state, people will engage in behaviors that demonstrate they

Psychological reactance: an unpleasant state in which people feel that their freedom is being restricted.

do have freedom in their actions. Often these behaviors will be opposite to those desired by the influencing agent. Pennebaker and Sanders (1976) looked at the effectiveness of two appeals to reduce the incidence of graffiti in public restrooms. Some of the subjects saw a sign that said "Please do not write on the walls" and was signed by the grounds committeeman. Other subjects saw a sign that said "Do NOT write on walls" and was signed by the chief of security. The second sign resulted in significantly more graffiti than did the first sign; the students appeared to be displaying reactance in response to the chief of security's heavy-handed tactics.

Most researchers believe that a change produced by reward or coercive social power represents compliance (Kelman, 1958, 1961); there is a change in overt behavior but not in actual beliefs. This change will usually cease if the influencing agent cannot watch the targets of the influence or loses the ability to reward or punish them.

Being Liked, Respected, or Admired

In chapter nine you read how people's reference groups influence their attitudes. People compare their attitudes to those of their reference group, and if there is a difference, they may change their attitudes to match those of the group. The reference group has the third characteristic that can produce social power, which French and Raven (1959) called **referent social power.** Referent social power does not require surveillance; for this reason, it is more efficient than reward or coercive social power. In many instances, influencing agents are not even aware that they have referent power over another person's behavior. For example, until my wife pointed it out, I was not aware that my son had become the only other living person besides me who *always* eats French vanilla ice cream cones.

Referent social power: the ability of an influencing agent to exert control over people because people like, respect, or admire the agent.

A change produced by referent social power is socially dependent, as is the case with reward and coercive social power, but less effort is required to maintain this change. However, referent social power does not produce true change or private acceptance. It produces something Kelman (1958, 1961) called **identification.** In identification, a change persists only as long as people remain attracted to the influencing agent and see the change as part of their relationship with the influencing agent. Kelman (1958, 1961) and Romer (1979) have demonstrated that identification and private acceptance are two distinct processes, caused by different types of social power. The type of social power French and Raven (1959) believed was responsible for private acceptance is expert social power.

Identification: a change in behavior or belief due to an attraction for or a desire to identify with the influencing agent.

Being an Expert

One attribute that enables an individual to influence people's private beliefs and that can cause permanent changes in behavior is **expert social power** (French and Raven, 1959). For example, if someone asked you to name the two theorists who proposed expert social power, you would say French and Raven. This is a correct answer but is it based solely on your assumption that the author of a social psychology textbook has expertise about this discipline. I can influence your beliefs and behavior.

Expert social power: the ability of an influencing agent to exert control over people because of the agent's expertise in the matter at hand.

Expert social power is a much more efficient means of control than is reward or coercive social power. Control is exerted without any surveillance, and it is not necessary that the targets of the influence attempt like or admire the influencing agent. All that is needed is that the targets believe the influencing agent is an expert and, thus, correct.

A dramatic illustration of the effects of expert social power was provided in a study by Naftulin, Ware, and Donelly (1973). A group of psychologists, educators, and college administrators listened to a lecture entitled "Mathematical Game Theory as Applied to Physical Education." The lecturer, Dr. Fox, had impressive academic credentials. After his presentation, Dr. Fox was evaluated by his audience. The evaluations were extremely positive. He was described as knowledgeable, articulate, and astute. The audience should have included one more word in their evaluations—phony. Dr. Fox was an actor, trained by Naftulin and his associates to use double-talk and nonsequiters and, in general, to make no sense. But the highly educated members of his audience were "seduced by the style of Dr. Fox's presentation" (Naftulin et al., 1973, p. 633).

The Dr. Fox study also points out that expert social power—like reward, coercive, and referent social power—produces behavior that is socially dependent. Dr. Fox was able to influence his audience only so long as they believed he was an expert. Once they learned who he really was, his power was gone.

In revisions of the original model of the bases of social power, Raven and his associates (Collins and Raven, 1969; Raven and Kruglanski, 1970) have drawn a distinction between expert social power and **informational social power.**

Informational social power: the ability to influence people based on the perceived correctness of the information contained in a message.

If people accept a message as true, they will be influenced. Influence due to informational social power is not socially dependent; it does not depend on the characteristics of another person. Despite this difference, the immediate effects of both expert and informational social power are the same; they produce true change or private acceptance.

Having the Right to Control

In any civilized society, there are positions of authority. People who occupy such positions are given the right to exercise control over other people. This is **legitimate social power.** Examples of people with legitimate social power are police officers, federal judges, the president of General Motors, the president of your university, a four-star general, and the Pope.

Legitimate social power: the ability of an influencing agent to exert control over people because people believe the agent has the right to do so.

All of these people could use reward or coercive social power to exert control, but because of the positions they occupy they do not have to. People accept their control because they accept the rules that say people in these positions have the right to control them. This right is not dependent on the referent or expert social power of the person who occupies the position. For instance, a lieutenant will take orders from a captain even if he dislikes the captain and considers him a dolt.

This is not to suggest that the other bases of social power are irrelevant to legitimate social power. In most instances, the legitimate social power of a position is derived from the fact that occupants of the position pre-

Topic Background

The Boy Will Come to Nothing

By and large, it makes sense to allow yourself to be influenced by expert social power; to listen to and follow the advice of experts. But experts are only human, and they do make mistakes. In their informative and entertaining book *The Experts Speak*, Christopher Cerf and Victor Navasky (1984) provide a "definitive compendium" of expert judgments which it would have been wise to ignore. Some excerpts from the book follow.

"Hurray boys, we've got them! We'll finish them up and then go home to our station." General George Custer when he first saw the Indian encampment in the Valley of the Little Big Horn. (1876)

"I'm sorry Mr. Kipling, but you just don't know how to use the English language." A newspaper editor informing Rudyard Kipling that an article Kipling had submitted to the paper would not be published. (1889)

"Forget it, Louis. No Civil War picture ever made a nickel." A production executive at Metro Goldwyn Meyer movie studio advising the president of the studio not to buy the film rights to the novel *Gone with the Wind*. (1936)

"[He] doesn't have the presidential look." An executive at United Artists movie studio explaining why he did not select Ronald Reagan for a role in a movie. (1964)

"You ain't goin' nowhere . . . son. You ought to go back to drivin' a truck." The manager of the Grand Ole Opry, explaining to Elvis Presley why he (Presley) was being fired after one performance. (1954)

"The singer will have to go." An early manager of the Rolling Stones evaluating Mick Jagger's value to the group. (1963)

"How can he call it a wonderful success when everyone acquainted with the subject will recognize it as a conspicuous failure?" A professor of physics evaluating Thomas Edison's invention, the electric light bulb. (1879)

"[He] made a great mistake when he gave up pitching. Working once a week, he might have lasted a long time and become a great star." A baseball manager commenting on Babe Ruth's decision to change from a pitcher to an outfielder. (1921)

"I think there is a world market for about five computers." The chairman of the board of International Business Machines (otherwise known as I.B.M.), commenting on the future of computers. (1943)

"The boy will come to nothing." Jakob Freud predicting the future of his son, Sigmund. (1864)

Despite his father's pessimistic prediction, Sigmund Freud went on to make something of himself.

viously exercised other forms of social power. For example, look at the type of power used by the Roman Catholic popes now and in the past. The pope recently asked Father Robert Drinnan to resign his seat in the United States House of Representatives. Father Drinnan complied with the pope's request not because he feared punishment or believed that the pope's prohibitions against priests in politics were correct, but because he believed in the church and in the pope's authority.

In a fictional but historically accurate novel, Umberto Eco describes how a fourteenth-century pope, Pope John XXII, dealt with an order of monks who disagreed with him over a matter of Church doctrine:

> When he was elected in 1316, he wrote to the King of Sicily telling him to expel those monks from his lands, where many had taken refuge; and [several were] put in chains. . . . For those who continued [to disobey] John was merciless, and he had them persecuted by the Inquisition and many were burned at the stake. (1983, p. 52)

Note how much easier it is for a modern pope to exert control over priests. In general, legitimate social power is much more efficient than reward, coercive, referent, or perhaps expert social power. It is hard to conceive a contemporary society that could function without legitimate social power. But can legitimate social power be carried too far? This is really what the prologue was all about.

Obedience to Authority   According to Meyer (1970), Milgram's research was largely motivated by his belief that cultures differ in the extent to which their members obey the commands of people in authority. Milgram believed that Germans were an extremely obedient people, more obedient than Americans. His original idea was to show that Americans would refuse to shock another person in the experiment, but Germans would follow the experimenter's orders. Then Milgram would study the variables that make members of one culture more obedient than members of another culture. But because of the extremely high level of obedience shown by his original subjects, Milgram never studied Germans; instead he studied the causes of obedience in Americans*. Three of the variables which received special attention were: salience of the victim; authority of the experimenter; and responsibility given to the subject.

Salience of the Victim   In the prologue experiment, the victim (the learner) sat in one room and the subject (the teacher) sat in another. Milgram proposed that if the victim's plight could be made more salient to the subjects, the subjects might be more willing to obey. To test this idea, Milgram compared the amount of obedience obtained in this experiment to the amount obtained in conditions in which the victim was made more salient. In the first condition, the victim was moved into the same room as the subject and placed in a chair a few feet from the subject. The subject could both see and hear the victim as the shock was increased. In the second condition the victim was also seated near the subject, but the shock was administered in a different manner. In the first condition, the victim (supposedly) received the shock through an electrode attached to his wrist. In the second condition the victim's arm was placed on an electrified plate. When the shock reached 150 volts, the victim removed his arm from the plate. The subject was ordered by the experimenter to place the victim's arm back on the plate. As Milgram had proposed, obedience declined as the salience of the victim increased. (See figure 11-2.)

Salience of the Experimenter   Milgram reasoned that if making the victim more salient would reduce obedience, making the experimenter less salient should also reduce obedience. He arranged another experiment, in which the experimenter gave the subjects their initial instructions and then left the room. For the remainder of the experimental session, the experimenter spoke with the subjects by telephone. Obedience decreased markedly; only 20 percent of the subjects administered the maximum shock.

---

*Levels of obedience similar to that obtained in the United States have been obtained in Australia (Kilham and Mann, 1974), Jordan (Shanab and Yahya, 1977), and West Germany (Mantell, 1977).

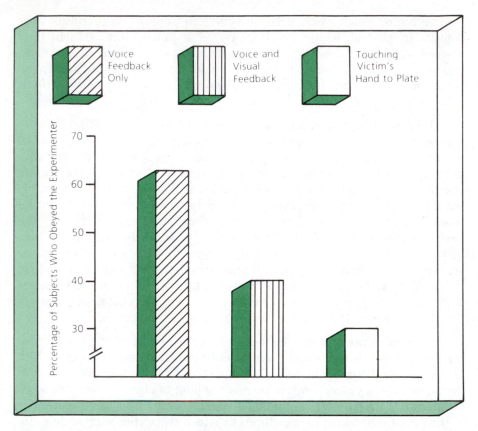

Figure 11-2. *As the victim became more salient, obedience declined.*
Source: Milgram (1974).

Authority of the Experimenter Milgram wondered how much of his subjects' obedience was due to the setting in which the experiments were conducted. Perhaps the subjects assumed that Yale, being a reputable university, would not allow any unethical or dangerous experiments. To determine if this explained at least part of the obedience, Milgram removed this source of experimenter authority. He moved the experiment from Yale University to a run-down office building in another city. As he expected, obedience was lower under these circumstances. But it did not disappear; 48 percent of the subjects who participated in the experiment went all the way to 450 volts.

Penner, Hawkins, Dertke, Spector, and Stone (1973) used another technique to reduce an experimenter's authority—they made him incompetent. That is, they had him do things such as start the experiment late, drop equipment, temporarily break the shock apparatus, and in general, play the fool. He was able to produce much less obedience than was a competent, self-assured experimenter. But this difference only emerged after the experimenter explicitly pointed out his mistakes to the subjects and explained his behavior by saying that he had conducted the experiment only twice before. Evidently, subjects are not easily convinced that authority figures do not know what they are doing.

Placing Responsibility on the Subject   In all of the variations of Milgram's procedure presented thus far, the experimenter has either implicitly or explicitly taken responsibility for what happened to the victim. If the responsibility for what happens to the victim is shifted to the subjects, few will deliver high levels of shock (Mantell, 1971; Milgram, 1974).

This finding led to Milgram's general explanation of obedience to authority. He proposed that if people accept the legitimate social power of a person and do what that person requests, they are in an **agentic state.** One psychological consequence of feeling as if one is merely an agent, carrying out someone else's orders, is a lowered sense of responsibility for the consequences of one's actions. Agents assume that responsibility lies with the person who gave the order. If a person can induce an agentic state in others, Milgram argued, then even good, caring, compassionate individuals are capable of committing atrocities against other humans.

Agentic state: a condition which people perceive themselves as agents of someone else.

Obedience in the Real World   Milgram's research evoked a good deal of criticism. Some critics questioned the ethics of putting people through such an ordeal (Baumrind, 1964), while others questioned whether the conditions Milgram created in his laboratory bore any relation to obedience in the real world.

At about the time Milgram was conducting this research, Israeli agents captured an escaped Nazi war criminal, Adolf Eichmann. Eichmann was said to have been responsible for transferring hundreds of thousands of Jews to Hitler's death camps and organizing the means of their destruction. For these crimes, he was tried by the Israeli government. At the trial, the following exchange took place between Eichmann and the prosecutor, Hausner:

> HAUSNER: Then you admit that you were an accomplice to the murder of millions of Jews?
>
> EICHMANN: That I cannot admit. I ask myself whether I am guilty as an accomplice from the human point of view. But I do not consider myself guilty from the legal point of view. I received orders and I executed orders. If the deportations which I carried out—the ones in which I had a part—led to death of some of these Jews, then the legal questions must be examined as to whether I am guilty in terms of responsibility. (Pearlman, 1963, p. 467)

Was this merely the self-serving statement of a man on trial for his life? In the judgment of noted historian Hannah Arendt, it was not. Arendt, herself a Jew, explained Eichmann's behavior as follow:

> This was the way things were, this was the new law of the land, based on the Fuhrer's order; whatever he did he did, as far as he could see, as a law-abiding citizen. He did his duty, as he told the police and the court over and over again; he not only obeyed orders, he also obeyed the law.

And just as the law in civilized countries assumes that the voice of conscience tells everybody "Thou shalt not kill," even though man's natural desires and inclinations may at times be murderous, so the law of Hitler's land demanded that the voice of conscience tell everybody; "Thou shalt kill." (1963, pp. 120, 134)

Arendt may have attributed Eichmann's behavior too much to legitimate social power, but there is validity in her explanation. Perhaps Milgram was not being extreme when he stated in a television interview that if he had to staff a nazi-type concentration camp, he could find more than enough guards in any middle-sized American town. Milgram's statement was based not on his perception of latent anti-Semitism among Americans, but on the strength of legitimate social power to produce obedience.

Individual Differences in Obedience to Authority The main lesson to be learned from studies of obedience is that under the right circumstances, almost anyone can be made to obey the orders of a person in authority. This does not mean that there are no individual differences in obedience to authority. The concept of the authoritarian personality, or **authoritarianism,** was introduced by Adorno and his associates in 1950. Since the defining characteristic of the trait of authoritarianism is the tendency to identify with or submit to the commands of authority figures, it is not surprising that researchers have studied the relationship between this trait and obedience. (See chapter nine for a further discussion of this trait.)

In the early 1970s, several researchers (for example, Granberg and Corrigan, 1972; Izzett, 1971) gave subjects a scale that measured authoritarianism and then determined each subject's willingness to oppose the United States government's policies on Vietnam. The rationale behind these studies was that authoritarian individuals would be less willing than others to challenge authority by protesting against their government. This prediction was supported. Other studies have found that authoritarian individuals are more favorably inclined toward the prosecution in a criminal trial than are nonauthoritarian individuals (Garcia and Griffitt, 1978), and Elms (1972) found greater obedience to the experimenter in Milgram's shock experiments among authoritarian subjects.

Tactics of Social Influence

In some instances, we comply to the requests of other people not because of their attributes but because of the tactics they use. For example, a person knocks on your door and shows you a picture of handicapped children, and you give him a three-dollar donation; a telephone solicitor persuades you to buy a three-year subscription to *Mountain Climber's Weekly* even though you break into a cold sweat if you go any higher than the second story of a building; a department store clerk gets you to buy the more expensive of two shirts you were considering.

One common tactic used to produce compliance is *reciprocity;* if someone does someone else a favor, the latter feels obliged to reciprocate. (See chapter six.) Thus, the act of doing a favor can be used as a social influence tactic. Cialdini (1984) claimed that businesses often use this tactic to get people to buy their products. He provided the example of a company that gives potential customers free samples of its products to use for a few days. When the salesperson returns to pick up the unused portion of the product, people usually purchase some—not necessarily because they like the product, but because they feel obligated to repay the favor.

Another tactic is *ingratiation*, in which one person attempts to gain control over another by agreeing with him. (See chapter six.) In recent years, social psychologists have focused their interest on other influence tactics, such as the foot-in-the-door technique and the low-ball technique.

Foot-in-the-Door Technique

When I was in college, I spent part of one summer working as a factory representative for the Auto-Magic Pen and Pencil Company of Detroit, Michigan. My job was that of a pitchman. I would stand in front of small crowds of people, or "tips" as pitchmen call them, and try to sell a $2.95 pen and pencil set. I was given a pitch to memorize and told never to deviate from it. An important aspect of my pitch was how it set people up for the "close"—the point at which the people are asked to buy something. Before I asked them for any money, I showed my audience a less expensive pen. I told them that this pen was not yet on the market. Then I said, "If it were for sale, how many of you would buy it? If you would, please raise your hand." At the close of the pitch, I asked them to do exactly the same thing, but this time people who raised their hands were agreeing to pay $2.95 for the set.

The logic behind this part of the pitch was that people who complied with a small request (like raising their hand) would be much more likely to comply with a later, larger one, like actually purchasing the product. Door-to-door salespeople call this the "foot-in-the-door" technique. They believe that if people will allow them in their homes, they are much more likely to agree with a request to buy something. Freedman and Fraser (1966) were the first to empirically test the efficacy of the *foot-in-the-door* influence tactic. They found that when people agreed to a small favor—placing a very small sign in their yards—the chances that they would agree with a later request to place a very large and ugly sign in their yards were dramatically increased. Since this study, the foot-in-the-door technique has been used to get people to do such things as sign a petition (DeJong, 1981) or donate money (Schwarzfeld, Bizman, and Raz, 1983), and it has been found effective in most instances (Beamen, Cole, Preston, Klentz, and Steblay, 1983).

The original explanation of why compliance with a small request produces compliance with a subsequent larger request was based on Bem's (1972) self-perception theory. (See chapters five and ten.) Basically, it was argued that as the result of compliance with the first request, people come to see themselves as helpful and thus are more likely to help in the future. This explanation was accepted for a long time, but recent research has raised some questions about whether self-perception can totally explain the effectiveness of the foot-in-the-door technique (Beamen et al., 1983;

DeJong, 1979). A study by Rittle (1981) suggested that compliance with the first request, in addition to changing self-perceptions, may also change people's perceptions of being compliant. As the result of complying and experiencing no negative consequences (and perhaps experiencing positive consequences), people's views of compliant behavior changes. As a result, they are more likely to help on subsequent occasions.

Low-Ball Technique

The family car is on its last legs—or wheels. Dad decides to purchase a new automobile. He goes to his favorite dealer and test drives a new station wagon. To his surprise, he discovers that (a) he really likes the station wagon and (b) he can purchase the car for about $10,000. Although the final papers are not signed, Dad and the salesperson agree on the final price, the color of the car, whether or not there will be a service contract, and so on. The car will be ready next Tuesday. On the appointed day, Dad packs the family into the soon-to-be-discarded family car and heads for the dealership. When he gets there, he is in for a surprise. The salesperson tells Dad that the boss will not approve the sale because there was a mistake in the calculations; the car will cost $11,000. When Dad protests, the sales-person points out that this is only a 10 percent increase in the cost of the car, and if Dad wants to investigate, he will find that this price is the same as other dealers are charging for this model. Dad knows this is true because he priced this model at other dealerships. If Dad pays $11,000 for the car—and he probably will—he has been influenced by a tactic car dealers call low-balling.

In a 1978 article, Cialdini and his associates (Cialdini, Cacioppo, Bassett, and Miller, 1978) studied the efficacy of the low-ball technique. They found that when people freely make a preliminary decision that would commit them to some course of action, they will engage in that course of action even when the costs of the action increase. **Low-balling** differs from the foot-in-the-door technique in the following respect: In the foot-in-the-door technique, the target behavior is different from the behavior that is initially requested; in low-balling, the target behavior is the same as that initially requested.

Pallack, Cook, and Sullivan (1980) used a variant of the low-ball pro-cedure to increase energy conservation. Homeowners were asked to reduce the amount of natural gas they used each month and told that if they did so, their names would appear in newspaper articles as public-spirited, civic-minded citizens. After a month of dutiful energy conservation, the homeowners learned that it would not be possible to publicize their names. Remarkably, they saved *more* gas after learning this than they had before.

Cialdini (1984) explained the success of low-balling by proposing that people become committed to the behavior, whether it is buying a car or conserving energy. Even when the costs increase or the rewards decrease, this commitment to the behavior motivates people to comply with the initial request.

Low-balling: an influence tactic wherein the costs or rewards for performing a behavior are changed after people agree to perform the behavior.

The tactic of low-balling is used by automobile dealers to get the buyer to pay more money for a car.

A study by Burger and Petty (1981) suggests that commitment to the person making the request may be more important than commitment to the behavior. Subjects who had already completed an experiment were asked to participate in a second experiment. One-third of them (the control group) were told that they would receive no additional extra credit for their participation in the second study. The remainder of the subjects were low-balled. They were initially told that they would receive extra credit points, but a few minutes after they had agreed, they learned that these points were not available. They were asked again if they wanted to participate in the second experiment. For half the subjects who were low-balled, the second request came from the same person who had asked them initially; for the other half of the low-balled subjects, the second request came from a different person. Thus Burger and Petty created three groups: (a) control, (b) low-ball, same requester, and (c) low-ball, different requester.

If the effectiveness of low-balling is due to a commitment to the behavior, it should have made little difference whether the second request came from the same or a different person. But if the effectiveness of low-balling depends on commitment to the person who elicited agreement with the initial request, then subjects who were asked twice by the same person should have complied more than those who were asked by different people. Compliance with the second request was greatest when it was made by the same person as had made the first request. (See figure 11-3).

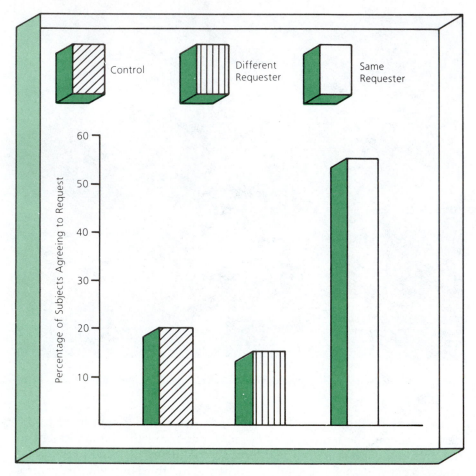

Figure 11-3. *The low-ball technique was most effective when the same person made both requests.*
Source: Burger and Petty (1981).

Research Highlight

Door-in-the-Face Technique

In his book *Influence*, Robert Cialdini (1984) tells about an incident in which he was approached by a Boy Scout and asked to purchase two five-dollar tickets to a charity circus that would be held the following Saturday night. Cialdini, who had better things to do with his time and money, refused. Then the Boy Scout asked him if he would buy some chocolate bars, which cost a dollar a piece. Cialdini bought two. What aroused Cialdini's interest was that he did not like chocolate. Why then did he buy the bars?

Before this question is answered, consider another example of the same influence tactic. Television producers often argue with network censors over what material can and cannot be used in a show. One technique producers have developed to manipulate the censors is to place lines in a script which they know the censors will cut. They then "retreat" to the lines they originally wanted. Gary Marshall, the producer of "Happy Days" and "Laverne and Shirley," described how he used this technique:

We had a situation where Squiggy's in a rush to get out of his apartment and meet some girls upstairs. He says: "Will you hurry up before I lose my lust?" But in the script we put something even stronger, knowing the censors would cut it. They did; so we asked innocently, well, how about "lose my lust?" "That's good," they said. Sometimes you gotta go at em backward.

On the "Happy Days" series, the biggest censorship fight was over the word "virgin." That time, says Marshall, "I knew we'd have trouble, so we put the word in seven times, hoping they'd cut six and keep one. It worked. We used the same pattern again with the word "pregnant." (Russell, 1978, cited in Cialdini 1984, pp. 51, 52)

Cialdini and his associates (Cialdini, Vincent, Lewis, Catalan, Wheeler, and Darby, 1975) called the tactic used by both the Boy Scout and the television producer the door-in-the-face technique and offered the following explanation of it. The Boy Scout's request was so unreasonable that Cialdini turned him down. Cialdini saw the second, smaller request as a concession made by the Boy Scout. Since the Boy Scout had conceded a little, so did Cialdini, and he ended up buying the unwanted candy bars. The door-in-the-face technique is almost exactly the opposite of the foot-in-the-door technique, in which compliance is produced by first making a large request and then making a smaller, more reasonable one.

Harari, Mohr, and Hosey (1980) examined the efficacy of the door-in-the-face technique. Unlike the subjects in most of the experiments you have read about, their subjects were not students but professors. These professors were asked by a student to spend two hours with him or her in a discussion of their department's value in the current educational system. For about half the professors, this request was preceded by a much larger request; they were asked to spend two hours a week for the next three weeks helping the student with a term paper on this topic. Seventy-eight percent of the professors who had previously received the large request and turned it down agreed to the second, smaller request; 57 percent of the professors who received only the small request agreed to it. The initial door in the face increased compliance with the second request.

SUMMARY

The study of social influence concerns what gives an individual or a group the ability to change people's beliefs or behavior. Certain attributes give individuals this ability, or social power. The first two of these attributes are being able to control whether people are rewarded and being able to control whether people are punished; these are called reward and coercive social power. These kinds of social power produce compliance rather than true change; if the influencing agent loses control of rewards and punishments, compliance disappears. Coercive social power can also produce psychological reactance, a negative reaction to being controlled.

The third attribute that provides social power is being liked, respected or, admired; this is called referent social power. People act in accord with the influencing agent because they identify with and want to be like him. The agent does not need to watch them to influence their actions. The fourth basis of social power is having expertise. If people believe that the change advocated by the influencing agent is the correct one, they will experience private acceptance of the agent's position.

The fifth basis of social power is the right to control another person, or legitimate social power. An agent has influence over people because they accept rules that say the agent can tell them what to do. In some situations, legitimate social power can produce socially undesirable behaviors. One situation is when people feel that they are not responsible for their own actions but are merely carrying out the orders of someone in authority.

The ability of people to control or change the actions of others may be based on the tactics they use rather than on their attributes. Two such tactics are the foot-in-the-door technique and the low-ball technique.

GROUP INFLUENCE ON THE INDIVIDUAL

The first section of this chapter focused on the attributes and tactics that give an individual the ability to influence another. In this section, the focus of attention turns to how and why groups influence an individual. The discussion of this topic begins with descriptions of some old but very important studies of group influences on individuals. It then turns to current explanations of why people sometimes yield to group pressure and sometimes resist group pressure.

Sherif's Research

In 1935, Muzafer Sherif reported on some of the first systematic studies of group influences on an individual's thoughts and actions. He presented subjects with an illusion known as the autokinetic phenomenon. If people are placed in a darkened room and asked to stare at a small spot of light projected onto a wall, they will see the light appear to move. In fact, the light is stationary and the apparent motion is due to the movement of the people's own eyes. Sherif asked subjects to estimate how many inches the light had moved. After a short period of time, subjects would settle on a consistent estimate. Once this had been established, Sherif exposed the subjects to a group of confederates who unanimously gave an estimate quite different from those given by the subjects. For example, if a subject said the light moved four inches, the confederates would say 16 inches. This caused the subjects to change their estimates. In this example, the subjects said the light moved 14 or 15 inches. The subjects were not displaying compliance; they did not say this only when the confederates were present. Subsequent research (Rohrer, Baron, Hoffman, and Swander, 1954; MacNeil and Sherif, 1976) found that subjects could be influenced by the confederates for a long time after the initial encounter.

Why did the judgments of the confederates have this impact? According to Sherif, they did not influence a subject's perception of how much the light had moved. Instead, they provided the subject with a frame of reference for how many inches this movement represented (Sherif, 1963). Suppose you are taken by three friends to see a professional volleyball game. You are amazed by the speed of play and by how hard the players hit the ball. This isn't the game you played in sixth grade. You say to your friends, "Boy, that ball must be going at least 20 miles an hour when someone slams it." Your friends laugh and tell you that 100 miles an hour is more like it. (This is, in fact, true.) From then on, you will estimate the speed of the ball quite differently.

In ambiguous situations or in situations in which a person has no previous experience, the judgments of others will establish a standard, or **norm,** for thoughts and actions. This norm will serve as a frame of reference when the person encounters the situation again (Wheeler, Deci, Reis, and Zuckerman, 1978). As Wheeler and his associates (1978) pointed out, Sherif's primary interest was in the product of group influence, or norms. He was not as interested in the process of group influence, the mechanism that leads people to change their judgments to fit those of the group. This question was addressed several years later by Solomon Asch.

Norm: a standard or guide for people's behavior and beliefs.

Asch's Research

Asch's view of social behavior was greatly influenced by the gestalt tradition in psychology. (See section on impression formation in chapter four.) The gestaltists said people actively process and organize the information they receive from others. Asch looked at the behaviors of Sherif's subjects and wondered how they processed the discrepant information they received from the confederates. The situation Asch (1951, 1952, 1955, 1957) created to answer this question was quite different from that created by Sherif. The stimuli Sherif's subjects were asked to judge were ambiguous; there was no correct answer to the question of how much the light had moved. But the stimuli Asch's subjects were asked to judge were clear-cut. The subjects were shown two cards. On one was a single vertical line called the standard line; on the other card were three vertical lines, called the comparison lines. Subjects were to say which of the comparison lines matched the standard line. This was a very easy task; when working by themselves, subjects rarely chose the wrong line. (See figure 11-4.)

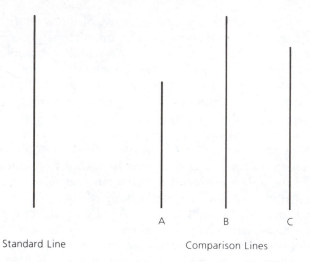

Standard Line   Comparison Lines

Figure 11-4. In Asch's experiment, subjects were to judge which of the three comparison lines matched the standard line.
Source: Asch (1951).

In the critical part of Asch's experiments, the subjects were not alone but were part of a small group. Each group member was asked to look at a set of cards and then say aloud which of the three lines matched the standard line. There were 18 sets of cards. There was nothing unusual about the group members' responses on the first two sets, but on the third set something strange happened. The first group member gave a clearly incorrect response, as did the second, third, and fourth members. These incorrect judgments continued until it was the last person's turn to respond. As you have probably figured out, the other group members did not just happen to make the same incorrect choice on this trial. They were confederates who had been instructed to make unanimously incorrect choices on certain sets of cards. They were to create a unanimously incorrect majority.

Asch had created a dilemma for the one true subject in the group. On the one hand, his eyes told him that, say, line C matched the standard line. But on the other hand, a group of his peers with vision at least as good as his had chosen a different line. Thus, the subject was subjected to "two contradictory and irreconcilable forces" (Asch, 1951).

Asch found that the group influenced the individual's choices. About 76 percent of the subjects went along at least once with an obviously incorrect choice of the unanimous majority. On the average, subjects agreed with the majority's judgment on about one-third of the trials.

Most people find Asch's results interesting, but some do not see the significance of his findings. Asch's experiment demonstrated a significant social phenomenon, **conformity.** He also showed that under conditions where people would not be expected to yield to group pressure, subjects did yield, or conform. Since Asch's original research, the process he identified has been found to affect behaviors ranging from how many people wait in line for a bus (Mann, 1977) to the solutions college students offer

Conformity: a change in behavior or belief that results from real or imagined group pressure.

for interpersonal problems (Santee and Maslach, 1982). You are exposed to group pressure almost every time you interact with other people. How you dress, what you say, and perhaps even what you think can be modified by the judgments of others.

A former student of Asch used the basic procedure developed by his teacher to demonstrate that group pressure could be used to induce behaviors that people would typically not perform. The former student was Stanley Milgram, the author of the experiment presented in the prologue.

Milgram (1964) investigated how group pressure would influence subjects' behaviors in another experiment using the situation described in the prologue.

Subjects were randomly assigned to either an experimental or a control group. Subjects in the control group received instructions about the purpose of the experiment, were assigned the role of teacher (the person who administered shock to the learner), and were told to decide for themselves how much shock the learner should receive after he made an error. Subjects in the experimental condition were subjected to group pressure. Two confederates were also assigned the role of a teacher. After the learner (also a confederate) made an error, the three teachers would together decide how much shock to give him. They were to use the following procedure: The first teacher would recommend a shock level, the second teacher would do the same, and then the third teacher would decide on the amount of shock to give the learner and would actually give the shock. It was made clear that the third teacher did not have to give the shock level recommended by the other teachers; he could choose one that was higher or lower. The one true subject was always assigned the role of the third teacher, and the two confederate teachers always unanimously recommended a 15-volt increase after an error. (See figure 11-5 for the results of this experiment.)

Of the 40 subjects in the control condition, two gave the learner more than 150 volts of electric shock. Twenty-five of the 40 subjects in the group-pressure condition gave more than 150 volts. Only one subject in the control condition gave the maximum shock, but seven in the group pressure condition did this.

Conformity

In a science, it is not enough to demonstrate the existence of some phenomenon—one must also explain why it occurs. One of the first attempts to explain why Asch's subjects acted as they did was made by Deutsch and Gerard (1955). They proposed that two separate influence processes could produce conformity: normative and informational.

Normative Social Influence

In **normative social influence,** people conform not because they believe in what they are saying or doing but because they think this is what expected of them. Deutsch and Gerard argued that conformity is not a true change because it is a change in behavior without a change in belief—in other words, it is compliance. Normative social influence causes people to do or

Normative social influence: a tendency to conform to a group norm because of the belief that this is what others desire.

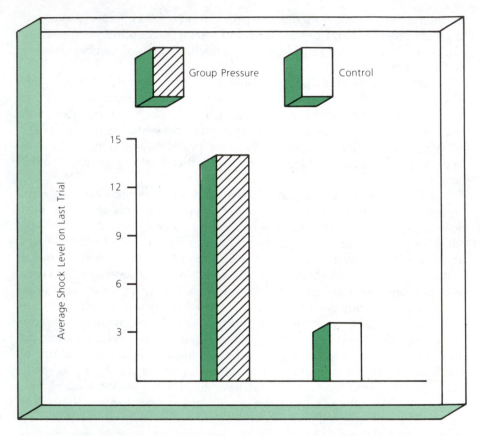

Figure 11-5. *Subjects shocked the victim much more in the group pressure condition than in the control condition.*
Source: Milgram (1964).

say things they do not believe for two reasons. People may fear the negative consequences of not conforming or they may conform because they are attracted to the group that advocates that behavior.

Fear of Negative Consequences   The fear that if one does not conform, one will experience negative consequences is similar to the reaction to coercive social power. But in most instances, group coercion is subtle or may only exist in the mind of the individual. This can be illustrated by my behavior on the day I attended my first class in graduate school. Until that day, my typical attire was a pair of very faded Levis, a torn and ragged flannel shirt, and a pair of loafers that had not been shined in months. But when I entered that class at 8:00 A.M., I wore a sport jacket, a clean white shirt, and a tie. I looked as if I were all set to sell life insurance. Why? Because I expected that this would be the norm in the class, and I did not want to stand out or look foolish. Unfortunately, the standard dress in class that first day was jeans, a flannel shirt, and unshined loafers.

The negative consequences in this example were self-generated. In some situations, however, groups do punish those who do not conform.

THE FAR SIDE   by Gary Larson

Laboratory peer pressure

Reprinted by permission of Chronicle Features, San Francisco.

According to Festinger (1950), groups prefer uniformity in the opinions and actions of their members; they desire adherence to the group norm. If someone deviates from the norm, a group's initial reaction is to try to persuade him to accept the norm. If persuasion fails, the group will often use less subtle means. It may ridicule (Asch, 1952) or punish the deviant. Freedman and Doob (1968) convinced a group that one of its members had consistently conformed to its norms while another had consistently deviated from its norms. The group was then asked to pick two of its members to take part in additional experiments. In one of these, the subjects would receive money; in another, the subjects would receive electric shock. The group chose the conformer for the money experiment and the deviant for the shock experiment.

If persuasion, ridicule, and punishment fail to change the deviant's position, the group will probably reject the deviant. This is especially likely when the group is close knit and uniformity is necessary for the group to reach its goals. Evidence suggests that deviants know they will be rejected without an explicit message from the group. Allen (1964) led subjects to believe that they either had or had not deviated from their group's norms. Deviants were much more likely to expect that they would be rejected from the group than were nondeviants.

In some circumstances, groups do not autmomatically punish or reject deviant members. One is when the member has achieved a good deal of status within the group. Gerson (1967) looked as how fraternity members reacted to behavior that deviated greatly from a group norm. They were told that someone in the fraternity had sold copies of the fraternity's test files to an outsider. Some were told that the guilty party was a high-status member of the fraternity, and others were told that the guilty party was a low-status member. The fraternity members recommended a written apology when this violation was committed by the high-status person, but recommended a one-semester suspension from the fraternity for the low-status member.

Idiosyncrasy credits: certain actions or characteristics which give people the ability to deviate from group norms and to avoid punishment.

Hollander (1971) attempted to explain the kind of response made to the high-status member by proposing the construct of **idiosyncrasy credits.** Hollander argued that group members who have contributed to the group in the past and have previously conformed to group norms build up credits in the same way that one builds up money in a bank account. When people deviate from the norm, these credits enable them to do so without any penalty. However, just as people who overdraw their bank accounts are punished, so are people who use up their idiosyncrasy credits punished or rejected by the group.

Attraction to the Group   It would be incorrect to conclude that normative social influence is always based on negative consequences. In some instances positive motivations cause a change in people's behavior without any change in their beliefs. For example, if group members are committed to helping their group reach some goal and believe that going along with the group norm will increase the chances that the group will reach that goal, they may engage in compliance. Consider the political party system in the United States. Each party has a primary election to choose its party's candidate. Once the primaries are over, the losers often promise their full support to the winners. The reason for this is not that the losers have changed their feelings about the winners, but that they believe any member of their own party would be a better office holder than a member of the other party. Therefore, they conform to the party norm.

Informational Social Influence

Informational social influence: a tendency to conform to a group norm because of the belief that the group norm is correct.

The other major process that Deutsch and Gerard (1955) believed produced conformity was called **informational social influence.** The change produced by informational social influence is basically the same sort of change produced by expert social power—a change in belief as well as behavior, or private acceptance, because people believe that the group's position is correct. If a task is difficult, if people are unsure of themselves, or if the group has expertise, people are likely to accept the group norm as correct and to conform (Allen, 1965).

The belief that the group norm is correct may also influence judgments on relatively simple tasks. Deutsch and Gerard (1955) repeated Asch's original experiment with one significant modification. In one condition of the experiment, subjects thought their answers would be anonymous. Thus, the normative social influences on them would be minimal; the other members of the group would not know which line they had chosen. Even in this condition, some of the subjects conformed to the group choice. Their behavior appeared to be due to informational social influence.

Put yourself in one subject's place. You are sure, but not *absolutely* sure, that you know which line matches the standard. These other folks, however, also seem sure that their choice is correct. You have learned from prior experience that the odds that everyone else is wrong and you are right are usually quite small. So even on this very simple task, you occasionally give the group's judgment more weight than yours. If the other people were not confederates, this would not be a bad strategy. Other people are a valuable source of information about reality, and it is often reasonable to accept their views of the world. Researchers have proposed two processes to explain why informational influence may lead people to conform: social comparison and cognitive restructuring.

Social Comparison   The idea that other people provide information about reality is at the core of Leon Festinger's (1954) **theory of social comparison processes.** Festinger proposed that people are interested in determining if their views of reality are valid. If the reality is physical, people do not need to turn to others for validation of their views, but if the reality is social, people often need to turn to others. For example, I do not need others to help me determine if dropping a priceless vase to the floor will cause it to break (physical reality). But I do need others to help me determine if dropping priceless vases to test my hypothesis is a good idea (social reality).

If people's view of social reality is not supported by others, they will do one of three things; they will try to change other people's view to match their own; they will disregard other people as sources of valid information about social reality; or, if they are unable or unwilling to do either of these, they will change their views to match those of others. If people change their own views, they are not engaging in spineless, wishy-washy behavior. They are merely accepting a reasonable source of information about the nature of social reality.

Cognitive Restructuring   A similar explanation of conformity has been offered by Allen and Wilder (1980). They argued that conformity may involve a two-step process. In the first step, people learn that their peers have made a unanimous judgment of some stimulus. This causes them to modify their own interpretations of the stimulus. When they have reinterpreted the stimulus in the manner suggested by the peers' judgment, the peers' position becomes more acceptable. As a result, the chances that people will conform increase greatly. For example, a person opposes gun control because he sees it as restricting everyone's right to own any kind of firearm. Then he is confronted by the fact that all of his peers favor gun control. This causes him to rethink what gun control means. He comes to see gun control as a way of keeping firearms out of the hands of criminals. As a result of this changed interpretation, he decides he favors gun control.

Allen and Wilder experimentally tested this proposal. Their subjects believed they were helping to develop a questionnaire by providing interpretations of phrases that would be used in it. Subjects were randomly assigned to one of three groups. Members of the control group read a statement such as "I would never go out of my way to help another person

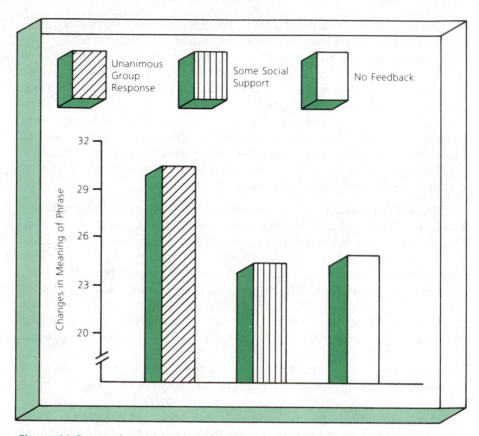

Figure 11-6. *Confronted with a unanimous response by their peers, subjects reinter-preted the stimulus presented to the peers such that their behavior now became understandable.*
Source: Allen and Wilder (1980).

if it meant giving up some personal pleasure." They were then asked to indicate what the phrase "go out of my way" meant in that sentence. They did this by looking at the following scale and circling the number that came closest to their understanding of the meaning of this phrase.

Be inconvenienced   1 2 3 4 5   Risk my life

Subjects in the second and third conditions were asked to do exactly the same thing, but first they learned how some of their peers had responded to the original statement. Subjects in the second condition learned that three out of four people who answered this question agreed that they would not go out of their way to help another person. Subjects in the third condition learned that all of their peers had answered that they would not go out of their way to help another person. Allen and Wilder proposed that these subjects would experience conflict, they would wonder how their peers could agree with such an unpopular position. To resolve this conflict, they would reinterpret the meaning of the phrase "go out of my way" such that it would explain their peer's behavior. They would be much more likely to believe that the phrase meant "risk my life" than would members of the other two groups. This is what happened. (See figure 11-6).

In a separate experiment, Allen and Wilder (1980) investigated how this reinterpretation would affect conformity. Half their subjects learned that their peers had interpreted the phrase "go out of my way" to mean "risk my life." The other half of the subjects did not receive this reinterpretation of the phrase. Subjects in the first group conformed significantly more than did subjects in the second group. Restructuring of reality affected the subjects' tendencies to conform.

Nonconformity

Not all of the subjects in Asch's original experiment conformed; 24 percent did not go along with the unanimous majority, and few conformed on every trial. A failure to change in response to group pressure is called nonconformity (Allen, 1975). Like conformity, nonconformity incorporates two separate processes. Forsyth (1983) called one **independence** and the other **anti-conformity.** A teenager who wears an unusual hairdo because he really likes this style is displaying independence; a teenager who wears an unusual hairdo because this drives his parents up a wall is displaying anticonformity. Given the value most people place on independence, one would think there would be considerable research on nonconformity. But researchers know a good deal more about why people yield to group pressure than why they resist it, although they have given some attention to social support for nonconformity.

Independence: people's expression of beliefs and behaviors that are consistent with their own standards.

Anti-conformity: the expression of beliefs and behaviors that are the opposite of the group norm.

In Asch's original series of experiments, he found that if a naive subject had an ally when confronted by the unanimous majority, conformity dropped from 33 percent to 5 percent. The social support another person provided all but eliminated conformity. The research of Vernon Allen and his colleagues (Allen, 1975) suggested that this is a generalizable finding. As a rule, the presence of someone who joins an individual in dissent from the majority reduces conformity. Bragg and Dooley (1972) found that the effects of social support for nonconformity remain even after the supporter has left the scene, and a study by Allen and Feldman (1971) suggested that social support from someone who is not physically present when the group pressure is exerted also reduces conformity.

Allen has proposed two general explanations of these findings. One is that people who have some degree of social support are less likely to believe that they will experience negative consequences for their dissent and, as a result, are less likely to conform. A study by Allen (1964) supported this proposal. Subjects who differed from a group norm were asked to estimate the likelihood they would be rejected from the group. When they were a lone dissenter, 69 percent estimated that they would be rejected. When they had an ally, only 30 percent estimated that this would happen. Newston, Allen, and Wilder (1973) found that subjects were less likely to attribute dissent to a personal characteristic when there was social

Although people often yield to group pressure, there are times when they refuse to go along with the crowd.

support for the dissent. This suggests that social support lessens the chances that people will be labeled as deviants or oddballs because they dissent from the majority view.

The other explanation for the effect of an ally's presence comes from Allen and Wilder's 1980 study presented earlier. In this study, when peers unanimously endorsed an unpopular statement, subjects reinterpreted the meaning of a key phrase in the statement. However, when one of the peers dissented the subjects did not reinterpret the statement. The fact that some-one else shared their views reduced the need to engage in cognitive re-structuring of reality.

Under some circumstances, the presence of an ally does not reduce conformity. One such circumstance is when people are more likely to iden-tify with the majority than with their fellow dissenters. Boyanowsky and Allen (1973) studied this. White subjects who were prejudiced against blacks were exposed to pressure from an all-white majority. Half of these subjects received support from another white person, while the other half received support from a black person. When the task concerned physical reality (the length of lines), black and white supporters were equally ef-fective in reducing conformity. But when the task concerned social reality (opinions or personal beliefs), the white supporter was much more effective than the black supporter. In this study, the support of a black person actually increased the prejudiced white subjects' tendencies to conform with the majority's position. Prejudiced white subjects agreed with the views of a black when they and a black person were alone, but they rejected a black person's position in the presence of other whites. Evidently, the subjects failed to accept social support offered by a black person because they were afraid they would be rejected by the other whites if they agreed with a black.

Individual Differences in Reactions to Group Pressure

When Asch first published his conformity research, many people found it hard to believe that "normal" individuals would act as his subjects did. They felt that his subjects must have yielded to the obviously incorrect judgments of others because of a basic weakness in their personality structures. But research failed to identify any personality variable or variables that were consistently associated with conformity.

The interactionist view of human social behavior may explain this failure. (See chapter three.) The interactionist view proposes that human social behavior is the product of interaction between both personal characteristics and the situations people encounter.

Research Highlight

A Voice in the Wilderness

Most researchers interested in social influence have studied the process whereby the minority is influenced by and conforms to the majority view. Part of the reason for this focus is that at the time Asch did his landmark studies there was considerable concern about majority suppression of minority dissent. In the late 1940s and early 1950s, the memory of Hitler's suppression of dissent in Germany was still fresh in people's minds and professors at American universities were losing their jobs because they expressed unpopular views.

Serge Moscovici acknowledged that majority influence on the minority is a valid phenomenon to study, but he argued that it is not the only kind of social influence in a group. In some instances, the majority may be influenced by the minority. Moscovici and his associates (Moscovici, 1980); Moscovici and Faucheux, 1972; Moscovici and Personnaz, 1980) have studied this minority influence.

Moscovici and Faucheux created a situation where four naive subjects and one confederate were asked to identify what characteristic a series of objects shared. The confederate consistently gave the wrong answer. The influence of his behavior on the majority was determined by comparing the majority's answer to that of a control group that did not contain a lone dissenter. Moscovici and Faucheux found that if the dissenter was highly consistent in his judgment, the majority was aware of this consistency and perceived the dissenter as having confidence in his judgments; they were influenced by him.

In later studies, Moscovici (1980) demonstrated another aspect of minority influence. Subjects were exposed to positions on social issues that were either moderate and reasonable (for example, automobile makers should put pollution control devices on the cars they produce) or extreme and unreasonable (for example, the government should close down any industry that causes pollution). These positions were attributed either to a majority or to a minority group. The subjects were then given a series os statements, some of which expressed sentiments consistent with but not identical to the positions they had just heard. Subjects indicated whether or not they agreed with these statements. Three weeks later, the subjects returned and did the same thing. The dependent measure was the extent to which the subjects agreed with these statements.

Initially, the reasonable majority had more influence on the subjects than did any other group. But when the subjects were retested three weeks later, a very different picture emerged. The unreasonable minority position had the greatest influence on the subjects' views. According to Moscovici, the reasonable majority had merely produced compliance. The unreasonable minority had produced conversion to its position.

While some researchers have questioned Moscovici's findings, minority influence on the majority probably merits more study. Most social movements begin with a small group of people who dissent from popular opinion. It would be interesting to learn why some succeed and others fail.

In different situations, different characteristics may be relevant to the behavior of interest. People may conform on one occasion because of normative social influence and on another because of informational social influence. A personality characteristic that predisposes people to yield to normative social influence probably would not also predispose people to yield to informational social influence. The effects of interaction between personal characteristics and situational factors can be seen in studies of sex differences in conformity.

Sex Differences

The initial research on individual differences in conformity suggested that although no "conforming personality" could be found, women conformed more than men (Allen and Crutchfield, 1963; Endler, 1966). The explanation for this was that women are socialized to be docile, compliant, and submissive; men are socialized to be strong and independent (Krech et al., 1962). Sistrunk and McDavid (1971) suggested that this may not be the only reason greater conformity had been found in women than in men. They believed that many conformity researchers may have used stimuli that were more interesting or familiar to men than to women. As a result, men were more likely to resist conformity pressures in those experiments.

Were the situation reversed, Sistrunk and McDavid argued, men would conform more than women because the key variable is not sex, but the type of material used.

To test this proposal, three sets of items were developed: male oriented, female oriented, and sex neutral. Male and female subjects were given all three sets of items and exposed to group pressure. On the sex-neutral items, women conformed slightly more than men; on the male-oriented items, women conformed much more than men, and on the female-oriented items, men conformed significantly more than women.

A more recent study (Eagly, Wood, and Fishbaugh, 1981) illustrated another way in which a situational variable may interact with a person's gender to affect conformity. The subjects were male and female college students who were asked to give their opinions on a number of different issues. The experiment was rigged so that before the subjects gave their own views, they were exposed to the unanimous opinions of a group of their peers. Half the subjects were assigned to a surveillance condition in which their peers would supposedly know how they had responded. The other half were assigned to a no-surveillance condition. (See figure 11-7 for the results.)

Females conformed more than men only in the surveillance condition. However, females conformed an equal amount in both conditions, whereas males conformed significantly less in the surveillance condition than in the no-surveillance condition. Why would men conform less when their peers would know how they had acted? Eagly and her associates offered an explanation based on the concept of impression management. (See chapter five.) Part of the male image, they argued, is that men remain strong and independent even in the face of group pressure. Actions inconsistent with this image would place a male subject in an unfavorable light; therefore, males were just as willing as females to yield to group pressure in the no-surveillance condition, but they protected their image in the surveillance condition and yielded less to group pressure.

Self-Presentation

The idea that responses to group pressure are often part of people's attempts to control the image they present to others led Santee and Maslach (1982) to study some other personality correlates of reactions to group pressure. They gave subjects scales that measured two separate aspects of impression management. The first was a desire to present oneself as a unique individual; the second was a concern with acting in a socially appropriate and acceptable manner. Santee and Maslach found a negative relationship between the first characteristic and conformity, but they found a positive relationship between the second characteristic and conformity. They also found that the strength of these relationships depended on certain situational variables. They exposed subjects to two types of majorities, one that was unanimous and another that was split in its opinions. Subjects who desired to present themselves as unique individuals were much more likely to dissent when the majority was unanimous than when

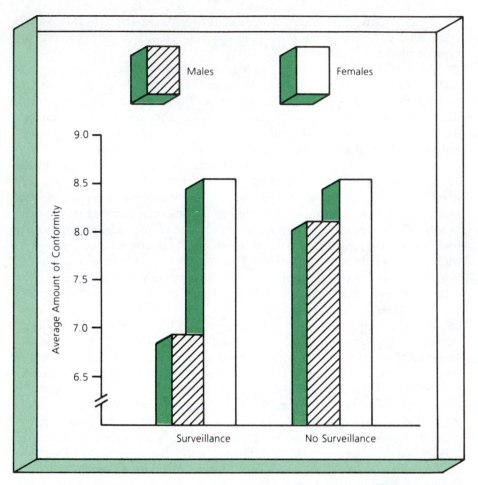

Figure 11-7. *In the surveillance condition males conformed much less than females, but in the no survellance condition males and females conformed a comparable amount.* Source: Eagly et al. (1981).

it was split. Why? According to Santee and Maslach, because a unanimous majority presented them with the clearest chance to show that they were unique individuals. This finding underscores a point made earlier. People's personal characteristics affect how they react to group pressure, but they do not operate independently of the situation in which group pressure is applied. Personal characteristics interact with situational variables to affect conforming behavior.

Deindividuation

The material presented thus far suggests that group membership can cause people to engage in behaviors they would not normally perform. With the exception of the Milgram experiments on shock, the behaviors have been pretty tame. But now consider this factual account of the Oneida commune led by John Noyes, a renegade preacher. This commune existed in upstate New York during the late sixties and early seventies.

When Noyes believed that certain of Oneida's young people were mature enough for their first sexual experience, community women volunteered to share their beds with teenaged boys, while Noyes or other older men of his choosing would indoctrinate the female virgins. In addition to pleasing the older people, Noyes believed that this system offered the young the benefit of more experienced lovers—and, since the older males had already proven themselves faithful to Noyes' policy of "male continence," there was little chance of unwanted pregnancies. Although the younger members would also be permitted to enjoy sex within their age group, there was constant community pressure against any sign of "exclusive" love.

   In the free-love system at Oneida, any man wishing to go to bed with a certain woman had to first submit his request to a Noyes-appointed intermediary, a senior woman who then relayed the "invitation" to the desired woman and ascertained whether or not the latter was willing. While any woman could refuse the propositions of any and all men, such rejections were generally not the rule in Oneida's sex-affirmative society; and the sexual records kept by Oneida's intermediaries indicated that most community women had an average of two or four lovers a week, and some of the younger women had as many as seven different lovers in a week. (Talese, 1980, pp. 341, 342, 364)

Oh well, another of those free-love communes from the crazy sixties. Yes, that's true—the *1860s*. The community at Oneida was founded by Noyes in 1849 and lasted until 1879. The residents of Oneida were not twentieth-century hippies, engaging in anticonformity. All members of the community worked six days a week; they ran a number of successful businesses, including a company that made tin-plated spoons (the Onieda silver company is still in operation); education was compulsory; and the most gifted children from Oneida attended colleges such as Columbia and Yale, where they were trained as doctors, laywers, and engineers. However, the sexual behavior of the people who lived in this commune was socially unacceptable in nineteenth-century America. Indeed, it would be socially unacceptable to most Americans today.

   This is an extreme example of how group membership can affect people's behavior. But considerable evidence suggests that under certain circumstances, group membership can result in an increase in socially unacceptable or even antisocial actions (Festinger, Pepitone, and Newcomb, 1952). Diener, Fraser, Beamen, and Kelem (1976) looked at the behavior of children who were out trick-or-treating. One of the homes the children visited was part of their experiment. When the children knocked on the door, they were shown into a room that contained a bowl of candy and a bowl of pennies. An adult told the children they should take only one piece of candy and then left the room. When the children were in a group, 60 percent of them either took more than one piece of candy or took some of the money; when the children were by themselves, only 20 percent did this. Other studies have shown that group membership can increase people's willingness to aggress (Prentice-Dunn and Rogers, 1983) and can lower inhibitors against socially inappropriate behaviors (Diener, 1980).

Deindividuation: a psychological state in which people have decreased senses of personal identity and responsibility.

Zimbardo (1970) proposed that the mechanism responsible for this is **deindividuation.** He believed that group membership may lead to deindividuation because people feel more anonymous in a group or because group members act in accord with the roles they have been assigned rather than their personal values.

Anonymity

In Diener and his associates' 1976 study of children's behavior while trick-or-treating the researchers also looked at how anonymity would affect the children's behaviors. They found that children who were required to identify themselves before the adult left the room were much less likely to commit a transgression than were children allowed to hide behind their Halloween masks. Rogers and Prentice-Dunn (1981) found that when subjects are made to feel anonymous, their levels of aggression increase.

Assignment of Roles

There are many instances of what appears to be deindividuated behavior in which people have little if any anonymity. In the Oneida commune, official records were kept of who slept with whom and how often. In the prologue experiment, Milgram's subjects were not anonymous, and yet they seemed to be willing to engage in antisocial, destructive behaviors.

An explanation was offered by Milgram: The subjects acted this way largely because they saw themselves as agents of a higher authority and because they felt that this authority responsible would take responsibility for their actions. They were just doing their jobs. Zimbardo (1973) made a similar analysis. People are assigned a role to play; their behaviors are the result of the requirements of that role rather than their beliefs, personality characteristics, or values,

Zimbardo provided a dramatic demonstration of what he proposed. He used newspaper advertisements to recruit 24 normal, college-age males. These men were told about the general purpose of the experiment and offered $15.00 per day to participate After they had agreed, a coin flip was used to decide who would be prisoners and who would be guards. The guards were given a general briefing about the dangers of being a prison guard but were given no specific instructions on how to act. It was left up to them to establish the prison's rules.

The experiment began with the prisoners being picked up unexpectedly at their homes. They were taken to a police station where they were fingerprinted and booked. Then they were taken to Zimbardo's mock jail. The prisoners were stripped, searched, deloused, and given uniforms with numbers on them. Then they were shown to the cells where they were to spend the next two weeks.

Six days later, the experiment was terminated because many of the guards had become excessively brutal in their treatment of the prisoners. They took pleasure in acts of cruelty and humiliation. The prisoners became "servile, dehumanized robots." They seemed to lose all sense of personal identity and social responsibility. Prisoners called each other by their numbers. On one occasion, they let a prisoner spend the night in a small closet rather than give up their blankets.

What caused these people to act as they did? Zimbardo argued that labeling people as guards and prisoners and putting them in a situation where the labels are relevant produced the pathological behavior observed among his subjects:

> The prison situation, as presently arranged, is guaranteed to generate severe enough pathological reactions in both guards and prisoners as to debase their humanity, lower their feelings of self-worth, and make it difficult for them to be part of a society outside of their prison. (1973, p. 164)

There is little question that in the case of prisoners, this dehumanization does occur. In the riot at Attica State Prison in 1971, the prisoners presented a list of demands that would have to be met before the riot would end. Consider the preamble to this list:

> We are MEN! We are not beasts and do not intend to be beaten or driven as such. The entire prison populace has set forth to change forever the ruthless brutalization and disregard for the lives of the prisoners here and throughout the United States. What has happened here is but the sound before the fury of those who are oppressed. (Cited in Wicker, 1975)

Deindividuation and Antisocial Behavior

Why should anonymity or assuming a role cause people to act in an extremely antisocial fashion? To answer this question, Diener (1980) and Prentice-Dunn and Rogers (1983) have used the construct of **self-awareness** (Wicklund, 1975). When people focus their attention on themselves as opposed to the world around them, they are in a state of self-awareness. (See chapter five.) One of the consequences of this is an increased awareness of their personal standards and values (Wicklund, 1975). When people focus their attention outward, their awareness of these internal standards decreases; as a result, the influence these standards exert over people diminishes and the influence certain aspects of the situation exert increases. If these situational cues suggest antisocial socially unacceptable behavior, the likelihood that such behavior will occur increases. It appears that group membership, anonymity, and assuming certain roles can all serve to reduce self-awareness, which can produce deindividuated actions.

Many antisocial actions can be explained by situational variables that produce diminished self-awareness and deindividuated behaviors, but this explanation can be overused. For example, Zimbardo's analysis of the problems in many prisons may not apply to all prisons. The physical conditions that exist in most prisons are atrocious; many prisoners are dehumanized before they are incarcerated; and prison guards are often poorly trained individuals who lack the characteristics needed to perform an adequate job (Wicker, 1971). Similarly, while common, ordinary, nonmalevolent people were willing to injure another person in the Milgram experiments, one should not conclude from this that Nazis like Eichmann were common, ordinary, nonmalevolent individuals. The point of the research on deindividuation and conformity is that under certain circumstances, people can be made to do things they would not otherwise do.

SUMMARY

One way groups influence an individual is by establishing norms and then putting pressure on the individual to adhere to them. A change in behaviors or beliefs as the result of this pressure is called conformity. It is believed that two separate processes lead to conformity. The first is called normative social influence. People often conform in response to normative social influence because they believe this will help a group reach its goals or because they fear negative personal consequences if they do not conform. These negative consequences can be self-generated—people conform to avoid looking foolish—or they can be generated by the group.

The second major influence that leads to conformity is called informational social influence, which produces true changes. It is likely to occur when a task is difficult or when there is no objective way of determining what is the correct position on an issue. In such instances, people use the group norm as information about reality.

Most of the pressure on group influence has focused on conformity. However, people do not invariably yield to group pressure. People may remain independent or even engage in anticonformity, in which they do exactly the opposite of the group norm. Collectively, these behaviors are known as nonconformity. Attempts to identify the personality characteristics that differentiate between conformers and nonconformers have not been successful This is probably because the same person may conform in different situations for different reasons.

Sometimes, as the result of group membership, people become deindividuated; they develop a decreased sense of personal identity and responsibility. As a result, they are capable of acting in socially unacceptable or antisocial ways. Two aspects of group membership that may be responsible for this are an increased sense of anonymity and an identification with the role assigned by the group.

Applications

Medical Regimens: Just What the Doctor Ordered

Most medical and behavioral researchers agree that certain psychological processes can play a role in the development of certain health problems. For example, it is believed that the Type A behavior pattern may be related to the incidence of coronary heart disease. (See the applications section of chapter three.) This section addresses another way in which social psychological processes can affect people's health.

People visit physicians because they want to prevent an illness or want a cure for an illness they already have. Unless the physician is a surgeon, it is unlikely that the physician will directly solve the medical problem or prevent its occurrence. For example, if the problem is high blood pressure, the doctor does not treat it during the visit, but prescribes medication and a special diet. Similarly, if the problem is an infection, the doctor usually prescribes an antibiotic that the patient should take for several days. In essence, patients usually pay for advice on how they themselves can treat or prevent an illness, and a cure largely depends on the extent to which they agree with and follow this advice. This is an example of the process of social influence.

According to Gachtel and Baum (1983), while the reasons people do or do not follow a medical professional's recommendation are the most thoroughly researched aspects of health-related behaviors, failure to comply with such recommendations remains a serious health problem. In the first part of this section, the extent of the problem and its causes and consequences are examined. Then the focus turns to ways by which the incidence of compliance may be increased.

COMPLIANCE WITH MEDICAL REGIMENS

A **medical regimen** can range from a suggestion that a person quit smoking to instructions on a bottle of pills. Here the term *compliance* means the act of accepting and following a medical regimen; noncompliance is the failure to accept and follow a medical regimen (Sackett and Haynes, 1976). Researchers have studied both the causes and the consequences of noncompliance.

Medical regimen: a course of action that a medical professional believes will positively affect people's health.

Causes of Noncompliance

Compliance rates as low as 8 percent and as high as 96 percent have been found in different studies. Most reviews of this research area conclude that, on the average, 40 to 50 percent of the people who are told to follow a medical regimen fail to do so (Sackett and Snow, 1979; Stone, 1979). These rates of noncompliance can even be found for regimens that are extremely simple and very important. Bergman and Werner (1963) looked at compliance rates among children who had seen a doctor and were supposed to take penicillin for ten days. By the third day, 56 percent of the children had stopped taking the pills; by the ninth day, the noncompliance rate was 82 percent. Other researchers have examined compliance with recommended self-examination. Breast cancer is the major cause of death for American women between the ages of 40 and 49. The earlier this form of cancer is discovered, the more favorable is the prognosis. Self-examination for breast cancer is simple, inexpensive, and noninvasive, but polls of American women indicate that over half either fail to conduct periodic self-examinations or conduct them incorrectly (Melamed, 1984).

In general, acute, serious illnesses that have painful or distressing symptoms produce the highest levels of compliance. The longer an illness lasts, however, the lower the rate of compliance. Charney (1972) reported that among diabetics, the incidence of noncompliance (identified as giving themselves the wrong dosage of insulin) was 30 percent for those who had had the disease for less than five years. The incidence of dosage errors was 80 percent for those who had had the disease for more than 20 years. In addition, complex regimens result in less compliance than simple regimens. And regimens with unpleasant side effects have lower compliance rates than those with no side effects (Hulka, Cassel, Kupper, and Burdette, 1976; Melamed, 1984).

One consistent finding has been that the more satisfied patients are with their health professionals, the more likely they are to comply with a regimen. Francis, Korsch, and Morris (1969) interviewed mothers who had taken their children to a physician and had had treatment regimens prescribed for those children. Francis and associates obtained data on satisfaction with the physician and compliance rates. As satisfaction increased, so did compliance rates. (See figure 11-8).

Some researchers have sought to identify the demographic or personality characteristics associated with compliance. According to Kasl (1975), there is no evidence that people differ in their willingness to comply with regimens as a function of demographic characteristics such as age, race, sex, social class, or marital status; nor have any personality differences between compliers and noncompliers been found.

Consequences of Noncompliance

The most obvious consequence of noncompliance is that an illness is either not prevented or not cured, but there are other consequences as well. For example, if a patient discontinues a medication without telling the physician or takes less of the medication than the physician has prescribed, the physician may conclude that the dosage prescribed was too low. As a result, the physician may later prescribe an inappropriately high level of the drug and overmedicate the patient (Stone, 1979).

An important aspect of medical treatment is getting a patient to comply with the doctor's recommendations.

INCREASING COMPLIANCE WITH MEDICAL REGIMENS

The first part of this chapter introduced the concept of social power—the ability to influence the thoughts or actions of another person. The ability to exert this influence depends on some characteristic that the influencer possesses or is believed to possess by the object of the influence attempt. It can be the ability to reward or punish the person (reward or coercive social power), being liked by the person (referent social power), or being correct (expert social power). It has been argued that since compliance with medical regimens is essentially a social influence process, it may greatly depend on the social power of health professionals. Patients may often fail to comply with a regimen because health professionals use the wrong types of social power when attempting to influence their patients or do not possess the characteristics that would give them social power over their patients (DiMatteo, 1979; Janis, 1982, 1983; Rodin and Janis, 1979, 1982; Stone, 1979).

Reward and Coercive Social Power

Most medical professionals have neither the time nor the inclination to constantly monitor the extent to which their outpatients comply with pre-scribed regimens. Thus, reward and coercive social power, both of which require surveillance to be effective, are usually of little value in producing compliance among outpatients (Janis, 1983; Rodin and Janis, 1979). However, certain treatments are conducted in the office and require considerable compliance and cooperation from the patient. One such treatment is that which dentists provide in their office. For dentists to effectively complete a procedure, their patients must comply with a series of requests. If the patients fail to comply, they may receive less than optimum treatment; they may also develop negative attitudes toward dental treatment and fail to seek it when needed. Melamed and her associates (1983) reported that as many as 12 million Americans avoid dental treatment every year because of negative feelings about it.

In a 1983 study, Melamed and her associates looked at the effects of rewards and punishments on children who had visited a dentist. The children were randomly assigned to one of four different conditions. In the first condition, the dentists verbally rewarded cooperative behavior and ignored uncooperative behavior. In the second condition, they ignored cooperative behavior and verbally punished uncooperative behavior. In the third condition, the dentists used both rewards for cooperation and punishments for uncooperation. In the fourth condition, a control condition, the dentists used neither reward nor punishment. Each child was seen four times by the same dentist, and at each visit the dentist rated the child's cooperativeness and level of fear.

The clearest differences between the four conditions were found during the first two visits. (See figure 11-9.) Children in the punishment condition were significantly more disruptive at these two visits than were children in the other conditions. By the fourth session, this difference had all but disappeared. However, one should not discount the potentially negative consequences of using only punishment (coercive social power) to try to induce compliance. The subjects in this experiment were forced to visit a dentist once a week for four weeks; they may have become accustomed to the dentist. Had the subjects been given a choice, those in the punishment condition probably would have avoided further visits to the dentist.

Instrumental Conditioning

The principles developed by learning theorists have been used by other researchers to engender compliance with medical regimens outside the doctor's office. Dworkin (1982), for example, has used instrumental conditioning to produce compliance among people suffering from curvature of the spine, or idiopathic scoliosis. This illness usually begins with a single curve in the spine. A second curve will often develop as the result of the person's attempts to compensate for the first curve. The traditional treatment for this illness is the Milwaukee brace. It basically encases the entire upper body and neck and, to be effective, it must be worn about twenty-three hours a day. People suffering from this illness, especially adolescents, fail to wear the brace.

Dworkin and his colleagues have developed a small device (about the size of a pack of cigarettes) that is worn by a person who has idiopathic scoliosis. The device detects changes in the length of the person's spine and gives off a signal that is audible only to that person. The person is

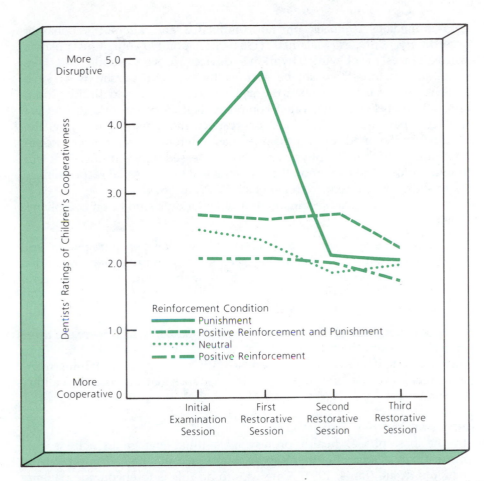

Figure 11-9. *Punishment produced the most disruptiveness at the time of the childrens' second visit to the dentist. Reprinted by permission of the publisher and the authors.* Source: Melamed et al. (1983).

then to adjust his posture to the correct position. If this is not done in twenty seconds, the signal becomes loud enough for others to hear. Dworkin and his associates found that ten of the 12 patients who used this device for two years showed an 8 percent reduction in the curvature of their spines. This was as much improvement as has been found among patients who wear the cumbersome Milwaukee brace.

Conditioning techniques have also been used to increase compliance among diabetics, people undergoing chemotherapy for cancer, and individuals on long-term weight-loss programs (Melamed, 1984).

Referent Social Power

The use of Dworkin's monitoring device increases the likelihood that a person with scoliosis will adhere to a treatment regimen. The person gets immediate feedback on noncompliance and alters his behavior accordingly. But, as Melamed (1984) has pointed out, the positive consequences of obeying Dworkin's device are very subtle and take some time before they can be seen. Why would a person wear such a device every day and obey the signal? Irving Janis and Judith Rodin (1979, 1982) believed that often compliant behaviors are due to the fact that the patients admire, like, or respect the person providing the treatment; the medical professional has referent social power. Rodin and Janis felt that "a physician who possessed referent social power would increase the likelihood that patients will feel personal responsibility in adhering to prescribed regimens" (1979, p. 64).

A quote from a subject in another of Dworkin's studies on compliance illustrates this point:

> I always depend very heavily on Barry Dworkin's encouragement and his personality . . . He not only seems aware of my general condition but he is never satisfied with less than my best and I cannot fool him. I feel we are friends and allies—it's really as though [we're doing this together]. (Cited in Jonas, 1972)

Rodin and Janis (1979) have proposed a model in which there are three critical phases in the health professional's use of referent social power to increase compliance with a regimen: acquiring, using, and retaining referent social power. Several studies provide evidence that supports the validity of this model.

Acquiring Referent Social Power

In the first phase, health professionals must engage in actions that make them *significant others,* people whose acceptance and approval the patients desire (Janis, 1983). One way to do this is to encourage patients to engage in self-disclosure and to provide understanding and acceptance when they do. The health-professional becomes someone patients can rely upon and trust; someone who will accept them with all their weaknesses and defects.

Research has shown, however, that the relationship between self-disclosure and adherence to a regimen is curvilinear; a moderate amount of self-disclosure between a medical professional and a patient produces more adherence than very little or a great deal of self-disclosure (Rodin and Janis, 1979; Janis, 1983). Janis and Quinlan (1982) proposed two possible explanations of why extremely high levels of self-disclosure produce less compliance than do moderate levels of self-disclosure. First, even though a medical professional provides support and understanding, excessive levels of disclosure about their weaknesses and defects demoralizes people and shakes their self-confidence. As a result, they come to doubt their abilities to adhere to a difficult regimen, such as an extended diet. Second, excessive levels of self-disclosure may make patients too dependent on the health professional and make them expect that the health professional will solve their problems for them.

Using Referent Power

Once medical professionals have acquired referent social power, they must use it to get patients to comply with their regimens. Janis (1982) lists several things that will serve this end. Patients must be given specific recommendations as to the actions in which they should engage. Patients must also become committed to these actions and see failure to engage in them as a violation of the norms of an important group. And patients must be given a sense that they can control and are responsible for whether or not they benefit from the regimen.

Retaining Referent Social Power after
Termination of Contact

At some point, the patients' regular contacts with their health professionals have to end. Rodin and Janis believed that it is crucial that compliance with the regimens continue. To achieve this continued compliance, they recommended that health professionals assure patients that there will be communication between them in the future; assure patients that they will continue to have positive regard for them; and attempt to increase patients' senses of responsibility and self-control.

Rodin and Janis's model makes sense and is consistent with research on the social influence process, but there have been no direct tests of its validity. However, a fair amount of evidence shows that the social support of a significant other will increase long-term compliance with both prevention and treatment regimens.

Janis and Hoffman (1982), for example, conducted a ten-year study of the effects of a treatment designed to reduce or stop smoking. People who had come to an antismoking clinic were randomly assigned to one of three conditions: a high-contact partner condition, in which they and another person going through the program were required to speak with each other every day for five weeks; a low-contact partner condition, in which individuals were assigned a partner but not required to keep in contact; and a no-partner control condition. One year later, the members of the control group were smoking 30 cigarettes per day; members of the low-contact group were smoking about 20 cigarettes per day; and members of the high-contact group were smoking five cigarettes per day. Ten years after the start of the program, people in the first two groups were smoking 20 to 25 cigarettes a day; members of the high-contact group were, on the average, smoking less than two cigarettes per day.

Janis and Hoffman believed that the high-contact partner provided the support and encouragement needed to get through the early stages of not smoking. Recordings of conversations between the partners disclosed that they praised one another's successes in cutting down and criticized one another for backsliding. Although informal contact between the partners continued for some time after treatment, the researchers do not believe social support can explain the differences one and ten years after the program had ended. They suggest that the presence of a partner caused the subjects to internalize the norms established in the program and diminished the impact of the formal end of the program.

Nowell and Janis (1982) used basically the same procedure in a program designed to help women lose weight. Women in the high-contact condition lost more weight and stayed with the program longer than did women in the low-contact and no-contact conditions.

Finally, Caplan, Harrison, Wellons, and French (1980) investigated the impact of social support provided by a nurse on compliance among people suffering from high blood pressure. Their major findings were that social support from the nurse produced increases in motivation to comply with the regimen; the increased motivation produced increases in compliance; and the increased compliance produced decreases in the patients' blood pressures.

Expert Social Power

Expert social power produces influence in the absence of surveillance, and most medical professionals possess this kind of social power. But, as Stone (1979) pointed out, physicians should not assume that their expertise alone will cause compliance with a regimen. They must also determine their patients' abilities to understand and carry out the instructions contained in a regimen, their patients' views of their personal responsibilities for successful treatment, and their patients' reactions to the physician's attempts to control their behaviors. Ley and Spelman (1967) analyzed the readability and understandability of instructions given to lower-economic-class hospital patients. Using a formula that provides a measure of reading ease, Ley and Spelman found that the hospital's instructions were much too difficult for these patients to understand.

The Return of Dr. Fox?

In general, people benefit from following their doctors' orders, and compliance is preferred to noncompliance. As a result, social psychologists and other scientists have been interested in ways by which compliance with medical regimens can be increased. But Irving Janis (1983), one of the leading researchers in this area, has sounded a cautionary note. He has pointed out that some medicines, despite the claims of their makers, are at best neutral and sometimes even harmful. Some medical professionals, despite their supposed expertise, make mistakes or are simply "quacks." Researchers interested in compliance may want to study ways by which people can intelligently decide to *not* comply with regimens that do not produce any benefits for them. Just as we must teach people not to be seduced by the style of phonies such as the Dr. Fox you read about earlier, so we must teach people not to be seduced by the style of an incompetent medical professional.

Chapter Twelve

Interdependent Social Behavior

Prologue

Joseph B. Sidowski, L. Benjamin Wyckoff, and Leon Tabory. (1956). The influence of reinforcement and punishment in a minimal social situation. *Journal of Abnormal and Social Psychology*, **52,** 115–119.

Background

This chapter examines social interactions in which the outcomes for the participants are jointly determined by their actions. Joseph Sidowski and his associates believed that the outcomes of such interactions are determined by the rewards and punishments each participant provides for the others and that, over time, participants will develop a pattern of interaction that is rational and mutually beneficial. Sidowski and his associates' problem was how to demonstrate that this pattern is due solely to the rewards and punishments, and is not due to more traditional social psychological constructs—such as how much the participants in the interaction like one another or what attributions they make about one another's behaviors. To solve this problem, the researchers created a situation which they said would "seem strange to most social psychologists"—the minimal social situation. In the minimal social situation, two people are unaware of each other's existence, but each has control over the rewards and punishments the other receives.

Hypothesis

The major hypothesis made by Sidowski and his associates was that over time, people in the minimal social situation will learn the behaviors that maximize the positive outcomes and minimize the negative outcomes from the interaction.

Subjects

The subjects were 40 male undergraduates at the University of Wisconsin.

Procedure

Two subjects participated in the experiment at the same time, but each was led to believe he was the only person in the experimental session. One subject was seated in front of a panel that contained shock electrodes, a counter, and two buttons. The electrodes were attached to the subject's left hand, and he was informed that during the experiment he would both receive shock through the electrodes and earn points. The number of points earned would be shown on the counter. The experiment would begin when a white light went on and end when the light went out.

While the light was on, the subject was to press either of the two buttons in any manner he wished and as frequently as he wanted to. The only restrictions were that the subject not press both buttons at the same time and not hold a button down once he had pushed it. The subject's goal was to earn as many points as he could. Although the relationship between the buttons and the shock or points was never discussed, most subjects believed that their own pattern of button pushing would affect whether they received points or shock.

This belief was not entirely correct. When the subject in one room (subject A) pushed the right-hand button, the subject in the other room (subject B) received one point; when subject A pushed the left-hand button, subject B received a shock. Subject A unknowingly had direct control over what happened to subject B. And subject B unknowingly had direct control over what happened to subject A. When subject B pushed the right-hand button, subject A received a shock; when subject B pushed the left-hand button, subject A received one point.

There were two conditions in this experiment. In the first condition, both of the subjects in an experimental session received weak shock; the shock was just strong enough for them to feel that they were receiving it. In the other condition, both of the subjects in an experimental session received strong shock; the shock was twice as strong as that received by subjects in the weak-shock group. The dependent measure for all subjects was the proportion of responses in which one subject gave the other subject a point rather than a shock.

Results

The results of this experiment are very simple and straightforward. (See figure 12-1.) By the time five minutes had elapsed, subjects in the strong-shock condition were pushing the buttons that gave each other points almost 70 percent of the time. In the weak-shock condition, the subjects chose this button about 40 percent of the time. Although they had no contact and were unaware of each other's existence, subjects in the strong-shock condition learned a pattern of interacting that was mutually beneficial.

Implications

When people first read about the minimal social situation, many wonder about its relevance to real-world social interactions in which people are aware of one another and have give-and-take exchanges. Sidowski and his associates would be the first to admit that these real interactions are much more complex than the minimal social situation. But the situation they created in their laboratory does contain the basic characteristics of any true social interaction: interdependence of the actions of the parties to the interaction and interdependence of the outcomes each party receives. In the first part of the chapter, this idea, as well as Sidowski and his associates' proposal that learning principles can be applied to social interactions, are examined. As the chapter progresses, the strengths and weaknesses of this approach to interdependent social behavior are discussed.

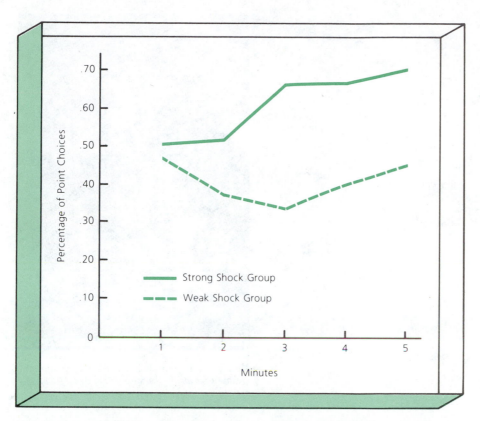

Figure 12-1.   *Within five minutes the subjects in the strong shock group were selecting the point button 70 percent of the time. Copyright (1956) American Psychological Association. Reprinted by permission of the authors.*
Source: Sidowski et al. (1956).

The fact that the minimal social situation was presented in the prologue suggests that many social psychologists—including me—consider it an important part of research on interdependent social behavior. Indeed, this is true (for example, Gergen, 1969; Raven and Rubin, 1983; Rosenbaum, 1980; Thibaut and Kelley, 1959). As noted in the presentation of this experiment, however, the minimal social situation is so unusual, so minimally social, that perhaps a more clear-cut illustration of interdependent social behavior is needed.

Chang and Eng Bunker were brothers who lived and worked in nineteenth-century America. As their first names suggest, they were of Chinese ancestry. They adopted the surname Bunker after they immigrated to the United States. Although they had almost no formal education and came from a very poor family, the Bunker brothers achieved considerable fame and fortune. They had a successful career in show business, after which

Chang and Eng Bunker. Their lives provided the ultimate example of interdependent social behavior.

Cooperation: behavior in which people work toward goals that will benefit themselves and other individuals.

Competition: behavior in which people work toward goals that will benefit only themselves.

they enjoyed considerable prosperity as farmers in a small North Carolina community. The brothers' brides were also sisters, Adelaide and Sarah Yates. The two families produced twenty-one children (Wallace and Wallace, 1978).

What makes the lives of Chang and Eng Bunker so remarkable and so relevant to this chapter is a physical characteristic they possessed: From their births in 1811 until their deaths in 1874, they were joined at the abdomen by a 5½-inch piece of ligament. Although their parents were Chinese, they were born in Siam. They were the original Siamese twins.

If one stops and thinks about how Chang and Eng Bunker must have had to live, one sees perhaps the ultimate example of social interdependence. This chapter addresses less extreme instances of interdependent social behavior than do either the minimal social situation or the lives of the Bunker brothers. But all interdependent social behaviors share these characteristics in common: first, the behavior of one party to an interaction affects the behavior of other parties to the interaction, and vice versa; second, each party's outcome from the interaction is at least partially determined by the other parties' outcomes; and third, parties to interdependent interactions are faced with a choice between **cooperation** and **competition.**

In the first section of this chapter, a general theory of the variables that determine people's interdependent social behaviors is presented and illustrated. In the second section, the discussion turns to interdependent social behavior where, unlike the situation that confronted the Siamese twins, there is a genuine conflict of interest between the parties involved. In the third section of the chapter, two questions are addressed: how people decide if they have been treated fairly in an interdependent interaction and what people do if they decide they have not. In the applications section, applications of these concepts to civil and international conflict are examined.

SOCIAL EXCHANGE

Many researchers use the term social exchange to describe the phenomenon of interest in this chapter (Homans, 1961; Gergen, 1969; Gergen, Greenberg, and Willis, 1980; Thibaut and Kelley, 1959). A social exchange is a give-and-take relationship between two or more people. The first question that can be asked about a social exchange is what principles guide people's behavior in such relationships.

Sidowski and his associates proposed that the basic principles of learning theory could explain their subjects' behavior in the minimal social situation. They argued that the subjects developed a mutually beneficial pattern of responding because it was rewarding to do so. Imagine that two minutes into the experiment both subjects have by chance chosen to push the button that gives the other one a shock. Thinking that their own behavior is responsible for the shock, each next chooses the other button. Both of them receive a reward, a point on the counter. Reinforcement theory says the point increases the probability this choice will be repeated. If it is repeated, both subjects receive another point, and soon they are locked in to a mutually cooperative strategy. The ability to develop this strategy depended on the joint efforts of the participants.

This idea is at the core of a much more elaborate theory of the causes of interdependent social behavior, John Thibaut and Harold Kelley's (1959) **social exchange theory.**

Social Exchange Theory

The basic premise of this and other exchange theories (for example, Homans, 1961) is that human interactions can be conceptualized as business transactions. People exchange resources with one another in the hope that they will earn profits. Suppose you have a midterm at 9:00 A.M., and you are staying up late to study. It's now 3:00 A.M. In addition to being sleepy, you are very hungry. A nice sausage pizza would really hit the spot. There is a problem, however; you have the money to buy a pizza, but the nearest pizzeria is three miles away, and last week your car went to the great car wash in the sky. You approach another student who is also staying up all night and has a car. You make her an offer: You will pay for the entire pizza and give her half, if she will drive to the pizzeria and pick it up. Since she is also hungry but broke, this sounds like a good deal.

Social exchange theory: the theory that participants in an interaction jointly determine the rewards and costs they receive from it.

But she has a question: "What will be on the pizza?" "Sausage, what else." "I hate sausage," she replies. "I want three-quarters of the pizza to be anchovies or there's no deal."

You are in a bind. You are so hungry, you could eat dirt—but not an anchovy. So you make a counteroffer; the pizza will be half sausage and half anchovy, and you will give her a dollar for gas money. She agrees. The pizza is ordered, picked up, and eaten, and you continue your studies with a full stomach.

Before considering the tactics you and the other person used to reach this agreement, examine a social exchange theory analysis of the interaction. Social exchange theory says that the quality of an interaction—how satisfied you and the other person are with your pizza arrangement—depends on the outcomes each participant receives. These outcomes are profitable for people if the rewards they receive are greater than the costs they incur. A reward is anything that gratifies people's needs; in this case, it was a pizza. A cost is anything people must sacrifice. In this case, your primary cost was money (and perhaps having to look at the anchovies). Your acquaintance's costs were time, a little effort, and some minimal automobile expenses. Perhaps the key aspect of this interaction was the interdependence of the two participants. If either of you had reneged on the deal, or broken off the negotiations on sausage versus anchovies, neither would have obtained what you wanted. Just as Sidowski and his associates' subjects jointly determined what happened to them, so the two of you jointly determined the outcome of your interaction. But this outcome was less than you originally wanted; your original offer was half a sausage pizza if the other person would pick it up, and you ended up paying an extra dollar and looking at a distasteful food. Was this outcome acceptable to you?

Comparison level: the level of satisfaction people expect from an exchange.

To answer this question, Thibaut and Kelley (1959) introduced the concept of a **comparison level.** People's comparison levels are the product of their past experiences with the other parties to the exchange, their past experiences in other similar exchanges, and their general views of what can be reasonably expected from the exchange. When actual outcomes drop below their comparison levels, people become dissatisfied and will try to change the outcomes. If they cannot change the outcomes, they *may* leave the relationship. However, people do not automatically leave or break off relationships when actual outcomes fall below their comparison levels. They also examine what the outcomes in the other relationships would be. For example, you may have felt dissatisfied with the arrangement for obtaining the pizza, but when you looked at your options, it was the best you could do. The only other person awake who had a car had the values of Darth Vadar and would have demanded at least $6.00 and three-fourths of the pizza. You decided to stay in this relationship because of your **comparison level for alternatives.** If the level of satisfaction in a current relationship, however bad, exceeds that which would be found in an alternative relationship, people will probably stay in the present relationship.

Comparison level for alternatives: a comparison between the level of satisfaction people are presently receiving and the level of satisfaction they would receive from alternative relationships.

The final characteristic of this episode is that it represents an exchange process; one person provided something and, in return, received something. In this exchange, you provided money; in return, you received half a pizza with sausage. The other person provided transportation and received half a pizza with anchovies and a dollar. This was essentially a business transaction with a tangible outcome, but even in social transactions with intangible outcomes, things are exchanged. Foa and Foa (1980) proposed that in all interpersonal relationships, there is an exchange of **resources.** They proposed that one can conceive of the resources people exchange as belonging to one of six classes. (See table 12-1.)

Resources: anything that can be transmitted from one person to another.

Table 12-1.   *The resources exchanged between people.*

Goods—any products or objects
Information—advice, opinion, or instructions
Love—affectionate regard, warmth, or comfort
Money—any coin or token that has some value
Services—activities of the body or belonging to the individual
Status—an evaluative judgment which conveys high or low prestige

Source: Fao and Fao (1974).

Some of the resources are concrete, such as money, and others are abstract, such as status. The specific kind of resource exchanged depends on the nature of the relationship. For example, money and goods are likely to be exchanged in a business transaction; love and status are likely to be exchanged in a social transaction (Buss, 1983; Clark and Mills, 1979). Exchanges are also more likely to occur within resource classes than between them. People are more likely to exchange love for love than love for money (Brinberg and Castell, 1982). (Unless that's how they earn their living.)

The minimal social situation, the lives of the Bunker brothers, and the pizza transaction all contain the same basic elements of a social exchange—interdependence and joint determination of the outcome. But the first two share a characteristic that is not shared by the third: complete mutual cooperation is needed to produce the best outcome. This is not to say that exchanges such as these are free from strife. Shock was used in Sidowski and his associates' experiment to teach the subjects to press the reward button. And things were not always peaceful between Chang and Eng. Once, when the brothers were helping to repair the roof of their church, Eng smashed Chang's fingers with a hammer. A fistfight ensued, which ended only when both (of course) brothers fell from the roof (Wallace and Wallace, 1978). But in the final analysis, there was no rational alternative to total cooperation for Eng and Chang.

In the pizza exchange, however, one participant did better for herself by trading her resources for a greater portion of the outcome and being slightly less cooperative. Humans do not spend a significant portion of their time arguing about the division of pizzas at 3:00 A.M., but they do spend a good deal bargaining about the outcomes of exchanges. The next section examines some of the variables which affect bargaining.

Bargaining

Bargaining: an activity in which parties to an exchange attempt to decide what each will give and what each will get.

The definition of **bargaining** used by most social psychologists is a good description of what happened in the pizza transaction. It can also describe exchanges between a professional athlete's agent and the owner of a team negotiating a salary, representatives of labor and management trying to avoid a strike, lawyers trying to work out a plea bargaining arrangement, two countries discussing a treaty to limit nuclear arms, and a couple writing a prenuptial divorce settlement (Rubin and Brown, 1975).

Rubin and Brown (1975) proposed that all such exchanges have certain characteristics. First, the exchange occurs because there is some conflict of interest and no simple, easily obtainable distribution of resources that all parties would see as meeting or exceeding their comparison level. Second, the goal of the exchange is the division or exchange of specific resources or the resolution of less tangible issues. The attempt to reach this goal usually involves some proposals or demands presented by one party, followed by evaluation of these by the other party, "followed by concessions and counterproposals" (Rubin and Brown, 1975, p. 14). And third, participation in the exchange is voluntary. Voluntary here does not mean that people get a warm glow when they think about the prospect of bargaining; in fact, they may find it quite distasteful. Participation in the exchange is voluntary because all parties believe there is more to gain than to lose if they negotiate or bargain with one another.

In recent years, some researchers have begun to study bargaining exchanges in naturalistic settings, but most of what is known about people's behavior in these exchanges comes from laboratory experiments. In these experiments, subjects are asked to play games that contain the basic elements of a bargaining exchange. One of the most widely used games is the *bilateral monopoly game* (Siegal and Fouraker, 1960). In this game, one person is the only seller of some commodity and one person is the only buyer of that commodity. The parties to the exchange are the only ones interested in the commodity, and they must reach a negotiated settlement or both lose.

Subjects are assigned the role of either the buyer or the seller and told that their goals are to achieve the maximum profit for themselves. Usually, the subjects' profits are points that can be exchanged for money at the end of the experiment. The conflict of interest comes from how each person will achieve a maximum profit. Their task is to use proposals, counterproposals, and concessions to arrive at an agreement both find acceptable.

The following example illustrates the elements of the bilateral monopoly game. Imagine a very small town with only one meat-packing company and only one restaurant that serves hamburgers. The meat-packing company wants to sell small quantities of hamburger meat at high prices per pound. The restaurant, which has to sell its hamburgers at a fixed price, wants to buy large quantities of hamburger at low prices per pound.

The game begins with the company offering to sell one hundred pounds of hamburger at two dollars a pound. The restaurant then makes a counterproposal, offering to buy two hundred pounds of meat at one dollar a pound. Offers and counteroffers are made until the parties reach an agreement or decide they want to break off negotiations. In this game, as in most social exchanges, situational variables and personality characteristics affect the parties' behavior.

Situational Influences on Bargaining Behavior

Researchers have used the bilateral monopoly game as well as other games to study how people bargain and to determine what influences a person's effectiveness in a bargaining exchange. Most of this research has focused on how situational variables can influence the manner in which people bargain and the outcomes of exchanges.

Site of the Negotiations Some negotiations, like those in a laboratory, take place in neutral sites, but many take place in the home territory of one of the parties to the exchange. Experts in international negotiations (Ball, 1972; Coffin, 1973) have argued that people who negotiate in their home territories may have a real advantage over their visitors, and the available research (Taylor and Lanni, 1981; Martindale, 1971) tends to support this argument. Martindale had subjects assume the role of either a defense attorney or a prosecuting attorney. Their task was to negotiate how much of a penalty the defense attorney's client should receive. Half of the bargaining sessions took place in the living quarters of the subjects who played the role of the defense attorney; half took place in the living quarters of the subjects who played the role of the prosecuting attorney. The dependent measure in the experiment was the amount of penalty the defendant received compared to an independent estimate of how much penalty the defendant should receive. Subjects who negotiated in their home territories talked more, were more dominant, and were more assertive than were their visitors. This was reflected in the outcomes of the exchanges. When the sessions took place in the defense attorney's living quarters, the penalty received by the defendant was less than the independent estimate; when the sessions took place in the prosecuting attorney's living quarters, the penalty received by the defendant was greater than the independent estimate.

Time Pressures It is August, and your favorite football team is in preseason training camp. Unfortunately for you and other fans, the team's star player has still not reported to camp. He has played out his contract, and his agent and the team owner cannot reach a new agreement. This situation frustrates you because the contract expired nine months ago. This is not unusual. Labor unions and management often do not start bargaining in earnest until a few hours before a scheduled strike. And if the experiences of my many divorced friends is representative, most negotiated divorce settlements do not occur until a day or two before a judge is supposed to hear the case.

If bargaining is to the mutual advantage of the participants, why do people often put it off until the eleventh hour? One reason is simple personal animosity; people get angry at one another and do not do the things that are in their best interests. Another reason is tactics; people believe that if they wait until the last minute, they will be able to wring more concessions out of the other participants to the exchange.

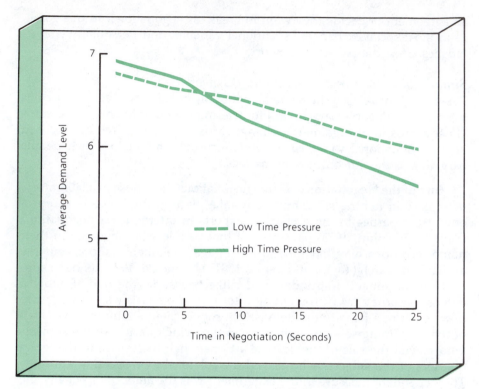

Figure 12-2. As time passed, subjects in the high time pressure condition began to demand less. Copyright (1982) American Psychological Association. Reprinted by permission of the authors.
Source: Smith et al. (1982).

A study by Smith, Pruitt, and Carnevale (1982) supports this belief. They had subjects play a game in which they would bargain over the division of a reward. On each of twelve trials, two subjects would try to reach an agreement on how to divide ninety cents between them. One subject would make an initial demand, say, 70 cents. The other subject would make a counterdemand, and they would go back and forth until either they reached agreement or the time for the exchange had ended. The dependent measure was what the subjects demanded over the course of an exchange. Half the subjects were allowed 90 seconds to reach an agreement (a low-time-pressure condition); half were allowed 45 seconds (a high-time-pressure condition). To make sure these differences in time pressure would be responsible for any differences in demands made by the subjects, Smith and his associates had a confederate pretend to be one of the subjects. Her behavior was exactly the same in both the high- and low-time-pressure conditions. (See figure 12-2 for the results of this experiment.)

Initially, subjects in the high-time pressure condition demanded just as much as did subjects in the low-time-pressure condition. But as the exchange continued, the effects of time emerged. Subjects in the high-time-

An auction is a bargaining exchange in which the auctioneer usually has the advantage. The bidder for an item must deal with other bidders as well as the auctioneer.

pressure condition began to demand less and less. The time pressure made them more willing to make concessions.

Knowing that time pressure may produce greater concessions might give a person an advantage in negotiations, but people must be very careful in using this strategy. If time runs out and no agreement has been reached, the result is usually worse than the outcome of any negotiated settlement.

Bargaining Strategies   Research on bargaining strategies has focused on questions such as whether a "tough" bargaining strategy will be more effective than a "soft" bargaining strategy. A tough bargainer is one who makes a small initial offer and concedes little during the course of the exchange. According to Rubin and Brown (1975), tough bargainers are more effective than soft bargainers.

Third-Party Intervention   Because of the inherent conflict of interest in any bargaining situation, sometimes the participants are unable or unwilling to accept an agreement that provides less than either desires, and they reach a stalemate. In such situations, it may be advantageous to ask a third person to mediate such disputes. Third parties are often called in to settle negotiations in large organizations. For example, many labor unions, especially those whose members work for government agencies, ask third-party mediators to settle labor contract disputes. And the contract between the Professional Baseball Player's Association and team owners requires that a third party mediate salary disputes. In recent years, an increasing number of disagreements that would previously have resulted in lawsuits are being referred to professional mediators. The goal of a mediator is to get parties to mutually agree to a resolution. What are the effects of these efforts?

Rubin (1980) suggested two consequences of third-party intervention. First, it provides the participants with a face-saving option; one party can make a concession to the other party, not because it is giving in, but because the third party suggested it. Second, the third party can identify the key issues in the dispute and determine where there is agreement and disagreement on those issues. The participants can then focus their efforts on specific points rather than on the dispute in general.

However, identifying the issues that separate the parties may have a less than beneficial effect. Erikson, Holmes, Frey, Walker, and Thibaut (1974) found that when a conflict between parties was intense, identification of the issues that divided them exacerbated rather than diminished the conflict. Evidently, identifying the issues reminded the participants of how serious their dispute really was.

Personality Variables and Bargaining Behavior

The question of how personal characteristics affect bargaining behavior has not received as much attention as has the question of how situational variables affect bargaining behavior. It is expected that bargaining, like other social behaviors, is influenced by the personal characteristics of the bargainers, and that these characteristics interact with situational factors to affect people's behavior in a bargaining exchange. Swap and Rubin, for example, (1982) have found that some people bargain in the same manner irrespective of their opponent's behavior, but that other people are sensitive to the behavior of their opponent and base their bargaining strategies on what their opponent does. A personality variable called **Machiavellianism** appears to be related to people's effectiveness in a bargaining exchange.

Machiavellianism: a personality trait that causes people to believe that others can be manipulated for their own ends and to have the desire to do this.

Niccolò Machiavelli was a sixteenth-century philosopher who wrote on the topic of power and how to obtain it. Machiavelli's advice to the rulers of Italy was simple: If you want power, you will need to manipulate others. Manipulation, deceit, and opportunism, he wrote, are acceptable strategies because "the ends justify the means." Machiavelli's point of view has long interested political scientists and social philosophers. In the late 1960s, it attracted the interest of some social and personality psychologists. They wondered if some people are more predisposed to accept Machiavelli's view of the world than others and, if so, how this predisposition would be manifested in social behavior.

This interest led Richard Christie and Florence Geis (1970) to develop a scale that measured the personality characteristic of Machiavellianism. (See table 12-2 for a few items from this scale.)

Table 12-2.   *Some items from the Machiavellianism (Mach V) scale. Someone with Machiavellian tendencies will give the answers indicated in the parentheses.*

1. The best way to handle people is to tell them what they want to hear. (True)
2. Honesty is the best policy in all cases. (False)
3. It is wise to flatter important people. (True)
4. Most people are basically good and kind. (False)

Source: Christie and Geis (1970).

In their 1970 book, *Studies in Machiavellianism,* Christie and Geis presented a number of studies that addressed the impact of Machiavellian tendencies on social behavior. One aspect of social behavior that received special attention was bargaining. Geis, Weinheimer, and Berger (1970) conducted a study on this topic. Before the actual study began, Geis and her associates generated a set of political positions that most college students opposed (raising the drinking age to twenty-five, for example). These issues were used later in the study.

Male subjects were given the Machiavellianism scale and divided into a high group and a low group on the basis of their scores. Then both groups were asked to play a game of "legislature." They were to play the roles of legislators and try to get certain bills through Congress. Successful passage of a bill resulted in a player earning votes from his constituents. The player who accumulated the most votes would win a prize. To get a bill passed, players would use a technique called logrolling; they would exchange their support for another player's bill for his support for their own bill. The game would begin with a player making a short speech on behalf of his bill, then a ten-minute bargaining session would take place; and following that a vote would be held. The dependent measure was the number of votes each player won by getting his bills passed.

Research Highlight

Consumer Protection

Most Americans have engaged in a bargaining exchange over the price of a car with an automobile salesperson—and most have lost something in this exchange. A field study by Cialdini, Bickman, and Cacioppo (1979) illustrates how a little tough bargaining by prospective buyers can greatly improve their outcomes in these transactions.

The subjects were salespeople at an automobile dealership. They were approached by confederates posing as prospective car buyers. The independent variable was whether these prospective buyers were tough or soft bargainers. It was manipulated by varying the confederates' behavior toward the salesperson's offers. In the tough condition, the confederate first asked about the price of an Impala; when he received the salesperson's initial offer, he protested and demanded a lower price. In the soft condition, the confederate also asked about the price of an Impala, but when he received the salesperson's initial offer, he responded positively. The confederates in both conditions then asked the price of a new Monte Carlo. After hearing the salesperson's initial offer, they asked for a better price on the car. The dependent measure was the salesperson's initial and subsequent offers on the Monte Carlo. The initial and subsequent offers the salespeople made to the tough bargainer were about $200 less than the offers made to the soft bargainer.

In a laboratory experiment conducted by Smith and his associates (1982), the researchers combined tough bargaining with high time pressure. They found that when both were present, subjects were most likely to make concessions. But before you dash out to get a good deal on a car, a word of caution: Tough bargaining and time pressures are not without risks. They may lead to a situation in which neither you nor the salesperson will concede, and you both lose—you lose a reasonable deal on a car you want, and the salesperson loses a reasonable sale he would like to make.

Two types of bills were considered. The first concerned neutral issues, such as changing the specifications for sewer pipes or moving a government office. The other concerned emotionally involving issues. Geis and her associates predicted that Machiavellian tendencies would interact with the type of bill under consideration to effect the subjects' effectiveness at log-rolling. They proposed that on bills concerned with neutral issues, high and low Machiavellians would not differ. On bills concerned with emotional issues, high Machiavellians would be more effective at using logrolling techniques than low Machiavellians. Low Machiavellians' personal feelings on the issues would interfere with their ability to argue and bargain for a bill they opposed, but high Machiavellians' feelings would not interfere with their ability to argue and bargain for a bill they opposed.

The researchers' predictions were fully supported (see figure 12-3). Low Machiavellians were slightly more effective than high Machiavellians on the neutral issues, but on the emotional issues they were much less effective. These results indicate that high Machiavellians are not, in general, more effective bargainers than low Machiavellians. Only when the object of the bargaining has certain characteristics do high Machiavellians outperform low Machiavellians.

Again, this study shows how personality and situational variables interact to affect social behavior. A more recent study by Geis and Moon (1981) suggested another reason Machiavellians might be effective in bargaining exchanges. These researchers found that when asked to lie, high-Machiavellian subjects were much more convincing than were low-Machiavellian subjects.

SUMMARY

Interdependent social behavior occurs when two or more people interact, and it has three distinguishing characteristics. First, the behavior of one person in the interaction affects and is affected by the behavior of the other people in the interaction. Second, each person's outcome from the interaction is at least partially determined by the other people's outcomes. And third, the people in the interaction have a choice of acting cooperatively or competitively. Most theories about social behavior in interdependent interactions are predicated on the assumption that these interactions are akin to business transactions, leading many theorists to call them social exchanges.

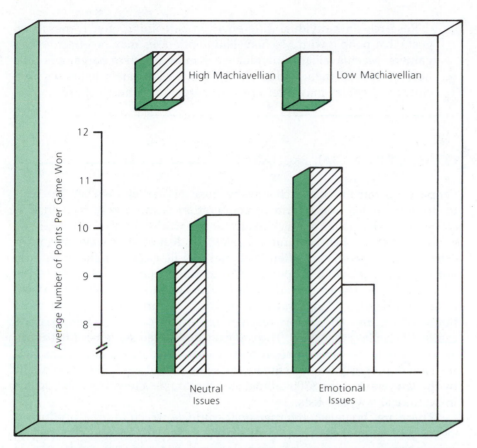

Figure 12-3. *While low machiavellians were slightly more effective bargainers than high machiavellians on neutral issues, the pattern was reversed on emotional issues.* Source: Geis et al. (1970).

People's evaluations of an interaction are based on their internal standards of what constitutes a satisfactory outcome from a social exchange. If an outcome falls below their standards, people will consider finding new social exchanges. However, before leaving the present exchange, they will compare their current outcomes with those likely in an alternative exchange. If the former exceeds the latter, they will stay in the present relationship.

One aspect of social exchanges that has attracted considerable research attention is bargaining, or negotiation, which occurs when people have to divide a resource or resolve an intangible issue. The situational variables that influence the outcome of a bargaining exchange include the site at which the bargaining takes place, time pressures on the participants, bargaining strategies used by participants, and third-party intervention. Third parties are sometimes brought in to mediate disagreements between parties to an exchange. If a disagreement is not too basic or too intense, third-party intervention usually increases the chances of a settlement.

Research on individual differences in bargaining effectiveness suggests that people with Machiavellian tendencies may be effective bargainers. Machiavellian individuals are more effective bargainers than non-Machiavellian individuals in situations where an individual's principles and values may interfere with bargaining effectiveness.

CONFLICT IN SOCIAL EXCHANGES

People cooperate in social exchanges because it is in their own best interests to do so; usually, some form of cooperation is more beneficial than is competition. However, a quick glance at the world shows that people do not always act in their best interests. A great deal of interpersonal conflict exists because people are often irrational and illogical. For example, a divorce attorney tells of a property settlement between a couple involved in a bitter divorce. The couple and their lawyers had to work out the division of several hundred thousand dollars worth of furniture, art, and other household items. The couple reached agreement on every item except a cabinet worth less than $300. The carefully developed settlement fell apart, and ultimately the division of property was decided by the court. The final division of property was essentially the same as that worked out originally by the lawyers, but the $300 cabinet cost the couple a few thousand dollars in additional lawyer's fees.

Interpersonal conflict: an exchange in which the participants have opposing goals and thus act competitively.

There are, however, **interpersonal conflicts** which are the product of logical and rational decisions on the part of the participants. This section examines two such conflicts, zero-sum and nonzero-sum, and ways to positively resolve them.

Zero-Sum Conflict

Zero-sum conflict: an exchange in which one participant's gains minus the other participant's losses always equals zero.

One exchange that almost always gives rise to interpersonal conflict is a **zero-sum conflict;** for example, a chess match, a poker game, or a fight between two children over a toy. There is a clear winner, and what she wins is taken from the loser. If one agrees to participate in a zero-sum conflict, it would be irrational not to compete. Indeed, in many of these exchanges (boxing matches, football games), laws have been passed that make it illegal for the participants not to be totally competitive.

Nonzero-Sum Conflict

Nonzero-sum conflict: an exchange in which one participant's gains minus the other's losses do not equal zero; both may win or both may lose.

Another exchange that leads to interpersonal conflict is a **nonzero-sum conflict,** which differs from a zero-sum conflict in the following respect: It is possible for all participants in a nonzero-sum conflict to lose. This can be seen by examining two nonzero-sum conflict games used by researchers, the prisoner's dilemma and the commons dilemma.

The Prisoner's Dilemma

The prisoner's dilemma game (Luce and Raffia, 1957) is based on the following hypothetical situation. Two people, suspected of a crime, are ar-

An athletic contest such as this football game is an example of a zero-sum conflict; there will be a winner and a loser. In a nonzero-sum conflict, both parties can be winners and both sides can be losers.

rested by the police. When they are brought to the station, they are separated and questioned by a district attorney. The district attorney is sure that the suspects are guilty, but does not have enough evidence to convict them. Therefore, she decides to try a ploy. The district attorney tells the first suspect that if she confesses and implicates her partner, she will receive a very light sentence—less than a year. The partner will get a much longer sentence—15 years. If the suspect refuses to confess, the district attorney will get her on some trumped-up charges, and she will get a five-year sentence. Thus, the first suspect has two possible choices: confess and receive less than a year sentence, or do not confess and receive a five-year sentence.

The suspect is about to confess her heart out, when it dawns on her that someone is probably making the same offer to her partner. She figures that if both confess, they will each get at least a ten-year sentence. Quickly figuring that five years is less than ten (she is dishonest but not stupid), she decides not to confess, but to keep her mouth closed and do her time. But if she does not confess and her partner does, she will get a 15-year sentence while her partner gets less than a year.

The pattern of outcomes for the two suspects is called a *payoff matrix*. (See the top portion of figure 12-4.) Typically, researchers re-create the prisoner's dilemma, but use points that can be exchanged for a prize in place of the jail sentences. (See the bottom portion of figure 12-4 for an example of this type of payoff matrix.)

The payoff matrix motivates each person to compete, yet in the final analysis, there is more to be gained by mutual cooperation. As Pruitt and Kimmel (1977) said, ''Individual rationality leads to collective irrationality.''

Figure 12-4. *The top payoff matrix is for two suspected criminals; the bottom payoff matrix is for two people playing the Prisoner's Dilemma Game.*

This situation is called a **mixed-motive game.** The word *game,* as it is used here, comes from the work of theoretical mathematicians who used it to describe similar situations (Tedeschi, Schlenker, and Bonoma, 1973); these games should not be confused with games like Scrabble or Trivial Pursuit. The nuclear arms race, for instance, is a nonzero-sum, mixed-motive game; there are reasons for the superpowers to engage in cooperative actions (reduce nuclear arsenals, develop treaties) and reasons to engage in competitive actions (develop new weapons, renege on old treaties). Competitive actions may produce gains for one country (more coercive power), but in the long run, mutual competition may well result in a situation where everyone is a loser.

For many years, the prisoner's dilemma game, or some variant of it, was the primary means social scientists used to study non-zero-sum interpersonal conflicts and ways to reduce them. But as time passed, the prisoner's dilemma research came under criticism for using an artificial situation and producing findings that were interesting but might not be relevant to real-word non-zero-sum conflicts (Nemeth, 1972). As a result of such criticisms, the amount of research using the prisoner's dilemma game has declined dramatically in recent years, and researchers have turned to other games. Some look at conflict resolution by examining people's behavior in bargaining exchanges; others study conflict in situations based on the "tragedy of the commons" (Hardin, 1968).

The Commons Dilemma

The citizens of early settlements in the northeastern United States sometimes found it financially advantageous to jointly own common grazing areas for their cattle. These grazing areas had a limited amount of vegetation. As long as the residents realized this and limited the number of cattle grazing on the commons, the system worked fine. However, a few greedy people invariably increased the number of their cattle grazing on the commons. Seeing this, other residents would increase the number of their cattle grazing on the commons. The vegetation could not support all the cattle, and the residents' cattle died. This situation is called the commons dilemma, or more generally, a **social trap.**

One does not have to return to eighteenth-century New England to find social traps. If you have ever worked in an office that had a coffee fund, you have been part of a potential social trap. It is in the coffee fund participants' best interests to drink as much coffee as they want and whenever possible contribute nothing to the fund. However, if everyone does this, the coffee is soon depleted and there is no money to replace it. For some people, this would be a tragedy equal to that of the commons dilemma. Whenever there is a limited supply of some resource (water, fossil fuels), there is a potential for a social trap.

Reducing Interpersonal Conflict

It is possible for one player in a mixed-motive game to use a totally competitive strategy and profit handsomely—possible, but unlikely. This would occur only if the player were lucky enough to be playing against a

Mixed-motive game: an exchange in which there is a rational reason to compete and a rational reason to cooperate.

Social trap: a situation in which competition produces short-term gains for an individual but long-term costs for all participants.

masochistic individual. Few people play games in this manner. In most instances, competition is costly to all participants. Therefore, it is beneficial to look for ways to reduce interpersonal conflict by decreasing competition and increasing cooperation.

Using Threats

One common response to conflict is for the parties to threaten one another. People use threats because they believe they can produce a quick end to the conflict and an outcome that is favorable to them (Frost and Wilmot, 1978). For example, labor unions threaten to strike, and management threatens to deunionize, and each side hopes that its threat will cause the other side to be a little more cooperative.

Deutsch and Krauss (1960) conducted a classic study on threat and how it impacts behavior in a social exchange. The subjects were asked to play the roles of the owners of two trucking companies, Acme and Bolt. The subjects (female telephone operators) were shown a map. (See figure 12-5.)

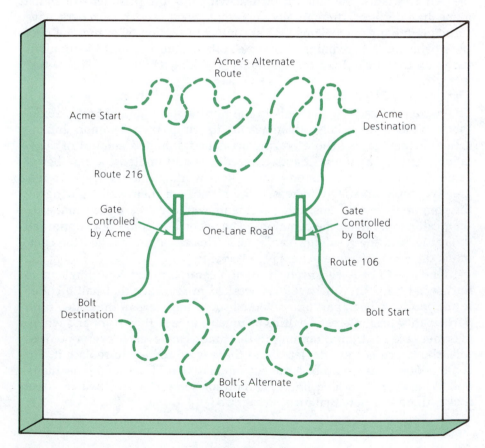

Figure 12-5.   *The road map used by Deutsch and Krauss to study threat in interpersonal conflicts.*
Source: Deutsch and Krauss (1960).

The players' goal was to get their trucks from the start box to the destination box as quickly as possible. They would receive 60 cents per trip less operating expenses, which were computed at a penny for each second a trip took. The trucks traveled at a fixed rate of speed. For both Acme and Bolt, the most profitable route was down the middle of the one-lane road—and therein lay the conflict. Acme and Bolt both wanted to use this road, but if they both insisted on using it, each would block the way of the other. The solution to this conflict was relatively simple: Acme could let Bolt use the one-way road on the first trip, and then Bolt could reciprocate the favor on the next trip. While neither will make as much as they would if there were no competition, they would still make some profit. Deutsch and Krauss did not let their subjects speak to one another, yet the subjects managed to work out this cooperative strategy. On the average, subjects earned from four to six cents per trip.

All this changed, however, when threat was introduced into the trucking game. Acme was given a gate which it could use to prevent Bolt from reaching its destination using the one-lane road. Thus, Acme could stop Bolt and while Bolt's truck was idle, Acme could use the alternate route. This route was costly (players who used the alternate route lost at least 10 cents per trip), but using this strategy would give Acme control over Bolt's outcomes. Conventional wisdom would lead to the prediction that Acme could quickly force Bolt into a subservient position and profit handsomely, but this wisdom would be wrong. Bolt lost a good deal of money when Acme could threaten to use the gate, but Acme suffered from the threat as well, losing about five cents per trip. This happened because Bolt responded to the threat by becoming a good deal *less* willing to cooperate on the use of the one-lane road. When Deutsch and Krauss gave both companies a gate, things got even worse. Then both companies averaged a loss of 20 cents per trip. Rather than increasing cooperation, threat increased competition.

In the years following Deutsch and Krauss's original study, there has been considerable controversy about whether the study's results are applicable to the real world. Perhaps the major criticism is of how threat was operationalized in this study. The subjects did not threaten to use the gate, they simply used it. In actual conflicts, people usually issue a warning before they use a gate or a similar means of control. Shomer, Davis, and Kelley (1966) found that when subjects in a trucking game could warn one another of their intentions, cooperation increased between the players. Similar results have also been found by others (for example, Moln, 1981).

This does not mean that Deutsch and Krauss's findings should be disregarded. Threat is, at best, a risky means to resolve interpersonal conflict. People often react negatively to coercive social power. (See chapter eleven.) If people perceive a threat to be an attempt at coercion, they may compete rather than cooperate. Jamison and Thomas (1974) found that threat often leads to distrust between the participants to an exchange. Studies of the factors that lead to war indicate that most wars are preceded by arms races—increases in each side's ability to threaten the other (Smith, 1980; Wallace, 1980).

Developing Cooperation

Pruitt and Kimmel (1977) and others (for example, Apfelbaum, 1974; McGrath, 1984) have argued that the first step to cooperation in a mixed-motive situation is for one participant to adopt the goal of mutual cooperation, realizing at some point in the exchange that the other participants cannot be exploited and that continued noncooperation is costing everyone a great deal (McGrath, 1984). This participant desires cooperation not because of an altruistic motivation, but because of enlightened self-interest—the understanding that cooperation will benefit the cooperator. This is the same thing that motivated the subjects in the minimal social situation; a desire for a profitable outcome. It is not enough, however, for a participant to adopt a goal of cooperation; the perceptions of the other participants must also be changed. The other participants must come to believe they have also adopted the goal of mutual cooperation. Participants in a social exchange, even those who desire cooperation, will not cooperate while believing that the other participants are going to compete. They realize the interdependence of outcomes and know that if they cooperate while others compete, they will be exploited. This section presents research on some of the factors which lead to both the adoption of the goal of mutual cooperation and the expectation that others have adopted this goal.

Communication   The findings on the effects of communication are straightforward: The ability to communicate increases cooperation in mixed-motive situations. Wichman (1969) had subjects play the prisoner's dilemma game under one of four conditions: isolated (subjects could neither see nor hear one another); visual communication (subjects could see but not hear one another); verbal communication (subjects could hear but not see one another); and complete communication (subjects could both see and hear one another). Cooperation was the greatest in the complete communication condition. (See figure 12-6.) Comparable results have been found in other studies (for example, Voissem and Sistrunk, 1971).

Strategies of Responding   In mixed-motive games, one aspect of players' behavior that has received attention is game strategies. The question of whether totally cooperative actions persuade an opponent to act in a similar manner has been studied. Most research suggests not; in fact, this strategy often invites exploitation (Pruitt and Kimmel, 1977; Rosenbaum, 1980). Research has also found that consistently competitive responses are usually reacted to with consistently competitive responses. However, the consequences of the tit-for-tat strategy are somewhat more positive.

Think back to the prologue. In the minimal social situation, subjects unknowingly developed the following strategy: If the other person shocks me when I have rewarded him, I will change buttons and shock him the next time, but if the other person rewards me, I will stay with the same button and reward him. This is the basic idea of a matching, or a **tit-for-tat strategy.** For example, on the first trial of a prisoner's dilemma game, player A competes (confesses) and player B cooperates (does not confess). On the second trial, player B competes and continues to compete until

Tit-for-tat strategy: a strategy in mixed-motive games wherein one player matches the other player's previous actions; cooperation is followed by cooperation, competition is followed by competition.

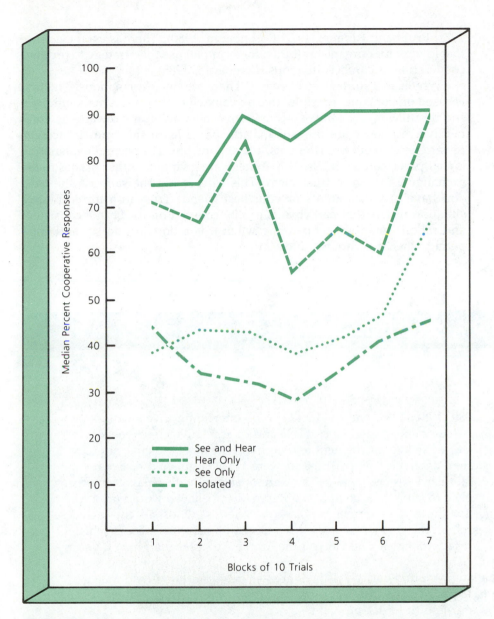

Figure 12-6. *Over trials, players who could communicate with one another cooperated more than those who were isolated from one another.*
Source: Wichman (1969).

there is a cooperative response from her opponent on trial 14. On trial 15, player B cooperates and continues to cooperate as long as player A does so. Any return to competition is matched by a competitive response on the following trial.

The tit-for-tat strategy, or some variant of it, is the most effective means for inducing cooperation in a mixed-motive game (Bixenstine and Gaebelin,

1971; Pruitt and Kimmel, 1977; Rosenbaum, 1980). There is even evidence that lower-order organisms (birds, for example) use this strategy to produce cooperation in conflict situations (Lombardo, 1985).

Why is this strategy so effective? There are two explanations. The first is based on the same principles that explain why the subjects in the minimal social situation cooperated—cooperative responses are rewarded, competitive responses are punished. Participants learn this and, to achieve rewards and avoid punishments, they cooperate. The second explanation is that participants who use this strategy are giving the other parties to the exchange a reason to trust them. This trust is not the same as the trust you have in your parents or your best friend. Trust in a mixed-motive situation means that participants can be counted on to act in a consistent and rational manner, cooperating when it is rational to do so, and competing when it is rational to do so.

Topic Background

And the Winner Is . . . .

Robert Axelrod (1980, 1984, 1985) has conducted some interesting investigations of the strategies people use in interpersonal conflicts and their relative effectiveness. In his first investigation, he held a tournament to determine the most effective strategy in the prisoner's dilemma game. The participants were 14 distinguished researchers, all of whom were familiar with this game. They were presented with a payoff matrix for the game and asked to submit the computer program they believed would produce the best outcome for them. The winner was a social scientist who had conducted considerable research on the game. His program consisted of just four lines, in which he outlined a tit-for-tat strategy. Cooperate on the first move; after that, match your opponent's previous move.

A short time later, Axelrod placed ads in computer magazines and held a bigger tournament with 62 participants from six countries. Again, the winner was the participant with the four-line tit-for-tat program.

In 1984, Axelrod devised a game for the readers of the magazine *Science '84*. The ad announcing the game and its rules appeared as follows:

Science 84 invites you to join in a cooperation experiment. We have designed a contest. No money will be awarded—but we would like you to play as if the offer were real. To participate, tear out the card, check the $20 or $100 box, and return it to *Science 84* by October 31. Under the terms of our hypothetical offer, participants get the amount of money they request. There is one catch, however: If more than 20 percent of the respondents ask for $100, no one receives anything.

What will you do? If everyone checks the $20 box then everyone gets rewarded. But there is also a rational argument for checking the $100 box. You could, in a sense, play as if everyone else had already made his or her choice. Because this experiment involves thousands of people, the chances are remote that you will tip the $100 responses over 20 percent. If the threshold has not been exceeded, you could get $100 without affecting the rewards of others. If the threshold has been passed already, your answer still won't make any difference.

This experiment mirrors the problems societies have with, for example, pollution. The individual benefits of polluting are greater than the individual costs of pollution because those costs are spread out among everybody. As long as the majority cooperates, a few can "cheat" without significantly affecting the others. Of course, cooperation is not always beneficial to society; business monopolies and organized crime depend on it.

Much of economic and social theory is based on how rationally people respond in such situations. A dilemma arises because rational thinking in individuals often leads to what might appear to be an irrational choice for the group. But there is no one right answer for all situations. What's your choice?

This was the commons dilemma. Over 30,000 people responded to the ad, including the noted scientist and author, Isaac Asimov. Sixty-five percent of these people chose $20.00 and the remainder chose $100.00. The question that Asimov and others raised was whether people would be so cooperative if the situation were real and they actually would receive money. What do you think?

These conclusions come primarily from research that has used the prisoner's dilemma game to study behavior in mixed-motive situations. In recent years, researchers have turned their interest more toward social traps, such as the commons dilemma. This research suggests that trust plays a role in people's willingness to cooperate to preserve scarce resources. Messick, Wilke, Brewer, Kramer, Zemke, and Lui (1983) divided subjects into groups of those who believed that others would exercise restraint in the use of a scarce resource (a limited pool of experimental points) and those who believed that others would not exercise such restraint. Subjects who trusted the other people decreased their own usage of the resource.

Group Identity The basic dilemma in a mixed-motive situation is clear. The consequences of everyone looking out for themselves are usually disastrous in the long run, no matter how successful in the short run. Hardin (1968) suggested that the most practical solution to this problem is to appoint a leader who can force people to act cooperatively. Messick and Brewer (1983) suggested another, less authoritarian remedy—increase the individual's sense of belonging to and identifying with an interdependent group. This might increase willingness to "exercise personal restraint in the interest of collective welfare" (Kramer and Brewer, 1984). An example of this strategy is the appeals made to Americans in the 1970s to conserve energy, which were based on the theme that energy conservation is a patriotic endeavor.

To test the effects of group identity, Kramer and Brewer used a laboratory version of the commons dilemma. The subjects were students who were told that they and five other people would be drawing from the same limited resource—a pool of 300 points worth five cents each. The subjects' task was to earn as many points as possible while making the resource last as long as possible. Subjects believed that their group would be comprised of six individuals; two other local college students and three elderly people who were linked to the three students through a computer system. The independent variable was administered by telling half the subjects that the experimenters were interested in comparing the behavior of the young with the behavior of the old members of the group, and telling the other half that the experimenters were interested in comparing the behavior of the entire group with the behavior of people from other cities. Thus a sense of group identity was created in the second half of the subjects.

All subjects received the same (false) feedback on how much the other group members were taking from the limited resource. The dependent measure was how many points subjects took over the course of an experiment session.

The independent variable had the predicted effect on the male subjects, but not on the female subjects; the males exercised considerably more restraint when they saw themselves as part of the entire group than when they saw themselves as part of a limited subgroup (See figure 12-7.) Subsequent studies have found no differences in the behavior of male and female subjects in the commons dilemma. These studies have shown that one possible solution to the commons dilemma may be to instill in people a sense of group identity.

SUMMARY

In some social exchanges, there are valid and logical reasons for the participants to be in conflict. One such situation is when two parties are competing for a prize, as is the case in a sports contest. Another situation that usually produces conflict is one in which there is a logical, rational reason to act in a competitive manner. However, if all the people involved in a conflict are competitive, the results will be disastrous. When there is one winner and one loser in a conflict, it is called a zero-sum conflict. In another kind of conflict, a nonzero-sum conflict, it is possible for all participants to win or all participants to lose.

Cooperation usually produces a better outcome than competition. Thus, research has focused on the factors which will produce cooperation in a nonzero-sum conflict. Researchers have developed experimental games to study this process. Among these are the prisoner's dilemma game, in which players must decide whether or not to confess to a crime and the commons dilemma game, in which players must decide how to divide up a limited resource.

One possible tactic to produce cooperation is threat. Research suggests, however, that threat often increases the level of competition and conflict. The key to developing cooperation appears to be that players

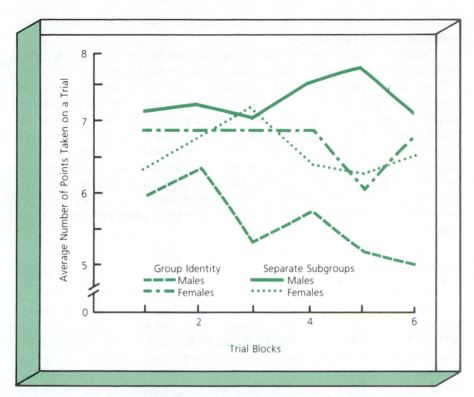

Figure 12-7. *When male subjects identified with the entire group, they were less selfish than when they saw themselves as a separate subgroup. Copyright (1984) American Psychological Association. Adapted by permission of the authors.*
Source: Kramer and Brewer (1984).

adopt the goal of cooperation and believe that others have adopted the same goal. One way in which this can be achieved is by allowing the participants to communicate with one another. Another way is by using certain strategies in mixed-motive games. The strategy that seems most effective is called matching, or tit for tat. Studies of games where the conflict is due to a scarcity of desired resources suggest that another way to engender cooperation is to create among the participants a sense of belonging to an interdependent group.

JUSTICE AND FAIRNESS

So far in this chapter, the message that has been communicated is that people are motivated to cooperate with each other only when it is in their self-interests to do so. But this is not all there is to interdependent social behavior; people are also often motivated by a sense of justice and fairness. Humans learned long ago—and continue to learn—that exchanges in which one participant totally exploits the other are doomed to failure and profit no one. Therefore, they have developed rules to govern people's behavior in social exchanges.

Participants act in accord with these rules for two reasons. First, other participants to an exchange either explicitly or implicitly insist on this; they will not knowingly and willingly let others exploit them. Second, the rules are such an integral part of human interactions that they have become societal norms and often personal norms. These norms provide both external and internal pressure to comply with the rules and motivate people to act fairly when they deal with others. People generally believe that the outcomes for the participants in an exchange should be fair, and just (Cook and Hegtvedt, 1983; Eckhoff, 1974; Gergen et al., 1980). This section presents a general theory of how people decide what is a fair or just outcome and then discusses what people do when the outcomes are not fair or just.

Equity Theory

Equity theory: the theory that people expect to receive outcomes from an exchange that are in keeping with their contributions to the exchange.

Equity theory is a general model of how people decide if an exchange is fair and what they do if it is not. There are two major situations in which equity theory is most relevant (Adams, 1965; Walster, Walster, and Berscheid, 1978). The first is called a mutual exchange and is a situation in which two people are directly involved in the exchange of valued resources. Examples of a mutual exchange range from a marriage in which one person gives the other fidelity and devotion in exchange for financial security to a company in which an employer gives employees a salary in exchange for their time and efforts. The second situation involving equity theory is when people have a limited resource and must decide how to distribute it. Examples of this range from winners of a world series deciding how to divide up the winner's pool to a judge deciding how much money a person injured in a traffic accident should receive.

In either type of situation, equity theory predicts that people will desire resources to be allocated in proportion to people's contributions; the more one gives, the more one gets—a simple and noncontroversial prediction. But the process of deciding the fair proportion can often be complex, and in some cases the prediction is not correct.

Equity in Mutual Exchanges
Current equity theory owes much to the work of J. Stacey Adams (1965; Adams and Freedman, 1976). Adams was intrigued by people who appeared to have been treated fairly in a mutual exchange, but were dissatisfied by the outcome of the exchange. For example, Stouffer and his colleagues (1949) investigated job morale among members of the army air corps (the predecessor of the air force) and the military police during the Second World War. Objectively, the promotion opportunities for the members of the air corps were much greater than for members of the military police, yet army air corps members were much *less* satisfied with their promotion opportunities.

Topic Background

Arabia's New Solomon

In Saudi Arabia, there are many legends about Abdul Aziz, the founder and first ruler of that country. This legend is intended to show his wisdom and sense of justice:

> A woman came to Abdul Aziz one day demanding the death sentence on the killer of her husband.
>
> "How did your husband die?" asked Abdul Aziz, who used to sit every day in his palace or tents to hear the cases that his people brought to him.
>
> "This man was picking dates in a palm tree when he fell down on my husband below," said the woman, "and now I come before you a widow."
>
> "Did this man fall down with malice?" asked Abdul Aziz. "Did he know your husband? Was it his intention, you believe, to break you husband's neck?"
>
> "I know not who he is nor why he fell," replied the widow. "But I do know that thanks to him I am now alone in the world and my children are fatherless. I demand my blood price."
>
> This was, by law, the widow's right, and Abdul Aziz could not deny it her. So he asked her in what form she would like to take her compensation.
>
> "His head," she said at once. "A life for a life. I will accept no less."
>
> Abdul Aziz remonstrated with the woman. What good was another man's death to her—or to her children? She needed money, and she would receive it, for even though the man clearly fell from the palm tree by accident, he was still bound to pay her husband's blood price.
>
> But the woman would not be dissuaded from vengeance, and so Abdul Aziz spoke again.
>
> "It is your right to take compensation, and it is your right to ask for this man's life. But it is my right, by God, to decide in what fashion he must die. And so now hear me well. You may take this man outside with you instantly and he shall be tied to the foot of a palm tree. Then you yourself shall climb to the top of that palm tree and drop down upon him from on high. Thus you may take his life as he took your husband's, and then you will have received what is rightfully yours."
>
> "Or perhaps," added the emir in the long pause that followed, "you would prefer to take the blood money, after all . . ." And so the widow took the blood money hurriedly, and all marvelled at the justice of Abdul Aziz. (Cited in Lacey, 1982)

Adams suggested that this was because the promotion chances for members of the military police were irrelevant to members of the air corps. He proposed that people in the air corps looked instead at the promotions of their fellow air corps members; in comparison to them, unpromoted air corps members saw themselves as being unfairly or unjustly treated. People compare their own outcomes in a relationship to the outcomes of relevant others, and they use this comparison as a basis for deciding whether or not they have been treated fairly.

Adams put his proposal into a formula. Equity exists when person A's outcomes ÷ person A's inputs = person B's outcomes ÷ person B's inputs. People estimate the ratio of what they have put into a relationship to what they have gotten out of it and compare this ratio to the ratio of others involved in the same relationship. If the other ratios are equal to their own, people feel they have been treated equitably or fairly; if the two ratios are unequal, people feel they have been treated inequitably or unfairly.

An exchange between Bud Abbott and Lou Costello illustrates the principles of equity theory. If you spend any time watching old movies on television, you have probably seen films starring this comedy team. At the time most of these films were made, Abbott and Costello were the leading box office attractions in the United States. By the mid-1940s, Abbott and Costello were both earning more than any other person in the United States, $470,000 per year (Thomas, 1977). (Today, an equivalent salary would be over $10 million a year.) But Costello was not satisfied; he felt that he was being treated inequitably. This feeling stemmed partly from an incident that occurred before the team had reached stardom: Abbott had demanded and gotten $10.00 of Costello's salary from an appearance. Contrary to his screen image of a sweet, gentle, unassuming man, Costello was an egotistical, hostile individual. These characteristics, in combination with the past slight, led to the following exchange with his manager, Eddie Sherman.

"Okay. Now you go tell Bud that from now on we split our movie dough sixty-forty or I don't work with him."

Eddie was stunned. Lou had never given the slightest hint that he would make such a demand. "Lou, you can't be serious," he said.

"You think I would kid about something like this?"

"No, I guess you wouldn't. But I wish you would think about it."

"I have been thinking about it," Lou said excitedly. "I've been thinking about it for five years now, ever since Bud [took the $10.00 from me]. Well, he's going to pay for it now."

"Lou, I gotta tell you I think you're completely off base. The money doesn't mean that much to you. You're gonna be making more money than you'll know what to do with. Think what this would do to Bud. He's got his pride, you know."

"Yeah? Well, he shoulda thought about mine five years ago."

"This could hurt the team very deeply. You need Bud, Lou."

"Bullshit. I could paint him on a backdrop, that's how much I need him."

"I wish you would change your mind."

"No chance. Now go to Bud and give him the news. And there's something else."

"What's that?"

Abbott and Costello fought about money in their movies and in real life. The reason appears to be Costello's belief that he was being treated inequitably.

"We're changing the billing. From now on it's Costello and Abbott."

"Change the billing!"

"Costello and Abbott. That's the way it's going to be."

"But that's impossible. Everybody knows you as Abbott and Costello."

"Not anymore. Now go deliver your message."

"Lou—"

"That's it, little man." (Thomas 1977, pp. 88–89)

When Abbott was informed of his partner's demand, he responded: "That ungrateful bastard. He'd still be doing pratfalls in burlesque if it wasn't for me. He'd be nothing without me" (Thomas, 1977, p. 90). But Abbott, faced with the break-up of the team, accepted the sixty-forty split. However, the studio that made Abbott and Costello's films quite reasonably threatened a lawsuit if the name were changed, and Costello reluctantly dropped that demand.

Costello's belief that he was being treated inequitably was based primarily on his perception of the relative contributions he and Abbott made to their comedy team. The fact that he was making more than millions of other people was irrelevant. What was relevant was Abbott's salary. According to Adams (1965), perceptions of equity and inequity are based not on absolute standards, but on a comparison between one's own input-to-outcome ratio and the input-to-input ratios of others in the exchange.

People's perceptions of the value of their own contributions to an exchange may differ greatly. For example, Costello saw Abbott as contributing little to the team—"I could just paint him on a backdrop." Abbott believed that Costello "would be nothing without me."

Costello's dissatisfaction with the fifty-fifty arrangement for distributing the team's salary illustrates that an *equalitarian* distribution of resources is not always seen as an equitable distribution of resources. Many people, like Costello, find it unfair to get an equal share of resources when they contributed an unequal share to the exchange. People become psychologically distressed when they believe they are in an inequitable exchange (Walster et al., 1978). They may react to this distress by demanding a more equitable distribution, as Costello did.

Inequity and Distress

Walster and her associates proposed that the more inequitably people are treated, the more distress they will experience. People who believe they are getting less than their share will experience distress, and people who receive more than their share will also experience distress (Adams, 1965; Walster el al., 1978). But people become more distressed when they feel they are victims of inequitable exchanges than when they feel they are beneficiaries (Lane and Mess'e, 1971).

In a study by Austin and Walster (1974), subjects were led to expect that they would be paid $2.00 per hour for performing a proofreading task. After the task was completed, all the subjects were told they had done a good job and were given envelopes with their pay. Some were overpaid—they received three dollars; some were underpaid—they received one dollar; and some received what they had expected—two dollars. Then subjects in all three groups filled out a scale that measured how contented or distressed they were. The subjects who received the expected amount, who were equitably treated, were far more contented than were those who were either overrewarded or underrewarded. (See figure 12-8.)

Similar findings were obtained by Pritchard, Dunnette, and Jorgenson (1972). They found that workers who believed they had been overcompensated for their work were less satisfied with their jobs than were those who believed they had been equitably compensated for their work.

Gergen (1969) used the terms **benign inequity** to describe a situation in which someone is overcompensated, and used the term **malignant inequity** to describe a situation in which someone is undercompensated. When either type of inequity occurs, people are motivated to eliminate it and restore equity.

Restoration of Equity

People can reestablish equity in one of two general ways. One, they can physically restore equity by changing their inputs to/or outcomes from the

Benign inequity: an exchange in which people get more than they deserve.

Malignant inequity: an exchange in which people get less than they deserve.

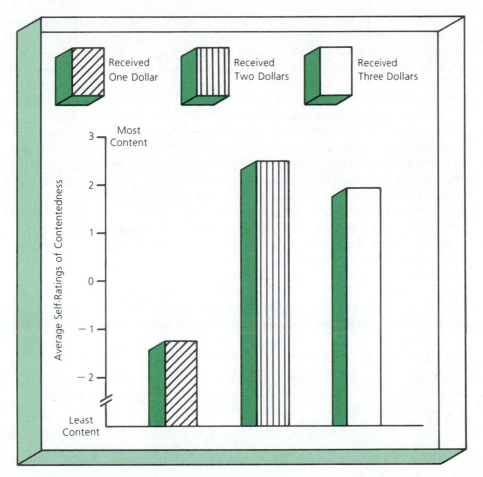

Figure 12-8. *Subjects were most contented when the pay they received matched their expectations.*
Source: Austin and Walster (1974).

exchange. Two, they can psychologically restore equity by restructuring their perceptions of the inputs and outcomes so that the ratios no longer appear inequitable to them. If people use one means to restore equity to an exchange, they will not use the other (Walster et al., 1978). If neither means works and the ratio is below people's own comparison levels and their comparison levels for alternatives, they are likely to leave the relationship (Adams, 1965). Equity theory's predictions about how people will physically or psychologically restore equity depend on whether the inequity is malignant or benign.

Physical Restoration of Equity   Studies have shown that people become distressed when they are overcompensated for their work. How will they attempt to physically restore equity and reduce distress when the inequity is benign? According to Adams (1965), they will either increase their inputs and so expend more in the relationship, or decrease their outcomes and so get less out of the relationship. The research that has tested this prediction has produced mixed results. Adams and his associates (Adams and Jacobsen, 1964; Adams and Rosenbaum, 1962) have found that workers who feel they are receiving more pay than they deserve will either increase their productivity or increase the quality of the product they produce or both. This result is logical and consistent with equity theory.

Other studies (Cook and Hegtvedt, 1983) have not found the same results, possibly because it may be more difficult to create a benign inequity than the theory suggests. Carrell and Dittrich (1978) pointed out that people are sensitive to the inequities created by underpayment, but insensitive to the inequities created by overpayment. Also, when people do experience distress due to things such as overpayment, their feelings of distress do not last very long. When the inequity is malignant, physical attempts to restore equity usually involve making demands for some sort of compensation that would make the exchange equitable or reducing inputs to the exchange (Adams, 1965; Walster et al., 1978).

An example of this latter technique of equity restoration is found in Studs Terkel's (1974) book *Working*. One woman in this book had once been a call girl and had received hundreds of dollars for her favors. But when Terkel interviewed her, she was a streetwalker who received five or ten dollars for the same activities. She attempted to restore equity by reducing her inputs, as this excerpt of her interview with Terkel shows:

> As a streetwalker, I didn't have to act. I let myself show the contempt I felt for the tricks. They weren't paying enough to make it worth performing for them. As a call girl, I pretended I enjoyed it sexually. You have to act as if you had an orgasm. As a streetwalker, I didn't. I used to lie there with my hands behind my head and do mathematics equations in my head or memorize the keyboard typewriter. (Terkel, 1974, p. 98)

Psychological restoration of equity: a distortion of reality that provides a justification of an inequity.

Psychological Restoration of Equity   When equity cannot be physically restored people will turn to the **psychological restoration of equity.** The following example illustrates this process when the inequity is benign. After considerable pleading, you have persuaded a classmate to lend you her lecture notes so you may study them for a few hours on the night before the examination. "You can have them," she says, "but please bring them back by 9:00 PM." You fall asleep, do not return the notes and your classmate receives a "D" on the examination. You cannot physically restore equity—the examination is over—but you can psychologically restore equity. One way to do this is to derogate the victim of your actions. For example, you could decide that if your classmate was stupid enough to give someone as irresponsible as you her notes, she deserves what happened to her. In this way, you devalue her inputs to the exchange and rationalize the treatment she received.

The victims of such actions—people who are experiencing malignant inequity—may also use psychological means to restore equity. For example, they may convince themselves that the other party deserved a better out-

Topic Background

Equity Theory at the Ball Park

If you asked owners of professional baseball teams to name the most significant change in the game in the last 25 years, they would probably identify the change in the reserve clause. From 1897 until 1975, the contract signed by a professional baseball player contained a clause that gave the owner rights to the player's services for as long as he played professional baseball. Unless the player was sold or traded, the team with which he signed was the only one for which he could play. In late 1975, this clause was ruled valid for only one year after the end of a player's contract. Thus, a player who played out his contract was obligated to play for that team for just one more season. After that, he would be a free agent; he could sign a contract with any team he wished. This change made several players almost instant millionaires, but it had a drawback: The owner was allowed to reduce the player's salary by 20 percent during that final year.

The change in the reserve clause had the potential of creating strong feelings of inequity among some players. Imagine two players, both of whom have played out their five-year contracts. The first player is offered a huge amount of money to sign a new contract with the team. The second player's performance was roughly equivalent to that of the first, but he is offered less money than he feels he is worth. He refuses to sign and will play his final year for that team with a 20 percent cut in pay.

Both players are involved in an exchange with the owner—their input (for example, driving in runs) is exchanged for an output (a salary). But when the unsigned player compares his input-to-outcome ratio for that final year to the ratio of his signed teammate or to his own input-to-outcome ratio during the previous year, he is likely to experience malignant inequity—to feel he is getting less than he deserves. How could he restore equity?

Quitting the game is not a reasonable strategy; then he would receive no money. He cannot play for another team; the new reserve clause prevents this. The salience of his reduced salary and his teammate's higher salary is such that the player would have difficulty psychologically restoring equity by distorting his perceptions of his outcome. According to equity theory, there is only one alternative: He can reduce his inputs until either the owner comes up with a reasonable contract or he signs with a new team.

Lord and Hohenfeld (1979) studied whether baseball players actually dealt with malignant inequities in this manner. Their subjects were 23 baseball players who had not signed a new contract before the beginning of the 1976 season. Ten of these players signed a new contract with their team during the course of the season; 13 did not. Lord and Hohenfeld obtained statistics on the players' batting averages, home runs, runs batted in, and runs scored from 1973 through 1977.

The statistics for runs batted in are presented in the following figure. Look at the records of players who signed during the season. Before they signed, the percentage of times they drove in a run was much lower than it had been in the previous years. But after they signed a new, more lucrative contract, their runs-batted-in percentages improved considerably. This pattern was found for batting averages and home runs as well. Signing the new contracts restored equity and increased outputs.

Now look at the statistics for the players who remained unsigned all season and signed with a new team in 1977. Their runs-batted-in percentages during 1976 were lower than they had been in the previous three years. It was not until 1977, when they signed a contract with another team for more money, that their batting performances improved.

Thus, even people who make hundreds of thousands of dollars can experience malignant inequity. But would a player who gets $800,000 a year and bats .187 experience benign inequity and return part of his salary?

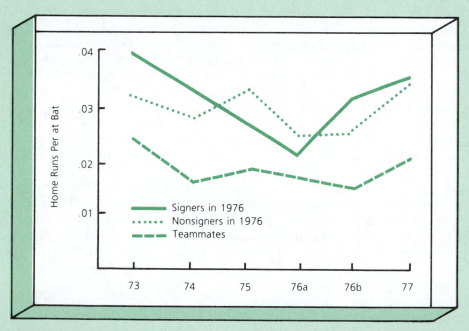

Baseball players apparently responded to inequitable treatment by lowering their productivity.
Source: Lord and Hohenfeld (1979).

come from the exchange, deny they were victimized, or rationalize that they merited the treatment they received. The unfortunate person who lent you her notes could psychologically restore equity by deciding that the grade was not important or that she was so stupid that she deserved what happened to her.

A number of factors can influence people's propensity to use psychological means to restore equity. For example, people who expect to be exploited even before an exchange begins are more likely to use these rationalizations than are people who do not have this expectation (Austin and Walster, 1974). Cohen (1982) has argued that people's perception of whether they are being treated inequitably, why, and what they can do about it depends greatly on the attributions they make about their own and other's behavior.

The Allocation of Resources

Another situation in which people are concerned with justice and fairness is in the allocation of resources. An employer must decide how much of a bonus each employee will receive; business partners must decide how to split their profits; the Jackson brothers must decide how to split the millions they earned from a concert tour—these are all instances of resource allocation. Leventhal (1976) said that people desire fairness in resource allocations; but again one must ask what rule for allocating resources is fair. There are a number of possibilities. Resources could be allocated on the basis of an **equity norm,** or on the basis of a **norm of need,** or on an **equalitarian norm.** Situational variables and individual differences affect which norms are used.

Equity norm: a rule that the amount of resources allocated to people should be proportional to their contributions.

Norm of need: a rule that the amount of resources allocated to people should be proportional to their needs.

Equalitarian norm: a rule that everyone should receive the same amount of resources.

Research Highlight

And Justice for All

The tendency to derogate the victim of a malignant inequity appears, on first inspection, to simply be a self-serving attempt to psychologically restore equity. But the work of Melvin Lerner and his colleagues (for example, Lerner, 1974, 1980; Lerner and Miller, 1978; Lerner and Simmons, 1966) suggests that it may also be due to people's views of the world and ideas about the natural order of things.

Lerner proposed that most people believe in a cosmic equity—that the world is a fair and just place, where the good are rewarded and the bad are punished. Sometimes this belief in a just world is violated, however, and bad things happen to good people. In such situations, others will try to restore equity by helping the victims. If this is impossible, then people may attempt to reconcile the conflict between their belief in a just world and the plight of good people in trouble by deciding that the victims were not good or deserving after all. People may engage in this kind of rationalization even when they are not responsible for the other people's troubles.

Lerner and Simmons had subjects watch a female confederate supposedly receiving painful electric shock. (In fact, they saw a videotape.) In one condition of this experiment, subjects were led to believe they could stop the shock and end the woman's discomfort. In another condition, they were led to believe that the woman would receive another series of painful shock. Subjects in a third condition were led to believe that the woman was afraid of shock but had agreed to be shocked so they could receive their experimental points.

Then subjects in all three conditions rated how attractive they found the woman's personality and how others would react to her. The results for the first dependent measure are presented in the following figure.

The woman was rated as less attractive when she was to receive further shocks than when the subjects could alleviate her suffering. When she took the role of a martyr, her ratings fell even more. The same results were found for the other dependent measure. According to Lerner, derogating this woman served to maintain the subject's belief in a just world.

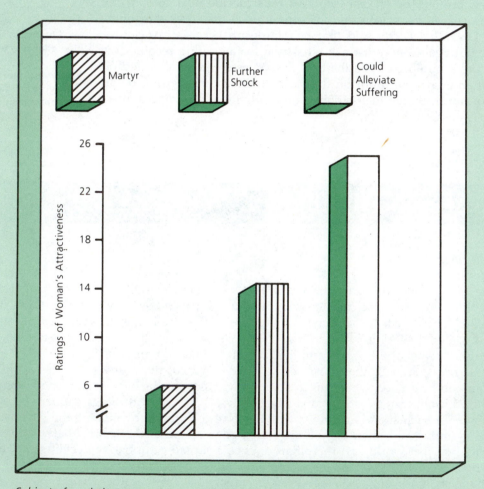

Subjects found the martyr least attractive and the person whose suffering could be stopped most attractive.
Source: Lerner and Simmons (1966).

Situational Variables

The original versions of equity theory (for example, Adams, 1965) proposed that people always prefer the equity norm when they allocate resources. A number of theorists have questioned this proposal (for example, Deutsch, 1975; Elliott and Meeker, 1984; Mikula, 1980; Sampson, 1975). It has been suggested that in different situations, different norms are preferred.

One thing that might influence the choice of a distribution scheme is what people hope to achieve by the allocation of resources (Cook and Hegtvedt, 1983). A study by Stake (1983) illustrates this point. Subjects were asked to play the role of a manager in a company and to decide how to distribute 50 dollars in bonus money to two people they supervised. The subjects were told that both workers deserved a bonus, but one had contributed about a third more to the company than had the other. Subjects were first asked to make a fair allocation of money; then they were asked to imagine that their primary goal was to promote good relationships between the two workers when making an allocation of bonus money; finally, the subjects were asked to imagine that their primary goal was to foster an increase in worker productivity when making the allocation. The dependent variable was the difference between the amount of bonus money awarded to each worker; the greater the difference, the less equal the distribution of money. (See figure 12-9.)

When the primary motivation was fairness, the more deserving worker received about $9.00 more in bonus money than the less deserving worker. When the primary motivation was the promotion of a good relationship between the workers, the more deserving worker received only about three dollars more. When the motivation shifted to productivity, the more deserving worker received over nine dollars more than the less deserving worker. Similar results have been reported by other researchers (Elliott and Meeker, 1984; Leventhal, Karuza, and Frey, 1980).

Social relationships between people may also affect how and why they allocate resources to one another. Groups composed of friends are more likely to use the norms of equality or need than are groups that comprise strangers (Austin, 1980). Also, when people are in long-term relationships, they are more likely to use the equality norm than are people in short-term relationships. When allocations are made on the basis of inputs, people may evaluate a friend's inputs differently than a stranger's—strangers allocate resources on the basis of ability; friends allocate awards on the basis of both ability and effort (Lamm and Kayser, 1978).

Individual Differences

As has been the case with almost every phenomenon presented in this book, there may be individual differences in preferences for different allocation schemes. Greenberg (1979) looked at how acceptance of the Protestant ethic would affect the manner in which people allocate resources. Since people who endorse this ethic believe in the value of hard work, it was predicted that they would base their allocations on an equity norm rather than on an equality norm. Greenberg found that people who scored high and low on a scale that measured acceptance of the Protestant ethic

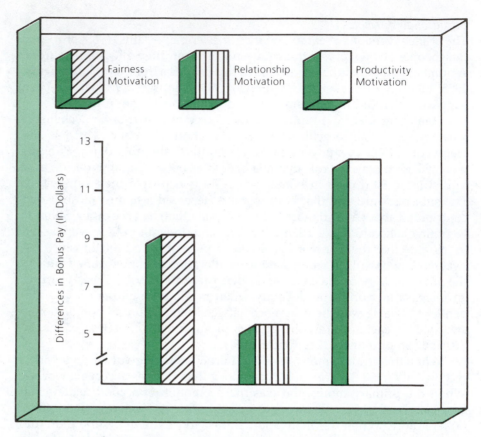

Figure 12-9. *The greatest discrepancy in bonus pay occurred when the allocator wanted to increase productivity.*
Source: Stake (1983).

did not differ in their preferences for either norm, but they did differ in what they considered in making allocations; high scorers were more likely to base their allocations on things like effort than were low scorers.

One characteristic that has received considerable research attention is the sex of the person who is allocating the resources. A large number of studies have found that women are more likely to distribute resources on the basis of an equality norm than are men; men tend to use an equity norm (Kahn, O'Leary, Krulewitz, and Lamm, 1980; Major and Deaux, 1982; Major and Adams, 1983). It is not clear why this difference exists, however. The most popular explanation has been that because women are more oriented toward maintaining harmony and peace in a group of people than are men, they are more inclined to use an equality norm (Kahn et al., 1980). Empirical tests of this explanation, however, have not supported it (Watts, Vallacher, and Messe, 1982; Major and Adams, 1983). Another approach has been to look at how people's preferences for one norm over another may be influenced by the interaction between sex and situational variables.

In the typical experiment on this topic a subject and other people work on a task in exchange for a reward given to the entire group. The subject is asked to decide how the reward should be divided among the people in the group. Reis and Jackson (1981) proposed that the tasks used in most experiments have been male oriented, and that this bias may have been reflected in sex differences when rewards were allocated. To investigate this idea, these researchers created tasks that were either male or female oriented, and they had males and females work on both kinds of tasks and then allocate rewards. Reis and Jackson (1981) hypothesized that both males and females would use the equity norm when the task was oriented toward their own sex, but would use the equality norm when it was oriented toward the other sex. As expected, both males and females used the equity norm when the task was oriented toward their own sex. However, males also use this norm when the task was female oriented; women who worked on a male-oriented task used the equality norm. Thus, Reis and Jackson's hypothesis was only partially confirmed. The sex role orientation of the task influenced the behavior of the female subjects but not the male subjects.

Sex composition of the group may also explain sex differences in reward allocation. In most sex-difference studies, same-sex groups have been used; males allocate rewards to males and females allocate rewards to females. At least two studies (Kahn, Nelson, and Gaeddert, 1979; Reis and Jackson, 1981) have found that women are more likely to *receive* resources on the basis of the equality norm. So sex differences may reflect, at least in part, the effect of who receives the resources rather than of who gives them.

These findings demonstrate that sex interacts with certain situational variables to produce differences in allocation schemes, but they do not explain other sex differences in reward allocations. Women accept less equitable payoffs for their work than do men, women work longer and harder for the same payoff than do men, and women expect a lower salary than do men with the same qualifications (Callahan-Levy and Messe, 1979; Major and Konar, In Press; Major, McFarlin, and Gagnon, 1982). A "weaker sense of own equity" (Callahan-Levy and Messe, 1979) may be responsible for some of the sex differences in resource allocations. This weaker sense may also be related to the fact that despite their increasing numbers in the work force, women remain underutilized and underpaid relative to their male co-workers. This finding does not suggest that women are responsible for these inequities, but that women may be more willing to accept them than are men.

Procedural Justice

In recent years, some researchers (for example, Leventhal et al., 1980; Thibaut and Walker, 1975) have proposed that there is more to people's perceptions of justice and fairness than the resources they receive from an exchange. In addition, people are influenced by the procedures used to produce the outcomes, or **procedural justice.** A procedure can be fair, but produce an unfair outcome. For example, imagine a production department holds a lottery to decide who gets what raise. This is a fair and unbiased procedure, but it could result in an unfair allocation of resources—the least productive person could get all the reward.

There is much less research on procedural justice than on other aspects of equity theory, but the results are intriguing. They suggest that often

Procedural justice: when the procedures used to reach an outcome are just and fair.

people's judgments of the overall fairness of an exchange may be more influenced by the fairness of the procedures used to determine the outcome of the exchange than by the actual outcome (Greenberg and Folger, 1983; Tyler and Folger, 1980). Perhaps the desire for fairness in social exchanges is more ingrained in people than earlier research would suggest.

SUMMARY

A desire for justice and fairness influences the outcomes of social interactions. People are motivated to act fairly, and they expect others to act in the same way. Equity theory proposes that people expect to receive outcomes from an exchange that are in keeping with their contributions to it. When people feel their input-to-outcome ratio is more than they deserve, they experience benign inequity; when people feel their input-to-output ratio is less than they deserve, they experience malignant inequity.

Equity can be restored either physically or psychologically. When an inequity is benign, physical restoration may be attempted by increasing one's contributions to the exchange or compensating the victim of the inequity. Psychological restoration when an inequity is benign often involves derogation of the victims of the inequity, which has the effect of justifying the treatment they have received. When an inequity is malignant, people may physically restore equity by reducing their contributions to the exchange or by demanding compensation. Psychological restoration of equity can involve people convincing themselves that no injustice was done or that they deserved the treatments they received.

Recent research on fairness in social exchanges has focused on the rules people use when they allocate resources. These allocations can be based on an equity norm—people receive an amount in proportion to their contributions; an equality norm—everyone gets the same amount irrespective of their contributions; or a norm of need—the neediest people get the most resources. The norm that guides a particular distribution of resources depends on what people hope to achieve by the resource allocation.

Sex differences have been found in how people allocate resources. In general, males tend toward an equity norm; females tend toward an equality norm. It appears that preference for a certain distribution scheme is influenced by the interaction between sex and certain situational variables, but some sex differences transcend situations. Women accept less equitable payoffs than do men, and they expect to have to do more to earn the same payoffs as men.

Most of the research on fairness has focused on people's reactions to the outcomes of an exchange, but the process that leads to these outcomes has also been researched. People may accept unfair outcomes if they believe the procedures that led to these outcomes were fair.

Applications

Civil and International Conflict

It is possible to apply the principles on exchanges between individuals to exchanges between groups of people. This section examines two particular kinds of intergroup exchanges: civil conflict—disputes that can lead to civilian protests or collective violence—and international conflicts. It presents theories on the causes of these conflicts, as well as some techniques that may lead to their resolution.

CIVIL CONFLICT

At the time that this book is being written, the United States is in a period of relative domestic tranquility. A president has been reelected by an overwhelming majority of voters, the economy appears strong, and few social problems seem capable of bringing large numbers of protesters into the streets. Nevertheless, civil conflict and even civil war are integral parts of this nation's history. One major cause of the War of Independence was discontent with the taxes the British government had levied on the citizens of its North American colonies. Less than 20 years after this war was over in 1794, the fledgling United States government found itself facing a rebellion over the same basic issue; President Washington sent troops into western Pennsylvania to put down a rebellion by farmers who were resisting a tax on homemade whiskey. The most violent of the draft protests of the 1960s would pale in comparison to a draft protest 100 years earlier in New York City; in July 1863, a riot broke out over the imposition of a new draft quota. During the four-day riot, 500 people were killed (Heaps, 1966).

Janowitz (1968) pointed out that the riots by black residents of America's ghettos in the 1960s were not the first incidents of collective racial violence in the United States. A race riot in 1917 between black and white residents of East St. Louis, Illinois, resulted in the deaths of 39 people, and a comparable number of people were killed in a race riot in Chicago two years later.

In many respects, the relative tranquility of the past few years is the exception rather than the rule. And the United States is not unique. The specific events that lead to a civil conflict differ across time and situations, but conflict theorists believe that many civil conflicts are due to the same factor, relative deprivation.

Relative Deprivation

Earlier this chapter introduced the roles justice and fairness play in social exchanges between individuals, and explained that people often determine

Civil disturbance and violence often result from the perception that relative to other groups one's own group is deprived.

whether or not they have been treated fairly by comparing their own situations to those of others. Many conflict theorists believe a similar process occurs at the group level. They propose that groups within a country use other groups as a reference to determine how they are being treated.

Sometimes members of a group will feel that relative to other groups in their country, they are faring badly. This leads to a feeling of **relative deprivation,** and relative deprivation can lead to civil conflict (Abeles, 1976; Gurr, 1970; Issac, Murtran, and Stryker, 1980). This proposal assumes that people rebel not because they are deprived in the absolute sense, but because they have compared their present status with what they believe they are entitled to and they feel deprived (Guimond and Dube'-Simond, 1983); they perceive a discrepancy between what "is" and what "ought to be."

Relative deprivation: people's feelings that they are deprived compared to the conditions of others or to their own expectations.

Relative deprivation is probably not the only cause of civil conflict (Obershall, 1978), but it does provide a good general explanation of this phenomenon. Theory and research on the different kinds of relative deprivation suggest that just as people react negatively when they experience malignant inequity, so groups react negatively when they experience relative deprivation.

Progressive Deprivation

Ted Robert Gurr (1970; Gurr and Duvall, 1976) has put forth a model of how relative deprivation can lead to civil conflict. Gurr proposed that relative deprivation produces anger and frustration among members of the affected group, which in turn increase the probability that members of the group will engage in aggressive acts such as rebellion or riots. Gurr believed that different conditions lead to different kinds of relative deprivation. Of most interest here are the conditions which Gurr said lead to *progressive deprivation*.

In his theory, Gurr called the events, objects, and conditions people desire and strive to obtain *values;* he termed the level of values a group believes it is entitled to possess *values expectations;* and he defined *value capabilities* as the level of values a group believes it can attain and maintain. These are based on group members' estimates of what they presently have and what they can expect in the future.

Progressive deprivation is usually preceded by a period of time in which a group experiences a significant increase in its standard of living or social status or both. As a result, both its value expectations and value capabilities increase. But when, for some reason, hard times occur, and the group's value capabilities level off or begin to decline, the resultant discrepancy between the rising expectations and the falling capabilities produces relative deprivation and the potential for civil conflict. (See figure 12-10 for a diagram of the conditions that lead to progressive deprivation.)

Progressive deprivation may explain why most revolutions occur when a long period of "economic and social development is followed by a short period of sharp reversal" (Davies, 1962, p. 6). Gurr (1970) suggested that progressive deprivation may, at least in part, explain the black protest movement of the 1960s. From the early 1940s until the mid-1950s, the income of blacks relative to those of whites with comparable education moved rapidly toward equality. But in the 1950s, black income began to decline, and by the 1960s, blacks had lost almost half the economic gains they had made. The feelings of relative deprivation this reversal created may have led to the riots in black ghettos in the 1960s.

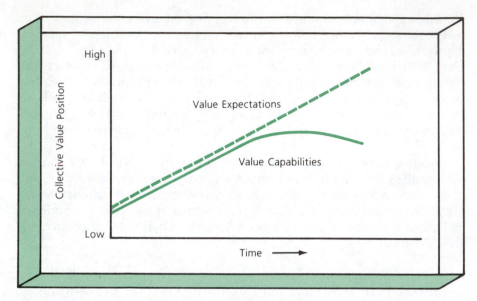

Figure 12-10.   *Gurr's model of the conditions which lead to Progressive Deprivation. Reprinted by permission of the publisher and the author.*
Source: Gurr (1970).

Personal versus Fraternal Deprivation

Abeles (1976) attempted to refine Gurr's ideas about the effects of progressive deprivation by distinguishing between *personal* and *fraternal relative deprivation*. Personal relative deprivation is the feeling that one personally is deprived in relation to other people; fraternal relative deprivation is the feeling that one's group is deprived in relation to other groups.

Abeles measured both personal and fraternal relative deprivation among a group of 950 black ghetto residents. Then he obtained their attitudes toward black militancy—the tendency to favor protest (both violent and nonviolent), increased political power for blacks, racial separatism, and ambivalent attitudes toward whites. As Abeles put it, high scores on the militancy measure indicated a willingness to move against the perceived oppressor.

He found that feelings of personal deprivation were unrelated to militancy, but that feelings of fraternal deprivation were related to militancy. Blacks were ready to protest not because they felt they personally had been treated unfairly, but because they felt their ethnic group had been treated unfairly.

A similar result was obtained by Guimond and Dube'-Simond (1983) in a study conducted in Canada. For many years, there has been a movement among French-speaking Canadians (Francophones) living in the Province of Quebec to remove Quebec from the rest of Canada or at least give it more autonomy from Canada's central government. These researchers wanted to know if relative deprivation was related to support for this political movement. They asked 80 Francophones to indicate how deprived they felt in relation to (a) other Francophones and (b) English-speaking Canadians, or Anglophones (fraternal relative deprivation). Personal deprivation was unrelated to support for the separatist movement, but fraternal deprivation was. The greater the perceived fraternal deprivation, the more the subjects supported autonomy for Quebec.

INTERNATIONAL CONFLICT

Conflict theorists believe they understand the causes of civil conflict and can create models that explain it. They are much less confident of their abilities to understand and explain international conflict. One noted conflict theorist, Anatol Rapoport (1976), suggested that it is not possible to develop theories or models of international conflict because there is no consistency or regularity between the causes of one war and the causes of another. However, some researchers have proposed that misperceptions are one cause of international conflicts.

Misperceptions

Rapoport's point of view is disputed by social psychologists such as Ralph K. White (1970, 1977). White acknowledged that no single theory could explain why nations go to war, but he believed that certain factors are common to most international conflicts. According to White, a decision to go to war is sometimes the result of an objective evaluation of the threats to a nation and the reality of the situation. In other instances, war is the result of a decision by an aggressive or power-hungry leader to satisfy these needs. Far more common than either of these situations, though, are situations in which two or more countries do not desire a conflict, yet end up at war with one another. How can this happen?

White believed the culprit was "black-and-white thinking . . . straining toward a black-and-white picture [of one's own and other countries] consciously or unconsciously distorting evidence, slanting and selecting it [such that it supports this viewpoint]" (1970, p. 243). In other words, the decision to wage war may be based on objectively incorrect or even distorted views of another country, the threat it poses, and the factors that motivate its actions. These **misperceptions** can increase the chances of a war no one wants or decrease the chances of a peace everyone wants.

White has analyzed four major conflicts in the twentieth century: (1) the conflict between Serbia and Austria, which led to World War I; (2) the conflict between Germany and Poland, which was a major cause of World War II; (3) the conflict between the United States and North Vietnam (and the Viet Cong), which led to the United States' long-term involvement in southeast Asia; and (4) the conflict between Israel and the Arab states, which led to four wars in the last 35 years. In all of these conflicts, he has found the same basic kinds of misperception: diabolical-enemy image, moral self-image, virile self-image, absence of empathy, military overconfidence, and selective inattention.

Misperceptions: incorrect or distorted views of another person or thing.

In this scene from the war between Iraq and Iran, Iraqi soldiers celebrate a victory over Iran. Like many wars in the Middle-East, this conflict was fueled by misperceptions on the part of both sides.

White acknowledged that misperceptions are probably not the original cause of a dispute between nations; the origins probably lie in some real conflict of interest between the goals of one nation and the goals of another. But when two countires are moving toward war, misperceptions serve to speed up the process. They reduce the chances of avoiding an armed conflict, which neither side may desire. And they make it more difficult for the countires to end an armed conflict. (See also the applications section of chapter thirteen.)

Diabolical-Enemy Image

In all of his analyses, White found evidence that at least one party to the conflict perceived the other as a diabolical entity with few if any redeeming qualities. Consider how the president of North Vietnam, Ho Chi Minh, and the president of the United States, Lyndon B. Johnson, characterized one another's actions. According to Ho, it was "crystal clear that the United States is the aggressor who is trampling under foot the Vietnamese soil" (cited in White 1970, p. 21). But according to Johnson, "In Vietnam, Communism seeks to impose its will by force of arms . . . It is this desire . . . for conquest . . . which moves . . . the enemy" (1970, p. 217).

A more recent analysis of statements made by the leaders of the United States and the Soviet Union showed exactly the same pattern (Plous and Zimbardo, 1984). For example, in March 1983, President Reagan described the Soviet Union as an "evil empire." A month later, the Soviet foreign minister said that the "table of evils [committed by the United States was] very long," (cited in Plous and Zimbardo, 1984).

Moral Self-image

Not only do parties in international conflict see one another as evil, they see themselves as the embodiments of good. Consider the Arab-Israeli conflict. The Arabs see themselves as the victims of "Zionist expansionism and aggression," while the Israelis see themselves as people who desire peace, but who have been forced into war by their Arab neighbors (White, 1977).

Virile Self-image

According to White, parties to an international conflict often see themselves not only as the embodiment of good, but as the embodiment of strength and virility. To back down in the face of another country's threats would be inconsistent with this self-image; "real" men don't run from a fight. White points out that before the First World War, the great powers seemed to be more afraid of being humiliated than of facing the consequences of war. Similarly, Hitler was obsessed with a need to demonstrate the strength and courage of the German people.

Absence of Empathy

Parties to an international conflict often display an inability to understand how the other side thinks and feels. Again, the Arab-Israeli conflict illustrates this. Psychologists who have interviewed Arab leaders such as Yasser Arafat (Kelman, 1982) have noted that these leaders are largely unaware of the impact that Hitler's holocaust against the Jews still has on the thinking of Israel's leaders and its people. The Israelis are equally unaware of the factors that impact the Arabs' thinking. Cohen, Kelman, Miller, and

Smith (1977) brought Israelis and Palestinians together to discuss the ways the conflict between them might be resolved. The Israelis were simply unable to understand the importance of a homeland to the Palestinians.

Military Overconfidence

In the period of time before a war breaks out, the parties often display an excessive amount of confidence in their abilities to win the coming war. Hitler, for example, invaded Poland even though England and France threatened war if he did; and in perhaps his greatest military blunder, he attacked his former ally, the Soviet Union, a year or so later. Histories of the American involvement in Vietnam suggest that until the late 1960s, the United States was sure it could achieve a military victory in that country (Halberstam, 1973).

Selective Inattention

White defined selective inattention as the "unconscious tendency not to pay attention to certain disturbing and embarrassing things, such as the human side of an enemy or the morally questionable aspects of the behavior of one's own country" (1977). In the case of the Arab-Israel conflict, White pointed out that most Arabs fail to see that their threats against Israel fuel Jewish fears of another holocaust and produce many of the actions the Arabs find most objectionable. For their part, the Israelis fail to see how natural it is for the Arabs to be angry with them for taking large amounts of land from them and how their behavior fuels this anger.

Reduction of International Conflict

As discussed earlier, a nonzero-sum, mixed-motive conflict, has two distinguishing characteristics. First, in contrast to a zero-sum conflict in which there is a clear winner and a clear loser, it is possible for all participants in a nonzero-sum game to win or for all participants to lose. Second, in a nonzero-sum conflict, there is a motivation to cooperate and a motivation to compete, but it is in both parties' best interests to cooperate. This is also a good description of the situation confronting two countries involved in an international dispute; theorists view international conflict as a nonzero-sum, mixed-motive conflict.

In the last 20 to 25 years, social scientists have begun to investigate whether the techniques that produce cooperation in laboratory studies of interpersonal conflict can be used to reduce real-world conflicts between nations.

The GRIT Strategy

GRIT strategy: a strategy for reducing the level of international conflict.

The GRIT approach to reducing the level of conflict between two nations had its origins in a noted psychologist's concerns about world peace. Charles Osgood (1959, 1962) was troubled by what he saw as the ever-increasing level of conflict between the United States and the Soviet Union. Osgood believed that this dangerous trend might be reversed by using the graduated reciprocation in tension reduction strategy, or the **GRIT strategy.**

Osgood proposed that neither GRIT nor any other strategy will work unless the nations involved in the conflict believe (1) that they will both derive considerable benefits from cooperation and (2) that because of the interdependence of outcomes, both will experience considerable losses from competition.

At the core of the GRIT strategy is a series of unilateral concessions one party makes to the other. These concessions have three characteristics. One, they should reduce the level of threat to the other party but not seriously weaken the position of the party that makes them. Two, they should not indicate weakness on the maker's part. And three, they should be concessions that can be reciprocated.

The first step in implementing the GRIT strategy is for the party that plans to use it to publicly announce its general intention to reduce tension and to point out to the target party the benefits of reciprocating (Osgood, 1974). Each specific concession should be announced before it is made, and the party using GRIT should make it clear that each concession is part of the overall strategy to reduce tension. After the first concession is made, reciprocation should be invited. Whether or not reciprocation occurs, the initiating party should engage in further unilateral concessions. The subsequent concessions should also be well publicized and their intents made clear. While these concessions are being made, the initiating party must respond firmly to any threatening actions of the other party. In other words, it must be made clear that while the initiating party is willing to cooperate, it will not be bullied.

There has been a good deal of laboratory research on the GRIT strategy. These studies indicated that GRIT can be effective in producing cooperation between two individuals engaged in a nonzero-sum, mixed-motive interpersonal conflict (Linskold, 1979). The question of interest is whether GRIT would reduce real-world, international conflict. At this point, the answer to this question is not known, but there are indications GRIT would work.

The strongest evidence comes from a series of events that occurred in the early 1960s. In mid-1963, President Kennedy gave a remarkable speech in which he suggested that the United States should consider ways to make mutual peace and cooperation attractive to the Soviet Union. Then he announced that the United States was halting atmospheric testing of nuclear weapons and that it would not resume testing unless another country resumed testing.

The Soviets responded almost immediately. They let Kennedy's speech be broadcast to eastern Europe. The next day at the United Nations, the Soviet Union dropped its objections to the placing of peace keepers in a Middle Eastern country. In response, the United States dropped its objections to full member status for Hungary, a Soviet ally.

These initial small concessions were followed by further acts of bilateral cooperation. The Soviet Union announced that it had halted production of strategic bombers, and the United States agreed, for the first time, to sell grain to the Soviet Union. The two countries agreed to the installation of a hotline between Moscow and Washington, a nuclear test ban treaty, a pact not to orbit nuclear weapons, and the establishment of direct commercial flights between the two countries (Etzioni, 1967).

This period of cooperation between the superpowers began to wind down in the fall of 1963. Kennedy was beginning his reelection campaign and was afraid he would appear "soft on communism." Shortly thereafter, Kennedy was assassinated; the chances of restarting the peace offensive died with him.

These historical incidents do not prove the utility of the GRIT strategy. In fact, some researchers have questioned whether President Kennedy and the Soviets were sincere in the concessions they made (Etzioni, 1967). But the incidents do suggest that GRIT is a strategy that merits further consideration.

Third-Party Intervention

If strategies such as GRIT offer promise for the reduction of international conflict, it seems reasonable to ask why so few countries have used them. A possible answer comes from White's work on misperceptions. Consider the war between Iran and Iraq, which has gone on for several years. Imagine that someone were trying to convince the Iranians to use the GRIT strategy to end the war. It is unlikely that Iran—which perceives Iraq as the diabolical enemy—would believe that any unilateral concessions it made to Iraq would be reciprocated. Even if Iran made such concessions, Iraq would probably misperceive the motivation behind them.

One way to reduce the level of conflict in an exchange between two individuals is to bring in a third party. The goal of this third party is to intervene in a way that helps the individuals reach a cooperative, mutually beneficial strategy. A number of conflict theorists believe that third parties can provide the key to the resolution of many international conflicts.

Researchers have identified two kinds of third-party intervention in international conflicts. One is mediation. According to Fisher (1983), mediators are primarily concerned with achieving an agreement on the specific causes of the dispute. They want the conflict resolved immediately and will use whatever tactics are needed to achieve this end—including deception and threat. The other kind of third-party intervention is as consultation. Consultants are primarily concerned with creating a situation that will lead to feelings of trust and to a willingness to cooperate. They are less concerned with the immediate resolution of the conflict than with the creation of a climate that will have long-term positive consequences. As a result, consultants are not likely to use the manipulative tactics of the mediator.

Mediation in the Middle East In the fall of 1973, the fourth Arab-Israeli war since 1948 broke out. The Arabs achieved more military success in this than in any of the previous wars, but eventually the Israelis gained the upper hand. By the second week of the war, the Israelis were driving on Cairo, the capital of Egypt, and Damascus, the capital of Syria. The Soviet Union threatened military intervention if the Israelis did not stop, and the United States forced Israel to accept a truce by withholding the delivery of weapons and ammunition that Israel desperately needed.

In the months that followed the war, something unique in the history of the Middle East happened. Both the Israelis and the Arabs accepted an agreement on the return of some land to the Arabs and on the establishment of permanent cease-fire lines. The man who accomplished this diplomatic coup was the United States secretary of state Henry Kissinger.

Pruitt (1983) analyzed Kissinger's activities and argued that he used several traditional mediation strategies to achieve the agreement. Rather than trying to get these bitter enemies to engage in face-to-face negotiations, Kissinger shuttled back and forth between them. This reduced the chances of angry exchanges which would harden each side's bargaining position.

When the Arabs and the Israelis were each asked to make concessions, these requests came from Kissinger rather than the opposing parties in the negotiation. This had two advantages. A concession requested by a mediator is more likely to be accepted than one made by an enemy, and if the requested concession provokes anger, this anger is directed at the mediator rather than at the opposing party.

When Kissinger was able to extract a concession from one side, he presented it to the other side as his own idea. This avoided the problem of one side being seen as soft or weak by the other because it had made a concession, which could have led to unreasonable demands. Also, by accepting a proposal made by Kissinger rather than one made by Israel, for example, the Arabs could make a concession and not lose face.

Kissinger was also able to develop alternatives not seen by either side. For example, the Syrians wanted the Israelis to withdraw from some of their land, but the Israelis did not want Syrian soldiers so close to their farming communities on the Israel-Syria border. This impasse was solved by Kissinger proposing that United Nations troops be placed on the land vacated by the Israelis.

Finally, by controlling the communications between the two countries, Kissinger could keep the momentum toward an agreement going. When the negotiations were stalled on a certain point, he could change the focus to a point that could be resolved. Thus, he could prevent either side from seeing the negotiations as pointless.

There is little question that the successful conclusion of these negotiations represented Kissinger's greatest diplomatic achievement (Sheehan, 1976). But advocates of the consultant role for third parties would raise some serious questions about the long-range value of Kissinger's effort. They would argue that by focusing only on the resolution of the very specific issues relating to the 1973 war and ignoring the more fundamental issues of the Arab-Israeli conflict (a homeland for the Palestinians, secure borders for the Israelis), Kissinger may have made the resolution of these fundamental issues more difficult (Fisher, 1983; Hoppman and Druckman, 1983). An enduring resolution of this international conflict may require consultation.

Consultation   Over the past several years, several social scientists have investigated the utility of having third parties intervene as consultants in civil and international conflicts. One notable attempt has been conducted by Herbert Kelman and his associates (Kelman, 1972, 1982, 1983; Kelman and Cohen, 1976; Cohen et al., 1977).*

In the early 1970s, Cohen and his associates were able to get several Israelis and Palestinians to participate in a pilot conflict resolution workshop. The goals of this workshop were to get the participants to view the Arab-Israel conflict as "conflict analysts" rather than as "combative representatives" of their respective groups, and to show the participants how their usual styles of interaction might be blocking conflict resolution between their respective groups in the world outside the workshop. The workshop staff made their roles as a third parties to the dispute quite clear. They were not judges who would decide which side was right or wrong. Their task was to facilitate communication between the participants. To this end, they tried to point out each side's possible misperceptions and attempted to get them to see the other's perspective. Cohen and his associates reported favorable responses from the workshop participants, but did not conduct a formal evaluation of its effect. Doob (1970), however, reported that consultation met with only limited success when it was used with representatives of several nations in Africa. Those studies which have examined its value in resolving civil conflicts report positive results. Thus, the results of studies on the effectiveness of this technique are mixed.

As Kelman (1982) and others have noted, it would be foolish to believe that complex, decades-old civil and international conflicts will be easily resolved by the GRIT strategy, third-party intervention, or any other technique. But he and the other researchers of these conflicts believed that resolution is possible. While many attempts will fail, it would seem that the costs of not trying are infinitely greater than those of trying.

---

*Kelman's work on social influence was discussed in chapter eleven.

Chapter Thirteen

Group Processes

by Paul E. Spector

Prologue

Michael A. Wallach, Nathan Kogan, and Daryl J. Bem (1962).
Group influence on individual risk-taking. *Journal of
Abnormal and Social Psychology*, **65,** 75–86.

Background

This chapter is concerned with the behavior of people in small groups. In
the 1960s, conventional wisdom held that people in groups make more
conservative decisions than do people alone. In 1961, a graduate student
at the Massachusetts Institute of Technology's (MIT's) business school directly tested this idea, using male business majors as his subjects. He found
that participation in a group discussion made his subjects take more risks
(Stoner, 1961). Michael Wallach and his associates wanted to find out if
these results would generalize to males and females who were not business
majors.

Hypothesis

These researchers did not propose a formal hypothesis. Instead, they asked
a research question: Do people make riskier decisions when they are members of a group than when they are alone?

Subjects

The subjects were 167 male and female undergraduates at the University
of Colorado.

Procedure

Subjects participated in the experiment with four or five other people of
the same sex. Each member of the group was given a questionnaire containing descriptions of 12 life situations in which the central person had
to make a decision about two courses of action. One choice, if successful, would be clearly more desirable than the other, but this course of action was the more risky. One example of these choice dilemmas is as
follows:

> Mr. B, a 45-year-old accountant, has recently been informed by his
> physician that he has developed a severe heart ailment. The disease
> would be sufficiently serious to force Mr. B to change many of his
> strongest life habits—reducing his work load, drastically changing his
> diet, giving up favorite leisure-time pursuits. The physician suggests
> that a delicate medical operation could be attempted which, if suc-
> cessful, would completely relieve the heart condition. But its success
> could not be assured, and in fact, the operation might prove fatal.

Subjects were then asked to imagine they were advising Mr. B and to indicate the lowest odds of success they would accept before they would recommend that Mr. B have the operation. The alternatives ranged from a 90 percent chance of success to a 10 percent chance of success, plus an additional alternative in which the subjects could refuse to recommend the operation no matter how likely it were to succeed. Subjects first filled out the questionnaire by themselves, not knowing that they would consider the dilemmas again in a group discussion. When they were finished, the experimenter asked them to discuss each dilemma as a group and come up with a group decision. The discussion of each dilemma continued until all group members could agree upon a choice. Other undergraduates served as a control group. They filled out the questionnaire by themselves twice.

Results

The effect of group discussion was determined by subtracting the subjects' first set of choices from their second set of choices. Because of the way the choices were worded, the more *negative* the difference, the larger the risky shift between the choices. (See figure 13-1 for the total difference scores for members of the experimental discussion group and the control group.)

Among the subjects who merely filled out the questionnaire twice by themselves, there was not significant change. Among the subjects who engaged in the group discussion before they made their second set of choices, there was a significant shift to the more risky alternatives.

Implications

The unexpected finding of greater riskiness in groups stimulated research on the causes of what came to be known as the risky-shift effect. In the 1960s and 1970s, this phenomenon was studied extensively. Subsequent research has led social psychologists to question the reasons why groups are sometimes riskier than individuals and the importance of the phenomenon, but Wallach and his associates' study has added to our knowledge of group processes. This study serves to illustrate one basic point of this chapter: In most instances, what a group is and what it does are more than the simple sum of its members' characteristics and abilities.

Groups: collections of two or more people who interact with and have influence on one another and who perceive themselves to be interrelated with one another.

The previous chapters have focused primarily on individuals—how they affect and are affected by others. This chapter turns its attention to the behavior of groups of people. Unless you are a hermit, you belong to social groups; in fact, most of us will belong to hundreds of such **groups** during our lifetimes. These groups are formed for many purposes, including work, study, recreation, and religion. Members of groups have shared or at least interrelated goals. Your social psychology class, for example, is a group, and you and most of your fellow students share the goal of passing the course.

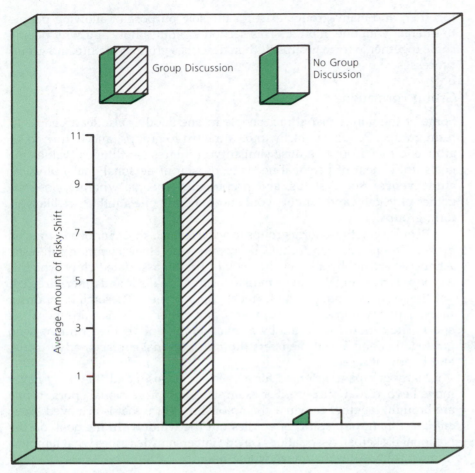

Figure 13-1. *Group discussion caused subjects to move their choices to riskier alternatives.*
Source: Wallach et al. (1962).

This chapter begins by explaining what the basic elements of a group are, why groups form, what they are, and how they operate. Then it examines the results of a group's efforts, or group performance. The factors that influence group performance are discussed, as is the issue of whether groups outperform individuals. Next, the topic of leadership—who becomes a leader and how the leader's actions affect a group—are considered. In the applications section, groups that make important decisions in the real world are examined.

NATURE OF GROUPS

In the prologue, the individual subjects formed a group because the experimenter told them to do so. In everyday life, no one has to tell people to form groups. Usually people form groups because they enjoy being together, and many groups exist for the sole purpose of allowing people to interact with one another. This section examines how and why people come together to form groups. It then describes group structure and group processes.

Group Formation

Some of the things that attract people to one another also lead people to form groups. People are likely to be attracted to groups, and in turn to be attractive to a group, because similarity of interests, attitudes, values, or goals; fulfillment of personal needs or pursuit of personal goals; physical attractiveness; social status; and propinquity—people who are close together physically and cannot avoid bumping into one another are likely to form groups.

People sometimes form groups to achieve goals that cannot be achieved alone. Groups are also formed by people who share common interests. Almost every hobby and leisure activity has an associated club, which is a group. For example, runners tend to be individualistic and inner-directed, yet they form running clubs in most communities. These clubs sponsor races, carbohydrate-loading dinners, and other activities around their sport. They are often started by a small number of devoted runners who get together and solicit members through personal contacts, advertising, and booths at races.

Many groups are formed for a specific purpose, and they may never move beyond that purpose. For example, some professional sports teams are brought together to win a championship. Once that is achieved, their *esprit de corp* (group spirit) often flies out the window. In his book on the National Basketball Association, David Halberstam describes what happens to most teams after they have won a title:

> Players were willing to sacrifice on the way to a championship, but once there, once at the top, it was a different matter. Agents and wives spoke of bigger salaries and of greater recognition, and of how much rival players, of lesser talent and playing on losing teams, were making. In Washington, runner-up the previous year, Bob Dandridge was said to be sulking; there was also dissidence from other players and Dick Motta, the coach, was reported to want out . . .
>
> Nor was it just the players who changed after victory. Sam Schulman, the Seattle owner, having finally won his championship, had chosen the night of the victory party to inform Paul Silas [an older player] that his salary, if he intended to return the following year, would have to be cut in half . . . With the championship achieved, Silas had become a luxury again. Even Silas, a rare expert on the lack of sentiment in the NBA, had been surprised by Schulman's way of rewarding him, of breaking the news. (Halberstam, 1981, pp. 90–91)

Other groups may move beyond one purpose or goal and develop other interests. For example, a group of friends might decide to go into business together, expanding their group's purpose from social to economic. Multipurpose groups that become cohesive may last a long time because their existence does not rely on one particular need or goal.

In the early stages of group existence, some common purpose or goal binds people together. Over time, people invest effort into a group and may find great satisfaction in being members. They may find that they like the other members and enjoy being with them. If this occurs—there is no guarantee that it will—the group becomes cohesive.

Groups expend effort in two major areas. The first area of effort is achievement of group goals or fulfillment of group purpose; in a work group, for example, this would involve doing productive work for the company. The second area of effort is maintenance of the group. Conflicts may arise among group members, members may find other groups to achieve their goals, and members may change their goals—all these possibilities create forces toward group dissolution. If group members wish to continue existing as a group, effort must be expended to keep them together. Such efforts are often expended by group leaders, who may mediate disputes between members, encourage people to stay in a group, and be strong proponents of a group's standards.

Group Structure

A group, a collection of interacting people, can vary considerably in size from two people (a *dyad*) to many people. The limit to group size is the limit of how many people can interact with one another. Clearly, 10,000 people cannot be a group because they cannot directly interact with one another.

Groups may begin as loose collections of people in which everyone is equal and contributes the same. As groups stay together over time, people's contributions to them tend to change and their influence becomes differentiated. The characteristics of groups also change. These characteristics of groups define **group structure.** Just as one can describe the structure of the human body, one can discuss the structure, or component parts, of groups. According to Stang and Wrightsman (1981), the components of group structure are roles, norms, status, and communication patterns. These structual characteristics enable psychologists to describe groups and to differentiate one group from another. They also enable psychologists to describe the relationships among group members.

Group structure: the arrangement of roles, norms, status, and communication patterns that emerges during group formation.

Roles

According to role theory, people's behaviors can be described and explained in terms of their roles, which define expected behaviors according to specified social positions. (See chapter one.) In other words, a given role, defines how a person should act. The roles actors and actresses play in movies are restrictive; they define what is to be said and how it should be said. Group roles are less restrictive, but they still set limits on behavior. One common role found in groups is that of the leader. A leader is expected to direct and coordinate the activities of the group members. If you are a group leader, other members of the group expect you to act like the leader: When a decision must be made, they expect you to make it; when a task has to be divided among people, they expect you to divide it. Most groups have three basic kinds of roles for their members. These can be illustrated by considering the structure of an unusual group.

Task-oriented role: behaviors directed toward the achievement of a group's goal.

Maintenance role: behaviors concerned with the relationships between group members.

On October 12, 1972, a plane carrying a group of athletes and their friends left from Montevideo, Uruguay, and headed for Santiago, Chile. The plane never arrived; it crashed in the Andes Mountains. For the next 10 weeks, the passengers endured starvation, illness, and constant subzero temperatures. Incredibly, 16 of the 45 passengers survived.

One role that emerged in this group was the **task-oriented role.** People who take this role try to direct and coordinate the activities of a group. Among the Andes survivors, this role was taken by Robert Canessa. Mr. Canessa kept the others from starving to death by convincing them that to survive they would have to eat the remains of their dead companions. He showed the group how to make blankets and create places to sleep. He was in charge of medical supplies. Mr. Canessa persuaded the group members that they must organize expeditions to find help rather than wait to be rescued, and he led the expedition that finally found help.

A second role that can be seen in these people's behaviors is the **maintenance role** (Bales, 1958, 1970). People who take this role are concerned with group morale; they attempt to keep thing harmonious and attend to the relationships between group members. Mr. Canessa played the task-oriented role well, but he cared little about maintenance. He was short-tempered and abusive toward the other people struggling to survive. The maintenance role was taken by Nando Parrado. Here is how Pier Paul Read, the author of a book describing the survivors' ordeal, described Mr. Parrado:

> Parrado . . . who before the accident had been a gawky, timid, would-be playboy, was now a hero. His courage, strength, and unselfishness made him the best loved of them all. He was always the most determined to brave the mountains and the cold and set out for civilization; and for this reason those who were younger, weaker, or had less determination placed all their faith in him. He also comforted them when they cried and took on himself much of the humdrum work around the plane from which, as an expeditionary, he was officially excused. He would never suggest a course of action without rising at the same time to put it into effect. One night, when part of the wall blew down in a strong wind, it was Parrado who climbed out from under the blankets to build it up again. When he returned he was so cold that those sleeping on either side of him had to punch and massage his body to bring back the circulation; but when half an hour later, the wall blew down again, Parrado once again rose to rebuild it. (1974, p. 127)

Finally, there is the individual role, or **self-oriented role.** People who take this role basically care only about themselves and often attempt to undermine the efforts of the people playing the task-oriented and maintenance roles. Among the Andes survivors, people who played this role were called parasites. They sat in the sun trying to keep warm while complaining about their plight. They did nothing to help the group reach its goal or to keep up group morale.

Just as people can be members of several different groups, they can also find themselves holding several different roles in one group. Faculty members have the role of teacher and the role of researcher. Students prefer that their professors spend their time in the teacher role, but large universities prefer that their faculty members spend their time doing research. As long as a faculty member can do both, everyone is satisfied. However, if students are waiting for their final exam grades and their professor has to meet a submission deadline for a grant proposal, a problem arises. Either the students do not get their grades on time or the professor does not get a research grant. Such situations create **role conflict.**

Role conflict leads to a number of problems for both the individual and the group, including dissatisfaction with the group, poor task performance, emotional strain, and withdrawal (Van Sell, Brief, and Schuler, 1981). As a result, in many areas in society, roles are separated to minimize role conflicts. Most companies, for example, have nepotism rules which prevent relatives from supervising one another on the job. And because of possible role conflict, the owners of a professional baseball team are never allowed to umpire a game.

Role conflict: a situation in which two or more roles compete for time and attention and make conflicting demands; often each role requires a behavior that cannot be tolerated by the other roles.

Norms

Roles are expectations for behavior based on people's social positions; **norms** are expectations for all group members irrespective of role or position. For example, work groups in factories decide how much each person should produce. These groups may encourage members to work hard and produce a lot, or they may demand that workers withhold output and goldbrick; they many adopt either high or low norms for productivity.

Norms: standards or guidelines for people's behaviors and beliefs.

The longer a group is in existence, the more set its norms and the more its norms separate and isolate the group from other people. Student groups, for example, often adopt specific dress norms which help give them identity and a sense of group existence. In the late 1960s, male students wore their hair long. In fact, many young national guardsmen wore short-hair wigs to camp so they did not have to cut their hair. But twenty years later, male students wear their hair short, and wig sales have definitely declined. A Mohawk haircut, spiked arm bracelet, dog collar, and torn T-shirt comprise the appropriate attire for admission into a group of punk rockers.

When group members detect a norm violation by another member, their first action is to inform the perpetrator that this behavior is out of line. Continued violation results in stronger and stronger pressure on the individual, which can include friendly and not-so-friendly reminders, nasty comments, threats, and aggressive responses. Factory workers are well known for their physical violence against performance-norm violators (Roethlisberger and Dickson, 1939). When continued efforts to gain compliance fail, the violator is excluded from the group and may be ostracized. This process is commonly called *peer pressure*—the social forces people apply to one another for norm adherence. (See the following cartoon.)

Status

Status implies an evaluation of people, including how attractive they are (not necessarily physically), how much influence they exert, and how favorable their positions in the group are. People high in status are respected by group members and are seen as being special. Status can come from

Status: the prestige people have in a group.

BEETLE BAILEY

people's positions or roles within a group, from their characteristics, or from their achievements. The leader role is held in high esteem, and people gain a certain amount of status from being a leader. People who are particularly successful in areas respected by group members are given high status. For example, if you join a bowling team and bowl a perfect game, you are assured high status in that group unless the rest of the members duplicate your feat and equalize status, or unless you go into a slump and fail to break 100, thereby losing status.

Communication Patterns

Another structural characteristic of groups is the communication patterns among members. In the prologue, the group members could engage in unrestricted communication with one another, but in many groups this is not the case. For example, factory workers often cannot talk freely with each other because of the physical characteristics of the assembly line. Workers must remain at their stations and may be unable to see or hear others, thus restricting communication. Your access to other social psychology class members is restricted at least during times the class is meeting.

In the early 1950s, researchers began to study how the pattern of communication among members of a group would affect the group's actions. Subjects were placed in groups of varying sizes and were given tasks to perform that required group effort. Communication patterns, or networks, were created by isolating group members in booths and allowing communication to flow only among certain booths. Communication was allowed only by passing notes, which were placed into slots leading from one partition to another. (See figure 13-2 for some examples of these networks.)

Each point represents a group member, and the lines joining the points show the allowable flow of communication. In the *circle* network, each person could pass a note only to the two people on either side. In the *common* network, each person could communicate directly with each other person in the group.

Centralization and its opposite, decentralization, are concepts that describe and categorize communication networks. Centralized networks, such as the wheel or Y, contain positions with more direct communication

Centralization: the extent to which some group members have greater access to communication and information channels than have others.

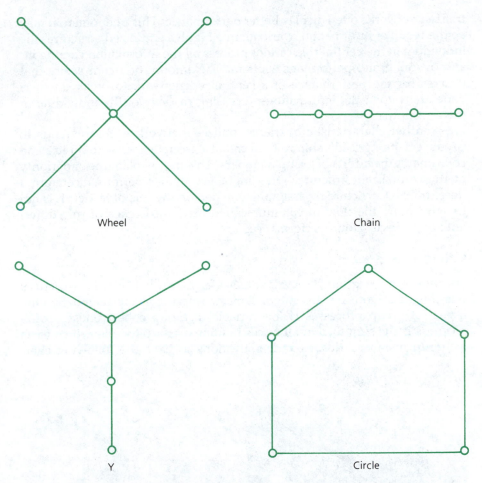

Wheel

Chain

Y

Circle

Figure 13-2. *Four of the communication networks studied by Leavitt.*

access than others. In the wheel network, only the person in the center can communicate with everyone else. In a decentralized network, such as the circle or chain, communication access is more equal. The degree of centralization can determine communication patterns among group members.

Leavitt (1951) studied four network patterns in five-person groups: the circle, chain, Y, and wheel. (See figure 13-2.) Each subject in the study was given a card with several symbols (square, diamond, asterisk). Only one of these symbols appeared on all of the cards, and the task was to discern which was the common symbol. Leavitt was interested in both task performance and group member enjoyment of the task. He found that the more centralized networks performed better than did the less centralized ones. However, group members in the decentralized networks enjoyed the task more than did members in the centralized networks.

Later research showed that the superiority of centralization may be limited to simple tasks, such as finding a common symbol (Shaw, 1964). On more complex tasks, such as solving mathematical problems, decentralized networks often display better performance. This phenomenon may be the result of information overload; in a highly centralized structure, the individual in the central role cannot process all the information coming in, and overall group performance suffers. The amount of a complexity that it takes for the performance of a centralized network to break down is dependent upon the information-processing capacity of the individual in the central role.

Another characteristic of the centralized network is that it tends to produce a strong leadership role, to create a group leader who directs and coordinates the efforts of group members. This may explain the superiority of the centralized structure. One might get similar performance from a decentralized structure by assigning one person the role of leader. It is not clear whether the flow of communication or the existence of role differentiation affects group performance.

Group Processes

To understand a group, one must consider more than just its structure; one must also consider the interactions among the group members. One aspect of group processes is the variable of group cohesiveness. **Cohesiveness** is the sum total of all forces holding a group together. It consists of group members' desires and motivations to have the following char-

A highly cohesive group such as this one will demand and achieve compliant behavior from its members.

acteristics: Group members like each other; group members are attracted to one another, nonsexually in most groups; group members enjoy being part of the group; group members share common goals; and group members want to keep the group together.

In other words high-cohesive groups have everything that the professional basketball teams described earlier did not have. Group cohesiveness is something that develops over time and requires a certain mixture of the right people and the right circumstances. Groups created in the laboratory for research purposes, such as the group in the prologue, rarely continue after the experiment is over. It is almost impossible to develop the kind of cohesiveness that will keep a group together over the short time span of a laboratory experiment.

Topic Background

Measuring Group Interaction

Researchers interested in studying group interactions have developed systems that enable them to record and classify the things people say when they are in a group. The most widely used coding system is interaction process analysis (IPA), developed by R.F. Bales in 1950 and revised by him in 1970.

A group interaction is recorded and each statement of each member is placed in one of the twelve categories presented in the following list.

Bales' Categories:

Seems Friendly
Dramatizes
Agrees

Gives Suggestions
Gives Opinion
Gives Information

Asks for Information
Asks for Opinion
Asks for Suggestion

Disagrees
Shows Tension
Seems Unfriendly

Categories one to three and ten to twelve reflect socioemotional or maintenance activities—activities that affect the personal relationships between members of the group. Some of these are positive and some are negative. The remaining categories reflect task-oriented activities—activities concerned with the group solving some problem or reaching some goal.

The placement of statements into categories is done by two observers who are well trained in recognizing the type of statements that should be placed in each category. These observers also indicate who makes each statement, to whom it is made, and how the recipient responds. Bale's coding system is complex and difficult to master, but well-trained observers can use it to provide a reliable and valid record of group interactions.

Recently, Bales (1980) has proposed a more complex, three-dimensional coding system. Each statement is classified in terms of where it falls on three dimensions: (1) dominance-submission, (2) friendly-unfriendly, and (3) task oriented–socioemotional oriented. He believed this new system provides a way of describing a group's structure as well as the pattern of interaction among its members.

Even work groups existing for many years will not necessarily become cohesive.

Group cohesiveness has implications for group behavior. Cohesive groups tend to have strong norms, and they tend to demand compliance to these norms because norm violations threaten group continuation. The stronger the motivation to continue a group, the stronger the effort to eliminate norm violations and, in the extreme, norm violators. On the other hand, the members of a cohesive group are motivated to remain in the group, and they are more likely to avoid norm violation out of fear of group rejection. Cohesive groups can be great homogenizers of their members' behavior, demanding and achieving consistent and expected behavior.

SUMMARY

Groups form naturally out of everyday interactions among people. They often develop around a common purpose or goal, such as the need for group effort to accomplish a task, or around common interests. Sometimes groups are formed for specific purposes and the groups do not move beyond those purposes. In other cases, groups become quite cohesive and their goals encompass areas beyond their original intents.

Group structure is composed of norms, roles, status, and communication networks. Roles are the behaviors expected of people because of their social position. Group members can hold task-oriented, maintenance, or self-oriented roles. Norms are behaviors expected of all individuals in a group. Status is the prestige that a person holds in a particular group. It develops from a person's attractiveness, abilities, accomplishments, and position in a group. Groups may have different communication patterns among their members. Whether or not communication is restricted and the pattern of who talks to whom defines group structure. With simple tasks, performance is superior when communication is restricted and flows through a central person; with complex tasks, the best performance results from open and unrestricted communication.

The glue that bonds group members is group cohesiveness. Cohesiveness is defined as the sum total of forces holding a group together. Cohesiveness is high when group members like each other; group members are attracted to one another; group members enjoy being part of the group; group members share common goals; and group members want the group to stay together. Cohesive groups tend to have strong norms and they work hard to ensure compliance to those norms. This means that groups with norms to be productive perform well on tasks, while groups with norms to be unproductive perform poorly.

GROUP PERFORMANCE

The experiment in the prologue demonstrated that people's decisions are riskier when they are in a group than when they are alone. Subsequent research has cast doubt on this general conclusion, but it does appear that people perform differently in groups than they do when they are alone. This section discusses some of the group influences on individuals that lead to this difference and then addresses the related issue of whether groups perform better on tasks than do individuals.

Group Influences on the Individual

If you have a task to do, will you perform it better if you are alone or with other people? These "others" can be simply watching you, in which case they are called an audience or observers; if they are performing the same task, but not interacting with or helping you, they are called coactors.

Social FacilitationTheory

Research on the simple presence of others goes back to the experiment which began chapter one. In 1898 Norman Triplett analyzed the records of professional cyclists who had raced under three different conditions; against an opponent, against pacers on tandem bicycles, and alone against the clock. The cyclists in the first two conditions (riding with others) turned in faster times than did the cyclists racing alone. Evidence of superior performance in the presence of others was found when Triplett devised a laboratory experiment in which children moved a spool around a small race course by turning a fishing reel. This phenomenon is called **social facilitation.**

Since Triplett's experiment, many others have been conducted with both observers and coactors and with many different tasks. The results of these studies have not all found the social facilitation effect. Sometimes people performed better in the presence of others, but sometimes they performed worse. Singerman, Borkovec, and Baron (1976) found that the presence of others inhibited learning of a complex maze task, a phenomenon called **social inhibition.**

It was not until 1965 that an explanation for the conflicting results of these studies was proposed. Robert Zajonc noted that when individuals

Social facilitation: the tendency for the presence of others to improve an individual's performance.

Social inhibition: the tendency for individuals to perform more poorly in the presence of others.

worked on relatively simple or well-known tasks—such as riding a bicycle, solving simple arithmetic problems, winding fishing reels—performance increased or was facilitated by the presence of others. However, when the tasks were complex or new—such as solving complex mathematics problems, memorizing written text, or solving logic problems—performance was hindered or inhibited by the presence of others. This led Zajonc to propose that the presence of others causes increased physiological arousal in humans performing a task. If success on a task requires that a person perform some simple behavior that has been well learned and well practiced (such as pedaling a bicycle), the arousal makes the behavior more likely and thus the presence of others improves performance. But if success on a task requires that a person perform some complex behavior that has not been well learned or well practiced (such as using a new chess strategy), the arousal makes the behavior less likely and thus the presence of others hurts task performance. Empirical research supports Zajonc's ideas about increases in arousal (Bond and Titus, 1983; Chapman, 1973; Borden, 1980; Martens, 1969), but as yet researchers do not know why the arousal occurs (Geen, 1980).

Social Impact Theory

Social impact theory: a model or theory of how the presence of others affects an individual.

Bibb Latan'e and his associates have developed the **social impact theory** to describe the effects of the presence of others on individuals (Latan'e, 1981; Latan'e and Nida, 1980). Impact is defined as the sum of social forces impinging upon a person from the presence of others. It is a psychological variable concerned with the perceived press of others. You may have felt this impact when making a presentation in class, performing on stage, or participating in an athletic event. Impact is determined by three variables— strength, immediacy, and number. Strength refers to the salience of the other people to the individual; it consists of status, power, influence, and overall social relationship. The instructor in your social psychology class probably has more strength to you than the other students in your class, unless you have special relationships with some of them. Furthermore, the instructor has more strength if he is a regular faculty member than if he is a graduate student. Immediacy has to do with the closeness in time and space of the other people. People are more immediate to you if they are physically present than if they are watching you on television or listening to you on the telephone. Finally, number refers simply to the number of others present.

Social impact theory says that as the strength, immediacy, or number of others increases, so does their impact, but that each increment in impact is less than the previous one. An increase in audience size from one to two people, for example, has more impact than does an increase from five to six people, and much more impact than an increase from ninety to one hundred people. This proposal is akin to the idea from economics that the first dollar poeple earn is worth more to them than the one hundredth dollar.

A study by Latan'e and Harkins (1976) provided support for this theory. Subjects were asked to imagine they were reciting a memorized poem in front of an audience. To simulate the audience, Latan'e and Harkins proj-

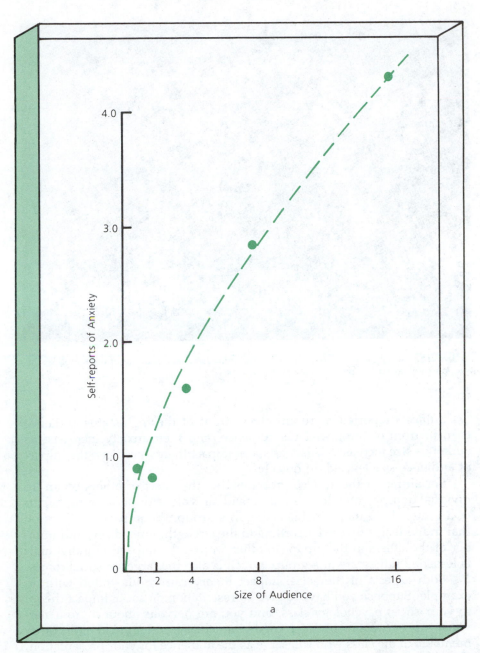

Figure 13-3. *As social impact theory predicts, the effect of audience size on anxiety diminished fairly quickly.*
Source: Latan'e and Harkins (1976).

ected faces on a screen in front of the subjects. They systematically manipulated the number of faces the subjects saw, and manipulated status by showing either teenaged or middle-aged faces. Subjects were asked to indicate how much anxiety they felt. (See figure 13-3 for the subjects' self-reports of anxiety.)

According to social impact theory, the strength, immediacy, and number of the people in the audience will affect the performance of this singer.

Subjects reported more anxiety in front of the high-status audience than in front of the low-status audience, and their anxiety increased as audience size increased. Also, as social impact theory predicts, the impact of audience size leveled off quickly.

Social impact theory also proposes that the effect of others on an individual depends on whether the individual is alone or performing as part of a group. If an individual is acting in a group, the impact of others on that individual is divided according to the strength, immediacy, and number of the others in the group. In other words, the impact on individuals is lessened if they are in a group, which is also the target of social forces.

Both aspects of the social impact theory can be illustrated with an example. Suppose you have to give a presentation on social impact theory to your social psychology class, and you are nervous about it. Your nervousness is a function of the strength, immediacy, and number of the other members of the class who will serve as the audience for your presentation, and of the instructor who will evaluate it. Your nervousness is less if your class is small than if it is large. In addition, if you are making a presentation as part of a group, your nervousness is less because the social impact of the audience is divided among the members of the group. The larger the presenting group, the more divided the audience impact—and the less you are affected.

In several studies, Latan'e and his associates have obtained data that support the theory. These studies have involved both the impact of observers on an individual and the division of impact on individuals in groups. For example, Freeman, Walker, Borden, and Latan'e (1975) studied tipping behavior in restaurants. They discovered that the bigger the party, the smaller the tip. When individuals dined alone, they tipped an average of 19 percent of the bill, but when individuals dined in groups of five or six, they tipped less than 13 percent of the bill. In a study of helping behavior, Latan'e and Dabbs (1975) had confederates ride elevators and accidentally drop a handful of coins or pencils in the presence of varying numbers of other passengers. They found that the more people present, the smaller the likelihood of people helping. About 40 percent helped when they were the only other person present; about 15 percent helped when they were among six others.

The more people that are present, the less compelled any individual feels to engage in helping. Does this sound familiar? It should, because it is similar to the concept of diffusion of responsibility. (See chapter eight.) Latan'e's pioneering work on diffusion of responsibility in helping led to the development of social impact theory.

Group Polarization

The effect of groups on individual decision making was identified primarily as the result of Wallach and his associates' research on the risky-shift effect. After they found that people in a group discussion made riskier decisions, a number of researchers began a search for the causes of this phenomenon. This search led to the discovery that group discussion does not always produce a risky shift. Nordhoy (1962) developed choice dilemmas that consistently generated cautious shifts. In a nonlaboratory study, Spector, Cohen, and Penner (1976) allowed students to choose one of eight grading systems for the entire class. The systems were scaled from a risky to a conservative likelihood to lead to high grades. Results showed a conservative shift; the groups chose options that were more certain to provide good grades.

Researchers have found both risky and conservative shifts in different studies and with different tasks, and they have found similar effects with decisions that do not involve risk. Studies have been conducted of jury decisions on innocence versus guilt and on the severity of punishment deserved. In general, it has been found that a group decision is more extreme than the average of individual decisions; this finding is called **group polarization** (Lamm and Myers, 1978; Moscovici and Zavalloni, 1969; Myers, 1983). In one study, Myers and Kaplan (1976) asked simulated juries to review hypothetical cases that varied in the likelihood that the defendant was guilty. Subjects were asked to rate the defendant's likelihood of guilt from 1 to 20 and the severity of punishment deserved from 1 to 7. (See figure 13-4 for the results.) When the defendant was likely to be guilty, groups polarized in the direction of greater guilt and more severe punishment. When the defendant was unlikely to be guilty, groups polarized in the direction of less guilt and less severe punishment.

It turns out that 11 of the 12 choice dilemmas used in Wallach and his associates' original experiment elicited initial risky tendencies, but one consistently generated a cautious shift (Davis, 1969). Had Nordhoy's (1962) choice dilemmas been used in the original experiment, the conclusion

Group polarization: an effect wherein group discussion does not change members' initial tendencies but makes them more extreme.

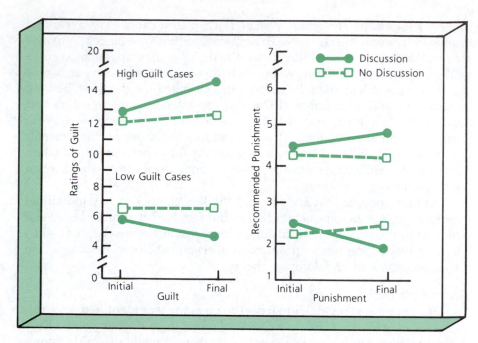

Figure 13-4. *Group discussion served to polarize the initial tendencies of the group members. Copyright (1976) American Psychological Association. Reprinted by permission of the authors.*
Source: Myers and Kaplan (1976).

would have been that the decisions made by individuals in groups are more conservative. Obviously, the risky shift effect is a special case of the more general groups' polarization phenomenon. What remains to be established is the mechanism that explains group polarization.

Lamm and Myers (1978) have suggested two mechanisms that account for group polarization both of which were presented in chapter eleven. First, group members influence each other by presenting logical and informational arguments that persuade each other. The content of these arguments might point out societal norms or focus on an argument other group members have not considered. For example, jurors might be reminded that the judicial system has a norm of innocent until proven guilty, or they might remind each other of crucial aspects of the testimony. The second mechanism has to do with normative social influence, or the tendency for people to conform to one another. It is an unusual individual who will hold onto a position that no one else holds, especially when being pressured.

Individual versus Group Performance

When human beings have a problem to solve or a goal to accomplish, they may puzzle over it for 30 seconds individually and then form a group. Jesus had a group of disciples to help him spread his message. The founders of the United States established a group to write the Declaration of Independence. Every president since George Washington has had a group of advisers to help him run the country. You may get a group of people together to study for the final examination in this course. Your instructor is not evaluated by one person but by a group of other professors. And so on. Is this faith in the superiority of groups over individuals justified?

This is a question that has been asked many times by social psychologists, and it has no simple answer. As Davis (1980) pointed out, the early research on groups suggested that groups perform better than individuals on many types of tasks. It was assumed that groups make rational decisions, based on the combined wisdom of its members, and that individual members inspire one another to be creative problem solvers. It is known today that these assumptions are not always true and that the relative effectiveness of groups versus individuals depends on a number of other variables, primarily on the type of task at hand. This section compares individual and group performance on three different types of task—additive, problem solving, and decision making. It then suggests ways in which group performance can be improved.

Additive Tasks

Additive tasks are those in which the group product is the sum of individual products. An example is a tug of war, in which the total pull is the sum of the individual pulls. Often additive tasks involve the manipulation of physical objects, as in the construction of a house or the raising of a barn. Some examples of tasks that have been used in research studies include building castles out of blocks, cheering and yelling, and playing tug of war.

In additive tasks, one would expect that a group of people can produce more than one individual, unless that individual was quite exceptional. However, will a group of five people produce five times as much as one person? In general, the answer to this question seems to be no: A five-person group will typically produce less than the combined output of five individuals working alone. One of the earliest demonstrations of this was an unpublished study by Ringelmann (Forsyth, 1983).

Ringelmann asked people individually and in groups to pull a rope attached to a gauge. Individuals pulled, on the average, with a force of 63 kilograms (about 130 pounds). When placed in groups of eight, they did not pull with a force equal to eight individuals pulls, which would have been 504 kilograms (about 1,040 pounds). Instead, they pulled with a force of 248 kilograms (about 520 pounds), which was less than half what would be expected. Two processes may account for this difference: social loafing and process loss.

Social Loafing   Latan'e and his associates (Latan'e, Williams, and Harkins, 1979) have termed the loss of individual productivity in groups **social loafing.** Social loafing is part of social impact theory, which describes how impact is divided among group members. When people have tasks to do, their efforts are divided in the same way impact is divided: The bigger the group, the less task effort exerted by each individual.

In studies by Latan'e and his associates, subjects were brought into the laboratory and asked to cheer and clap in response to a signal given

Social loafing: the tendency for people to exert less effort when they are in a group.

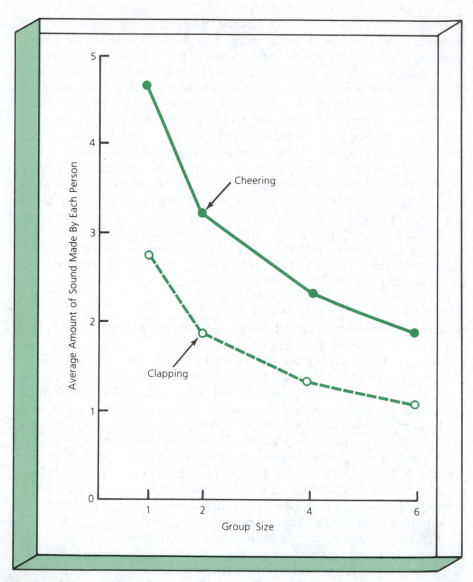

Figure 13-5. *As group size increased, the amount of effort expended by group members decreased.*
Source: Latan'e et al. (1979).

by the experimenter. The size of the group in which individuals performed the task was manipulated, and ranged from one to six. (See figure 13-5 for the effects of this manipulation.) The larger the group, the less the average sound per subject—or the more individual group members loafed (Latan'e et al., 1979).

Recently, Prestholdt (1984) demonstrated that this kind of social loafing occurs among teams whose job it is to yell or cheer. He found that high school cheerleaders cheered less loudly when together than when alone.

The social loafing effect disappears when individuals believe their own performances can be monitored. In another cheering study, Williams, Harkins, and Latan'e (1981) hooked subjects to a microphone and told them the microphone recorded how loud they were cheering. The subjects ceased to loaf. It appears people loaf when they feel that nobody can tell they are not exerting maximum effort. When their individual effort is apparent to others, the social impact upon them is more immediate, and they exert themselves. Loafing is a good name for this phenomenon.

Process Loss   When group members work on a task together, they often interfere with one another. You may have experienced this type of interference while having an assistant—possibly a child—help you with a task. If you know how to do a task and your assistant does not, you may spend more time explaining what to do than it would take to do the task yourself. Interference of this type leads to **process loss.** Process loss occurs because of interference resulting from a lack of coordinated effort, group conflict, or maintenance efforts. It may also occur because of intentional interference, which results when some group members would rather do something else or when group members are in competition with one another. Process loss is not necessarily loafing. People may interfere with one another even when they are all working as hard as possible on a task. The nature of a task dictates the extent to which joint efforts interfere with one another. In a yelling task, there would be little interference, but in a construction task where everyone works on part of a whole structure, there is considerable opportunity for interference.

Process loss: the tendency for group interaction to produce a decline in efficiency.

Research Highlight

Were the Beatles Social Loafers?

Few songwriters have had more influence on contemporary music than John Lennon and Paul McCartney. Between 1963 and 1970, they wrote 162 songs. Seventy were written by Lennon, 45 by McCartney, and 47 by both. The quality of these songs varied. Two social psychologists who were also Beatles fans wondered whether the concept of social loafing might explain why some songs were better than others. Jackson and Padgett (1982) investigated whether the songs co-written by Lennon and McCartney would, as social loafing would predict, be of lower quality than those written by either Lennon or McCartney.

These reseachers' hypothesis was complicated. One explanation of social loafing is that people feel less identifiable when they are in a group than when they are alone. Jackson and Padgett believed that in the early part of Lennon's and McCartney's careers—until about 1967—they probably did not feel any less identifiable when they produced a joint product than when they wrote alone. The Beatles were a cohesive unit, "sharing their music and their lives with one another." (Jackson and Padgett, 1982). Thus, it did not matter whether the song was by Lennon, McCartney, or Lennon and McCartney. But after 1967, the relationships among the Beatles began to sour, and each began to emerge as a separate, identifiable personality. They and their fans became aware of who contributed what to the group. This difference led Jackson and Padgett to predict that they would not find evidence of social loafing in the pre-1967 jointly written songs, but that they would find it in the post-1967 jointly written songs.

Social loafing produces reduced effort and reduced effort usually produces a lower-quality product, so the researchers attempted to measure the quality of the songs of interest. One way they did this was to determine whether a song had been released as a single or placed on an album. The Beatles and the executives of their record company evaluated their recordings and chose what they believed were the better ones for release as singles; the poorer recordings would then appear only on albums. A second measure was the sales of single releases written either by one of the two or both of them.

The analyses of the number of songs released as singles and as part of an album supported Jackson and Padgett's hypothesis. Before 1967, songs written by either Lennon or McCartney were less likely to be released as singles than were co-written songs. After 1967, individually written songs were more likely to be released as singles than were co-written songs. Essentially the same pattern was found in the sales of single records.

There is an alternate explanation of these findings. The relationship between Lennon and McCartney cooled considerably in the late 1960s. Thus, the lower quality on the post-1967 joint efforts may have reflected a lack of coordination or the existence of competition between them. In other words, process loss rather than social loafing may have been responsible for the poorer quality of the combined efforts on later songs.

In a study by Rosenbaum, Moore, Cotton, Cook, Hieser, Shovar, and Gray (1980), subjects constructed towers out of building blocks, performing the task either alone or in groups. Rosenbaum and his associates manipulated the motivational set of the subjects in the groups by giving a monetary reward based either on the best single performance in the group (competition) or on the overall group product (cooperation). When there was a cooperative set among the group members, they performed as well as did the individuals. But when there was a competitive set, group performance was much poorer. (See figure 13-6.)

Problem-solving Tasks

A second kind of task that often confronts groups is to find the solution or solutions to a problem. If you have been a member of a group trying to figure out how to raise money for a charity, planning a social or athletic event, or attempting to complete a class assignment, you have engaged in group problem solving. Sometimes the problems to be solved can be

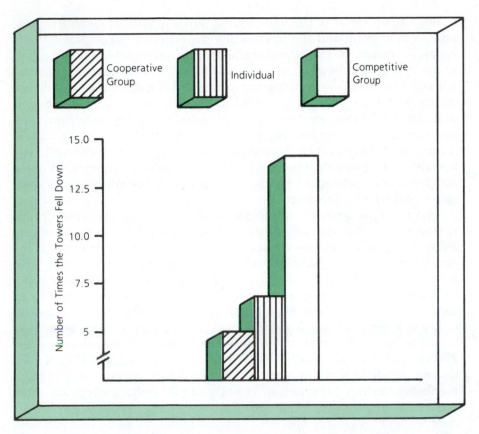

Figure 13-6. *When subjects were part of a competitive group they performed worse than did either a cooperative group or subjects working alone.*
Source: Rosenbaum et al. (1980).

simple—what is the shortest route for a homecoming parade, for example. Sometimes they can be complex—how to improve interracial relations on a campus, for example. Government agencies make extensive use of group problem solving. For instance, the American scientists who worked to develop the first atomic bomb during the Second World War were engaged in group problem solving (how to harness atomic power) as were the members of Congress who investigated the Watergate scandal. Research on group problem solving has focused on how the nature of the problem and the tactics used to solve it can affect group effectiveness and efficiency. The problems studied range from simple judgments, like guessing someone's weight, to complex tasks like solving mathematical equations or logic problems.

Simple Judgments Simple judgment tasks are those in which individuals or groups must make a judgment or guess about something, typically a physical characteristic of a person or thing. Some examples are guessing the number of beans in a bottle, someone's weight, or the temperature of a room. Groups are compared to individuals in judgment tasks in one of two ways. In the first method, an individual is given the same task as is a group and the individual's performance is compared to the group judgment. In the second method, the same number of individuals as are in a group are given the task, but these individuals do not interact with one another. The pseudogroup composed of individuals who do not interact is called a *staticized*, or *nominal*, group. The judgments of individuals in a staticized group are combined and compared to the judgment of an interacting group. Suppose five people are asked to independently guess a number of beans. Their guesses are 342, 567, 291, 400, and 450. The average of the five judgments is 410. This average is then compared to the judgment of an interacting group of five people to see which group came closer to the correct answer.

With simple quantitative judgments, both real and staticized groups perform better than do individuals, and staticized groups usually perform better than do real groups (Davis, 1969). One reason for this is that the average of several judgments is more accurate than a single estimate. This comes from psychological test theory and it is why tests usually have many items. Any single item alone is not a good measure of the student's performance: A poor student might get lucky and happen to know the answer or guess it correctly, and a good student might forget a particular answer or make an error; however, lucky guesses and unfortunate errors will average out in a total score based on many items. In fact, you do not need several people to find this effect. If a single person makes multiple judgments of something, that person's combined judgments are typically more accurate than most of the individual guesses, as long as the person makes independent judgments and does not just guess the same quantity over and over. (See the discussion of concept of reliability presented in chapter two.)

You can test this phenomenon with a simple experiment. Ask 10 people to guess your weight. The people can be friends or strangers, as long as they do not already know your weight. You will find that the average of the 10 guesses is reasonably close to your actual weight, and that it is closer than most of the individual guesses. Furthermore, you will find that the range of guesses is considerable. For someone with a weight of 150 pounds, estimates of 130 to 170 pounds would not be unusual. If you get a larger number of estimates, you will find that the average will get closer to the real value. In general, the larger the number of estimates, the closer the average to the true value.

Complex Tasks   Complex tasks include logic problems, math problems, and mental puzzles. Many of these problems have one obvious correct answer—obvious, that is, once you find the solution. These are called *eureka* problems; once you finally solve them, you immediately realize they are solved. An example of a typical eureka problem follows.

Three Missionaries and three Cannibals are on the A-side of the river. Get them across to the B-side by means of a boat which holds only two at one time. All the Missionaries and one Cannibal can row. Never under any circumstances or at any time may the Missionaries be outnumbered by the Cannibals. (Davis, 1969, p. 38)

This problem is difficult to solve for most people. Try it and you will undoubtedly find it takes some time. However, once you find the solution, you will have a sudden feeling of insight. You will say to yourself, "Of course, the answer is really very simple!" or simply, "Eureka!" (Hint: A cannibal who has been taken to side B may return to side A.)

This type of problem has been used to compare the performance of groups to that of individuals. Comparisons have been made of the number of problems solved, the time taken for solution, and the correctness of solutions. In general, groups are better able to find a correct solution than is a single individual. Here is the reason why.

Suppose the missionary-cannibal problem can be solved in 20 minutes by 33 percent of all individuals. If the problem is given to 30 people to solve on their own, probability theory would predict that 10 (33 percent) will be able to solve it in 20 minutes. If 30 people are randomly divided into 10 groups of three, the law of probability predicts that seven groups (70 percent of the 10 groups) will include at least one individual who can solve the problem in 20 minutes. Thus, 70 percent of the groups will reach the correct answer in 20 minutes, compared to 33 percent of the individuals.

However, if interacting groups are compared to staticized groups, they usually do poorer than the staticized groups (Davis, 1980). The reason for this is that the group process interferes with the problem solving of individuals (process loss). Thus, not all 10 of the individuals who could solve the problem alone in 20 minutes could do so in a group. One mechanism put forth to explain why this process loss occurs is the *equalitarian hypothesis* (Davis, 1980; Restle and Davis, 1962). According to this hypothesis, each individual in a group receives a proportionate amount of the group's time, even though some individuals cannot solve the problem. Groups spend much of their problem-solving time discussing the partial solutions of people who cannot solve the problem. An individual capable of solving the problem may be distracted by less-capable individuals who ask for opinions, advice, or assistance. Furthermore, the individual with the correct solution must compete for the attention of other group members to present the solution and convince them it is correct. Thus, groups do not perform as well as, theoretically, they should.

The ability to solve problems is only one aspect of group effectiveness. Another is efficiency of resource utilization. This is of particular concern to groups of employees, whose tasks are the jobs they are being paid to do. Assuming comparability of salaries, it costs more to have a group work on a problem than to have an individual work on a problem; thus, the question becomes whether it takes fewer person-hours to have employees solve a problem alone or in a group. On this score, groups lose their advantage.

The main advantage of a group over individuals is that a group is more likely to contain a skilled problem solver than a single individual is to be a skilled problem solver. The most skilled problem solver in a group determines how quickly the group solves a problem, but typically the group slows this person down. In addition, if, say, five people are in a group, five people are spending time and effort working on a problem that a single person will eventually solve; the efforts of four people are wasted.

In terms of resource utilization, it is often better to assign a problem to one individual and to spend the efforts of others on other tasks—assuming that it is possible to determine who would be capable of solving the problem. This procedure is followed in naturally occurring groups. For example, in business and government, many individuals are hired as consultants to solve problems alone.

Resource utilization may be more efficient if a group is working on a task that can be subdivided. If a complex problem or task has several parts, groups could regain efficiency by having a different group member solve each part.

Topic Background

An Exercise in Group Problem Solving

The studies of group problem solving suggest that the advantages of using a group approach to solve a problem depend largely on the problem itself. Here is a task on which groups usually do better than individuals. You will need to ask two or three friends to help you.

Imagine that you and your friends are space explorers, and you have escaped from a dangerous enemy. You were to have met some allies on the lighted side of Earth's moon. Unfortunately, your spaceship crash-lands 200 miles from their ship. You find an abandoned capsule and four spacesuits from the United States moon exploration program. Only the following items in the capsule are in usable condition:

A box of matches
Fifty feet of nylon rope
Five gallons of water
A first aid kit with medicine and needles for injections
Food concentrate
A magnetic compass
One case of dehydrated milk
Parachute silk
Signal flares
A stellar map of the moon's constellation
A solar-powered FM receiver-transmitter
A portable solar-powered heater
Two .45-caliber pistols
Two 100-pound canisters of oxygen
A self-inflating life raft

Your survival depends on reaching the other ship, so you must choose the items that will be most valuable on the 200-mile trip. Have each member of the group rank these fifteen items in order of their importance. Do this individually; avoid any group discussion. Then get together and come up with a group decision. In reaching this decision, avoid simply arguing for your own individual rankings. Avoid getting stalemated on any one item, but at the same time, do not give in just to avoid conflict. Most important, seek out differences of opinion; solicit information from all the group members.

The average rankings of a group of National Aeronautics and Space Administration (NASA) scientists who worked on the Apollo program are presented below. Add up the absolute differences between each of your individual rankings and those of the NASA scientists. Then do the same for the rankings arrived at by your group. The difference between your group's decision and the scientists' rankings should be much smaller. Your group should have done better than any individual member because the group discussion enabled people with different viewpoints and types of information to interact (Hall, 1971).

NASA Scientists' Rankings:
1. Oxygen (without it, you will never reach the ship)
2. Water (to replace the loss of body liquids on the lighted side of the moon)
3. Map (to navigate)
4. Food (to supply energy for you and others)
5. Receiver-transmitter (to communicate with the other ship; works only within short ranges)
6. Nylon rope (to scale cliffs)
7. First aid kit (contains vitamins and medicines; NASA space suits have special openings for injections)
8. Parachute silk (to protect from sun's rays)
9. Self-inflating life raft (the carbon monoxide bottle used to inflate the raft could be used for propulsion)
10. Signal flares (to send up a distress signal when you see the ship)
11. Pistols (to possibly use for propulsion)
12. Dehydrated milk (too bulky a form of food)
13. Heating unit (not needed unless you are on the moon's dark side)
14. Magnetic compass (totally worthless; the magnetic field on the moon is not polarized)
15. Matches (there is no oxygen on the moon to sustain a flame)

Brainstorming Other problems unlike eureka problems do not have one correct answer. For these, each member of a group may come up with a different solution—in some tasks, the goal is to come up with as many solutions as possible. For example, the budget deficit dilemma, which the president and his advisers face annually, probably has no single solution; successful group performance requires the generation of a number of different ideas for reducing the budget deficit.

A common approach to generating problem solutions or potential decision choices is brainstorming. **Brainstorming** is based upon the assump-

Brainstorming: a structured group technique for generating a large number of valid solutions to a problem.

Small groups, such as this one, must often decide which of a number of possible solutions to a problem it will adopt.

tions that groups can be efficient problem solvers and that group members inspire one another's performances. It is expected that the inspiration group members give each other will stimulate solutions that might otherwise have been missed.

In a typical brainstorming session, group members are asked to generate as many solutions as possible. For example, people might be asked to generate all the possible uses for a toothpick. Osborn (1963) gave certain rules for running a brainstorming session. These rules specify that solutions should not be criticized, no matter how ridiculous; group members should give solutions, no matter how silly they might seem; members should generate as many solutions as they can; and members should feel free to play off each other's ideas.

The idea of brainstorming makes intuitive sense, and it has been a popular technique. Unfortunately, the research on the technique does not

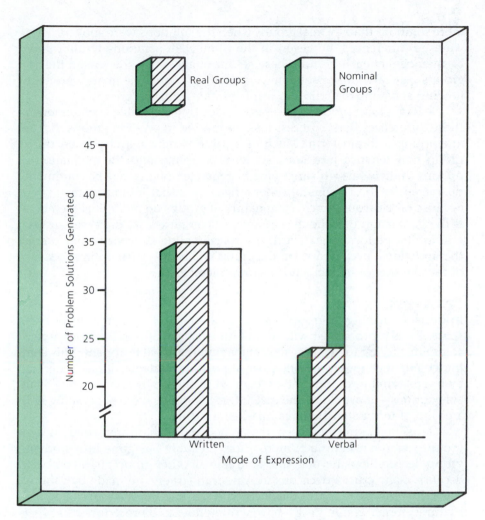

Figure 13-7. *When subjects wrote their solutions, real and nominal groups produced the same number; but when they said them, nominal groups produced many more.*
Source: Philipsen et al. (1979).

support its use (Forsyth, 1983). Groups fail to generate more options than an equivalent number of individuals working alone (a staticized group), and they often generate fewer options (Lamm and Trommsdorff, 1973). It is not clear why this occurs, but Lamm and Trommsdorff argue that part of the reason is **evaluation apprehension;** group members are hesitant to give options that seem silly or foolish because they are afraid the other members will think bad of them.

A study by Philipsen, Mulac, and Dietrich (1979) provides support for this explanation. Philipsen and his associates had real and staticized groups brainstorm solutions to a problem. In the staticized groups, individuals read their solutions into a tape recorder. In the real groups, solutions were said aloud. After this process, all subjects were asked to write down their selections. (See figure 13-7 for the results.) The staticized groups generated

Evaluation apprehension: a state of concern, anxiety, or apprehension because of anticipated evaluation of one's performance by other people.

more solutions than the real groups when the solutions were spoken. There were no differences, however, in the number of solutions written down by members of each group. These results suggest that the reason the real groups generated fewer solutions was that individual members were withholding solutions they did not want to share with the group.

Several group process concepts provide other possible explanations of these differences. First, process loss is expected to occur in groups that are attempting to brainstorm. Much of a group's time may be taken up by group maintenance functions, strategy planning, and the evaluation of options. Individuals who are trying to generate options may be continually distracted by the options of others. Second, social inhibition may occur because of the arousal-increasing nature of groups on individual members. If the generation of options is a novel or complex task, increased arousal will inhibit performance. Third, the social loafing concept would predict that individual performance in the group will be less than optimal because of the division of impact among group members.

Decision-making Tasks

In decision making, a group must decide which of a number of possible solutions to a problem it will adopt. An example of this is a government committee trying to find ways to combat international terrorism. This committee might choose from a number of possible strategies it has generated by brainstorming, or it might be required to choose from only a few available options—as would be the case if the committee were negotiating with a group of terrorists who have hijacked a plane.

Decision-making has been researched more than any other area of group performance; in fact, more effort probably has gone into studying group decision making than into studying all other group tasks combined because many crucial decisions in American society are made by groups.

Many groups adopt formal decision rules, and many—clubs, state legislatures, formal committees—have written rules and procedures that specify their decision-making processes. *Robert's Rules of Order* specifies the procedures many groups adopt for allowing group members to participate in the decision process and for voting on decisions. In American society, one popular decision scheme or rule is the majority vote. This is a particularly good procedure if a group is considering relatively few different options and if every group member is supposed to have equal influences on the decision. However, most groups' decisions are complex, requiring members to choose from many options and to make decisions on several points, and some decisions are made by groups whose members do not have equal influence. For example, the role of leader usually gives the group member holding that position more influence than other group members. A strong group leader may be able to sway the group in one direction or the other. When groups with strong leaders use majority vote to make a decision, they often do not allow the leaders to vote except to break a tie.

Groups that do not have formal decision rules reach decisions by using social influence and discussion to consider the options, eventually eliminating all but one. Two subgroups may emerge, each arguing for its choice, but eventually one subgroup wins out over the other. An impasse may occur, and a group may fail to reach consensus, but usually this does not happen. Especially in a cohesive group where everyone is motivated to avoid intragroup conflict and damage to the group, group members will give in to one another and reach a consensus.

Improving Group Performance

Irrespective of the benefits derived from group decision making or problem solving, most humans simply prefer to form groups when there is a problem to solve or a decision to make. The effectiveness of groups' procedures for accomplishing these activities may be improved through team building and nominal group techniques.

Team-Building

One tactic for improving group performance is team building (Beer, 1976; Huse, 1975). This procedure is used a great deal in companies to create effective work groups. The groups can range from the lowest to the highest levels of an organization, and they may be formed any place where employees must work together.

Team building is actually a family of techniques that generally involve conducting an analysis of the processes within groups and presenting a series of exercises designed to improve group functioning. The purpose of some exercises is to build group cohesiveness and get people used to working together. Other exercises focus on teaching group members to work effectively together. They may involve having a trainer lead a group in discussions that focus on group processes, effective group strategies, intragroup conflict resolution, goal setting, planning, and group effort coordination. They may also involve having group members work on tasks designed to give them practice in group techniques for goal setting and problem solving or on improving the group itself.

Research on the effectiveness of team building is sparse (Beer, 1976), but Friedlander (1967) compared the performance of four groups trained in team building to eight untrained control groups. The results showed that team building increased problem-solving effectiveness, mutual influence, and personal involvement among members, as well as the leader's approachability.

Nominal Group Technique

Another effective technique for improving group performance is the **nominal group technique** (NGT). (This technique should not be confused with the nominal or staticized groups, which are used to compare individual and group problem-solving performances.) The NGT is a structured method for running a problem-solving and decision-making group. It is based on the research findings of several group processes, and it is an attempt to combine individual and group processes in a way that capitalizes on the strengths of both.

Nominal group technique: a technique for improving group performance.

The NGT is described in detail by Delbecq, Van de Ven, and Gustafson (1975). For it to work, a group of individuals must agree to run a problem-solving meeting according to NGT rules. The procedure recognizes that this sort of task has three phases: generation of potential solutions, evaluation of solutions, and choice of final solution. The first phase is best done by individuals alone. The second phase can be done effectively by groups if some of the negative aspects of unstructured group interactions (process loss, for example) can be controlled. The third phase can be accomplished by a group if a scheme is devised for combining differing individual opinions into a single choice.

These three phases may be applied as follows: First, the problem is presented to the group and individuals are instructed to generate as many solutions as possible in a given amount of time, with no interaction among members. (This is the same procedure used to establish nominal, or staticized, groups.) Each individual works independently, and negative group effects are reduced. The only group effect that might occur is the presence of others (facilitation or inhibition), since the individuals are often in the same room. But with everyone working on his own tasks, this effect should be minimal. When the solution-generation phase is completed, each person's solutions are shared with the group. At this point there is no discussion or evaluation. Usually someone designated as a recorder goes around the room recording one solution from each individual, continuing to make rounds until all options have been given.

In the second phase, each option is taken in order from the list and discussed. The strengths and weaknesses of each option are presented and clarification and modification can take place. When all options have been evaluated, the second phase is over.

In the third phase, members vote on their choices. A formal voting procedure greatly simplifies this process and avoids wasting time on further group interaction. Typically, if there is an initial majority choice, that majority will carry a final consensus.

The research on the NGT is supportive; it seems that this approach is effective with solution-generation and problem-solving tasks (Van de Ven and Delbecq, 1971). Gustafson, Shukla, and Delbecq (1973) tried out different methods for solving judgment tasks. Subjects worked alone, in unstructured groups, or in groups using a variation of NGT. The problems the subjects were given to solve involved calculating the likelihood of certain outcomes—for example: The observed height of a person is 68 inches. Is the person more likely to be a male or female? How much more likely? (Gustafson et al., 1973) This sort of problem has one correct solution, but it is not a eureka problem because the correct answer is not obvious. When Gustafson and his associates compared the conditions, they found that the modified NGT was the best, and the unstructured group was the worst.

SUMMARY

Group performance covers two interrelated topics: how groups influence individuals' behavior and whether groups and individuals differ in the quality of their performance. A good deal of evidence indicates that people's behavior changes when they enter a group. Several constructs and theories have been developed to explain the effects of a group on the individual. One is social facilitation—the theory that improvement in performance is the result of the mere presence of others. Another is group polarization—the theory that participation in a group discussion results in a strengthening of the individual's dominant tendencies. Social impact theory attempts to describe how people's performances change as the result of the size of a group and the status of its members.

The question of whether groups perform better or worse than individuals depends to a certain extent on the kind of task that confronts a group. On additive tasks, the group effort is the sum of individual member efforts, and social loafing is a common phenomenon. With problem-solving tasks, groups have an advantage over individuals in that they are more likely to have a member who can solve a problem than an individual is likely to be able to solve the problem. A group, however, is inefficient in its use of human resources, and often a skilled individual does better alone than in a group. With complex problem-solving tasks that involve the generation of multiple solutions, group performance is often considerably poorer than individual performances. Brainstorming was at one time considered a way of improving group problem solving, but research has shown that it is not effective and may actually inhibit problem solving.

Decision making in groups is a complex process that involves choosing between several alternative solutions to a problem. Again there is evidence to suggest that groups make less than optimum decisions. Because of this, certain strategies have been proposed to improve group performance, including the team building technique and the nominal group technique. Team building is a procedure used in work organizations to build effective work groups. The nominal group technique is a procedure that attempts to combine the best features of individual and group performance in a way that will improve the final product. It is of particular value with tasks that involve both the generation of potential problem solutions and the choice of a solution.

LEADERSHIP

The groups studied by Wallach and his associates in the prologue were created as leaderless discussion groups, and they did not stay together long enough for a leader to emerge. But most groups have a leader, and this leader has a disproportionate amount of **social power**—the ability to influence the thoughts and actions of other group members. A leader's power can be legitimate, based on the formal control given to the position, such as the elected president of a club or it can be another form of social power, based on such attributes as being liked or seen as an expert. Certain functions in a group are generally given to its leader, including directing the group's efforts toward goals and maintaining the group's existence. Perhaps more than any other member, the leader represents and reflects the goals and collective positions of the group. This section addresses the questions of who becomes a leader and what makes a good leader. It presents the trait, leader behavior, contingency, and social interaction approaches to answering these questions.

Trait Approach

The earliest approach to the study of leadership was the trait approach (called the great man approach in more sexist times). This point of view was based upon the premise that good leaders are born, not made; leadership is inherent in the individual. Two assumptions of the trait approach are that leadership is a basic part of an individual's personality, and that it is not feasible to train a person to be a good leader; instead, you must find people with certain traits and put them in leadership roles.

It follows that much of the trait approach research involved attempts to describe the characteristics of good leaders. One way this was done was to find a group of good leaders and a group of bad leaders and compare the characteristics of the two. An example of this approach is a massive study by Randle (1956), who studied 1,427 executives from 25 different companies. Randle analyzed the background of each executive, obtaining ratings of the executive's effectiveness from five peers in the company, administering a battery of psychological tests, and interviewing each subject for one and a half to three hours. It required over 2000 thousand hours to conduct all the interviews. Randle then placed the executives into three categories: good, mediocre, and bad leadership. He found 30 traits that seemed to differentiate the groups of executives. The good executives had more drive, intelligence, initiative, motivation, and creativity than the other two categories of executives.

These results seem to make sense, but several problems with the trait approach led to its eventual abandonment. First, the traits identified in different studies were not consistent; for example, one study might find that creativity is important and another would find it is not. Second, many of the traits studied were ambiguous and overlapping—in Randle's study, for example, what is the difference between motivation and drive? Third, the relationship between traits and leadership is not very strong; good leaders might be somewhat more intelligent than poor leaders, but the differences are not likely to be large. Fourth, the leadership process seems to be much more complex than indicated in trait studies, and there does not seem to be a set of characteristics that predicts leadership in all situations. An individual who is a good leader in one setting will not necessarily be a good leader in another. For example, the characteristics of the Ayatollah Khomeni made him a popular and effective leader in Iran, but it is unlikely that these same characteristics would make him either popular or effective in a North American or European country.

Leader Behavior Approach

The failure of the trait approach to explain the success or failure of leaders led some psychologists to try another approach. Rather than looking at leaders' traits, they looked at their behavior when they led a group. A basic assumption of this approach was that leaders are made, not born, and that good leadership is a cluster of behaviors which you can train a person to perform. The methodology used in studies of leader behavior was to describe what leaders do and to then determine the effects of that behavior on followers or subordinates.

One concept that came from this approach was **leadership style.** This style appeared as a consistent approach to group decision making across a wide variety of decision tasks and with a wide variety of decision groups. Fleishman (1953) found that some leaders adopt a task-oriented style; they are primarily interested in moving a group toward its goal and they spend most of their time organizing and structuring a group. Other leaders adopt a person-oriented style. These leaders are concerned mainly with the individual needs of the members. They attempt to generate trust, warmth, and respect among the group members, and they are considerate (Fleishman and Harris, 1962; Halprin and Winer, 1952, 1957).

Leadership style: the characteristic way a leader deals with followers.

Perhaps the most extensive leader behavior research program was the Ohio State Studies conducted in the 1950s. The researchers' purpose was to describe the behaviors of supervisors and to reduce a large number of individual behaviors to a small number of dimensions or styles (Hemphill and Coons, 1957). They began with a careful analysis of leader behaviors in work settings. An initial list of 1,800 specific behavioral incidents was compiled and then distilled to a list of 150 behaviors. The final list was put into a questionnaire format and administered to employees for rating their supervisors. This scale became the Leader Behavior Description Questionnaire (LBDQ), which has been used in dozens of leadership studies (Stogdill, 1963).

Using the LBDQ scale, the Ohio State research group found that leaders showed two basic kinds of behavior. The first was called *consideration.* Consideration is a set of person-oriented behaviors that demonstrate a caring for subordinates. The supervisor treats employees as valuable people whose feelings and well-being are important. The second kind was called *initiating structure.* It is a set of task-oriented behaviors that demonstrate a concern for getting work done. The supervisor coordinates efforts, sets goals, checks to be sure tasks are being accomplished, and urges people toward greater task effort. These two kinds of behavior correspond to the two leadership styles mentioned above and to the primary roles people take in groups. A leader who primarily engages in consideration is a person-oriented leader, or takes a maintenance-oriented role; one who engages in initiating structure is a task-oriented leader, or takes a task-oriented role. However, it is possible for a leader to display both kinds of behavior, to be both person and task oriented. Some theorists argue that this is the best kind of leader (Blake and Mouton, 1978).

Once these dimensions of leader behavior had been identified, the Ohio State studies focused on how they affected followers. Fleishman and

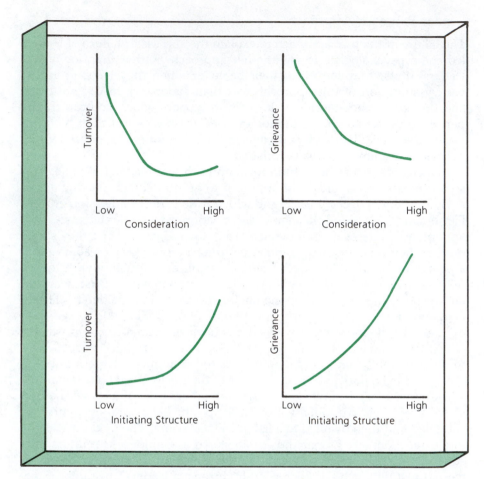

Figure 13-8. *The effects of consideration and initiating structure of turnover and worker grievances.*
Source: Fleishman and Harris (1962).

Harris (1962) described the results of one study that examined how the consideration and the initiating structures of supervisors affected the grievance and turnover rates of employees. This study was conducted in a truck assembly plant among supervisors and assembly workers. Fifty-seven work groups, each consisting of one supervisor and several subordinates, served as subjects in the study. (See figure 13-8 for a summary of the results.)

Compared to supervisors with low levels of consideration, supervisors who exhibited high levels had subordinates who filed fewer grievances and were less likely to quit. The opposite results were found for initiating structure. It would seem that initiating structure, or trying to coordinate and facilitate task performance, is counterproductive; however, Fleishman and Harris also found that high consideration counteracted the negative effects of high initiating structure. In other words, supervisors can push subordinates to greater efforts as long as they show consideration. This finding is consistent with the finding that the best leadership style may be one that is both person and task oriented (Blake and Mouton, 1964, 1978).

The leader behavior approach has also been shown to be too simplistic. Not every subordinate responds the same way to supervisors, and no one style is effective with all subordinates. Also, characteristics of situations determine in part what leadership approaches are effective. It is doubtful, for example, that the same leadership style would be effective for the captain of a softball team and the captain of a nuclear submarine. Social situations, being very complex, must be described and studied using complex methods.

Contingency Approach

The contingency approach is far more complex than the leader behavior or trait approaches and contains elements of both. It is based on the assumption that the best style of leadership depends or is contingent upon the situation. Simply put, leadership effectiveness is determined by both a leader's behavior and the situation in which the leadership takes place. For a specific situation, it may be possible to define the traits needed for effective leadership and it may be possible to define leader behaviors that are called for by the demands of a certain situation. This approach, however, recognizes that no specific leadership characteristics or behaviors are always effective.

The most popular version of a contingency approach is Fiedler's contingency theory. Fiedler (1978) has proposed a model of leadership effectiveness based on the characteristics of the supervisor, the tasks that the group must accomplish, and the social relationships between the leader and followers. Fiedler, like other leadership researchers, believed that the two basic leadership styles were task oriented and person oriented. He also believed that people with certain personality characteristics were more likely to adopt one style over the other. To identify these people, he developed the **Least-Preferred Co-worker Scale** (LPC scale).

The LPC scale is based on the idea that how people view other people indicates something about their personalities and, thus, their leadership styles. To fill out the scale, supervisors think about the person they find the hardest to work with and rate that person on 18 different characteristics. Fiedler said that leaders who are very task oriented will tend to rate a difficult co-worker as negative on the scale; these leaders are called low-LPC leaders. Person-oriented leaders will tend to see a difficult co-worker in a more favorable light; these leaders are called high-LPC leaders. Thus, the LPC scale may indicate if a leader is task or person oriented (Fishbein, Landy, and Hatch, 1969). Other researchers disagree. Mitchell (1970) presented evidence that the LPC scale measures how complex a view of the world a person has. Whatever it measures, the LPC scale seems to be important in the leadership process, as we will see below.

Fiedler proposed that leaders' effectiveness depends on their LPC scores and on three characteristics of the situation in which they are supposed to lead. The first of these characteristics is *task structure*, which refers to several features of a task, including the number of correct solutions to the task, the clarity of the task's requirements, and the number of ways the task can be accomplished. For instance, a highly structured task has one correct solution, one way of accomplishing the task, and clear task

Least-preferred co-worker scale: a scale that asks leaders to rate the characteristics of their least-preferred co-worker.

requirements. The second characteristic is *position power;* the control a leader has over rewards and punishments. A powerful leader is able to administer significant rewards and punishments. The third situational characteristic is *leader-member relations,* which concerns how much the group members like the leader. Good relations exist when the leader is liked and trusted and commands the respect and loyalty of the group.

Fiedler also referred to situations as either favorable (high control) or unfavorable (low control) to the leader. In the most favorable situation, the task is highly structured, the leader's power is strong, and the leader-member relations are good. In the most unfavorable situation, the task is loosely structured, the leader's power is weak, and the leader-member relations are bad. In very favorable and very unfavorable situations, a low-LPC leader does best. In intermediate situations, a high-LPC leader does best.

A summary of some of Fiedler's (1971) results with actual groups shows the relationship between LPC scores and group performance when leader-member relations were very good, very bad, and moderate. (See figure 13-9.) Groups led by low-LPC leaders did best in the extremely favorable and extremely unfavorable situations. Groups led by high-LPC leaders did best in moderate situations.

Support has been found for Fiedler's model (Fiedler, 1978; Peters, Hartke, and Pohlman, 1985), but there have also been many criticisms (e.g., Graen, Alvares, Orris, and Martella, 1970; Shiflett, 1973). The most serious concerns involve the lack of clarity about what the LPC scale measures. Apparently, high- and low-LPC leaders do differ in their behavior, but it is not currently known how they differ. Furthermore, there is uncertainty about the personal characteristics of high- and low-LPC leaders.

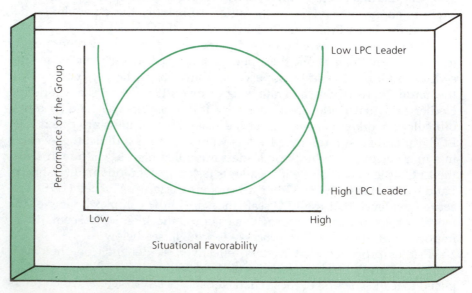

Figure 13-9. When the situation is extremely favorable or unfavorable, the low LPC leader is more effective than the High LPC leader.
Source: Fiedler (1971).

Leadership effectiveness seems to depend on the interaction between the characteristics of a leader and the characteristics of the people in the group.

Social Interaction Approach

The trait, leader behavior, and contingency approaches all ignore the follower in the leadership process. However, leadership is a two-way street; the leader role exists only if it is recognized by followers. Recently, some work has viewed leadership as an interaction between leaders and followers, in which the follower is as important to understanding the process as is the leader. The behavior of followers affects the behavior of their leaders, and often a leader behaves differently with different followers.

A number of studies have investigated the effects of subordinate behavior on supervisory style. For example, Lowin and Craig (1968) conducted a simulation study in which they hired subjects to be office managers. The subjects were unaware that their subordinates were confederates. Some confederates purposely performed their jobs competently, and some performed incompetently. The results showed that the performance of the subordinates influenced the style the supervisor used with them. High-performing subordinates were treated with a high level of consideration and a low level of initiating structure, and were not supervised closely. Low-performing subordinates were treated with a low level of consideration and a high level of initiating structure, and were supervised closely. Thus, rather than supervisor style causing performance on the job, performance may cause supervisor style.

Other research has shown that people differ in the supervisory style they prefer from their leaders. Spector (1982) summarized research on the personality variable *locus of control*. (See chapter five.) He concluded that people who believe they control their own fates (have an internal locus-of-control orientation) prefer and probably perform better with nondirective supervision. People who believe that others control their fates (have an external locus-of-control orientation) prefer and probably perform better with directive supervision.

If leaders are going to be effective, they must have the flexibility to respond appropriately to each follower, even if this means treating each follower differently. The result of many years of leadership research has shown that leadership is a complex process, involving characteristics of supervisors, their particular behaviors, the leadership situation, and characteristics of followers. Furthermore, it is a process that takes place at the level of the leader-follower dyad. There is no one best way to lead. Leaders must consider both the situation and the individuals involved.

SUMMARY

In most groups, the leader is an individual group member to whom group members give a disproportionate amount of social influence. The leader uses this power to perform vital functions for the group.

Researchers have approached the questions of who becomes a leader and what makes an effective leader from several different perspectives. The first of these was the trait approach, in which attempts were made to identify the personality characteristics that distinguish good from bad leaders. The search for the definitive list of these characteristics has not been successful; it has found that the relationships between traits and leadership success are rarely strong.

The leader behavior approach to this issue was an attempt to describe exactly what leaders do and how their behavior is related to the behavior of subordinates. The concept of leadership style, an overall description of a leader's behavior, resulted from this approach. This research effort identified the basic elements of leaders' behavior—consideration and initiating structure—but it failed to show that any one set of behaviors was invariably more successful than another.

The contingency approach was based on the assumption that characteristics of good leaders depend upon the situation; leader characteristics and behaviors that are effective in one setting are not necessarily effective in another. This can be seen in the best-known contingency approach, which proposes that the best leadership style when situational factors are very positive or very negative is not the best style when a situation is moderately positive or moderately negative.

The social interaction approach reduces the leadership process to the level of an interaction between an individual leader and a follower. Research based on this approach has shown that leaders with multiple followers often treat each follower differently. One variable that determines treatment is the follower's task performance. This research has shown that leadership is a complex process that can be understood only by studying jointly the influence of supervisor characteristics, subordinate characteristics, the situation, and the behavior of supervisors and subordinates.

Applications

Decision Making in Actual Groups

This chapter began with the suggestion that hermits are unaffected by the activities of groups. This is probably not true; if hermits were to be forced from their places of isolation, it probably would be as the result of a group decision.

All of us are affected by the decisions of groups whose members we may not know. Sometimes we are not even aware that these groups exist. This section examines decision making in two different kinds of everyday group. The first is composed of individuals who earn their livings making decisions, government policy makers. The second is composed of people who are placed in their roles by the legal system jurors. The examination of these two groups illustrate how many of the principles of group processes can be used to understand and perhaps improve the decision-making process.

GOVERNMENT DECISION MAKING

At about the time the subjects in the prologue experiment were discussing whether Mr. B should take a risky or conservative course of action, another group of people was involved in a similar process in Washington, D.C. These people were not, however, college students in an experiment; they were advisers to President John F. Kennedy. The problem that confronted Kennedy and his advisers was whether or not to carry through on a Central Intelligence Agency (CIA) plan, developed before Kennedy took office, to organize and support a full-scale invasion of Cuba by exiles from that country. To help him make difficult decisions such as this, Kennedy had assembled an outstanding group of people. They represented the best minds from academia and business. Some have described them as "the best and the brightest" people ever to advise a president. But their decision to go ahead with the invasion has been characterized as one of the "worst fiascoes ever perpetrated by a responsible government" (Janis, 1972, p. 14).

These advisers believed that no one would ever know the United States had organized the invasion; that the Cubans would rise up and overthrow Fidel Castro at the first sign of resistance; and that an invasion force of 1400 men could land on the beach at the Bay of Pigs and overwhelm Cuba's weak army and air force. All of these assumptions were wildly wrong. Despite the considerable planning that went into the actual invasion, it was a disastrous military operation. The invaders landed without adequate supplies and air cover. The invasion plan called for the invaders to take the beach; if this failed, they were to retreat and join forces with other anti-Castro groups in the nearby mountains. However, the mountains were 80 miles away and the landing area was surrounded by miles of jungle and snake-infested swamps. As Janis (1972) pointed out, an examination of any map of Cuba would have shown this.

Of the original 1400 invaders, 1200 were captured by Cuban forces. Eventually, these were ransomed by the United States in exchange for $50 million dollars in food and medical supplies (Houseman, 1981). How could this have happened? How could people with the experience, knowledge, and ability of Kennedy's advisers have made such a wrong decision? Most analysts agree that when the decision was made to invade Cuba and the invasion plan was developed, any reasonably knowledgeable and objective person could have seen that the decision was wrong and the invasion would fail. What went wrong in the decision-making process?

In the early 1970s, Irving Janis (1972) began an attempt to answer this question. One of the first things Janis found was that the Bay of Pigs disaster was not the first such instance of competent government officials acting in incompetent ways. Consider the actions of Admiral H.E. Kimmel and his staff in the days shortly before the Japanese attack on Pearl Harbor on December 7, 1941. The issue of how much warning the American forces had is still a matter of debate among military historians, but it is clear that Kimmel and his staff had had reason to be concerned. United States intelligence had broken the Japanese government's secret codes and had informed Kimmel that the Japanese navy was planning an attack somewhere in the Pacific. Six days before the attack on Pearl Harbor, the American forces at Pearl Harbor lost contact with several Japanese carriers, and someone suggested they might be headed for the American base. Kimmel treated this as a joke; he and his staff decided it "couldn't happen there" and took no security precautions (Janis, 1972). It was not until 8:00 A.M. on December 7, when the Japanese planes began bombing Pearl Harbor, that an alarm was sounded. Over 2000 Americans were killed and 15 American ships were destroyed.

Janis (1972) and Janis and Mann (1977) cited two more recent examples of the same phenomenon: the decision to escalate the United States' involvement in Vietnam made by President Johnson and his advisers, and the decision to commit the Watergate break-in and the attempt to cover up their involvement in this crime by President Nixon and his advisers. Janis (1972, 1979) believed that the same underlying process was at work in all these examples; he called this process **groupthink.**

Groupthink

Groupthink does not happen only among political and military leaders. Janis (1972) cited the decision of the Ford Motor Company in 1956 to produce the Edsel as another example of groupthink. The decision to market this new and unwanted automobile cost Ford three hundred million dollars. Groupthink is likely to occur when the following conditions exist: first, the group is highly cohesive and there is a strong norm to go along with group decisions; second, the group, either on purpose or by accident, becomes isolated from objective and unbiased information about the issue at hand; and third, the leader of the group is seen as someone who will give strong

Groupthink: a situation in which group pressure produces a deterioration of mental efficiency, reality testing, and moral judgment among members of a group.

support to the decisions made by its members. Janis has proposed six specific symptoms of groupthink.

Symptoms of Groupthink

First, an *illusion of invulnerability* is shared by the group's members, which leads to risk taking. Theodore White provided an illustration of this with his characterization of the people involved in Watergate:

> There was probably little doubt in the minds of any of the culprits that their superiors stretching up through the Committee to Re-Elect [the president] to the former Attorney General, who was now about to become executive director of this sprawling underground, could surely arrange for their release and after appropriate explanation, cover up the episode. (1975, p. 160)

Second, when groupthink occurs, members of the group will *rationalize* or discount warnings. Admiral Kimmel, for example, had a conversation the night before the Japanese attack with the wife of another admiral. She warned him that the Japanese would probably attack Pearl Harbor. This woman had extensive knowledge of the area and of Japanese intentions, yet she was described as "crazy" by Kimmel and his advisers.

Third, considerable *pressure* is put on members who disagree with the group's decision. For example, when one of President Kennedy's advisers began to have doubts about the invasion plan, the president's brother Robert Kennedy told him, "You may be right or wrong, but the President has made up his mind. Don't push it any further" (cited in Janis, 1972, p. 42).

Pressures such as these produce a fourth symptom of groupthink, *self-censorship;* group members are hesitant to express doubts about the group decision. Consider the recent disclosure that by 1965, the United States secretary of defense had believed the war in Vietnam was not winnable. He evidently had not shared this belief with the other members of President Johnson's cabinet.

As a result of pressures and self-censorship, a fifth symptom of groupthink emerges, the *illusion of unanimity;* the group members believe that everyone else agrees with the group decision. The sixth symptom of groupthink is the emergence of members who act as *self-appointed mind guards,* who prevent negative information from reaching the group.

Studies of Groupthink

Janis's analyses of historical incidents and his proposals about the causes and symptoms of groupthink are impressive. Empirical studies of groupthink provide some degree of support for Janis's ideas. Janis had identified certain United States government leaders as either suffering or not suffering from groupthink. Tetlock (1979) examined public statements made by those leaders and rated them for symptoms of groupthink. As Janis would have predicted, leaders identified as suffering from groupthink gave more simplistic analyses of the problem at hand and were more positive about members of their own groups than were leaders identified as not suffering from groupthink. The groupthink leaders were not, however, more negative about their opponents.

Other researchers have attempted to test Janis's ideas by observing groups of college students in laboratory settings. Because these groups were composed of people who had met only a few minutes earlier and who were not confronted with actual problems, the results of these studies must be treated with extreme caution. Courtright (1978) found that both cohesiveness and the need to arrive at a solution to a problem quickly caused group members to produce fewer different solutions and lower-quality solutions. In a somewhat more elaborate study, Flowers (1977) manipulated group cohesiveness and the degree to which a group's leader was open to different solutions to a problem confronting the group. Unlike Courtright, Flowers found no effect of group cohesiveness, but she did find that groups with open leaders produced higher-quality solutions than did groups with leaders who were not open to different solutions.

Avoiding Groupthink

In the aftermath of the Bay of Pigs disaster, President Kennedy ordered an in-house study of why he and his advisers had performed so poorly. The study group's analysis of the problem led Kennedy to drastically change the procedures he and his advisors used to make decisions. When the Cuban missile crisis took place 16 months later, the performance of Kennedy and his advisers was brilliant (Abel, 1966; Janis, 1972; Janis and Mann, 1977). They were able to force the Soviet Union to remove its missiles from Cuba and to avoid a nuclear war. Janis's analysis of the differences between the Bay of Pigs disaster and the Cuban missile crisis, as well as other incidents of group decision making, led to the following recommendations to avoid groupthink and improve group decision making.

First, the group must establish rules that encourage the examination of all possible solutions to the problem and that discourage premature agreement on one solution. To achieve this, group leaders must be open to disagreement from the group's members and must not state their own views too forcefully. President Kennedy went so far as to designate his brother Robert Kennedy as a devil's advocate, to challenge the ideas presented by group members or their leader.

Second, the group must not fall victim to misperceptions of themselves or their adversary, and they must carefully evaluate the consequences of their actions. The first part of this recommendation is essentially the same point as that made by Ralph White (1970) regarding misperceptions and international conflict. (See chapter twelve).

Third, Janis believed that Kennedy and his advisors were successful in the Cuban missile crisis because they used effective decision-making techniques. He concluded that an effective group develops a set of alternative solutions and carefully evaluates the pros and cons of each until it reaches a consensus on the best solution. Before the decision is imple-

After falling victim to groupthink during the invasion of the Bay of Pigs in 1961, President Kennedy changed the way he and his advisors made decisions. This enabled them to avoid groupthink and improve the quality of their decisions.

mented, the group adjourns to give everyone a second chance to consider the decision. These procedures produce commitment to the final choice and adherence to it once the plan is implemented. This strategy may sound familiar; it is similar to the nominal group technique (NGT). Both procedures can be used to improve the quality of group decisions.

JURY DECISION MAKING

In Chapter four, the perceptual processes that might influence a juror's decision were discussed. A trial was conceptualized as an experiment, with an independent variable (the true facts) and a dependent variable (the juror's decision). The goal of our legal system, it was proposed, is to make sure a trial is internally valid—that the independent variable and only the independent variable causes the dependent variable. This earlier discussion stopped at the level of an individual juror's judgment of what the true facts were. It assumed that the final decision of a jury would simply reflect the sum of jurors' individual judgments, and did not examine the possible effects of group structure and processes on the final decision. In many instances, this is a safe assumption. Penrod and Hastie (1980) present data that suggest jurors are unanimous on their first ballot about a third of the time. And Kalven and Zeisel (1966) reported that over half of the juries they studied reached a decision within one hour of the time they began their deliberations. These facts suggest that there is relatively little time for

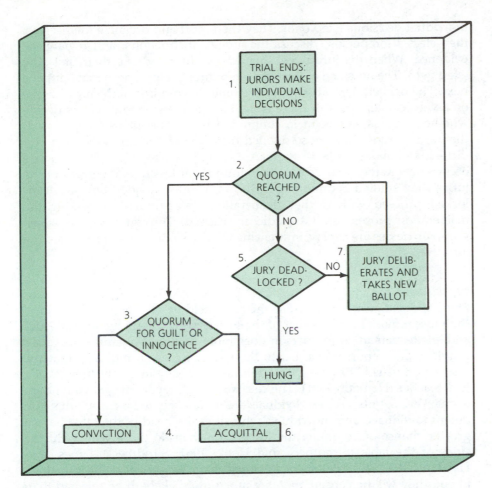

Figure 13-10. *A model of jury decision making. Copyright (1980) American Psychological Association. Reprinted by permission of the authors.*
Source: Penrod and Hastie, (1980).

group factors to affect a jury's decision. Yet, in some situations, as in the experiment presented in the prologue, being in a group changes the decisions people make. Thus, a jury's final decision may not be the simple sum or average of the decisions of the individual jurors.

One such situation was the trial of John Mitchell and Maurice Stans, two members of President Nixon's cabinet who were indicted for illegal campaign activities. When the jurors took their first vote, eight favored and four opposed a guilty verdict. After several days of deliberations, they voted for acquittal. This section considers how the variables that affect group processes might affect jury deliberations and thus, possibly, the internal validity of a trial.

Jury Deliberations

Penrod and Hastie conceptualized jury decision making as a series of steps. (See figure 13-10.) When a trial has ended, the jurors have made their individual decisions (step one). They then meet and organize themselves; they elect a foreperson, discuss the judge's instructions, and review the evidence. When the jurors feel they are ready, they take their first vote (step two). The outcome of this vote (step three) determines what happens next. The deliberations are over at this time if two-thirds of the jurors agree on a verdict (step four). If there is not sufficient agreement, jurors decide whether there is any point in continuing the deliberations (step five). If the jurors decide they are so divided that they will never agree on a verdict—they are deadlocked—they are a hung jury (step six). (This is a rare occurrence. Kalven and Zeisel (1966) found that less than 6 percent of the juries they studied became hung.) Jurors who are divided but not deadlocked proceed with further deliberations (step seven), repeating the deliberation process until a verdict is reached. Throughout these steps, group processes are at play, influencing the decisions of individuals and the jury.

Structure

One aspect of group structure is the roles held by its members. In a jury, the most important role is that of the foreperson, who is the jury's leader and spokesperson. A foreperson does more than just organize the jury's activities and report its verdict to the judge. Research indicates that the foreperson usually has the greatest influence of any juror on the verdict a jury reaches (Nemeth, 1981). The selection of a foreperson is not a random event. Verbal, outspoken individuals are more likely to be chosen than are quiet individuals, and individuals who sit at the head of the table have a greater chance of becoming the foreperson than do those who sit at the sides of the table (Strodtbeck and Hook, 1961; Strodtbeck, James, and Hawkins, 1957). Jury members' personal characteristics also affect the likelihood they will be chosen; men are much more likely to be selected than are women, and businesspeople are more likely to be selected than are clerical workers or laborers (Simon, 1967; Strodtbeck et al., 1957).

Size

Historically, juries in criminal trials have been composed of 12 people. In the last 15 to 20 years, a number of states have passed laws that allow smaller juries. These states argued that the number of people on a jury is irrelevant to their final decision, and smaller juries can save a state time and money.

In the late 1960s, Florida decided to use six-person juries in some trials. This decision was challenged in *Williams versus Florida*. In 1970, the Supreme Court issued a historic ruling on the constitutionality of six-person juries. The court concluded that a six-person jury is no less likely to be fair and impartial than a 12-person jury, and that given the same facts, the different-size juries would reach the same verdict. The Court let the Florida law stand.

The Supreme Court did not carefully consider the social psychological literature on the relationship between group size and the quality of group performance in making its ruling. In the years following its decision, lawyers challenged the ruling and turned to social psychology for help. The literature on this question is complex and occasionally confusing. On the one hand, research suggests that the more people there are in a group, the more likely a group member is to correctly recall the facts of the issue at hand, and that large groups often cancel errors in individual judgments (Lorge et al., 1958; Kelley and Thibaut, 1969). There is, however, more equal participation in smaller groups, which *may* produce fairer decisions (Nemeth, 1981).

The Supreme Court also assumed that if there were a minority position in a jury, the pressure on it to conform would be greater in a twelve-person jury than in a six-person jury. Research has suggested that this assumption was incorrect. Latan'e's social impact theory and Asch's conformity research (see chapter eleven) both indicated that pressure to conform remains essentially constant once a group reaches a certain size—usually four people. Also, as Forsyth (1983) pointed out, people are less likely to conform when they have an ally, and the existence of an ally is less likely in a six-person jury than in a twelve-person jury. In addition, Saks (1977) discovered that six-person juries were not as representative of a community as twelve-person juries, and that using smaller juries significantly reduced the number of minority group members who served on juries in some communities.

These and other research findings were considered in 1978 when the Supreme Court was asked to rule on the constitutionality of five-person juries. The Court concluded these were not constitutional, but six-person juries were. Justice Harry Blackmun's opinion could have been written by a social psychologist for a research journal:

> Statistical studies suggest that the risk of convicting an innocent person (Type 1 Error) rises as the size of the jury diminishes. Because the risk of not convicting a guilty person (Type 2 Error) increases with the size of the panel, an optimal jury size can be selected as a function of the interactions between the two risks. Nagel and Neef (1975) concluded that the optimal size for the purpose of avoiding errors should vary with the importance attached to these two types of mistakes . . . As the size diminished to five and below, the weighted sum of errors increased because of the enlarging risk of the conviction of innocent defendants. (Cited in Loftus and Monahan, 1980, p. 270)

Other research has supported Justice Blackmun's conclusion and has also suggested that the Supreme Court might want to reconsider its ruling on six-person juries. Padawer-Singer, Singer, and Singer (1977) found that six-person juries were significantly more likely to have a predeliberation consensus than were 12-person juries. Valenti and Downing (1975) found that when *apparent* guilt was high, six-person juries were more likely to convict than were twelve-person juries. And Kerr and MacCoun (1985) reported that when a case was close, the more people there were on the jury, the more likely the jury was to be hung (unable to reach a verdict).

Decision-making Procedures

When a group must reach a decision, it must first determine what constitutes a group decision, or what percentage of group members must agree to a course of action before it is taken. In common law, the rule has historically been that every juror must agree with the verdict. In 1972, the Supreme Court was asked to rule on whether decision rules that required less than unanimity were constitutional. It decided they were, and suggested that if 75 percent or more of the jurors agree on a verdict, a defendant's constitutional rights have not been violated.

The question of whether this rule change has produced changes in the decisions juries reach has been extensively studied. Most evidence suggests that its effects are negligible. James Davis and his colleagues (Davis, Kerr, Atkin, Holt, and Meek, 1975) examined the behavior of juries who were instructed to use a unanimity decision rule. They found that despite this instruction, juries often acted as if there were a two-thirds rule: If eight of the twelve jurors agreed, the others went along with the decision. Also, a minority of jurors is rarely able to convert the majority to its position; Penrod and Hastie (1979) estimated this occurs in less than 3 percent of jury deliberations.

The change in the decision rule does make a hung jury more unlikely (Kerr, Atkin, Stasser, Meeker, Holt, and Davis, 1976). Some have suggested that juries using the less restrictive decision rule base their decisions on weaker evidence than do juries using the unanimity rule (Saks and Hastie, 1978). If this is true, widespread use of the 75 percent decision rule may result in increased numbers of internally invalid jury decisions.

The Value of Jury Research

Given the large amount of interest in the legal system among social psychologists and the resulting large amount of research, it is reasonable to briefly consider the value of this research. The first point that must be made is that science for the sake of science is, in the judgment of social psychologists, a valuable and worthwhile enterprise. Much of the research on juries is not intended to solve problems in the legal system, but to advance social psychologists' basic understandings of how groups operate. Such basic research must continue if social psychology is to survive.

The topic of this research does, however, lead one to ask whether social psychological research on juries has served to improve the legal system. Excuse the pun but, the jury is still out on this question. An examination of the Supreme Court's ruling of the constitutionality of five-person juries reveals that the Court used research literature to make its decision (Loftus and Monahan, 1980). But the Court apparently ignored the research literature that suggested six-person juries may have similar drawbacks. A cynic might suggest that the Court used social psychological research when it served its purposes, and ignored it when it did not. Perhaps the problem is that social scientists have not yet acquired the ability to get the courts to listen to what they have learned about how juries make decisions.

Chapter Fourteen

Environmental Influences on Social Behavior

by Paul E. Greenbaum

Prologue

John B. Calhoun (1962). Population Density and Social Pathology. *Scientific American*, **206,** 139–148.

Background

The study of environmental influences on social behavior dates back to at least the mid-1940s. Interest in the field increased dramatically during the 1960s and early 1970s as the result of studies by ethologists and biologists on the physical and psychological effects of overcrowding. Most of these studies were naturalistic observations of how animals reacted to excessive population density. However, John Calhoun decided to study overpopulation in a more systematic way by manipulating the characteristics of an environment so that he could cause overcrowding. For ethical, legal, and moral reasons, Calhoun did not conduct his study with humans; his subjects were a colony of rats.

Hypotheses

Calhoun's major hypothesis was that when the rats became overcrowded, there would be a breakdown in the social order and a resultant increase in social pathology. A secondary hypothesis was that the physical characteristics of the rats' environment would moderate the effects of excessive population density.

Subjects

The subjects were 48 male and female Norway breed laboratory rats.

Procedure

Calhoun built a ten-by-fourteen-foot enclosure. (See figure 14-1.) The rats' environment was divided into pens which were connected by ramps. Pens two and three were accessible from all the other pens; pens one and four were accessible only from pens two and three.

   Calhoun placed the rats in the four pens. Each pen contained an ample supply of food and water and a place where nests could be built for newborn rats. In the absence of natural predators, the population of rats grew rapidly, and soon there were 80 animals in the enclosure. Calhoun stopped the population explosion at 80 rats by removing additional offspring from the enclosure.

   Calhoun observed and recorded the behavior of the rats before and after they became overcrowded. Of special interest to him was the behavior of the animals in the most accessible pens, two and three.

Results

Before the colony became overcrowded, the male rats engaged in normal

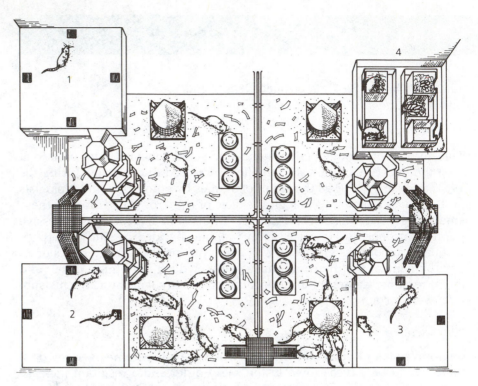

Figure 14-1.
Source: Calhoun (1962).

behaviors. They spent much of their time gathering females into harems, mating with them, and protecting their territories. They were sociable, did not move much from their territories, were generally nonaggressive, and rarely made sexual advances toward females in other harems.

After conditions became overcrowded, the males in the less accessible pens, especially dominant males, continued to act more or less in the same manner. The behavior of males in the most accessible pens changed dramatically. Some became hypersexual, attempting to mate with receptive and nonreceptive females both inside and outside their harems. Some also become hyperactive and hyperaggressive, and engaged in acts of cannibalism and homosexuality (abnormal behaviors among rats). Other males in the most accessible pens became completely passive and socially withdrawn.

Among females in the most accessible pens, normal sexual and maternal behaviors almost disappeared when the conditions became overcrowded. The females were unable to build nests or nurse their infants, and as a result, over 80 percent of the rat pups died before weaning. In contrast, the infant mortality rate was 50 percent in the less accessible pens. Sufficient food and water were available at all times, but the rats all attempted to eat and drink at the same time. As a result, several rats died of hunger or thirst.

Implications

As is the case with many of the studies presented in this chapter, Calhoun's study had both theoretical and practical implications. At the theoretical level, it demonstrated in a controlled environment how overcrowding could create social pathologies among animals. Much of the research in the second section of this chapter is concerned with whether this effect is also found among humans. The practical implication is that if humans do react to overcrowding as did Calhoun's rats, then we must look for ways to alleviate overcrowding in our environment.

The topic addressed in this chapter is the ways in which environmental variables affect human social behavior. This is part of a branch of psychology called **environmental psychology.** Many of the people who study environmental effects on human behavior are or have been social psychologists, although their focus of interest differs somewhat from that of most social psychologists. Most social psychological research concerns how social stimuli affect human behavior, and the independent variables used are usually social variables. The independent variable in environmental psychological research is the environment itself.

For example, in the prologue, the immediate cause of pathological behaviors among the rats was the presence of too many other rats, but this overpopulation was due to the nature of the environment in which the rats had been placed. Had they been free to roam, rather than being enclosed in a ten-by-fourteen-foot enclosure, or had there been less food, or had natural enemies been present, this overpopulation would not have occurred. Also, the structure of the pens—some were completely accessible, some were not—had consequences for the rats. The independent variable was the environment itself.

This chapter presents three interrelated topics in environmental psychology. The first section considers the effects of urban environments on social behavior. The second section focuses on perhaps the most salient characteristic of the urban environment, the presence of large numbers of people living in close proximity to one another. In this section, people's attempts to control and regulate the physical space around them and their reactions to excessive population densities are examined. The third section addresses the effects of man-made, or built, environments on social behavior. Unlike previous chapters, this one does not contain a separate applications section. This is because most of the research and theory in environmental psychology is motivated by actual social problems and attempts to remediate them—in a way, the entire chapter is an applications section.

So much of what interests environmental social psychologists occurs in the real world that they find the laboratory is often not a suitable place to conduct research; instead, they frequently use natural settings. Rather

Environmental psychology: the study of how natural and created environments affect and are affected by human behavior.

than trying to control all the variables in these natural settings, environmental researchers have developed research strategies that let them enter real-world settings. Thus, much of the research described in this chapter takes place in schools, in offices, on public streets and in public places, and in people's homes and neighborhoods. This is not to say that laboratory experimentation is never used to study the environment's impact on social behavior; it remains an important tool in the environmental researcher's arsenal, and is used to study environmental stress effects (for example, crowding, heat, noise) or personal space violations. Field research in non-laboratory settings, however, takes on added importance in this area of psychology, which attempts to study human social behavior in the natural environment.

THE URBAN ENVIRONMENT

The pathologies observed among Calhoun's rats were due to too many animals and not enough space. The rats were unable to effectively cope. Some people argue that humans confront a similar problem as a result of the growth in the world's population. It took from the beginning of human existence to the year 1650 for the number of people on earth to reach 500 million. In the next 200 years, the world's population doubled to one billion, a **doubling time** of 200 years. By 1930, there were two billion people on earth; the doubling time had dropped to 80 years. And by 1970, the population was four billion, a doubling time of 40 years (Altman, 1975; Ehrlich, 1968). As the world's population increases, the doubling time decreases.

Doubling time: the length of time it takes for the world's population to double.

But humans are not running out of living space. Population growth is being brought under control, and there is plenty of available land. If humans were evenly distributed across all the land on earth, every man, woman, and child alive would have 10 acres of land on which to live (Freedman, 1975). This is hardly the situation confronted by Calhoun's rats. The problem is that humans do not live on all the available land; out of choice or necessity, they tend to concentrate in certain areas. For example, more people live in six square miles of New York City than in the 100,000 square miles of Wyoming; there are 70,000 people per square mile in the center of New York City.

Urbanism: the movement of people from rural to urban areas.

One of the most consistent trends in human history is the increase in the number of people who live in the same location, or **urbanism.** The origins of urbanism lie in Mesopotamia and the Nile River Valley. Approximately 10,000 years ago, humans in this area shifted from hunting and gathering as their primary means of acquiring food to growing and harvesting crops. The existence of a more or less stationary food supply increased the number of people who chose to settle in one location. The next significant phase of urbanism was the Industrial Revolution of the 18th and 19th centuries, when the existence of large factories further increased the tendency of people to settle together in one location. The extent to which humans have become urbanized has risen rapidly since the Industrial Revolution. In 1790, only 5 percent of all Americans lived in cities;

One consequence of living in big cities is a lessened concern with the welfare of others.

today the figure is 70 percent (United States Department of Commerce, 1981).

The next section examines the effects of urban environments on social behavior and presents two concepts which have been proposed as explanations of these effects: stimulus overload and environmental stressors.

The Effects of Urban Living on Social Behavior

Most theorists agree that compared to people who live in nonurban areas, such as small towns and suburbs, urbanites are less friendly, less polite, and less civil. A number of studies have looked at the comparative helpfulness of people who live in cities and of those who live in small towns; small-town residents have been found to be more helpful (Korte, 1981). Altman, Levine, Nadien, and Villena (1969) had confederates knock on the doors of city and small-town residents and ask if they could use the telephone. In a small town, 50 percent of the males and 94 percent of the females who made this request were allowed into the subjects' homes. In a city, the percentages were less than half of these.

These differences might be due to a greater fear of crime among city dwellers, but other studies also suggest that urbanites are less helpful. Korte (1978, 1980) has summarized the findings from several studies of urban-nonurban differences in helping. Compared to small-town residents, urban residents are less likely to help a person who has called a wrong number, to mail a letter they have found on the street, to do a favor for a stranger, to correct a financial error that benefited them, to cooperate with an interviewer, and to assist a lost child. Also, big-city bank tellers are more likely to double-check the amount of money deposited by customers. Urbanites also report that they are less well acquainted and have fewer contacts with their neighbors than do people from suburbs and small towns (Korte, 1981).

A dramatic illustration of the differences between people who live in small and large cities was provided by Zimbardo (1973b). He placed apparently abandoned cars on streets in New York City, New York, and Palo Alto, California. The license plates were removed and the hoods were raised as an invitation to vandals. In New York City, 10 minutes after the car had been placed on the street, a couple and their nine-year-old son approached. While the woman served as a lookout, the father and son deftly removed the radiator and the battery from the car. This family's actions were not unique. Within 24 hours, the car had been stripped of every movable part. During the next two days, the tires were slashed, all the windows were broken, and stones and metal bars were used to smash the doors, fenders, and hood. By the end of the three-day period, the car was an unmovable hunk of metal. The car placed in Palo Alto was untouched, except that one considerate person lowered the hood to protect the engine from damage in the rain.

One might think that the devastation of the car in New York City was the work of street gangs, which are more common there than in Palo Alto. But the majority of the looters were well-dressed adults. Zimbardo believed that the New Yorkers' behaviors were due largely to the social anonymity that is part of urban life. People "don't know who you are and don't care and you don't know who they are and don't care" (Zimbardo, 1973b, p. 411). Something about urban life makes people less human.

Stanley Milgram (1970) has offered the following analysis of the effects of urban living. People, Milgram pointed out, can process only a limited number of stimuli or inputs from their environment. The size, density, and diversity of urban populations may result in an excessive amount of social and nonsocial stimuli impinging on people which creates **stimulus overload.** Because they cannot process all these stimuli, city dwellers have developed a number of mechanisms that help them reduce or cope with the excessive stimulation.

Stimulus overload: a condition in which the inputs people receive from the environment exceed their capacities to process them.

Empirical research suggests that urbanites do engage in behaviors that are consistent with Milgram's proposal. For example, bus drivers put limits on their social exchanges with riders by not making change. People use blocking and filtering devices to minimize the level of social stimuli. These devices include such things as unlisted phone numbers and answering machines to screen out unwanted callers, and unfriendly or rude behavior to discourage conversational encounters.

Bornstein (1979) looked at the relationship between city size and the walking speed of its residents. In general, the larger the city, the faster people walked. How does walking fast reduce stimulus overload? It decreases the possibility that someone will stop a person and engage in conversation.

Another way to reduce the number of unwanted social interactions is to avoid displaying nonverbal behavior that would invite them. Newman and McCauley (1977) and McCauley, Coleman, and DeFusco (1978) have looked at urban-nonurban differences in the amount of eye contact a person makes with a stranger. In their first study, a confederate approached residents of a small town, a suburb, or a large city. The amount of eye contact made with the stranger was greatest in the small town and least in the city.

On first inspection, these results seem to support Milgram's proposal that city dwellers attempt to reduce the level of their social input; but there is an alternate explanation of the difference. Perhaps the kind of people who choose to live in a city are simply less friendly than those who choose to live in the suburbs or in small towns. To test this possibility, McCauley and his associates (1978) conducted a second study in which the subjects were people who lived in a suburb but commuted by train to their jobs in a large city. As these people approached an express train which linked the suburb and the city, confederates attempted to make eye contact with them. This was done both when the commuters were at the suburban train station and when they were at the city train station. Any differences between eye contact in the two stations would be explained by differences between the two locations, since the same set of people were observed at both locations. McCauley and associates found that there was less eye contact in the city station.

Environmental Stressors and Urban-Nonurban Differences

Environmental stressors are negative or unpleasant aspects of a person's environment, such as excessive temperature, noise, and air pollution. (See chapter seven.) Some theorists have proposed that urban-nonurban differences in social behavior are, at least in part, due to the greater incidence of environmental stressors in urban settings.

The level of environmental stressors is usually greater in large cities than in small towns. For example, noise levels increase with community size (Dillman and Tremblay, 1977), as does air pollution. According to Rotton (1978), just living in New York City and breathing its air is equivalent to smoking 38 cigarettes a day. The people, automobiles, and industries concentrated in cities produce heat, and the large buildings and pollution trap this heat; thus, cities are usually warmer than surrounding areas (Fisher, 1976). Also, because of their high buildings, heat, and air pollution, urban areas have less sunshine, more wind, and more rain (Fisher, Bell, and Baum, 1984). And there are other stressful consequences of living in a large city, such as traffic jams and high crime rates.

The question is not whether the urban environment is more stressful than the nonurban environment, but how environmental stressors affect human behavior. Hans Selye (1956) and other researchers have developed a model of how humans and other organisms react to stress. Selye's model is called the **general adaptation syndrome;** it proposes that there are three stages in the reaction to stress.

General adaptation syndrome: a pattern of responses to continued stress.

The first stage is called an *alarm reaction*. During this stage, an organism is initially exposed to a stressor and mobilizes its resources to deal with the problem; the organism's physiological systems are activated. This is followed by the second stage, *resistance*; the organism becomes physiologically aroused and actively attempts to cope with or adapt to the threat. If resistance is effective, the organism's physiological arousal returns to normal and it survives. If resistance is ineffective, the third stage, *exhaustion*, occurs. In research with animals, Selye found that the exhaustion stage of the general adaptation syndrome was often accompanied by disease or death.

It has been suggested that the level of environmental stressors present in urban settings is such that city dwellers are constantly forced to try to cope with them. Thus, these people may be chronically aroused, as in the resistance stage of Selye's model. Chronic physiological arousal may have three negative consequences for social behavior. One, it may create excessive levels of stimulation, or stimulus overload, which people seek to reduce by becoming less social. Two, even if the exhaustion stage does not occur, continued arousal is an unpleasant experience and may produce negative moods in people; this too would affect their interactions with others. Three, high levels of arousal interfere with performance on complex tasks; this may frustrate people and make it more likely they will act in an unpleasant manner.

The general adaptation syndrome has been used to explain the effects of several environmental stressors on human social behavior. Three stressors that have received considerable attention are temperature, noise, and air pollution.

Temperature

Researchers have conducted both laboratory and field studies on the effects of high temperatures on aggression. (See chapter seven.) The laboratory experiments have usually obtained a curvilinear relationship—people are more likely to engage in hostile aggression in a warm environment (72 to 86 degrees Fahrenheit) than in a cool (64-degree) or hot (93-degree) environment (Bell and Baron, 1977). Field studies suggest that as temperature increases, the incidence of violent crimes also increases. For example Harris and Stadler (1983) computed a daily discomfort index of temperature and humidity in Dallas, Texas, and correlated this with the number of assaults that occurred each day. As the discomfort index went up, so did the number of assaults. Other research has examined the effects of temperature on sociability and helping behavior.

Sociability Bell (1980) investigated the effects of temperature on mood and found that college students who were insulted by an experimenter in a hot room evaluated the experimenter more negatively than did those who were insulted in a cool room. These results suggest that people are less attracted to one another in a hot than in a comfortable environment. Griffitt (1970) placed subjects in either a comfortably cool or an uncomfortably hot room while they worked on simple tasks. The subjects were then given a description of another person and asked to indicate how much they liked this person. Greater interpersonal attraction was found among subjects in the cool than in the hot room.

Griffitt and Veitch (1971) conducted a similar experiment in which they systematically varied how hot the room was, how crowded the room was, and whether the other person was similar or dissimilar to the subjects. (Generally, people are more attracted to similar than to dissimilar others—see chapter six.) Griffitt and Veitch found that all three variables affected interpersonal attraction. The least interpersonal attraction occurred when the subjects evaluated a dissimilar person in a hot and crowded room.

Baron and Bell (1974, 1976), however, failed to find that heat reduces attraction. And Kenrick and Johnson (1979) have raised questions about whether Griffitt and Veitch's results would have been obtained if their subjects had engaged in face-to-face interactions with the other person.

Helping   Other researchers have looked at how heat might affect helping behavior. The results of their studies have also been inconsistent. Some (Cunningham, 1979; Page, 1978) found less helping in hot, uncomfortable environments than in cool, comfortable ones. But Schneider, Lesko, and Garrett (1980) examined helping in four situations: a disabled person had dropped a book, someone had lost a contact lens, someone had dropped a bag of groceries, and a person needed help in completing a survey. They found that temperature did not affect helping in any of these situations.

Extreme cold is also an environmental stressor. Perhaps because of the rigors of conducting a field study in subzero weather, there have been relatively few studies on how cold affects social behavior. The few studies that have been done have examined helping. Bennet, Rafferty, Canivez, and Smith (1983) found more helping in cold, harsh environments, and they suggested that in such environments there may be a norm to help others.

These results are interesting, but they do not provide enough consistent findings to draw any strong conclusions about the effects of temperature on helping. It may well be that the relationship depends on other as yet unidentified factors.

Noise

Noise, or noise pollution, is an inevitable consequence of living in an urban environment. The Environmental Protection Agency (1972) estimated that the quietest times in an inner-city apartment are noisier than the noisiest times in small-town living areas. Research on how noise affects people's behaviors has focused on the quality of social interactions, helping, academic performance, and adapting to noise.

Noise: excessively loud, uncontrollable, unpredictable, or unwanted sounds.

Quality of Social Interactions   Noise has a number of effects on social behavior. It can make people anxious, irritable, and aggressive (Donnerstein and Wilson, 1976; Korte and Grant, 1980; Matthews and Canon, 1975; Page, 1977; Ward and Suedfeld, 1973). Ward and Suedfeld placed a sound truck outside a college dormitory. For three days and nights the unfortunate residents of the dorm were bombarded with the recorded sounds of a busy highway. The behavior of the students during this time period was compared to their behavior during a normal three-day period. During the noisy period, the residents became more tense, disagreed with one another more often during discussions, and in general showed a deterioration in their social relations. They were so angry about the noise that on two occasions they cut the power lines to the truck, and they threatened to destroy the equipment if the sound were not turned off.

Noise also affects social interactions in more indirect ways. It causes people to narrow their focus of attention, to focus on the most salient stimuli in their environment and block out or ignore less salient stimuli (Broadbent, 1971, 1979; Cohen and Weinstein, 1981). Theorists do not fully agree on why this narrowing of attention occurs. Broadbent (1979) proposed that it is a consequence of the heightened arousal noise produces. Cohen (1978) used the notion of stimulus overload to explain narrowing of attention. He argued that noise in combination with other ongoing stimuli may overload a person's processing capacity, and that people narrow their attention to reduce this overload.

Several studies have investigated how the narrowing of attention might affect social behavior. Korte and Grant (1980) studied the effects of traffic noise on people's awareness of what was going on around them. As pedestrians walked in the shopping district of a large city in Scotland, they encountered some unusual stimuli placed there by the experimenters. Some of these people passed a woman wearing a large pink hat and later passed a bunch of brightly colored balloons tied to a tree or a lamp post. Others encountered a large sign and a woman holding a yellow teddy bear. These stimuli were placed in the shopping district during a time of high and a time of low traffic noise. After the subjects had passed the stimuli, they were stopped by an interviewer and asked if they had seen anything unusual as they walked along the street. If they said no, then the interviewer would show them a list of objects and ask if they had seen any of them. Subjects in the low-noise condition were significantly more likely to be aware of the unusual stimuli than were those in the high-noise condition (56 percent versus 35 percent).

Other findings from this study merit mention. Milgram proposed that urbanites walk rapidly and avoid eye contact with others as a means of dealing with stimulus overload. Korte and Grant measured these two variables and found that people exposed to the high level of traffic noise did walk faster and make less eye contact than those exposed to the low level of traffic noise. Evidently, noise pollution leads to stimulus overload and, as a result, causes people to be less aware of social stimuli and less likely to engage in social interactions.

A study by Appleyard and Lintell (1972) supported this conclusion. Appleyard and Lintell observed and interviewed residents of areas where the traffic noise levels were either low, moderate, or high. They found that people in the low-noise areas were quite likely to engage in casual social interactions on the sidewalks, but that people in the high-noise areas rarely did so. People in the noisy area described it as a lonely place to live; the residents of the quiet area described it as friendly and sociable. People in the low-noise area reported having three times as many friends and twice as many acquaintances as did those in the high-noise area.

Helping   In general, studies have found that noise reduces people's willingness to offer help (Fisher et al., 1984). Two explanations have been offered. One explanation is that noise puts people in bad moods and that these negative moods often reduce people's willingness to offer help. (See chapter eight.) The other explanation, based on the concept of narrowing of attention, suggests that people may help less under conditions of high noise because they became less aware of the victim's need for help. A study by Matthews and Canon (1975) supported this idea. The subjects were people who passed a confederate who had dropped a stack of books as he was getting out of a car. Two variables were manipulated. The first was the confederate's supposed need for help; for half the subjects, the confederate wore a cast on his arm, for the other half he did not. The second variable was noise; as half the subjects approached the confederate, another confederate started a lawn mower that did not have a muffler; the lawn mower was not started for the other half of the subjects. The dependent measure was the percentage of subjects who offered help. (See figure 14-2 for the results.)

Subjects in the low-noise condition responded differently depending on the confederate's need. They helped significantly more in the high-need (cast) than in the low-need (no-cast) condition. But subjects in the high-noise condition did not appear to notice the difference in the confederate's need. They were no more likely to help in the high-need than in the low-need condition. One reasonable explanation of this finding is that subjects narrowed their attention in the high-noise condition.

Academic Performance   A number of environmental psychologists have proposed that noise may interfere with academic performance (Cohen and Weinstein, 1981). This proposal is based on two interrelated assumptions: one, an integral part of learning is communication between teachers and their students, and high noise interferes with this communication; two, noise is an environmental stressor, which causes an increase in physiological arousal. If physiological arousal is too high, it interferes with performance on complex tasks, such as the kind a student may encounter in a classroom.

Bronzaft and McCarthy (1975) studied the academic performances of children whose elementary schools were located within two hundred feet of an elevated train track. The noise made by a train passing on those tracks made it impossible for people to hear each other unless they shouted. Some of the children in these schools were in classrooms that did not face the tracks and were somewhat shielded from the noise; others were in classrooms that directly faced the tracks. Bronzaft and McCarthy compared the reading achievement scores of these two groups of children. In the lower grades, children from the noisy side of the school were two to three months behind those from the relatively quiet side. In the sixth grade, the difference was as great as 11 months.

Cohen, Evans, Krantz, Stokols, and Kelly (1981) compared the performances of children whose schools were in a busy air traffic corridor with those of children in schools outside the corridor. Cohen and his associates found that third and fourth graders in the noisy schools performed significantly worse on simple and complex puzzles than did children from the quiet schools.

Adapting to Noise   Selye's model of reactions to stress, the general adaptation syndrome, proposed that organisms can adapt to and cope with environmental stressors. This may be true for some environmental stressors, but it does not appear to be true for noise. Physiological arousal declines as noise continues, but people do not become less aware of the noise (see Borsky, 1961; Glass and Singer, 1972; Morgan and Dirks, 1973; Stern et al., 1970). Indeed, there is reason to believe that people become *more* annoyed with noise as time passes (Jonsson and Sorenson, 1973; Weinstein, 1978). Jonsson and Sorenson found that complaints by residents about noise from a highway were more frequent one year after it opened than six months after it opened, suggesting that a short-term attempt to deal with noise by reducing social contacts may not be effective when noise becomes chronic. The inability of people to adapt to noise suggests that it is an extremely potent environmental stressor.

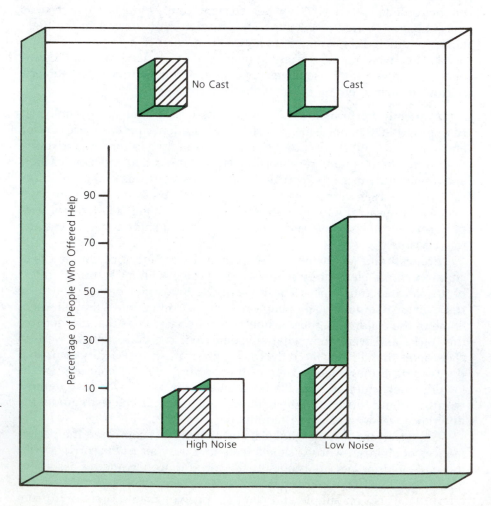

Figure 14-2.   Under conditions of high noise the cast had no effect on helping, but under conditions of low noise the person wearing the cast received significantly more help.
Source: Matthews and Canon (1975).

What is noise to one person may be beautiful music to another.

Research Highlight

Reducing Noise in Schools

Bronzaft and McCarthy did not study the effects of noise on school children's performances out of idle curiosity; they were employed by agencies responsible for establishing policies on noise control. Their finding that children in noisy classrooms were falling behind those in less noisy classrooms led the New York Transit Authority, the agency that ran the trains, to begin an experimental noise abatement program. The site of this program was public school (PS) 98, where the trains passed every four and a half minutes. This was the same school Bronzaft and McCarthy had used in their original study.

The transit authority used two techniques to reduce the noise levels in the classrooms that faced the train tracks—they installed sound-absorbing accoustical ceilings and placed rubber padding on the tracks outside the classrooms. These efforts produced about a 10 percent reduction in the noise levels in the classrooms—a difference easily noticed by the average person.

Bronzaft (1981) tested the reading achievement of children in the noisy and quiet classrooms before the noise abatement program was instituted. As in the study she had conducted six years earlier, the students on the noisy side showed significantly worse performances. Some children were as much as a year behind. For these children, being taught in a noisy classroom was comparable to being demoted.

The children of PS 98 were tested and compared again two to three years after the noise abatement program was instituted. This time there were no significant differences in test scores between the quiet and noise-abated classrooms. All of the classes were performing at or above their grade-level norms, suggesting that the abatement program was effective. Based on these findings the transit authority sought additional funding to reduce noise along the entire 60 miles of elevated track, to reduce the noise level for one-half million people.

At about the time that Bronzaft was conducting her research, the Los Angeles school system filed a lawsuit against the Los Angeles International Airport for the level of noise pollution air traffic caused in some of the local schools. Within the airport landing corridor, a plane flew over the affected schools every two and a half minutes, and the noise level created by the planes was 20 percent higher than that caused by the trains in New York City. The Los Angeles school system won its suit and used money from the settlement to implement a variety of noise abatement measures, which significantly reduced the noise levels in the classrooms.

Cohen, Evans, Krantz, Stokols, and Kelly (1981) studied the effects of this reduction. They compared the children in the noise-abated classrooms to children in classrooms that continued to be noisy and in classrooms that had always been quiet. The results were similar to those found in New York, although not as dramatic. Children in the noise-abated rooms performed better than those in the noisy rooms, but not as well as those in the quiet rooms. Cohen and his associates suggested that the Los Angeles school children did not benefit as much from noise abatement as did the New York school children because of the pervasiveness of the noise from the airport. The excessive airplane noise did not occur in just the classroom; it occurred in the students' homes as well. Thus, the Los Angeles school children had a much harder time escaping noise pollution.

Air Pollution

Air pollution occurs when the air we breath contains toxic gases or airborne solid particles. The effects of air pollution on people's physical health has been well documented. It can cause respiratory disorders such as asthma and bronchitis, heart problems, and neurological problems. It is estimated that in the United States, over 200 million dollars is spent each year on health care problems caused by air pollution (Evans and Jacobs, 1981).

Much less is known about the psychological effects of air pollution, but it appears that these also may be negative. For example, it has been found that compared to people in environments with clean air, people in polluted environments are less cooperative, less friendly, and more irritable (Cunningham, 1979; Evans and Jacobs, 1981). Rotton, Frey, Barry, Milligan, and Fitzpatrick (1979) conducted a laboratory experiment on how air pollution affects aggression. They found the same curvilinear relationship between air pollution and aggression as Baron and Bell (1975) found between heat and aggression; people aggressed more in rooms with moderately polluted air than in rooms with either clean or extremely polluted and unpleasant air. This again suggests that when the discomfort created by environmental stressors gets too high, people may attempt to avoid increasing their discomfort by refraining from aggression. Before concluding that extreme air pollution might inhibit aggression, however, field studies must be conducted. (Remember, Baron and Bell's laboratory findings on heat and aggression have not been supported in nonlaboratory settings.)

While chronic exposure to polluted air is medically harmful, people appear to psychologically adapt to it. Evans, Jacobs, and Frager (1982) examined two groups of people who had recently moved to an area that had high levels of smog. One group had lived in another smoggy area for at least five years; the other had lived in a relatively smog free environment. Newcomers reported more respiratory problems than long-term smog breathers. Also, when both groups were shown pictures of urban settings that contained smog, the long-term residents saw less smog in the pictures than did the newcomers.

In Defense of Urban Living

This review has focused almost exclusively on the negative aspects of urban living and has ignored possible positive aspects of urban enivronments. This focus reflects the problem-oriented nature of environmental research and public opinion. Korte (1980) reported that only 13 percent of all United States citizens and 21 percent of all urbanites say that they would prefer

The level of pollution and other environmental stressors is higher in urban areas than in rural areas.

to live in cities. However, it is necessary to at least mention some alternative views of the urban environment.

Descriptions of life in urban centers in the eighteenth, nineteenth and early twentieth centuries suggest that in many ways living conditions in cities have improved. Also, urbanization is not the only cause of environmental stressors like air pollution. For example, in 1972, anthropologists found the frozen body of an Eskimo woman who had died about 1600 years earlier, long before urban centers existed. They were able to perform an autopsy and found that she had black lung disease, caused by breathing highly polluted air (Fisher et al., 1984).

Several environmental psychologists reject the notion that life in a large city is inherently pathological, and some even argue for the benefits of urban living. In his book *Crowding and Behavior,* Jonathan Freedman (1975) included a chapter entitled "In Praise of Cities." He points out the cultural, economic, and social opportunities offered by cities, which are not available in nonurban areas. Proshansky (1976), another noted environmental psychologist, proposed that the diversity of the urban experience may make people more adaptable. And some writers (for example, Creekmore, 1985; Geller, 1980) have argued that for some people, urban living does not create stimulus overload but rather a desired level of stimulation.

SUMMARY

Environmental psychologists study how the environment affects an organism's behavior. Environmental variables can affect both nonsocial and social behaviors, but most environmental psychologists have studied their effects on social behavior. Much of their research has focused on the direct and indirect consequences of living in an urban environment.

Studies of the social behavior of people who reside in urban environments indicate that compared to people who live in nonurban environments, urbanites are less polite, less friendly, and less civil. One major explanation of this is based on the concept of stimulus overload—urban living may create more stimulation than people can effectively process. To reduce the level of inputs from their environment to a manageable level, urbanites may reduce the number of their social interactions by engaging in behavior that make them less sociable.

Another related explanation of urban-nonurban differences is based on the concept of environmental stressors, which are more prevalent in an urban environment. Environmental stressors cause physiological and psychological stress, which in turn affects people's social behavior. Research on environmental stressors has focused primarily on the effects of temperature, noise, and air pollution. It has been found that increases in ambient temperature may negatively affect people's moods and may make them less attracted to others. Research on the relationship between heat and aggression has produced differing results.

Noise is defined as any unwanted sound. Prolonged exposure to noise has direct and indirect effects on social behavior. People in a noisy environment become anxious, irritable, and aggressive. They may also experience stimulus overload and, as a result, engage in behaviors that discourage social interactions with others.

Little research has been done on the social effects of air pollution, but it appears that they are comparable to those of noise. However, while people appear to be able to psychologically adjust to air pollution, they are unable to adjust to noise pollution.

THE PRESENCE OF OTHERS

Readers who live in small towns or suburbs may be feeling pretty good right now. Life in a small town is not as stimulating as life in a big city, but small-town residents do not have to worry about noise, air pollution, crime, and the most salient characteristic of urban life—the presence of large numbers of other people in the same environment. It seems it is the urbanites who live like Calhoun's rats.

As your sixth grade teacher would say, wipe that smile off your face. Wherever humans live, they must cope with the presence of other people. For example, you attend school in a small town, far away from a metropolitan center, but you probably find yourself in close proximity to other people. You may have to share a bathroom with several individuals, eat in a dining hall with hundreds of diners, and study in a room filled with students. The presence of others is an inescapable fact of modern life.

Calhoun's rats were unable to cope with the presence of other members of their species, and they became pathological. Is the same true of humans? This section addresses that question by first describing how people attempt to control and regulate the use of the space around them. Then the section examines what happens when people are unable to control the use of these spaces and conditions become overcrowded.

Personal Space

Put this book down and find another person. Approach this person, move to within a foot of her, and watch what she does. (It is probably a good idea not to grin or drool while you do this.) Unless this person is involved in an intimate or romantic relationship with you, she will probably wince a bit, hunch up her shoulders, look terribly uncomfortable, say something like "What are you doing?" and take several steps backward. It will be clear this person does not want you so close. You will have invaded an invisible zone, called **personal space.** When someone violates your personal space, you feel uncomfortable and take actions to remove the intruder from this zone.

When Hall (1959) first began to write about personal space, he conceived it as a circle which surrounds a person. Recently, Hayduk (1978)

Personal space: an invisible zone around a person which others may not enter.

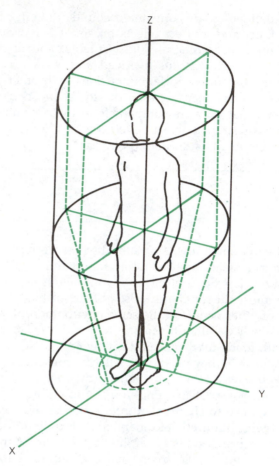

Figure 14-3. *Hayduk's model of personal space. Copyright (1978) American Psychological Association. Reprinted by permission of the author.*
Source: Hayduk (1978).

proposed that personal space is more like a three-dimensional figure. (See figure 14-3.)

The exact physical boundaries of a person's personal space differ across situations. For example, if two people are engaged in an intimate activity such as making love, a distance between them of less than a foot will not create discomfort; but if two people are engaged in an impersonal business transaction, a distance of less than four feet may create discomfort (Hall, 1963). Research has used several measurement techniques to study individual differences in personal space requirements.

Measurement
Personal space is an unobservable, hypothetical construct, and most people are not aware of the size of their personal space. It has therefore been necessary to develop techniques that measure this construct. Some researchers use *naturalistic observation*—they observe and record social inter-

In intimate interactions such as this one, people's personal space can be invaded without creating discomfort.

actions in real-world settings and measure the distance between people in these interactions. Others use the *stop-distance procedure*—they approach a subject and stop at the point where the subject reports feeling uncomfortable; the distance from this point to the subject defines personal space. Many researchers find it difficult or time-consuming to directly measure personal space in laboratory or field settings, so they use a *simulation*, or *projective*, technique to measure personal space. Kuethe (1962, 1964) was the first to use simulation to measure personal space. He gave his subjects cutouts of human figures and asked them to place the cutouts on a felt-covered board. By examining the distances between the figures representing the subjects and those representing other people, he estimated the subjects' personal space.

The simulation technique may be the easiest way to measure personal space, but it may also be the least valid. Hayduk (1983) reviewed 37 studies that had used both naturalistic observation and simulation to measure people's personal spaces. On the average, the correlation between the two techniques was only .39; less than 16 percent of the differences in the size of people's personal space could be predicted from the simulation procedure. In light of this, Hayduk and others (for example, Holahan, 1982) argued that naturalistic observations are the most desirable way to measure personal space, followed by the stop-distance procedure. Only if neither is possible should simulations be used.

Individual Differences

All humans appear to have a personal space, which vary greatly in size from person to person and from culture to culture. In general, people from northern European cultures have much larger personal space than do people from Mediterranean or Arab cultures (Holahan, 1982). Even people within the same country display cultural differences in the sizes of their personal spaces. For example, Hispanic-Americans stand closer to one another than do Anglo-Americans (Ford and Graves, 1977). These kinds of differences can create some interesting cross-cultural differences. I* experienced such a difference when I directed the doctoral dissertation of a Cuban-American student, David. Every time David and I met to discuss the project, David would place his chair about two feet from mine. I would subtly move my chair backward, but David would soon follow. One morning, we moved our chairs almost the length of an eight-foot table. This continued until one day a friend of David's, also a Cuban-American, looked at us and said, "David, stop sitting so close to Penner. You know Anglos can't handle that." Only then could we both acknowledge this cultural difference in our spatial behavior.

There are also sex differences in personal space. The personal space of men is usually larger than that of women (Wittig and Skolnick, 1978). When men interact with women, the distances between them are usually less than when men interact with other men. It appears that this is because the women move closer to the men (Edwards, 1972).

Some evidence suggests racial differences in personal space also exist—blacks tend to interact at closer distances than whites. Some researchers believe that in the United States, socioeconomic variables may explain these differences (Hayduk, 1978; Patterson, 1974).

Invasions

When someone attempts to invade people's personal space, they usually first change their posture or gestures in an attempt to block the invasion. I,* for example, rocked back in my chair when David entered my personal space. If this is not effective, people will move even farther away or, if possible, leave the scene.

Sommer (1969) demonstrated this with subjects who appeared oblivious to the environment around them—psychiatric patients at a mental hospital. When Sommer saw a male patient sitting alone on a bench on the hospital grounds, he walked over and sat down six inches from the patient. If the patient moved, so did Sommer. (See figure 14-4 for the effects of this invasion.)

Within one minute, 20 percent of the invaded individuals had fled the area. Within eight minutes, 50 percent had been driven away. Control subjects—patients sitting in the same area whose personal space was not invaded—remained seated on the benches.

---

*Coauthor Penner.

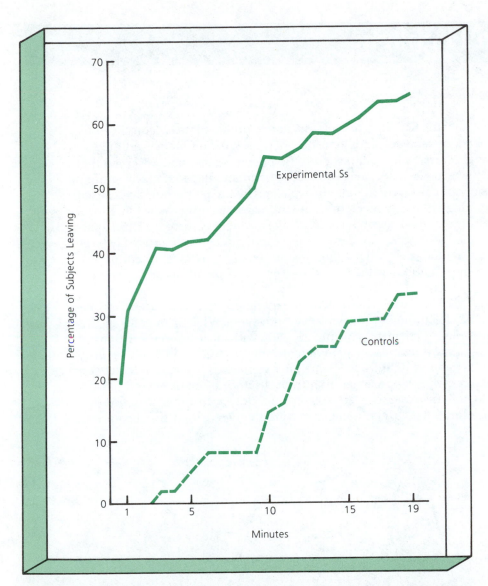

Figure 14-4. *Psychiatric patients reacted to invasions of their personal space by leaving the area.*
Source: Sommer (1969).

Consequences of Invasions

People often find themselves in situations where they cannot prevent violation of their personal space and cannot flee the scene. Most theorists believe that the invasion of someone's personal space creates stress and increased physiological arousal (Fisher et al., 1984; Holahan, 1982)

A study by Middlemist, Knowles, and Matter (1976) illustrated this process. Their subjects were males who were using the urinals in a lavatory. As the men approached a urinal, a confederate took a place either quite

Research Highlight

Personal Space of Violent Prisoners

In the late 1960s, Augustus Kinzel, a psychiatrist at the United States Medical Center for Federal Prisoners, investigated another aspect of individual differences in the size of people's personal space. In his daily work at the prison, Kinzel had observed that physical proximity was often associated with abrupt and spontaneous fights among the inmates. These outbreaks were frequently explained by the perpetrators as caused by the victims "getting up in my face" or "messing with me." Yet, as far as Kinzel could see, no violations of normal conversational distance had occurred. Kinzel speculated that these violent episodes may have involved individuals with unusually large interpersonal space boundaries; what other people would consider a comfortable conversational distance might have been perceived by these people as an invasion of their space.

To test this idea, Kinzel (1970) conducted an experiment that measured the personal space zones of violent and nonviolent male prisoners. Violent inmates in this study had life histories of frequent violent behavior with at least one incident of physical assault or fighting in prison. Nonviolent inmates were minimum-security prisoners with no histories of fighting. Each prisoner was asked to stand in the center of a room. The experimenter approached him from distance of eight feet and asked the inmate to say when the experimenter had come too close, causing discomfort (the stop-distance procedure). The experimenter measured and recorded the distance at

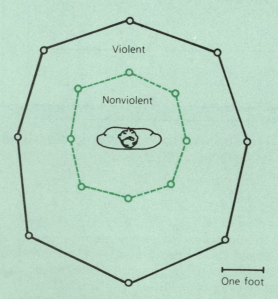

One foot

The personal spaces of violent and nonviolent prisoners.
Source: Kinzel (1970).

which each inmate stopped him. This procedure was repeated until measures from eight different points around a prisoner were obtained.

The following figure shows Kinzel's results. As expected, the violent inmates had a much larger personal space zone. The average area for these men was 29.3 square feet, compared to 7.0 square feet for the nonviolent men.

A second and more subtle difference between the groups can also be seen in the composite figure. In the violent group, the personal space area in back of the prisoner was larger than that in the front. For the nonviolent inmates, there was no such difference. The violent inmates were also more sensitive to people approaching them from their blind sides. Kinzel explained this difference as being derived primarily from the violent prisoners' concerns with homosexuality. For the violent group, he suggested, the rear body area is seen as highly vulnerable. This interpretation is plausible in view of the widespread occurrence of sexual attacks in prison; however, the violent prisoners may have been concerned about nonsexual assaults as well. It is probably not a good idea for violent individuals in a hostile environment to let others come up on them from behind, which is why gunslingers in the Old West liked to sit with their backs to the wall. Failure to do this cost violent men such as Billy the Kid and Jesse James their lives.

close to them or at a moderate distance. In the control condition, no confederate was present. The dependent measures were the lengths of time it took the subjects to begin to urinate and the lengths of time they urinated. These measures were used because stress and arousal delay the onset of urination and shorten its duration. The measures were observed and recorded using a periscope device hidden in the bathroom.

As the arousal-stress view would predict, the closer the confederate stood to the subjects, the longer the delay before they began to urinate and the shorter the time they urinated. The conclusion suggested by these results—that people invariably react negatively to invasions of their personal spaces—is not supported by other research. For example, Storms and Thomas (1977) systematically manipulated the distance confederates stood from a subject and whether the confederates acted in a positive and friendly or negative and unfriendly manner. If the confederates acted in a friendly manner, subjects liked them more when they stood six inches away from them than when they stood 30 inches away. If the confederates acted in an unfriendly manner, the reverse was true. In other words, the invasion of the subjects' personal space served primarily to intensify normal reactions to the confederates' behavior.

In a related experiment, Baron (1978) found that when there was a high need for help, people were more willing to assist someone who stood about a foot away than someone who stood three to four feet away. The reverse was true when there was a low need for help. These findings also suggest an intensification of the subjects' dominant response.

Territoriality

Most animals display territorial behaviors, and some theorists (Ardrey, 1966; Lorenz, 1966) propose that humans also have an instinctual drive to identify a physical area as their own and to defend it from intruders. Although other theorists question whether this behavior has an instinctual cause, they do agree that humans display **territoriality.** Altman (1975) has identified three types of territories used by humans. The first he called a *primary territory.* This is a place, such as a home or office, that belongs to a specific person who attempts to control its use by others. A *secondary territory* is an area that is not owned by anyone but is used regularly by a certain group of people who control its use. A classroom and the lounge in a dormitory are examples of this kind of territory. *Public territories* are places, such as beaches, shopping malls, or public parks, that do not appear to belong to anyone and to which access and use are uncontrolled. The ways in which people mark their territories and the effects of territoriality on social behavior have attracted the attention of some researchers.

Territoriality: the identification of certain physical areas as being owned or controlled by a specific person or group.

"And now, Randy, by use of song, the male sparrow will stake out his territory...an instinct common in the lower animals."

Reprinted by permission of Chronicle Features, San Francisco.

Marking

Humans use various means to communicate that a territory belongs to them and should not be entered without their permission. Street gangs spray paint their names on buildings and sidewalks; homeowners mark their property with hedges, fences, and No Trespassing signs; and library patrons mark their chairs with jackets and books.

People's social behavior appears to differ as a function of how well they mark their primary territories. In a study of suburban homes, Edney (1972), found that the more well marked their boundaries were, the longer the owners had lived in them and the longer they intended to stay in them. Also, the owners of well-marked homes answered their door bells more rapidly, suggesting heightened concern about defending their territories.

Markers are not used simply to reduce social contacts with others. In a study of an inner-city neighborhood, Greenbaum and Greenbaum (1981) found that homeowners whose porches, yards, and sidewalks were well marked were more likely to be selected as acquaintances by their neighbors than were homeowners with less well marked territories.

Effects on Social Behavior

Humans feel more comfortable when they are in their primary territories than when they are in a secondary of public territory (Altman, 1975). Edney and his associates (Edney, 1975; Edney and Uhlig, 1977) have found that college students rate themselves and are rated by others as calmer and more relaxed when they are in their own dormitory rooms (their primary territories) than when they are in someone else's room. Studies of residents in institutions indicate that the better established the territories within the institutions, the lower the level of violence (O'Neill and Paluck, 1973).

Another finding from territory research is that people appear to perform better when they are in their own territories than when they are visiting someone else's territory. (See the discussion of bargaining in chapter twelve.) Martindale (1971) found that college students were more successful in negotiations that took place in their own rooms. Edney (1975) found that people were better able to resist the attempts of others to control them when they were in their own territories than when they were in the territory of a person attempting to exert control. And Taylor and Lanni (1981) examined the amount of influence people exerted in three-person conversations. They found that when people were in their own territories (their own rooms in a dormitory), they were the most influential member of the triad. This was true even among people who normally were not dominant individuals.

Crowding

While the study in the prologue is the most well known study on the effects of overcrowding on animals, it was not the only one to find these results. Similar effects have been found in such varied species as elephants, fish, monkeys, and rabbits (Galle, Gove, and McPherson, 1972). The research that followed these studies attempted to determine if similar effects would be found among humans.

One of the first things researchers realized when they turned their attention to humans was that population density could not be equated with crowding as it could in animal research (Stokols 1972). The term **density** is a physical concept arrived at by counting the number of people in a specified area. **Crowding** is a psychological concept. Excessive density does not automatically lead to crowding.

Density: the number of people per unit of space.

Crowding: a subjective feeling that there are too many people in an environment.

Topic Background

Home, Sweet Home—Maybe

Most athletes and their fans believe that home teams have a sizable advantage over their visiting opponents. Professional football teams try to make the play-offs, and to compile records that will enable them to play their play-off games at home. Most college basketball conferences have each team play another twice, once at each team's home school, to eliminate the home-court advantage. Bookmakers usually take the home-team advantage into account when they set odds on a sporting event, and the people who patronize bookmakers take it into account when they make their bets. Is the widespread belief in a home-team advantage justified?

Schwartz and Barsky (1977) conducted research designed to determine if the home-court advantage affects a team's record of wins and losses. They examined the performances of home and visiting teams in a variety of sports, including major league baseball, basketball, football, and hockey. Their results supported the idea of a home-court advantage. In each sport, over half of all victories were found to occur at home. They also found that this advantage is apparently greater for some sports than for others. The largest difference was found in hockey, where the home teams won 64 percent of their games. In baseball, the home teams won 53 percent of their games, only 3 percent more than would be expected if the location of the game had no effect on winning. Professional football teams won 58 percent of their home games; college football teams won 60 percent of their home games. Schwartz and Barsky believed that the home-court advantage is a potent influence in hockey because hockey is played indoors, where crowd support is amplified. Consistent with this explanation was their finding that when a crowd had something to cheer about, the larger the crowd, the greater the home-field advantage.

Improved performance by the home team is not the only result of the home-court advantage. The visiting players are often adversely affected by the audience's behavior in support of the home team. Greer (1983) observed both home and visiting college basketball teams for the five-minute period following sustained booing from the fans. He recorded the number of points scored, number of fouls or violations called, and number of turnovers or changes in the possession of the ball. He found that booing affected all of these measures. Following a bout of audience booing, the home team's scoring improved and its number of turnovers and fouls decreased. The visiting team, on the other hand, showed reduced performance rates in all of these categories during the five minutes after it was booed. Greer suggested that the crowd's booing increased stress in the visiting team. Just as loud and uncontrollable noises have been shown to produce a narrowing of attention which leads to reduced task performance in the laboratory (Glass and Singer, 1972), the crowd's booing may have disrupted the visitors' attention to their performances.

Ironically, the intense support of the home team's fans may turn into a disadvantage. Baumeister and Steinhilber (1984) hypothesized that during crucial games, a supportive crowd might cause players to have high levels of self-attention that would interfere with performance. Rather than paying attention to critical aspects of the game, the players' concerns with "looking good" for fans and others may draw their attention away from events on the court or field. Baumeister and Steinhilber evaluated the tendency for home teams to "choke" by examining the records of the world series from 1924 to 1982 and of the National Basketball Association championship series from 1967 to 1982.

In the world series, the home team won 60 percent of the early games but only 39 percent of the deciding seventh games. A similar pattern was found for basketball; the home team won 70 percent of the early games but only 46 percent of the last games played at home. This early-late game difference appeared to be due to a decline in the performance of the home team. For example, the number of errors committed by the home team increased from the early to late games in the world series; the number of errors by the visitors did not change. The same thing happened in basketball. Free throw accuracy declined among the home-team basketball players in the final game, but not among the visitors.

So there is strong evidence to support the belief that home teams often experience a natural advantage because they are playing on their own turf and have a supportive crowd behind them. However, odds makers might also wish to consider Baumeister and Steinhilber's finding that this advantage can turn into a handicap when the pressure to perform and win is unusually high.

When researchers talk about density in a certain environment, they usually distinguish between inside and outside density. *Inside density* is the number of people per spatial unit within a dwelling unit; the number of people per room in a house, for example. *Outside density* is the number of people per geographic region; the number of people living on a block or in a neighborhood, for example. High outside density does not automatically lead to high inside density. Assume someone lives in a luxury apartment in the middle of New York City. Hundreds of other residents live in her building and thousands of other residents live on her block. Consequently, her outside density is high. However, her apartment contains 15 rooms, which she shares with two other people. Thus, her inside density is low. Conversely, suppose an unemployed coal miner in rural Appalachia lives in the only house in a valley, and shares this three-room house with nine other people. The outside density is low, while the inside density is high.

It is also necessary to distinguish between *social* and *spatial density*. Social density refers to the number of people in a given area; spatial density refers to the available space in a given area (Holahan, 1982). Most researchers agree that the subjective experience of crowding is most likely to occur when there is high inside, social density. However, not all researchers agree on the cause and effects of crowding.

Causes
The three theories presented below all assume that humans come to feel

crowded when they attribute a negative state or event to the presence of others.

Stress Theory　The first general theory is that the presence of others is a stressor which activates the general adaptation syndrome and creates unpleasant levels of arousal in humans (Holahan, 1982). This stress can be created by the excessive stimulation that often accompanies the presence of large numbers of people in an area, or it may be created by the arousal accompanying the invasion of people's personal space. Worchel and Teddlie (1976) compared the reactions of subjects who had been randomly assigned to one of two environments—two small rooms. The overall population densities in the rooms were identical, but the seating arrangements were different. In one room, subjects sat in chairs that were touching one another; in the other room, the subjects sat in chairs that were two feet apart. Subjects in the first environment were more likely to report feeling crowded. Evidently, this was due to the invasion of their personal space.

Control Theory　The control theory also considers crowding to be a stress reaction, but suggests a different cause for the stress—people's lack of control over their environment. This loss of control can be manifested when people are not free to do the things they want to do or when they are forced into doing things they do not want to do (Baum and Valins, 1979).

Consider the environment created for a large number of agricultural workers in southern Florida (Woodard v. Fowler, 1979). These workers had little money and could find no public housing in the city where they lived, so they rented ten-by-ten-foot rooms in small apartment buildings. The rooms leased for approximately one hundred dollars per month, and were each occupied by families of four to eight people. There were eight rooms on each floor of the building, and the rooms had no sinks or bathrooms.

According to the control theory of crowding, an excessive number of people in a small area causes the loss of control over one's environment and the experience of being crowded.

The 30 to 60 residents on each floor shared one sink, two toilets, and one shower.

If residents of these buildings wished to take a shower, read a book, or just sleep, they needed the cooperation of those with whom they shared the room and the floor. Similarly, the residents could not avoid social interaction with others and were not free to choose with whom they interacted. This objective loss of control should lead to the subjective experience of crowding (Proshansky, Ittelson, and Rivlin, 1970; Zlutnick and Altman, 1972).

Ecological Theory The ecological view of crowding considers how overpopulation can affect the social and physical ecology of a group's environment. As long as high density levels do not disrupt a group's social organization or ability to attract resources, group members are able to adjust and do not experience crowding. But when high density levels produce negative consequences, people experience crowding (Barker, 1968; Wicker, 1979). For example, people living in a densely populated area would not feel crowded unless the level of population density became so great that they could not find a place to live or could not obtain food for their families.

Effects on Human Social Behavior

Does the subjective experience of crowding lead to negative consequences among humans? A social scientist's answer to this question depends, to a certain extent, on the methods used to answer it.

The initial studies of crowding among humans used a correlational approach. Galle and his associates (1972) obtained census tract data on population density and then correlated density figures with juvenile delinquency rates, mental hospital admission rates, and other social pathology indexes. These correlational studies provided some valuable data, but they were deficient in several respects. Many did not distinguish between inside and outside densities in the areas they studied (Altman, 1975). More importantly, they did not determine whether the people in the areas they studied felt crowded; the researchers assumed that people who lived in densely populated areas felt crowded and thus displayed certain behaviors, but did not interview these people to verify their assumption. Finally, these studies did not consider that population density is often highly associated with socioeconomic factors. Poor people, for example, tend to live in crowded areas; thus, any correlation between population density and crime rates, for instance, may be as much due to a high level of poverty in an area as it is to the number of people living in the area.

Later correlational studies used statistical techniques to control for, or eliminate, the effects of variables other than crowding. Some researchers felt that the best strategy was to study crowding in a laboratory setting where they could systematically manipulate the variables of interest and directly measure people's responses, or feelings of being crowded. They achieved this control and precision at some cost. People do not react the same to being in a room with 10 other people for 60 minutes as they do to spending every day in an apartment with 10 other people. Also, it is believed that prolonged loss of control leads to the feeling of crowding, but the experimenters were legally and ethically required to inform their subjects that they could leave the experiment whenever they desired. Thus, unlike people in the outside world, most subjects in the laboratory crowding experiments had a good deal of control over their environment.

Quasi-experiment: an experiment, usually conducted in a nonlaboratory setting, in which subjects cannot be randomly assigned to different conditions.

These problems caused many researchers to investigate crowding by conducting **quasi-experiments,** in which they compared the behaviors of groups of people who, because of some naturally occurring event, differed in the population density of their environments or in their feelings of being crowded. For example, Rodin (1976) examined children who lived in same-size apartments in the same housing project, but who shared their apartments with different numbers of people. These children were brought into a laboratory where the effects of these differences in inside densities on their social behavior were examined. Rodin found that children from high-density apartments were less likely to try to exert control over what happened to them than were children from low-density apartments.

In another part of the same study, Rodin examined how children in low- and high-density apartments reacted to an unsuccessful experience. Half the children were given an easy problem to solve and half were given a problem that was unsolvable. Then both groups were given a second, solvable problem, and the number who solved this second problem was recorded. (See figure 14-5 for the results.) Among children in low-density apartments, prior success or failure had no effect on their performance on the second problem. But among children in high-density apartments, failure on the first problem resulted in less success on the second problem. These children appeared to give up in the face of an initial failure.

Having defined the constructs of density and crowding and having examined the manner in which social psychologists study them, the discussion returns to the question that began this chapter: Do these variables affect the behaviors of humans? Laboratory and field research suggest that when people feel crowded, certain aspects of their social behavior and health may be affected.

Sociability   In general, it appears that when people find themselves in an overcrowded environment, they become less friendly and less sociable (Baum and Valins, 1979; Epstein, 1981). Baron, Mandel, Adams, and Griffen (1976) studied these effects in a natural setting. In the early 1970s, the admissions office at a large state university underestimated the number of students who would accept admission to the university. As a result, there was a serious shortage of dormitory space, and three students were assigned to a number of rooms designed to hold only two students. Baron and his associates studied the crowding in this environment. They found that compared to the students in the doubles, those assigned to the triples felt more crowded, less in control of their environments, less satisfied with their rooms, and less satisfied with their roommates. They preferred to socialize with people other than their roommates. (By the way, in this and other studies [for example, Karlin, Epstein, and Aiello, 1978], students

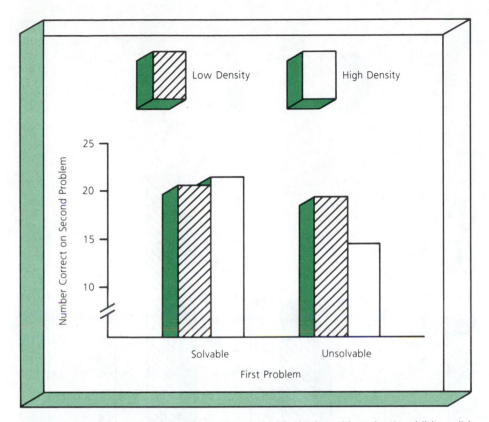

Figure 14-5. *When the first problem was solvable, high and low density children did equally well on the second problem; but when the first problem was unsolvable, the low density children were more successful.*
Source: Rodin (1976).

assigned to triple rooms also had lower grade point averages than those assigned to double rooms.)

Baum and Valins (1979) conducted a study at a university where the architectural designs of the dormitories caused some students to feel crowded while others did not. Students who felt crowded tended to avoid being in places where they would have to interact with others; they tended to both physically and psychologically withdraw from others. For example, in one part of this quasi-experiment, crowded and noncrowded students were asked to sit at a table while they waited for an experiment to begin. Subjects waited either alone or with a confederate. Baum and Valins measured how far the subjects sat from the confederate, how much the subjects looked at the confederate, and how much discomfort the subjects felt while waiting. There were no differences between the crowded and noncrowded subjects when they were alone, but there were differences between the two groups when they were with the confederate. Subjects who felt crowded in their dormitories sat farther away from the confederate, looked at him less, and were more uncomfortable than were subjects who did not feel crowded in their dormitories. (See figure 14-6.)

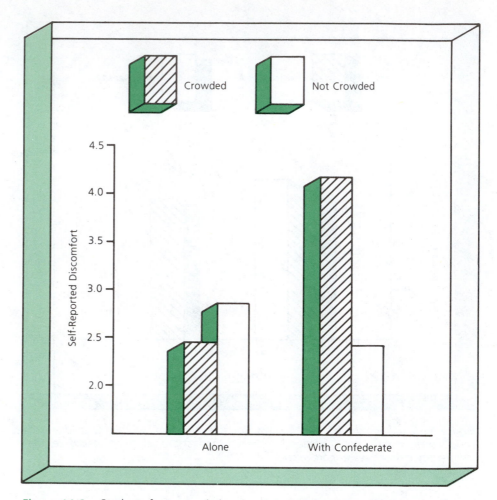

Figure 14-6. *Students from crowded and uncrowded dormitories felt the same when alone, but students from the crowded dormitories felt more discomfort in the presence of the confederate.*
Source: Baum and Valins (1979).

These findings are consistent, but it should not be assumed that excessive density always makes people less sociable. Epstein (1981) pointed out that if people are in an overpopulated environment but can retain a sense of control over that environment, they will show less of a tendency to feel crowded and, thus, may not become less sociable. Epstein also argued that the nature of the relationships between the people in a crowded environment may affect their feelings of being crowded. If they have a cooperative relationship, the effects of density and crowding may be greatly reduced.

In a study of the residents of Hong Kong, one of the most densely populated places on earth, Mitchell (1971) obtained data that supported this proposal. In Hong Kong, it is not uncommon for ten people to share a 400-square-foot apartment, which means that each person has less than 40 square feet of living space. This is an extremely high level of inside density; most Americans live in homes that allow each family member at least 400 to 500 square feet of living space. Some of the apartments in Hong Kong are shared by one family, but many are shared by two unrelated families. Mitchell found the most adverse reactions to crowding among people who lived in apartments that contained unrelated families and who could not easily leave their apartments. Epstein proposed that the family-nonfamily difference was due to the family members' abilities to develop cooperative arrangements with one another.

Aggression   Research on the effects of crowding on aggression assumes that crowding is a stressor and that stressors increase the likelihood of aggression. Empirical studies have not always supported these assumptions. Some have found increases in aggression as the result of increases in density (Hutt and Vaizey, 1966; Ginsberg, Pollman, Wauson, and Hope, 1977); others have found no relationship (Loo, 1972; Price, 1971).

In an attempt to reconcile these conflicting results, it has been proposed that other factors may moderate the relationship between crowding and aggression. Rohe and Patterson (1974) found that increased density did not lead to more aggression among children if they had an adequate number of toys with which to play. If there were not enough toys, increases in density produced increases in aggression. This finding is consistent with the ecological theory of crowding; if there are adequate resources, overcrowding does not affect people's social behavior.

There may also be individual differences in how people react to excessive density. When conditions become crowded, men tend to become more aggressive and competitive, but women often become more positive and cooperative (Saegert, MacIntosh, and West, 1975; Stokols, Rall, Pinner, and Schopler, 1973). It has been suggested that this difference may be explained by differences in how males and females react to stress. Freedman (1975) proposed that women are socialized to respond to others in a friendly and positive manner, while men are socialized to be more hostile and competitive. The stress engendered by crowding exacerbates these differences.

Health   Overpopulated environments may also affect people's psychological and physical health. Baum and Valins (1979) found that when people feel crowded for some period of time, they often develop the belief that they are unable to control or change their environment. This sense of learned helplessness lowers a person's self-esteem and may affect a person's physical health. (See the applications section of chapter five.) Perhaps this partially explains Cox, Paulus, McCain, and Karlovac's (1982) finding that as prison populations became more dense, suicide and death rates for older inmates increased. Cox and his associates also noted that the more prisoners per cell, the greater the number of illness complaints. Other researchers have identified specific physical consequences of overcrowding. And D'Atri (1975) and Paulus, McCain, and Cox (1978) found higher blood pressure in more socially crowded prisons.

While this research suggests some rather consistently negative consequences of crowding, it must be put in context. Humans appear to be less vulnerable to the effects of excessive population densities than are other species. Humans are intelligent, adaptable creatures who can exist in a host of different environments. And humans can mitigate the effects of an environment on its inhabitants by the structures they build. So, without claiming, as some do, that there are no inherently negative consequences of crowding (for example, Freedman, 1975), we cannot agree with those who see humans ending up like Calhoun's rats.

SUMMARY

Humans attempt to regulate and control the behavior of people with whom they share living or work space; they like to keep a certain amount of physical distance between themselves and others in their environment. This distance is called personal space. The size of people's personal space varies as a function of the situation they are in and their prior social experiences. Invasion of people's personal space produces physiological arousal and stress, but does not usually produce negative social behavior.

Another means of control and regulation is the establishment of territories; certain areas are identified as being owned and controlled by a person or a group of persons. Most people identify their homes or the places they work as their own territories. People are prepared to defend their territories, and they are calmer and more relaxed when they are in their home territories than when they are visitors in other people's territories. One major consequence of this is that people are often more interpersonally effective when they interact in their own territories.

Sometimes people find themselves in densely populated environments. Such settings can cause stress, reduce the levels of control people have over their environment, and reduce the availability of needed resources. If these or any other negative events are seen as caused by the presence of others, people will feel crowded. This feeling has consequences for human social behavior; when people are crowded, their moods worsen, they become less friendly and less sociable, they are less helpful, and if they are males, they become more aggressive. Finally, crowding may negatively affect people's physical and mental health.

THE BUILT ENVIRONMENT

Built environment: an environment designed and shaped by humans.

When people discuss the results of the study in the prologue, they tend to concentrate on the disastrous impact of overcrowding on the rats and to ignore another interesting finding: The design of the pens, or the **built environment,** mitigated somewhat the effects of excessive population density. All the rats suffered from overcrowding, but the most dramatic effects were found among rats whose pens were connected with ramps to all the other pens. The rats whose pens were connected with ramps to only two other pens were relatively better off. This final section considers how the aspects of the environment humans have designed and shaped—their built environment—affects social behavior.

Psychologists who study this topic are interested in specifics such as how the architectural designs of buildings or the physical characteristics of rooms in buildings influence the behavior of those who live and work in them. These researchers do not believe that the characteristics of people's built environments totally determine their behavior; instead, they espouse a point of view called **environmental probabilism** (Fisher et al., 1984; Porteus, 1977). This point of view is similar to that proposed by Kurt Lewin approximately 50 years ago in his general theory about the causes of social behavior. (See chapters one and three.) Lewin proposed that social behavior is caused by, or is a function of, both the person and the environment— $B = f(p,e)$. Given their interest in the impact of the environment on social behavior, it is not surprising that Lewin and his students were among the first psychologists to study how the physical characteristics of buildings could affect social behavior.

Environmental probabilism: the theory that the personal characteristics of people, the behavior of others, and the characteristics of the built environment make some behaviors more probable than others.

Building Design and Social Relationships

In the mid 1940s, Lewin and several of his students were involved in a large research project on group behavior. As part of this project, three students, Leon Festinger, Stanley Schachter, and Kurt Back (1950) conducted a now-classic investigation of how the design of buildings affected the development of friendships.

Friendship Development

The research project was housed at the Massachusetts Institute of Technology (MIT). In 1946, MIT opened two housing projects to accommodate the large number of married veterans who had entered this school after World War II. One of the projects consisted of 100 single-family houses arranged around nine courts. The other consisted of 17 buildings, each divided into 10 apartments that opened onto a common balcony. Certain features of the housing projects made them a good place to study the effects of architectural design on the development of friendships. First, the residents did not know one another before they moved into the projects, and they all moved in at the same time. Second, the residents were quite similar to one another; they were all married veterans, majoring in engineering. Third, the residents were randomly assigned to their new apartments. These features made the housing project much like a controlled laboratory setting in which people are randomly assigned to different conditions.

Festinger and his associates (1950) believed that two aspects of the students' living arrangements would influence the development of friendships. The first independent variable was the physical distance between their apartments; the less the distance between them, the more likely they were to become friends. This prediction was based on the commonsensical notions that for two people to become friends, they must have the chance to interact, and that the less the physical distance between two people, the greater the chance for interaction.

The second independent variable was something Festinger and his colleagues called the *functional distance* between apartments—the extent to which social contacts between residents were encouraged or discouraged. Imagine two apartment buildings. One building has only one staircase, located in the middle of the building; the other building has a staircase at each end of the building. The functional distance between the first- and second-floor end apartments in the first building is much less than the functional distance between the first- and second-floor end apartments in the second building. As a result, Festinger and his associates would predict that first- and second-floor end-apartment residents in the first building would be more likely to become friends than would first- and second-floor end-apartment residents in the second building.

The researchers let sufficient time elapse for the residents to get to know one another, and then asked the residents to name the three people they "saw most of socially." The residents' responses provided data on the relationship between the two kinds of distance and friendship development. As predicted, physical distance affected social preferences. The closer the students in the single-family homes lived to one another, the more likely they were to interact socially. No students whose homes were more than 180 feet apart named one another as social contacts. The same results were found among the students who lived in apartments. (See figure 14-7.) The closer two apartments were, the more likely students were to name one another as social contacts. This was true whether they lived on the same floor or on different floors, and whether they lived in the same building or in different buildings.

Functional distance also affected the development of friendships; the less the functional distance was, the more likely people were to become friends. For example, when the staircases between the second and ground floors were located at the ends of a balcony on each apartment building, second-floor residents were more likely to encounter residents of first-floor end apartments than to encounter residents of other first-floor apartments. As a result, second-floor residents selected first-floor end-apartment residents more than other first-floor residents.

The setting studied by Festinger and his associates was unusual; typically, people who live in the same area are not as demographically similar as were the veterans in the MIT project. But subsequent research has suggested that their findings are generalizable. Greenbaum and Greenbaum (1981) found that architectural design affected social choices in an inner-city area populated by different ethnic groups. Nahemow and Lawton (1976) found the same thing among residents of high-rise apartments.

A recent study by Case (1981) examined the long-term effects of architectural design on social relationships. Case's subjects were residents of two all-male freshman dormitories at Princeton University. His findings agreed with those of earlier researchers: The less the physical and functional distance between people, the more likely they were to become friends. But

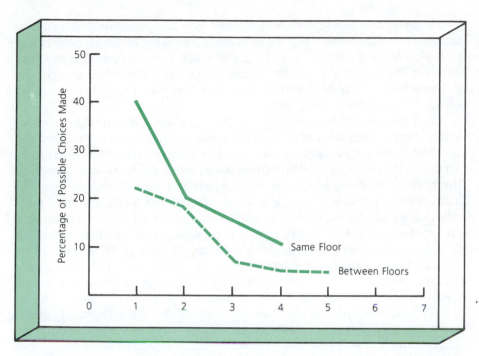

Figure 14-7. *The less the distance between students' apartments, the more likely they were to choose one another as friends. Reprinted by permission of the publisher and the authors.*
Source: Festinger et al. (1950).

Case did not stop there, he went on to ask, "How long do these relationships exist?"

To answer this question, Case obtained data on the students' choices of roommates when they were in their second year of college and no longer living in a dormitory. Over 80 percent of the students studied by Case chose a roommate from the people they had identified as acquaintances in their freshman dormitories. Even when these students were seniors, 50 percent of their roommates were individuals they had identified as acquaintances in their freshman year.

Interior Design and Social Behavior

The general structure is not the only aspect of a building that affects the behavior of those who live or work there. The physical arrangements of the rooms within it and the manner in which these rooms are furnished also influence behavior.

Furniture Arrangement

According to Reusch and Kees (1956), the manner in which furniture is arranged affects the quantity and quality of social interactions that occur within a setting. *Sociopetal* arrangements are open and encourage social interactions; *sociofugal* arrangements are closed and discourage social interactions.

Sommer and Ross (1958) investigated how the placement of furniture affected interactions between the patients of a geriatric hospital. If the chairs in the social area were placed along the walls, there was little interaction between the patients. When the chairs were clustered in small groups, the patients began to interact with one another. Holahan (1972) found similar effects in a psychiatric hospital.

Zweigenhaft (1976) examined the effects of furniture arrangement in a setting with which you are probably familiar, the office of a college instructor. The question of interest was whether the way in which instructors arranged the furniture in their offices might affect students' evaluations of the professors. Zweigenhaft recorded where in their offices instructors at a small college placed their desks. Some placed their desks against a wall, where the desk did not act as a barrier to interaction between the instructor and a student visitor. Others placed their desks in front of them, where the desk did act as a barrier. After recording which arrangement an instructor had, Zweigenhaft obtained student evaluations of that instructor's courses. As expected, instructors in the barrier offices received lower ratings than did instructors in the open offices.

These findings do not allow one to conclude that the desk arrangements caused the student evaluations. It is just as possible that low student evaluations over several years had caused certain instructors to place a barrier between themselves and students. To determine the true cause-and-effect relationship between desk placement and student reactions, Campbell and Herren (1978) conducted the following experiment. Students interacted with an instructor whom they had never met before. These interactions took place in either a barrier or a no-barrier environment. No differences were found in the students' ratings of the instructor. Thus, it would seem that desk placement alone was not the cause of the lower student evaluations received by some of the instructors in Zweigenhaft's study.

Hensley (1982) proposed that the manner in which instructors placed their desks and the evaluations they received may have both been reflections of the same underlying variable, their attitudes toward teaching. Hensley's data supported this proposal. Instructors with traditional views about teaching and about relationships between teachers and students were more likely than instructors with nontraditional views to have office furniture arrangements in which a desk was used as a barrier. It was also found that the placements of the instructors' desks were influenced by other variables, including the number of student advisees the instructors had. The more advisees they saw, the less likely they were to place their desks between themselves and visitors to their offices. This was true whether instructors held traditional or nontraditional views of teaching. The reason for this open furniture arrangement was simply that it made it possible to process more student advisees at a faster rate.

Classroom Ecology

Robert Sommer (1967, 1969) has investigated something he called *classroom ecology*, or how the physical characteristics of a classroom affect students' behavior and performance. In the first of several studies on this topic,

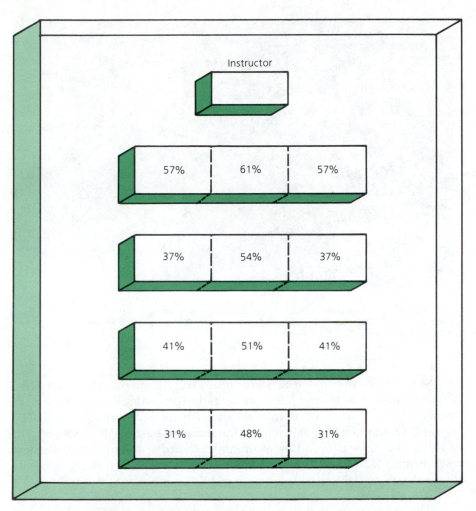

Figure 14-8. *The numbers in the boxes represent the percentage of students partic-ipating in class discussion. Students in the front row and center aisle were most likely to participate in class discussions.*
Source: Sommer (1967).

Sommer (1967) investigated the effects that student seating in a classroom had on class participation. The subjects were college students enrolled in an introductory psychology course. As part of the course, they participated in small discussion groups each week. Sommer recorded the locations of students' seats and how much they interacted with the person who led the discussion sections. He predicted that the easier it was for students to make visual contact with the instructor, the more they would participate in classroom discussions. In a traditionally arranged classroom, with rows and aisles, students in the front rows and center aisles would participate more than those in the back rows and side aisles. As predicted, the per-centage of students who participated in classroom discussions differed as a function of the rows in which they were seated and whether they were in the center or sides of a row. (See figure 14-8.)

The research on classroom ecology suggests that where students sit in a classroom affects their behavior. Note that the children directly facing the teacher are more responsive than those off to either side.

Students in the first row were more likely to participate than were students in any other row, and students in the center of each row were more likely to participate than were those at the sides of each row. The easier it was to make visual contact, the more interaction. Further support for this finding was found by examining other discussion sections which met around tables in seminar rooms. Students who sat directly opposite the instructor participated more than did those who sat to the right or left of the instructor.

The students in this study were not randomly assigned to their seats; thus, it is not known whether (a) the seating arrangement caused differences in participation or (b) those students most interested in classroom participation chose seats where it would be easiest to make visual contact with the instructor. A subsequent study by Becker, Sommer, Bee, and Oxley (1973) suggested that both processes are at work. Students who desire active participation in a class choose the front or center seats; once in these locations, physical aspects of the seating arrangements affect the students' behavior.

A study by Rosenfeld, Shea, and Greenbaum (1979) demonstrated how seating arrangements subtly influence the degree to which students participate in class. Students were shown videotapes of a teacher whose nonverbal behaviors (primarily facial expressions) indicated that an answer to a question was right or wrong. They viewed these videotapes from different perspectives. Some saw the teacher's reactions from the perspective of a student seated in the front row of a classroom; others saw the reactions from the perspective of someone seated in a rear row or side aisle. Students with the latter perspective tended to have more difficulty in correctly judging the teacher's reactions. This diminished ability to get accurate feedback on a teacher's reactions would probably inhibit classroom participation.

Other research (for example, Koneya, 1976; Levine et al., 1982; Stires, 1982) has indicated that, as Lewin suggested many years earlier, classroom behavior is influenced by both the characteristics of the student and the physical characteristics of the environment. Koneya had students participate in a class where they were seated in a circle around the instructor and, thus, all had an equal chance to interact with her. On the basis of their behavior, students were classified as high, medium, or low verbalizers. Then the students were randomly assigned to seats in a traditionally arranged classroom. High and medium verbalizers who were assigned to central seats participated more than did high and medium verbalizers who were assigned to peripheral seats. Seat assignment did not affect the behavior of low verbalizers; they were equally unlikely to participate wherever they sat. Thus, classroom seating arrangements interacted with the personality of the students to determine their behavior.

Built Environments and Reactions to the Presence of Others

Humans, like Calhoun's rats, share their built environments with other members of their species. And just as the rats' built environment affected their reactions to others, so humans' built environment affects their reactions to others.

One study of this relationship, conducted by Baum, Reiss, and O'Hara (1974), focused on invasions of personal space. As discussed earlier, personal space is an invisible boundary around people which they do not want others to enter. People attempt to avoid situations in which their personal spaces will be invaded and to leave situations in which such invasions occur. Baum and his associates were interested in how the design of an environment might help people protect their personal spaces.

The subjects were community college students who approached drinking fountains in two campus buildings. One fountain was in an alcove recessed about eight inches into the wall; the other was flush to the side of the wall. Baum and his colleagues had two experimental conditions in which they placed a confederate either one foot or five feet from the fountains. They also had one control condition in which no confederate was present. They then recorded the number of people who drank from each fountain and for how long. (See figure 14-9 for the number of people who drank from the two fountains under these three conditions.)

No differences were found in the confederate-absent (control) condition, but in the other two conditions, about twice as many students drank from the recessed fountain. Why? According to Baum and his colleagues, the presence of the confederate at the nonrecessed fountain constituted a threat to the subjects' personal space, so they avoided that fountain. But in the case of the recessed fountain, the wall surrounding it provided a barrier or shield which the subjects saw as protecting their personal space; thus, subjects were much more willing to approach and use the recessed fountain.

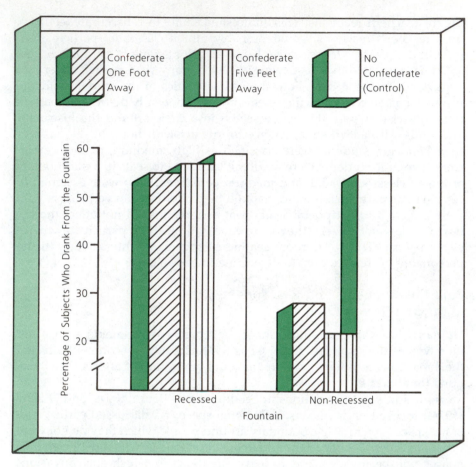

Figure 14-9.   *The presence of a confederate had no effect with the recessed fountain, but reduced drinking with the non-recessed fountain.*
Source: Baum et al. (1974).

The Built Environment and Crowding

Among humans, excessive population density does not automatically lead to the negative feeling of being crowded. If two people were in different environments of comparable densities, one may feel crowded and the other may not. Research conducted in the last 10 to 15 years strongly suggests that the architectural design of built environments is a major determinant of whether people feel crowded, and that changes in design can decrease people's feelings of being crowded.

Architecture Design

In the early 1970s, Andrew Baum and Stuart Valins (1977, 1979) found a situation that provided them with an excellent opportunity to study the relationship between architectural design and perceived crowding. Students at a northeastern university were randomly assigned to one of two dormitories. The designs and arrangements of the rooms in these two

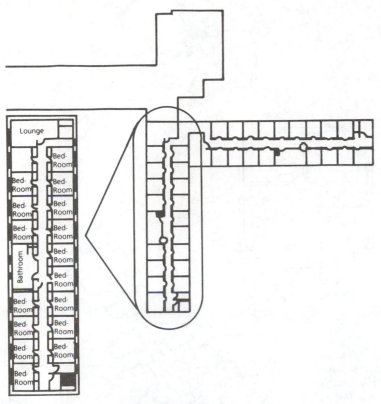

Figure 14-10a. *Floor plan of the corridor design dormitory. Reprinted by permission of the publisher and the authors.*
Source: Baum and Valins (1977).

dormitories differed radically. Baum and Valins called the first a corridor design (see figure 14-10a.) This design had 17 rooms to a floor, with each room opening on the same corridor. At the center of the corridor was a bathroom, which was shared by the 34 people who lived on the floor, and at the end of the floor was a lounge-study area. This design allowed approximately 155 square feet of living space per person.

The design of the other dormitory was called a suite design. (See figure 14-10b.) The students lived in small four- to six-person suites, each with its own bathroom and lounge. This dormitory also housed 34 students to a floor and allowed approximately 155 square feet of living space per person.

Baum and Valins (1977) proposed that people experience the sense of being crowded when they feel they are unable to control or regulate the number of unwanted social contacts they have. This lack of control, Baum and Valins reasoned, should be much greater in the corridor dorm than in the suite dorm. Imagine someone who lives in the corridor dormitory needs to use the bathroom. To do this, she must leave her room and enter the corridor, where she is likely to encounter several of the 33 other people who live on her floor. Since she does not know them very well, she is

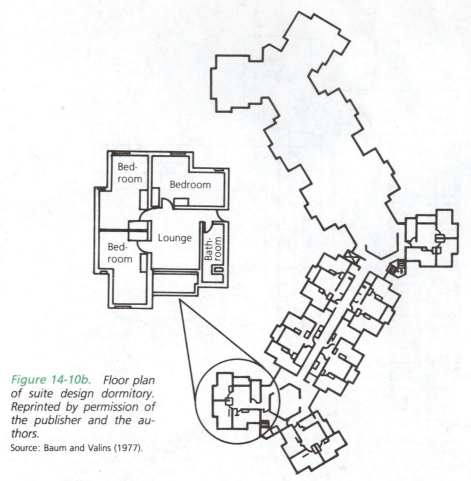

Figure 14-10b. *Floor plan of suite design dormitory. Reprinted by permission of the publisher and the authors.*
Source: Baum and Valins (1977).

unable to predict the nature of her interactions with them and thus does not desire these interactions. Once she reaches the bathroom, she will encounter still other people and, perhaps, be forced to interact with them. Now imagine that someone who lives in the suite dormitory needs to use the bathroom. It is not necessary to enter the corridor; all she must do is pass through the lounge. In the lounge will be at most four or five people whom she knows well. Thus, she has a good sense of what to expect from them. Once she reaches the bathroom, she can shut out other people.

The corridor and suite residents experience the same level of physical density, but the suite resident has much more control over social contacts than does the corridor resident. As Baum and Valins predicted, the corridor residents were more likely than the suite residents to describe themselves as crowded, lacking privacy, and wanting to avoid contact with others. The corridor residents tended to avoid areas where it was likely they would come into contact with others, while suite residents seemed to prefer such areas. As a result, when corridor residents were alone, they stayed in their rooms, but suite residents stayed in the lounge areas of their suites. (Calhoun observed a comparable behavior among his rats; animals in the most crowded pens often sought places where the probability of future social

Topic Background

Public Housing: A Good Idea Gone Bad?

In 1954, a housing project was opened in St. Louis, Missouri, which it was hoped would be a model of how to meet the housing needs of low-income inner-city residents. The Pruitt-Igoe project consisted of 43, 11-story buildings containing over 2,700 apartments. Twelve thousand people moved into this project.

Pruitt-Igoe was a disaster. Within a few years of its opening, the playgrounds and parking lots were covered with broken glass and most of the elevators were filled with human excrement and garbage and were unworkable. Gangs waited in the stairwells to attack the residents, so no one would live on the upper floors. By 1970, 27 of the original 43 buildings were vacant. In 1972, they were demolished by the city of St. Louis.

A number of environmental psychologists have argued that the disaster of Pruitt-Igoe was due to its architectural design. Oscar Newman (1973) identified a series of structural arrangements in the design of buildings that tend to increase the likelihood of crime. He argued that crime is encouraged in places that are seen as not belonging to anyone in particular, such as lobbies and walkways. Newman described such spaces as undefended because they have no provision for limiting access to outsiders. Such zones offer convenient opportunities for vandalism, assaults, and other types of crime. Newman pointed to the Pruitt-Igoe housing project as a prime example of undefended space. There were so many residents in the project that it was impossible for everyone to know each other; residents could not distinguish other residents from potentially dangerous outsiders. The boundaries of the complex were not clearly defined, making it difficult to regulate intrusions. There were no surveillance features at building entrances and in elevator lobbies; the Pruitt-Igoe lobbies had multiple entranceways and no windows to let those outside see what was going on inside. This arrangement provided outsiders easy access to a relatively concealed space which offered optimal conditions for criminal activity.

Many of Newman's ideas were supported by a survey of residents from Pruitt-Igoe and nearby tenement buildings (Yancey, 1972). Pruitt-Igoe residents, when compared to their neighbors, were more satisfied with the interior spaces of their apartments (78 percent versus 55 percent), but were less satisfied with the surrounding environment (53 percent versus 74 percent). The most frequent reasons given for dissatisfaction with the environment were (1) an inability to see their children when they were outdoors and thus an inability to supervise their play; (2) a mistrust of others in the building; and (3) the fear of robbery or assault outside the apartment.

Newman's ideas have been controversial, and more recent findings have cast doubt on his proposal that defensible space prevents urban crimes. Newman and Franck (1982) found that as building size increased, use of space, social interaction, and control of space all decreased, while fear of crime increased. However, the actual personal crime rate, as measured by robberies and assaults per 1,000 residents, was not found to be affected by building size.

Farley (1982) computed the rate of violent and nonviolent crimes over a seven-year period, from 1971 to 1977, in 10 public housing developments and surrounding houses located in St. Louis. Included in these housing developments were both low- and high-rise buildings. These areas contained all of the large public housing developments within the city. There were no differences in crime rates between the high- and low-rise buildings. Moreover, the crime rates for the high-rise public housing were not higher than for the rest of the city, and they were not higher than would be expected for the location of the housing within the city and the type of residents. Farley contended that conventional wisdom has overstated the extent of crime in and near public housing. However, his finding does not totally disprove the defended-space concept. Crimes associated with youth, such as vandalism, minor assaults, and victimless crime, were not considered in Farley's study, and these crimes may occur at higher rates in high-rise public housing.

The lack of defensible space was probably not the only cause of the failure of Pruitt-Igoe. However, the subsequent studies of this project's failure suggest that urban planners must do more than simply build buildings; they must also consider how the designs of these buildings will affect the behavior of their residents.

encounters was the lowest.) This social withdrawal was also found when the students were outside their dormitories (Baum, Harper, and Valins, 1975).

These findings were replicated at another university where students lived in either a long-corridor-design dormitory (40 people sharing a common corridor) or a short-corridor-design dormitory (20 people sharing a common corridor) (Baum and Valins, 1979). At this second university, Baum and Valins found further differences between those students whose environment made them feel crowded and those whose environment did not. For example, when confronted with difficult but solvable anagrams, the long-corridor (crowded) residents gave up more quickly than did the short-corridor (uncrowded) residents.

Rodin and Baum (1978) had subjects in a similar study play a variant of the prisoner's dilemma game (see chapter twelve), in which they could either act cooperatively, act competitively, or withdraw from the game. They found that long-corridor residents were significantly more likely to withdraw from the game than were short-corridor residents.

These two sets of findings led Baum and Valins to propose that one consequence of perceived crowding is an increased sense of lack of control and increased helplessness. Their conclusion is significant because it is based on studies of a group of young college students who had lived in the dormitories for less than a year. One can only imagine the effects of crowding on economically disadvantaged individuals who must endure crowding year after year.

Changing Architectural Design
The results of Baum and Valins's research, studies of the effects of built environments such as the work on classroom ecology by Sommer, and

other studies have led environmental psychologists to explore ways to change and improve existing built environments and to become involved in the design of new built environments. Some examples of what has been done in this area are changes in the designs of dormitories and institutions.

These two offices create very different environments for the workers in them. In which would you prefer to work?

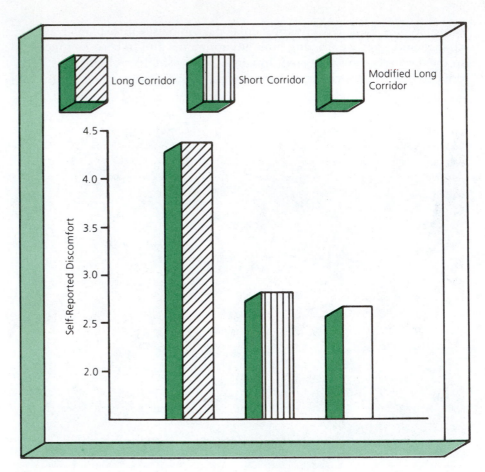

Figure 14-11. *When the long corridor was modified subjects acted like the short corridor residents, showing little discomfort in the presence of the confederate.*
Source: Baum and Davis (1980).

Dormitories Baum and Davis (1980) were able to use a simple structural modification to convert a long-corridor dormitory floor into a short-corridor floor. About halfway down the long corridor, two sets of unlocked doors were constructed. These divided the 20 rooms on the floor into two sets of ten rooms each. Students who lived on this floor were compared to those who lived on a long-corridor floor and on a true short-corridor floor. Students were randomly assigned to the dormitory floors, so differences between them could be reasonably attributed to differences in design.

This simple change produced the desired effects. Students on the modified-long-corridor floor, compared to those on the long-corridor floor, felt more in control of their environment and more able to regulate their social experiences. Students on both the modified-long-corridor and the true short-corridor floors became more social as the semester progressed, while students on the long-corridor floor became less social. And the behavior of the three groups differed when they were placed in a waiting room with a confederate. (See figure 14-11.) Both the modified-long-corridor and the short-corridor residents sat closer to the confederate and looked at her more than did the long-corridor residents. The first two groups also reported less discomfort while they waited.

The effects of other architectural designs can also be reduced. Baum and Davis (1976) found that light-colored dormitory rooms were seen as less crowded than dark-colored rooms. Wicker (1979) examined ways to reduce the difficulties experienced by the large number of tourists who waited to board shuttle buses at a national park. Chain-linked iron posts which served to force people into a waiting line decreased the amount of competition to get on the buses and made the wait more pleasant for the tourists. And Desor (1972) has conducted laboratory studies in which using partitions in work or living areas reduced the levels of perceived crowding among subjects, as did reducing the number of doors.*

Institutions   Zimring, Weitzer, and Knight (1982) described a project in which the interior design of a large institution for "severely and profoundly retarded individuals" was completely renovated and redesigned. The major goal of this effort was to increase the level of social interactions among the residents of the institution. To achieve this, Zimring and his associates believed that they needed to create living and social areas which gave the clients a greater sense of privacy and control over their environment.

Before the renovations, residents slept in large rooms or wards with walls or partitions between their beds and no space or objects they could call their own. For some of the residents, these areas were redesigned into an arrangement almost identical to the short-corridor dormitory design studied by Baum and Valins. Twelve two-person bedrooms opened onto a common corridor, and the resident shared a large bathroom and a lounge area.

Zimring and his colleagues observed the behavior of the residents before and after these renovations had been made. At the end of two and a half years, the rate of interaction between the residents had increased significantly; they were more verbal, more alert, and less withdrawn. Also, staff members became less likely to intrude into the residents' personal or private space. Similar, though less dramatic, effects were obtained in another building at the institution when the sleeping arrangements were changed from 20-person open rooms to suites of three two-person rooms.

Zimring and his colleagues attributed the improvement observed among the residents to a greater sense of control over their environment—sense of control that was largely produced by changes in the interior design of the institution. Thus, it appears that while humans may react to their built environment in a manner akin to Calhoun's rats, there is one important difference between the species: Humans, unlike rats, can modify and improve their built environment.

---

*However, Stokols, Smith, and Proster (1976) were unable to replicate this finding in a field experiment, and partitions had no effects in a later study by Zimring, Weitzer, and Knight (1982).

SUMMARY

The built environment is that part of the environment which is designed and shaped by humans. Research suggests that the interior and exterior designs of built environments in which people live or work can affect social behavior.

With regard to the exterior design, the structure of a building influences the chances that people will come into contact and become friends. The less the physical distance between two people who inhabit the same structure, the more likely they are to become friends. Of comparable importance is the functional distance between people, which refers to the extent to which a building's design or structure encourages or discourages social contact between two people. The less the functional distance, the greater the likelihood of friendship development. These social relationships continue long after the parties have left the building.

The interior design of a structure can affect both the quantity and quality of social interactions. Some furniture arrangements, for example, facilitate social interactions, while others inhibit social interactions. One setting in which the effects of interior design have been extensively studied is the classroom. The seats taken by students affect the degree to which they participate in class and, perhaps, their classroom performance. These effects are strengthened by the fact that students do not randomly choose where they sit. Outgoing students select seats that make eye contact with an instructor most likely; thus, an instructor is more likely to encourage participation from them.

A structure's interior design can also affect people's reactions to others. In some structures, the design allows people to have little control over the number of social contacts they have; in other structures, the design permits considerable control. Even if the two types of structure provide the same amount of living space for residents, those in the former will feel more crowded than those in the latter. As a consequence of feeling crowded, residents become socially withdrawn and display signs of helpnessness. These findings have led environmental psychologists to work with architects to remediate the effects of certain built environments or to design environments that facilitate desirable social behavior.

REFERENCES

Abel, C.G., Becker, J.V., and Skinner, L.J. (1980). Aggressive behavior and sex. *Psychiatric Clinics of North America, 3*, 133–151.

Abel, E. (1966). *The missile crisis.* New York: Lippincott.

Abeles, R.P. (1976). Relative deprivation, rising expectations, and black militancy. *Journal of Social Issues, 32*, 119–138.

Abramson, L.Y., Seligman, M.E., and Teasdale, J.D. (1978). Learned helplessness in humans: Critique and reformulation. *Journal of Abnormal Psychology, 87*, 49–74.

Adair, J.G. (1973). *The human subject: The social psychology of the psychological experiment.* Boston, MA: Little Brown.

Adair, J.G. (1980). Psychology at the turn of the century: Crises, challenges, promises. *Canadian Psychology, 21*, 165–178.

Adams, J.S. (1965). Inequity in social exchanges. In L. Berkowitz (Ed.), *Advances in experimental social psychology* (Vol. 2). New York: Academic Press.

Adams, J.S., and Freedman, S. (1976). Equity theory revisited: Comments and annotated biliography. In L. Berkowitz and E. Walster (Eds.), Advances in experimental social psychology (Vol. 9). New York: Academic Press.

Adams, J.S., and Jacobsen, P.R. (1964). Effects of wage inequities on work quality. *Journal of Abnormal and Social Psychology, 69*, 19–25.

Adams, J.S., and Rosenbaum, W.B. (1962). The relationship of worker productivity to cognitive dissonance about wage inequities. *Journal of Applied Psychology, 46*, 161–164.

Adorno, T.W., Frenkel-Brunswik, E., Levinson, D.J. and Sanford, N.R. (1950). The authoritarian personality. New York: Harper Row.

Ainsworth, M.D.S. (1969). Object relations, dependency, and attachment: A theoretical review of the mother-infant relationship. *Child Development, 40*, 969–1025.

Ajzen, I., and Fishbein, M. (1977). Attitude-behavior relations: A theoretical analysis and review of empirical research. *Psychological Bulletin, 84*, 888–918.

Ajzen, I., and Fishbein, M. (1980). *Understanding attitudes and predicting social behavior.* Englewood Cliffs, NJ: Prentice Hall.

Allen, V.L. (1964). Group reaction to an opinion deviate: The deviate's expectations. Unpublished manuscript, University of Wisconsin.

Allen, V.L. (1965). Situational factors in conformity. In L. Berkowitz (Ed.), *Advances in experimental social psychology* (Vol. 2). New York: Academic Press.

Allen, V.L. (1975). Social support for nonconformity. In L. Berkowitz (Ed.), *Advances in experimental social psychology* (Vol. 8), New York: Academic Press.

Allen, V.L., and Crutchfield, R.S. (1963). Generalization of experimentally reinforced conformity. *Journal of Abnormal and Social Psychology, 67*, 326–333.

Allen, V.L., and Feldman, R.S. (1971). The role of a nonpresent partner in reducing conformity. Unpublished manuscript, University of Wisconsin.

Allen, V.L., and Wilder, D.A. (1980). The impact of group consensus and social support on stimulus meaning: Mediation of conformity by cognitive restructuring. *Journal of Personality and Social Psychology, 34*, 1116–1124.

Allport, G.W. (1935). Attitudes. In C. Murchison (Ed.), *Handbook of social psychology* (Vol. 2). Worcester, MA: Clark University Press.

Allport, G.W. (1954). *The nature of prejudice.* Reading, MA: Addison-Wesley.

Allport, G. (1968). The historical background of modern social psychology. In G. Lindzey and E. Aronson (Eds.), *The handbook of social psychology* (2nd ed., Vol. 1). Reading, MA: Addison-Wesley.

Allport, G.W., and Postman, L. (1947). *The psychology of rumor.* New York: Henry Holt and Co.

Altman, D., Levine, M., Nadien, M., and Villena, J. (1969). Trust of the stranger in the city and the small town. Unpublished manuscript. New York University.

Altman, I. (1975). *The environment and social behavior.* Monterey, CA: Brooks/Cole.

Altman, I., and Taylor, D.A. (1973). *Social penetration: The development of interpersonal relationships.* New York: Holt, Rinehart & Winston.

Altman, I., Vinsel, A., and Brown, B.B. (1981). Dialetic conceptions in social psychology: An application to social penetration and privacy regulation. In L. Berkowitz (Ed.), *Advances in experimental social psychology* (Vol. 14). New York: Academic Press.

Anderson, C.A., and Anderson, D.C. (1984). Ambient temperature and violent crime: Tests of the linear and curvilinear hypothesis. *Journal of Personality and Social Psychology, 46*, 91–97.

Anderson, N.H. (1965). Adding versus averaging as a stimulus combination rule in impression formation. *Journal of Experimental Psychology, 70*, 394–400.

Apfelbaum, E. (1974). On conflicts and bargaining. In L. Berkowitz (Ed.), *Advances in experimental social psychology* (Vol. 7). New York: Academic Press.

Appleyard, D., and Lintell, M. (1972). The environmental quality of city streets: The residents' viewpoint. *Journal of the American Institute of Planners, 38*, 84–101.

Archer, R.L. (1979). Role of personality and the social situation. In G.J. Chelune (Ed.), *Self-disclosure.* San Francisco, CA: Jossey-Bass.

Archer, R.L., Diaz-Loving, R., Gollwitzer, P. Davis, M.H., and Foushee, H.C. (1981). The role of dispositional empathy and social evaluation in empathic mediation of helping. *Journal of Personality and Social Psychology, 40*, 786–796.

Ardrey, R. (1966). *The territorial imperative.* New York: Antheneum.

Arendt, H. (1963). *Eichmann in Jerusalem.* New York: Viking.

Arnold, E. (1967). *A night of watching.* New York: Fawcett.

Aronfreed, J., and Paskal, V. (1965). Altruism, empathy and the conditioning of positive affect. Unpublished manuscript. University of Pennsylvania.

Aronfreed, J., and Paskal, V. (1966). The development of sympathetic behavior in children: An experimental test of a two-phase hypothesis. Unpublished manuscript. University of Pennsylvania.

Aronson, E. (1969). The theory of cognitive dissonance: A current perspective. In L. Berkowitz (Ed.), *Advances in experimental social psychology* (Vol. 4). New York: Academic Press.

Aronson, E., and Carlsmith, J.M. (1968). Experimentation in social psychology. In G. Lindzey and E. Aronson (Eds.), *The handbook of social psychology* (2nd ed. Vol. 2). Reading, MA: Addison-Wesley.

Aronson, E., and Cope, V. (1968). My enemy's enemy is my friend. *Journal of Personality and Social Psychology, 8*, 8–12.

Aronson, E., and Osherow, N. (1980). Cooperation, prosocial behavior and academic performance. In L. Bickman (Ed.), *Applied social psychology annual* (Vol. 1). Beverly Hills, CA: Sage.

Aronson, E., Stephan, C., Sikes, J., Blaney, N., and Snapp, M. (1978). *The jigsaw classroom.* Beverly Hills, CA: Sage.

Aronson, E., Turner, J., and Carlsmith, J.M. (1963). Communicator credibility and communication discrepancy as determinants of opinion change. *Journal of Abnormal and Social Psychology, 67*, 31–36.

Aronson, E., Willerman, B., and Floyd, J. (1966). The effect of a pratfall on increasing interpersonal attractiveness. *Psychonomic Science, 4*, 227–228.

Asch, S.E. (1946). Forming impressions of personality. *Journal of Abnormal and Social Psychology, 41*, 258–290.

Asch, S.E. (1951). Effects of group pressure on the modification and distortion of judgments. In H. Guetzkow (Ed.), *Groups, leadership, and men*. Pittsburgh, PA: Carnegie Press.

Asch, S.E. (1952). *Social psychology*. Englewood Cliffs, NJ: Prentice Hall.

Asch, S.E. (1955). Opinions and social pressures. *Scientific American*, **193**, 31–35.

Asch, S.E. (1957). An experimental investigation of group influence. In *Symposium on preventive and social psychiatry*. Walter Reed Army Institute of Research. Washington, D.C.: U.S. Government Printing Office.

Ashmore, R.D., and Del Boca, F.K. (1976). Psychological approaches to understanding group conflicts. In P.A. Katz (Ed.), *Toward the elimination of racism*. New York: Pergamon Press, 1976.

Atkin, C.K. (1975). *Effects of television advertising on children: Second year experimental evidence* (Report No. 2). East Lansing, MI: Michigan State University Press.

Atkin, C.K. (1977). Effects of campaign advertising and newscasts on children. *Journalism Quarterly*, **54**, 503–508.

Atkin, C.K. (1980). Effects of television advertising on children. In E.L. Palmer and A. Dow (Eds.), *Children and the faces of television: Teaching, violence, selling*. New York: Academic Press.

Austin, W., and Walster, E. (1974). Reactions to confirmations and disconfirmations of expectancies of equity and inequity. *Journal of Personality and Social Psychology*, **30**, 208–216.

Austin, W. (1980). Friendship and fairness: Effects of type of relationship and task performance on choice of distribution rules. *Personality and Social Psychology Bulletin*, **6**, 402–408.

Ax, A.F. (1953). The physiological differentiation between fear and anger in humans. *Psychosomatic Medicine*, **15**, 433–444.

Axelrod, R. (1980). Effective choice in the prisoner's dilemma game. *Journal of Conflict Resolution*, **24**, 3–27.

Axelrod, R.A. (1984). Cited by W.F. Allman in Nice guys finish first. *Science 84*, October, 31, 25–30.

Axelrod, R.A. (1985). Cited by W.F. Allman in ''The Science '84 cooperation experiment-the results.'' *Science 85*, February, 20.

Backman, C.W., and Secord, P. (1959). The effect of perceived liking on interpersonal attraction. *Human Relations*, **12**, 379–384.

Baekeland, F., and Lundwall, L. (1975). Dropping out of treatment: A critical review. *Psychological Bulletin*, **82**, 738–783.

Bagozzi, R.P. (1981). Attitudes, intentions, and behavior: A test of some key hypotheses. *Journal of Personality and Social Psychology*, **41**, 607–627.

Baker, L.D., and Reitz, J. (1978). Altruism toward the blind: Effects of sex of helper and dependency of victim. *Journal of Social Psychology*, **104**, 19–28.

Bales, R.F. (1950). *Interaction process analysis: A method for the study of small groups*. Cambridge, MA: Addison-Wesley.

Bales, R.F. (1958). Task roles and social roles in problem-solving groups. In E.E. Maccoby, T. Newcomb, and E. Hartley (Eds.). *Readings in social psychology*. New York: Holt, Rinehart, & Winston.

Bales, R.F. (1970). *Personality and interpersonal behavior*. New York: Holt, Rinehart & Winston.

Bales, R.F. (1980). *SYMLOG case study kit*. New York: Free Press.

Bales, R.F., and Hare, A.P. (1965). Diagnostic use of the interaction profile. *Journal of Social Psychology*, **67**, 239–258.

Ball, A.W. (1973). Nixon's appointment in Peking-Is this trip necessary? *New York Times Magazine*, Feb. 13, 11, 50–55.

Ball-Rokeach, S.J., Rokeach, M., and Grube, J.W. (1984). The great American values test. *Psychology Today*, **18**, 34–41.

Bandler, R.J., Madaras, G.R., and Bem, D.J. (1968). Self-observation as a source of pain perception. *Journal of Personality and Social Psychology*, **9**, 205–209.

Bandura, A. (1960). *Relationship of family patterns to child behavior disorders. Progress Report*, Stanford University Project No. M-1734, United States Health Service.

Bandura, A. (1965). Influence of models' reinforcement contingencies on the acquisition of imitative responses. *Journal of Personality and Social Psychology*, **1**, 589–595.

Bandura, A., (1969), *Principles of behavior modification*. New York: Holt Rinehart and Winston.

Bandura, A. (1973). *Aggression: A social learning analysis*. Englewood Cliffs, NJ: Prentice-Hall, Inc.

Bandura, A., (1977), *Social learning theory*, Englewood Cliffs NJ: Prentice-Hall.

Bandura, A. (1983). Psychological mechanisms of aggression. In R. Geen & E. Donnerstein (Eds.), *Aggression: Theoretical and empirical reviews* (Vol. 1). New York: Academic Press.

Bandura, A., Ross, D., and Ross, S.A. (1963). Imitation of film mediated aggressive models. *Journal of Abnormal and Social Psychology*, **66**, 3–11.

Bandura, A., and Walters, R.H. (1959). *Adolescent aggression*. New York: Ronald Press.

Bandura, A., and Walters, R.H. (1963). *Social learning and personality development*. New York: Holt, Rinehart, and Winston.

Barash, D.P. (1977). *Sociobiology and behavior*. New York: Elsevier.

Barker, R.G. (1968). *Ecological psychology: Concepts and methods for studying the environment of human behavior*. Stanford, CA: Stanford University Press.

Baron, R.A. (1974a). Aggression as a function of victim's pain cues, level of prior anger arousal, and exposure to an aggressive model. *Journal of Personality and Social Psychology*, **29**, 117–124.

Baron, R.A. (1974b). Sexual arousal and physical aggression: The inhibiting influence of cheesecake and nudes. *Bulletin of the Psychonomic Society*, **29**, 217–219.

Baron, R.A. (1976). The reduction of human aggression: A field study of incompatible reactions. *Journal of Applied Social Psychology*, **6**, 260–274.

Baron, R.A. (1977). *Human aggression*. New York: Plenum.

Baron, R.A. (1978). Invasions of personal space and helping: Mediating effects of invader's apparent need. *Journal of Experimental Social Psychology*, **14**, 304–312.

Baron, R.A. (1979). Heightened sexual arousal and physical aggression: An extension to females. *Journal of Research in Personality*, **13**, 91–102.

Baron, R.A. (1983). The control of human aggression. In R. Geen and E. Donnerstein (Eds.), *Aggression: Theoretical and empirical reviews* (Vol. 2), New York: Academic Press.

Baron, R.A., and Ball, R.L. (1974). The aggression-inhibiting influence of nonhostile humor. *Journal of Experimental Social Psychology*, **10**, 23–33.

Baron, R.A., and Bell, P.A. (1975). Aggression and heat: Mediating effects of prior provocation and exposure to an aggressive model. *Journal of Personality and Social Psychology*, **31**, 825–832.

Baron, R.A., and Bell, P.A. (1976). Aggression and heat: The influence of ambient temperature, negative affect, and a cooling drink on aggression. *Journal of Personality and Social Psychology*, **33**, 245–255.

Baron, R.A., and Ransberger, V.M. (1978). Ambient temperature and the occurrence of collective violence: The long hot summer revisited. *Journal of Personality and Social Psychology*, **36**, 351–360.

Baron, R.M., Mandel, D.R., Adams, C.A., and Griffen, L.M. (1976). Effects of social density in university residential environments. *Journal of Personality and Social Psychology*, **34**, 434–446.

Barthe, D.G., and Hammen, C.L. (1981). The attributional model of depression: A naturalistic extension. *Personality and Social Psychology Bulletin*, **7**, 53–58.

Batson, C.D. (1983). Sociobiology and the role of religion in promoting prosocial behavior: An alternative view. *Journal of Personality and Social Psychology, 45,* 1380–1385.

Batson, C.D., Cochran, P.J., Biederman, M.F., Blosser, J.L., Ryan, M.J., and Vogt, B. (1978). Failure to help when in a hurry: Callousness or conflict? *Personality and Social Psychology Bulletin, 4,* 97–101.

Batson, C.D., and Coke, J.S. (1981). Empathy: A source of altruistic motivation? In J.P. Rushton & R.M. Sorrentino (Eds.), *Altruism and helping behavior.* Hillsdale, NJ: Erlbaum.

Batson, C.D., Duncan, B., Ackerman, P., Buckley, T., and Birch, K. (1981). Is empathic emotion a source of altruistic motivation? *Journal of Personality and Social Psychology, 40,* 290–302.

Batson, C.D., O'Quin, K., Fultz, J., Vanderplas, M., and Isen, A.M. (1983). Influence of self-reported distress and empathy on egoistic versus altruistic motivation to help. *Journal of Personality and Social Psychology, 43,* 706–718.

Batson, C.D., O'Quin, K., and Pych, V. (1982). An attribution theory analysis of trained helpers' inferences about clients' needs. In T.A. Wills (Ed.), *Basic processes in helping relationships.* New York: Academic Press, 1982.

Baum, A., and Davis, G.E. (1976). Spatial and social aspects of crowding perception. *Environment and Behavior, 8,* 527–545.

Baum, A., and Davis, G.E. (1980). Reducing the stress of high-density living: An architectural intervention. *Journal of Personality and Social Psychology, 38,* 471–481.

Baum, A., Harper, J., and Valins, S. (1975). The role of group phenomena in the experience of crowding. *Environment and Behavior, 7,* 185–198.

Baum, A., Reiss, M., and O'Hara, J. (1974). Architectural variants of reaction to spatial invasion. *Environment and Behavior, 6,* 91–100.

Baum, A., and Valins, S. (1977). *Architecture and social behavior: Psychological studies in social density.* Hillsdale, NJ: Lawrence Erlbaum.

Baum, A., and Valins, S. (1979). Architectural mediation of residential density and control: Crowding and the regulation of social contact. In L. Berkowitz (Ed.), *Advances in experimental social psychology* (Vol. 12). New York: Academic Press.

Baumrind, D. (1964). Some thoughts on ethics of research: After reading Milgram's Behavioral study of 'obedience'. *American Psychologist, 19,* 421–423.

Baumeister, R.F., and Steinhilber, A. (1984). Paradoxical effects of supportive audiences on performance under pressure: The home field disadvantage in sports championships. *Journal of Personality and Social Psychology, 47,* 85–93.

Beach, F. (1969). Its all in your mind. *Psychology Today, 3,* 33–35.

Beamen, A.L., Cole, C.M., Preston, M., Klentz, B., and Steblay, N.M. (1983). Fifteen years of foot-in-the-door research: A meta-analysis. *Personality and Social Psychology Bulletin, 9,* 181–186.

Becker, F.D., Sommer, R., Bee, J., and Oxley, B. (1973). College classroom ecology. *Sociometry, 36,* 514–525.

Beckham, B., and Aronson, H. (1978). Selection of jury foremen as a measure of the social status of women. *Psychological Reports, 43,* 475–478.

Beer, M. (1976). The technology of organizational development. In M.D. Dunnette (Ed.), *Handbook of industrial and organizational psychology.* Chicago: Rand McNally.

Bell, P.A. (1980). Effects of heat, noise, and provocation on retaliatory evaluative behavior. *Journal of Personality and Social Psychology, 40,* 97–100.

Bell, P.A., and Baron, R.A. (1974). Environmental influences on attention: Effects of heat, attitude similarity, and personal evaluations. *Bulletin of the Psychonomic Society, 4,* 479–481.

Bell, P.A., and Baron, R.A. (1976). Aggression and heat: The mediators role of negative affect. *Journal of Applied Social Psychology, 6,* 18–30.

Bell, P.A., and Baron, R.A. (1977). Aggression and ambient temperature: The facilitating and inhibiting effects of hot and cold environments. *Bulletin of the Psychonomic Society, 4,* 443–445.

Bellezza, F.S., and Bower, G.H. (1981). Person stereotypes and memory for people. *Journal of Personality and Social Psychology, 41,* 856–865.

Bem, D.J. (1967). Self-perception: An alternative explanation of cognitive dissonance phenomena. *Psychological Review, 74,* 183–200.

Bem, D.J. (1970). *Beliefs, attitudes, and human affairs.* Belmont, CA: Brooks/Cole.

Bem, D.J. (1972). Self-perception theory, In L. Berkowitz (Ed.), *Advances in experimental social psychology* (Vol. 6). New York: Academic Press.

Bem, D.J., and Allen, A. (1974). On predicting some of the people some of the time: The search for cross-situational consistency. *Psychological Review, 81,* 506–520.

Bennet, R., Rafferty, J.M., Canivez, G.L., and Smith, J.M. (1983). The effects of cold temperature on altruism and aggression. Paper presented at annual meeting of the Midwestern Psychological Association.

Berglas, S., and Jones, E.E. (1978). Drug choice as a self-handicapping strategy in response to noncontingent success. *Journal of Personality and Social Psychology, 36,* 405–417.

Bergman, A.B., and Werner, R.T. (1963). Failure of children to receive penicillin by mouth. *New England Journal of Medicine, 268,* 1334–1338.

Berkowitz, L. (1962). *Aggression: A social psychological analysis.* New York: McGraw-Hill.

Berkowitz, L. (1965). The concept of aggressive drive. In L. Berkowitz (Ed.), *Advances in experimental social psychology* (Vol. 2). New York: Academic Press.

Berkowitz, L. (1968). Impulse, aggression and the gun. *Psychology Today, 2,* 16–22.

Berkowitz, L. (1969). The frustration-aggression hypothesis revisited. In L. Berkowitz (Ed.), *Roots of aggression.* New York: Atherton Press.

Berkowitz, L. (1971). The contagion of violence: An S-R, mediational analysis of some effects of observed aggression. In W. Arnold & M. Page (Eds.), *Nebraska symposium on motivation.* Lincoln, NB: University of Nebraska Press.

Berkowitz, L. (1974). Some determinants of impulsive aggression: Role of mediated associations with reinforcements for aggression. *Psychological Review, 81,* 165–176.

Berkowitz, L. (1983). The experience of anger as a parallel process in the display of impulsive "angry" aggression. In R. Geen & E. Donnerstein (Eds.), *Aggression: Theoretical and empirical reviews* (Vol. 1). New York: Academic Press.

Berkowitz, L., and Alioto, J.T. (1973). The meaning of an observed event as a determinant of its aggressive consequences. *Journal of Personality and Social Psychology, 28,* 206–217.

Berkowitz, L., and Donnerstein, E. (1982). External validity is more than skin deep: Some answers to criticisms of laboratory experiments. *American Psychologist, 37,* 245–257.

Berkowitz, L., and Geen, R.C. (1967). Stimulus qualities of the target of aggression: A further study. *Journal of Personality and Social Psychology, 5,* 364–368.

Berkowitz, L., and Knurek, D.A. (1969). Label-mediated hostility generalization. *Journal of Personality and Social Psychology, 13,* 200–206.

Berkowitz, L., and LePage, A. (1967). Weapons as aggression-eliciting stimuli. *Journal of Personality and Social Psychology*, **7**, 202–207.

Berscheid, E., Dion, K., Walster, E. and Walster, G.W. (1971). Physical attractiveness and dating choice: A test of the matching hypothesis. *Journal of Experimental Social Psychology*, **7**, 173–189.

Berscheid, E. and Walster, E. (1969). *Interpersonal attraction*. Reading, MA: Addison-Wesley.

Berscheid, E., and Walster, E. (1972). Beauty and the best. *Psychology Today*, **6**, 42–46, 74.

Bersheid, E., and Walster, E. (1974a). A little bit about love. In T.L. Huston (Ed.), *Foundations of interpersonal attraction*. New York: Academic Press.

Berscheid, E., and Walster, E. (1974b). Physical attractiveness. In L. Berkowitz (Ed.), *Advances in experimental social psychology* (Vol. 7). New York: Academic Press.

Berscheid, E., and Walster, E. (1978). *Interpersonal attraction* (2nd Ed.). Reading, MA: Addison-Wesley.

Berscheid, E., Walster, E., and Bohrnstadt, G. (1973). Body image. *Psychology Today*, **7**, 119–131.

Beuf, A. (1974). Doctor, lawyer, and household drudge. *Journal of Communication*, **24**, 142–145.

Bickman, L., and Kamzan, M. (1973). The effect of race and need on helping behavior. *Journal of Social Psychology*, **89**, 73–77.

Birchler, C.R., Weiss, R.L., and Vincent, J.P. (1975). Multimethod analysis of social reinforcement exchange between maritally distressed and nondistressed spouse and stranger dyads. *Journal of Personality and Social Psychology*, **31**, 349–360.

Bixenstine, V.E., and Gaebelin, J.N. (1971). Strategies of "real" opponents in eliciting cooperative choice in a prisoner's dilemma game. *Journal of Conflict Resolution*, **15**, 157–166.

Blake, R.R., and Mouton, J.S. (1964). *The managerial grid*. Houston, TX: Gulf.

Blake, R.R., and Mouton, J.S. (1978). *The new managerial grid*. Houston, TX: Gulf.

Blalock, H.M. (1967). *Toward a theory of minority group relations*. New York: Wiley.

Blaney, N.T., Stephan, C., Rosenfield, D., Aronson, E., and Sikes, J. (1977). Interdependence in the classroom: A field study. *Journal of Educational Psychology*, **69**, 139–146.

Bobo, L. (1983). Whites' opposition to busing: Symbolic racism or realistic group conflict? *Journal of Personality and Social Psychology*, **45**, 1196–1210.

Bochner, S., and Insko, C. (1966). Communicator discrepancy, source credibility, and influence. *Journal of Personality and Social Psychology*, **4**, 61.

Bogart, K., Loeb, A., and Rittman, J. (1969). Behavioral consequences of cognitive dissonance. Paper presented at annual meeting of the Eastern Psychological Association.

Boggiano, A.K., and Ruble, D.N. (1979). Competence and the overjustification effect: A developmental study. *Journal of Personality and Social Psychology*, **37**, 1462–1468.

Bond, C.F. (1981). Dissonance and the pill: An interpersonal simulator. *Personality and Social Psychology Bulletin*, **7**, 398–403.

Bond, C.F., and Titus, L.J. (1983). Social facilitation: A meta-analysis of 241 studies. *Psychological Bulletin*, **94**, 265–292.

Borden, R.J. (1980). Audience influence. In P.B. Paulus (Ed.), *Psychology of group influence*. Hillsdale, NJ: Lawrence Erlbaum.

Bornstein, M.H. (1979). The pace of life revisited. *International Journal of Psychology*, **14**, 83–90.

Bowlby, J. (1973). *Attachment and loss* (Vol. 2): *Separation*. London: Hogarth.

Boyanowsky, E.O., and Allen, V.L. (1973). Ingroup norms and self-identity as determinants of discriminatory behavior. *Journal of Personality and Social Psychology*, **23**, 408–418.

Bragg, B.W.E., and Dooley, S.I. (1972). Generalization of resistance in conformity pressure. *Proceedings of the 80th Annual Convention of the American Psychological Association*, **7**, 167–168.

Bramel, D.A. (1962). A dissonance theory approach to defensive projection. *Journal of Abnormal and Social Psychology*, **69**, 121–129.

Brehm, J. (1960). A dissonance analysis of attitude-discrepant behavior. In M.J. Rosenberg, C.I. Hovland, W.J. McGuire, R.P. Abelson, and J.W. Brehm, (Eds.), *Attitude organization and change: An analysis of consistency among attitude components*. New Haven, CT: Yale University Press.

Brehm, J. (1966). *A theory of psychological reactance*. New York: Academic Press.

Brehm, J., and Cohen, A. (1962). *Explorations in cognitive dissonance*. New York: Wiley.

Brehm, S.S., and Brehm, J.W. (1981). *Psychological reactance: A theory of freedom and control*. New York: Academic Press.

Brewer, M. (1979). The role of ethnocentrism in intergroup conflict. In W.C. Austin and S. Worchel (Eds.), *The social psychology of intergroup relations*. Monterey, CA: Brooks/Cole.

Brewer, M., Dull, V., and Liu, L. (1981). Perceptions of the elderly: Stereotypes as prototypes. *Journal of Personality and Social Psychology*, **41**, 656–670.

Brigham, J.C., Maass, A., Snyder, L.D., and Spaulding, K. (1982). Accuracy of eyewitness identifications in a field setting. *Journal of Personality and Social Psychology*, **42**, 673–681.

Brinberg, D., and Castell, P. (1982). A resource exchange theory approach to interpersonal interactions: A test of Foa's theory. *Journal of Personality and Social Psychology*, **43**, 260–269.

Broadbent, D.E. (1971). *Decision and stress*. New York: Academic Press.

Broadbent, D.E. (1979). Human performance and noise. In C.M. Harris (Ed.), *Handbook of noise control*. New York: McGraw-Hill.

Brock, T.C., and Shavitt, S. (1983). Cognitive-response analysis in advertising. In L. Percy and A.C. Woodside (Eds.), *Advertising and consumer psychology*. Lexington, MA: Heath and Company.

Brodt, E.E., and Zimbardo, P.G. (1981). Modifying shyness-related behavior through symptom misattribution. *Journal of Personality and Social Psychology*, **41**, 437–449.

Bronzaft, A.L. (1981). The effect of a noise abatement program on reading ability. *Journal of Environmental Psychology*, **1**, 215–222.

Bronzaft, A.L., and McCarthy, D.P. (1975). The effect of elevated train noise on reading ability. *Environment and Behavior*, **7**, 517–528.

Brotman, H. (1974). The fastest growing minority: The aging. *American Journal of Public Health*, **64**, 249–252.

Brown, B. (1974). Depression roundup. *Behavior Today*, **5**, 117.

Brown, J. (1985). Mock segregation real for some. *Atlanta Constitution*, January 6.

Brown, P., and Elliott, R. (1965). Control of aggression in a nursery school class. *Journal of Experimental Child Psychology*, **2**, 103–107.

Brundage, L.E., Derlega, V.J., and Cash, T.F. (1977). The effects of physical attractiveness and need for approval on self-disclosure. *Personality and Social Psychology Bulletin*, **3**, 63–66.

Brunson, B.I., and Matthews, K.A. (1981). Type A coronary-prone behavior pattern and reactions to uncontrollable events: An analysis of learned helplessness. *Journal of Personality and Social Psychology*, **40**, 906–918.

Bryan, J.H., and Walbek, N.H. (1970). The impact of words and deeds concerning altruism upon children. *Child Development*, **41**, 747–757.

Buckhout, R. (1980). Nearly 2000 witnesses can be wrong. *Bulletin of Psychonomic Society*, **16**, 307–310.

Burger, J.M., and Petty, R.E. (1981). The low-ball compliance technique: Task or person commitment? *Journal of Personality and Social Psychology*, **40**, 492—499.

Burgess, F.W., and Wallin, P. (1953). Homogamy in social characteristics. *American Journal of Sociology*, **49**, 109–124.

Burnam, M.A., Pennebacker, J.W., and Glass, D.C. (1975). Time consciousness, achievement striving, and the coronary-prone behavior pattern. *Journal of Abnormal Psychology*, **84**, 76–79.

Burt, M.R. (1980). Cultural myths and supports for rape. *Journal of Personality and Social Psychology*, **38**, 217–230.

Buss, A.H. (1971). Aggression pays. In J.L. Singer (Ed.), *The control of violence and aggression*. New York: Academic Press.

Buss, A.H. (1980). *Self-consciousness and social anxiety*. San Francisco, CA: Freeman.

Buss, A.H. (1983). Social rewards and personality. *Journal of Personality and Social Psychology*, **44**, 553–563.

Buss, A.H., Booker, A., and Buss, E. (1972). Firing a weapon and aggression. *Journal of Personality and Social Psychology*, **22**, 196–202.

Byrne, D. (1971). *The attraction paradigm*. New York: Academic Press.

Byrne, D., and Clore, G.L. (1970) A reinforcement model of evaluative responses. *Personality: An International Journal*, **1**, 103–128.

Byrne, D., and Nelson, D. (1965). Attraction as a linear function of proportion of positive reinforcements. *Journal of Personality and Social Psychology*, **1**, 659–663.

Byrne, D., and Wong, T.J. (1962). Racial prejudice, interpersonal attraction, and assumed similarity of attitudes. *Journal of Abnormal and Social Psychology*, **65**, 246–252.

Cacioppo, J.T., and Petty, R.E. (1980). Persuasiveness of communication is affected by exposure frequency and message quality: A theoretical and empirical analysis of persisting attitude change. In J.H. Leight and C.R. Martin (Eds.), *Issues and research in advertising*: Ann Arbor, MI: University of Michigan Press.

Calder, B.J., and Ross, M. (1973). *Attitudes and behavior*. Morristown, NJ: General Learning Press.

Calder, B.J., and Sternthal, B. (1980). Television commercial wearout: An information processing view. *Journal of Marketing Research*, **17**, 173–186.

Calhoun, J.B. (1962). Population density and social pathology. *Scientific American*, **206**, 139–148.

Callahan-Levy, C.M., and Messe, L.A. (1979). Sex differences in allocation of pay. *Journal of Personality and Social Psychology*, **37**, 433–446.

Campbell, D.E., and Herren, K.A. (1978). Interior arrangement of the faculty office. *Psychological Reports*, **43**, 234.

Campbell, D.T. (1947). The generality of social attitudes. Unpublished doctoral dissertation. University of California, Berkeley.

Campbell, D.T. (1963). Social attitudes and other acquired behavioral dispositions. In S. Koch (Ed.), *Psychology: A study of science* (Vol. 6). New York: McGraw-Hill.

Campbell, D.T., and Fiske, D.W. (1959). Convergent and discriminant validation by the multitrait multimethod matrix. *Psychological Bulletin*, **56**, 81–105.

Campbell, D.T., and Stanley, J. (1966). *Experimental and quasi-experimental designs for research*. Chicago: Rand McNally.

Cannell, C.F., and Kahn, R.L. (1968). Interviewing. In G. Lindzey and E. Aronson (Eds.), *Handbook of social psychology* (2nd ed. Vol. 2). Reading, MA: Addison-Wesley.

Cantor, J.R., Zillman, D., and Bryant, J. (1975). Enhancement of sexual arousal in response to erotic stimuli through misattribution of unrelated residual arousal. *Journal of Personality and Social Psychology*, **32**, 69–75.

Cantor, N., and Mischel, M. (1979). Prototypes in person perception. In L. Berkowitz (Ed.), *Advances in experimental social psychology* (Vol. 12). New York: Academic Press.

Caplan, R.D., Harrison, R.V., Wellons, R.V., French, J.R.P. (1980). Social support, person-environment fit, and coping. In L. Furman and J. Gordis (Eds.), *Mental health and the economy*, Kalamazoo, MI: Upjohn.

Carlsmith, J.M., and Anderson, C. (1979). Ambient temperature and the occurrence of collective violence: A new analysis. *Journal of Personality and Social Psychology*, **37**, 337–344.

Caroll, J.S., and Payne, J.W. (1979). Crime seriousness, recidivism risk, and causal attributions in judgments of prison term by students and experts. *Journal of Applied Psychology*, **62**, 595–602.

Carter, R. (1975). *The sixteenth round: From number 1 contender to number 45472*. New York: Warner Books.

Cartwright, D. (1979). Contemporary social psychology in historical perspective. *Social Psychology Quarterly*, **42**, 82–93.

Cartwright, D., and Harary, F. (1956). Structural balance: A generalization of Heider's Theory. *Psychological Review*, **63**, 277–293.

Carver, C.S., and Glass, D.C. (1978). Coronary prone behavior pattern and interpersonal aggression. *Journal of Personality and Social Psychology*, **36**, 361–366.

Carver, C.S., and Scheier, M.F. (1978). Self focusing effects of dispositional self-consciousness, mirror presence, and audience presence. *Journal of Personality and Social Psychology*, **36**, 324–332.

Case, F.D. (1981). Dormitory architecture influences: Patterns of student social relations over time. *Environment and Behavior*, **13**, 23–41.

Cash, T.F., Gillen, B., and Burns, S.D. (1977). Sexism and "beautyism" in personnel consultant decision making. *Journal of Applied Psychology*, **62**, 301–310.

Cattell, R.B., and Nesselroade, J.R. (1967). Likeness and the completeness theories examined by sixteen personality factor measures on stably and unstably married couples. *Journal of Personality and Social Psychology*, **7**, 351–361.

Cerf, C., and Navasky, V. (1984). *The experts speak: A definitive compendium of authoritative misinformation*. New York: Pantheon.

Chaffee, S.H., Jackson-Beeck, M., Durall, J., and Wilson, D. (1977). Mass communication in political communication. In S.A. Renshon (Ed.), *Handbook of political socialization: Theory and research*. New York: Free Press.

Chaiken, A.L., and Derlega, V.J. (1974). Liking for the norm breaker in self-disclosure. *Journal of Personality*, **42**, 117–124.

Chaiken, S. (1979). Communicator physical attractiveness and persuasion. *Journal of Personality and Social Psychology*, **37**, 1387–1397.

Chaiken, S. (1983). Physical appearance variables and social influence. In C.P. Hermann, E.T. Higgins, and M. Zanna (Eds.), *Physical appearance, stigma, and social behavior: The third Ontario symposium*. Hillsdale, NJ: Erlbaum Associates.

Chaiken, S., and Eagly, A.H. (1983). Communication modality as a determinant of persuasion: The role of communicator salience. *Journal of Personality and Social Psychology*, **45**, 241–256.

Chance, J.E. (1972). Academic correlates and maternal antecedents of children's belief in external or internal control of reinforcements. In J.B. Rotter, J.E. Chance, and E.J. Phares (Eds.), *Applications of a social learning theory of personality*. New York: Holt, Rinehart and Winston.

Chapman, A.J. (1973). An electromyographic study of apprehension about evaluation. *Psychological Reports*, **33**, 811–814.

Charney, E. (1972). Patient-doctor communications: Implications for the clinician. *Pediatric Clinics of North America*, **19**, 263–279.

Check, J.V.P., and Malamuth, N. (1983). Sex role sterotyping and reactions to depictions of stranger versus acquaintance rape. *Journal of Personality and Social Psychology*, **45**, 344–356.

Cheek, J. (1982). Aggregation, moderator variables, and the validity of personality tests: A peer-rating study. *Journal of Personality and Social Psychology*, **43**, 1254–1269.

Christie, R., and Geis, F.L. (1970). *Studies in Machiavellianism*. New York: Academic Press.

Cialdini, R.B. (1984). *Influence: How and why people agree to things*. New York: Morrow.

Cialdini, R.B., Baumann, D.J., and Kenrick, D.T. (1981). Insights from sadness: A three step model of the development of altruism as hedonism. *Developmental Review*, **1**, 207–223.

Cialdini, R.B., Bickman, L,, and Cacioppo, J.T. (1979). An example of consumeristic social psychology: Bargaining tough in the new car showroom. *Journal of Applied Social Psychology*, **9**, 115–126.

Cialdini, R.B., Borden, R.J., Thorne, A., Walker, R.M., Freeman, S., and Sloan, R.E. (1976). Basking in reflected glory: Three football field studies. *Journal of Personality and Social Psychology*, **34**, 366–375.

Cialdini, R.B., Cacioppo, J.T., Bassett, R., and Miller, J.A. (1978). Low-ball procedure for producing compliance: Commitment then cost. *Journal of Personality and Social Psychology*, **36**, 463–477.

Cialdini, R.B., Darby, B.L., and Vincent, J.E. (1973). Transgression and altruism: A case for hedonism. *Journal of Experimental Social Psychology*, **9**, 502–516.

Cialdini, R.B., and Kenrick, D.T. (1976). Altruism as hedonism: A social development perspective on the relationship of negative mood state and helping. *Journal of Personality and Social Psychology*, **34**, 907–914.

Cialdini, R.B., Kenrick, D.T., and Baumann, D.J. (1982). Effects of mood on prosocial behavior in children and adults. In N. Eisenberg-Berg (Ed.), *Development of prosocial behavior*. New York: Academic Press.

Cialdini, R.B., Petty, R.E., and Cacioppo, J.T. (1981). Attitude and attitude change. *Annual Review of Psychology*, **32**, 357–404.

Cialdini, R.B., Vincent, J.E., Lewis, S.K., Catalan, J., Wheeler, D., and Darby, B.L. (1975). Reciprocal concessions procedure for inducing compliance. The door in the face technique. *Journal of Personality and Social Psychology*, **31**, 206–215.

Clark, M.S., and Mills, J. (1979). Interpersonal attraction in exchange and communal relationships. *Journal of Personality and Social Psychology*, **37**, 12–24.

Clifford, M.M., and Walster, E. (1973). The effects of physical attractiveness on teacher expectation. *Sociology of Education*, **46**, 248–258.

Clore, G.L., and Byrne, D. (1974). A reinforcement-affect model of attraction. In T.L. Huston (Ed.), *Foundations of interpersonal attraction*. New York: Academic Press.

Coch, L., and French, J.R.P., Jr. (1948). Overcoming resistance to change. *Human Relations*, **1**, 512–532.

Coffin, R.A. (1973). *The negotiator: A manual for winners*. New York: Amacom.

Cohen, R.L. (1982). Perceiving injustice: An attributional perspective. In J. Greenberg and R.L. Cohen (Eds.), *Equity and justice in social behavior*. New York: Academic Press.

Cohen, S. (1978). Environmental load and the narrowing of attention. In A. Baum, J.E. Singer and S. Valins (Eds.), *Advances in environmental psychology* (Vol. 1). Hillsdale, NJ: Erlbaum.

Cohen, S., Evans, G.W., Krantz, D.S., and Stokols, D. (1980). Physiological, motivational, and cognitive effects of aircraft noise on children. *American Psychologist*, **35**, 231–243.

Cohen, S., Evans, G.W., Krantz, D.S., Stokols, D., and Kelly, S. (1981). Aircraft noise and children: Longitudinal and cross-sectional evidence on adaptation to noise and the effectiveness of noise abatement. *Journal of Personality and Social Psychology*, **40**, 331–345.

Cohen, S., and Weinstein, N. (1981). Nonauditory effects of noise on behavior and health. *Journal of Social Issues*, **37**, 36–70.

Cohen, S.P., Kelman, H.C., Miller, F.D., and Smith, B.L. (1977). Evolving intergroup techniques for conflict resolution: An Israeli-Palestinian pilot workshop. *Journal of Social Issues*, **33**, 165–189.

Coke, J.S., Batson, C.D., and McDavis, K. (1978). Empathic mediation of helping: A two-stage model. *Journal of Personality and Social Psychology*, **36**, 752–766.

Coleman, J.C., Butcher, J.N., and Carson, R.C. (1980). *Abnormal behavior and modern life*. Glenview, IL: Scott, Foresman and Co.

Collins, B.E., and Raven, B.H. (1969). Group structure: Attraction, coalitions, communication, and power. In G. Lindzey and E. Aronson (Eds.), *The handbook of social psychology* (2nd ed. Vol. 4). Reading, MA: Addison-Wesley.

Collins, J.K. (1981). Self-recognition of the body and its parts during adolescence. *Journal of Youth and Adolescence*, **10**, 243–254.

Comstock, G., Chafee, S., Katzman, N., McCombs, N., and Roberts, D. (1978). *Television and human behavior*. New York: Columbia University Press.

Connell, R.W. (1972). Political socialization in the American family: The evidence reexamined. *Public Opinion Quarterly*, **36**, 323–333.

Conroy, W.J., Katkin, F.S., and Barnette, W.L. (1973). Modification of smoking behavior by use of a self-confrontation technique. Paper presented at annual meeting of the Southeastern Psychological Association.

Cook, K.S., and Hegtvedt, K.A. (1983). Distributive justice, equity, and equality. *Annual Review of Sociology*, **9**, 217–241.

Cook, S. (1979). Social science and school desegregation: Did we mislead the supreme court? *Personality and Social Psychology Bulletin*, **5**, 420–437.

Cook, S. (1984). The 1954 social science statement and school desegregation: A reply to Gerard. *American Psychologist*, **39**, 819–832.

Cook, T.D., and Campbell, D.T. (1979). *Quasi-experimentation: Design and analysis issues for field settings*. Boston, MA: Houghton Mifflin.

Cook, T.D., and Flay, B.R. (1978). The persistence of experimentally induced attitude change. In L. Berkowitz (Ed.), *Advances in experimental social psychology* (Vol. 11). New York: Academic Press.

Cooley, C.H. (1922). *Human nature and the social order*. New York: Charles Scribner's Sons.

Cooper, H.M. (1979). Statistically combining independent studies: Meta-analysis of sex differences in conformity. *Journal of Personality and Social Psychology*, **37**, 131–146.

Cooper, H.M., Burger, J.M., and Good, T.L. (1981). Gender differences in academic locus of control beliefs of young children. *Journal of Personality and Social Psychology*, **40**, 562–572.

Cooper, J. (1980). Reducing fears and increasing assertiveness: The role of dissonance reduction. *Journal of Experimental Social Psychology*, **16**, 558–593.

Cooper, J., and Axsom, D. (1982). Effort justification in psychotherapy. In G. Weary and H.L. Mirels (Eds.), *Integrations of clinical and social psychology*. New York: Oxford University Press.

Cooper, J., and Croyle, R.T. (1984). Attitudes and attitude change. *Annual Review of Psychology*, **35**, 395–426.

Cooper, J., and Worchel, S. (1970). Role of undesirable consequences in arousing cognitive dissonance. *Journal of Personality and Social Psychology*, **16**, 199–206.

Corning, P.A., and Corning, C.H. (1972). Toward a general theory of violent aggression. *Social Science Information*, **11**, 7–35.

Costanzo, P.R., Coie, J.D., Grumet, S.F., and Farnill, D.A. (1973). A reexamination of intent and consequence on childrens' moral judgments. *Child Development*, **44**, 154–161.

Cottrell, N.B. (1972). Social facilitation. In C.G. McClintock (Ed.), *Experimental social psychology*. New York: Holt, Rinehart, and Winston.

Courtney, A.E., and Whipple, T.W. (1983). *Sex stereotyping in advertising*. Lexington, MA: Lexington Books.

Courtright, J.A. (1978). A laboratory investigation of groupthink. *Communication Monographs*, **43**, 229–246.

Cowen, E.L. (1982). Help is where you find it: Four informal helping groups. *American Psychologist*, **37**, 385–395.

Cowen, E.L., Gesten, E.L., Boike, M., Norton, P., Wilson, A.B., and deStefano, M.A. (1979). Hairdressers as caregivers I: A descriptive profile of interpersonal help giving involvements. *American Journal of Community Psychology*, **7**, 633–648.

Cowan, E.L., Gesten, E.L., Davidson, E.R., and Wilson, A.B. (1981a). Hairdressers as caregivers II: Relationship between helper-characteristics and help-giving behavior and feelings. *Journal of Prevention*, 1, 225–239.

Cowen, E.L., McKim, B., and Weissberg, R.P. (1981b). Bartenders as informal interpersonal help-agents. *American Journal of Community Psychology*, **9**, 715–729.

Cox, V.C., Paulus, P.B., McCain, G., and Karlovac, M. (1982). The relationship between crowding and health. In A. Baum and S. Valins (Eds.), *Advances in environmental psychology* (Vol. 4). Hillsdale, NJ: Erlbaum.

Crandall, V.C. (1973). Differences in parental antecedents of internal-external control in children and young adulthood. Paper presented at annual meeting of the American Psychological Association.

Creekmore, C.R. (1985). Cities won't drive you crazy. *Psychology Today*, **19**, 46–53.

Crowne, D.P., and Marlowe, D. (1964). *The approval motive*. New York: Wiley.

Croyle, R.T., and Cooper, J. (1983). Dissonance arousal: Physiological evidence. *Journal of Personality and Social Psychology*, **45**, 782–791.

Cunningham, M.R. (1979). Weather, mood, and helping: Quasi-experiments with the sunshine Samaritan. *Journal of Personality and Social Psychology*, **37**, 1947–1956.

Cunningham, M.R., Steinberg, J., and Grev, R. (1980). Wanting to and having to help: Separate motivations for positive mood and guilt induced helping. *Journal of Personality and Social Psychology*, **38**, 181–192.

D'Atri, D.A. (1975). Psychophysiological responses to crowding. *Environment and Behavior*, **7**, 237–252.

Daniels, L.A. (1982). In defense of busing. *New York Times Magazine*, April 17, 34–37, 92–98.

Dansereau, F. Jr., Graen, G., and Haga, W.J. (1975). A vertical dyad linkage approach to leadership within formal organizations: A longitudinal investigation of the role making process. *Organizational Behavior and Human Performance*, **13**, 46–78.

Darley, J.M., and Batson, C.D. (1973). From Jerusalem to Jericho: A study of situational and dispositional variables in helping behavior. *Journal of Personality and Social Psychology*, **27**, 100–108.

Darley, J.M., and Goethals, G.R. (1980). People's analysis of the causes of ability linked performance. In L. Berkowitz (Ed.), *Advances in experimental social psychology* (Vol. 13). New York: Academic Press.

Darley, J.M., and Latané, B. (1968). Bystander intervention in emergencies: Diffusion of responsibility. *Journal of Personality and Social Psychology*, **8**, 377–383.

Darwin, C. (1859). *On the origin of the species by means of natural selection*. London: Murray.

Davidson, A.R., and Jaccard, J. (1979). Variables that moderate the attitude-behavior relation: Results of a longitudinal survey. *Journal of Personality and Social Psychology*, **37**, 1364–1376.

Davies, J.C. (1962). Toward a theory of revolution. *American Sociological Review*, **27**, 5–19.

Davis, J.H. (1969). *Group performance*. Reading, MA: Addison-Wesley.

Davis, J.H. (1980). Group decision and procedural justice. In M. Fishbein (Ed.), *Progress in social psychology* (Vol. 1). Hillsdale, NJ: Erlbaum.

Davis, J.H., Kerr, N.L., Atkin, R., Holt, R., and Meek, D. (1975). The decision processes of 6- and 12-person juries assigned unanimous and two-third majority rules. *Journal of Personality and Social Psychology*, **32**, 1–14.

Davis, K.E., and Jones, E.E. (1960). Changes in interpersonal perception as a means of reducing cognitive dissonance. *Journal of Abnormal and Social Psychology*, **61**, 402–410.

Davis, M.H. (1980). Measuring individual differences in empathy. *JSAS Catalog of Selected Documents in Psychology*, **10**, 85.

Davis, M.H. (1983). Empathic concern and the muscular dystrophy telethon: Empathy as a multidimensional construct. *Personality and Social Psychology Bulletin*, **9**, 223–229.

Davis, W.L., and Phares, E.J. (1969). Parental antecedents of internal-external control of reinforcement. *Psychological Reports*, **24**, 427–436.

Dawkins, R. (1976). *The selfish gene*. Oxford: Oxford University Press.

de Charms, R. (1972). Personal causation training in the schools. *Journal of Applied Social Psychology*, **2**, 95–113.

Deaux, K. (1978). Sex related patterns of social interaction. Paper presented at annual meeting of the Midwestern Psychological Association.

Deci, E.L., and Ryan, R.M. (1980). The empirical exploration of intrinsic motivational processes. In L. Berkowitz (Ed.), *Advances in experimental social psychology* (Vol. 13). New York: Academic Press.

Defoe, D. (1719). *Robinson Crusoe* (Reprinted 1948). New York: Modern Library.

De Jong, W. (1979). An examination of self-perception mediation of the foot in the door effect. *Journal of Personality and Social Psychology*, **37**, 2171–2180.

De Jong, W. (1981). Consensus information and the foot in the door effect. *Personality and Social Psychology Bulletin*, **7**, 423–430.

Delbecq, A.L., Van de Ven, A.H., and Gustafson, D.H. (1975). *Group techniques for program planning*. Glenview, IL: Scott, Foresman.

Delgado, J.M. (1967). Social rank and radio-stimulated aggressiveness in monkeys. *Journal of Nervous and Mental Disease*, **144**, 383–390.

Dengerink, H.A., and Bertilson, H.A. (1975). Psychopathy and physiological arousal in an aggressive task. *Psychophysiology*, **12**, 682–684.

Derlega, V.J., Harris, M.S., and Chaikin, A.L. (1973). Self-disclosure reciprocity, liking, and the deviant. *Journal of Experimental Social Psychology*, **9**, 277–284.

Derlega, V.J., Wilson, M., and Chaikin, A.L. (1976). Friendship and disclosure reciprocity. *Journal of Personality and Social Psychology*, **34**, 578–582.

Desor, J.A. (1972). Toward a psychological theory of crowding. *Journal of Personality and Social Psychology*, **21**, 79–83.

Deutsch, M. (1975). Equity, equality, and need: What determines which value will be used as the basis of distributive justice? *Journal of Social Issues*, **31**, 137–149.

Deutsch, M., and Gerard, H. (1955). A study of normative and informational social influences upon individual judgment. *Journal of Abnormal and Social Psychology*, **51**, 629–636.

Deutsch, M., and Krause, R.M. (1960). The effect of threat on interpersonal bargaining. *Journal of Abnormal and Social Psychology*, **61**, 181–189.

Devlin, P. (1976). *Report to the secretary for the home department of the departmental committee on evidence of identifications in criminal cases.* London: Her Majesty's Stationary Office.

Diener, E. (1980). Deindividuation: The absence of self-awareness and self-regulation in group members. In P. Paulus (Ed.), *The psychology of group influence.* Hillsdale, NJ: Erlbaum.

Diener, E., and De Four, D. (1978). Does television violence enhance program popularity? *Journal of Personality and Social Psychology*, **36**, 333–341.

Diener, E., Fraser, S.C., Beamen, A.L., and Kelem, R.T. (1976). Effects of deindividuation variables on stealing among Halloween trick or treaters. *Journal of Personality and Social Psychology*, **33**, 497–507.

Dillman, D.A. (1978). *Mail and telephone surveys: The total design method.* New York: Wiley-Interscience.

Dillman, D.A., and Tremblay, K., Jr. (1977). The quality of life in rural America. *Annals of the American Academy of Political and Social Sciences*, **429**, 115–129.

Di Matteo, M.R. (1979). A social psychological analysis of physician patient rapport: Toward a science of the art of medicine. *Journal of Social Issues*, **35**, 12–33.

Dion, K.K. (1973). Young children's stereotyping of facial attractiveness. *Developmental Psychology*, **9**, 183–188.

Dion, K.K., Berschied, E., and Walster, E. (1972). What is beautiful is good. *Journal of Personality and Social Psychology*, **24**, 285–290.

Directory of the American Psychological Association (1986). Washington, DC.: American Psychological Association.

Doherty, W.J. (1983). Impact of divorce on locus of control orientation in adult women: A longitudinal study. *Journal of Personality and Social Psychology*, **44**, 834–840.

Dollard, J., Doob, L., Miller, N., Mower, O.H., and Sears, R.R. (1939). *Frustration and aggression.* New Haven, CT: Yale University Press.

Donnerstein, E. (1980). Aggressive erotica and violence against women. *Journal of Personality and Social Psychology*, **39**, 269–277.

Donnerstein, E. (1983). Erotica and human aggression. In R. Geen and E. Donnerstein (Eds.), *Aggression: Theoretical and empirical reviews* (Vol. 2). New York: Academic Press.

Donnerstein, E., and Berkowitz, L. (1981). Victim reactions in aggressive-erotic films as a factor in violence against women. *Journal of Personality and Social Psychology*, **41**, 710–724.

Donnerstein, E., and Wilson, D.W. (1976). Effects of noise and perceived control on ongoing and subsequent aggressive behavior. *Journal of Personality and Social Psychology*, **34**, 774–781.

Doob, L.W. (1970). *Resolving conflict in Africa: The Fermeda workshop.* New Haven, CT: Yale University Press.

Dovidio, J. (1984). Helping behavior. In L. Berkowitz (Ed.), *Advances in experimental social psychology* (Vol. 17). New York: Academic Press.

Dowd, M. (1984). 20 years after Kitty Genovese's murder, experts study bad Samaritanism, *New York Times*, March 21, B1, B4.

Driscoll, R., Davis, K.E., and Lipitz, M.E. (1972). Parental interference and romantic love: The Romeo and Juliet effect. *Journal of Personality and Social Psychology*, **24**, 1–10.

Duncan, B.L. (1976). Differential social perception and attribution of intergroup violence: Testing the lower limits of stereotyping of blacks. *Journal of Personality and Social Psychology*, **34**, 590–598.

Durkheim, E. (1893). *The division of labor in society.* New York: Free Press.

Dutton, P., and Aron, A. (1974). Some evidence for heightened sexual attraction under conditions of high anxiety. *Journal of Personality and Social Psychology*, **30**, 510–517.

Duval, S., and Wicklund, R.A. (1972). *A theory of objective self-awareness.* New York: Academic Press.

Dworkin, B.G. (1982). Instrumental learning for the treatment of disease. *Health Psychology*, **1**, 45–61.

Eagly, A.H. (1978). Sex differences in influenceability. *Psychological Bulletin*, **85**, 86–116.

Eagly, A.H. (1983). Who says so? The processing of communicator cues in persuasion. Paper presented at annual meeting of the Eastern Psychological Association.

Eagly, A.H., and Carli, L.L. (1981). Sex of researchers and sex typed communications as determinants of sex differences in influenceability: A meta-analysis of social influence studies. *Psychological Bulletin*, **90**, 1–20.

Eagly, A.H., and Chaiken, S. (1984). Cognitive theories of persuasion. In L. Berkowitz (Ed.), *Advances in experimental social psychology* (Vol. 16). New York: Academic Press.

Eagly, A., Chaiken, S., and Wood, W. (1981). An attribution analysis of persuasion. In J.H. Harvey, W.J. Ickes and R.F. Kidd (Eds.), *New directions in attribution research* (Vol. 3). Hillsdale, NJ: Erlbaum.

Eagly, A., and Himmelfarb, S. (1973). *Readings in attitude change.* New York: John Wiley & Son.

Eagly, A.H., and Himmelfarb, S. (1978). Attitudes and opinions. *Annual review of psychology*, **29**, 517–544.

Eagly, A.H., and Warren, R. (1976). Intelligence, comprehension, and opinion change. *Journal of Personality*, **44**, 226–242.

Eagly, A., Wood, W., and Chaiken, S. (1978). Causal inferences about communicators and their effect on opinion change. *Journal of Personality and Social Psychology*, **36**, 424–435.

Eagly, A., Wood, W., and Fishbaugh, L. (1981). Sex differences in conformity: Surveillance by the group as a determinant of male nonconformity. *Journal of Personality and Social Psychology*, **40**, 384–394.

Ebbesen, E.B., Duncan, B., and Konečni, V. (1975). Effects of content of verbal aggression on future verbal aggression: A field experiment. *Journal of Experimental Social Psychology*, **11**, 192–204.

Ebbesen, E.B., Kjos, G.L., and Konečni, V.J. (1976). Spatial ecology: Its effect on the choice of friends and enemies. *Journal of Experimental Social Psychology*, **12**, 505–518.

Eckhoff, T. (1974). *Justice: Its determinant in social interaction.* Rotterdam: Rotterdam Press.

Eco, U. (1983). *In the name of the rose.* London: Pan Books Ltd.

Edney, J.J. (1972). Property, possession, and permanence: A field study in human territoriality. *Journal of Applied Social Psychology*, **2**, 275–282.

Edney, J.J. (1975). Territoriality and control: A field experiment. *Journal of Personality and Social Psychology*, **31**, 1108–1115.

Edney, J.J., and Uhlig, S.R. (1977). Individual and small group territories. *Small Group Behavior*, **8**, 457–468.

Edwards, D.J.A. (1972). Approaching the unfamilar: A study of human interaction distances. *Journal of Behavioral Sciences*, **1**, 249–250.

Ehrhardt, A.A., Epstein, R., and Money, J. (1968). Fetal androgens and female gender identity in early-treated adrenogenital syndrome. *Johns Hopkins Medical Journal*, **122**, 160–167.

Ehrlich, P. (1968). *The population bomb.* New York: Ballantine.

Eisenberg, N. (1983). The relation between empathy and altruism: Conceptual and methodological issues. *Academic Psychology Bulletin*, **5**, 195–208.

Elliott, G.C., and Meeker, B.F. (1984). Modifiers of equity effect: Group outcome and causes for individual performance. *Journal of Personality and Social Psychology, 46,* 586–597.

Ellison, K.W., and Buckhout, R. (1981). *Psychology and criminal justice.* New York: Harper Row.

Elms, A.C. (1972). *Social psychology and social relevance.* Boston, MA: Little Brown.

Endler, N.S. (1966). Conformity as a function of different reinforcement schedules. *Journal of Personality and Social Psychology, 4,* 175–180.

Endler, N.S., and Magnusson, D. (1976). *Interactional psychology and personality.* Washington, D.C. : Hemisphere Publishing.

Environmental Protection Agency (1972). *Report to the President and Congress on noise.* Washington, D.C.: U.S. Government Printing Office.

Epstein, L.H., and Cluss, P.A. (1982). A behavioral medicine perspective on adherence to long-term medical regimens. *Journal of Consulting and Clinical Psychology, 50,* 950–971.

Epstein, S. (1973). The self-concept revisited: Or a theory of a theory. *American Psychologist, 28,* 404–416.

Epstein, S. (1979). Stability of behavior: I On predicting most of the people much of the time. *Journal of Personality and Social Psychology, 37,* 1097–1126.

Epstein, S. (1980). The stability of behavior: II Implications for psychological research. *American Psychologist, 35,* 790–806.

Epstein, Y.M. (1981). Crowding, stress, and human behavior. *Journal of Social Issues, 37,* 1126–1144.

Epton, N. (1959). *Love and the French.* Cleveland, OH: World.

Erikson, B., Holmes, J.G., Frey, R., Walker, L., and Thibaut, J. (1974). Functions of a third party in the resolution of a conflict: The role of judge in pretrial conferences. *Journal of Personality and Social Psychology, 30,* 293–306.

Erikson, E.H. (1968) *Identity youth and crisis,* New York: Norton.

Erikson, E.H. (1969) *Ghandi's truth,* New York: Norton.

Eron, L.D. (1982). Parent-child interaction, television violence, and aggression of children. *American Psychologist, 37,* 197–211.

Eron, L.D., Huesman, L.R., Lefkowitz, M.M., and Walder, L.O. (1972). Does television violence cause aggression? *American Psychologist, 47,* 382–389.

Etzioni, A. (1967). The Kennedy experiment. *The Western Political Quarterly, 20,* 361–380.

Evans, G.W., and Jacobs, S.V. (1981). Air pollution and human behavior. *Journal of Social Issues, 37,* 95–125.

Evans, G.W., Jacobs, S.V., and Frager, N.B. (1982). Adaptation to air pollution. *Journal of Environmental Psychology, 2,* 99–108.

Evans, R.I. (1980a). Behavioral medicine: A new applied challenge to social psychologists. In L. Bickman (Ed.), *Applied social psychology annual* (Vol. 1). Beverly Hills, CA: Sage.

Evans, R.I. (1980b). *The making of social psychology.* New York: Gardner Press Inc.

Evans, R.I., Rozelle, R.M., Mittlemark, M.B., Hansen, W.B., Bane, A.L., and Havis, J. (1978). Determining the onset of smoking in children: Knowledge of immediate physiological effects and coping with peer pressure, media pressure, and parent modeling. *Journal of Applied Social Psychology, 8,* 126–135.

Fagot, B.I. (1974). Sex differences in toddler's behavior and parental reaction. *Developmental Psychology, 10,* 554–558.

Fanselow, M.S., and Buckhout, R. (1976). Nonverbal cueing as a source of biasing information in eyewitness identification testing. *Center for Responsive Psychology* Monograph, CR–26.

Fantino, E. (1973). Aversive control. In T. Nevin and C. Reynolds (Eds.), *The study of behavior: Learning, motivation, emotion, and instinct.* Glenview, IL: Scott, Foresman.

Faranda, J.A., Kaminski, J.A., and Giza, B.K. (1979). An assessment of attitudes toward women with the bogus pipeline. Paper presented at annual meeting of the American Psychological Association.

Farley, J.E. (1982). Has public housing gotten a bum rap? *Environment and Behavior,14,* 443–477.

Fazio, R.H., Effrein, E.A., and Falender, V.J. (1981). Self-perceptions following social interactions. *Journal of Personality and Social Psychology, 41,* 232–242.

Fazio, R.H., and Zanna, M.P. (1981). Direct experience and attitude-behavior consistency. In L. Berkowitz (Ed.), *Advances in experimental social psychology* (Vol. 14). New York: Academic Press.

Fazio, R.H., Zanna, M.P., and Cooper, J. (1977). Dissonance and self-perception: An integrative view of each theory's proper domain of application. *Journal of Experimental Social Psychology, 13,* 464–479.

Fenigstein, A. (1979a). Does aggression cause a preference for viewing media violence? *Journal of Personality and Social Psychology, 37,* 2307–2317.

Feningstein, A. (1979b). Self-consciousness, self-attention, and social interaction. *Journal of Personality and Social Psychology, 37,* 75–86.

Fenigstein, A. (1984). Self-consciousness and the overperception of self as target. *Journal of Personality and Social Psychology, 47,* 860–871.

Fenigstein, A., Scheier, M.F., and Buss, A.H. (1975). Public and private self-consciousness. *Journal of Consulting and Clinical Psychology, 43,* 522–527.

Feshbach, S., and Singer, R.D. (1972). Television and aggression: A reply to Liebert, Sobol, and Davidson. In J.P. Murray, E. Rubinstein and G. Comstock (Eds.), *Television and social behavior* (Vol. 5): *Television's effects: Further explorations.* Washington, D.C.: National Institute of Mental Health.

Feshbach, S., Stiles, W.B., and Bitter, E. (1967). The reinforcing effect of witnessing aggression. *Journal of Experimental Research in Personality, 2,* 133–139.

Festinger, L. (1950). Informal social communication. *Psychological Review, 57,* 271–282.

Festinger, L. (1953). An analysis of compliant behavior. In M. Sherif and M.O. Wilson (Eds.), *Group relations at the crossroads.* New York: Harper.

Festinger, L. (1954). A theory of social comparison processes. *Human Relations, 7,* 117–140.

Festinger, L. (1957). *A theory of cognitive dissonance.* Stanford, CA: Stanford University Press.

Festinger, L. (1964). Behavioral support for opinion change. *Public Opinion Quarterly, 28,* 404–417.

Festinger, L. (1980). *Retrospections on social psychology.* New York: Oxford University Press.

Festinger, L., and Carlsmith, J.M. (1959). Cognitive consequences of forced compliance. *Journal of Abnormal and Social Psychology, 58,* 203–210.

Festinger, L., Pepitone, A., and Newcomb, J. (1952). Some consequences of deindividuation in a group. *Journal of Abnormal and Social Psychology, 47,* 382–389.

Festinger, L., Riecken, H.W., and Schachter, S. *When prophecy fails.* Minneapolis, MN: University of Minnesota Press, 1965.

Festinger, L., Schachter, S., and Back, K. (1950). *Social pressures in informal groups.* New York: Harper.

Field, M. (1974). Power and dependency: Legitimization of dependency condition. *Journal of Social Psychology, 92,* 31–37.

Fiedler, F.E. (1971). Validation and extension of the contingency model of leadership effectiveness: A review of empirical findings. *Psychological Bulletin*, **76**, 128–148.

Fiedler, F.E. (1978). The contingency model and the dynamics of the leadership process. In L. Berkowitz (Ed.), *Advances in Experimental Social Psychology* (Vol. 11). New York: Academic Press.

Findley, M.J., and Cooper, H.M. (1983). Locus of control and academic achievement: A literature review. *Journal of Personality and Social Psychology*, **44**, 419–427.

Fishbein, M. (1963). An investigation of the relationship between beliefs about an object and attitudes toward that object. *Human Relations*, **16**, 233–239.

Fishbein, M. (1966). Sexual behavior and propositional control. Paper presented at annual meeting of the Psychonomic Society.

Fishbein, M. (1967). Attitude and the prediction and behavior. In M. Fishbein (Ed.), *Readings in attitude theory and measurement.* New York: Wiley.

Fishbein, M., and Ajzen, I. (1972). Attitudes and opinions. *Annual Review of Psychology*, **23**, 487–544.

Fishbein, M., and Ajzen, I. (1975). *Belief, attitude, intention, and behavior: An introduction to theory and research.* Reading, MA: Addison-Wesley.

Fishbein, M., Ajzen, I., and Hinkle, R. (1980). Predicting and understanding voting in American elections: Effects of external variables. In I. Ajzen and M. Fishbein (Eds.), *Understanding attitudes and predicting human behavior.* Englewood Cliffs, NJ: Prentice-Hall.

Fishbein, M., Bowman, C.H., Thomas, K., Jaccard, J.J., and Ajzen, I. (1980). Predicting and understanding voting in British elections and American referenda: Illustrations of the theory's generality. In I. Ajzen and M. Fishbein (Eds.), *Understanding attitudes and predicting human behavior.* Englewood Cliffs, NJ: Prentice-Hall.

Fishbein, M., and Coombs, F.S. (1974). Basis for decision: An attitudinal analysis of voting behavior. *Journal of Applied Social Psychology*, **4**, 95–124.

Fishbein, M., and Feldman, S. (1963). Social psychological studies in voting behavior: I. Theoretical and methodological considerations. *American Psychologist*, **18**, 388.

Fishbein, M., Landy, E., and Hatch, G. (1969). A consideration of two assumptions underlying Fiedler's Contingency Model for prediction of leadership effectiveness. *American Journal of Psychology*, **82**, 457–473.

Fisher, C.S. (1976). *The urban experience.* New York: Harcourt Brace Jovanovich.

Fisher, J.D., Bell, P.A., and Baum, A. (1984). *Environmental psychology.* New York: Holt, Rinehart & Winston.

Fisher, R. (1983). Playing the wrong game. In J.Z. Rubin (Ed.), *The dynamics of third party intervention in the middle east.* New York: Praeger.

Fisher, R.J. (1983). Third party consultation as a method of intergroup conflict resolution. *Journal of Conflict Resolution*, **27**, 301–334.

Fisher, W.F. (1963). Sharing in pre-school children as a function of amount and type of reinforcement. *Genetic Psychology Monographs*, **68**, 215–245.

Fiske, E.B. (1983). Campus computers reshape social life and work habits. *New York Times*, January, 2, 1, 20.

Fiske, S.T., and Taylor, S.E. (1984). *Social cognition.* Reading, MA: Addison-Wesley.

Fleishman, E.A. (1953). Leadership climate, human relations training, and supervisory training. *Personnel Psychology*, **23**, 52–75.

Fleishman, E.A., and Harris, E.F. (1962). Patterns of leadership behavior related to employee grievances and turnover. *Personnel Psychology*, **15**, 43–56.

Floody, O.R., and Pfaff, D.W. (1974). Steroid hormones and aggressive behavior. Approaches to the study of hormone sensitive brain mechanisms for behavior. In S.H. Frazier (Ed.), *Aggression research publications for research in nervous and mental disease* (Vol. 52), Baltimore, MD: Williams and Wilkins.

Flowers, M.L. (1977). A laboratory test of some implications of Janis' groupthink hypothesis. *Journal of Personality and Social Psychology*, **35**, 888–896.

Foa, E.B., and Foa, U.G. (1974). *Societal structures of the mind.* Springfield, IL: Charles C. Thomas.

Foa, E.B., and Foa, U.G. (1980). Resource theory: Interpersonal behavior as exchange. In K.J. Gergen, M.S. Greenberg, and R.H. Willis (Eds.), *Social exchange: Advances in theory and research.* New York: Plenum.

Foelker, G. (1985). The role of psychological variables as determinants of fear of crime in the elderly. Unpublished doctoral dissertation. University of South Florida.

Follett, K. (1984). *On the wings of eagles.* London: William Collins.

Ford, J.G., and Graves, J.R. (1977). Differences in Mexican-American and white children in interpersonal distance and social touching. *Perceptual and Motor Skills*, **45**, 779–785.

Forsyth, D.R. (1983). *An introduction to group dynamics.* Monterey, CA: Brooks/Cole.

Francis, V., Korsch, B.M., and Morris, M.J. (1959). Gaps in doctor-patient communication. *New England Journal of Medicine*, **280**, 535–540.

Francoeur, R. (1984). *Becoming a sexual person.* New York: John Wiley & Sons.

Frankenhauser, M. (1980). Psychoneuroendocrine approaches to the study of stressful person-environment transactions. In H. Selye (Ed.), *Selye's guide to stress research* (Vol. 1). New York: Van Nostrand-Reinhold.

Franklin, C.W. II (1982). *Theoretical perspectives in social psychology.* Boston, MA: Little Brown and Company.

Fredericks, A.J., and Dorsett, D.L. (1983). Attitude-behavior relations: A comparison of the Fishbein-Ajzen and the Bentler-Speckart models. *Journal of Personality and Social Psychology*, **45**, 501–512.

Freedman, D.G. (1974). *Human infancy: An evolutionary perspective.* Hillsdale, NJ: Lawrence Erlbaum Associates.

Freedman, J.L. (1975). *Crowding and behavior.* San Francisco: W.H. Freeman.

Freedman, J.L., and Doob, A.N. (1968). *Deviancy: The psychology of being different.* New York: Academic Press.

Freedman, J.L., and Frazer, S.C. (1966). Compliance without pressure: The foot in the door technique. *Journal of Personality and Social Psychology*, **4**, 195–202.

Freeman, S., Walker, M., Borden, R., and Latané, B. (1975). Diffusion of responsibility and restaurant tipping: Cheaper by the bunch. *Personality and Social Psychology Bulletin*, **1**, 584–587.

French, J.R.P., and Raven, B. (1959). The bases of social power. In D. Cartwright (Ed.), *Studies in social power.* Ann Arbor, MI: Institute for social research.

Freud, S. (1920). *A general introduction to psychoanalysis.* New York: Boni & Liverant.

Freud, S. (1933). *Why war? Open letter series* (Vol. II). Paris: League of Nations International Institute of Intellectual Cooperation.

Freuh, T., and McGhee, P.E. (1975). Traditional sex role development and the amount of time spent watching television. *Developmental Psychology*, **11**, 109.

Friedlander, F. (1967). The impact of organizational training laboratories upon the effectiveness and interaction of ongoing work groups. *Personnel Psychology*, **20**, 289–307.

Friedman, M., and Rosenman, R. (1974). *Type A behavior and your heart,* New York: Knopf.

Frieze, I., and Weiner, B.H. (1971). Cue utilization and attributional judgments for success and failure. *Journal of Personality,* **39,** 591–605.

Frodi, A. (1975). The effect of exposure to weapons on aggressive behavior from a cross-cultural perspective. *International Journal of Psychology,* **10,** 283–292.

Frodi, A. (1977). Sexual arousal, situational restrictiveness, and aggressive behavior. *Journal of Research in Personality,* **11,** 48–58.

Frost, J.H., and Wilmot, W.N. (1978). *Interpersonal conflict.* Dubuque, IA: W.C. Brown.

Gachtel, R.J., and Baum, A. (1983). *An introduction to health psychology.* Reading, MA: Addison-Wesley.

Gaertner, S.L., and Dovidio, J.F. (1977). The subtlety of white racism, arousal, and helping behavior. *Journal of Personality and Social Psychology,* **35,** 691–707.

Gaertner, S.L., Dovidio, J.F., and Johnson, G. (1979a). Race of victim, non-responsive bystanders, and helping behavior. Paper presented at annual meeting of the American Psychological Association.

Gaertner, S.L., Dovidio, J.F., and Johnson, G. (1979b). The sublety of white racism. The effects of the race of the prevailing authority, opportunity for diffusion of responsibility, and race of victim on helping behavior. Unpublished manuscript. University of Delaware.

Galle, O.R., Gove, W.R., and McPherson, J.M. (1972). Population density and pathology: What are the relationships for man? *Science,* **176,** 23–30.

Gallup, G.G., Jr. (1970). Chimpanzees: Self recognition. *Science,* **167,** 86–87.

Gallup, G.G., Jr. (1977). Self-recognition in primates. A comparative approach to the bidirectional properties of consciousness. *American Psychologist,* **32,** 329–338.

Gara, M.A., and Rosenberg, S. (1981). Linguistic factors in implicit personality theory. *Journal of Personality and Social Psychology,* **41,** 450–457.

Garcia, L., and Griffitt, W. (1978). Evaluation and recall of evidence. Authoritarianism and the Patty Hearst case. *Journal of Research in Personality,* **12,** 57–67.

Geen, R.G. (1978). Effects of attack and uncontrollable noise on aggression. *Journal of Research in Personality,* **12,** 15–29.

Geen, R.G. (1980). The effects of being observed on performance. In P.B. Paulus (Ed.), *Psychology of group influence.* Hillsdale, NJ: Lawrence Erlbaum.

Geen, R.G. (1983). Aggression and television violence. In R. Geen and E. Donnerstein (Eds.), *Aggression: Theoretical and empirical reviews* (Vol. 2). New York: Academic Press.

Geen, R.G., and O'Neal, E.C. (1969). Activation of cue elicited aggression by general arousal. *Journal of Personality and Social Psychology,* **11,** 289–292.

Geen, R.G., and Quanty, M.B. (1977). The catharsis of aggression. In L. Berkowitz (Ed.), *Advances in experimental social psychology* (Vol. 10). New York: Academic Press.

Geen, R.G., Stonner, D., and Shope, G.L. (1975). The facilitation of aggression by aggression: A study in response inhibition and disinhibition. *Journal of Personality and Social Psychology,* **31,** 721–726.

Geer, J.H., and Jarmecky, L. (1973). The effect of being responsible for reducing another's pain on subject's response and arousal. *Journal of Personality and Social Psychology,* **26,** 232–237.

Geffner, R. (1978). The effects of interdependent learning on self-esteem, inter-ethnic relations, and intra-ethnic attitudes of elementary school children: A field experiment. Unpublished doctoral dissertation, University of California, Santa Cruz.

Geis, F.L., and Moon, T.H. (1981). Machiavellianism and deception. *Journal of Personality and Social Psychology,* **41,** 766–775.

Geis, F.L., Weinheimer, S., and Berger, D. (1970). Playing legislature: Cool heads and hot issues. In R. Christie and F.L. Geis (Eds.), *Studies in Machiavellianism.* New York: Academic Press.

Geller, D.M. (1980). Responses to urban stimuli: A balanced approach. *Journal of Social Issues,* **36,** 86–100.

Gerard, H.B. (1983). School desegregation: The social science role. *American Psychologist,* **38,** 869–877.

Gerard, H.B., and Mathewson, G. (1966). The effects of severity of initiation on liking for a group: A replication. *Journal of Experimental Social Psychology,* **2,** 278–287.

Gerard, H.B., and Miller, N. (1975). *School desegregation.* New York: Plenum.

Gerbasi, K.C., Zuckerman, M., and Reis, H.T. (1977). Justice needs a new blindfold: A review of mock jury research. *Psychological Bulletin,* **84,** 323–345.

Gerbner, G. (1982). Cited in Life according to TV. *Newsweek,* December 6, 1982.

Gergen, K.J. (1969). *The psychology of behavior exchange.* Reading, MA: Addison-Wesley.

Gergen, K.J. (1978). Experimentation in social psychology: A reappraisal. *European Journal of Social Psychology,* **36,** 1344–1360.

Gergen, K.J., Gergen, M.M., and Meter, K. (1972). Individual orientations to prosocial behavior. *Journal of Social Issues,* **8,** 105–130.

Gergen, K.J., Greenberg, M.S., and Willis, R.H. (1980). *Social exchange: Advances in theory and research.* New York: Plenum.

Gerson, L.W. (1967). Punishment and position: The sanctioning of deviants in small groups. *Case Western Reserve Journal of Sociology,* **1,** 54–62.

Giarrcisso, R., Johnson, P., Goodchilds, J., and Zellman, G. (1979). Adolescent cues and signals: Sex and assault. Paper presented at annual meeting of the Western Psychological Association.

Gibbons, F.X., Carver, C.S., Scheier, M.F., and Hormuth, S.E. (1979). Self-focused attention and the placebo effect: Fooling some of the people some of the time. *Journal of Experimental Social Psychology,* **15,** 263–274.

Gillig, P.M., and Greenwald, A. (1974). Is it time to lay the sleeper effect to rest? *Journal of Personality and Social Psychology,* **29,** 132–139.

Gillin, J.C., and Ochberg, F.M. (1970). Firearms control and violence. In D. Daniels, M. Gilula, and F. Ochberg (Eds.), *Violence in the struggle for existence.* Boston, MA: Little Brown.

Gilmour, R., and Duck, S. (1980). *The development of social psychology.* London: Academic Press.

Ginsburg, H.J., Pollman, V.A., Wauson, M.S., and Hope, M.L. (1977). Variation of aggressive interaction among male elementary school children as a function of changes in spatial density. *Environmental Psychology and Nonverbal Behavior,* **2,** 67–75.

Gittleson, B. (1975). *Biorhythm—A personal science.* New York: Arco.

Glass, D.C. (1977). *Behavior patterns, stress, and coronary.* Hillsdale, NJ: Erlbaum.

Glass, D.C., and Singer, J.E. (1972). *Urban stress.* New York: Academic Press.

Glass, D.C., Snyder, M.L., and Hollis, J. (1974). Time urgency and the Type A coronary prone behavior pattern. *Journal of Applied Social Psychology,* **4,** 125–140.

Goethals, G.R., and Nelson, R.E. (1973). Similarity in the influence process: The belief-value distinction. *Journal of Personality and Social Psychology*, **25**, 117–122.

Goffman, E. (1959). *The presentation of self in everyday life.* Garden City, NY: Doubleday Anchor.

Goffman, E. (1963). *Behavior in public places.* New York: Free Press.

Goffman, E. (1971). *Relations in public.* New York: Basic Books.

Goldband, S. (1980). Stimulus specificity of physiological response to stress and the Type A coronary-prone behavior pattern. *Journal of Personality and Social Psychology*, **39**, 670–679.

Goldberg, L.R. (1981). Unconfounding situational attributions from uncertain, neutral, and ambiguous ones: A psychometric analysis of descriptions of oneself and various types of others. *Journal of Personality and Social Psychology*, **41**, 517–552.

Goldberg, M.E., and Gorn, G.J. (1974). Children's reactions to television advertising: An experimental approach. *Journal of Consumer Research*, **1**, 69–75.

Goldstein, M. (1974). Brain research and violent behavior. *Archives of Neurology*, **30**, 1–34.

Golightly, C., and Byrne, D. (1964). Attitude statements as positive and negative reinforcements. *Science*, **146**, 798–799.

Gonzales, M.H., Davis, J.M., Loney, G.L., Lu Kens, C.K., and Junghans, C.M. (1983). Interactional approach to interpersonal attraction. *Journal of Personality and Social Psychology*, **44**, 1192–1197.

Goranson, R.E., and King, D. (1970). Rioting and daily temperatures: Analysis of U.S. riots in 1967. Unpublished manuscript. York University.

Gormly, J. (1983). Predicting behavior from personality trait scores. *Personality and Social Psychology Bulletin*, **9**, 267–270.

Gouaux, C. (1972). Induced affective states and interpersonal attraction. *Journal of Personality and Social Psychology*, **24**, 53–58.

Gouldner, A.W. (1960). The norm of reciprocity: A preliminary statement. *American Sociological Review*, **25**, 161-178.

Graen, G., Alvares, K.M., Orris, J.B., and Martella, J.A. (1970). Contingency model of leadership effectiveness: Antecedent and evidential results. *Psychological Bulletin*, **74**, 285–296.

Granberg, D., and Corrigan, G. (1972). Authoritarianism, dogmatism, and orientations toward Vietnam War. *Sociometry*, **35**, 468–476.

Greenbaum, C.W. (1979). The small group under the gun: Uses of small groups in battle conditions. *Journal of Applied Behavioral Science*, **15**, 392–405.

Greenbaum, P.E., and Greenbaum, S.D. (1981). Territorial personalization: Group identity and social interaction in a Slavic-American neighborhood. *Environment and Behavior*, **5**, 574–589.

Greenberg, J. (1979). Group vs individual equity judgments: Is there a polarization effect? *Journal of Experimental Social Psychology*, **15**, 204–212.

Greenberg, J., and Folger, R. (1983). Procedural justice, participation, and the fair process effects in groups and organizations. In P.B. Paulus (Ed.), *Basic group processes.* New York: Springer-Verlag.

Greene, D., Sternberg, B., and Lepper, M.R. (1976). Overjustification in a token economy. *Journal of Personality and Social Psychology*, **34**, 1219–1234.

Greenstein, T.N. (1976). Behavior change through value self-confrontation: A field experiment. *Journal of Personality and Social Psychology*, **34**, 254–262.

Greenwald, A. (1966). Effects of prior commitment on behavior change after a persuasive communication. *Public Opinion Quarterly*, **29**, 595–601.

Greenwald, A. (1968). Cognitive learning, cognitive responses to persuasion, and attitude change. In A. Greenwald, T. Brock and T. Ostrom (Eds.), *Psychological foundations of attitudes.* New York: Academic Press.

Greenwald, A., Baumgardner, M.H., and Lippe, M.R. (1979). In search of reliable persuasion effects: III The sleeper effect is dead. Long live the sleeper effect! Unpublished manuscript, Ohio State University.

Greer, D.L. (1983). Spectator booing and home advantage: A study of social influence in the basketball arena. *Social Psychology Quarterly*, **46**, 252–261.

Griffitt, W. (1970). Environmental effects on interpersonal affective behavior: Ambient effective temperature and attraction. *Journal of Personality and Social Psychology*, **15**, 240–244.

Griffitt, W., and Veitch, R. (1971). Hot and crowded: Influences of population density and temperature on interpersonal affective behavior. *Journal of Personality and Social Psychology*, **17**, 92–98.

Gross, A.E., Wallston, B.S., and Piliavin, J.M. (1975). Beneficiary attractiveness and cost as determinants of responses to routine requests for help. *Sociometry*, **38**, 131–140.

Groth, A.N., Burgess, A., and Hohlstrom, L.L. (1977). Rape: Power, anger, and sexuality. *American Journal of Psychiatry*, **134**, 1239–1243.

Grusec, J.E. (1981). Socialization processes and the development of altruism. In J.P. Rushton and R.M. Sorrentino (Eds.), *Altrusim and helping behavior: Social, personality, and developmental perspectives.* Hillsdale, NJ: Erlbaum.

Grush, J.E. (1980). Impact of campaign expenditures, regionality, and prior outcomes on the 1976 Democratic presidential primaries. *Journal of Personality and Social Psychology*, **38**, 337–347.

Guimond, S., and Dubé-Simond, L. (1983). Relative deprivation and the Quebec nationalist movement. The cognition-emotion distinction and the personal-group deprivation issue. *Journal of Personality and Social Psychology*, **44**, 526–535.

Gurin, G., Veroff, J., and Feld, S. (1960). *Americans view their mental health: A nationwide interview survey.* New York: Basic Books.

Gurr, T.R. (1970). *Why men rebel.* Princeton, NJ: Princeton University Press.

Gurr, T.R., and Duvall, R. (1976). Introduction to a formal theory of conflict within social systems. In L.A. Coser and O.N. Larsen (Eds.), *The uses of controversy in sociology.* New York: Free Press.

Gustafson, D.H., Shukla, R.K., Delbecq, A., and Walster, G.W. (1973). A comparative study of differences in subjective likelihood estimates made by individuals, interacting groups, delphic groups, and nominal groups. *Organizational Behavior and Human Performance*, **9**, 280–291.

Haberman, P.M., and Baden, M.M. (1978). *Alcohol, other drugs, and violent death.* New York: Oxford University Press.

Hackman, J.R., and Oldham, G.R. (1980). *Work redesign.* Reading, MA: Addison-Wesley.

Halberstam, D. (1973). *The best and the brightest.* Greenwich, CT: Fawcett.

Halberstam, D. (1981). *The breaks of the game.* New York: Ballantine.

Hall, C.S., and Lindzey, G. (1978). *Theories of personality.* New York: Wiley.

Hall, E.T. (1959). *The silent language.* New York: Doubleday.

Hall, E.T. (1963). A system for the notation of proxemic behavior. *American Anthropologist*, **65**, 1003–1026.

Hall, J. (1971). Decisions, decisions, decisions. *Psychology Today*, **5**, 51–54, 86–88.

Halprin, A.W., and Winer, B.J. (1952). *The leadership behavior of the airplane commander.* Columbus, OH: Ohio State University Research Foundation.

Halprin, A.W., and Winer, B.J. (1957). A factorial study of leader behavior descriptions. In R.M. Stogdill and A.C. Coons (Eds.), *Leader behavior: Its description and measurement*. Columbus, OH: Ohio State University.

Hamilton, D.L. (1979). A cognitive-attributional analysis of stereotyping. In L. Berkowitz (Ed.). *Advances in experimental social psychology* (Vol. 12). New York: Academic Press.

Hamilton, D.L., and Gifford, R.K. (1976). Illusory correlation in interpersonal perception: A cognitive basis of stereotypic judgments. *Journal of Personality and Social Psychology*, **12**, 392–407.

Hamilton, D.L., and Rose, T. (1978). Illusory correlation and maintenance of stereotypic beliefs. Unpublished manuscript. University of California at Santa Barbara.

Hamilton, D.L., Dugan, P.M., and Troller, T.K. (1985). The formation of stereotypic beliefs: Further evidence for distinctiveness-based illusory correlations. *Journal of Personality and Social Psychology*, **48**, 5–18.

Hamilton, G.V., and MacGowan, K. (1929). *What is wrong with marriage?* New York: Albert and Charles Boni.

Hamilton, T.P., Swap, W.C., and Rubin, J.Z. (1980). Predicting the effects of anticipated third party intervention: A template matching approach. *Journal of Personality and Social Psychology*, **41**, 1141–1152.

Hamilton, V.L. (1980). Intuitive psychologist or intuitive lawyer? Alternative models of the attribution process. *Journal of Personality and Social Psychology*, **39**, 767–772.

Hamilton, W.D. (1972). Altruism and related phenomena, mainly in social insects. *Annual Review of Ecology and Systematics* **3**, 193–232.

Haney, C., and Manzolati, J. (1981). Television criminology? Network illusions of criminal justice realities. In E. Aronson (Ed.), *Readings about the social animal* (3rd Edition). San Francisco: Freeman.

Harari, H., Mohr, D., and Hosey, K. (1980). Faculty helpfulness to students: A comparison of compliance techniques. *Personality and Social Psychology Bulletin*, **6**, 373–377.

Hardin, G.J. (1968). The tragedy of the commons. *Science*, **162**, 1243–1248.

Harding, J., Proshansky, H., Kutner, B., and Chein, I. (1968). Prejudice and ethnic relations. In G. Lindzey and E. Aronson (Eds.) *Handbook of Social Psychology* (2nd ed. Vol. 5). Reading, MA: Addison-Wesley.

Hare, A.P. (1976). *Handbook of small group research* (2nd ed.). New York: Free Press.

Hare, R.D. (1970). *Psychopathy: Theory and research*. New York: Wiley.

Harlow, H.F. (1961). The development of affectional patterns in infant monkeys. In B.M. Foss (Ed.), *Determinants of infant behavior*. New York: Wiley.

Harris, K.D., and Stadler, S.J. (1983). Determinism revisited: Assault and heat stress in Dallas, 1980. *Environment and Behavior*, **15**, 235–256.

Harris, M., and Huang, L. (1974). Aggression and the attribution process. *Journal of Social Psychology*, **92**, 209–216.

Harris, M.B. (1977). Effects of altruism on mood. *Journal of Social Psychology*, **102**, 197–208.

Harris, M.B., and Samorette, G.C. (1976). The effect of actual and attempted theft, need, and a previous favor on altruism. *Journal of Social Psychology*, **99**, 193–202.

Hartman, D.P. (1969). Influence of symbolically modeled instrumental aggression and pain cues on aggressive behavior. *Journal of Personality and Social Psychology*, **11**, 280–288.

Harvey, J.H., Town, J.P., and Yarkin, K.L. (1981). How fundamental is the "Fundamental Attribution Error"? *Journal of Personality and Social Psychology*, **40**, 346–349.

Hastie, R., Landsman, R., and Loftus, E.F. (1978). Eyewitness testimony: The dangers of guessing. *Jurimetrics Journal*, **19**, 1–8.

Hastorf, A., and Cantril, H. (1954). They saw a game: A case study. *Journal of Abnormal and Social Psychology*, **49**, 129–134.

Hatfield, E., Traupmann, J., and Walster, G.W. (1979). Equity and premarital sex. In M. Cook and G. Wilson (Eds.), *Love and attraction*. New York: Pergamon.

Hatfield, E., Utne, M.K., and Traupman, J. (1979). Equity theory and intimate relationships. In R.L. Burgess and T.L. Huston (Eds.), *Social exchange in developing relationships*. New York: Academic Press.

Hatfield, E., Walster, G.W., and Traupmann, J. (1979). Equity and extramarital sex. In M. Cook and G. Wilson (Eds.), *Love and attraction*. New York: Pergamon.

Hayduk, L.A. (1978). Personal space: An evaluative and orienting overview. *Psychological Bulletin*, **85**, 117–134.

Hayduk, L.A. (1983). Personal space: Where we now stand. *Psychological Bulletin*, **94**, 293–335.

Heaps, W.A. (1966). *Riots USA 1765–1965*. New York: Seabury Press.

Heider, F. (1958). *The psychology of interpersonal relationships*. New York: Wiley.

Hendrick, C., and Brown, S.R. (1971). Introversion, extraversion, and interpersonal attraction. *Journal of Personality and Social Psychology*, **20**, 31–36.

Hendrick, C., and Hendrick, S. (1983). *Liking, loving, and relating*. Monterey, CA: Brooks/Cole.

Hennigan, K.M., DelRosario, M.L., Heath, L., Cook, T.D., Wharton, J.D., and Calder, B.J. (1982). Impact of television on crime in the United States: Empirical findings and theoretical implications. *Journal of Personality and Social Psychology*, **42**, 461–477.

Hensley, W.E. (1982). Professor proxemics: Personality and job demands as factors of faculty office arrangements. *Environment and Behavior*, **14**, 581–592.

Higbee, K.L., Millard, R.J., and Folkman, J.R. (1982). Social psychology research in the 1970s: Predominance of experimentation and college students. *Personality and Social Psychology Bulletin*, **8**, 180–183.

Higgins, E.T., and Bryant, S.L. (1982). Consensus information and the fundamental attribution error: The role and development of ingroup vs. out-group knowledge. *Journal of Personality and Social Psychology*, **43**, 889–900.

Hill, C.E. (1974). A comparison of perceptions of a therapy session by clients, therapists, and objective judges. *JSAS Catalog of Selected Documents in Psychology*, **4**, 16.

Hill, S.D., Bundy, R.A., Gallup, G.G., Jr., and McClure, M.K. (1970). Responsiveness of young and nursery reared chimpanzees to mirrors. *Proceedings of the Louisiana Academy of Sciences*, **33**, 77–82.

Himmelfarb, S., and Lickteig, C. (1982). Social desirability and the randomized response technique. *Journal of Personality and Social Psychology*, **43**, 710–717.

Himmelweit, H.T., Swift, B., and Jolger, M.E. (1980). The audience as critic: A conceptual analysis of television entertainment. In P.H. Tannenbaum (Ed.), *The entertainment functions of television*. Hillsdale, NJ: Erlbaum.

Hiroto, D.S. (1974). Locus of control and learned helplessness. *Journal of Experimental Psychology*, **102**, 187–113.

Hobfoll, S.E., and Penner, L.A. (1978). The effect of physical attractiveness on therapists' initial judgments of a person's self-concept. *Journal of Clinical and Consulting Psychology*, **46**, 200–201.

Hochreich, D.J. (1972). Internal-external control and reaction to the My Lai court martials. *Journal of Applied Social Psychology*, **2**, 319–325.

Hoffman, M.L. (1975). Altruistic behavior and the parent child relationship. *Journal of Personality and Social Psychology*, **31,** 937–943.

Hoffman, M.L. (1981). Is altruism part of human nature? *Journal of Personality and Social Psychology*, **40,** 121–137.

Hogarty, G.E. and associates (1973). Drug and sociotherapy in the aftercare of the schizophrenic patients: One year relapse rates. *Archives of General Psychiatry*, **31,** 603–608.

Hokanson, J.E. (1970). Psychophysiological evaluation of the catharsis hypothesis. In E. Megargee and J. Hokanson (Eds.), *The dynamics of aggression*. New York: Harper and Row.

Hokanson, J.E., and Burgess, M. (1962). The effects of three types of aggression on vascular processes. *Journal of Abnormal and Social Psychology*, **64,** 446–449.

Hokanson, J.E., Willers, K.R., and Korupsak, E. (1968). The modification of autonomic responses during aggressive exchanges. *Journal of Personality*, **36,** 386–404.

Holahan, C.J. (1972). Seating patterns and patient behavior in an experimental dayroom. *Journal of Abnormal Psychology*, **80,** 115–124.

Holahan, C.J. (1982). *Environmental psychology*. New York: Random House.

Hollander, E.P. (1971). *Principles and methods of social psychology* (2nd ed.) New York: Oxford Press.

Hollister, L. (1975). The mystique of social drugs and sex. In M. Sandler and G.L. Gessa (Eds.), *Sexual behavior: Pharmacology and biochemistry*. New York: Raven Press.

Holmes, D.S. (1978). Projection as a defense mechanism. *Psychological Bulletin*, **85,** 677–688.

Holmes, D.S., Curtright, C.A., McCaul, K.D., and Thissen, D. (1980). Biorhythms: Their utility for predicting post-operative time, death, and athletic performance. *Journal of Applied Psychology*, **65,** 233–236.

Homans, G.C. (1961). *Social behavior: Its elementary forms*. New York: Harcourt Brace Jovanovich.

Hoppman, P.T., and Druckman, D. (1983). Henry Kissinger as strategist and tactician in the middle east. In J.Z. Rubin (Ed.), *Dynamics of third party intervention*. New York: Praeger.

Hornstein, H.A. (1970). The influence of social models on helping. In J. Macauley and L. Berkowitz (Eds.), *Altruism and helping behavior*. New York: Academic Press.

Horowitz, L.M., French, R., and Anderson, C.A. (1982). The prototype of the lonely person. In L.A. Peplau and D. Perlman (Eds.), *Loneliness: A sourcebook of current theory, research, and therapy*. New York: Wiley Interscience.

House, T.H., and Milligan, W.L. (1976). Autonomic responses to modelled distress in prison psychopaths. *Journal of Personality and Social Psychology*, **34,** 556–560.

Houston, L.N. (1981). Romanticism and eroticism among black and white college students. *Adolescence*, **16,** 263–272.

Hovland, C.I., and Janis, I. (1959). *Personality and persuasibility*. New Haven, CT: Yale University Press.

Hovland, C.I., Janis, I., and Kelley, H.H. (1953). *Communication and persuasion*. New Haven, CT: Yale University Press.

Hovland, C.I., Lumsdaine, A.A., and Sheffield, F.D. (1949). Experiments on mass communication. Princeton, NJ: Princeton University Press.

Hovland, C.I., and Sears, R.R. (1940). Minor studies of aggression: Correlation of lynchings with economic indices. *Journal of Psychology*, **9,** 301–310.

Hovland, C.I., and Weiss, W. (1951). The influence of source credibility on communication effectiveness. *Public Opinion Quarterly*, **15,** 635–650.

Hulka, B.S., Cassel, J.C., Kupper, L.L., and Burdette, J.A. (1976). Communication, compliance and concordance between physicians and patients with prescribed medications. *American Journal of Public Health*, **66,** 847–853.

Hunt, M. (1974). *Sexual behavior in the 1970s*. Chicago: Playboy Press.

Huse, E.F. (1975). *Organizational development and change*. St. Paul, MN: West.

Huston, T.L. (1983). Men and women in marriage: A behavioral profile. Paper presented at annual meeting of the Society of Experimental Social Psychologists.

Huston, T.L., and Levinger, G. (1978). Interpersonal attraction and relationships. *Annual Review of Psychology*, **29,** 115–156.

Huston, T.L., Geis, G., and Wright, R. (1976). The angry samaritans. *Psychology Today*, June, 61–64, 85.

Hutt, C., and Vaizey, M.J. (1966). Differential effects of group density on social behavior. *Nature*, **209,** 1371–1372.

Ickes, W., and Barnes, R.D. (1978). Boys and girls together—and alienated: On enacting sex role stereotypes in mixed-sex dyads. *Journal of Personality and Social Psychology*, **36,** 669–683.

Ineichen, B. (1979). The social geography of marriage. In M. Cook and G. Wilson (Eds.), *Love and attraction*. New York: Pergamon.

Insko, C. (1967). *Theories of attitude change*. New York: Appleton-Century Crofts.

International Association of Police Chiefs (1967). *Witness perceptions*. Washington, D.C.: International Association of Police Chiefs.

Isen, A.M. (1970). Success, failure, attention, and reaction to others: The warm glow of success. *Journal of Personality and Social Psychology*, **15,** 294–301.

Isen, A.M., and Levin, P.F. (1972). Effects of success and failure on children's generosity. *Journal of Personality and Social Psychology*, **21,** 384–388.

Isen, A.M., Shalker, T.E., Clark, M., and Karp, L. (1979). Affect accessibility of material in memory and behavior: A cognitive loop? *Journal of Personality and Social Psychology*, **36,** 1–12.

Isen, A.M., and Simonds, S.F. (1978). The effect of feeling good on a helping task that is incompatible with good mood. *Journal of Personality Social Psychology*, **41,** 346–349.

Issac, L., Murtran, E., and Stryker, S. (1980). Political protest orientations among black and white adults. *American Sociological Review*, **45,** 191–213.

Istvan, J., and Griffitt, W.C. (1980). Effects of sexual experience on dating desirability and marriage desirability: A social profile. *Journal of Marriage and Family*, **42,** 377–385.

Izzett, R.R. (1971). Authoritarianism and attitudes toward the Vietnam War as reflected in behavioral and self-report measures. *Journal of Personality and Social Psychology*, **17,** 145–148.

Jackson, J.J., and Padgett, V.R. (1982). With a little help from my friends: Social loafing and the Lennon-McCartney songs. *Personality and Social Psychology Bulletin*, **88,** 672–677.

Jacobs, P.A., Brunton, M., and Melville, M.M. (1965). Aggressive behavior, mental subnormality, and the XYY male. *Nature*, **208,** 1351–1352.

James, W. (1884). What is an emotion? *Mind*, **9,** 188–205.

Janda, L.H., O'Grady, K.E., and Barnhart, S.A. (1980). Effects of sexual attitudes and physical attractiveness on person perception of men and women. *Sex Roles*, **7,** 189–199.

Janis, I.L. (1968). Attitude change via role playing. In R. Abelson, E. Aronson, W. McGuire, T. Newcomb, M. Rosenberg, and P. Tannenbaum (Eds.), *Theories of cognitive consistency: A sourcebook*. Chicago: Rand-McNally.

Janis, I.L. (1972). *Victims of groupthink*. Boston, MA: Houghton Mifflin.

Janis, I.L. (1979). Preventing groupthink in policy-planning groups: Theory and research perspectives. Paper presented at annual meeting of the International Society of Political Society.

Janis, I.L. (1982). *Counseling on personal decisions: Theory and research on short term helping relationships*. New Haven, CT: Yale University Press.

Janis, I.L. (1983). The role of social support in adherence to stressful decisions. *American Psychologist, 38,* 143–160.

Janis, I.L., and Feshbach, S. (1953). Effects of fear arousing communications. *Journal of Abnormal and Social Psychology, 48,* 78–92.

Janis, I.L., and Hoffman, D. (1982). Effective partnerships in a clinic for smokers. In I.L. Janis (Ed.), *Counseling on personal decisions: Theory and research on short-term helping relationships.* New Haven, CT: Yale University Press.

Janis, I.L., and King, B.T. (1954). The influence of role-playing on opinion change. *Journal of Abnormal and Social Psychology, 49,* 211–218.

Janis, I.L., and Mann, L. (1977). *Decision making: A psychological analysis of conflict, choice and commitment.* New York: Free Press.

Janis, I.L., and Quinlan, D.M. (1982). What disclosing means to the client: Comparative case studies. In I.L. Janis (Ed.), *Counseling on personal decisions: Theory and research on short-term helping relationships.* New Haven, CT: Yale University Press.

Janowitz, M. (1969). Patterns of collective racial violence. In H. Graham and T. Gurr (Eds.), *Violence in America: Historical and comparative perspectives.* Washington, D.C.: National Commission on the Causes and Prevention of Violence.

Jarvik, L.F., Klodin, V., and Matsuyama, S.S. (1973). Human aggression and the extra Y chromosome: Fact or fantasy? *American Psychologist, 28,* 674–682.

Jellison, J.M., and Green, J. (1981). A self-presentational approach to the fundamental attribution error. The norm of internality. *Journal of Personality and Social Psychology, 40,* 643–649.

Jenkins, C.D. (1976). Recent evidence supporting psychologic and social risk factors for coronary disease. *New England Journal of Medicine, 294,* 987–994, 1033–1038.

Jenkins, C.D., Rosenman, R.H., and Zyzanski, S.J. (1974). Predictions of clinical heart disease by a test for the coronary prone behavior pattern. *New England Journal of Medicine, 33,* 1271–1275.

Jennings, M.K., and Niemi, R.G. (1968). The transmission of political values from parent to child. *American Political Science Review, 62,* 564–575.

Johnson, D.W., and Johnson, R.T. (1981). Effects of cooperative and individualistic learning experiences on inter-ethnic interaction. *Journal of Educational Psychology, 73,* 444–449.

Jonah, B.A., Bradley, J.S., and Dawson, N.E. (1981). Predicting individual subjective responses to traffic noise. *Journal of Applied Psychology, 66,* 490–501.

Jonas, G. (1972). Profiles: Visceral learning I. Dr. Neal E. Miller. *New Yorker, 48,* 34–57.

Jones, E.E. (1964). *Ingratiation.* New York: Appleton-Century-Crofts.

Jones, E.E., and Berglas, S. (1978). Control of attributions about the self through self-handicapping strategies: The appeal of alcohol and the role of under-achievement. *Personality and Social Psychology Bulletin, 4,* 200–206.

Jones, E.E., and Davis, K.E. (1965). From acts to dispositions: The attribution process in person perception. In L. Berkowitz (Ed.), *Advances in experimental social psychology* (Vol. 2). New York: Academic Press.

Jones, E.E., Gergen, K.J., and Jones, R.G. (1963). Tactics of ingratiation among leaders and subordinates in a status hierarchy. *Psychological Monographs, 77,* (3 Whole No. 566).

Jones, E.E., and Goethals, G.R. (1972). Order effects in impression formation: Attribution context and the nature of the entity. In E.E. Jones, D.E. Kanouse, H.H. Kelley, S. Valins, and B. Weiner (Eds.), *Attribution: Perceiving the causes of behavior.* Morristown, NJ: General Learning Press.

Jones, E.E., and Harris, V.A. (1967). The attribution of attitudes. *Journal of Experimental Social Psychology, 3,* 1–24.

Jones, E.E., and McGillis, D. (1976). Correspondent inferences and the attribution cube: A comparative reappraisal. In J.H. Harvey, W.J. Ickes, and R.F. Kidd (Eds.), *New directions in attribution research* Vol. 1. Hillsdale, NJ: Erlbaum.

Jones, E.E., and Nisbett, R.E. (1971). *The actor and the observer: Divergent perceptions of the causes of behavior.* Morristown, NJ: General Learning Press.

Jones, E.E., Rhodewalt, F., Berglas, S., and Skelton, J.A. (1981). Effects of strategic self-presentation on subsequent self-esteem. *Journal of Personality and Social Psychology, 41,* 407–421.

Jones, E.E., and Sigall, H. (1971). The bogus pipeline: A new paradigm for measuring affect and attitude. *Psychological Bulletin, 76,* 349–364.

Jones, E.E., and Wortman, C. (1973). *Ingratiation: An attributional approach.* Morristown, NJ: General Learning Press.

Jones, J. (1981). *Bad blood: The Tuskegee syphilis experiment.* New York: Free Press.

Jones, R. (1971). Cited in: Work with marijuana: I Effects, S.S. Snyder. *Psychology Today, 14,* 64.

Jones, W.H. (1982). Loneliness and social behavior. In L.A. Peplau and D. Perlman (Eds.), *Loneliness: A sourcebook of current theory, research, and therapy.* New York: Wiley Interscience.

Jonsson, E., and Sorenson, S. (1973). Adaptation to community noise: A case study. *Journal of Sound and Vibration, 26,* 571–575.

Jorgenson, D.O., and Lange, C. (1975). Graffiti content as an index of political interest. *Perceptual and Motor Skills, 45,* 630.

Joseph, N. (1981). *Campus, couples, and violence.* New York: New York Times.

Jourard, S.M. (1964). *The transparent self.* Princeton, NJ: Van Nostrand, Rheinhold.

Judd, C.M., and Johnson, J.T. (1981). Attitudes, polarization, and diagnosticity: Exploring the effect of affect. *Journal of Personality and Social Psychology, 41,* 26–36.

Judd, C.M., Kenny, D.A., and Krosnick, J.A. (1983). Judging the positions of political candidates: Models of assimilation and contrast. *Journal of Personality and Social Psychology, 44,* 952–963.

Judd, C.M., and Kulik, J.A. (1980). Schematic effects of social attitudes on information processing and recall. *Journal of Personality and Social Psychology, 38,* 569–578.

Kahn, A., Nelson, R.E., and Gaeddert, W.P. (1979). Sex of subject and sex composition of group as determinants of reward allocation. *Journal of Personality and Social Psychology, 38,* 737—750.

Kahn, A., O'Leary, V.E., Krulewitz, J.E., and Lamm, H. (1980). Equity and equality: Male and female means to a just end. *Basic and Applied Social Psychology, 1,* 173–197.

Kahneman, D., and Tversky, A. (1973). On the psychology of prediction. *Psychological Review, 80,* 237–251.

Kalven, H., Jr., and Zeisel, H. (1966). *The American jury.* Boston, MA: Little Brown and Company.

Kamin, E.J. (1967). Reference groups and sex conduct norm violations. *Sociological Quarterly, 8,* 495–504.

Kamin, E.J., and Parcell, S.R. (1977). Sexual aggression: A second look at the offended female. *Archives of Sexual Behavior, 6,* 67–76.

Kaplan, M.F., and Kemmerick, G.D. (1974). Juror judgment as information integration: Combining evidential and nonevidential information. *Journal of Personality and Social Psychology*, **30**, 493–499.

Kaplan, M.F., and Miller, L.E. (1978). Reducing the effects of juror bias. *Journal of Personality and Social Psychology*, **36**, 1443–1455.

Kaplan, M.F., and Schersching, C. (1978). Reducing juror bias: An experimental approach. In P.D. Lipsitt and B.D. Sales (Eds.), *New directions in psycholegal research*. New York: Van Nostrand Rheinhold.

Karlin, R.A., Epstein, Y.M., and Aiello, J.R. (1978). Strategies for the investigation of crowding. In A. Esser and B. Greenbie (Eds.), *Design-for-community-and-privacy*. New York: Plenum Press.

Karylowski, J. (1982). Two types of altruistic behavior: Doing good to feel good or to make the other feel good. In V.J. Derlega and J. Grzelak (Eds.), *Cooperation and helping behavior: Theories and research*. New York: Academic Press.

Kasl, S.V. (1975). Issues in adherence to health care regimens. *Journal of Human Stress*, September, 5–17, 48.

Kassarjian, H.H. (1982). Consumer psychology. *Annual Review of Psychology*, **33**, 619–650.

Katz, D. (1960). The functional approach to the study of attitudes. *Public Opinion Quarterly*, **24**, 163–204.

Kelley, H.H. (1972a). Attribution in social interaction. In E.E. Jones and D.E. Kanouse, H.H. Kelley, S. Valins, B. Weiner (Eds.), *Attribution: Perceiving the causes of behavior*. Morristown, NJ: General Learning Press.

Kelley, H.H. (1972b). Causal schemata and the attribution process. In E.E. Jones, D.E. Kanouse, H.H. Kelley, S. Valins, B. Weiner (Eds.), *Attribution: Perceiving the causes of behavior*. Morristown, NJ: General Learning Press.

Kelley, H.H. (1973). The process of causal attributions. *American Psychologist*, **28**, 107–128.

Kelley, H.H. (1978). A conversation with Edward E. Jones and Harold H. Kelley. In J.H. Harvey, W. Ickes and R.F. Kidd (Eds.), *New directions in attribution research* (Vol. 2). Hillsdale, NJ: Erlbaum Associates.

Kelley, H.H., and Thibaut, J.W. (1969). Group problem solving. In G. Lindzey and E. Aronson (Eds.), *The handbook of social psychology* (2nd ed. Vol. 4). Reading, MA: Addison-Wesley.

Kelman, H.C. (1958). Compliance, identification, and internalization. *Journal of Conflict Resolution*, **2**, 51–60.

Kelman, H.C. (1961). Processes of opinion change. *Public Opinion Quarterly*, **25**, 57–78.

Kelman, H.C. (1972). The problem solving workshop in conflict resolution. In R.L. Merritt (Ed.), *Communication in international politics*. Urbana, IL: University of Illinois Press.

Kelman, H.C. (1982). Creating the conditions for Israeli-Palestinian negotiations. *Journal of Conflict Resolution*, **26**, 39–75.

Kelman, H.C. (1983). Conversations with Arafat: A social-psychological assessment of the prospects for Israeli-Palestinian Peace. *American Psychologist*, **38**, 203–216.

Kelman, H.C., and Cohen, S.P. (1976). The problem-solving workshop: A social-psychological contribution to the resolution of international conflicts. *Journal of Peace Research*, **13**, 79–90.

Kelman, H.C., and Hovland, C.I. (1953). "Reinstatement" of the communicator in the delayed measurement of opinion change. *Journal of Abnormal and Social Psychology*, **48**, 327–335.

Kendrick, A. (1969). *Prime time: The life of Edward R. Murrow*. New York: Avon.

Kenrick, D.T., and Cialdini, R.B. (1977). Romantic attraction: Misattribution versus reinforcement explanations. *Journal of Personality and Social Psychology*, **35**, 381–391.

Kenrick, D.T., Cialdini, R.B., and Linder, D.E. (1979). Heterosexual attraction and attributional processes in fear producing situations. In M. Cook and G. Wilson (Eds.), *Love and attraction*. New York: Pergamon.

Kenrick, D.T., and Johnson, G.A. (1979). Interpersonal attraction in aversive environments: A problem for the classical conditioning paradigm? *Journal of Personality and Social Psychology*, **37**, 572–579.

Kerlinger, F.N. (1979). *Behavioral research: A conceptual approach*. New York: Holt, Rinehart and Winston.

Kerner, J.F., and Stephens, L. (1983). Attributions and arousal as mediators of mitigation's effect on retaliation. *Journal of Personality and Social Psychology*, **45**, 335–343.

Kerr, N.L., Atkin, R.S., Stasser, G., Meeker, D., Holt, R.W., and Davis, J.H. (1976). Guilt beyond a reasonable doubt: Effect of concept definition and assigned decision rule on judgments of mock jurors. *Journal of Personality and Social Psychology*, **34**, 282–294.

Kerr, N.L., and MacCoun, R.J. (1985). The effects of jury size and polling method on the process and product of jury deliberation. *Journal of Personality and Social Psychology*, **48**, 349–363.

Kessler, J.B. (1977). The social psychology of jury deliberations. In R.J. Simon (Ed.), *The jury system in America*. Beverly Hills, CA: Sage.

Kidder, L.H. (1981). *Research methods in social relations*. New York: Holt, Rinehart and Winston.

Kilham, W., and Mann, L. (1974). Level of destructive obedience as a function of transmitter and executant roles in the Milgram obedience paradigm. *Journal of Personality and Social Psychology*, **29**, 696–702.

Kilpatrick, D.G., Resick, P., and Veronen, L. (1981). Effects of a rape experience: A longitudinal study. *Journal of Social Issues*, **37**, 105–122.

Kinder, D.R., and Sears, D.O. (1981). Symbolic racism versus threats to the good life. *Journal of Personality and Social Psychology*, **40**, 414–431.

Kinsey, A.C., Pomeroy, W.B., and Martin, C.E. (1948). *Sexual behavior in the human male*. Phildelphia: W.B. Saunders.

Kinsey, A.C., Pomeroy, W.B., Martin, C.E., and Gebhard, P.H. (1983). *Sexual behavior in the human male*. Philadelphia: Saunders.

Kinzel, A.S. (1970). Body buffer zone in violent prisoners. *American Journal of Psychiatry*, **127**, 59–64.

Klein, E.B. (1963). Stylistic components of response as related to attitude change. *Journal of Personality*, **31**, 38–51.

Klein, D.C., Fencil-Morse, E., and Seligman, M.E. (1976). Learned helplessness, depression, and the attribution of failure. *Journal of Personality and Social Psychology*, **33**, 508–516.

Kluger, R. (1976). *Simple justice*. New York: Knopf.

Knight, J.A., and Vallacher, R.R. (1981). Interpersonal engagement in social perception: The consequences of getting into the action. *Journal of Personality and Social Psychology*, **40**, 990–999.

Kogan, N., and Wallach, M.A. (1964). *Risk taking: A study in cognition and personality*. New York: Holt, Rinehart & Winston.

Kohlberg, L. (1966). A cognitive-developmental analysis of children's sex role concepts and attitudes. In E. Maccoby (Ed.), *The development of sex differences*. Stanford, CA: Stanford University Press.

Kohlberg, L. (1969). Stage and sequence: The cognitive developmental approach to socialization. In D.A. Goslin (Ed.) *Handbook of socialization theory and research*. Chicago: Rand McNally.

Kolditz, T.A., and Arkin, R.M. (1982). An impression management interpretation of the self-handicapping strategy. *Journal of Personality and Social Psychology*, **43**, 492–502.

Koller, M.R. (1962). Residential and occupational propinquity. In R. Winch, R. McGinnis, and H.R. Barringer (Eds.), *Selected studies in marriage and the family*. New York: Holt.

Konečni, V. (1975). The mediation of aggressive behavior: Arousal level vs anger and cognitive labeling. *Journal of Personality and Social Psychology, 32,* 706–712.

Koneya, M. (1976). Location and interaction in row-and-column seating arrangements. *Environment and Behavior, 8,* 265–282.

Korte, C. (1978). Helpfulness in the urban environment. In A. Baum, J. Singer, and S. Valins (Eds.), *Advances in environmental psychology* (Vol. 1). Hillsdale, NJ: Erlbaum.

Korte, C. (1980). Urban-nonurban differences in social behavior and social psychological models of urban impact. *Journal of Social Issues, 36,* 29–51.

Korte, C., and Grant, R. (1980). Traffic noise, environmental awareness, and pedestrian behavior. *Environment and Behavior, 12,* 408–420.

Kramer, R.M., and Brewer, M.B. (1984). Effects of group identity on resource use in a simulated commons dilemma. *Journal of Personality and Social Psychology, 46,* 1044–1057.

Krebs, D. (1975). Empathy and altruism. *Journal of Personality and Social Psychology, 32,* 1134–1146.

Krech, D., Crutchfield, R., and Ballachey, E. (1962). *Individual in society.* New York: McGraw-Hill.

Kryter, K.D. (1970). *The effects of noise on man.* New York: Academic Press.

Kuehn, L.L. (1974). Looking down a gun barrel: Person perception and violent crime. *Perceptual and Motor Skills, 39,* 1154–1164.

Kuethe, J.L. (1962). Social schemas. *Journal of Abnormal and Social Psychology, 64,* 31–38.

Kuethe, J.L. (1964). Prejudice and aggression: A study of specific social schemata. *Perceptual and Motor Skills, 18,* 107–115.

Kuiper, N.A. (1978). Depression and causal attributions for success and failure. *Journal of Personality and Social Psychology, 36,* 236–246.

Lacey, R. (1981). *The kingdom: Arabia and the house of Sa'ud.* New York: Harcourt, Brace and Jovanovich.

Lamb, M.E. (1984). Social and emotional development in infancy. In M.H. Bornstein and M.E. Lamb (Eds.), *Development psychology: An advanced text.* Hillsdale, NJ: LEA.

Lamb, M.E., and Urberg, K.A. (1978). The development of gender role and gender identity. In M.E. Lamb (Ed.) *Social and personality development,* New York: Holt, Rinehart and Winston.

Lamm, H., and Kayser, E. (1978). The allocation of monetary gain and loss following dyadic performance: The weight given effort and ability under conditions of low and high intradyadic attraction. *European Journal of Social Psychology, 8,* 275–278.

Lamm, H., and Myers, D.G. (1978). Group-induced polarization of attitudes and behavior. In L. Berkowitz (Ed.), *Advances in experimental social psychology* (Vol. 11). New York: Academic Press.

Lamm, H., and Trommsdorff, G. (1973). Group versus individual performance on tasks requiring ideational proficiency (brainstorming): A review. *European Journal of Social Psychology, 3,* 361–388.

Landy, D., and Mettee, D. (1969). Evaluation of an aggressor as a function of exposure to cartoon humor. *Journal of Personality and Social Psychology, 12,* 66–71.

Lane, I.M., and Messé, L.A. (1971). Equity and the distribution of rewards. *Journal of Personality and Social Psychology, 20,* 1–17.

Langer, E.J., Blank, A., and Chanowitz, B. (1978). The mindlessness of ostensibly thoughtful action. *Journal of Personality and Social Psychology, 36,* 635–642.

Langer, E., and Rodin, J. (1976). The effects of choice and enhanced personal responsibility for the aged: A field experiment in an institutional setting. *Journal of Personality and Social Psychology, 34,* 191–198.

Langlois, J.H., and Stephen, C.W. (1981). Beauty and the beast: The role of physical attractiveness in the development of peer re-

lations and social behavior. In S.S. Brehm, S.M. Kassin, F.X. Gibbons (Eds.), *Developmental social psychology.* New York: Oxford.

La Piere, R. (1934). Attitudes vs actions. *Social Forces, 13,* 230–237.

Latan'e, B. (1981). The psychology of social impact. *American Psychologist, 36,* 343–356.

Latan'e, B., and Bidwell, L.D. (1977). Sex and affiliation in college cafeterias. *Personality and Social Psychology Bulletin, 3,* 571–574.

Latan'e, B., and Dabbs, J. (1975). Sex, group size, and helping in three cities. *Sociometry, 38,* 180–194.

Latan'e, B., and Darley, J.M. (1970). *The unresponsive bystander: Why doesn't he help?* New York: Appleton-Century-Crofts.

Latan'e, B., and Darley, J. (1976). *Help in a crisis: Bystander response to an emergency.* Morristown, NJ: General Learning Press.

Latan'e, B., and Harkins, S. (1976). Cross-modality matches suggest anticipated stage fright a multiplicative power function of audience size and status. *Perception and Psychophysics, 20,* 482–488.

Latan'e, B., and Nida, S. (1980). Social impact theory and group influence: A social engineering perspective. In P.B. Paulus (Ed.), *Psychology of group influence.* Hillsdale, NJ: Erlbaum.

Latan'e, B., and Nida, S. (1981). Ten years of research on group size and helping. *Psychological Bulletin, 89,* 308–324.

Latan'e, B., Williams, K., and Harkins, S. (1979). Many hands make light the work: The causes and consequences of social loafing. *Journal of Personality and Social Psychology, 37,* 822–832.

Lau, R.R., and Russell, D. (1980). Attributions in sports pages. *Journal of Personality and Social Psychology, 39,* 29–38.

Layden, M.A. (1978). Attributional retraining for low self-esteem women. Unpublished manuscript. University of Wisconsin.

Leavitt, H.J. (1951). Some effects of certain communication patterns on group performance. *Journal of Abnormal and Social Psychology, 46,* 38–50.

Lefcourt, H. (1973). The function of the illusion of control and freedom. *American Psychologist, 28,* 417–425.

Lefcourt, H.M. (1976). *Locus of control: Current trends in theory and research.* Hillsdale, NJ: Erlbaum.

Lefkowitz, M.M., Eron, L.D., Walder, L.O., and Huesmann, L.R. (1977). *Growing up to be violent.* New York: Pergamon.

Lehrman, D.S. (1953). A critique of Konrad Lorenz's theory of instinctive behavior. *Quarterly Review of Biology, 28,* 337–363.

Lepper, M.R., Greene, D., and Nisbett, R.E. (1973). Undermining children's intrinsic interest with extrinsic rewards: A test of the overjustification hypothesis. *Journal of Personality and Social Psychology, 28,* 129–137.

Lerner, M.J. (1975). The justice motive in social behavior: Introduction. *Journal of Social Issues, 31,* 1–20.

Lerner, M.J. (1980). *The belief in a just world: A fundamental delusion.* New York: Plenum.

Lerner, M.J., and Miller, D. (1978). Just world research and the attribution process: Looking back and ahead. *Psychological Bulletin, 85,* 1030–1051.

Lerner, M.J., and Simmons, C.H. (1966). Observer's reactions to the "innocent victim": Compassion or rejection. *Journal of Personality and Social Psychology, 4,* 203–210.

Leventhal, G.S. (1976). The distribution of rewards and resources in groups and organizations. In L. Berkowitz (Ed.), *Advances in experimental social psychology* (Vol. 9). New York: Academic Press.

Leventhal, G.S., Karuza, J., and Frey, W.R. (1980). Beyond fairness: A theory of allocation preferences. In G. Mikula (Ed.), *Justice and social interaction.* New York: Springer.

Leventhal, H. (1970). Findings and theory in the study of fear communications. In L. Berkowitz (Ed.) *Advances in experimental social psychology* (Vol. 5). New York: Academic Press.

Leventhal, H., and Cleary, P.D. (1980). The smoking problem: A review of the research and theory in behavioral risk modification. *Psychological Bulletin*, **88**, 370–405.

Levin, G.R., and Simmons, J.J. (1962). Response to food and praise by emotionally disturbed boys. *Psychological Reports*, **11**, 539–546.

Levine, D.W., McDonald, P.J., O'Neal, E.C., and Garwood, S.G. (1982). Classroom seating effects: Environment or self-selection-neither, either, or both. *Personality and Social Psychology Bulletin*, **8**, 365–369.

Levine, D.W., O'Neal, E.C., Garwood, S.G., and McDonald, P.J. (1980). Classroom ecology: The effects of seating position and grades and participation. *Personality and Social Psychology Bulletin*, **6**, 409–412.

Levine, R.A., and Campbell, D.T. (1972). *Ethnocentrism: Theories of conflict, ethnic attitudes, and group behavior*. New York: Wiley.

Levinger, G. (1979). A social exchange view on the dissolution of pair relationships. In R.L. Burgess and T.L. Huston (Eds.), *Social exchange in developing relationships*. New York: Academic Press.

Levinger, G., Senn, D.J., and Jorgenson, B.W. (1970). Progress toward permanence in courtship: A test of the Kerckhoff-Davis hypotheses. *Sociometry*, **33**, 427–443.

Levinger, G., and Snoek, J.D. (1972). *Attraction in relationship: A new look at interpersonal attraction*. Morristown, NJ: General Learning Press.

Lewicki, P. (1982). Social psychology as viewed by its practitioners. *Personality and Social Psychology Bulletin*, **8**, 409–446.

Lewin, K. (1936). *Principles of topological psychology*. New York: McGraw-Hill.

Lewin, K. (1943). Forces behind food habits and methods of change. *Bulletin of National Research Council*, **108**, 35–65.

Ley, P., and Spelman, M.S. (1967). *Communicating with the patient*. London: Staples Press.

Leyens, J.P., and Parke, R.E. (1975). Aggressive slides can induce a weapons effect. *European Journal of Social Psychology*, **32**, 346–360.

Liebert, R.M., and Baron, R.A. (1972). Some immediate effects of televised violence on children's behavior. *Developmental Psychology*, **6**, 469–475.

Likert, R.A. (1932). A technique for the measurement of attitudes. *Archives of Psychology*, **140**, 1–55.

Linder, D.E., Cooper, J., and Jones, E.E. (1967). Decision freedom as a determinant of the role of incentive magnitude in attitude change. *Journal of Personality and Social Psychology*, **6**, 245–254.

Lindsey, R. (1979). *The falcon and the snowman*. New York: Simon and Schuster.

Lindsey, R.C.L., Wells, G.L., and Rumpel, C.M. (1981). Can people detect eyewitness-identification accuracy across and within situations? *Journal of Applied Psychology*, **66**, 79–88.

Linskold, S. (1979). Managing conflict through announced conciliatory initiatives backed with retaliatory capability. In W.G. Austin and S. Worchel (Eds.), *The social psychology of inter-group relations*. Monterey, CA: Brooks/Cole.

Lippa, R. (1976). The effect of expressive control on expressive consistency and on the relation between expressive behavior and personality. *Journal of Personality*, **46**, 438–461.

Lippitt, R., and White, R.K. (1947). An experimental study of leadership and group life In T.M. Newcomb and E.L. Hartley (Eds.), *Readings in social psychology*. New York: Holt, Rinehart, and Winston.

Loftus, E.F. (1979). *Eyewitness testimony*. Cambridge MA: Harvard University Press.

Loftus, E.F. (1983). Whose shadow is crooked? *American Psychologist*, **38**, 576–577.

Loftus, E., and Monahan, J. (1980). Trial by data: Psychological research as legal evidence. *American Psychologist*, **35**, 270–283.

Loftus, E.F., and Palmer, J.C. (1974). Reconstruction of automobile destruction: An example of the interaction between language and memory. *Journal of Verbal Learning and Verbal Behavior*, **13**, 505–589.

Loftus, E.F., and Zanni, G. (1975). Eyewitness testimony: The influence of the wording of a question. *Bulletin of the Psychonomic Society*, **5**, 86–88.

Lombardo, M.P. (1985). Mutual restraint in swallows: A test of the Tit for Tat model of reciprocity. *Science*, **227**, 1363–1365.

London, P. (1970). The rescuers: Motivational hypotheses about Christians who saved Jews from the Nazis. In J. Macauley and L. Berkowitz (Eds.), *Altruism and helping behavior*. New York: Academic Press.

Loo, C. (1972). The effects of spatial density on the social behavior of children. *Journal of Applied Social Psychology*, **4**, 372–381.

Lord, R.G., and Hohenfeld, J.A. (1979). Longitudinal assessment of equity effects on the performance of major league baseball players. *Journal of Applied Psychology*, **64**, 19–26.

Lorenz, K.S. (1966). *On aggression*. New York: Harcourt Brace Jovanovich.

Lorge, I., Fox, D., Davitz, J., and Brenner, M. (1958). A survey of studies contrasting the quality of group performance and individual performance. *Psychological Bulletin*, **55**, 337–372.

Lorion, R.P. (1974). Patient and therapist variables in treatment of low income patients. *Psychological Bulletin*, **81**, 344–354.

Lott, A.J., and Lott, B.E. (1974). The role of reward in the formation of positive interpersonal attitudes. In T.L. Huston (Ed.), *Foundations of interpersonal attraction*. New York: Academic Press.

Lowin, A., and Craig, J.R. (1968). The influence of level of performance on managerial style: An experimental object lesson in the ambiguity of correlational data. *Organizational Behavior and Human Performance*, **3**, 440–458.

Loye, D., Gorney, R., and Steele, G. (1977). Effects of television: An experimental field study. *Journal of Communication*, **27**, 206–216.

Luborsky, L., Chandler, M., Auerbach, A.H., Cohen, J., and Bachrach, H.M. (1971). Factors influencing the outcome of psychotherapy: A review of quantitative research. *Psychological Bulletin*, **75**, 145–185.

Luce, R.D., and Raiffa, H. (1957). *Games and decisions: Introduction and critical survey*. New York: Wiley.

Lucker, G.W., Rosenfield, D., Sikes, J., and Aronson, E. (1977). Performance in the interdependent classroom: A field study. *American Educational Research Journal*, **13**, 115–123.

Lumsdaine, A.A., and Janis, I.L. (1953). Resistance to "counterpropaganda produced by one-sided and two-sided propaganda" presentations. *Public Opinion Quarterly*, **17**, 311–318.

Maccoby, E.E., and Jacklin, C.N. (1974). *The psychology of sex differences*. Stanford, CA: Stanford University Press.

MacDonald, A.P. (1971). Internal-external locus of control: Parental antecedents. *Journal of Consulting and Clinical Psychology*, **37**, 141–147.

MacNeil, M.K., and Sherif, M. (1976). Norm change over subject generation as a function of arbitrariness of norms. *Journal of Personality and Social Psychology*, **34**, 762–773.

Maddux, J.E., and Rogers, R.W. (1980). Effects of source expertness, physical attractiveness and supporting arguments on persuasion: A case of brains over beauty. *Journal of Personality and Social Psychology*, **39**, 235–241.

Mahoney, E.R. (1979). Patterns of sexual behavior among college students. Unpublished manuscript. Western Washington University.

Mahoney, E.R. (1983). *Human sexuality*. New York: McGraw-Hill.

Maier, N.R.F., and Solem, A.R. (1952). The contribution of a discussion leader to the quality of group thinking: The effective use of minority opinions. *Human Relations*, **5**, 277–288.

Major, B., and Adams, J.B. (1983). Role of gender, interpersonal orientation, and self-presentation in distributive-justice behavior. *Journal of Personality and Social Psychology*, **45**, 598–608.

Major, B., and Deaux, K. (1982). Individual differences in justice behavior. In J. Greenberg and R.L. Cohen (Eds.), *Equity and justice in social behavior*. New York: Academic Press.

Major, B., and Konar, E. (In Press). An investigation of sex differences in pay expectations and their possible causes. *Academy of Management Journal*.

Major, B., McFarlin, D., and Gagnon, D. (In Press). Overworked and underpaid: On the nature of gender differences in personal entitlement. *Journal of Personality and Social Psychology*.

Malamuth, N. (1981). Rape proclivity among males. *Journal of Social Issues*, **37**, 138–157.

Malamuth, N. (1983). Factors associated with rape as predictors of laboratory aggression. *Journal of Personality and Social Psychology*, **45**, 432–443.

Malamuth, N., and Check, J.V.P. (1980a). Penile tumescence and perceptual responses to rape as a function of victim's perceived reactions. *Journal of Applied Social Psychology*, **10**, 528–547.

Malamuth, N., and Check, J.V.P. (1980b). Sexual arousal to rape and consenting depictions: The importance of the woman's arousal. *Journal of Abnormal Psychology*, **89**, 763–766.

Malamuth, N., and Check, J.V.P. (1981a). The effects of exposure to aggressive-pornography: Rape proclivity, sexual arousal, and beliefs in rape myths. Paper presented at annual meeting of the American Psychological Association.

Malamuth, N., and Check, J.V.P. (1981b). The effects of mass media exposure on acceptance of violence against women. *Journal of Research in Personality*, **15**, 436–444.

Malamuth, N., and Donnerstein, E. (1983). The effects of aggressive-pornographic mass media stimuli. In L. Berkowitz (Ed.), *Advances in experimental social psychology* (Vol. 15). New York: Academic Press.

Malamuth, N., Haber, S., and Feshbach, S. (1980). Testing hypotheses regarding rape: Exposure to sexual violence, sex differences, and the normality of rape. *Journal of Research in Personality*, **14**, 121–137.

Malamuth, N., Heim, M., and Feshbach, S. (1980). The sexual responsiveness of college students to rape depictions: Inhibitory and disinhibitory effects. *Journal of Personality and Social Psychology*, **38**, 399–408.

Malpass, R.S., and Devine, P.G. (1981). Eyewitness identification: Lineup instructions and absence of the offender. *Journal of Applied Psychology*, **66**, 482–491.

Malpass, R.S., and Kravitz, J. (1969). Recognition for faces of own and other races. *Journal of Personality and Social Psychology*, **13**, 330–334.

Mann, L. (1981). The baiting crowd in episodes of threatened suicide. *Journal of Personality and Social Psychology*, **41**, 703–709.

Mann, R. (1977). The use of social indicators in environmental planning. In I. Altman and J.F. Wohlwill (Eds.), *Human behavior and environment* (Vol. 2). New York: Plenum.

Mantell, D. (1971). The potential for violence in Germany. *Journal of Social Issues*, **27**, 101–112.

Marks, E.L., Penner, L.A., and Stone, A.V.W. (1982). Helping as a function of empathic responses and sociopathy. *Journal of Research in Personality*, **16**, 1–20.

Marston, M. (1970). Compliance with medical regimens. *Nursing Research*, **19**, 312–323.

Martens, R. (1969). Palmar sweating and the presence of an audience. *Journal of Experimental Social Psychology*, **5**, 371–374.

Martin, G.B., and Clark, R.D. III (1982). Distress crying in neonates: Species and peer specificity. *Developmental Psychology*, **18**, 3–9.

Martindale, D.A. (1971). Territorial dominance in dyadic verbal interactions. *Proceedings of the 79th Annual Convention of American Psychological Association*, **6**, 305–306.

Massie, R.K. (1980). *Peter the Great: His life and world*. New York: Ballantine Books.

Masters, W.H., and Johnson, V.E. (1966). *Human sexual response*. Boston, MA: Little Brown.

Mathes, F.W., and Edwards, L.I. (1978). Physical attractiveness as an input in social exchanges. *Journal of Psychology*, **98**, 267–275.

Matthews, K.A. (1977). Caregiver-child interactions and the Type A coronary-prone behavior pattern. *Child Development*, **48**, 1752–1756.

Matthews, K.A. (1981). 'At a relatively early age . . . the habit of working the machine to its maximum capacity': Antecedents of the Type A coronary prone behavior pattern. In S.S. Brehm, S.M. Kassin, and F.X. Gibbons (Eds.), *Developmental social psychology* New York: Oxford.

Matthews, K.A. (1982). Psychological perspectives on the type A behavior pattern. *Psychological Bulletin*, **91**, 293–323.

Mathews, K.E., and Canon, L.K. (1975). Environmental noise level as a determinant of helping behavior. *Journal of Personality and Social Psychology*, **32**, 571–577.

McAlister, A., Puska, P., Koskela, K., Pallonen, V., and Maccoby, N. (1980). Mass communications and community in public health education. *American Psychologist*, **35**, 375–379.

McArthur, L.Z. (1972). The how and what of why: Some determinants and consequences of causal attribution. *Journal of Personality and Social Psychology*, **22**, 171–193.

McArthur, L.Z., and Post, D.L. (1977). Figural emphasis and person perception. *Journal of Experimental Social Psychology*, **13**, 520–535.

McCagny, C.H. (1980). *Crime in American society*. New York: Macmillan.

McCarty, D., Diamond, W., and Kaye, M. (1982). Alcohol, sexual arousal, and the transfer of excitation. *Journal of Personality and Social Psychology*, **42**, 977–988.

McCauley, C., Coleman, G., and DeFusco, P. (1978). Commuters' eye contact with strangers in city and suburban train stations: Evidence of short-term adaptation to interpersonal overload in the city. *Environmental Psychology and Nonverbal Behavior*, **2**, 215–225.

McDermott, J. (1979). *Rape victimization in 26 American cities*. Washington, D.C.: U.S. Department of Justice, Law Enforcement and Assistance Administration.

McFarland, C., and Ross, M. (1982). Impact of causal attributions on affective reactions to success and failure. *Journal of Personality and Social Psychology*, **43**, 937–946.

McGinniss, J. (1971). *The selling of a president*. New York: Trident Press.

McGovern, L.P. (1976). Dispositional social anxiety and helping behavior under three conditions of threat. *Journal of Personality*, **44**, 84–97.

McGrath, J.E. (1984). *Groups: Interaction and performance*. Englewood Cliffs, NJ: Prentice Hall.

McGuire, W.J. (1964). Inducing resistance to persuasion: Some contemporary approaches. In L. Berkowitz (Ed.), *Advances in experimental social psychology* (Vol. 1). New York: Academic Press.

McGuire, W.J. (1968). Personality and susceptibility to social influence. In E.F. Borgatta and W.W. Lambert (Eds.), *Handbook of personality theory and research*. Chicago: Rand McNally.

McGuire, W.J. (1969). The nature of attitudes and attitude change. In G. Lindzey and E. Aronson (Eds.), *The handbook of social psychology* (2nd ed., Vol. 3). Reading, MA: Addison-Wesley.

McGuire, W.J. (1973). The yin and yang of progress in social psychology. *Journal of Personality and Social Psychology*, **26**, 446–456.

McGuire, W.J., and Papageorgis, D. (1961). The relative efficacy of various types of prior belief-defense in producing immunity against persuasion. *Journal of Abnormal and Social Psychology*, **62**, 327–337.

Mehrabian, A., and Epstein, N. (1972). A measure of emotional empathy. *Journal of Personality*, **40**, 525–543.

Melamed, B.G., and associates (1983). Dentists' behavior management as it affects compliance and fear in pediatric patients. *Journal of American Dental Association*, **106**, 324–330.

Melamed, B.G. (1984). Health intervention: Collaboration for health and science. In B.L. Hammonds and C.J. Scheirer (Eds.), *The master lecture series* (Vol. 3). Washington, D.C.: American Psychological Association.

Messe, L.A., and Watts, B.L. (1983). Complex nature of the sense of fairness: Internal standards and social comparisons as bases for reward evaluations. *Journal of Personality and Social Psychology*, **45**, 84–93.

Messick, D.M., and Brewer, M.B. (1983). Solving social dilemmas: A review. In L. Wheeler and P. Shaver (Eds.), *Review of personality and social psychology* (Vol. 4). Beverly Hills, CA: Sage.

Messick, D.M., Wilke, H., Brewer, M.B., Kramer, R.M., Zemke, P., and Lui, L. (1983). Individual adaptations and structural change as solutions to social dilemmas. *Journal of Personality and Social Psychology*, **44**, 294–309.

Mewborn, C.R., and Rogers, R.W. (1979). Effects of threatening and reassuring components of fear appeals on physiological and verbal measures of emotion and attitudes. *Journal of Experimental Social Psychology*, **15**, 242–253.

Meyer, A.J., Nash, J.D., McAlister, A.L., Maccoby, N., and Farquhar, J.N. (1980). Skills training in a cardiovascular health education campaign. *Journal of Consulting and Clinical Psychology*, **48**, 129–242.

Meyer, P. (1970). If Hitler asked you to electrocute a stranger, would you? Probably. *Esquire*, **74**, 73, 128–132.

Middlemist, R.D., Knowles, E.S., and Matter, C.F. (1976). Personal space invasions in the lavatory: Suggestive evidence for arousal. *Journal of Personality and Social Psychology*, **33**, 541–546.

Midlarsky, E., and Bryan, J.H. (1967). Training charity in children. *Journal of Personality and Social Psychology*, **5**, 408–415.

Midlarsky, E., and Bryan, J.H. (1972). Affect expressions and children's imitative altruism. *Journal of Experimental Research in Personality*, **6**, 195–203.

Midlarsky, E., Bryan, J.H., and Brickman, P. (1973). Aversive approval: Interactive effects of modeling and reinforcement on altruistic behavior. *Child Development*, **44**, 321–328.

Midlarsky, E., and Midlarsky, M. (1973). Some determinants of aiding under experimentally induced stress. *Journal of Personality*, **41**, 305–327.

Mikula, G. (1980). On the role of justice in allocation decisions. In G. Mikula (Ed.), *Justice and social interaction*. New York: Springer-Verlag.

Milgram, S. (1964). Group pressure and action against the person. *Journal of Abnormal and Social Psychology*, **69**, 137–143.

Milgram, S. (1965). Some conditions of obedience and disobedience to authority. *Human Relations*, **18**, 57–76.

Milgram, S. (1969). The lost-letter technique. *Psychology Today*, **2**, 30–33.

Milgram, S. (1970). The experience of living in cities. *Science*, **167**, 1461–1468.

Milgram, S. (1974). *Obedience to authority: An experimental view*. New York: Harper & Row.

Miller, D.T. (1976). Ego involvement and attributions for success and failure. *Journal of Personality and Social Psychology*, **34**, 901–906.

Miller, D.T., Norman, S.A., and Wright, E. (1978). Distortion in person perception as a consequence of the need for effective control. *Journal of Personality and Social Psychology*, **36**, 598–607.

Miller, D.T., and Porter, C.A. (1980). Effects of temporal perspective on the attribution process. *Journal of Personality and Social Psychology*, **39**, 532–541.

Miller, D.T., and Ross, M. (1975). Self-serving biases in the attribution of causality: Fact or fiction? *Psychological Bulletin*, **82**, 213–225.

Miller, L.C., and Cox, C.L. (1982). For appearance's sake: Public self-consciousness and makeup. *Personality and Social Psychology Bulletin*, **8**, 748–751.

Miller, M. (1971). *On being different*. New York: Random House.

Miller, N.E. (1941). The frustration aggression hypothesis. *Psychological Review*, **48**, 337–342.

Miller, R.L., Brickman, P., and Bolen, D. (1975). Attribution versus persuasion as a means of modifying behavior. *Journal of Personality and Social Psychology*, **1975, 31**, 430–441.

Mischel, W. (1968). *Personality and assessment*. New York: Wiley.

Mischel, W. (1969). Continuity and change in personality. *American Psychologist*, **24**, 1012–1018.

Mischel, W. (1979). On the interface of cognition and personality: Beyond the person-situation debate. *American Psychologist*, **34**, 740–754.

Mischel, W. (1984). Convergences and challenges in the search for consistency. *American Psychologist*, **39**, 351–364.

Mitchell, R.E. (1971). Some implications of high density housing. *American Sociological Review*, **36**, 18–29.

Mitchell, T.R. (1970). Leader complexity and leadership style. *Journal of Personality and Social Psychology*, **16**, 166–174.

Moe, J.L., Nacoste, R.W., and Insko, C.A. (1980). Belief versus race as determinants of discrimination: A study of adolescents in 1966 and 1979. *Journal of Personality and Social Psychology*, **41**, 1031–1050.

Moln, L.D. (1981). The conversion of power imbalance to power use. *Social Psychology Quarterly*, **44**, 151–163.

Money, J. (1965). Psychosexual differentiation. In J. Money (Ed.) *Sex research, new developments*. New York: Holt, Rinehart, and Winston.

Money, J., and Ehrhardt, A. (1972). *Man and woman: Boy and girl*. Baltimore: Johns Hopkins Press.

Money, J., Hampson, J.G., and Hampson, J.L. (1957). Imprinting and the establishment of gender role. *Archives of Neurological Psychiatry*, **77**, 333–336.

Monson, T.C. (1985). Situational constraints, self-selection of settings and the prediction of behavior. Paper presented at annual meeting of the Southeastern Psychological Association.

Montague, A. (1976). *The nature of human aggression*. New York: Oxford University Press.

Mook, D.G. (1983). In defense of external validity. *American Psychologist*, **38**, 379–387.

Moore, B.S., Underwood, B., and Rosenhan, D.L. (1973). Affect and altruism. *Developmental Psychology*, **8**, 99–104.

Morgan, D.E., and Dirks, D.D. (1973). Suprathreshold loudness adaptation. *Journal of the Acoustical Society of America*, **53**, 1560–1564.

Moriarity, D., and McGabe, A.E. (1977). Studies of television and youth sport. In *Ontario Royal Commission on Violence in the Communications Industry Report* (Vol. 5). Toronto, OT: Queens Printer for Ontario.

Morse, S., and Gergen, K.J. (1970). Social comparison, self-consistency, and the concept of self. *Journal of Personality and Social Psychology*, **16**, 148–156.

Moscovici, S. (1980). Toward a theory of conversion behavior. In L. Berkowitz (Ed.), *Advances in experimental social psychology* (Vol. 13). New York: Academic Press.

Moscovici, S., and Faucheux, C. (1972). Social influence, conformity bias, and the study of active minorities. In L. Berkowitz (Ed.), *Advances in experimental social psychology* (Vol. 6). New York: Academic Press.

Moscovici, S., and Personnaz, B. (1980). Studies in social influence V. Minority influence and conversion behavior in a perceptual task. *Journal of Experimental Social Psychology*, **16**, 270–282.

Moscovici, S., and Zavelloni, M. (1969). The group as a polarizer of attitudes. *Journal of Personality and Social Psychology*, **12**, 125–135.

Moskowitz, J.M., and Wortman, P.M. (1981). Reassessing the impact of school desegregation. In R.F. Boruch, P.M. Wortman, and D.S. Cordray (Eds.), *Reanalyzing program evaluations*. San Francisco, CA: Jossey-Bass.

Mosteller, F., and Wallace, O.L. (1963). Inference in an authorship problem: A comparative study of discrimination methods applied to the authorship of the Federalist Papers. *Journal of American Statistical Association*, **58**, 275–309.

Mueller, C.W. (1983). Environmental stressors and aggressive behavior. In R. Geen and E. Donnerstein (Eds.), *Aggression: Theoretical and empirical reviews* (Vol. 2). New York: Academic Press.

Mueller, C.W., and Donnerstein, E. (1977). The effects of humor-induced arousal upon aggressive behavior. *Journal of Research in Personality*. **11**, 73–82.

Mueller, C.W., Donnerstein, E., and Hallam, J. (1983). Violent films and prosocial behavior. *Personality and Social Psychology Bulletin*, **9**, 83–89.

Murphy, G., Murphy, L.B., and Newcomb, T.M. (1937). *Experimental social psychology*. (Rev. Ed.) New York: Harper.

Murray, J.P., and Ahammer, I.M. (1977). Kindness in the kindergarten: A multidimensional program for faciliatory altruism. Paper presented to the biennial meeting of the Society for Research in Child Development.

Murstein, B.I. (1972). Physical attraction and marital choice. *Journal of Personality and Social Psychology*, **22**, 8–12.

Murstein, B.I. (1974a). *Whom will marry whom?* New York: Springer

Murstein, B.I. (1974b). *Love, sex, and marriage through the ages*. New York: Springer.

Murstein, B.I. (1976). *Who will marry whom: Theories and research in marital choice*. New York: Springer.

Murstein, B.I., and Christy, P. (1976). Physical attractiveness and marriage adjustment in middle aged couples. *Journal of Personality and Social Psychology*, **34**, 537–542.

Myers, D.G. (1983). *Social Psychology*, New York: McGraw-Hill.

Myers, D.G., and Kaplan, M.F. (1976). Group-induced polarization in simulated juries. *Personality and Social Psychology Bulletin*, **2**, 63–66.

Naftulin, D.H., Ware, J.E., and Donelly, F.A. (1975). The Doctor Fox lecture: A paradigm of educational seduction. *Journal of Medical Education*, **48**, 630–635.

Nahemow, L., and Lawton, M.P. (1976). Similarity and propinquity in friendship formation. *Journal of Personality and Social Psychology*, **32**, 205–213.

Navasky, V.S. (1981). *Naming names*. New York: Penguin Books.

Nemeth, C. (1972). A critical analysis of research utilizing the prisoner's dilemma paradigm for the study of bargaining. In L. Berkowitz (Ed.), *Advances in experimental social psychology* (Vol. 6). New York: Academic Press.

Nemeth, C.J. (1981). Jury trials: Psychology and law. In L. Berkowitz (Ed.), *Advances in experimental social psychology* (Vol. 14). New York: Academic Press.

Nemeth, C.J., Endicott, J., and Wachtler, J. (1976). From the '50s to the '70s: Women in jury deliberations. *Sociometry*, **39**, 293–304.

Nemeth, C.J., and Wachtler, J. (1974). Creating the perceptions of consistency and confidence: A necessary condition for minority influence. *Sociometry*, **37**, 529–540.

Newcomb, T.M. (1943). *Personality and social change*. New York: Dryden.

Newcomb, T.M. (1961). *The acquaintance process*. New York: Holt, Rinehart, and Winston.

Newcomb, T.M. (1978). The acquaintance process: Looking mainly backward. *Journal of Personality and Social Psychology*, **36**, 1075–1083.

Newcomb, T.M., Koenig, K.E., Flacks, R., and Warwick, D.P. (1967). *Persistence and change: Bennington College and its students after 25 years*. New York: Wiley.

Newman, J., and McCauley, C. (1977). Eye contact with strangers in city, suburb, and small town. *Environment and Behavior*, **9**, 547–558.

Newman, O. (1973). *Defensible space*. New York: Macmillan.

Newman, O., and Franck, K.A. (1982). The effects of building size on personal crime and fear of crime. *Population and Environment*, **5**, 203–220.

Newston, D., Allen, V.L., and Wilder, D.A. (1973). Attribution of cause of dissent. Unpublished manuscript. University of Wisconsin.

Nisbett, R.E. (1980). The trait construct in lay and professional psychology. In L. Festinger (Ed.), *Retrospections on social psychology*. New York, Oxford.

Nisbett, R.E., and Borgida, E. (1975). Attribution and the psychology of prediction. *Journal of Personality and Social Psychology*, **32**, 932–943.

Nordhoy, F. (1962). Group interaction in decision making under risk. Unpublished Master's thesis. Massachusetts Institute of Technology.

Norman, W.T. (1963). Toward an adequate taxonomy of personality attributes: Replicated factor structure in peer nomination personality ratings. *Journal of Abnormal Social Psychology*, **66**, 574–583.

Norvell, N., and Worchel, S. (1981). A reexamination of the relation between equal status contact and intergroup attraction. *Journal of Personality and Social Psychology*, **41**, 5, 902–908.

Novak, D.W., and Lerner, M.J. (1968). Rejection as a function of perceived similarity. *Journal of Personality and Social Psychology*, **9**, 147–152.

Nowell, C., and Janis, I.L. (1982). Effective and ineffective partnerships in a weight-reduction clinic. In I.L. Janis (Ed.), *Counseling on personal decisions: Theory and research on short-term helping relationships*. New Haven, CT: Yale University Press.

Nowicki, S., and Strickland, B.R. (1973). A locus of control scale for children. *Journal of Clinical and Consulting Psychology*, **40**, 148–154.

O'Bryant, S.L., and Corder-Bolz, C.R. (1978). The effects of television on children's stereotyping of women's work roles. *Journal of Vocational Behavior*, **12**, 233–243.

O'Leary, V.E. (1974). Some attitudinal barriers to occupational aspirations in women. *Psychological Bulletin*, **81**, 809–826.

O'Neill, S.M., and Paluck, R.J. (1973). Altering territoriality through reinforcement. *Proceedings of the 81st Annual Convention of the American Psychological Association*, **8**, 901–902.

Obershall, A. (1978). Theories of social conflict. *Annual Review of Sociology*, **4**, 291–313.

Orne, M.T. (1969). Demand characteristics and the use of quasi-controls. In R. Rosenthal and R.L. Rosnow (Eds.), *Artifact in behavioral research*. New York: Academic Press.

Osborn, A.F. (1963). *Applied imagination* (3rd ed.). New York: Charles Scribner's Sons.

Osgood, C.E. (1959). Suggestions for winning the real war with communism. *Journal of Conflict Resolution*, **3**, 295–325.

Osgood, C.E. (1962). *An alternative to war or surrender*. Urbana, IL: University of Illinois Press.

Osgood, C.E. (1965). Cross cultural comparability of attitude measurement via multi-lingual semantic differential. In I.S. Steiner and M. Fishbein (Eds.), *Recent studies in social psychology*. New York: Holt, Rinehart, and Winston.

Osgood, C.E. (1974). GRIT for MBFR: A proposal for unfreezing force-level postures in Europe. Unpublished manuscript, University of Illinois.

Osgood, C.E., Suci, G.F., and Tannenbaum, P. (1957). *The measurement of meaning*. Urbana, IL: University of Illinois Press.

Oskamp, S. (1977). *Attitudes and opinions*. Englewood Cliffs, NJ: Prentice Hall.

Oskamp, S. (1984). *Applied social psychology*. Englewood Cliffs. NJ: Prentice-Hall.

Padawer-Singer, A.M., and Barton, A.H. (1975). The impact of pretrial publicity on jurors' verdicts. In R. Simon (Ed.), *The jury system in America*. Beverly Hills, CA: Sage.

Padawer-Singer, A.M., Singer, A.N., and Singer, R.L.J. (1977). An experimental study of twelve vs. six member juries under unanimous vs. nonunanimous decision. In B.D. Sales (Ed.), *Psychology in the legal process*. New York: Spectrum.

Page, R.A. (1977). Noise and helping behavior. *Environment and Behavior*, **9**, 311–334.

Page, R.A. (1978). Environmental influences on prosocial behavior: The effect of temperature. Paper presented at annual meeting of the Midwestern Psychological Association.

Pallack, M.S., Cook, D.A., and Sullivan, J.J. (1980). Commitment and energy conservation. *Applied Social Psychology Annual*, **1**, 235–253.

Pandey, J., and Griffitt, W. (1974). Attraction and helping. *Bulletin of Psychonomic Society*, **3**, 123–124.

Papageoris, D., and McGuire, W.J. (1961). The generality of immunity to persuasion produced by pre-exposure to weakened counterarguments. *Journal of Abnormal and Social Psychology*, **62**, 475–481.

Park, B., and Rothbart, M. (1982). Perception of out-group homogeneity and levels of social categorization: Memory for the subordinate attributes of in-group and out-group members. *Journal of Personality and Social Psychology*, **42**, 1031–1068.

Parker, D.R., and Rogers, R.W. (1981). Observation and performance of aggression: Effects of multiple models and frustration. *Personality and Social Psychology Bulletin*, **7**, 302–308.

Parlee, M.B. (1979). The friendship bond. *Psychology Today*. **13**, 43–54, 113.

Patterson, A.H. (1974a). Factors affecting interpersonal spatial proximity. Paper presented at annual Meeting of the American Psychological Association.

Patterson, A.H. (1974b). Hostility catharsis: A naturalistic quasi-experiment. Paper presented at annual meeting of the American Psychological Association.

Patterson, R.L., Dupree, L.W., Eberly, D.A., Jackson, G.M., O'Sullivan, M.J. Penner, L.A., and Dee-Kelly, C.D. (1982). *Overcoming the deficits of aging: A behavioral approach*. New York: Plenum.

Patterson, R.L., Penner, L.A., Eberly, D.A., and Harrell, T.L. (1983). Behavioral assessments of intellectual competence, conversational skills, and personal hygiene skills. *Behavioral Assessment*, **5**, 207–218.

Paulus, P.B., McCain, G., and Cox, V.C. (1978). Death rates, psychiatric commitments, blood pressure, and perceived crowding as a function of institutional crowding. *Environmental Psychology and Nonverbal Behavior*, **3**, 107–116.

Pearlman, M. (1963). *The capture and trial of Adolf Eichmann*. New York: Simon and Schuster.

Pennebaker, J.N., Dyer, M.A., Caulkins, R.S., Litowitz, D.L., Ackerman, P.L., Anderson, D.B., and McGraw, K.M. (1979). Don't girls get prettier at closing time: A country and western application to social psychology. *Personality and Social Psychology Bulletin*, **5**, 122–125.

Pennebaker, J., and Sanders, D.Y. (1976). American graffitti: Effects of authority and reactance arousal. *Personality and Social Psychology Bulletin*, **2**, 264–267.

Penner, L.A. (1971). Interpersonal attraction toward a black person as a function of value importance. *Personality: An International Journal*, **2**, 175–187.

Penner, L.A., Dertke, M.C., and Achenbach, C. (1974). The 'Flash' system: A field study of altruism. *Journal of Applied Social Psychology*, **3**, 362–378.

Penner, L.A., Hawkins, H.L., Dertke, M.C., Spector, P.E., and Stone, A.V.W. (1973). Obedience as a function of experimenter competence. *Memory and Cognition*, **1**, 241–245.

Penner, L.A., Summers, L., Brookmire, D.A., and Dertke, M.C. (1976). The lost dollar: Situational and personality determinants of a pro- and anti-social behavior. *Journal of Personality*, **44**, 274–293.

Penrod, S., and Hastie, R. (1979). Models of jury decision making: A critical review. *Psychological Bulletin*, **86**, 462–492.

Penrod, S., and Hastie, R. (1980). A computer simulation of jury decision making. *Psychological Review*, **87**, 133–159.

Peplau, L.A., and Perlman, D. (1979). Blueprint for a social psychological theory of loneliness. In M. Cook and G. Wilson (Eds.), *Love and attraction*. New York: Pergamon.

Peplau, L.A., Rubin, Z., and Hill, C.T. (1977). Sexual intimacy in dating relationships. *Journal of Social Issues*, **33**, 86–107.

Perlman, D. (1980). Attributions in the criminal justice process: Concepts and empirical illustration. In P.D. Lipsett and B.D. Sales (Eds.), *New directions in psycholegal research*. Beverly Hills, CA: Sage.

Perlman, D., and Oskamp, S. (1971). The effects of picture content and exposure frequency on evaluations of Negroes and whites. *Journal of Experimental Social Psychology*, **7**, 503–514.

Perlman, D. and Peplau, L.A. (1981). Toward a social psychology of loneliness. In S.W. Duck and R. Gilmour (Eds.), *Personal relationship in disorder*. London: Academic Press.

Perlman, D., and Peplau, L.A. (1982). Loneliness research: Implications for interventions. Paper presented at annual meeting of the American Psychological Association.

Perls, F. (1969). *Ego, hunger, and aggression*. New York: Random House.

Pesch, M. (1981). Sex role stereotypes on the air waves of the eighties. Paper presented at annual meeting of the Eastern Communication Association.

Peters, L.H., Hartke, D.D., and Pohlman, J.T. (1985). Fiedler's contingency model of leadership: An application of the meta-analysis procedures of Schmidt and Hunter. *Psychological Bulletin*, **97**, 274–285.

Petty, R.E., and Cacioppo, J.T. (1981). *Attitudes and persuasion: Classic and contemporary approaches*. Dubuque, IA: William C. Brown.

Petty, R.E., and Cacioppo, J.T. (1983). Central and peripheral routes in persuasion: Application to advertising. In L. Percy, and A. Woodside (Eds.), *Advertising and consumer psychology*. Lexington, MA: D.C. Heath.

Petty, R.E., and Cacioppo, J.T. (1984). The effects of involvement on responses to argument quantity and quality: Central and peripheral routes to persuasion. *Journal of Personality and Social Psychology*, **46**, 69–81.

Petty, R.E., and Caccioppo, J.T. (1985). The elaboration model of persuasion. In L. Berkowitz (Ed.), *Advances in experimental social psychology* (Vol. 18). New York: Academic Press.

Petty, R.E., Cacioppo, J.T., and Schumann, D. (1983). Central and peripheral routes to advertising effectiveness: The moderating role of involvement. *Journal of Consumer Research*, **10**, 134–148.

Petty, R.E., Ostrom, T.M., and Brock, T.C. (1981). *Cognitive responses in persuasion*. Hillsdale, NJ: Erlbaum Associates.

Phares, E.J. (1976). *Locus of control in personality*. Morristown, NJ: General Learning Press.

Philipsen, G., Mulac, A., and Dietrich, D. (1979). The effects of social interaction on group idea generation. *Communication Monographs*, **46**, 119–125.

Piaget, J. (1965). *The psychology of intelligence*. London: Routledge and Kegan Paul.

Piliavin, I.M., Piliavin, J.A., and Rodin, J. (1975). Costs, diffusion, and the stigmatized victim. *Journal of Personality and Social Psychology*, **32**, 429–438.

Piliavin, J.A., Dovidio, J.F., Gaertner, S.L., and Clark, R.D. III (1981). *Emergency intervention*. New York: Academic Press.

Piliavin, J.A., and Piliavin, I.M. (1972). The effects of blood on reactions to a victim. *Journal of Personality and Social Psychology*, **23**, 253–261.

Piliavin, J.A., Piliavin, I.M., and Truddell, B. (1974). Incidental arousal, helping, and diffusion of responsibility. Unpublished manuscript. University of Wisconsin.

Plous, S., and Zimbardo, P.C. (1984). The looking glass war. *Psychology Today*, **18**, 48–59.

Pope, D.C. (1983). *The making of modern advertising*. New York: Basic Books.

Porter, H. (1939). Studies in the psychology of stuttering: XIV. Stuttering phenomena in relation to size and personnel of audience. *Journal of Speech Disorders*, **4**, 323–333.

Porteus, J.D. (1977). *Environment and behavior*. Reading, MA: Addison-Wesley.

Prentice-Dunn, S., and Rogers, R.W. (1983). Deindividuation in aggression. In R. Geen and E. Donnerstein (Eds.), *Aggression: Theoretical and empirical reviews* (Vol. 2). New York: Academic Press.

Prestholdt, P.H. (1984). Yea team: Social loafing and team performance. Paper presented at annual meeting of the Southeastern Psychological Association.

President's Commission on Mental Health (1978). *Report to the President*. Washington, D.C.: U.S. Government Printing Office.

Pressley, S.A. (1984). How one man helps others. *Parade Magazine*, March 25, 4–6.

Price, J.L. (1971). The effects of crowding on the social behavior of children. Unpublished doctoral dissertation. Columbia University.

Price, R.A., and Vandenberg, S.G. (1979). Matching for physical attractiveness in married couples. *Personality and Social Psychology Bulletin*, **5**, 398–400.

Pritchard, R.D., Dunnette, M.D., and Jorgenson, D.O. (1972). Effects of perceptions of equity and inequity on worker performance and satisfaction. *Journal of Applied Psychology*, **56**, 75–94.

Proshansky, H.M. (1976). City and self-identity. Paper presented at annual meeting of the American Psychological Association.

Proshansky, H.M., Ittelson, W.H., and Rivlin, L.G. (1970). Environmental psychology: Man and his physical settings. New York: Holt, Rinehart, and Winston.

Pruitt, D.G. (1983). Kissinger as a traditional mediator with power. In J.Z. Rubin (Ed.), *The dynamics of third party intervention: Kissinger in the Middle East*. New York, Praeger.

Pruitt, D.G., and Kimmel, M.J. (1977). Twenty years of experimental gaming: Critique, synthesis, and suggestions for the future. *Annual Review of Psychology*, **28**, 363–392.

Pruitt, D.J., and Insko, C.A. (1980). Extension of the Kelley attribution model: The role of comparison-object, target-object consensus, distinctiveness and consistency. *Journal of Personality and Social Psychology*, **39**, 39–58.

Pryor, J.B., Gibbons, F.X., Wicklund, R.A., Fazio, R.H., and Hood, R. (1977). Self-focused attention and self-report validity. *Journal of Personality*, **45**, 514–527.

Quattrone, G.A. (1983). Overattribution and unit formation: When behavior engulfs the person. *Journal of Personality and Social Psychology*, **42**, 593–607.

Randle, C.W. (1956). How to identity promotable executives. *Harvard Business Review*, **34**, 122–134.

Rangel, J. (1985). Statistically at least, it is rather safe down there. *New York Times*, February 10, E7.

Rapoport, A. (1976). Mathematical models in theories of international relations: Expectations, caveats, and opportunities. In D.A. Zinnes and J.V. Gillespie (Eds.), *Mathematical models in international relations*. New York: Praeger.

Raven, B.H., and Kruglanski, A.W. (1970). Conflict and power. In P. Swingle (Ed.), *The structure of conflict*. New York: Academic Press.

Raven, B.H., and Rubin, J.Z. (1983). *Social Psychology*, New York: John Wiley and Son.

Rawlings, E.I. (1968). Witnessing harm to another: A reassessment of the role of guilt in altruistic behavior. *Journal of Personality and Social Psychology*, **10**, 377–380.

Read, P.P. (1974). *Alive*. New York: Avon Books.

Regan, D.T., and Fazio, R.H. (1977). On the consistency of attitudes and behavior: Look to the method of attitude formation. *Journal of Experimental Social Psychology*, **13**, 38–45.

Regan, D.T., Williams, M., and Sparling, S. (1972). Voluntary expiation of guilt: A field experiment. *Journal of Personality and Social Psychology*, **24**, 42–45.

Reis, H.T., and Jackson, L.A. (1981). Sex differences in reward allocation: Subjects partners and tasks. *Journal of Personality and Social Psychology*, **3**, 465–478.

Reis, H.T., Wheeler, L., Spiegal, N., Kernis, M.H., Nezlak, J., and Perri, M. (1982). Physical attractiveness in social interaction: II Why does appearance affect social experience? *Journal of Personality and Social Psychology*, **43**, 979–996.

Reisenzein, R. (1983). The Schachter theory of emotion: Two decades later. *Psychological Bulletin*, **94**, 239–264.

Reiss, M., Kalle, R.J., and Tedeschi, J. (1981). Bogus pipeline attitude measurement, impression management, and misattribution in induced compliance settings. *Journal of Social Psychology*, **115**, 247–258.

Reiss, M., Rosenfeld, P., Melburg, V., and Tedeschi, J.T. (1981). Self-serving attributions: Biased private perceptions and distorted public descriptions. *Journal of Personality and Social Psychology*, **41**, 224–231.

Restle, F., and Davis, J.H. (1969). Success and speed of problem solving by individuals and groups. *Psychological Review*, **69**, 520–536.

Reusch, J., and Kees, W. (1956). *Nonverbal communication: Notes on the visual perception of human relations.* Berkeley, CA: University of California Press.

Rice, M.E., and Grusec, J.E. (1975). Saying and doing: Effects on observer performance. *Journal of Personality and Social Psychology*, **32**, 584–593.

Richardson, D.C., and Campbell, J.L. (1982). Alcohol and rape: The effect of alcohol on attributions of blame for rape. *Personality and Social Psychology Bulletin*, **8**, 468–476.

Richardson, D.C., Vandenburg, R.J., and Humphries, S.A. (1983). Gender versus power: A new approach to the study of sex differences in retaliative aggression. Unpublished Manuscript, University of Georgia.

Riger, S., and Gordon, M.T. (1981). The fear of rape: A study in social control. *Journal of Social Issues*, **37**, 71–92.

Riordan, C.A., and Tedeschi, J.T. (1983). Attraction in aversive environments: Some evidence for classical conditioning and negative reinforcement. *Journal of Personality and Social Psychology*, **44**, 683–692.

Rittle, R.H. (1981). Changes in helping behavior: Self versus situational perceptions as mediators of the foot in the door effects. *Personality and Social Psychology Bulletin*, **7**, 423–430.

Rodin, J. (1976). Crowding, perceived choice and response to controllable and uncontrollable outcomes. *Journal of Experimental Social Psychology*, **12**, 564–578.

Rodin, J., and Baum, A. (1978). Crowding and helplessness: Potential consequences of density and loss of control. In A. Baum and Y. Epstein (Eds.), *Human response to crowding.* Hillsdale, NJ: Erlbaum.

Rodin, J., and Janis, I.L. (1979). The social power of health-care practitioners as agents of change. *Journal of Social Issues*, **35**, 60–81.

Rodin, J., and Janis, I.L. (1982). The social influence of physicians and other health care practitioners as agents of change. In H.S. Friedman and M.R. DiMatteo (Eds.), *Interpersonal Issues in health care.* New York: Academic Press.

Rodin, J., and Langer, E. (1977). Long-term effects of a control-relevant intervention with the institutionalized aged. *Journal of Personality and Social Psychology*, **35**, 897–902.

Rodin, J., and Langer, E. (1980). Aging labels: The decline of control and the fall of self-esteem. *Journal of Social Issues*, **36**, 12–29.

Roethlisberger, F.J., and Dickson, W.J. (1939). *Management and the worker.* Cambridge, MA: Harvard University Press.

Rogers, M., Miller, N.F., Mayer, S., and Duval, S. (1982). Personal responsibility and salience of the request for help: Determinants of the relation between negative affect and helping behavior. *Journal of Personality and Social Psychology*, **43**, 956–970.

Rogers, R.W. (1975). A protection motivation theory of fear appeals and attitude change. *Journal of Psychology*, **91**, 93–114.

Rogers, R.W., and Prentice-Dunn, S. (1981). Deindividuation and anger-mediated interracial aggression: Unmasking regressive racism. *Journal of Personality and Social Psychology*, **41**, 63–73.

Rohe, W., and Patterson, A.H. (1974). The effects of varied levels of resources and density on behavior in a day care center. Paper presented at meeting of the Environmental Design Research Association.

Rohner, R.P. (1976). Sex differences in aggression: Phylogenetic and enculturation perspectives. *Ethos*, **4**, 57–72.

Rohrer, J.H., Baron, S.H., Hoffman, E.L., and Swander, D.V. (1954). The stability of autokinetic judgments. *Journal of Abnormal and Social Psychology*, **49**, 595–597.

Rokeach, M. (1960). *The open and closed mind.* New York: Basic Books.

Rokeach, M. (1964). *The three christs of Ypsilanti.* New York: Knopf.

Rokeach, M. (1967). *The Value Survey.* Sunnydale, CA: The Halgren Press.

Rokeach, M. (1968). *Beliefs, attitudes and values.* San Francisco: Jossey Bass.

Rokeach, M. (1971). Long term experimental modification of values, attitudes and behavior. *American Psychologist*, **26**, 453–459.

Rokeach, M. (1973). *The nature of human values.* New York: Free Press.

Rokeach, M. (1979). *Understanding human values.* New York: Free Press.

Rokeach, M., Homant, R., and Penner, L. (1970). A value analysis of the disputed federalist papers. *Journal of Personality and Social Psychology*, **16**, 245–251.

Rokeach, M., and Kliejunas, P. (1972). Behavior as a function of attitude-toward-object and attitude-toward-situation. *Journal of Personality and Social Psychology*, **22**, 194–201.

Rokeach, M., and Mezei, L. (1966). Race and shared belief as factors in social choice. *Science*, **151**, 167–172.

Rokeach, M., and Rothman, G. (1965). The principle of belief congruence and the congruity principle as models of cognitive interaction. *Psychological Review*, **72**, 128–142.

Rokeach, M., Smith, P.W., and Evans, R.I. (1960). Two kinds of prejudice or one? In M. Rokeach (Ed.), *The open and closed mind.* New York: Basic Books.

Romer, D. (1979). Internalization versus identification in the laboratory: A causal analysis of attitude change. *Journal of Personality and Social Psychology*, **37**, 2171–2180.

Rook, K.S., and Hammen, C.L. (1977). A cognitive perspective on the experience of sexual arousal. *Journal of Social Issues*, **33**, 7–29.

Rorer, L.G. (1965). The great response style myth. *Psychological Bulletin*, **63**, 129–156.

Rosen, P.L. (1972). *The supreme court and social science.* Urbana, IL: University of Illinois Press.

Rosenbaum, M.E., Moore, D.L., Cotton, J.L., Cook, M.S., Hieser, R.A., Shovar, M.N., and Gray, M.J. (1980). Group productivity and process: Pure and mixed reward structures and task interdependence. *Journal of Personality and Social Psychology*, **39**, 626–642.

Rosenbaum, M.E. (1980). Cooperation and competition. In P.B. Paulus (Ed.), *The psychology of group influence.* Hillsdale, NJ: Erlbaum.

Rosenberg, M.J. (1960). An analysis of affective-cognitive consistency. In M.J. Rosenberg, C.I. Hovland, W.J. McGuire, R.P. Abelson, and J.W. Brehm (Eds.), *Attitude organization and change: An analysis of consistency among attitude components.* New Haven, CT: Yale University Press.

Rosenberg, M.J. (1969). The conditions and consequences of evaluation apprehension. In R. Rosenthal and R.L. Rosnow (Eds.), *Artifact in behavioral research.* New York: Academic Press.

Rosenberg, M.J., and Hovland, C.I. (1960). Cognitive, affective, and behavioral components of attitude. In M.J. Rosenberg, C.I. Hovland, W.J. McGuire, R.P. Abelson, and J.W. Brehm (Eds.),

Attitude organization and change: An analysis of consistency among attitude components. New Haven, CT: Yale University Press.

Rosenberg, S., Nelson, C.E., and Vivekananthan, P.S. (1968). A multidimensional approach to the structure of personality impressions. *Journal of Personality and Social Psychology.* **9**, 283–294.

Rosenberg, S., and Sedlak, A. (1972). Structural representations of implicit personality theory. In L. Berkowitz (Ed.), *Advances in experimental social psychology* (Vol. 6). New York: Academic Press.

Rosenfeld, H.M., Shea, M., and Greenbaum, P. (1979). Facial emblems of "right" and "wrong": Topographical analysis and derivation of a recognition test. *Semiotica*, **26**, 15–34.

Rosenhan, D. (1970). The natural socialization of altruistic autonomy. In J. Macauley and L. Berkowitz (Eds.), *Altruism and helping behavior.* New York: Academic Press.

Rosenhan, D.L. (1973). On being sane in insane places. *Science*, **179**, 250–258.

Rosenhan, D.L., Karylowski, J., Salovey, P., and Hargis, K. (1981). Emotion and altruism. In J.P. Rushton and R.M. Sorrentino (Eds.), *Altruism and helping behavior: Social, personality, and developmental perspectives.* Hillsdale, NJ: Erlbaum.

Rosenman, R.H. (1978). The interview method of assessment of the coronary prone behavior pattern. In T.M. Dembroski, S.M. Weiss, J.L. Shields, S.G. Haynes, and M. Feinlieb (Eds.), *Coronary-prone behavior.* New York: Springer-Verlag.

Rosenman, R.H., Brand, R.J., Scholtz, R.I., and Friedman, M. (1976). Multivariate prediction of coronary heart disease during 8.5 year follow-up in the Western Collaborative Group Study. *American Journal of Cardiology*, **37**, 903–910.

Rosenthal, R. (1966). *Experimenter effects in behavioral research.* New York: Appleton-Century-Crofts.

Rosenthal, R. (1969). Interpersonal expectations. In R. Rosenthal and R.L. Rosnow (Eds.), *Artifact in behavioral research.* New York: Academic Press.

Rosenthal, R., and Fode, K.L. (1963). Three experiments in experimenter bias. *Psychological Reports*, **12**, 491–511.

Rosenthal, R., and Jacobson, L. (1968). *Pygmalian in the classroom.* New York: Holt, Rinehart and Winston.

Rosenthal, R., and Rosnow, R.L. (1975). *The volunteer subject.* New York: Wiley.

Ross, E.A. (1908). *Social psychology: An outline and source book.* New York: Macmillan.

Ross, L. (1977). The intuitive psychologist and his shortcomings: Distortions in the attribution process. In L. Berkowitz (Ed.), *Advances in experimental social psychology* (Vol. 10). New York: Academic Press.

Ross, M., McFarland, C., and Fletcher, G.J.O. (1981). The effect of attitudes on the recall of personal histories. *Journal of Personality and Social Psychology*, **40**, 627–635.

Ross, M., McFarland, C., Conway, M., and Zanna, M.P. (1983). Reciprocal relation between attitudes and behavior recall: Committing people to newly formed attitudes. *Journal of Personality and Social Psychology*, **45**, 257–267.

Rotter, J.B. (1966). Generalized expectancies for internal versus external control of reinforcement. *Psychological Monographs*, **80**, (1 Whole No. 609).

Rotton, J. (1978). Air pollution is no choke. Unpublished manuscript. University of Dayton.

Rotton, J., Frey, J., Barry, T., Milligan, M., and Fitzpatrick, M. (1979). The air pollution experience and interpersonal aggression. *Journal of Applied Social Psychology*, **9**, 397–412.

Rouse, B., and Ewing, J. (1973). Marijuana and other drug use by women college students: Associated risk taking and coping activities. *American Journal of Psychiatry*, **130**, 486–491.

Rovario, S.E., and Holmes, D.S. (1980). Arousal transfer: The influence of fear arousal on subsequent sexual arousal for subjects with high and low sex guilt. *Journal of Research in Personality*, **14**, 307–320.

Royko, M. (1982). Harry wins 'Gun Owner of Year' award. *Tampa Tribune*, December 30, 25.

Rubenstein, C.M., and Shaver, P. (1982). The experience of loneliness. In L.A. Peplau and D. Perlman (Eds.), *Loneliness: A sourcebook of current theory, research and therapy.* New York: Wiley Interscience.

Rubenstein, C., Shaver, P., and Peplau, L.A. (1979). Loneliness. *Human Nature*, February, 58–65.

Rubin, A.M. (1978). Child and adolescent television use and political socialization. *Journalism Quarterly*, **55**, 125–129.

Rubin, J.Z. (1980). Experimental research on third party interventions in conflict: Toward some generalization. *Psychological Bulletin*, **87**, 379–392.

Rubin, J.Z., and Brown, B.R. (1975). *The social psychology of bargaining and negotiation.* New York: Academic Press.

Rubin, Z. (1970). Measurement of romantic love. *Journal of Personality and Social Psychology*, **16**, 265–273.

Rubin, Z. (1973). *Liking and loving: An invitation to social psychology.* New York: Holt, Rinehart, and Winston.

Ruble, D.N. (1984). Sex role development. In M.H. Bornstein and M.E. Lamb (Eds.), *Developmental psychology: An advanced textbook.* Hillsdale, NJ: LEA.

Ruble, D.N., Balaban, T., and Cooper, J. (1981). Gender constancy and the effects of sex-typed televised toy commercials. *Child Development*, **52**, 667–673.

Ruble, D.N., Feldman, N.S., Higgins, E.T., and Karlovac, M. (1979). Locus of causality and the use of information in the development of causal attributions. *Journal of Personality*, **47**, 595–614.

Rushton, J.P. (1975). Generosity in children: Immediate and long term effects of modeling, preaching, and moral judgment. *Journal of Personality and Social Psychology*, **31**, 459–466.

Rushton, J.P. (1979). Effects of prosocial television and film material on the behavior of viewers. In L. Berkowitz (Ed.), *Advances in experimental social psychology* (Vol. 12). New York: Academic Press.

Rushton, J.P. (1980). *Altruism, socialization, and society.* Englewood Cliffs, NJ: Prentice-Hall.

Rushton, J.P., and Littlefield, C. (1979). The effects of age, amount of modeling, and a success experience on seven- to eleven-year-old children's generosity. *Journal of Moral Education*, **9**, 55–56.

Rushton, J.P., and Owen, D. (1977). Immediate and delayed effects of TV modeling and preaching on children's generosity. *British Journal of Clinical and Social Psychology*, **14**, 309–310.

Rushton, J.P., and Teachman, G. (1978). The effects of positive reinforcement, attributions, and punishment on model induced altruism in children. *Personality and Social Psychology Bulletin*, **4**, 322–325.

Russell, D., Peplau, L.A., and Cutrona, C.E. (1980). The revised UCLA loneliness scale: Concurrent and discriminant validity evidence. *Journal of Personality and Social Psychology*, **39**, 472–480.

Rutherford, E., and Mussen, P. (1968). Generosity in nursery school boys. *Child Development*, **39**, 755–765.

Rutman, L. (1977). *Evaluation research methods: A basic guide.* Beverly Hills, CA: Sage.

Ryckman, R.M., Sherman, M.F., and Burgess, G.D. (1973). Locus of control and self-disclosure of public and private information by college men and women: Brief note. *Journal of Psychology*, **84**, 317–318.

Sackett, D.L., and Haynes, R.B. (1976). *Compliance with medical regimens.* Baltimore, MD: Johns Hopkins Press.

Sackett, D.L., and Snow, J.C. (1979). The magnitude of compliance and non-compliance. In R.B. Haynes, D.W. Taylor, and D.L. Sackett (Eds.), *Compliance in health care*. Baltimore, MD: The Johns Hopkins Press.

Saegert, S., Mac Intosh, E., and West, S. (1975). Two studies of crowding in urban public spaces. *Environment and Behavior, 7*, 159–184.

Saegert, S., Swap, W., and Zajonc, R.B. (1973). Exposure, context and interpersonal attraction. *Journal of Personality and Social Psychology, 25*, 234–242.

Sahakian, W.S. (1974). *Systematic social psychology*. New York: Chandler.

Saks, M.J. (1977). *Jury verdicts*. Lexington, MA: D.C. Heath and Co.

Saks, M.J., and Hastie, R. (1978). *Social psychology in court*. New York: Van Nostrand Rheinhold.

Sampson, E.E. (1975). On justice as equality. *Journal of Social Issues, 31*, 45–64.

Santee, R.T., and Maslach, C. (1982). To agree or not agree: Personal dissent amid social pressure to conform. *Journal of Personality and Social Psychology, 42*, 690–700.

Sargant, W. (1957). *Battle for the mind: A physiology of conversion and brainwashing*. Garden City, NY: Doubleday.

Sarnoff, I., and Zimbardo, P.G. (1961). Anxiety, fear, and social affiliation. *Journal of Abnormal and Social Psychology, 62*, 356–363.

Saulnier, K., and Perlman, D. (1981). The actor-observer bias is alive and well in prison: A sequel to Wells. *Personality and Social Psychology Bulletin, 7*, 559–564.

Schachter, S. (1951). Deviation, rejection, and communication. *Journal of Abnormal and Social Psychology, 46*, 190–207.

Schachter, S. (1959). *The psychology of affiliation*. Stanford, CA: Stanford University Press.

Schachter, S. (1964). The interaction of cognitive and physiological components of emotional state. In L. Berkowitz (Ed.), *Advances in experimental social psychology* (Vol. 1). New York: Academic Press.

Schachter, S. (1971). *Emotion, obesity, and crime*. New York: Academic Press.

Schachter, S., and Gross, L. (1968). Manipulated time and eating behavior. *Journal of Personality and Social Psychology, 10*, 98-106.

Schachter, S., and Singer, J.E. (1962). Cognitive, social and physiological determinants of emotional state. *Psychological Review 69*, 379-399.

Schantz, C.V. (1975). The development of social cognition. In. E.M. Hetherington (Ed.), *Review of Child Development Research* (Vol. 5). Chicago, IL: University of Chicago Press.

Scheier, M.F., Buss, A.H., and Buss, D.M. (1978). Self-consciousness, self-report of aggressiveness, and aggression. *Journal of Research in Personality, 12*, 133–140.

Schellenberg, J.A. (1978). *Masters of social psychology*. New York: Oxford.

Schlenker, B.R. (1980). *Impression management*. Monterey, CA: Brooks/Cole.

Schlenker, B.R. (1985). *The self and the social self*. New York: McGraw Hill.

Schneider, D.J., Hastorf, A.H., and Ellsworth, P.C. (1979). *Person perception* (2nd Ed.). Reading, MA: Addison-Wesley.

Schneider, F.W., Lesko, W.A., and Garrett, W.A. (1980). Helping behavior in hot, comfortable, and cold temperatures: A field study. *Environment and Behavior, 12*, 231–240.

Schultz, D.P. (1981). *A history of modern psychology* 3rd ed. New York: Academic Press.

Schulz, R. (1976). The effects of control and predictability on the psychological and physical well-being of the institutionalized aged. *Journal of Personality and Social Psychology, 35*, 897–902.

Schultz, R., and Hanusa, B.H. (1980). Experimental social gerontology: A social psychological perspective. *Journal of Social Issues, 36*, 30–46.

Schwartz, B., and Barsky, S.F. (1977). The home advantage. *Social Forces, 55*, 641–661.

Schwartz, S.H. (1973). Normative explanations of helping behavior: A critique, proposal, and empirical test. *Journal of Experimental Social Psychology, 9*, 349–364.

Schwartz, S.H. (1977). Normative influences on altruism. In L. Berkowitz (Ed.), *Advances in experimental social psychology* (Vol. 10). New York: Academic Press.

Schwartz, S.H., and Fleischman, J.A. (1982). Effects of negative personal norms on helping. *Personality and Social Psychology Bulletin, 8*, 81–86.

Schwartz, S.H., and Howard, J. (1982). Helping and cooperation: A self-based motivational model. In V.J. Derlaga and J. Grzelak (Eds.), *Cooperation and helping behavior: Theories and research*. New York: Academic Press.

Schwarzfeld, J., Bizman, A., and Raz, M. (1983). The foot in the door paradigm: Effects of second request size on donation probability and donor generosity. *Personality and Social Psychology Bulletin, 9*, 443–450.

Scott, J.P. (1958). *Aggression*. Chicago, IL: University of Chicago Press.

Scott, J.P. (1972). Hostility and aggression. In B. Wolman (Ed.), *Handbook of genetic psychology*. Englewood Cliffs, NJ: Prentice Hall.

Sears, D.O., Lau, R.R., Tyler, T.R., and Allen, H.M. (1980). Self interest or symbolic politics in policy attitudes and presidential voting. *American Political Science Review, 74*, 670–684.

Seashore, S.E. (1954). Group cohesiveness as a factor in industrial morale and productivity. *American Psychologist, 8*, 468.

Seaver, W.B. (1973). Effects of naturally induced teacher expectancies. *Journal of Personality and Social Psychology, 28*, 333–342.

Segal, M.W. (1974). Alphabet and attraction: An unobtrusive measure of the effect of propinquity in a field setting. *Journal of Personality and Social Psychology, 30*, 654–657.

Seidenberg, B., and Snadowsky, A. (1976). *Social psychology: An introduction*. New York: Free Press.

Seligman, M.E. (1975). *Helplessness: On depression, development, and death*. San Francisco: Freeman.

Seligman, M.E. (1981). A learned helplessness point of view. In L.P. Rehm (Ed.), *Behavior therapy for depression*. New York: Academic Press.

Selye, H. (1956). *The stress of life*. New York: McGraw-Hill.

Serrin, W. (1981). Sex is a growing multimillion dollar business. *New York Times*, February 9, B1–B6.

Seyfried, B.A., and Hendrick, C. (1973). When do opposites attract? When they are opposite in sex and sex-roles. *Journal of Personality and Social Psychology, 25*, 15–20.

Shaffer, D.R. (1979). *Social and personality development*. Monterey, CA: Brooks/Cole.

Shaffer, D.R., and Case, T. (1982). On the decision to testify in one's own behalf: Effects of withheld evidence, defendant's sexual preference, and juror dogmatism on juridic decisions. *Journal of Personality and Social Psychology, 42*, 335-346.

Shanab, M.E., and Yahya, L.A. (1977). A behavioral study of obedience in children. *Journal of Personality and Social Psychology, 35*, 530–536.

Shaw, M.E. (1964). Communication networks. In L. Berkowitz (Ed.), *Advances in experimental social psychology* (Vol. 1). New York: Academic Press.

Shaw, M.E., and Costanzo, P.R. (1982). *Theories of social psychology*. New York: McGraw-Hill.

Sheehan, E.R.F. (1976). How Kissinger did it: Step by step in the middle east. *Foreign Policy*, **22**, 3–70.

Sherif, C.W., Sherif, M., and Nebergall, R. (1965). *Attitude and attitude change*. Philadelphia, PA: Saunders.

Sherif, M. (1953). A study of some social factors in perception. *Archives of Psychology*, **27**, No. 187.

Sherif, M. (1963). *The psychology of social norms*. New York: Harper and Row. (Originally published 1936).

Sherif, M., Harvey, O.J., White, B.J., Hood, W.R., and Sherif, C. (1961). *Intergroup conflict and cooperation: The robber's cave experiment*. Norman, OK: University of Oklahoma Press.

Sherif, M., and Sherif, C.W. (1967). Attitude as the individual's own categories: The social judgment-involvement approach to attitude change. In C.W. Sherif and M. Sherif (Eds.), *Attitude, ego-involvement, and change*. New York: Wiley.

Sherif, M., and Sherif, C.W. (1969). *Social psychology*. New York: Harper.

Sherman, S., Presson, C.C., Chassin, L., Bensenberg, M., Corty, E., and Olshavsky, R.W. (1982). Smoking intentions in adolescents: Direct experience and predictability. *Personality and Social Psychology Bulletin*, **8**, 376–383.

Sherwin, A.L., Robb, J.P., and Lechter, M. (1973). Improved control of epilepsy by monitoring plasma ethosuximide. *Archives of Neurology*, **28**, 178–181.

Shiflett, S.C. (1973). The contingency model of leadership effectiveness: Some implications of its statistical and methodological properties. *Behavioral Science*, **18**, 429–440.

Shomer, R.W., Davis, A.H., and Kelley, H.H. (1966). Threat and the development of coordination: Further studies of the Deutsch and Krauss trucking game. *Journal of Personality and Social Psychology*, **4**, 119–126.

Shotland, R.L., and Yankowski, L.D. (1982). The random response method: A valid and ethical indicator of the "truth" in reactive situations. *Personality and Social Psychology Bulletin*, **8**, 174–179.

Should the punishment fit the crime? (1983). *Newsweek*, June 13, 22.

Shupe, L.M. (1954). Alcohol and crimes: A study of urine alcohol concentration found in 882 persons arrested during or immediately after the commission of a felony. *Journal of Criminal Law and Criminology*, **44**, 661–665.

Shweder, R. (1975). How relevant is an individual difference theory of personality? *Journal of Personality*, **43**, 455–484.

Sidowski, J.B., Wyckoff, B., and Tabory, L. (1956). The influence of reinforcement and punishment in a minimal social situation. *Journal of Abnormal and Social Psychology*, **52**, 115–119.

Siebenaler, J.B., and Caldwell, D.K. (1956). Cooperation among adult dolphins. *Journal of Mammology*, **37**, 126–128.

Siegal, S., and Fouraker, L.E. (1960). *Bargaining and group decision making: Experiments in bilateral monopoly*. New York: McGraw-Hill.

Sigall, H., and Ostrove, N. (1975). Beautiful but dangerous: Effects of offender attractiveness and nature of crime on juric judgment. *Journal of Personality and Social Psychology*, **31**, 410–414.

Sigall, H., and Page, R. (1971). Current stereotypes a little fading, a little faking. *Journal of Personality and Social Psychology*, **18**, 247–255.

Simmer, M. (1971). Newborn's response to the cry of another infant. *Developmental Psychology*, **45**, 136–150.

Simon, W., and Gagnon, J. (1977). Psychosexual development. In D. Byrne and L.A. Byrne (Eds.), *Exploring human sexuality*. New York: Crowell.

Simon, R.J. (1967). *The jury in the defense of insanity*. Boston, MA; Little, Brown.

Singer, J.D., and Small, M. (1970). *The wages of war 1816–1965: A statistical handbook*. New York: Wiley.

Singer, J.L., and Singer, D.G. (1982). Television viewing, family style, and aggressive behavior in preschool children. In M. Green (Ed.), *Violence and the American family*. Washington, DC.: American Association for the Advancement of Science.

Singerman, K.J., Borkovec, T.D., and Baron, R.S. (1976). Explorations in the drive theory of social facilitation. *Journal of Social Psychology*, **99**, 259–271.

Sistrunk, F., and McDavid, J. (1971). Sex variables in conforming behavior. *Journal of Personality and Social Psychology*, **17**, 200–207.

Slaby, R.G., Quarforth, G.R., and McConnachie, G.A. (1976). Television violence and its sponsors. *Journal of Communication*, **26**, 88–96.

Smith, P.C., Kendall, L.M., and Hulin, C.L. (1969). *The measurement of satisfaction in work and retirement*. Chicago, IL: Rand McNally.

Smith, D.L., Pruitt, D.G., and Carnevale, P.J.D. (1982). Matching and mismatching: The effect of own limit, other's toughness, and time pressure on concession rate in negotiation. *Journal of Personality and Social Psychology*, **42**, 876–883.

Smith, D.S., and Hindus, M.S. (1975). Premarital pregnancy in America 1640-1971: An overview and interpretation. *Journal of Interdisciplinary History*, **4**, 537–570.

Smith, M.B., Bruner, J.S., and White, R.W. (1956). *Opinions and personality*. New York: Wiley.

Smith, M.L., and Glass, G.V. (1977). Meta-analysis of psychotherapy outcome studies. *American Psychologist*, **32**, 752–760.

Smith, T.C. (1980). Arms race unstability and war. *Journal of Conflict Resolution*, 24, 253–284.

Snyder, C.R., and Shenkel, R.J. (1975). The P.T. Barnum effect. *Psychology Today*, **8**, 52–55.

Snyder, M. (1974). The self-monitoring of expressive behavior. *Journal of Personality and Social Psychology*, **30**, 526–537.

Snyder, M. (1979). Self-monitoring processes. In L. Berkowitz (Ed.), *Advances in experimental social psychology* (Vol. 12). New York: Academic Press.

Snyder, M. (1981). Impression management. In L. Wrightsman and K. Deaux (Eds.), *Social psychology in the 80's*. Monterey, CA: Brooks Cole.

Snyder, M., and Monson, T.C. (1975). Persons, situations, and the control of social behavior. *Journal of Personality and Social Psychology*, **32**, 637–644.

Snyder, M., and Swann, W.B., Jr. (1976). When actions reflect attitudes: The politics of impression management. *Journal of Personality and Social Psychology*, **34**, 637–644.

Snyder, M., and Tanke, E. (1976). Behavior and attitude: Some people are more consistent than others. *Journal of Personality*, **44**, 510–517.

Snyder, M., Tanke, E., and Berscheid, E. (1977). Social perception and interpersonal behavior: On the self-fulfilling nature of social stereotypes. *Journal of Personality and Social Psychology*, **35**, 656–666.

Snyder, M., and Uranowitz, S.W. (1978). Reconstructing the past: Some cognitive consequences of person perception. *Journal of Personality and Social Psychology*, **36**, 941–950.

Sobel, R.S. (1974). The effects of success, failure, and locus of control on postperformance attribution of causality. *Journal of General Psychology*, **91**, 29–34.

Sogi, A., and Hoffman, M. (1976). Empathic distress in the newborn. *Developmental Psychology, 12,* 175–176.

Sommer, R. (1967). Classroom ecology. *Journal of Applied Behavioral Science, 3,* 489–503.

Sommer, R. (1969). *Personal space.* Englewood Cliffs, NJ: Prentice-Hall.

Sommer, R., and Ross, H. (1958). Social interaction on a geriatric ward. *International Journal of Social Psychiatry, 4,* 128–133.

Sosa, J.N. (1968). Vascular effects of frustration on passive and aggressive members of a clinical population. Unpublished Masters Thesis. Florida State University.

Sosis, R.H. (1974). Internal-external control and the perception of responsibility of another for an accident. *Journal of Personality and Social Psychology, 30,* 393–399.

Soutter, B.R., and Kennedy, M.C. (1974). Patient compliance assessment in drug trials: Usage and methods. *Australia, New Zealand Journal of Medicine, 4,* 360–364.

Spanier, G.B. (1983). Married and unmarried cohabitation in the United States 1980. *Journal of Marriage and the Family. 45,* 277–288.

Spector, P.E. (1983). Behavior in organizations as a function of employee's locus of control. *Psychological Bulletin, 91,* 482–497.

Spector, P.E., Cohen, S.L., and Penner, L.A. (1976). The effects of real vs. hypothetical risk on group choice shifts. *Personality and Social Psychology Bulletin, 2,* 290–293.

Spielberger, C.D., O'Hagen, S.E.J., and Kling, J.K., (1978). Dimensions of the psychopathic personality: Anxiety and sociopathy. In R. Hare and D. Schalling (Eds.), *Psychopathy and behavior.* New York: Wiley.

Spielberger, C.D., and London, P. (1982). Rage boomerangs: Lethal Type A anger. *American Health, 1,* 52–56.

St. John, N.H. (1975). *School desegregation: Outcomes for children.* New York: Wiley.

Staats, A.W., and Staats, C.K. (1958). Attitudes established by classical conditioning. *Journal of Abnormal and Social Psychology, 57,* 37–40.

Staats, A.W., Staats, C.K., and Crawford, H.L. (1962). First-order conditioning of meaning and the parallel conditioning of a GSR. *Journal of General Psychology, 67,* 159–167.

Stake, J.E. (1983). Factors in reward distribution: Allocator motive, gender, and protestant ethic. *Journal of Personality and Social Psychology, 44,* 410–418.

Stang, D.J., and Wrightsman, L.S. (1981). *Dictionary of social behavior and social research methods.* Monterey, CA: Brooks/Cole.

Staub, E. (1978). *Positive social behavior and morality,* Vol. 1: *Social and personality influences.* New York: Academic Press.

Steinem, G. (1980). Erotica and pornography: A clear and present difference. In L. Lederer (Ed.), *Take back the night: Women on pornography.* New York: Morrow.

Stephan, W.G. (1978). School desegregation: An evaluation of predictions made in Brown v. Board of Education. *Psychological Bulletin, 85,* 217–238.

Stephen, W.G., Rosenfield, D., and Stephan, C. (1976). Egotism in males and females. *Journal of Personality and Social Psychology, 34,* 1161–1167.

Sterling, B. (1977). The effects of anger, ambiguity, and arousal on helping behavior. Unpublished doctoral Dissertation, University of Delaware.

Stern, R.M., Gaupp, L., and Leonard, W.C. (1970). A comparison of GSR and subjective adaptation to stressful stimuli. *Psychophysiology, 7,* 3–9.

Stires, L.K. (1982). Classroom seating location, order effects, and reactivity. *Personality and Social Psychology Bulletin, 8,* 362–363.

Stogdill, R.M. (1963). *Manual for the Leader Behavior Description Questionnaire—Form XII.* Columbus, OH: Ohio State University.

Stokols, D. (1972). On the distinction between density and crowding: Some implications for future research. *Psychological Review, 79,* 275–278.

Stokols, D., Rall, M., Pinner, B., and Schopler, J. (1973). Physical, social, and personal determinants of the perception of crowding. *Environment and Behavior, 5,* 87–117.

Stokols, D., Smith, T., and Proster, J. (1976). The perception of crowding as a function of architectural variations in natural settings. *American Behavioral Scientist, 18,* 792–814.

Stone, G.C. (1979). Patient compliance and the role of the expert. *Journal of Social Issues, 35,* 34–59.

Stoner, J.A.F. (1961). A comparison of individual and group decisions involving risk. Unpublished master's thesis. Massachusetts Institute of Technology.

Storms, M.D., and Thomas, G.C. (1977). Reactions to physical closeness. *Journal of Personality and Social Psychology, 35,* 412–418.

Stouffer, S.A., Suchman, E.A., DeVinney, L.C., Starr, S.A., and Williams, R.M., Jr. (1949). *The American soldier: Adjustment during Army life* (Vol. 1). Princeton, NJ: Princeton University Press.

Straus, M.A., Gelles, R.J., and Steinmetz, S.K. (1980). *Behind closed doors. Violence in the American Family.* New York: Doubleday.

Strickland, B. (1977). Internal-external control of reinforcement. In T. Blass (Ed.), *Personality variables in social behavior.* Hillsdale, NJ: Lawrence Erlbaum Associates.

Strodtbeck, F.L., and Hook, L.H. (1961). The social dimensions of a twelve-man jury table. *Sociometry, 24,* 397–415.

Strodtbeck, F.L., James, R., and Hawkins, C. (1957). Social status in jury deliberations. *American Sociological Review, 22,* 713–718.

Swap, W.C., and Rubin, J.Z. (1982). Measurement of interpersonal orientation. *Journal of Personality and Social Psychology. 44,* 208–219.

Swart, C., and Berkowitz, L. (1976). The effects of a stimulus associated with a victim's pain on later aggression. *Journal of Personality and Social Psychology, 33,* 623–631.

Sweeney, P.D., and Gruber, K.L. (1984). Selective exposure: Voter information preferences and the Watergate affair. *Journal of Personality and Social Psychology, 46,* 1208–1221.

Sweeney, P.D., Schaeffer, D., and Golin, S. (1982). Attribution about self and others in depression. *Personality and Social Psychology Bulletin, 8,* 37–42.

Tajfel, H. (1982). Social psychology of intergroup relations. *Annual Review of Psychology, 33,* 1–41.

Tajfel, H., Billig, M.G., Bundy, R.P., and Flament, C. (1971). Social categorization and intergroup behavior. *European Journal of Social Psychology, 1,* 149–178.

Talese, G. (1980). *Thy neighbor's wife.* New York: Doubleday & Company.

Tampa Tribune, April 3, 1985.

Tarde, G. (1899). *Social laws.* New York: Macmillan.

Tavris, C., and Sadd, S. (1977). *The Redbook report on female sexuality.* New York: Delacorte.

Taylor, D.A. (1979). Motivational bases. In G.J. Chelune (Ed.), *Self-disclosure.* San Francisco, CA: Jossey-Bass.

Taylor, R.B., and Lanni, J.C. (1981). Territorial dominance: The influence of the resident advantage in triadic decision-making. *Journal of Personality and Social Psychology, 41,* 909–915.

Taylor, R.B., DeSoto, C.B., and Lieb, R. (1979). Sharing secrets: Disclosure and discretion in dyads and triads. *Journal of Personality and Social Psychology, 37,* 1196–1203.

Taylor, S.E. (1975). On inferring one's attitudes from one's behavior: Some determining conditions. *Journal of Personality and Social Psychology, 31,* 126–131.

Taylor, S.E., and Fiske, S.T. (1978). Salience, attention and attribution: Top of the head phenomena. In L. Berkowitz (Ed.), *Advances in Experimental Social Psychology* (Vol. 11). New York: Academic Press.

Taylor, S.P., and Gammon, C.B. (1975). Effects of type and dose of alcohol on human physical aggression. *Journal of Personality and Social Psychology, 32,* 169–175.

Taylor, S.P., and Leonard, K.E. (1983). Alcohol and human physical aggression. In R. Geen and E. Donnerstein (Eds.), *Aggression: Theoretical and empirical reviews* (Vol 2). New York: Academic Press.

Taylor, S.P., Vardaris, R.M., Rawitch, A.B., Gammon, C.B., Cranston, J.W., and Labetkin, A.J. (1976). The effects of alcohol and delta-9-tetrahydrocannabinol on human physical aggression. *Aggressive Behavior, 2,* 153–161.

Tedeschi, J.T. (1981). *Impression management theory and social psychological research.* New York: Academic Press.

Tedeschi, J.T., and Rosenfeld, P. (1981). Impression management in the forced compliance rituals. In J. Tedeschi (Ed.), *Impression management theory and social psychological research.* New York: Academic Press.

Tedeschi, J.T., Schlenker, B.R., and Bonoma, T.V. (1973). *Conflict, power, and games.* Chicago: Aldine.

Teresa, V. (1973). *My life in the mafia.* Greenwich, CT: Fawcett.

Terkel, S. (1974). *Working.* New York: Pantheon Books.

Tesser, A., and Brodie, M. (1971). A note on the evaluation of a "computer date." *Psychonomic Science, 23,* 300.

Tetlock, P.E. (1979). Identifying victims of groupthink from public statements of decision makers. *Journal of Personality and Social Psychology, 37,* 1314–1324.

The man with 105 wives. (1983). *Newsweek,* February, 21, 43.

Thibaut, J.W., and Kelley, H.H. (1959). *The social psychology of groups.* New York: Wiley.

Thibaut, J.W., and Walker, L. (1975). *Procedural justice: A psychological analysis.* Hillsdale, NJ: Lawrence Erlbaum Associates.

Thomas, B. (1977). *Bud and Lou: The Abbott and Costello story.* New York: J.B. Lippincott Company.

Thomas, R.M. (1979). *Comparing theories of child development.* Monterey, CA: Wadsworth.

Thomas, W.I., and Znaniecki, F. (1918). *The polish peasant in Europe and America* (Vol. 1). Boston, MA: Badger.

Thompson, W.C., Fong, G.T., and Rosenhan, D.L. (1981). Inadmissible evidence and juror verdicts. *Journal of Personality and Social Psychology, 40,* 453–464.

Thurstone, L.L. (1928). Attitudes can be measured. *American Journal of Sociology, 33,* 529–544.

Thurstone, L.L., and Chave, E.J. (1929). *The measurement of attitude.* Chicago, IL: University of Chicago Press.

Timmerman, J. (1981). *Prisoner without a name, cell without a number.* New York: Knopf.

Toi, M., and Batson, C.D. (1982). More evidence that empathy is a source of altruistic motivation. *Journal of Personality and Social Psychology, 43,* 281–292.

Torrence, E.P. (1954). Some consequences of power differences on decision making in permanent and temporary three-man groups. *Research Studies, Washington State College, 22,* 130–140.

Tourangeau, R., and Ellsworth, P.C. (1978). The role of facial response in the experience of emotion. Unpublished manuscript. Yale University.

Triandis, H.C. (1961). A note on Rokeach's theory of prejudice. *Journal of Abnormal and Social Psychology. 62,* 184–186.

Triandis, H.C. (1980). Values, attitudes and interpersonal behavior. In H. Howe, and M. Page (Eds.), *Nebraska Symposium on Motivation* (Vol. 27). Lincoln, NE: University of Nebraska Press.

Triandis, H.C., and Davis, E. (1965). Race and belief as determinants of behavioral intention. *Journal of Personality and Social Psychology, 2,* 715–725.

Triplett, N. (1897). The dynamogenic factors in pacemaking competition. *American Journal of Psychology, 9,* 507–533.

Trivers, R.L. (1971). The evolution of reciprocal altruism. *Quarterly Review of Biology, 46,* 35–37.

Tunnell, G.R. (1977). Three dimensions of naturalness: An expanded definition of field research. *Psychological Bulletin, 84,* 426–437.

Turnbridge. R. (1970). Reliability costs of diabetic diets. *British Medical Journal, 2,* 78–80.

Turner, R.G. (1978). Consistency, self-consciousness, and the predictive validity of typical and maximal personality measures. *Journal of Research in Personality, 12,* 117–132.

Tversky, A., and Kahneman, D. (1973). Availability: A heuristic for judging frequency and probability. *Cognitive Psychology, 5,* 207–232.

Tversky, A., and Kahneman, D. (1974). Judgments under uncertainty: Heuristics and bias: *Science, 185,* 1124–1131.

Tyler, T.R., and Folger, R. (1980). Distributional and procedural aspects of satisfaction with citizen police encounters. *Basic and Applied Social Psychology, 1,* 281–292.

Underwood, B., Froming, W.J., and Moore, B.S. (1977). Mood, attention, and altruism: A search for mediating variables. *Developmental Psychology, 13,* 541–542.

Underwood, B., and Moore, B.S. (1981). Perspective taking and altruism. *Psychological Bulletin, 91,* 143–173.

Ungar, R.K., Hilderbrand, M., and Madar, T. (1982). Physical attractiveness and assumptions about social deviance: Some sex-by-sex comparisons. *Personality and Social Psychology Bulletin, 8,* 293–301.

United Methodist Women's Television Monitoring Project (1976). Reported at meeting of women's division of the Board of Global Ministries.

United States Department of Commerce. *Social indicators, 1976: Selected data on social conditions and trends in the United States,* Washington, D.C.: U.S. Government Printing Office.

United States Department of Justice (1983). *Violent crime in the United States.* Washington, D.C.: Bureau of Justice Statistics.

Valenti, A.C., and Downing, L.L. (1975). Differential effects of jury size on verdicts following deliberation as a function of the apparent guilt of the defendant. *Journal of Personality and Social Psychology, 32,* 655–663.

Valins, S. (1966). Cognitive effects of false heart-rate feedback. *Journal of Personality and Social Psychology, 4,* 400–408.

Valins, S., and Nisbett, R.E. (1972). Atribution process in the development and treatment of emotional disorders. In E.E. Jones, D.E. Kanouse, H.H. Kelley, R.E. Nisbett, S. Valins, and B. Weiner (Eds.), *Attribution: Perceiving the causes of behavior.* Morristown, NJ: General Learning Press.

Van de Ven, A., and Delbecq, A.L. (1971). Normal versus interacting group processes for committee decision-making effectiveness. *Academy of Management Journal, 14,* 203–212.

Van Egeren, L.F. (1979). Social interactions, communications, and the coronary prone behavior pattern: A psychophysiological study. *Psychosomatic Medicine, 41,* 2–18.

Van Sell, M., Brief, A.P., and Schuler, R.S. (1981). Role conflict and role ambiguity: Integration of the literature and directions for future research. *Human Relations*, **34**, 43–71.

Van Zelst, R.H. (1952). Sociometrically selected work teams increase production. *Personnel Psychology*, **5**, 175–185.

Vidmar, N., and Laird, N. (1983). Adversary social roles: Their effects on witnesses' communication of evidence and the assessments of adjudicators. *Journal of Personality and Social Psychology*, **44**, 888–898.

Voissem, N.H., and Sistrunk, F. (1971). Communication schedules and cooperative game behavior. *Journal of Personality and Social Psychology*, **19**, 160–167.

Wallace, I., and Wallace, A. (1978). *The two*. New York: Simon and Schuster.

Wallace, M. (1980). Some persisting findings: A reply to Professor Wilde. *Journal of Conflict Resolution*, **24**, 289–293.

Wallach, M.A., Kogan, N., and Bem, D.J. (1982). Group influence on individual risk-taking. *Journal of Abnormal and Social Psychology*, **65**, 75–86.

Walster, E., Aronson, E., and Abrahams, D. (1966). On increasing the attractiveness of a low prestige communicator. *Journal of Experimental Social Psychology*, **2**, 235–242.

Walster, E., Aronson, V., Abrahams, D., and Rotterman, L. (1966). The importance of physical attractiveness in dating behavior. *Journal of Personality and Social Psychology*, **4**, 508–516.

Walster, E., Berscheid, E., and Walster, G.W. (1973). New directions in equity research. *Journal of Personality and Social Psychology*, **25**, 151–176.

Walster, E., and Walster, G.W. (1978). *A new look at love*. Reading, MA: Addison-Wesley.

Walster, E., Walster, G.W., and Berscheid, E. (1978). *Equity: Theory and research*. Boston, MA: Allyn and Bacon.

Walters, R.H. (1969). Implications of laboratory studies of aggression for the control and regulation of violence. *Annals of the American Academy of Political and Social Science*, **364**, 60–72.

Ward, L.M., and Suedfeld, P. (1973). Human responses to highway noise. *Environemntal Research*, **6**, 306–326.

Warner, K.E. (1977). The effects of anti-smoking campaign on cigarette consumption. *American Journal of Public Health*, **67**, 645–650.

Warner, L.G., and DeFleur, M.L. (1969). Attitude as an interactional concept: Social constraint and social distance as intervening variables between attitudes and action. *American Sociological Review*, **34**, 153–169.

Warwick, P.P., and Lininger, C.A. (1975). *The sample survey: Theory and practice*. New York: McGraw-Hill.

Washburn, S., and De Vore, I. (1962). The social life of baboons. In C.H. Southwick (Ed.), *Primate social behavior*. Princeton, NJ: Van Nostrand.

Washington Post, January 23, 1982.

Watson, D. (1982). The actor and observer: How are their perceptions of causality divergent? *Psychological Bulletin*, **92**, 682–700.

Watson, J.B. (1925). *Behaviorism*. New York: W.W. Norton and Co., Inc.

Watts, B.L., Vallacher, R.R., and Messe, L.A. (1982). Toward understanding sex differences in pay allocations: Agency, communion, and reward distribution behavior. *Sex Roles*, **12**, 1175–1188.

Weary, G. (1980). Affect and egotism as mediators of bias in causal attributions. *Journal of Personality and Social Psychology*, **38**, 348–357.

Webb, E.T., Campbell, D.T., Schwartz, R.D., Sechrest, L., and Grove, J.B. (1981). *Nonreactive measures in the social sciences* (2nd ed.). Boston, MA: Houghton Mifflin.

Weigel, R.H., Loomis, J.N., and Soja, M.J. (1980). Race relations on prime time television. *Journal of Personality and Social Psychology*, **39**, 884–893.

Weigel, R.H., and Newman, L.S. (1976). Increasing attitude-behavior correspondence by broadening the scope of the behavioral measure. *Journal of Personality and Social Psychology*, **33**, 793–802.

Weigel, R.H., Vernon, D.T.A., and Tognaci, L.N. (1974). Specificity of the attitude as a determinant of attitude-behavior congruence. *Journal of Personality and Social Psychology*, **30**, 724–728.

Weiner, B.H., Frieze, I., Kukla, L., Reed, L., Rest, S. and Rosenbaum, R.M. (1972a). Perceiving the causes of success and failure. In E.E. Jones, D.E. Kanouse, H.H. Kelley, S. Valins, and B. Weiner (Eds.), *Attribution: Perceiving the causes of behavior*. Morristown, NJ: General Learning Press.

Weiner, B.H., Heckhausen, H., Meyer, W.V., and Cook, R.E. (1972b). Causal ascriptions and achievement behavior: A conceptual analysis of effort and a reanalysis of locus of control. *Journal of Personality and Social Psychology*, **21**, 239–248.

Weinstein, N.D. (1978). Individual differences in reactions to noise: A longitudinal study in a college dormitory. *Journal of Applied Psychology*, **63**, 458–466.

Weiss, R.F., Boyer, J.L., Lombardo, J.P., and Stitch, M.H. (1973). Altruistic drive and altruistic reinforcement. *Journal of Personality and Social Psychology*, **25**, 390–400.

Weiss, R.F., Buchanan, W., Alstatt, L., and Lombardo, J.P. (1971). Altruism is rewarding. *Science*, **171**, 1262–1263.

Weiss, R.S. (1974). The provisions of social relationship. In Z. Rubin (Ed.), *In doing unto others*. Englewood Cliffs, NJ: Prentice-Hall.

Weiss, W. (1968). Modes of resolution and reasoning in attitude change experiments. In R. Abelson, E. Aronson, W. McGuire, T. Newcomb, M. Rosenberg, and P. Tannenbaum (Eds), *Theories of cognitive consistency: A sourcebook*. Chicago, IL: Rand-McNally.

Wells, G.L., and Harvey, J.H. (1977). Do people use consensus information in making attributions? *Journal of Personality and Social Psychology*, **35**, 279–293.

West, S.G., Gunn, S.P., and Chernicky, P. (1975). Ubiquitous Watergate: An attributional analysis. *Journal of Personality and Social Psychology*, **32**, 55–65.

West, S.G., and Wicklund, R.A. (1980). *A primer of social psychological theories*. Monterey, CA: Brooks/Cole.

Wheeler, L. (1974). Social comparison and selective affiliation. In T.L. Huston (Ed.), *Foundations of interpersonal attraction*. New York: Academic Press.

Wheeler, L., Deci, E.L., Reis, H.T., and Zuckerman, M. (1978). *Interpersonal influence* (2nd ed.) Boston, MA: Allyn and Bacon.

White, G.L., Fishbein, S., and Rutstein, J. (1981). Passionate love and the misattribution of arousal. *Journal of Personality and Social Psychology*, **41**, 56–62.

White, J. (1983). Sex and gender issues in aggression research. In R. Geen and E. Donnerstein (Eds.), *Aggression: Theoretical and empirical reviews* (Vol. 2). New York: Academic Press.

White, L.S. (1979). Erotica and aggression: The influence of sexual arousal, positive affect and negative affect on aggressive behavior. *Journal of Personality and Social Psychology*, **37**, 591–611.

White, R.K. (1959). Motivation reconsidered: The concept of competence. *Psychological Review*, **66**, 297–233.

White, R.K. (1970). *Nobody wanted war: Misperception in Vietnam and other wars*. New York: Doubleday/Anchor.

White, R.K. (1977). Misperception in the Arab-Israeli conflict. *Journal of Social Issues*, **33**, 190–221.

White, T.H. (1975). *Breach of faith: The fall of Richard Nixon*. New York: Atheneum.

Wichman, H. (1969). Effects of isolation and communication on cooperation in a two-person game. Paper presented at annual meeting of the Western Psychological Association.

Wicker, A.W. (1969). Attitudes versus actions: The relationship of verbal and overt behavioral responses to attitude objects. *Journal of Social Issues*, **25**, 41–78.

Wicker, A.W. (1979). Ecological psychology: Some recent and prospective developments. *American Psychologist*, **34**, 755–765.

Wicker, T. (1975). *A time to die*. New York: Ballantine.

Wicklund, R.A. (1975). Objective self-awareness. In L. Berkowitz (Ed.), *Advances in experimental social psychology* (Vol. 8). New York: Academic Press.

Wicklund, R.A. (1978). Three years later. In L. Berkowitz (Ed.), *Cognitive theories in social psychology*. New York: Academic Press.

Wicklund, R.A., and Duval, S. (1971). Opinion change and performance facilitation as the result of objective self-awareness. *Journal of Experimental Social Psychology*, **7**, 319–342.

Wicklund, R.A., and Frey, D. (1980). Self-awareness theory: When the self makes a difference. In D.M. Wegner and R.R. Vallacher (Eds.), *The self in social psychology*. New York: Oxford University Press.

Wildman, R.W., Wildman, R.W. II, Brown, A., and Trice, C. (1976). Note on males' and females' preference for opposite sex body parts, bust size, and bust revealing clothing. *Psychological Reports*, **38**, 485–486.

Will, J.A., Self, P.A., and Datan, N. (1976). Maternal behavior and perceived sex of infant. *American Journal of Ortho-psychiatry*, **46**, 135–139.

Williams, K., Harkins, S., and Latane, B. (1981). Identifiability as a deterrent to social loafing: Two cheering experiments. *Journal of Personality and Social Psychology*, **40**, 303–311.

Williams, T.M. (1978). Differential impact of TV on children: A natural experiment on communities with and without TV. Paper presented at meeting of the International Society for Research on Aggression.

Wills, T.A. (1978). Helpers' perceptions of clients. *Psychological Bulletin*, **85**, 968–1000.

Wilson, E.O. (1975). *Sociobiology: The new synthesis*. Cambridge, MA: Harvard University Press.

Wilson, E.O. (1978). The genetic evolution of altruism. In L. Wispe (Ed.), *Altruism, sympathy, and helping*. New York: Academic Press.

Winch, R.F. (1954). The theory of conplementary needs in mate-selection. *American Sociological Review*, **19**, 241–249.

Winch, R.F. (1958). *Mate-selection: A study of complementary needs*. New York: Harper.

Wishner, J. (1960). Reanalysis of "Impressions of Personality." *Psychological Review*, **67**, 96–112.

Witkin, H.A. et al. (1976). Criminality in XYY and XXY men. *Science*, **196**, 347–555.

Wittig, M.A., and Skolnick, P. (1978). Status versus warmth as determinants of sex differences in personal space. *Sex Roles*, **4**, 493–503.

Wolchik, S.A., Beggs, V.E., Wincze, J.R., Sakheim, D.K., Barlow, D.H., and Mavissakalian, M. (1980). The effect of emotional arousal on subsequent sexual arousal in men. *Journal of Abnormal Psychology*, **89**, 595–598.

Wolfe, J., and Barker, V. (1980). Characteristics of imprisoned rapists and circumstances of the rape. In C.G. Warner (Ed.), *Rape and sexual assault*. Germantown, MD.: Aspen Systems Co.

Wolfe, T. (1979). *The right stuff*. New York: Farrer, Straus, Giroux.

Wolfgang, M.E., and Strohm, R.B. (1974). The relationship between alcohol and criminal homicide. *Quarterly Journal of Studies on Alcohol*, **17**, 411–425.

Woodside, A.G. (1983). Message-evoked thoughts: Consumer thought processing as a tool for making better copy, In L. Percy and A.G. Woodside (Eds.), *Advertising and consumer psychology*. Lexington, MA: D.C. Heath and Company.

Worchel, S., Axsom, D., Ferris, F., Samaha, G., and Schweitzer, S. (1978). Factors determining the effect of intergroup cooperation on intergroup attraction. *Journal of Conflict Resolution*, **22**, 429–439.

Worchel, S., and Teddlie, C. (1976). The experience of crowding: A two-factor theory. *Journal of Personality and Social Psychology*, **34**, 30–40.

Worthy, M., Gary, A.L., and Kahn, G.M. (1969). Self-disclosure as an exchange process. *Journal of Personality and Social Psychology*, **13**, 59–63.

Wright, P.L. (1980). Message-evoked thoughts: Persuasion research using thought verbalizations. *Journal of Consumer Research*, **7**, 151–175.

Wright, P.L. (1981). Cognitive responses to mass media advocacy. In R.E. Petty, T.M. Ostrom, T.C. Brock (Eds.), *Cognitive responses in persuasion*. Hillsdale, NJ: Erlbaum.

Wright, T.L., Holman, T., Steele, W.G., and Silverstein, G. (1980). Locus of control and mastery in a reformatory: A field study of defensive externality. *Journal of Personality and Social Psychology*, **38**, 1005–1013.

Yancey, W.L. (1972). Architecture, interaction, and social control: The case of a large scale housing project. In J.F. Wohlwill and D.H. Carson (Eds.), *Environment and the social sciences: Perspectives and applications*. Washington, D.C.: American Psychological Association.

Yarrow, M.R., Scott, P.M., and Waxler, C.Z. (1973). Learning concern for others. *Developmental Psychology*, **8**, 240–260.

Zajonc, R.B. (1965). Social facilitation. *Science*, **149**, 269–274.

Zajonc, R.B. (1968). Attitudinal effects of mere exposure. *Journal of Personality and Social Psychology*, **9**, Monograph 1–29.

Zanna, M.P., and Cooper, J. (1974). Dissonance and the pill: An attribution approach to studying the arousal properties of dissonance. *Journal of Personality and Social Psychology*, **29**, 703–709.

Zanna, M.P., Kiesler, C.A., and Pilkonis, P.A. (1970). Positive and negative attitudinal effect established by classical conditioning. *Journal of Personality and Social Psychology*, **14**, 321–328.

Zanna, M.P., Olson, J.M., and Fazio, R.H. (1980). Attitude-behavior consistency: An individual difference perspective. *Journal of Personality and Social Psychology*. **38**, 432–440.

Zanna, M.P., and Pack, S.J. (1975). On the self-fulfilling nature of apparent sex differences in behavior. *Journal of Experimental Social Psychology*, **11**, 583–591.

Zillman, D. (1971). Excitation transfer in communication-mediated aggressive behavior. *Journal of Experimental Social Psychology*, **12**, 419–434.

Zillman, D. (1978). Attribution and misattribution of excitatory reactions. In J.H. Harvey, W.J. Ickes, and R.F. Kidd (Eds.), *New directions in attribution research* (Vol. 2). Hillsdale, NJ: Erlbaum.

Zillman, D. (1979). *Hostility and aggression*. NJ: Erlbaum.

Zillman, D. (1983). Arousal and aggression. In R. Geen and E. Donnerstein (Eds.), *Aggression: Theoretical and empirical reviews* (Vol. 1). New York: Academic Press.

Zillman, D., Baron, R., and Tamborini, R. (1981). Social costs of smoking: Effects of tobacco smoke on hostile behavior. *Journal of Applied Social Psychology*, **6**, 548–561.

Zillman, D., Johnson, R.C., and Day, K.D. (1974). Attribution of apparent arousal and proficiency of recovery from sympathetic activation affecting excitation transfer to aggressive behavior. *Journal of Experimental Social Psychology*, **10**, 503–515.

Zillman, D., Katcher, A.H., and Milavsky, B. (1972). Excitation transfer from physical exercise to subsequent aggressive behavior. *Journal of Experimental Social Psychology*, **8**, 247–259.

Zimbardo, P.G. (1970). The human choice: Individuation, reason, and order versus deindividuation, impulse, and chaos. In W.J. Arnold and D. Levine (Eds.), *Nebraska symposium on motivation*. Lincoln, NE: University of Nebraska Press.

Zimbardo, P.G. (1973a). The psychological power and pathology of imprisonment. In E. Aronson and R. Helmreich (Eds.), *Social psychology*. New York: Van Nostrand.

Zimbardo, P.G. (1973b). Vandalism: An act in search of a cause. In P. Zimbardo and C. Maslach (Eds.), *Psychology for our times*. Glenview, IL: Scott Foresman.

Zimbardo, P.G. (1977). *Shyness: What it is what to do about it*. Reading, MA: Addison-Wesley.

Zimring, C.M., Weitzer, W., and Knight, R.P. (1982). Opportunity for control and the designed environment: The case of an institution for the developmentally disabled. In A. Baum and J. Singer (Eds.), *Advances in environmental psychology*, (Vol. 4). Hillsdale, NJ: Erlbaum.

Zinner, D.A. (1980). Why war: Evidence on the outbreak of international conflict. In T. Gurr (Ed.), *Handbook of political conflict*. New York: Free Press.

Zlutnick, S., and Altman, I. (1972). Crowding and human behavior. In J. Wohlwill and D. Carson (Eds.), *Environment and the social sciences: Perspectives and applications*. Washington, D.C.: American Psychological Association.

Zweigenhaft, R. (1976). Personal space in the faculty office: Desk placement and the student-faculty interaction. *Journal of Applied Psychology*, **61**, 529–532.

Name Index

Abel, C., 301
Abel, E., 609
Abeles, R., 554
Abrahams, D., 234, 409
Abramson, L., 202, 203
Achenbach, C., 320
Ackerman, P., 46, 215, 324
Adams, C., 646
Adams, J., 536–538, 540–542, 547
Adams, J. B., 548
Adler, A., 204
Adorno, T., 18, 357, 368, 370, 377, 380–382, 385, 386, 394, 472
Ahammer, I., 316
Aiello, J., 646
Ainsworth, M., 215
Ajzen, I., 357, 368, 370, 380–382, 385, 386
Alioto, J., 287
Allen, A., 103, 108
Allen, H., 396
Allen, W., 250, 253
Allen, V., 482, 485–488, 490
Allport, G., 14, 15, 157, 354, 398
Alstatt, L., 307
Altman, I., 220
Alvares, K., 603
Altman, I., 620, 640, 645
Anderson, C., 213, 282, 283
Anderson, D., 215, 282, 283
Anderson, N., 130
Apfelbaum, E., 530
Appleyard, D., 626
Archer, R., 220, 338
Ardrey, R., 640
Arendt, H., 472
Aristotle, 14
Arnold, E., 342
Arkin, R., 195, 196
Aron, A., 209, 210, 211, 240, 241
Aronfreed, J., 314
Aronson, E., 56, 230, 399, 409, 415, 426
Aronson, V., 234
Asch, S. E., 121, 122, 125, 127, 131, 479–481, 483, 613
Ashmore, R., 395
Astell, M., 242
Atkin, C., 374
Atkin, R., 614
Auerbach, A., 348
Austin, W., 540, 545
Axelrod, R., 532
Axsom, D., 396, 430, 431

Bachrach, H., 348
Back, K., 651
Backman, C., 228
Baden, M., 283
Baekeland, F., 343
Bajo, M., 69
Baker, L, 330
Balaban, T., 97
Bales, F., 570, 575, 576
Ball, A., 517
Ball-Rokeach, S., 439
Ballachey, E., 355
Bandler, R., 169
Bandura, A., 25, 88, 89, 90, 264, 265, 269, 270, 271,

273, 274, 286, 287
Bane, A., 453
Barash, R., 33
Barker, V., 300
Barlow, D., 251
Barnes, R., 235
Barnette, W., 440
Barnhart, S., 249
Barnum, P. T., 101, 102
Baron, R. A., 261, 268, 273, 274, 281, 282, 285, 287, 292, 293, 294, 295, 624, 630, 639
Baron, R. M., 646
Baron, R. S., 577
Baron, S., 479
Barry, T., 630
Barsky, S., 642
Barthe, D., 203
Barton, A., 160
Bassett, R., 474
Batson, C., 46, 311, 323, 324, 326, 348, 349
Baum, A., 497, 623, 644, 646–650, 657–665
Baumeister, R., 642
Baumann, D., 317
Baumgardner, M., 414
Baumrind, D., 471
Beach, F., 264
Beamen, A., 473,493
Becker, F., 656
Becker, J., 301
Bee, J., 656
Beer, M., 595
Beggs, V., 251
Bell, P., 281, 623, 624, 630
Bellezza, F., 149
Bem, D., 103, 108, 169, 170, 171, 178, 370, 371, 434, 435, 473, 565
Bennet, R., 625
Bensenberg, M., 385
Berger, D., 521
Berglas, S., 190, 195
Bergman, A., 498
Berkowitz, L., 57, 268, 274, 275, 277–280, 285, 287, 304, 305
Berscheid, E., 123, 124, 126, 224, 227, 234, 236–237, 238, 240, 241, 246, 253, 536
Bertilson, H., 340
Bettelheim, B., 204
Beuf, A., 392
Bickman, L., 331, 521
Bidwell, L., 4
Biederman, M., 326
Billig, M., 394
Birch, K., 46, 324
Birchler, C., 464
Bitter, E., 268
Bixenstine, V., 531
Bizman, A., 473
Blake, R., 599
Blalock, H., 391
Blaney, N., 399
Blank, A., 459
Blosser, J., 326
Bobo, L., 395, 397
Bochner, S., 415
Bogart, K., 436
Boggiano, A., 436
Bohrnstadt, G., 237

Boike, M., 349
Bolen, D., 93
Bond, C., 435, 578
Bonoma, T., 527
Booker, A., 278
Borden, R., 37, 578, 581
Borgida, E., 141
Borkovec, T., 577
Bornstein, M., 622
Borsky, L., 629
Bower, G., 149
Bowlby, J., 215
Bowman, C., 382
Boyanowsky, E., 488
Boyce, C., 429
Boyer, J., 307
Bragg, B., 487
Braid, J., 17
Bramel, D., 144
Bramson, L., 262
Brehm, J., 239, 357, 433, 464
Brehm, S., 464
Brewer, M., 133, 393, 533–535
Brickman, P., 93, 314
Brief, A., 571
Brigham, J., 155, 157
Brinberg, D., 515
Broadbent, D., 626
Brock, T., 446, 449
Brodie, M., 234
Brodt, E., 173, 174, 175
Bronzaft, A., 627
Brookmire, D., 342
Brotman, H., 204
Brown, A., 250
Brown, B., 201, 516, 519
Brown, B. B., 220
Brown, J., 9
Brown, P., 286
Brown, S., 227
Brundage, L., 220
Bruner, J., 374
Brunson, B., 115
Brunton, M., 265
Bryan, J., 314, 315, 316
Bryant, J., 251
Buchanan, W., 307
Buckhout R., 154, 156, 157
Buckley, T., 46, 324
Bundy, R., 91, 394
Burdette, J., 498
Burger, J., 185, 475
Burgess, A., 298
Burgess, F., 234
Burgess, G., 220
Burgess, M., 257, 258, 291
Burnam, M., 115
Burns, S., 125
Burt, P., 297, 298, 299, 300
Buss, A., 105, 107, 197, 272, 278, 515
Buss, D., 107
Buss, E., 278
Butcher, J., 201
Byrne, D., 224, 231, 232, 240, 241

Caldwell, D., 311
Calhoun, J., 617–619, 633, 665

Cacioppo, J., 384, 385, 408, 413, 420, 421, 434, 437, 445–449, 474, 521
Calder, B., 59, 382, 437, 440
Callahan-Levy, C., 549
Campbell, D., 51, 52, 53, 59, 67, 77, 356, 383, 393, 395
Campbell, D. E., 654
Campbell, J., 49, 50
Canivez, G., 625
Cannell, C., 64
Cannon, W., 165
Canon, L., 625
Cantor, N., 132, 251
Cantrill, H., 143
Caplan, R., 506
Carli, L., 422
Carlsmith, J., 56, 282, 403–405, 415, 425
Carmichael, L., 69
Carnevale, P., 518
Carrell, S., 542
Carter, R., 269
Carroll, J., 163
Carson, R., 201
Carsten, J., 69
Cartwright, D., 18, 230
Carver, C., 115, 116, 176, 178
Case, F., 652, 653
Case, T., 162
Cash, T., 125, 220
Cassel, J., 498
Castell, P., 515
Catalan, J., 477
Cattell, R., 245
Caulkins, R., 215
Cerf, C., 46
Chaffee, S., 282, 374
Chaikin, A., 221, 228
Chaikin, S., 409, 412, 415
Chance, J., 185
Chandler, M., 348
Chanowitz, B., 459
Chapman, A., 578
Charney, E., 498
Chassin, L., 385
Chave, E., 361
Check, J., 300, 301
Chein, I., 390
Chernicky, P., 163
Christie, R., 520
Christy, P., 234
Cialdini, R., 37, 41, 59, 68, 237, 241, 317, 318, 335, 437, 459, 474, 476, 477, 521
Clark, M., 334, 515
Clark, R., 314
Cleary, P., 451, 453, 454
Clifford, M., 124
Clore, G., 231, 232
Cluss, P., 500
Cochran, P., 326
Coffin, R., 517
Cohen, A., 433
Cohen, J., 348
Cohen, R., 545
Cohen, S., 557, 562, 626, 629, 630
Coie, J., 87
Coke, J., 323, 324, 348
Cole, C., 473
Coleman, G., 623
Coleman, J., 201
Collins, B., 466
Collins, J., 250
Comstock, G., 287
Comte, A., 16
Connell, R., 373
Conroy, W., 440, 441
Conway, M., 375

Cook, D., 474
Cook, K., 536, 547
Cook, M., 586
Cook, S., 397–399
Cook, T., 52, 53, 59, 414, 440, 442
Cooley, C., 32
Coombs, F., 357
Coons, R., 599
Cooper, J., 97, 185, 186, 422, 427, 428, 432, 434, 437
Cope, V., 230
Corning, C., 264
Corning, P., 264
Corrigan, G., 472
Corty, E., 385
Costanzo, P., 6, 7, 8, 12, 27, 87
Cotton, J., 586
Courtney, A., 391
Courtright, J., 609
Cowen, E., 349–351
Cox, C., 198
Cox, V., 649
Craig, J., 603
Crandall, V., 185
Cranston, J., 284
Crawford, H., 370
Creekmore, C., 632
Crown, D., 199
Croyle, R., 427, 428, 434, 437
Crutchfield, R., 355, 490
Cunningham, M., 334, 335, 625, 630
Curtright, C., 102
Cutrona, C., 214

D'Atri, D., 649
Dabbs, J., 581
Daniels, L., 146
Darby, B., 318, 477
Darley, J., 196, 310, 320, 322, 328, 329, 330
Datan, N., 95
Davidson, A., 382, 385
Davidson, E., 349
Davies, J., 553
Davis, A., 529
Davis, E., 395
Davis, J., 225, 581, 588, 589, 614
Davis, K., 138, 139, 145, 239, 433
Davis, M., 323, 338
Davis, W., 185
Dawkins, R., 312
Day, K., 275
Deaux, K., 4, 548
de Charms, R., 187
Deci, E., 436, 479
Defoe, D., 212, 216, 242
DeFour, D., 287
DeFleur, M., 383
DeJong, W., 473
DeFusco, P., 623
Delbecq, A., 596
Del Boca, F., 395
Delgado, J., 264
Del Rosario, M., 59
Dengerink, H., 340
Derlega, V., 220, 221, 228
Dertke, M., 320, 342, 470
Desor, J., 665
Desoto, C., 221
DeStefano, M., 349
Deutsch, M., 481, 484, 528, 529, 547
Devine, P., 157
Devlin, P., 155
DeVore, I., 263
Diamond, W., 251
Diaz-Loving, R., 338

Dickson, W., 571
Dietrich, D., 593
Diener, E., 287, 493–495
Dillman, D., 64, 623
DiMatteo, R., 501
Dion, K., 124, 234
Dirks, D., 629
Dittrich, M., 542
Doherty, W., 187
Dollard, J., 266
Donelly, A., 466
Donnerstein, E., 57, 294, 303, 304, 323, 625
Doob, A., 483
Doob, L., 266, 562
Dooley, S., 487
Dorsett, D., 382
Dovidio, J., 310, 311, 322, 323, 324, 328, 334
Dowd, M., 320
Downing, L., 613
Driscoll, R., 239
Druckman, D., 561
Duck, S., 57
Dube'-Simond, L., 553, 554
Dugan, P., 132
Dull, V., 135
Duncan, B., 46, 291, 324
Dunnette, M., 540
Dupree, L., 76
Durkheim, E., 16, 243
Durall, J., 374
Dutton, P., 209, 210, 211, 240, 241
Duval, S., 105, 176, 177, 335
Duvall, R., 553
Dworkin, B., 502–504
Dyer, M., 215

Eagly, A., 406, 409, 412, 413, 418, 491, 492
Ebbesen, E., 224, 291
Eberly, D., 76, 77
Eckhoff, T., 536
Eco, U., 467
Edney, J., 641
Edwards, D., 636
Edwards, L., 250
Effrein, E., 170
Ehrhardt, A., 95, 264, 265
Ehrlich, P., 620
Eisenberg, N., 338
Elliott, G., 547
Elliott, R., 286
Ellison, K., 154
Ellsworth, P., 126
Elms, A., 472
Endler, N., 109, 490
Epstein, L., 500
Epstein, N., 338
Epstein, R., 264
Epstein, S., 90, 104, 105, 108, 110, 152
Epstein, Y., 646
Epton, N., 242
Erickson, B., 520
Erikson, E., 84, 85, 86
Eron, L., 266, 287, 288, 289
Etzioni, A., 560
Evans, G., 629–631
Evans, R., 26, 29, 30, 216, 394, 453, 454
Ewing, J., 215

Fagot, B., 96
Falender, V., 170
Fanselon, M., 157
Fantino, E., 286
Faranda, J., 363
Farley, J., 662
Farquhar, J., 452
Farnill, D., 87

Faucheux, C., 489
Fazio, R., 81, 108, 170, 384, 435
Feld, S., 349
Feldman, N., 87
Feldman, R., 487
Feldman, S., 357
Fencil-Morse, E., 203
Fenigstein, A., 107, 178, 197, 198, 288
Ferrare, T., 205
Ferris, F., 396
Feshbach, S., 268, 286, 300, 303, 418
Festinger, L., 28, 29, 67, 232, 403–405, 425–427,
  434, 442, 483, 651
Fiedler, F., 601–603
Field, M., 331
Findley, M., 186
Fishbaugh, L., 491
Fishbein, M., 357, 358, 368, 370, 380–382, 385, 386,
  601
Fishbein, S., 239
Fisher, R., 560, 623, 632, 651
Fisher, W., 314
Fiske, S., 131, 150
Fitzpatrick, M., 630
Flacks, R., 373
Flament, C., 394
Flay, B., 414, 440, 442
Fleishman, E., 599, 600
Fleischman, J., 339
Fletcher, G., 375
Floody, O., 264
Flowers, M., 609
Foa, E., 515
Foa, V., 515
Fode, K., 54, 55
Foelker, G., 7
Folger, R., 550
Folkman, J., 17
Follett, K., 372, 373
Fong, G., 161
Ford, J., 636
Forsyth, J., 487, 583, 559
Foster, J., 99
Foushee, H., 338
Fouraker, L., 516
Frager, N., 631
Franck, K., 661
Francoeur, R., 297, 298
Francis, V., 498
Frankenhauser, M., 114
Franklin, C., 28
Fraser, S., 473, 493
Freedman, D., 391
Freedman, J., 473, 483, 620, 632
Freedman, L., 290
Freedman, S., 536
Freeman, S., 37, 536, 581
Fredricks, A., 382
French, J., 461, 462, 465, 506
French, R., 213
Frenkel-Brunswick, E., 19, 377, 394
Freud, A., 84
Freud, S., 15, 83, 84, 99, 257, 261, 262, 267, 271,
  425
Freuh, T., 392
Frey, D., 175
Frey, R., 520
Frey, J., 630
Frey, W., 547
Friedlander, F., 595
Friedman, M., 112
Frieze, I., 141
Frodi, A., 278, 294
Frost, J., 528
Froming, W., 335
Fultz, J., 326

Gaebelin, J., 531
Gaertner, S., 314, 322, 323, 324, 328
Gachtel, R., 497
Gaeddert, W., 549
Gagnon, D., 549
Gagnon, J., 253
Galle, O., 641, 645
Gallup, G., 91, 92
Gammon, C., 283, 284
Gara, M., 132
Garcia, L., 472
Garfunkel, A., 377
Garrett, W., 625
Gary, A., 221
Gebhard, L., 248
Geis, F., 520
Geis, G., 345
Geffner, R., 400
Geen, R., 273, 290, 292, 293, 578
Geer, J., 322
Geller, D., 632
Gelles, R., 260
Gerard, H., 398, 430, 481, 484
Gerbner, G., 287
Gergen, K., 57, 194, 337, 511, 513
Gergen, M., 337
Gerson, L., 483
Gesten, E., 349
Giarrusso, R., 299
Gibbons, F., 81, 178
Gifford, R., 134
Gillen, B., 125
Gillig, P., 414
Gilmour, R., 57
Ginsberg, H., 649
Gittleson, B., 102
Giza, B., 363
Glass, D., 115, 117, 629, 642
Glass, G., 348
Goethals, G., 131, 196, 262
Gottman, E., 188, 189, 191
Goldband, S., 114
Goldstein, M., 264
Goethals, G., 413
Goldberg, M., 374
Golightly, C., 232
Golin, S., 203
Gollwitzer, P., 338
Gonzales, M., 224, 225, 232
Good, T., 185
Goodchilds, J., 299
Goranson, R., 282
Gormly, J., 109
Gorn, G., 374
Gorney, R., 317
Gouaux, C., 231
Gouldner, A., 228
Gove, W., 641
Graen, G., 603
Granberg, P., 472
Grant, R., 625
Graves, J., 636
Gray, M., 586
Green, J., 193
Greenberg, M., 513, 547, 550
Greenbaum, P., 641, 656
Greenbaum, S., 641
Greene, D., 436
Greenstein, T., 440
Greenwald, A., 414, 442
Greer, P., 642
Grev, R., 335
Griffin, L., 646
Griffitt, W., 232, 249, 331, 472, 624
Gross, A., 331
Gross, L., 69

Grosslight, B., 69
Groth, A., 298
Grove, J., 67
Grube, J., 439
Gruber, K., 376
Grumet, J., 87
Grusee, J., 314, 315
Grush, J., 68, 223, 371
Guimond, S., 553, 554
Gunn, S., 163
Gurin, G., 349
Gurr, T., 553, 554
Gustafson, D., 596

Haber, S., 303
Haberman, P., 283
Halberstam, D., 558, 568
Hall, C., 84, 85
Hall, E., 633
Hall, J., 591
Hallam, J., 323
Halprin, A., 599
Hamilton, D., 132, 133, 134
Hamilton, G., 243
Hamilton, V., 152
Hamilton, W., 312
Hammen, C., 203, 251
Hampson, J. G., 95
Hampson, J. L., 95
Haney, C., 4
Hansen, W., 453
Hanusa, B., 204
Harari, H., 477
Harary, F., 230
Hare, R., 340
Hardin, G., 527, 533
Harding, J., 390
Hargis, K., 334
Harkins, S., 578, 579, 583, 585
Harlow, H., 215
Harper, J., 662
Harrell, T., 77
Harris, E., 599, 600
Harris, K., 624
Harris, M., 221, 335
Harris, V., 148
Harrison, R., 506
Hartke, D., 603
Hartman, D., 268
Harvey, J., 141, 152
Harvey, O., 395
Hastie, R., 155, 158, 610, 611
Hastorf, A., 126, 143
Hatch, G., 601
Hatfield, E., 245, 253, 254
Havis, J., 453
Hawkins, C., 612
Hawkins, H., 470
Hayduk, L., 633–635
Haynes, S., 496
Heaps, W., 551
Heath, L., 59
Heider, F., 26, 27, 29, 30, 123, 136, 150, 227, 229,
  230, 426
Heim, M., 300
Hegtvedt, K., 536, 547
Hellman, L., 464
Hemphill, B., 599
Hendrick, C., 227, 242
Hendrick, S., 242
Hennigan, K., 59, 60
Hensley, W., 654
Herren, K., 654
Hieser, R., 586
Higbee, K., 17
Higgins, E., 87

Hildebrand, M., 124
Hill, C., 247, 252, 253, 348
Hill, S., 91
Himmelfarb, S., 364, 406, 418
Himmelweit, H., 287
Hindus, M., 249
Hinkel, R., 382
Hiroto, D., 200
Hobfoll, S., 124, 125
Hochreich, D., 186
Hoffman, D., 505
Hoffman, E., 479
Hoffman, M., 313, 314, 321, 344, 345
Hogarty, G., 500
Hohenfeld, J., 543, 544
Hohlstrom, L., 298
Hokanson, J., 257, 258, 291
Holahan, C., 635, 637, 644
Holines, J., 520
Hollander, E., 484
Hollis, J., 115
Hollister, L., 251
Holman, T., 186
Holmes, D., 102, 144, 251
Holt, R., 614
Homans, G., 513
Homant, R., 67
Hood, R., 81
Hood, W., 395
Hook, L., 612
Hope, M., 649
Hoppman, P., 561
Hormoth, S., 178
Hornstein, H., 320
Horowitz, L., 213
Hosey, K., 477
House, T., 340
Houseman, R., 607
Hovland, C., 355, 385, 406, 407, 413, 414, 424, 425,
    440, 441, 454
Howard, J., 339
Huesmann, L., 287
Hulka, B., 498
Humphries, S., 266
Hunt, M., 248, 249
Hull, C., 24
Huse, E., 595
Huston, T., 232, 238, 253, 345, 346
Hutt, C., 649

Ickes, W., 235
Ineichen, B., 243
Insko, C., 141, 395, 415, 425
Isen, A., 326, 334
Issac, A., 553
Istvan, J., 249
Ittelson, W., 645
Izzett, R., 472

Jaccard, J., 382, 385
Jacklin, C., 96, 264
Jackson, G., 77
Jackson, J., 585, 586
Jackson, L., 549
Jackson-Beeck, M., 374
Jacobs, P., 265
Jacobs, S., 630
Jacobsen, P., 542
Jacobson, L., 55
Jaeger, M., 287
James, R., 612
James, W., 165
Jamison, L., 529
Janda, L., 249
Janis, I., 406, 417, 418, 501, 504–506, 606–610
Janowitz, M., 551

Jarmecky, L., 322
Jarvik, I., 265
Jellison, I., 193
Jenkins, C., 112, 113, 114
Jennings, M., 373
Johnson, D., 400
Johnson, G., 241, 322, 625
Johnson, J., 375
Johnson, P., 299
Johnson, R., 275
Johnson, T., 400
Johnson, V., 251
Jonas, G., 504
Jones, E., 103, 131, 138, 139, 145, 148, 190, 194,
    195, 363, 432
Jones, J., 72
Jones, R., 53, 194, 398
Jones, W., 213, 214
Jonsson, E., 629
Jorgenson, B., 245
Jorgenson, D., 363, 540
Joseph, N., 298
Jourad, S., 220
Judd, C., 375, 416
Junghans, C., 224

Kahn, A., 548
Kahn, R., 64
Kahmeman, D., 146
Kalle, R., 435
Kalven, H., 154, 610
Kamin, E., 298
Kaminski, J., 363
Kamzan, M., 331
Kaplan, G., 372
Kaplan, M., 130, 161, 162, 381
Karlin, R., 646
Karlovac, M., 87, 649
Karp, L., 334
Karuza, J., 547
Karylowski, J., 334, 339
Kasl, S., 498
Kasserjian, H, 446
Katcher, A., 276
Katkin, F., 440
Katz, D., 374, 375
Katzman, N., 287
Kaye, M., 251
Kayser, E., 547
Kees, W., 653
Kelem, R., 493
Kelley, H., 137, 138, 140, 142, 163, 406, 511, 513,
    514, 529, 613
Kelly, S., 629, 630
Kelly-Dee, C., 76
Kelman, H., 408, 413, 414, 465, 557, 562
Kemmerick, G., 130
Kendrick, A., 374
Kennedy, M., 499
Kenny, D., 375
Kenrick, D., 237, 241, 317, 318, 625
Kernis, M., 236
Kerr, N., 613, 614
Kessler, S., 155
Kidder, L., 10, 71, 359
Kiesler, C., 370
Kilham, W., 469
Kilpatrick, D., 297
Kimmel, M., 525, 530, 532
Kinder, D., 396
King, B., 425
King, D., 282
Kinsey, A., 248, 249
Kinzel, A., 638, 639
Kjos, G., 224
Klein, D., 203, 394

Klentz, B., 473
Kliejunas, P., 383, 384
Kling, J., 101
Klodin, V., 265
Kluger, R., 397
Knarek, D., 278
Knight, J., 144
Knight, R., 665
Knowles, E., 637
Koenig, K., 373
Kogan, N., 565
Kohlberg, L., 87, 88
Kolditz, T., 195, 196
Koller, M., 243
Konar, E., 549
Konečhi, V., 224, 291, 335
Koneya, M., 657
Koropsak, E., 291
Korsch B., 498
Korte, C., 621, 622, 625
Koskela, K., 452
Kralewitz, J., 548
Kramer, R., 533–535
Krantz, D., 629, 630
Krauss, R., 528, 529
Kravitz, J., 157
Kuethe, J., 635
Krebs, D., 322, 323, 327, 331, 348
Krech, D., 355, 490
Kremer, J., 277
Krosnick, J., 375
Kruglanski, A., 466
Kuehn, L., 158
Kuhn, G., 221
Kuiper, N., 202
Kukla, L., 141
Kulik, J., 375
Kupper, L., 498
Kutner, B., 390

Labetkin, A., 284
Lacey, R., 537
Laird, N., 161
Lamb, M., 83, 96
Lamm, H., 547, 581, 582, 593
Landsman, R., 158
Landy, D., 294
Landy, F., 601
Lane, I., 540
Lange, C., 363
Langer, E., 204, 206, 459
Langlois, J., 126
Lanni, J., 517, 641
LaPiere, R., 353, 354, 379, 383, 385
Latane, B., 4, 310, 320, 322, 328, 329, 330, 578–
    581, 583, 584, 613
Lau, R., 68, 180, 396
Lawson, E., 126, 131, 137, 138, 145
Lawton, M., 652
Layden, M., 204
Leavitt, H., 573
LeBon, G., 16
Lechter, M., 500
Lee, D., 429
Lefcourt, H., 186, 204
Lefkowitz, M., 287
Lehrman, D., 264
Leonard, K., 283
Lesko, W., 625
LePage, A., 278
Lepper, M., 436, 437
Lerner, M., 227, 545, 546
Leventhal, G., 545, 547, 549
Leventhal, H., 418, 451, 453, 454
Levin, G., 286
Levin, P., 334

Levine, D., 657
Levine, M., 621
Levine, R., 393, 395
Levinger, G., 218, 219, 232, 245, 246
Levinson, D., 19
Levinson, R., 377, 394
Lewicki, P., 29
Lewis, S., 477
Lewin, K., 27, 28, 29, 30, 110, 425, 426, 651
Ley, P., 506
Leyens, J., 278
Lichtenstein, V., 242, 243
Lickteig, C., 364
Lieb, R., 221
Liebert, R., 287
Likert, R., 360
Linder, D., 237, 241, 432
Lindsey, R., 429
Lindsey, R. C., 157
Lindzey, G., 84, 85
Lininger, C., 62
Linskold, S., 559
Lintell, M., 626
Liptz, M., 239
Lippa, R., 197
Lippe, M., 414
Litowitz, D., 215
Littlefield, C., 315
Locke, J., 242
Loels, A., 436
Loftus, E., 155, 158, 159, 613
Lombardo, J., 307
Lombardo, M., 532
Loo, C., 649
Loomis, J., 391
London, P., 112, 343
Loney, G., 224
Lord, R., 543, 544
Lorenz, K., 261, 262, 263, 264, 267, 271, 286, 641
Lorge, I., 613
Lorion, R., 347
Lott, A., 231
Lott, B., 231
Lowin, A., 603
Loye, D., 317
Luborsky, L., 348
Luce, R., 524
Lucker, G., 399
Lui, L., 135, 533
LuKens, C., 224
Lumsdaine, A., 406, 417
Lundwald, L., 348

Maass, A., 155
Maccoby, E., 96, 264
Maccoby, N., 452
MacGoun, R., 613
MacGowan, K., 243
MacNeil, M., 479
Madar, T., 124
MacIntosh, E., 649
Madaras, G., 169
Maddux, J., 408
Maederer, C., 69
Magnusson, D., 109
Mahoney, E., 249, 253, 298, 299, 301
Major, B., 548, 549
Malamuth, N., 300, 301, 302, 303, 304
Malpass, R., 157
Mandel, D., 646
Mann, L., 469, 607, 609
Mann, R., 480
Mantell, D., 469, 471
Manzolati, J., 4
Marks, E., 323, 340, 341
Marlowe, D., 199

Martella, J., 603
Martens, R., 578
Martin, C., 248
Martin, G., 314
Martindale, D., 517, 641
Maslach, C., 481, 491
Massie, R., 99, 100
Masters, W., 251
Mathes, F., 250
Mathewson, G., 430
Matsuyama, S., 265
Matter, C., 637
Matthews, K., 115, 117, 118, 625
Mavissakalian, M., 251
May, F., 232
Mayer, S., 335
McAlister, A., 432
McArthur, L., 141, 150
McCabe, A., 316
McCagny, 299
McCain, G., 649
McCarthy, D., 251, 627
McCaul, K., 102
McCauley, C., 623
McCombs, N., 287
McClure, M., 91
McConnachie, G., 287
McDavid, J., 422, 490
McDavis, K., 324
McDermott, J., 297
McFarland, C., 181, 182, 375
McFarlin, D., 549
McGhee, P., 392
McGillis, D., 139
McGinness, J., 362
McGovern, L., 326
McGrath, J., 530
McGraw, K., 215
McGuire, W., 45, 368, 417, 425, 454
McPherson, J., 641
Mead, G., 16, 17, 30
Meek, D., 614
Meeker, B., 547
Meeker, D., 614
Mehrabian, A., 338
Melamed, B., 498, 502–504
Melburg, V., 181
Melville, M., 265
Messé, L., 540, 548, 549
Messick, D., 533
Meter, K., 337
Mettee, D., 294
Meyer, A., 452
Mewborn, C., 418
Meyer, P., 469
Mezzi, L., 394
Middlemist, R., 637
Midlarsky, E., 314, 315, 326, 345
Midlarsky, M., 326
Mikula, G., 547
Milausky, B., 276
Milgram, S., 363, 457, 458, 460, 461, 469, 481, 482, 492, 494, 622, 626
Millard, R., 17
Miller, D., 150, 180, 543
Miller, F., 557
Miller, J., 474
Miller, L., 161, 162, 198
Miller, N., 266, 335, 398
Miller, R., 93, 94
Milligan, M., 630
Milligan, M., 340
Mills, J., 515
Mischel., W., 102, 103, 132
Mitchell, R., 648
Mittlemark, M., 453

Mitchell, T., 601
Moe, J., 395
Mohr, D., 477
Molm, L., 529
Monahan, J., 613
Money, J., 95, 264
Monson, T., 108, 109, 197, 198, 384
Montague, A., 272
Mook, D., 57
Moore, B., 335, 338
Moore, D., 586
Moon, T., 522
Morgan, D., 629
Moriarity, D., 316
Morris, M., 498
Moscovici, S., 489, 490, 501
Moskowitz, J., 398
Moskowitz, R., 69
Mosteller, F., 68
Mouton, J., 599
Mowrer, O., 266
Mueller, C., 281, 294, 323
Mulac, A., 593
Murphy, G., 17
Murphy, I., 17
Murray, J., 316
Murstein, B., 234, 241, 242, 245
Murtran, E., 553
Mussen, P., 315
Myers, D., 110, 581, 582

Nacoste, R., 395
Nadien, M., 621
Naftulin, D., 466
Nahemow, L., 652
Nash, J., 452
Navasky, V., 464, 468
Nebergall, R., 415
Nelson, R., 549
Nelson, D., 225
Nelson, R., 413
Nemeth, C., 154, 527, 613
Nesselroade, J., 245
Newcomb, J., 493
Newcomb, T., 17, 224, 227, 230, 373
Newman, J., 623
Newman, L., 386
Newman, O., 661
Newston, D., 487
Nezlek, J., 236
Nias, S., 243
Nida, S., 328, 578
Niemi, R., 373
Nisbett, R., 103, 141, 348, 436
Nordhoy, F., 581
Norman, S., 150
Norton, P., 349
Norwell, N., 396
Novak, D., 227
Nowell, C., 506
Nowicki, S., 187

O'Grady, K., 249
O'Hagen, S., 101
O'Hara, J., 657
O'Leary, V., 185, 548
O'Neal, E., 278
O'Neill, S., 641
O'Quin, K., 326, 348
O'Sullivan, M., 76
Obershall, L., 553
Olshavsky, R., 385
Olson, J., 108, 384
Orne, M., 53
Orris, J., 603

Osborn, A., 592
Osgood, C., 361, 558, 559
Osherow, N., 399
Oskamp, S., 368–370, 373, 374, 384, 451
Ostrom, T., 446
Ostrove, N., 125
Owen, D., 316
Oxley, B., 656

Pack, S., 135
Padawer-Singer, A., 160, 613
Padgett, V., 585, 586
Page, R., 363, 625
Pallack, M., 474
Pallonen, V., 452
Palmer, J., 158
Paluck, R., 641
Pandey, J., 331
Papageorgis, D., 417
Parcell, S., 298
Park, B., 394
Parke, R., 278
Parker, D., 288, 290
Parlee, M., 212
Paskal, V., 314
Patterson, A., 290, 636, 649
Patterson, R., 76, 77
Paulus, P., 649
Payne, J., 163
Pearlman, M., 471
Pennebaker, J., 115, 215, 465
Penner, L., 69, 77, 78, 124, 125, 320, 323, 341, 470, 581
Penrod, S., 155, 610, 611
Pepitone, A., 493
Peplau, L., 212, 213, 214, 215, 246, 252, 253
Perlman, D., 150, 163, 212, 213, 215, 370
Perls, F., 290
Personnaz, B., 489
Perri, M., 237
Pesch, M., 392
Peters, L., 603
Petty, R., 384, 385, 408, 413, 420, 421, 434, 437, 445–449, 475
Pfaff, D., 264
Phares, E., 183, 185, 186
Philipsen, G., 593
Piaget, J., 86
Piliavin, I., 323, 332
Piliavin, J., 314, 322, 323, 326, 327, 328, 330, 331, 332, 337, 344, 348
Pilkonis, P., 370
Pinner, B., 649
Plous, S., 557
Pomeroy, W., 248
Porteus, J., 651
Pohlman, J., 603
Pope, D., 445
Pollman, V., 649
Porter, C., 150
Post, D., 150
Postman, L., 157
Prentice-Dunn, S., 284, 493, 494
Pressley, S., 337
Presson, C., 385
Prestholdt, P., 584
Preston, M., 473
Price, J., 649
Price, R., 234
Pritchard, R., 540
Proshansky, H., 390, 632, 645
Pruitt, D., 141, 518, 525, 530, 532, 561
Pryor, J. B., 81, 106, 176
Puska, P., 452
Pych, V., 348

Quantz, M., 290, 292, 293
Quarforth, G., 287
Quattrone, G., 150
Quinlan, D., 504

Rafferty, J., 625
Raffia, H., 524
Rall, M., 649
Randle, C., 598
Rangel, J., 261
Ransberger, V., 282
Rapoport, A., 555
Rarvitch, A., 284
Raven, B., 461, 462, 465, 466, 511
Rawlings, E., 335
Raz, M., 473
Read, P., 570
Reagan, R., 99
Reed, I., 141
Regan, D., 384
Reis, H., 236, 237, 479, 549
Reisenzein, R., 173
Reiss, M., 181, 435, 657
Reitz, J., 330
Resick, P., 297
Rest, S., 141
Restle, F., 589
Reusch, J., 653
Rhodewalt, F., 190
Richardson, D., 49, 50, 266, 267
Rice, M., 324
Riecken, H., 67
Ringelmann, H., 583
Riordan, C., 241
Rittle, R., 474
Rittman, I., 436
Rivlin, L., 645
Robb, J., 500
Roberts, D., 287
Rodin, J., 204, 206, 332, 501, 504, 505, 646, 647, 662
Roethlisberger, F., 571
Rogers, M., 335, 336
Rogers, R., 284, 288, 290, 408–418, 493–495
Rohe, W., 649
Rohner, R., 264
Rohrer, J., 479
Rokeach, M., 67, 130, 355, 377–379, 383, 384, 386, 394, 395, 438–440, 442
Romer, D., 465
Rook, K., 251
Rorer, L., 64
Rose, T., 135
Rosen, P., 397
Rosenbaum, M., 511, 532, 586
Rosenbaum, R. 141
Rosenberg, M., 53, 355, 357
Rosenberg, S., 132
Rosenfeld, H., 656
Rosenfeld, P., 181, 438
Rosenfield, D., 180, 399
Rosenhan, D., 109, 110, 113, 161, 334, 335, 345
Rosenthal, R., 53, 54, 57
Rosnow, R., 57
Ross, D., 269
Ross, E., 16
Ross, L., 146, 149
Ross, H., 654
Ross, M., 180, 181, 375, 382, 439, 440
Ross, S., 269
Rothbart, M., 394
Rothman, G., 130
Rotter, J., 184, 186
Rotterman, L., 234
Rouse, B., 215
Rotton, J., 623, 630

Rovario, D., 251
Royko, M., 278, 279
Rozelle, R., 453
Rubenstein, C., 212, 214
Rubin, J., 462, 511, 516, 519, 520
Rubin, Z., 237, 246, 252, 253, 374
Ruble, D., 87, 95, 97, 436
Rumpel, C., 156
Rushton, J., 314, 315, 316
Russell, D., 69, 180, 214
Russell, L., 477
Rutherford, E., 315
Rutman, L., 76, 77
Rutstein, J., 239
Ryan, M., 326
Ryan, R., 436
Rychman, R., 220

Sackett, D., 497, 498
Sadd, S., 250
Saegert, S., 222, 649
Sagi, R., 314
Sahakian, W., 14, 15
Sakheim, D., 251
Saks, M., 613
Salovey, P., 334
Samaha, G., 396
Samorette, G., 335
Sampson, E., 547
Sanders, D., 465
Sanford, N., 19, 377, 394
Santee, R., 481, 491
Sargant, W., 369
Sarnoff, I., 217
Saulier, K., 150
Schachter, S., 67, 68, 69, 165–167, 172, 173, 179, 209, 216, 217, 239, 240, 251, 274, 651
Schantz, C., 87
Scheier, M., 107, 176, 178
Schersching, C., 161
Schlenker, B., 31, 32, 90, 93, 167, 188, 189, 190, 191, 199, 527
Schneider, D., 126, 127, 130, 132, 625
Schneider, F., 625
Schopler, J., 649
Schuler, R., 571
Schulz, R., 205, 206
Schultz, D., 15, 17, 27
Schumann, D., 447
Schwartz, B., 642
Schwartz, R., 67
Schwartz, S., 322, 339, 344
Schwarzfeld, J., 473
Schweder, R., 103
Schweitzer, S., 396
Scott, J., 264
Scott, P., 315
Sears, D., 396
Seaver, W., 55
Sechrest, L., 67
Secord, P., 228
Sedlak, A., 132
Segal, M., 222, 223
Seidenberg, B., 6
Self, P., 95
Seligman, M., 201, 202, 203, 204
Selye, H., 623, 624
Senn, D., 245
Serrin, W., 301
Shaeffer, D., 203
Shaffer, D., 84, 162
Shalker, T., 334
Shanab, M., 469
Shaver, P., 212, 214
Shavitt, S., 449
Shaw, M., 6, 7, 8, 12, 27, 573

Shea, M., 656
Sheehan, E., 561
Sheffield, F., 406
Shenkel, R., 101, 102
Sherif, C., 395, 396, 415, 416
Sherif, M., 395, 396, 415, 478, 479
Sherman, M., 220
Sherman, S., 385
Sherwin, A., 500
Shiftlett, S., 603
Shomer, R., 529
Shope, G., 292
Shovar, M., 586
Shotland, R., 365
Shukla, R., 596
Shupe, L., 283
Sidowski, J., 509–511, 513
Siegal, S., 516
Sienbenalar, J., 311
Sigall, H., 125, 363
Sikes, J., 399
Simmer, M., 314
Simmons, C., 545, 546
Simmons, J., 286
Simon, P., 377
Simon, R., 612
Simon, W., 253
Simonds, S., 334
Singer, A. N., 613
Singer, D. G., 288
Singer, J., 165, 166, 167, 172
Singer, J. D., 272
Singer, J. E., 629, 642
Singer, J. L., 288
Singer, R., 286
Singer, R. L., 613
Silverstein, G., 186
Singerman, K., 577
Sistrunk, F., 422, 490, 530
Skelton, J., 190
Skinner, B., 15, 24, 26
Skinner, L., 301
Skolnick, P., 636
Slaby, R., 287
Sloan, L., 37
Small, M., 272
Smith, B., 558
Smith, D., 249, 518, 522
Smith, J., 625
Smith, M., 348, 374, 375
Smith, P., 362, 394
Smith, T., 529
Snadowsky, A., 6
Snapp, M., 399
Snoek, J., 218, 219
Snow, J., 498
Snyder, C., 101, 102
Snyder, L., 155
Snyder, M., 107, 108, 115, 126, 148, 149, 197, 198, 384
Sobel, R., 186
Soja, M., 391
Sommer, R., 636, 654–657
Sorenson, S., 629
Sosa, J., 291
Sosis, R., 186
Soutter, B., 499
Spanier, G., 241
Spaulding, K., 155
Spector, P., 470, 581, 604
Spelman, M., 506
Spiegel, N., 236
Spielberger, C., 101, 112
Staats, A., 23, 370
Staats, C., 23, 370
Stadler, S., 624

Stake, J., 547
Stang, D., 167, 262, 569
Stanley, J., 51, 77
Stasser, G., 614
Staub, E., 338
Steblay, N., 473
Steele, G., 317
Steele, W., 186
Steinberg, J., 335
Steinem, G., 302
Steinmetz, S., 260
Steinhilber, A., 642
Stephan, C., 126, 180
Stephan, W., 180, 398, 399
Stephans, L., 277
Sterling, B., 322
Stone, A., 323, 470
Stone, G., 498, 501, 506
Stoner, J., 565
Stonner, D., 292
Storms, M., 639
Stouffer, S., 536
Strauss, M., 260, 291
Strickland, B., 185, 187, 199
Strodtbeck, F., 612
Strohm, R., 283
Stryker, S., 553
Suci, G., 361
Suedfeld, P., 4, 625
Sullivan, J., 474
Summers, L., 341
Stern, R., 629
Sternberg, B., 436
Sternthal, B., 449
Stiles, W., 268
Stires, L., 657
Stitch, M., 307
St. John, N., 398
Stogdill, R., 599
Stokols, D., 629, 641, 649
Swander, D., 479
Swann, W., 108
Swap, W., 222, 520
Swart, C., 279, 280
Sweeney, P., 203, 376
Swift, B., 287

Taborg, L., 509
Tajfel, H., 394, 396
Talese, G., 493
Tanke, E., 108, 126, 384
Tannenbaum, P., 361
Tarde, G., 15, 25
Tavris, C., 250
Taylor, D., 220, 221
Taylor, R., 221, 517, 641
Taylor, S., 131, 150, 171, 282, 284
Teachman, G., 314
Teasdale, J., 202
Teddlie, C., 644
Tedeschi, J., 181, 241, 435, 438, 527
Teresa, V., 273
Tesser, A., 234
Terkel, S., 542
Tetlock, P., 608
Thibaut, J., 511, 513, 514, 549, 613
Thissen, D., 102
Thomas, B., 539
Thomas, F., 529
Thomas, G., 639
Thomas, K., 382
Thomas, R., 84
Thomas, W., 354
Thompson, W., 161
Thorne, A., 37
Thurstone, L., 360, 361, 368

Timmerman, J., 389
Titus, L., 578
Tognaci, L., 385
Toi, M., 325, 326
Town, J., 152
Traupmann, J., 246, 253
Tremblay, K., 623
Triandis, H., 384, 395
Trice, C., 250
Triplett, N., 3, 4, 8, 12, 17, 577
Trivers, R., 312
Trolier, T., 132
Trommsdorff, G., 593
Truddell, B., 323
Turner, J., 415
Tversky, A., 146
Tyler, T., 396, 550

Uhlig, S., 641
Ulanoft, J., 444
Ungar, R., 124
Underwood, B., 335, 338
Uranowitz, S., 148, 149
Urberg, K., 96
Utne, M., 246

Vaizey, M., 649
Valenti, A., 613
Valins, S., 171, 348, 644, 646, 650, 658–662
Vallacher, R., 144, 145, 548
Vandenburg, R., 266
Van de Ven, A., 596
Van Egeren, L., 116
Van Sell, M., 571
Vandenberg, S., 234
Vanderplas, M., 326
Vandaris, R., 284
Veitch, R., 625
Vernon, D., 385
Veroff, J., 349
Veronen, L., 297
Vidmar, N., 161
Villena, J., 621
Vincent, J., 318, 465, 477
Vinsel, A., 220
Vogt, B., 326
Voissem, N., 530

Walbek, N., 316
Walder, L., 287
Walker, L., 520, 549
Walker, M., 37, 581
Wallace, A., 512, 515
Wallace, I., 512, 515
Wallace, M., 529
Wallace, O., 68
Wallach, M., 565
Wallin, P., 234
Wallston, B., 331
Walster, E., 123, 124, 224, 227, 234, 236, 237, 238, 240, 241, 246, 409, 410, 536, 540, 545
Walster, G., 234, 237, 238, 536, 596
Walters, R., 25, 269, 285
Ward, L., 625
Ware, J., 466
Warner, I., 383
Warner, K., 453
Warwick, D., 373
Warwick, P., 62
Washburn, S., 263
Watson, D., 150, 169
Watson, J., 354
Watts, B., 548
Wauson, M., 649
Waxler, C., 315
Weary, G., 181

Webb, E., 67, 363, 366
Weber, M., 16
Weigel, R., 385
Weiner, B., 141, 142, 182
Weinheimer, S., 521
Weinstein, N., 626
Weiss, R., 216, 307, 308, 309, 310, 323, 464
Weiss, W., 407, 446
Weissberg, R., 349
Weitzer, W., 665
Wellons, R., 506
Wells, G., 141, 157
Werner, R., 498
West, S., 163, 649
Wharton, J., 59
Wheeler, D., 477
Wheeler, L., 218, 236, 479
Whipple, T., 391
White, B., 395
White, G., 239, 240
White, J., 264
White, L., 294
White, R., 232, 374, 555, 558, 609
White, T., 608
Wichman, H., 530, 531
Wicker, A., 380, 665
Wicker, T., 495
Wicklund, R., 81, 105, 175, 176, 177, 495
Wilder, D., 485, 488
Wildman, R. W., 250
Wildman, R. W., II, 250

Wilke, H., 533
Will, G., 406
Will, J., 95
Willers, K., 291
Williams, K., 583, 585
William, T., 288
Willis, R., 513
Wills, T., 347, 349
Wilmot, W., 528
Wilson, A., 349
Wilson, D., 374, 625
Wilson, E., 33, 312, 391
Wilson, M., 228
Winch, R., 245, 246
Wincze, J., 251
Winer, B., 599
Wishner, J., 131
Witkin, H., 265
Wittig, M., 636
Wolchik, S., 251
Wolfe, J., 300
Wolfe, T., 192, 193
Wolfgang, M., 283
Wong, T., 227
Wood, W., 409, 422, 491
Woodside, A., 446
Worchel, S., 396, 434, 644
Worthy, M., 221
Wortman, C., 194
Wortman, P., 398

Wright, E., 150
Wright, P., 446
Wright, R., 345
Wright, T., 186
Wrightsman, L., 167, 262, 569
Wyckoff, L., 509

Yahya, L., 469
Yancey, W., 661
Yankowski, L., 365
Yarkin, K., 152
Yarrow, M., 315
Young, M., 69

Zajonc, R. 222, 370, 577
Zanna, M., 108, 135, 370, 375, 384, 395, 435
Zanni, G., 159
Zavalloni, M., 581
Zeisel, H., 154
Zellman, G., 299
Zemke, P., 533
Zeisel, H., 610
Zillman, D., 239, 251, 275, 276, 286, 292
Zimbardo, P., 173, 174, 175, 217, 494, 557, 562
Zimring, C., 665
Zlutnick, S., 645
Znaniecki, F., 354
Zuckerman, M., 479
Zyzanski, S., 113
Zweigenhaft, R., 654

Subject Index

Boldface numbers indicate the page on which the description or definition of the term appears.

Absence of empathy, 557
Academic achievement,
    and jigsaw technique, 399
    and locus of control, 186, 187
    racial differences in, 398
    and school desegregation, 398
    and teacher's expectancies, 55, 56
Acme trucking, 528
Active participation
    and attitude change, 424–442
    and cognitive dissonance, 403–405, 426–438
    and value confrontation, 438–441
Additive tasks **583, 597**
    and group performance, 583–586
    and process loss, 585
    and social loafing, 583–585
Advertising, 444–449. *See also* Advertising effectiveness
    history of, 444, 445
Advertising effectiveness
    and persuasive messages, 445–450
    and central route, 446, 447
    and peripheral route, 446, 447
    and repitition, 448, 449
    and thinking, 446, 447
Adze razor, 447, 448
Affective component, **355,** 367, 390
    and behavioral component, 357
    and cognitive component, 357
Affiliation, 215–218
    and classical conditioning, 215
    and embarrassment, 217
    and fear, 216, 217
    and instrumental conditioning, 216
Agentic state, **471**
    and deindividuation, 494
    and obedience, 471

Aggression, **259.** *See also* Angry aggression
    and biological orientation, 264–266
    control of, 286–295
    and frustration, 257–259, 266–268
    kinds of, 272, 273
    and social learning theory, 268–272, 285–286
Aggression-eliciting stimuli, 277–280, 284
    and angry aggression, 277–279
    and classical conditioning, 279, 280
    and weapons, 278, 279
Aggression instigators, 273, 274, 284
Aggressive cues. *See* Aggression-eliciting stimuli
Aggressive energy. *See also* Angry aggression
    and catharsis, 257–259
Aggressive pornography, **302**
    and aggression against women, 303, 304
    and attitudes toward sexual assaults, 303
    versus soft-core pornography, 301, 302
Air Florida, 6, 321
Air pollution, **630**
    and aggression, 630
    adaptation to, 631, 633
    in ancient times, 632
Alcohol
    and angry aggression, 281–284
    and self-awareness, 284
    and violent crimes, 283
Alcoholics Anonymous, 442
Allocation of Resources
    individual differences in, 547, 548
    motivations for, 547
    sex differences in, 548, 549
    situational influences on, 547
    strategies of, 545
Altruism, 310–312. *See also* Bystander intervention; Helping; Strong altruism
American Psychological Association, 9
Analysis of variance, 48

Androgens, 264
Androgyny, **97**
    and romantic attraction, 235
Anglophones, 555
Angry aggression
    and arousal, 257–259, 291
    and aggression eliciting stimuli, 277–279, 284
    control of, 286
    and crowding, 649
    definition of, 272
    and drugs, 281–284
    and environmental stressors, 280, 281, 284, 624, 625
    and excitation transfer, 275
    and incompatible responses, 291–294
    instinctual theories of, 273, 274, 284
    and noise, 625
    and two-factor theory, 275
    versus instrumental aggression, 273
Anthropology
    and social psychology, 12, 14
Anti-conformity, 487
Anti-semitism, 19, 344, 389. *See also* Jews
    in Germany, 393, 394
    in United States, 393, 394, 472
Antismoking campaigns, *See* Smoking prevention
Apartheid, 391
Applied research, **10, 11**
    versus basic research, 11, 13
Arab/Israeli conflict,
    and misperceptions, 555–558
    and third party-intervention, 560–562
Arabs, 389
Architectural design, *See also* Building design; Dormitory design; Institutional design; Interior design
    and crowding, 659–664, 666
    and invasion of personal space, 658

Archival studies, 68, 73
Arousal, *See also* Catharsis; Love
  and angry aggression, 257–259, 291
  and bystander intervention, 322, 323, 333
  and cognitive dissonance, 427
  and excitation transfer, 239, 275, 276
  and general adaptation syndrome, 624
  and sexual attraction, 239–241, 249–252
  and social facilitation, 578
Assaults
  aggravated, 259, 260
  characteristics of, 260, 261
  sexual, 297–303
Assimilation, **375**
  and latitude of acceptance, 416
  versus contrast, 375
Association, 194
Attica State Prison, 495
Attitude, **355**. *See also* Attitude change
  and behavior, 353, 354, 379–388
  formation of, 368–374
  functions of, 375–379
  measurement of, 358–367
  structure of, 355–358
Attitude-behavior relationship, 380–387
  methodological explanations, 385–387
  strength of, 379–380
  theoretical explanation, 380–385
Attitude change
  and active participation, 403–405, 424–438
  and behavior change, 440–443, 454, 455
  persistence of, 442
  and persuasive messages, 406–424
  and value change, 438–440
Attitude discrepant behavior, 403, 429
  and choice, 432
  and commitment, 432, 433
  and impact on others, 434
  and reward, 403–405
Attitude formation, 368–374, 379
  and classical conditioning, 369, 370
  and direct experiences, 368–370
  and mere exposure, 370, 371
  and self-perception theory, 370, 371
Attitude functions
  and ego protection, 377, 379
  and knowledge, 374, 375, 379
  and needs, 375, 376, 379
  and values, 377–379
Attitude measurement. *See also* Attitude scales
  and attitude-behavior relationship, 385
  direct measures, 358–362, 368
  indirect measures, 362–368
  specificity of, 386, 387
Attitude scales, **359**–362
  and reactivity, 362, 363
  semantic differential, 361, 362
  summative, 360, 361
  Thurstone, 359, 360
Attitude toward behavior, 380–382
Attitude toward object, 384
Attitude toward situation, 384
Attitudes toward
  birth control, 382
  busing, 397
  Chinese, 353, 354, 358, 379, 383, 385
  civil rights, 439
  communism, 379
  dentists, 369
  gun control, 360–362
  job, 362
  lawyers, 356–358
  rape, 299
  religion, 361, 373
  sexual activities, 248, 249
  smoking, 384

  urban/rural environments, 631, 632
  war in Vietnam, 472
Attribution
  actor-observer differences, 149–151
  biases in, 145, 147, 148, 151–153
  fundamental attribution error, 149–151
  internal versus external, 136
  and legal system, 163
  models of, 137–141
Authoritarianism, 472. *See also* Authoritarian personality
Authoritarian personality
  and anti-semitism, 393, 394
  and attitudes, 472
  and ethnocentrism, 394
  and obedience, 472
  scale, 394
Autokinetic phenomenon, 478
Autonomy, 84
Availability heuristic, 146
Averaging model, 127, 128
Awareness of norms, 318

B = f (p,e) 28, 110, 651
Baboons
  aggression among, 263
Balance theory
  of friendship, 229–231
  and p-o-x triad, 230, 231
Bargaining, **516**
  and Machiavellianism, 520–523
  location of, 517, 523, 641
  strategies of, 519, 521–523
  situational influences on, 517–520
  and third-party intervention, 519, 520, 523
  and time pressure, 517–519, 523
Barnum effect, 101, 102
Bartenders
  as nonprofessional helpers, 349–351
Baseball players, 543, 544
Basic research, **10**
  versus applied research, 10, 13
Basking in reflected glory, 37–39
Bay of Pigs invasion, 607
Behavior change
  and attitude change, 440–443
  consequences of, 442
Behavior measurement
  and attitude-behavior relationship, 385–387
  and multiple-act criterion, 385–387
Behavioral component, **356**, 357, 367, 390
  and affective component, 357
  and cognitive component, 357
Behavioral intentions, 380–382, 387
Benign inequity, **540**
  physical reduction of, 541, 542
  psychological reduction of, 542, 544
Bias
  in attributions, 145, 147, 148, 151–153
  information processing, 145–150
  motivational, 143–145
  and persuasive messages, 409
  versus error, 151–152
Bicycle racing, 3
Bilateral monopoly game, 516, 517
Biological orientation,
  and aggression, 264–266, 271
  and helping, 311, 312, 319
  and prejudice, 391
  and sex role behaviors, 94, 95
  and social behavior, 33
Biorhythms, 102
Black protest
  and deprivation, 554
Bogus pipeline, **363**, 368, 545
  and attitude measurement, 363
  versus unobtrusive measures, 363

Bolt trucking, 529
Brainstorming, **591**
  effectiveness of, 592–294, 597
  and evaluation apprehension, 593, 594
  and problem solving tasks, 591–594
Building design. *See also* Architectural design;
    Dormitory design; Institutional design; Interior design
  and friendship, 651–653
  and functional distance, 652, 653
Built environment, **650**–666. *See also* Architectural design; Building design; Dormitory design; Interior design; Institutional design
Bureau of Census, 445
Busing
  attitudes toward, 397
  incidence of, 146
Bystander intervention, **320**–333
  and arousal, 322, 323
  and costs, 327–333
  and diffusion of responsibility, 328–330, 332
  and emotions, 323–326
  and reward/cost matrix, 331–333
  and victim characteristics, 330, 331

Campaign expenditures, 371
Canada
  effects of television in, 288
  separatist movement in, 554, 555
Cancer, 450, 498
Category-based expectations, 139
Catharsis
  and aggressive energy, 257–259
  and control of aggression, 286–293, 296
  ethological theory of, 261–264
  hypothesis, 257–259, 286–293, 296
  and physical aggression, 257, 292, 293
  and sports participation, 290
  and substitute aggression, 291, 296
  and television violence, 288–290
  and verbal aggression, 257, 292, 296
Catholic church, 390, 429
Causal hypothesis, 44, 45
Causal schemata, 140
Central Intelligence Agency, 606
Central route, **420**
  and advertising effectiveness, 446, 447
  and attitude change, 420–423
  and involvement, 447, 448
  versus peripheral route, 420
Central traits, 131, 132
Centralization, **573**
  and communication patterns, 572–574
Chain communication pattern, 573
Chimpanzees
  helping in, 311
  self-concept of, 91, 92
  self-recognition in, 91, 92
Chinese
  attitudes toward, 353, 354
  confused with Japanese, 354, 397
Christians
  stereotypes among, 390
Circle communication pattern, 573
Civil conflict. *See also* Deprivation
  causes of, 551–555
  in United States, 551
Civil rights supporters
  characteristics, 344, 345
  and crime stoppers, 346
Classical conditioning, 22, 23
  and affiliation, 215
  and aggression eliciting stimuli, 279, 280
  and attitude formation, 369, 370
  and empathy, 313, 314
  and interpersonal attraction, 231–233

Classroom ecology, 654–657
Coercive social power
  basis of, 463, 464
  and compliance, 464, 478
  and marital distress, 464
  and medical regimens, 501–503
  as socially dependent, 464
Cognitions, 26, 426
Cognitive component, **356**, 367, 390
  and affective component, 357
  and behavioral component, 357
Cognitive dissonance
  and attitude change, 426–438, 442
  causes of, 427, 428
  and counterattitudinal advocacy, 403–405
  current status of, 434
  limitations of, 431–434
  reduction of, 427, 428
  versus impression management, 435, 436
  versus learning management, 432, 436
  versus self-perception, 434, 435
  and weight reduction, 430, 431
Cognitive orientation
  and field theory, 27, 28
  and Gestalt psychology, 26, 27
  and social behavior, 26–30, 34
  versus learning orientation, 28–30
Cognitive developmental theory, 86–88
Cognitive theories
  of attitude change, 426–442
Cohesiveness, **574**
  and group processes, 576, 577
Coitus
  and emotional intimacy, 252
  importance of, 253
  in romantic relationships, 252, 253
Commercials. See also Advertising; Advertising effectiveness
  and attitude formation, 374, 392
  and portrayals of women, 392
Commons dilemma, **527**
  and group identity, 533–535
  as mixed motive game, 533
  as social trap, 527
Communication networks. See Communication patterns
Communication patterns
  and centralization, 572
  and group structure, 572–574
  kinds of, 573
Communicator characteristics. See Source characteristics
"Communist menace," 464
Community interventions
  and smoking prevention, 452, 453
Companionate love, 238
Comparison level, **514**
  and social exchange theory, 514, 515
  versus comparison level for alternatives, 514
Comparison level for alternatives, **514**
  and social exchange theory, 514
  versus comparison level, 514
Comparative appraisal, 93
Competition, **512**
  in international conflicts, 558
  in interpersonal conflicts, 530–535
  and prejudice, 395–397
Complementarity theory, 244, 245
Compliance, **459**
  and coercive social power, 463, 464
  and medical regimens, 491–506
  and reward social power, 462
  versus private acceptance, 459
Computers, 4
Conditioning
  classical, 22, 215, 231–233, 279, 280, 313, 314, 369, 370

higher order, 22, 23, 372
  instrumental, 24, 33, 216, 268, 269, 307–309, 314, 319, 502, 503
Conflict
  civil, 551–555
  international, 555–562
  interpersonal, 524–535
  nonzero-sum, 524
  zero-sum, 524
Conflict resolution. See International conflict; Third party intervention
Conformity, **480**
  and group influence, 480–487, 496
  and informational social influence, 484, 485
  and jury decisions, 613
  and normative social influence, 481–484
  sex differences in, 490, 491
Consensus, **137**
  and attributions, 137
  and social desirability, 138
Consideration, 599, 600
Consistency
  and attribution, 137
  and cognitive dissonance, 426
  in social behavior, 104–109, 152
Construct validity, **43, 45**
  of attitude scales, 359
  of experiments, 52–56, 61
  of personality scales, 101
  threats to, 53–56
Consultation
  and reduction of conflicts, 561, 562
  versus mediation, 560
Content analysis, 67, 73
Contingency theory, **601, 602**
  and leadership effectiveness, 601–604
  and least-preferred co-worker, 601
Contrast, **375**
  and latitude of rejection, 416
  versus assimilation, 375
Control of aggression
  and arousal, 292, 293
  and catharsis, 286–293
  and television, 286–290
  and social learning theory, 286, 288
  and sports, 290
Control condition, 47
Control theory
  and crowding, 644, 650
Cooperation, **512**
  in classroom, 399, 400
  experiment on, 532, 533
  in international conflicts, 558
  in interpersonal conflicts, 530–535
  and prejudice, 395–397
Coronary heart disease
  and smoking, 450, 452
  and Type A behavior, 112–114
  treatment of, 500
Coronary prone behavior pattern, 113
Correlation coefficient, **65, 66, 73**
  between attitudes and behavior, 380
  between traits and behavior, 103
Correlational studies, 645
Correspondent inferences, 138–140
  bias in, 145
Costs
  and bystander intervention, 326–333
  of helping, 332, 333
  of not helping, 332, 333
Counterattitudinal advocacy, **425**
  and cognitive dissonance, 403–405, 425, 427
  and incentives, 425
  and self-perception theory, 435
Credibility
  and sleeper effect, 413, 414
  and source characteristics, 407–411, 423

Crime stoppers
  characteristics of, 345, 346
  and civil rights supporters, 346
  and rescuers of Jews, 346
Crowding, **641**
  and aggression, 649
  and architectural design, 658–664
  causes of, 643–645
  and learned helplessness, 646, 662
  and health, 649, 650
  and problem solving, 646
  in rats, 617–619
  and sociability, 646–650
  and social pathology, 617–619, 645
  versus density, 641
Crowding and behavior, 632
Cuban missile crisis, 609
Covariation model, 137, 138
  and attributions of success and failure, 141, 142
  and perceptions of crime, 163
Curvilinear relationship, **281**, 282, **415**, 416, 630, 631

Dating, 234–241
  and matching, 235, 237
Debriefing, 48, 73
Decision making
  and the government, 606–610
  and groupthink, 607–610
  and juries, 610–615
Decision-making tasks, **594, 597**. See also Groupthink
  decision rules in, 594, 595
Declaration of Independence, 406
Defense reaction, 322
Delusions, 386
Demand characteristics, **53**
  and construct validity, 53, 61
  and placebo effects, 53
Deindividuation, **494**
  and anonymity, 494
  and antisocial behavior, 495, 496
  and group membership, 493, 496
  and roles, 494–496
Density, **643**
  kinds of, 643
  versus crowding, 641
Dental care, 502, 503
Dependent variable, 46, 61
Depression
  and attributional style, 201, 202
  incidence of, 201
  and learned helplessness, 201
  neurotic, 201
  treatment of, 203, 204
Deprivation
  and black protest, 554
  and civil conflict, 551–555
  fraternal, 554, 555
  personal, 554, 555
  progressive, 553, 554
  relative, 551–553
  and Quebec separatist movement, 554, 555
Descriptive approach, 62–74. See also Observational methods; Surveys
  versus experimental approach, 70, 71
Diabetes, 498
Diabolical enemy image, 557
Diffusion of responsibility, **328**
  and bystander intervention, 328–330, 332
  and social impact theory, 581
Direct experience
  and attitude-behavior relationship, 384, 385, 387
  and attitude formation, 368–370
Discounting principle, 140

Discrimination, 390, 391
Distinctiveness, 138
Divorce
    and locus of control, 187
Door-in-the-face, 476, 477
Dormitory design. *See also* Architectural design;
    Building design; Interior design; Institutional
    design
    and crowding, 659–662
    changes in, 663–666
    long corridor, 659, 662, 664
    short corridor, 662, 664
    suite, 660
Doubling time, 620
Draft riots, 551
Dramatized performance, 190
Drive theory
    and aggression, 25
    and primary drives, 24
    and secondary drives, 24
    and social behavior, 24, 25, 34
Drugs
    and angry aggression, 281–284
E = mc², 355

Ecological theory
    and crowding, 645, 650
Ego despair, 86
Ego integrity, 86
Elderly
    and fear of crime, 6
    and locus of control retraining, 205, 206
    problems of, 204
    self-attributions of, 204–207
    and sense of control, 204, 205
    treatment programs for, 75–78
Emotion
    labeling of, 165–167
    two factor theory of, 165–167, 172, 173, 216
Empathic concern, **323**
    and helping, 323–325
    versus personal distress, 323, 326
Empathic response, 313. *See also* Empathy
Empathy
    costs, 327, 328
    and classical conditioning, 313, 314
    and helping, 313, 322–325, 327, 328, 338
    in infants, 314
    scale, 338
    and sociopathy, 340
    versus psuedo-empathy, 313
Energy conservation
    and group identity, 533
    and low balling, 474
Environmental probabilism, 651
Environmental Protection Agency, 625
Environmental psychology, **619**
    and social behavior, 617–666
Environmental stressors, **281, 623**. *See also* Air pol-
    lution; Noise; Temperature
    and angry aggression, 280–281, 284
    and urban/rural differences, 623–632
Epileptic seizure, 328, 500
Equal status contact, 398
Equalitarian norm, **545**
    and resource allocation, 545, 547, 550
Equality, 379, 439
Equity, **246**
    and extramarital affairs, 254
    and marital choice, 246
    physical restoration of, 541, 542
    and sexual activity, 253, 254
Equity norm, **545**
    and resource allocation, 545, 547, 550
Equity theory, **536**. *See also* Equity; Inequity
    and allocation of resources, 545–550
    and mutual exchanges, 536–540

Equalitarian hypothesis, 589
Eros, 262
Espionage, 429
Ethics. *See* Research ethics
Ethnic prejudice, 390. *See also* Racism
Ethnocentrism, **393**
    and authoritarian personality, 393, 394
    and group membership, 394
Ethological theory
    of aggression, 261–264
Ethology, 262
Eureka problem, 589
Evaluation apprehension, **53**
    and construct validity, 53, 61
Evolution. *See also* Kin selection; Reciprocal altru-
    ism
    and helping, 311, 312
Exchange theory. *See* Social exchange theory
Excitation transfer, **239**
    and angry aggression, 275
    and bystander intervention, 323
    and sexual attraction, 239–240
Expectancy-value model, **357, 358, 367**
    versus three-component model, 358
Experimental approach, 45–61. *See also* Field ex-
    periments; Laboratory experiments; Quasi-
    experiments
    versus descriptive approach, 70, 71
Experimental condition, 47
Experimental psychology
    and social psychology, 17, 20
Experimental realism, 56
Experimenter effects, **54**
    and construct validity, 54, 61
    and teacher's expectancies, 55, 56
Expert social power, **465**
    basis of, 465, 466, 478
    and Dr. Fox, 466
    and medical regimens, 506
    and private acceptance, 466
    as socially dependent, 466
Expertise
    and social power, 465, 466
    and source characteristics, 408–410, 423
    versus trustworthiness, 409–411
Exploratory affective exchange stage, 220
External validity, **56**
    of descriptive approaches, 70, 71
    of an experiment, 56, 57, 70, 71
Extreme group technique, 101
Extrinsic interest, 436
Extroversion, 171, 220
Eyewitness testimony, 155–160
    accuracy of, 155, 156
    importance of, 155, 159
    influences on, 157
    and memory, 158, 159
    and stress, 158

Factorial design, 49
Fahrenheit scale, 41, 42
Failure
    attributions of, 141, 142
    and self-attributions, 179, 180
Fairness. *See* Justice
Fear
    and affiliation, 216, 217
    and sexual attraction, 209–211, 240, 241
Fear-arousing messages, **418, 423**
    effectiveness of, 418, 419, 441
Federal Bureau of Investigation, 429
Federal Communications Commission, 59, 60
Federal Elections Commission, 68
Federalist papers, 67, 68
Field experiments, **57**
    versus laboratory experiments, 58

Field studies, 67, 73
Field theory, 27, 28, 34, 110
Fifth ammendment rights, 162
Fighting instinct, 262, 263, 271
Finland
    and smoking prevention, 452
    and television, 287
Flight, 90, 327, 330
Foot in the Door, 473, 474, 478
    and self-perception theory, 473, 474
    versus low balling, 474
Forced compliance
    and attitude change, 403–405
Francophones, 554, 555
Fraternal deprivation, 555
Freedom, 439
Friendships
    and building design, 651–653
    and liking, 227
    and propinquity, 222–224, 227
    and reciprocity, 228
    and similarity, 224–227
    theories of, 228–223
Frustration
    and aggression, 257–259
    aggression hypothesis, 266–268, 271
    and arousal, 258
    and violent television, 288, 290
Frustration-aggression hypothesis, 266–268, 271
Functional distance
    and friendship, 652, 653, 666
Functional relationship, 44
Fundamental attribution error, **149**
    and actor-observer differences, 147–149

Gender constancy, 97
Gender differences. *See* Sex differences
General adaptation syndrome, **623**
    and arousal, 624
    and environmental stressors, 623, 624, 632
Generalizability. *See* External validity
Generalized helping personality, 337
Generativity, 86
Genocide, 343
Gestalt psychology
    and field theory, 27, 28, 34
    and impression formation, 127
    influence on social psychology, 18, 26, 27
Government decision making, 606–610. *See also*
    Groupthink
Graduated reciprocation in. *See also* International
    conflict
    tension reduction strategy, 558
Graffitti, 363, 465
Great man approach, 598
Grit strategy, **558**
    and international conflict, 558, 560
    and President Kennedy, 559, 560
Group formation, 568, 569
Group identity. *See also* Commons dilemma
    and mixed motive game, 533–535
Group influence
    and conformity, 480–487
    and deindividuation, 492–495
    and nonconformity, 487–489
    and obedience, 481
    and risk taking, 565–567
Group influence
    and group polarization, 581, 582
    and social facilitation, 577, 578
    and social impact theory, 578–581
    and social loafing, 583–585
Group membership
    and ethnocentrism, 394
Group performance
    on additive tasks, 583–586

on decision making tasks, 594
improvements in, 595–596
on problem solving tasks, 586–594
Group polarization, **581**
explanation of, 582, 597
and jury decisions, 582
and risk taking, 581, 582
Group pressure. *See* Group influence
Group processes
and cohesiveness, 574, 576, 577
and group interactions, 575, 576
Group size
and bystander intervention, 328
Group structure, **569**
and communication patterns, 572, 574
and norms, 571
and roles, 569–571
and status, 571, 572, 576
Groups, 565, **566**, 567–615. *See also* Group formation; Group influence; Group processes; Group performance; Leadership
Groupthink. *See also* Decision making tasks; Nominal group technique
causes of, 607, 608
and decision making, 607–610
reduction of, 609, 610
symptoms of, 608
Guilt
and helping, 334, 335, 342
and personality, 85
Gun control, 360–362
Gun owner of the year, 278
Guttenberg printing press, 444

Hairdressers
as nonprofessional helpers, 349–351
Hawaiian culture
sexual arousal in, 250
Hedonic relevance, 145, 163
Hedonism, **15**
and industrial revolution, 15
and social psychology, 15, 20
Helping, **310**. *See also* Altruism; Bystander intervention
and biological orientation, 311, 312
and bystander intervention, 320–333
costs of, 327–331
developmental changes in, 317–319
and empathy, 313
experiment on, 46–49
individual differences in, 333–342
and mood, 318, 334, 335
and noise, 627
nonprofessional, 349–351
professional, 349–351
and similarity, 331
and social learning theory, 313–319
and temperature, 625
urban/rural differences in, 621
Hermaphroditism, 95
Heuristics, 146
Higher order conditioning, 22, 23, 372
Hitler, Adolph, 18, 19, 86, 342, 457, 471, 557
Holocaust, 393, 471
Home court advantage, 517, 642, 643
Homocides
and alcohol, 283
in United States, 260
Homogamy, 243, 244
Homosexuals
perceptions of, 27, 124, 148, 149
Hypotheses, **22**
kinds of, 44, 45
versus theories, 39
Hypothetical construct, 355

Idealized performance, 190
Identification, **465**
and referent social power, 465
Identity crisis, **85**
and personality, 85
Idiopathic scoliosis, 502–504
Idiosyncrasy credit, 484
Illusion of invulnerability, 608
Illusion of unanimity, 608
Illusory correlation, 134, 135
Imitation
and observational learning, 25
and social behavior, 15, 16, 20
Implicit decision rules, 146, 147
Implicit personality theory, 132
Impression formation, 123–136
and central traits, 131, 132
experiment on, 121–123
Gestalt explanation of, 127
and physical appearance, 123–126
linear combination explanation of, 127–130
Impression management, 38, **188**–199
and cognitive dissonance, 435–437
among pilots, 192, 193
individual differences in, 196–199
tactics of, 193–196
Incentives, **406**
and attitude change, 406, 407
and role playing, 425
Incompatible responses
and angry aggression, 291–294
Independence, 487
Independent variable, **46, 61**
and control condition, 47
and experimental condition, 47
Indirect intervention, 330, 331
Individual differences
in bargaining, 520–523
in conformity, 489–492
in helping, 333–342
in impression management, 196–199
in personal space, 636
in resource allocation, 547, 548
Individual influence. *See also* Social power
and social power, 461–472
tactics of, 472–478
Industrial revolution, 15, 620
Industry, 83
Inequity
among baseball players, 543, 544
and distress, 540
kinds of, 540
Inferiority, 85
Influence, 459
Influencing agent, 462
Informational social influence, **484**
and cognitive restructuring, 485–487
and conformity, 484, 485, 496
and social comparison, 485
Informational social power, 466
Informed consent, 73
Ingratiation, **194**
and impression management, 194
and social influence, 473
Initiating structure, 599, 600
Initiative, 85
Inoculation theory, 417
and smoking prevention, 454
Input-outcome ratio, 538
Inside density, 643, 649
Instinctual theories
and aggression, 261–265, 271
Institutional aggression, **272**
versus interpersonal aggression, 272
Institutional design. *See also* Architectural design; Building design; Dormitory design; Interior design

changes in, 665
Instrumental aggression, **272**
versus angry aggression, 273
Instrumental conditioning, 24, 33
and affiliation, 216
and aggression, 268, 269
and helping, 307–309, 314, 319
and medical regimens, 502, 503
Instrumental values, 377
Interaction process analysis, 575, 576
Interactionism
and causes of social behavior, 109, 110
Interactions
black-white, 365, 366, 391
male-female, 235
professor-student, 654, 655
statistical, 49–51
teacher-student, 655, 656
Interdependent social behavior
and conflict, 524–535, 551–562
justice in, 535–550
and social exchange, 513–523
Interior design. *See also* Architectural design; Building design; Dormitory design; Institutional design
of classrooms, 654, 655, 666
of offices, 654, 666
of rooms, 653, 654
Interjudge reliability, 43
Internal validity, **51**
of descriptive approaches, 70
of an experiment, 52, 61, 70
of jury trials, 154, 610
of treatment programs, 75
and random assignment, 52
Internalization, 318
International conflict. *See also* GRIT; Third party intervention
and misperceptions, 555–558
reduction of, 558–562
Interpersonal aggression, **272**. *See also* Angry aggression; Catharsis
versus institutional aggression, 272
Interpersonal attraction, 209, 210, **211**, 212–254. *See also* Friendships; Love; Romantic attraction
mere exposure and, 222, 223
theories of, 228–233
Interpersonal conflict, **524**
kinds of, 524–527
reduction of, 527–535
Interviews, 64
Intimacy, 86
Intrinsic interest, 436
Isolation, 86
Israeli/Arab conflict. *See* Arab/Israeli conflict

Japanese
attack on Pearl Harbor, 607
confused with Chinese, 354, 390
prejudice toward, 390, 391, 397
war against, 406
Jenkins Activity Survey, 113
Jesus Christ, 386, 582
Jews. *See also* Anti-semitism
in German universities, 18
genocide against, 18, 343, 471, 472
prejudice against, 389, 393
prejudice among, 372, 391
stereotypes of, 391
Jigsaw technique, **399**
effects of, 399, 400
and school desegregation, 399, 400
Jobs
attitude toward, 362
Juries. *See also* Jury decision making
and fifth ammendment, 162

and inadmissable evidence, 161
and pretrial publicity, 160
and testimony of witnesses, 161, 164
validity of decisions, 154, 155, 163, 610–614
Jury decision making. *See also* Juries
and decision rules, 614
and group polarization, 582
model of, 611
and size, 612, 613
and structure, 612
Jury size, 612, 613
Jury structure, 612
Just world hypothesis, 545, 546
Justice
and allocation of resources, 545–550
and equity theory, 535–545
procedural, 549, 550

Kennedy, John F., 559, 560, 606
and groupthink, 608, 609
Kin selection, 312
Knowledge bias, 409

Laboratory experiments
conditions in, 46
on crowding, 645, 646
execution of, 47, 48
on helping, 46–49
validity of, 51–57
value of, 57
versus field experiments, 58
versus quasi-experiments, 59
Latitude of acceptance, **415**
and assimilation, 416
and attitude change, 415, 416
and ego-involvement, 415
Latitude of rejection, **415**
and attitude change, 415, 416
and contrast, 416
and ego-involvement, 415
Lawyers
attitudes toward, 356–358
Leader behavior
and leader effectiveness, 599–601, 604
and leadership style, 599
Leader effectiveness, **597, 598**
contingency theory explanation, 601–604
leader behavior explanation, 599–601, 604
trait explanation, 598, 604
social interaction explanation, 603, 604
Leadership, 597–605. *See also* Leader effectiveness;
Leadership style; Social power
Leadership style, **599**
effects of, 600
kinds of, 599
and least-preferred co-worker scale, 601
and locus of control, 604
Learned helplessness, **201**
and crowding, 649
and depression, 201, 202
Learning orientation. *See also* Conditioning; Drive
theory; Observational learning
and social behavior, 22–26, 33, 523
versus cognitive orientation, 28–30
Learning theory
of friendship, 231–233
Least-preferred co-worker scale, **601**
and contingency theory, 601
and leadership style, 602–603
Legitimate social power, **466**
bias of, 466, 467, 478
and obedience, 469–472
of Pope, 467
Life space, 28
Likableness, 412
Liking. *See* Friendship

Linear combination model, 127–130
Locus of control
and academic achievement, 186, 187
changes in, 187
among the elderly, 205, 206
and leadership style, 604
racial differences in, 185
among prisoners, 186, 187
scale, 184
and self-attribution, 183–186
sex differences in, 185
and self-disclosure, 220
and divorce, 187
Logrolling, 521, 522
Loneliness, 212–215
scale, 214
Looking glass self, 32
Lost letter technique, 363
Love
in ancient Greece, 241
companionate, 238
courtly, 242, 243
and marriage, 241–243
and parental interference, 239
passionate, 238
and two-factor theory of emotion, 238
versus liking, 237–241
Love, Sex and Marriage through the ages, 241
Low-balling, **474**
effectiveness of, 474, 475, 478
and energy conservation, 474
versus foot in the door, 474

Machiavellianism, **520–523**
and bargaining, 520–522
scale, 520, 521
Mafia, 273
Main effects, **49**
and interactions, 49, 50
Maintenance role, **570**
effects of, 600
and group structure, 570
Malignant inequity, **540**
among baseball players, 543, 544
and distress, 540
physical reduction of, 541, 542
psychological reduction of, 542, 544
Marijuana
and aggression, 284
effects of, 53
Marital choice
theories of, 243–246
Marriage. *See also* Marital choice
and love, 241–243
Matching
of assets, 236
of attributes, 234, 237
and dating, 234–237
Mathematical ability, 359
Media. *See* Television
Mediation
and reduction of conflicts, 560, 561
versus consultation, 560
Medical regimens, **491**
benefits of compliance to, 500
causes of noncompliance to, 491, 492
consequences of noncompliance to, 499, 500
and social power, 501–506
Mere exposure
and attitude formation, 370, 371
and interpersonal attraction, 222–224
Message characteristics, 414–423
and amount of change advocated, 415–417
and fear-arousing messages, 418–420
and one-sided/two-sided messages, 417
versus message characteristics, 420–423

Middle East conflict. *See* Arab/Israeli conflict
Military overconfidence, 558
Minimal social situation, 509–511, 532
Minority influence, 489, 490
Mirrors
and self-awareness, 176, 177
and self-knowledge, 81, 82
and self-recognition, 91, 92
Misperceptions, **555**
and Arab/Israeli conflict, 555–558
definition of, 555
and War in Vietnam, 555, 556
and World War I, 555
and World War II, 555
Mississippi
murders in, 344
Mixed motive game, **527**. *See also* Common's dilemma; Prisoner's dilemma
cooperation in, 530–535
and group identity, 533–535
strategies in, 530–535, 559
and threats, 528, 529
Models, 88. *See also* Observational learning
and aggression, 270, 271
and helping, 314–316
Moderator variables
and attitude-behavior relationship, 384, 385,
387
and trait behavior relationship, 105–109
Mood
and helping, 319, 334–336, 342
Moral self-image, 557
Multiple-act criterion, 385–387
Mundane realism, 56
Murder Inc., 273
Mutuality, 218
My Lai, 186

National Commission on Obscenity and Pornog-
raphy, 301
Natural selection, 33, 311, 312
Natural social behavior, 66
Naturalistic observation, 635
Nazism, 344, 393, 394
Need for approval, 199
Needs
and attitude functions, 375, 376, 379
and drive theory, 24
Negative state relief hypothesis, 318, 335
Negotiations. *See* Bargaining
New School of Social Research, 29
New York City, 121, 320, 330, 629, 630
Niagara Falls
as aggression eliciting stimulus, 278
Nobel Prize, 263
Noise, **625**
and academic performance, 627, 629, 630
adaptation to, 629
and aggression, 625
and helping, 627
and social interactions, 625, 626, 633
and stimulus overload, 626
Nominal group, 588
Nominal group technique, **595**
effectiveness of, 596, 597
and group performance, 595, 596
and groupthink, 609, 610
versus nominal groups, 595
Nominal scale, 42
Noncausal hypotheses, 44
Noncommon effects, 139, 140
Noncompliance
to medical regimens, 491, 492, 499, 500
Nonconformity, 487–492
and anti-conformity, 487
causes of, 487, 488, 496
and independence, 487

Nonprofessional helpers, 349–351
Nonverbal behavior, 365, 366
    urban/rural differences, 622, 623
Nonzero sum conflict, **524.** *See also* Commons di-
    lemma; Prisoner's dilemma
    and international conflict, 558–560
    and interpersonal conflict, 524–535
Norm, **228, 339, 479, 571**
    and group structure, 571, 576
    personal and helping, 339
    reciprocity, 228
    social and helping, 339
Norm of need, **545**
    and resource allocation, 545, 547, 550
Normative social influence, **481**
    and attraction to group, 484
    and conformity, 481–484
    and group polarization, 582
    and negative consequences, 482, 483
Norway breed rats, 617
Nuclear freeze, 8
Nuclear test ban treaty, 559
Null hypothesis, 44, 45
Nursing homes, 205, 206

Obedience, 457–459, 469–472
    and agentic state, 471
    and authoritarianism, 472
    cross-cultural studies of, 469
    and group pressure, 481
    and legitimate social power, 469–472
Obesity, 68, 69
Observational learning, **88**
    and aggression, 269–272
    and helping, 314, 315, 319
    and imitation, 25
    and social behavior, 25, 26
    stages in, 88, 89
    and Type A behavior, 117
Observational methods
    archival studies, 68
    content analysis, 67
    field studies, 67
    simple observation, 68
Oedipus complex, 243
One-sided message, **417,** 423
    and innoculation, 417
    versus two-sided message, 417
Oneida commune, 493
Operational definition, **41**
    uses of, 41, 42, 45
Operationalization, 41, 45
Ordinal scale, 42
Order effects, 131
Orientation stage, 220
Orienting reaction, 322
Outcome evaluation, 77, 78
Outside density, 643
Overcrowding. *See* Crowding
Overjustification effect, 436, 437

P-O-X triad, 230, 231
Palestinians, 558, 561
Parental influences
    on aggression, 270–272
    on attitudes, 372, 373, 378
    on helping, 344, 345
    on sex role behaviors, 95–97
    on Type A behavior, 117, 118
Participant observers, 67
Passionate love, 238
Passive aggression, 261
Patient satisfaction. *See also* Medical regimens
    and noncompliance, 498, 499
Payoff matrix, 525, 526

Pearl Harbor, 607
Peer influence, 373
Peer pressure, 571
Performances
    and impression management, 189–191
    kinds of, 190
    and self-esteem, 190, 191
Peripheral route, **420**
    and advertising effectiveness, 446, 447
    and attitude change, 420–423
    and involvement, 447, 448
    versus central route, 420
Person-oriented leader, 601
Personal costs, **328**
    and bystander intervention, 328
Personal deprivation, 555
Personal distress, **323**
    and bystander intervention, 323, 324, 333
    versus empathic concern, 323, 326
Personal norm. *See* Norm
Personal space, **633**
    cultural differences in, 636
    individual differences in, 636
    invasions of, 636–639, 650
    measurement of, 634, 635
    model of, 634
    and violent prisoners, 638, 639
Personalism, 145
Personality, **99.** *See also* Traits
    development, 84–86
    and helping, 336–342
    scales, 100, 101
    trait approach to, 99–102, 104–109
Personality development. *See also* Socialization
    process
    Erikson's theory of, 84-86
Persuadability
and sex differences, 422
Persuasive messages, **405**
    and advertising, 445–450
    and attitude change, 405–424
    and message characteristics, 414–424
    and smoking prevention, 452, 453
    and source characteristics, 405–414
Philosophy
    and social psychology, 14–16
Photospread, 155
Physical aggression
    and catharsis, 257, 292, 293
Physical appearance
    and attitude change, 412, 413, 423
    and impression formation, 123–126
    and social behavior, 126
    and social popularity, 236, 237
Physical disfigurement
    and bystander intervention, 332
Placebo effects, 53, 500
Political science
    and social psychology, 12, 14
Populations, 62
Position power, 603
Positivism, **17**
    influence on social psychology, 18
Pornography
    kinds of, 302, 303
    and sexual violence, 301–305
Prediction of behavior
    and attitudes, 379–387
    and interactionism, 109, 110
    and situations, 102, 103
    and traits, 99–102, 104–109
Prejudice, 388–389, **390,** 391–400
    causes of, 390–397
    and conformity, 488, 489
    and discrimination, 390

    ethnic, 390
    and needs, 376
    pervasiveness of, 389
    race, 394, 395
    sex, 389, 391, 392
Presence of others. *See* Crowding; Personal space;
    Territory
Presidential elections
    1972, 376
    1976, 382
Presocialization stage, 316
Primacy effects, 131
Primary drives, 24
Primary elections, 371
Primary territory, 640
Prison guards, 494, 495
Prisoners, 494, 495
    personal space of, 638, 639
    self-attributions of, 151
Prisoner's dilemma, **524–527**
    and communication, 530, 531
    and crowding, 662
    as mixed motive game, 527
    and payoff matrix, 525, 526
    strategies in, 530–532
    and threat, 528, 529
Private acceptance, **459**
    and expert social power, 465, 466
Private self-consciousness, **107**
    and consistency of behavior, 107
    and self-perceptions, 178
    versus public self-consciousness, 197
Problem solving tasks, **586, 597**
    and brainstorming, 591–594
    complex, 588–591
    exercise, 590, 591
    and group versus individual performance, 586–
    594
    and group versus individual performance, 586–
    594
    simple, 587, 588
Procedural justice, 549, 550
Process evaluation, 76, 77
Process loss, **585**
    and additive tasks, 585
    and the Beatles, 586
Professional helpers, 347–349
Program evaluation, **10**
    illustration of, 75–78
Progressive deprivation, 553, 554
Projection, 144
Projection techniques, 635
Propinquity, **222**
    and friendship, 222–224
Prosocial behavior, 306–351. *See also* Altruism; By-
    stander intervention; Helping
Protestant ethic, 547
Prototypes, **132**
    of grandmothers, 133
    and impression formation, 132
Pruitt-Igoe project, 661, 662
Psuedogroup, 588
Psuedo-inconsistency, 383
Psychiatric patients, 636, 637
Psychoanalytic theories
    of aggression, 261, 262
    of marital choice, 243
    of socialization, 83–86
Psychological reactance. *See* Reactance
Psychology Today, 254
Psychotherapy. *See* Professional helpers; Therapy
    approach
Public health approach
    and smoking prevention, 451–455
    and community interventions, 452, 453
    and school intervention, 453, 454

Public housing
    and defensible space, 661
    problems in, 661, 662
Public opinion polling, 359, 360
Public self-consciousness, 197, 198
Public school, 98, 629
Public territory, 640
Punishment
    and control of aggression, 285, 286
    and dental care, 502, 503
    in minimal social situation, 510, 511

Quasi-experiments, 59–61
    on crowding, 646
    on impression management, 37–39
    and program evaluation, 77, 78
    on television, 59–61, 288
    versus laboratory experiment, 59
Quebec separatist movement, 554, 555
Questionnaires, 64

Race
    and shared belief, 394, 395
Race riots, 551
Racial differences
    in academic achievement, 398
    in income, 553
    in locus of control, 185
    in personal space, 636
    in self-esteem, 398
Racial prejudice. See Racism
Racism. See also Prejudice; School desegregation
    and ethnic prejudice, 390
    in Israel, 389
    and perceptions, 156, 157
    and school desegregation, 394
    in South Africa, 390
    symbolic, 396
    in United States, 18, 72, 344, 388, 551
    and violence, 281
Random assignment, 52
    and internal validity, 52
    versus random sampling, 52, 64
Random sampling, 62
    and surveys, 61–63
    versus random assignment, 52, 64
Randomized response technique, 364, 365
Rape
    attitudes toward, 297–300
    depictions of, 303–305
    incidence of, 297, 298
    motives for, 298
    myths about, 299, 300
    perceptions of, 50, 51
Rapists. See also Rape
    characteristics of, 301
Rats
    crowding among, 617–619
Reactance, 239, 464, 478
    and coercive power, 464, 465
Reactivity, 66
    and attitude scales, 362, 363
Realistic group conflict, 395
    versus symbolic racism, 396, 397
Recency effects, 131
Reciprocal altruism, 312
Reciprocity, 228
    and friendships, 228
    norm of, 228
    and self-disclosure, 221
    and social influence, 472
Reference group, 373
    and attitude formation, 373, 379
Referent social power, 465
    basis of, 465

and identification, 465, 478
and medical regimens, 503–506
as socially dependent, 465
Reflected appraisal, 90
Reinforcement, 89
    and aggression, 269
    direct, 89
    and helping, 307–309
    and minimal social situation, 513
    negative, 307
    positive, 307
    self, 89
    vicarious, 89
Reinforcement affect theory, 231
    and friendship, 231, 232
    and sexual attraction, 240
Relatedness model, 218
Relative deprivation, 551–553
Reliability, 43
    and attitude scales, 359
    kinds of, 43
    and personality scales, 100, 101
Repetition, 448, 449
Reporting bias, 409
Representativeness heuristics, 146
Rescuers of Jews
    characteristics of, 343, 344
    and crime stoppers, 346
Research ethics, 71–74
    and deception, 71
    guidelines for, 71
    and harm, 71, 72
    and invasion of privacy, 73
Reserve clause, 543, 544
Resources, 515
Response set, 64
Responsibility denial scale, 339
Retaliation. See Control of aggression
Rewards. See also Incentives
    and attitude change, 405, 428–433
    and minimal social situation, 510, 511
Reward/cost matrix, 332
    and bystander intervention, 331–333
Reward social power
    basis of, 462
    and compliance, 462, 478
    and medical regimens, 506
    as socially dependent, 462
Risky-shift effect, 565–567, 581
    and group polarization, 581, 582
Role conflict, 571
Role confusion, 85
Role playing, 425
Role theory, 32, 569, 570
Roles
    and conflict, 571
    and deindividuation, 494, 495
    and group structure, 569–571
    maintenance, 570
    self-oriented, 570
    task-oriented, 570
Romantic attraction, 233–246
    and androgyny, 235
    dating, 234–241
    marriage, 241–246
Rural/urban differences. See Urban/rural differences

Salient stimuli, 150
Sample, 62
Scale value, 360
Scales, 41
    attitude, 360–362
    Fahrenheit, 41
    kinds of, 42, 43, 45

personality, 100, 101
and variables, 41–43
Schizophrenia, 500
School desegregation
    effects of, 397–399
    and social scientists, 397
    and supreme court, 397
School intervention
    and smoking prevention, 453, 454
Secondary drive, 24
Secondary territory, 640
Selective exposure, 376, 377
Selective inattention, 558
Self, 167
    attributions, 179–187
    perceptions of, 168–179
Self-appointed mind guards, 608
Self-attributions
    of athletes, 180
    belief in, 181
    and depression, 201–204
    of elderly, 204–207
    and locus of control, 183–185
    of success and failure, 180–181
    reactions to, 181–182
Self-awareness, 105, 176
    and aggression, 284
    and consistency of behavior, 105–107
    and deindividuation, 495
    individual differences, 106, 107, 178
    and mirrors, 176, 177
    and self-perceptions, 176–178
    theory of, 175, 176
Self-censorship, 608
Self-concept, 90
    in chimpanzees, 91, 92
    and comparative appraisal, 93
    development of, 90, 92, 93
    and reflected appraisal, 90
    and value change, 439, 440
Self-consciousness scale, 107. See also Private; Public self-consciousness; Self-awareness
Self-disclosure, 220
    and compliance, 504
    and extroversion, 220
    and locus of control, 220
    and reciprocity, 221
Self-esteem
    and school desegregation, 398
Self-handicapping, 194
Self-knowledge, 167
    and mirrors, 81, 82
    and self-awareness, 175–177
Self-monitoring, 107
    and attitude-behavior relationship, 384
    and consistency of behavior, 107–109
    and impression management, 197
Self-oriented role, 570
Self-perception, 165–188. See also Self-perception theory
    and health, 201–206
Self-perception theory
    and attitude formation, 370, 371
    and foot-in-the-door, 473, 474
    and overjustification effect, 436, 437
    versus cognitive dissonance, 434, 435, 443
Self-presentation, 167, 188–200. See also Impression management
    and conformity, 491, 492
Self-recognition
    in chimpanzees, 91, 92
Self-theory, 32, 34
Semantic differential, 361, 362
Sentiment relationship, 229
Seventh Day Adventists, 343

Sex differences
in aggressiveness, 264–267, 271
in attitudes toward coitus, 253
in conformity, 490, 491
in locus of control, 185
in personal space, 636
in persuadibility, 422
in reactions to crowding, 648
in resource allocation, 548, 549
in salary, 549
Sex role behavior, **94**
and biological orientation, 94, 95
cognitive development explanations of, 96, 97
and gender constancy, 97
social learning theory explanation of, 95, 96
Sex role stereotypes, **97, 300**
in magazines, 69
and sexual violence, 300
study of, 19
Sexism. *See also* Prejudice
and racism, 391
study of, 19
and television, 391, 392
in the United States, 389, 390
Sexual activities
attitudes toward, 248, 249
and equity, 253, 254
and religious preferences, 252
and romantic attraction, 252–254
sex differences in, 253
Sexual arousal
and aphrodisiacs, 251, 252
and excitation transfer, 251
and sexual attraction, 239–241, 249–252
Sexual attraction
and arousal, 239–241, 249–252
and excitation transfer, 239–240
and body parts, 250
and two factor theory of emotion, 239
Sexual violence. *See* violence
Similarity
and source characteristics, 413
as cause of friendship, 224–227
as consequence of friendship, 227, 347, 348
and helping, 331
and racial prejudice, 227, 394, 395
Simple observation, 68
Situationism, **102**
and social behavior, 102, 103
and interactionsim, 109
versus trait approach, 104–109
Sleeper effect, 413, 414
Smoking. *See also* Smoking prevention
and coronary heart disease, 452
dangers of, 450
incidence of, 450
and intentions, 385
Smoking prevention
public health approach, 451-455
therapy approach, 451, 505, 506
and value confrontation procedure, 440, 441
Sociability
and crowding, 646–648, 650
and noise, 625, 626, 633
in urban environments, 621–623
Social cognition, **87, 121, 122**–163
accuracy of, 143–152
and the legal system, 154–163
and professional helpers, 348–349
and socialization, 87, 88
Social comparison process, **232**
and friendship, 232
and informational social influence, 485
Social density, 643
Social desirability
and attributions, 138, 139

and consensus, 138
and impression management, 199
and perceptions of crime, 163
scale, 199
Social exchange. *See* Bargaining; Conflict; Justice;
Social exchange theory
Social exchange theory, **513**
analysis of interactions, 514, 515
and bargaining, 516–522
and marital choice, 246
and minimal social situation, 515
Social facilitation, 3, 4, **577**, 578
and arousal, 578
explanation of, 578, 597
versus social inhibition, 577
Social impact theory, **578-580, 612**
and diffusion of responsibility, 581
and social loafing, 583–585
and tipping, 581
Social influence, **459**
and group influence, 478–496
and individual influence, 459–472
tactics of, 459, 472–478
Social inhibition, **577, 578**
versus social facilitation, 577
Social interaction
and leadership effectiveness, 603, 604
Social judgment theory, 415, 416, 423
Social learning theory
and causes of aggression, 268–272
and control of aggression, 285, 286
and helping, 313–319
and prejudice, 391, 392
and sex role behavior, 95, 96
and socialization, 88–90
Social loafing, **583**
and additive tasks, 583–585, 597
and the Beatles, 585, 586
and social impact theory, 583, 584
Social marginality, 343, 344
Social norm. *See* Norm
Social penetration model, 220
Social popularity
and physical appearance, 236, 237
Social power, **461**
coercive, 463, 464
expert, 465, 466, 478
informational, 466
and leadership, 597
legitimate, 466–472, 478
and medical regimens, 501–506
referent, 465, 478
reward, 462, 463, 478
Social psychologists
activities of, 9, 10
occupations of, 11
and research, 10, 11, 14
training of, 11
Social psychology, **6**
and experimental psychology, 17, 20
and gestalt psychology, 18
and history, 18–20
and other branches of psychology, 13, 14
and philosophy, 14–16, 20
and other social sciences, 12, 13
and sociology, 16, 20
Social schemata, 131–135
and attitudes, 375–377
and central traits, 131, 132
and implicit personality theory, 132
and prototypes, 132
and stereotypes, 132, 133
Social science statement, 397
Social stimuli, **7**
kinds of research on, 7, 8, 13

Social support
and medical regimens, 505, 506
and nonconformity, 487
and smoking prevention, 453
Social trap, **527**. *See also* Commons dilemma
Socialization, 82–97
cognitive developmental theories of, 86–88
psychoanalytic theories of, 83–86
and self-concept, 90–93
and sex differences, 93–97
social learning theories of, 88–90
and Type A behavior, 117–118
Socially dependent, 462
Sociobiology, 33, **311**
and helping, 311, 312, 319
Socioemotional activities, 575
Sociofugal arrangements, 653
Sociopetal arrangements, 653
Sociology
and social psychology, 12, 14, 16
Sociopathy, 101, **340**
and empathy, 340
and helping, 340–342
Soft-core pornography, 301, 302
Source characteristics, 407–414
attractiveness, 412, 413, 423
credibility, 407–411, 423
expertise, 408–410, 423
likableness, 412, 413, 423
versus message characteristics, 420–423
similarity, 413, 423
trustworthiness, 408–410, 423
Soviet Union
and GRIT, 559
Spacial density, 643
Sports
and angry aggression, 290, 296
Spurious relationship, 44
Stable exchange stage, 220
Stagnation, 86
Statistical group, 588, 594
Statistical significance, 48
Status, **571**
and group structure, 571, 572, 576
Stereotypes, **132**. *See also* Prejudice
cognitive explanations of, 132–134
about Jews, 390
and prejudice, 390
sex role, 97
Stimulus overload, 622, 623, 632
Stimulus-value-role theory, 245
Stop-distance procedure, 635
Strain toward symmetry, 227
Stress theory
and crowding, 644, 650
Strong altruism, **310**
biological factors, 311, 312
evolution of, 311, 312
and kin selection, 312
and reciprocal altruism, 312
Subjective norm, 381–382
Substitute aggression
and catharsis, 291
Subways
helping in, 332, 333
violent crimes in, 261
Success
attributions, 141, 142
and self-attributions, 181–183
Student activism
and social psychology, 19
Studies in Machiavellianism, 521
Summation model, 127, 128
Summative scale
construction of, 360, 361

example of, 362
versus Thurstone scale, 360
Supreme Court
and Edward Lawson, 126, 137
and jury size, 613
and school desegregation, 397
Surface contact, 218
Surveys, 62–65, 73
Symbolic interactionism, 20, 34, 91
and role theory, 32, 33
and self-concept, 90, 92
and self theory, 32
and social behavior, 30–33
Symbolic racism, **396**
versus realistic group conflict, 396, 397

Target-based expectations, 139
Task-oriented leader, 599, 601. *See also* Task-oriented role
Task-oriented role, **570**
and group structure, 570
Task structure, 601
Team-building, 595, 597
Television
and aggression, 286–290
and attitude formation, 4, 373, 374, 378
and catharsis, 288–290
and crime, 59–61
and frustration, 288–317
and helping, 316, 317
and program popularity, 287
portrayal of races on, 391
portrayal of women on, 391, 392
and smoking prevention, 452, 453
and value change, 439
violence on, 286, 287
Temperature
and aggression, 281–283, 624
and helping, 625
and sociability, 624, 625
Terminal values, 377
Territoriality, **640**
and marking, 640
effects on social behavior, 641, 650
Test-retest reliability, 43
Thanatos, 262
Theory, 22, 39
versus hypotheses, 39
Theory of reasoned action, 380–382, 387
Therapy approach
and smoking prevention, 451
Third Party Intervention
and bargaining, 519, 520, 523
and international conflict, 560–562
kinds of, 561, 562
Third Reich, 343
Threat, 529. *See also* Mixed motive game
Three component model, **355–357**
and prejudice, 390
versus expectancy-value model, 358
Thurstone scale
construction of, 360
and scale values, 360
example of, 361
versus Summative scale, 360
Time pressure
and bargaining, 519, 520, 523
Tit for tat strategy, **530**
among birds, 532
effectiveness of, 530–533
as tournament winner, 532
Tragedy of the commons, 527. *See also* Commons dilemma

Traits, **99**
and interactionism, 109
and leadership effectiveness, 598
of King Augustus, 100
and moderator variables, 105–109
of Peter the Great, 99, 100
and social behavior, 99–102, 104–109
and stability of behavior, 104, 105
versus situationism, 102, 103
Trucking game, 528
True affective exchange stage, 220
Trust, 84
Trustworthiness, 408–411
Tuskegee syphilis experiment, 72
Two-sided message, 417, 423
versus one-sided message, 417
Two factor theory of emotion, 165–167, **172**, 173, 216
and angry aggression, 275
and excitation transfer, 239
and love, 238
and sexual arousal, 239
and shyness, 173, 174
versus self-perception theory, 172
Type I error, 613
Type II error, 613
Type A behavior, 112–118, **497**
and aggressiveness, 115, 116
and coronary heart disease, 112–114
origins of, 117, 118
measurement of, 113, 114
and physiological responses, 114
and social behavior, 115, 116
and Type B behavior, 112–118
Type B behavior. *See* Type A behavior

Unilateral awareness, 218
Unit relationship, 229
Unit of analysis
in social psychology, 7, 8
United Nations, 561
United States
anti-semitism in, 393, 394, 472
and civil conflict, 551
communist scare in, 464
constitution, 154
racism in, 18, 72, 344, 388, 551
sexism in, 389, 390
Unobtrusive measures, 363–367
Urban environment
benefits of, 631, 632
compared to rural environment, 621–623
effects on social behavior, 621–623
and environmental stressors, 623–632
and stimulus overload, 622, 633
Urban riots, 282, 283
Urban/rural differences
in environmental stressors, 623, 632
in social behavior, 621–623, 632
Urbanism, 620

Validity, **43**. *See also* Construct validity; External validity; Internal validity
and extreme group technique, 101
kinds of, 43
Value change, 438–440. *See also* Value confrontation procedure
and attitude change, 439
Value confrontation procedure, 438, 439, 443
effects of, 439
and smoking cessation, 440, 441
and teacher's behavior, 440
via television, 439
versus cognitive dissonance, 438

Values
and attitudes, 377–379
instrumental, 377, 378
terminal, 377, 378
Vandalism, 622
Variables, **40**
and operationalization, 41, 42
and scales, 42, 43
relationships between, 44, 45
Variability. *See* Variance
Variance, 49
Vascular processes
and aggression, 257–259
Verbal aggression
and catharsis, 291, 292
Victim characteristics
and bystander intervention, 330, 331
Vietnam, 415
and groupthink, 607
and misperceptions, 555, 556
Violence
in family, 260, 261, 291, 292
and personal space invasions, 638, 639
and program popularity, 287
racial, 281
sexual, 261
on television, 286–290
Violent crimes
and alcohol, 283
incidence of, 259, 260, 273
in subway, 261
Virile self-image, 557

War
death toll from, 272
incidence of, 272
and instrumental aggression, 272
War of Independence, 551
Washington, D.C., 327
Watergate, 163, 376, 377
and groupthink, 608
Weak altruism. *See* Bystander intervention; Helping; Strong altruism
Weapons
as aggression eliciting stimuli, 278
Weapon focus, 158
Wear out, 448
Weight loss
and cognitive dissonance, 430, 431
Weighted averaging model, 127–130
and juror bias, 161
Wheel communication pattern, 573
Whiskey rebellion, 551
Williams versus *Florida*, 612
Woodward versus *Fowler*, 644
Working, 542
World War I
and misperceptions, 555
and theories of aggression, 262
World War II
and attitude research, 406
helpers in, 343, 344
and holocaust, 393, 394
and misperceptions, 555
and social psychology, 18

XYY syndrome, 265, 266

Y communication pattern, 573
Yooups, 9

Zero contact, 218
Zero-sum conflict, 524